Black Baseball's National Showcase

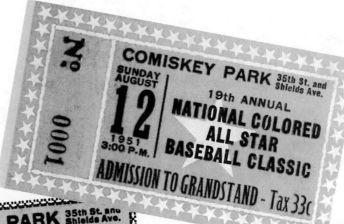

Black

THE EAST-WEST ALL-STAR GAME, 1933–1953

Baseball's

LARRY LESTER   WITH A FOREWORD BY JOE BLACK

National

University of Nebraska Press   Lincoln & London

Showcase

∞

Library of Congress
Cataloging-in-Publication Data
Lester, Larry.
Black baseball's national showcase : the East-West All-Star
Game, 1933–1953 / Larry Lester ; with a foreword
by Joe Black.
    p. cm.
Includes bibliographical references.
ISBN 0-8032-8000-9 (pbk. : alk. paper)
1. East-West All-Star Game (Baseball game)—History.
2. Negro leagues—History.   I. Title.
GV878.2 .L47 2001
796.357'648'08996073—dc21   2001027064

East-West game tickets (1945–59) courtesy of
Dennis Goldstein.

"N,"

Dedicated to:

My Mother, Casteline Williams, who fusses at me for
throwing away my treasure of baseball cards.

And to My Father, George Lester, who always made sure
I had tickets when the Yankees came to town.

Baseball in its time has given employment to known epileptics, kleptomaniacs,
and a generous scattering of saints and sinners. A man who is totally lacking in
character has often turned up to be a star in baseball. A man whose skin is white
or red or yellow has been acceptable. But a man whose character may be of the
highest and whose ability may be Ruthian has been barred completely from the
sport because he is colored.
—Sportswriter Sam Lacy, my mentor and inspirational leader

Contents

Photographs

Foreword Joe Black

BALTIMORE ELITE GIANTS AND BROOKLYN DODGERS

Baseball, considered by many to be America's number one pastime, has been a thriving recreational and employment aspect of this nation since 1839. Young men, black and white, could be seen cavorting on fields and in the streets as they endeavored to perfect their skills in catching, throwing, and hitting a baseball. It was exciting fun because many were hoping that one day they would be playing Major League Baseball. However, for one segment of the population, for many years this was an impossible dream. For many, many years those in power positions in baseball thought that skin pigmentation was more important than skill and deemed that Major League Baseball was for white males only.

However, a ray of sunshine penetrated the bitter disappointment of black males when in 1920 Rube Foster developed the Negro Major Leagues. Of course this venture was belittled by skeptics who wanted to label Foster's efforts as "sandlot" or "semipro" baseball. Nevertheless, that thought is a lie when a comparison shows that the Major Leagues and the Negro Leagues had the same two essential "showpieces," an All-Star Game and a World Series. The pages of sports history attest that players in both leagues had excellent skills. Although a separate entity, the players in the Negro Leagues displayed the same pride and athleticism as they competed for these prestigious rewards. The one difference was the fact that the Negro All-Star Game was called the East-West Game. The owners wanted the best based upon geographical locations of the teams. The first East-West Game was played in 1933 and it was a monumental success on the field and in the stands with multi-thousands spectators.

The players eagerly embraced this chance to be among the numbered few who would be on display in this special extravaganza. The players coveted this honor to be selected to show their baseball efficiency. I envy those fans who attended the early East-West Games because I did not have an opportunity to see the capabilities of Martin Dihigo, Bullet Rogan, Willie Foster, Oscar Charleston, Dick Lundy, and Turkey Stearnes, to name a few.

It was during my tenure with the Baltimore Elite Giants (1943–50) that I observed the baseball supremacy of Satchel Paige, Josh Gibson, Buck Leonard, Cool Papa Bell, Bill Byrd, Willie Wells, Verdell Mathis, Roy Campanella, Monte Irvin, Ray Dandridge, Max Manning, Hilton Smith, Double Duty Radcliffe, and Impo Barnhill. These players were superstars among the array of stars in the Negro Leagues. Competition was tough for the esteemed honor of being chosen to play in the East-West Game. I give you an example: Roy Campanella, a member of Baseball's Hall of Fame, was the number two catcher behind Josh Gibson.

The players who were chosen to play felt "special," and it also gave them an extra payday. However, after 1945 there was an added incentive, because all the players hoped their abilities would impress the baseball scouts enough to give them a chance to follow in the footsteps of Jackie Robinson and Larry Doby.

I was no exception. I was consumed with the desire to participate in the East-West Game. However, I could accept the fact that the talent of other players made me wait seven years before I gained the honor of playing in a East-West Game.

Acknowledgments

My support group consisted of many dedicated friends, family members, historians, and sports fans. I owe my biggest appreciation for the editing and proofreading jobs by Dick Clark (Ypsilanti MI) and the late Jerry Malloy (Mundelein IL). They encouraged me to take this project to the next level of research. I also owe a tremendous thanks to my daughters, Tiffany, Marisa, and Erica, for their assistance in typing the manuscript.

However, they were not alone in their input and commitment to a better book on the subject. I also give thanks to the following researchers and historians:

Luis Alvelo (Caguas PR)
Larry Bennett (Grand Junction CO)
Dr. Peter Bjarkman (Lafayette IN)
Charles Blockson (Philadelphia PA)
Todd Bolton (Smithsburg MD)
Bob Browning (Westtown PA)
Dr. Alice Carter (Pittsburgh PA)
Jim Chappell (North Kansas City MO)
Robin Clemmons (Alexandria VA)
Ricky Clemons (New York NY)
Phillip Collins (Dallas TX)
Deborah L. Dandridge (Lawrence KS)
Allen Davis (Cleveland OH)
Paul Debono (Indianapolis IN)
Bob Dolgan (Cleveland OH)
Jeff Eastland (Falmouth VA)
Morris Eckhouse (Cleveland OH)
Joellen ElBashir (Washington DC)
Eric Enders (Cooperstown NY)
Leo Ernstein (Kansas City MO)
Lisa Feder (Deerfield IL)
Kevin Fitzpatrick (New York NY)
Dr. Larry Gerlach (Salt Lake City UT)
Dennis Goldstein (Atlanta GA)
Al Gordon (Pittsburgh PA)
Dr. Leslie Heaphy (Canton OH)
Dr. Bob Hieronimus (Baltimore MD)
John B. Holway (Springfield VA)
April and Shawn Hughes (Kansas City MO)
Lou Hunsinger (Williamsport PA)
Merl Kleinknecht (Galion OH)
Ted Knorr (Lancaster PA)
Signe Knutson (Madison WI)
Michael Kollett (Au, Switzerland)

Neil Lanctot (King of Prussia PA)
Norman Lyons (Arlington TX)
David Andrew Leonard Marasco
  (Evanston IL)
Martin Socarras Matos (Havana, Cuba)
Ralph Maya (Miami FL)
Patricia McGlothen (Kansas City MO)
Sammy J. Miller (Florence KY)
Scot Mondore (Cooperstown NY)
Rick Morris (King of Prussia PA)
Eric Newland (Larchmont NY)
JaiElyn Obey (Washington DC)
Jim Overmyer (Lenox MA)
Theresa Pacheco (Kansas City MO)
Kelly Pangrac (Kansas City MO)
Robert Peterson (Ramsey NJ)
David Pietrusza (Scotia NY)
Bill Plott (Wilton AL)
Dr. Layton Revel (Carrollton TX)
Dr. Harry Robinson (Dallas TX)
Patrick Rock (Kansas City MO)
Mark Rucker (Boulder CO)
Jay Sanford (Arvada CO)
Kazuo Sayama (Tanabe, Japan)
Corey Seeman (Cooperstown NY)
Keith Smith (Kansas City MO)
Theora Stevenson (Kansas City KS)
Wayne Stivers (Evergreen CO)
Patricia Torres (Kansas City MO)
Gregg Truitt (Hockessin DE)
Eduardo Valero (Santurce PR)
Sharon Verminski (Pittsburgh PA)
Normal "Tweed" Webb (St. Louis MO)
Roger Webb (St. Louis MO)

Tim Wiles (Cooperstown NY)
Sheryl Williams (Lawrence KS)
Leslie Willis (Philadelphia PA)
Lyle Wilson (Mill Creek WA)
John Zajc (Cleveland OH)

Thanks to the following members of the baseball family for their contributions.

Sandra Quinn Bankhead
Joe Black
Donald Boyd
Sherwood Brewer
Bonnie Serrell Carr
Bill Cash
Julia Crutchfield
Geraldine Day
Jimmy Dean
Larry Doby
Mahlon Duckett
Wilmer Fields
Luis Garcia
Stanley "Doc" Glenn
Willie Grace
Teenie Harris
Sammie Haynes
Margaret Hedgepath
Herman "Doc" Horn
Hornsby Howell

Monte Irvin
Connie Johnson
Toni Johnson
Ethel M. Klep
Sam Lacy
Jim LaMarque
Max Manning
Jim Marshall
Bob Mitchell
Bob Motley
Christy Norris
Pamela Paige O'Neal
John "Buck" O'Neil
Robert Paige
Dick Powell
Ted "Double Duty" Radcliffe
Booker T. Robinson
Lester Rodney
Wilbur and Maxine Rogan
Terrence Scantlebury
Dewitt and Barbara Smallwood
DeMorris and Anna Smith
Malva Powell Smith
Alfred "Slick" and Tommie Surratt
Estelle Taylor
Quincy Trouppe Sr.
Leonard Wiggs

Black Baseball's National Showcase

Introduction

Until recently, even avid fans knew little of Negro League history or the rich culture of black baseball that preceded the Jackie Robinson era in Major League Baseball. Few fans knew that for more than half a century, some of the greatest ballplayers excelled behind an artificial but very solid color line. Behind the color barrier were quality championship teams like the Kansas City Monarchs, the Homestead Grays, the Pittsburgh Crawfords, the Chicago American Giants, the Newark Eagles, the Cleveland Buckeyes, and other top professional teams. They had players with catchy names like Buck and Mule, Turkey and Rabbit, the Rev and the Devil, Cool Papa and Pop, Schoolboy and Sonnyman, Smokey and Satch, coming in all shades and sizes to play a game between the white foul lines. Only now can we examine their true greatness without racial blinders.

The pinnacle of any Negro League season was the East-West All-Star Game. It was an all-star game and a world series all wrapped in one spectacle. Starting in 1933, the game was played annually at Chicago's Comiskey Park, with additional appearances in other parks in selected years. It brought thousands of fans to the Grand Hotel in Chicago and became the single most important black sporting event in America. The horrendous economic conditions of the 1930s and disagreement among league officials on a World Series format from 1928 to 1941 precluded any annual championship series, making the East-West All-Star Game black baseball's grandest attraction.

Eventually, All-Star attendance grew to over 50,000, often outdrawing its major league counterpart during the early to mid-1940s. Generally speaking, many historians, players, and fans argued that the overall success of the Chicago all-star games was one of the most important factors in the integration of Major League Baseball.

The fans chose teams by voting through the nation's two largest black newspapers, the *Chicago Defender* and the *Pittsburgh Courier*, voice of the voiceless people. Both papers were weeklies that owed much of their success to excellent political and sports coverage. These papers and smaller black presses promoted the East-West classics, giving fans across the country an opportunity to discover many stars—the batting power of Buck Leonard, George "Mule" Suttles, and Norman "Turkey" Stearnes; the lightning speed of James "Cool Papa" Bell, Willie "The Devil" Wells, and Sam Jethroe; and the pitching magic of Leon Day, Hilton Smith, and Leroy "Satchel" Paige. This abundance of talent raised optimism that black players were ready for the white majors. With black league play normally ignored by the white press, the East-West attraction offered an excuse for white America to see black baseball's best performers under one tent.

Except for a radio broadcast of a Joe Louis fight, this game was the biggest sporting event in black America. In 1995, at the 75th anniversary dinner held by the Negro Leagues Baseball Museum in Kansas City, Missouri, Monte Irvin, a 22-year-old outfielder for the Newark Eagles in 1941, recalled the tingle that surrounded the game:

> One of Kansas City's greatest was Satchel Paige. Satchel and I became great friends after a lot of turmoil in the beginning. Satch was the center of attention, and he knew it. As we stood around the batting cage, he'd say, "Fellas, the East-West Game belongs

1. The charismatic Satchel Paige often entertained his entourage before and after a big game. Here, Satchel spins wisdom at the Crawford Grill. Courtesy of Pamela Paige O'Neal.

to me. I don't have to pitch but two or three innings, so I'm gonna be very stingy today. In fact, I'm givin' up nothin'. When I get around to the Grand Hotel tonight, I'll buy you a beer. But today, nothin'. Zero!" You know something. He was right!

On a hot Sunday afternoon, around the eighth inning the whole stadium started chanting, "Satchel, Satchel, we want Satchel!" Satchel got up and warmed up and took that long loping stride of his across the outfield grass to the pitcher's mound. My buddy and teammate Len Pearson was the first hitter. I leaned over to him and said, "Lenny, I feel sorry for you!" He said, "Why?" "You're the first hitter and you know what Satchel wants to do to the first hitter?" He went and took his swings and came back and sat down. I said, "How did he look?" Lenny replied, "I don't know, I haven't seen him yet." Satchel pitched the eight and ninth, and the only hit we got off of him was a swinging bunt by Roy Campanella.

Irvin recalled another story: "In the 1939 East-West All-Star Game, the bases were loaded and we were behind by a couple of runs. Up comes Mule Suttles, a big home run hitter just like Babe Ruth. He came to the plate and on a 3–2 pitch, he popped the ball up for the third out. At the Grand Hotel that night, about four o'clock in the morning, Mule said, 'If I had that pitch just one more time, I'm sure I could do something with it.' After another four or five more beers, he said, 'I wish I had that pitch one more time.'"[1]

Another player, John "Buck" O'Neil, recalls his experience at the classic:

Let me tell you a little bit about the East-West game, because for a black ballplayer and black baseball fans, that was something special. Gus Greenlee began the game in 1933, the same year that the major leagues began their all-star game, and in the same ball-park, Comiskey Park in Chicago. That was the greatest idea Gus ever had, because it made black people feel involved in baseball like they'd never been before. While the big leagues left the choice of players up to the sportswriters, Gus left it up to the fans. After reading about great players in the *Defender* and *Courier* for so many years, they could cut out that ballot in the black papers, send it in, and have a say. That was a pretty important thing for black people to do in those days, to be able to vote, even if it was just for ballplayers, and they sent in thousands and thousands of ballots. It was like an avalanche!

. . . Right away it was clear that our game meant a lot more than a big-league game. Theirs was, and is, more or less an exhibition. But for black folks, the East-West Game was a matter of racial pride. Black people came from all over to Chicago every year—that's why we outdrew the big-league game some years, because we always had fifty thousand people at ours, and almost all of them were black people; not until after Jackie Robinson [played] did any whites come out.

In fact, we kept the game in Chicago because it was in the middle of the country, and people could get there from all over. The Illinois Central Railroad would put on a special coach from New Orleans to Chicago. They would pick up people all through Mississippi and Tennessee, right on into Chicago. The Sante Fe Chief would be picking up people in Wichita and Kansas City. The New York Central would come in from the East.

. . . This was "the" weekend. It was near the last weekend before school started, so a lot of kids would save up their nickels and dimes. In Chicago, all the black stores would sell tickets to the game. I remember in '42 box seats went for $1.65, grandstand seats for $1.10, and it was fifty-cents for a bleacher seat. And those stores on the South Side, from 40th to 50th Streets, like the Ben Franklin Department Store, Monarch Tailors, Harry's Men Shop, the South Center Department Store, they'd all have a big sign out, EAST-WEST TICKETS SOLD HERE. Because that would get people into the stores. A guy would come in and buy a ticket, and while he was there he might buy a hat or a pair of shoes.

The weekend was always a party. All the hotels on the South Side were filled. All the big nightclubs were hopping. Lena Horne was at the Regal club, and all the pubs had live entertainment. At the '42 game, Marva Louis, Joe Louis' wife and a wonderful singer, threw out the first ball with all the big shots there, you know what the atmosphere was like for us in Chicago. If you were anybody, you were at the East-West Game. And for many of us, if you were coming to Chicago, you would also be picking up your fall wardrobe.[2]

Sam Lacy, a writer for the *Baltimore Afro-American,* fondly remembers his days at black baseball's biggest event. Now 94, Lacy recalls:

It was a holiday for at least 48 hours. People would just about come from everywhere, mainly because it was such a spectacle. It was better than our present all-star game because the interest was focused purely on black folks.

Train, bus, automobile, very little flying, somehow fans managed to get there. I would go on my vacation during all-star week so that I could be there the entire week. I didn't want to miss anything!

In those days we played ball to win. It was not an exhibition game like it is today. It wasn't just a case of showing up. Guys would vie for positions on the team. And the audi-

2. Scribes from the various black weeklies at work in the press box. In the front row, right to left, are Arthur Greene (paper unknown), Cleveland Jackson (Cleveland Call-Post), and Art Carter and Sam Lacy (both from the Baltimore Afro-American). Courtesy of Sam Lacy.

ence participation was much more rabid than it is now. Much more rabid! Nowadays, attention is so divided among so many people.

For example, there was a game played here recently in Washington [DC] and [National League president] Bill White had me in his box. It was different! Just different! People didn't go overboard and get excited about the play on the field. At the East-West game, we just raised hell from the first pitch, right on through to the end of the game. It was a case where it was much more enjoyable. More like a picnic.[3]

On July 8, 1933, the *Pittsburgh Courier*'s John L. Clark, later an officer in the Negro National League, wrote about the current state of Negro League baseball. His text in part read:

Strange as it seems, the [white] dailies agreed almost unanimously that the status of leading Negro clubs was on a par with major league clubs. The players have just about done their part. They have played to win, kept in reasonably good physical shape and showed the fire and temperament of big league showmen. The owners, unfortunately, have closed shop on the idea. They no doubt are willing and glad to receive the honor and profit which goes with the improved status, but seem to have nothing to contribute.

Many inconsistencies continue to exist in the business administration of Negro baseball. [Black] owners will put out large amounts of money for uniforms, automobiles and buses, pay high salaries to managers and business agents. They will equip the team properly and provide transportation facilities, hire men to direct strategy and men to collect their share of the money; but the majority will not spend 60 cents or $1 for a score book. Nor will they pay to have records kept and transmitted of the games played.

3. John L. Clark (left), fine Pittsburgh Courier writer, stands by his friend Oscar Charleston, Crawfords outfielder and future Hall of Famer. Clark's 1933 editorial inspired me to write this historical tribute to the East-West games. Courtesy of Dick Clark.

Posters, placards and other forms of announcements are brought to advertise games to be played. But owners seem to have adopted a public-be-damned policy on reporting the outcome of the games. Very seldom do we find one man out of 16 or 18 who has time to visit a telegraph office and inform the "stay-at-homes" whether the team won or lost. And in those rare cases when this is done, the local newspapers must guess at hits, runs, errors, doubles, triples, strikeouts, stolen bases and the many other things which happen in a ball game—and which make records.

Owners have refused to recognize those factors, which make records, and in turn are deaf, dumb and blind to the fact that status is based on records of performance, good or bad. They seem to discount the fact that interest can be stimulated, maintained or killed outright by records alone. Worst of all, they are unfair to the public by withholding this information. Their general conduct is more like first-year sandlot promoters than big league owners.

Because this phase of the game has gone unrecognized is one of the genuine reasons why the status of Negro players cannot be proved. If we cannot prove by facts, we surely should not expect the other fellow to accept by oral commendation. Figures mean rating when available for comparison. But when one side produces figures and the other relies on memory and imagination, the comparison is unfair and unacceptable.

It might not happen this year. Nor next year. But some of these days a few men who venture to gamble thousands of baseball players will wake up. They will discover in the awakening that the only way to put Negro baseball on a par with what we call major leagues is to keep records of performances, relay the same information to the public and play fair with the press.

When this is done the status of clubs, leagues and players will approach the major league level.

Theories abound as to why statistical information was not provided to the public or the media on a regular basis. First, many owners were not willing to incur the additional expense of compiling statistics. Some owners also felt that players might use seasonal statistics as leverage in salary negotiations. Without the statistics, players would not be able to justify asking for a raise because they could not demonstrate statistically how well they performed on the field. Another theory is that the lack of statistics allowed owners to argue at season's end over which team was the league champion, with the most influential owner arguing and filibustering a path to the league crown. This practice was never more evident than at the end of the 1933 season. Finally, newspapers printed box scores that lacked individual runs scored or runs batted in to promote the concept of "winning as a team." It was not until 1944 that the Negro American League hired the Elias Bureau to compile league statistics. (See the chapter on the 1944 season for details.)

In the bitter depression year of 1932, eager to have a championship team, East-West All-Star Game creator Gus "Big Red" Greenlee raided rival teams of their top performers for his Pittsburgh Crawfords. Cum Posey's Homestead Grays lost catcher Josh Gibson, pitcher Ted "Double Duty" Radcliffe, outfielders Ted Page and Cool Papa Bell, plus first baseman Oscar Charleston, to Big Red's team. Greenlee also added third baseman Judy Johnson from the Hilldale Club of Philadelphia. Yet, the talent-rich Crawfords struggled to third place with a won-lost record of 32–26 in the short-lived East-West League of 1932. The next season they joined the newly organized Negro National League. In a split season, the Crawfords lost the first half to the Chicago American Giants by one game, and the American Giants also claimed the second half of the season. Greenlee challenged the validity of some of the league games played in the second half by the Chicago club. After considerable debate, league president Greenlee declared his team the Negro National League Champions for 1933.

With this legacy of sparse data in mind, this book attempts the difficult feat of presenting complete box scores for every East-West All-Star Game from 1933 to 1953. Seven previously unpublished game records are shown: the second games of 1939, 1947, and 1948 (in New York City); 1942 (Cleveland); and 1946 (Washington DC); plus newly rediscovered All-Star Games played in 1951, 1952, and 1953. Corrections have been made to previously published box scores: the spellings of player names are repaired, and revised totals for at bats, hits, and runs scored and batted in are presented. Added to each pitcher's totals are earned runs, hit batsmen, and wild pitches. Calculations of team batting averages, slugging percentages, earned run averages, and other previously unpublished statistics are used to determine all-time leaders.

In addition, the appendixes list day-by-day batting and pitching records, the leaders in batting and pitching for team and individual honors, plus all-time team rosters, personal all-star team selections, and other vital statistics and historical trivia about the classics. Unfortunately, some box scores do not show attendance, time length of game, men left on base, managers and coaches, or other statistics.

Every attempt has been made to ensure the accuracy of the data by comparing them with articles written by the leading sportswriters from the period. Despite an attempt for a complete statistical analysis of the East-West games, missing data may remain lost. As the eminent scientist Albert Einstein once said, "Not everything that counts can be counted; not everything that is counted is worth counting."

Financial reports are presented verbatim from the official league records. The reports, by the various league secretaries, appear as they were originally typed, including misspellings, incorrect totals, and format abnormalities.

Finally, comparative game accounts from the *Chicago Defender,* the *Pittsburgh Courier,* and other selected newspapers are provided to give readers a view of how the games were reported through the eyes of writers in their own cities.

WEDDING BANQUET IN HONOR OF PITTSBURGH CRAW...

The Guiding Light of Modern Negro Baseball
William Augustus Greenlee

BORN: THURSDAY, DECEMBER 26, 1895, MARION NC

DIED: MONDAY, JULY 7, 1952, PITTSBURGH PA

Many know of Rube Foster and his dictatorial rule of Western League baseball, but few know of his counterpart, Gus Greenlee, kingpin of the Eastern League. Although historians have given Foster the title "The Father of Black Baseball," Greenlee could fairly stake a claim to this epithet with the resurgence of interest in black baseball after Foster's death in 1930. When the two major leagues folded during the Great Depression, it was godfather Greenlee who resurrected the leagues to unprecedented popularity in the mid-1930s, and so Greenlee can be rightly called the "Guiding Light of Modern Negro Baseball" as well.[1]

During his lifetime, Greenlee was called a baseball executive, a boxing promoter, a nightclub owner, a numbers runner, a banker, and also an entertainment entrepreneur. All these monikers are correct. Richard Powell, former business manager for the Baltimore Elite Giants, recalled: "Well, Gus was a [George] Steinbrenner-type fellow. Gus wanted to be the big shot, where everyone would say, 'There goes Gus.' There was nothing reserved in his attitude. In fact, he wanted to run the league, so to speak. 'Larry, call so-and-so and tell them Gus told you so-and-so,' and you would relay that message. That type of foolishness. But he wasn't a bad fellow. Many of us have our egos."

Powell added, "If it were not for people like Gus Greenlee, there would have been no Jackie Robinsons, no Roy Campanellas or Don Newcombes. Because they [the owners] put their money in it to keep it going."[2]

Greenlee was born in Marion, North Carolina, a small textile town about 30 miles east of Asheville, in the western corner of the state. While his two brothers, Charles and Jack, were formally educated and became medical doctors, the truant Gus learned the trades of the streets to become just as financially prosperous.

The son of a brick mason, Greenlee joined the Great Migration movement in 1916. At age 20, catching a train to Pittsburgh, he arrived at his uncle's home with few material possessions. He worked at various menial jobs, including shining shoes and working as a construction laborer, before the U.S. Army called on October 30, 1917.[3]

After stopping a piece of shrapnel in his left leg at St. Mihiel, France, Private Greenlee, the World War I machine gunner for the famed 367th Regiment (92nd Division), was discharged on March 20, 1919,[4] and shipped back to Pittsburgh.[5] With the country in the midst of Prohibition, the six-foot-three, 200-pound "Big Red" (as light-complexioned blacks are often called) sold bootlegged whiskey from the trunk of his taxicab. Around town, he was known as "Gasoline Gus," selling to satellite mill towns like Homestead, Oakland, and Homewood.

Later, Gus opened several nightclubs. The first was called the Paramount, a dance hall featuring the Paramount Inn Orchestra, reputed by the *Courier* to be the city's best band. The club was shut down by the police in 1922.[6] And then there was the bohemian Sunset Café, which featured pianist Duke Ellington on occasion. Greenlee also owned the swanky

4. Greenlee Field hosting the Homestead Grays and Nashville Elite Giants on Opening Day, May 6, 1933. Note the towering lights used for night baseball and other events. Lights were installed in August 1932, several years before stadium lights appeared in major league ballparks. Courtesy of the Papers of Art Carter, Moorland-Spingarn Research Center, Howard University.

Working Man's Pool Hall on Fullerton Street. Of course, the immensely popular Crawford Grill was Greenlee's signature club. Greenlee, a local numbers baron, ran his office from above the Grill on Wylie Avenue, a mecca or "Little Harlem" for great jazz and appetizing food. The Grill was the nightspot for hanging out with Pittsburgh's biggest celebrities, athletes, politicians, and musicians. The Grill catered to the black Pittsburgh bourgeoisie, and the list of notable jazz musicians who visited the Grill includes drummer Max Roach and horn men Miles Davis, Dizzy Gillespie, and Louis Armstrong.

The Pittsburgh Crawfords were formed in the mid-1920s. Named after the Crawford Bath House, a celebrated gathering place for African-Americans, they were originally a local amateur team organized by Charles "Teenie" Harris, Johnny Moore, and brothers Raymond and Willie Harris (no relationship to Teenie). Teenie later became the *Pittsburgh Courier*'s eminent photographer and historian. In 1926, the Crawfords became champions of the city's racially mixed Recreation League. As their reputations grew as a quality team, they caught the attention of Gus "Big Red" Greenlee.

Soon after the depression, Teenie Harris, who had managed the semipro Crawfords A. C. (Athletic Club) since 1926, approached Greenlee as a sponsor. Teenie, 88 years old, remembered: "When I called him up and said I wanted some suits [uniforms] for the team, he said just go down to Honus Wagner [sporting goods store on Liberty Avenue]. He said, 'I'll call and let them know you're coming.' And he did! He paid for all the suits that day." Teenie added, "When I quit the Crawfords, I went to Gus and said, 'You can have the team and make a "big" team out of it.' And that's just what he did."[7] For the price of

5. The original Crawford Grill on Wylie Avenue, a mecca for great jazz and tasty delights that served black Pittsburgh. Gus Greenlee's office was located upstairs. The Grill was destroyed by fire in 1951. Courtesy of Teenie Harris.

6. A meeting of the minds that were instrumental in the creation of the East-West All-Star Game. Seated, left to right: club official Charles Tyler (Newark Eagles), owner Alejandro Pompez (New York Cubans), owner Gus Greenlee (Pittsburgh Crawfords), owner Effa Manley (Newark Eagles), and catcher Josh Gibson (Pittsburgh Crawfords). Standing, left to right: writer John L. Clark (Pittsburgh Courier), owner Jim "Soldier Boy" Semler (New York Black Yankees), owner Abe Manley (Newark Eagles), outfielder Oscar Charleston (Pittsburgh), and Roy Sparrow (Pittsburgh Crawfords secretary). Courtesy of the Papers of Art Carter, Moorland-Spingarn Research Center, Howard University.

uniforms and some baseball equipment, Greenlee purchased the Crawford "franchise." In 1930, under Greenlee's ownership, the Crawfords became a professional independent team, playing local and professional teams at Ammons Field and occasionally at Forbes Field, home of the Pirates. After two seasons of strong independent play, the Crawfords joined Cum Posey's newly organized East-West League in 1932.

The new league consisted of the Baltimore Black Sox, the Cuban Stars of New York, the Washington (DC) Pilots, Hilldale from Darby (Pennsylvania), the Cleveland Stars, the Newark Browns, Greenlee's Crawfords, and the Detroit Wolves (who later that year merged with the Homestead Grays, shortly before the league folded). Incomplete standings show that the Black Sox were leading the league with a 20–9 won-lost record. Greenlee's Craw-fords were third, behind the Detroit Wolves/Homestead Grays, with a 32–26 won-lost record. After the failure of the short-lived East-West League, Greenlee took club secre-tary Roy Sparrow's suggestion of an East-West All-Star Game showcasing the best players from the league.

This promotional idea was not without critics, however. In an undated 1934 editorial by W. Rollo Wilson called "Sports Shots," Wilson offered his support of Greenlee: "They knocked him, they said he wanted to be a czar but they neglected to say, also, that it was his money that was paying salaries for other owners, that he was assuming bills for clubs other than the Crawfords. He conceived the idea of an East-West game, the players to be selected by the vote of the fans and he had to put $2,500 on the line weeks before the date of the game. All that he has received for his efforts has been ill-advised criticism from those unacquainted with the facts and even from the very men who accepted his money to pay their personal bills."

The *Pittsburgh Post-Gazette* reported in 1932 that Greenlee said, "If it hadn't been for the numbers, my people would have been a lot worse off then they were." His numbers game was similar to today's lottery, albeit on a much smaller scale. His brother Charles stated that Gus and Alex Pompez (pronounced "Pom-Pay"), owners of the New York Cubans, had discovered the numbers game while vacationing in Cuba.[8] Teenie added that Gus shared the numbers with his older brother Woogy and, together, Gus and Woogie controlled the lottery game around the tri-state area.[9]

Greenlee's most popular game was to pick three numbers and hope for a match. He often used the last three digits of the last Wall Street Exchange bid for "butter and eggs" commodities. Or he would switch to something like a ballplayer's batting average.[10] His weekly take was roughly $1,500, from about 70 active gamblers.[11] Charles remembered, "I've seen some money now! We had walk-in safes, and I've seen the money stacked up taller than me, and I'm six feet tall."[12] Teenie Harris added, "I remember one time we had a number to hit pretty hard. We had two safes in the cellar that were full of money. The money had been in there so long it just stunk. Oh, what a terrible smell. But it was good money and we had to pay it out."[13]

Yet Greenlee was not only a taker but also a giver. When black families or business asso-ciates needed cash to buy coal for the winter cold, or pay a doctor's bill, or acquire basic staples like food, Greenlee was free with the loans. He advanced money for college tuition and provided start-up funds for small businesses like eateries, barbershops, and haber-dashers. Many unsecured loans were never repaid. With the collapse of Steel City Bank on 5th and Grant, in 1925, black patrons on the Hill were without a bank. Big Red generously became black Pittsburgh's new pawn broker and loan agent. "I knew he was a nice fellow," recalled Teenie Harris. "If you wanted some money or something like that, he would give it to you. Him and Woogy were the same way. Always giving out money."[14]

Greenlee's kindness continued during the holiday seasons, as he customarily gave away turkeys and hams during Thanksgiving and Christmas. And he financed a soup line for the Hill's homeless during the post-depression days. Food not sold at the Grill was donated to the soup line on Wylie Avenue.

Greenlee also held benefit games for various organizations. In 1931, he played the North Side Buicks in a benefit game for the Livingstone Memorial Hospital, with proceeds going to the ladies' auxiliary.[15] He leased his park to the Triangle Club, a group of Scottish Rite Masons, for a charity baseball game.[16] Greenlee also promoted games between the third and fifth voting wards as a political favor.[17] He later played a charity game against the Bacharach Giants in Columbus, Ohio, to raise monies for the NAACP defense fund.[18] The local press called him "friend of the little man."[19]

Eager to have a championship team of his own, Greenlee raided teams of their top performers. He lured pitcher Sam Streeter from the Birmingham Black Barons, John Henry Russell from the Detroit Stars, and Ted Page from the New York Black Yankees. Cum Posey's Grays lost catcher Josh Gibson, pitcher Double Duty Radcliffe, outfielder Cool Papa Bell, and first baseman Oscar Charleston to the lure of Big Red. Greenlee also added third baseman Judy Johnson and pitcher Rev Cannady from Hilldale to complete the coup. Despite the amassed talent, the Crawfords struggled to third place with a 32–26 won-lost record in the short-lived league of 1932. With regular attendance of between 5,000 and 10,000 each game, Greenlee sought to capitalize on the team's popularity and increase revenues by building his own park.

Greenlee justified his reasons for a new park in an open letter to the *Courier,* stating: "Having seen good colored teams visit Pittsburgh, following the Homestead Grays to Forbes Field and out of town points we inquired about the percentage to be divided at Forbes Field. We also noticed as the years past, the number of colored patrons increased. And above all we reckoned with the location of Forbes Field and relative disadvantage which our people had to undergo in reaching it. With these facts constantly before us, it followed quite naturally that a park more centrally located among Negroes would have better patronage."[20]

After six months of construction, on April 29, 1932, the new and fashionable Greenlee Field on the Hill opened its gates at 2400 Bedford Avenue.[21] Before an estimated crowd of 4,000 fans, Greenlee's Crawfords tasted a 1–0 defeat by the New York Black Yankees. Despite 10 strikeouts by Satchel Paige, Black Yankee Ted Page scored the game's only run, in the ninth. Page singled, stole second, went to third on catcher Cy Perkins's throwing error, and scored on a Texas League single by Clint Thomas. Jesse "Mountain Man" Hubbard of the New York Black Yankees held the Craws to three singles, fanning four. Withstanding last-minute heroics, Hubbard escaped the threatening ninth inning when he kept Oscar Charleston's blast to left field and Josh Gibson's drive to center field in the ball park.[22] Attorney Robert L. Vann, owner of the *Pittsburgh Courier,* tossed the ceremonial first pitch.[23] Ches Washington wrote in his column "Sez Ches" that "all the color, glamour and picturesqueness that usually attends the opening of a big league ball park was in evidence as Goodsen's New York Black Yankees helped the popular Pittsburgh Crawfords dedicate the attractive Greenlee Park here Friday. Photos of both teams were taken. The band played. An impressive dedicatory speech was made by R. L. Vann, during which the spectators stood to pay homage to Gus Greenlee, builder of the park."[24]

The Field claimed an estimated seating capacity of 6,000 for baseball and 10,000 for boxing. At the time, the modern brick and concrete structure was the largest stadium ever built that was maintained and owned by a black man. William Nunn of the *Courier* wrote of the stadium: "Pittsburgh has a new ball park, erected by a Negro, for Negroes, and with Negroes as participating factors. It is one of the finest independent ball parks in the country. With a left field longer than that at Forbes Field, and a right field which has yet to succumb to a home run wallop. It stands as a monument of progress."[25] Stadium architect L. A. Bellinger released figures showing that 14 carloads of cements, 1,100 lineal feet of steel fencing, and approximately 75 tons of steel were used. The Bedford Land Improvement Company estimated the total cost to build the red-brick stadium to be between $75,000 and $100,000. Future plans called for seating to increase to 15,000 for baseball and 20,000 for football. Gus proudly boasted that Greenlee Field's left-field line was 350 feet 3 inches long (reportedly 23 feet longer than Forbes Field) and that the field was the largest in western Pennsylvania.[26]

On Thanksgiving Day 1932, the mythical black collegiate football champion Wilberforce College (Ohio) played the West Virginia State Yellowjackets.[27] That day, amid motorcades and marching bands, Greenlee Field became a focal point for black fans, earning the park the title "Pittsburgh's Sports Center."[28]

Even the white press expressed praise for the mammoth structure. *Pittsburgh Post-Gazette* writer Harvey J. Boyle, in his column "Mirrors of Sport," claimed:

> A casual survey of the baseball park in Bedford Avenue, where the Crawfords will play their home games, indicates the general optimism of the men behind the project and their particular enthusiasm for semi-professional baseball and boxing.
>
> There must be a number of minor league ball parks scattered throughout the land far less pretentious than the Bedford Avenue establishment.
>
> A concrete and steel grandstand; well-constructed bleachers, and barring one stretch, a fence that itself cost a sizable sum [combine] to make this field one of the finest in Western Pennsylvania. The amount of grading necessary, on top of the construction, probably run the operation into $50,000.
>
> A special setup for boxing has been arranged, with seats on the field, and with the ring to be pitched where the greatest number of fans can see the show. It is one of the biggest operations around here.
>
> Ticket windows and entrances have been well laid out and a large crowd will be handled with a minimum amount of confusion.
>
> For baseball the foul lines are longer than at Forbes Field. The Philadelphia National League park could be put inside the Bedford plant.
>
> All that is necessary now is to get the crows, which the weather and the current times being what they are [post-depression era], may prove to be a big problem.[29]

In the first year of operation, 119,384 patrons passed through Greenlee's gates. Baseball accounted for 69,229 fans, with 22,081 fans seeing boxing events and another 21,639 fans enjoying football games. Another 6,435 fans witnessed soccer games at the Field. In August 1932, floodlights were installed, making Greenlee Field the first stadium in the country to feature nocturnal baseball.[30] The estimated cost to install the lighting fixtures was $6,000.[31]

The first nighttime contest was played against the bewhiskered House of David team on August 13, 1932.[32] The Craws won 6–3, behind William Bell's 6-hitter and 10 strikeouts. Newly acquired outfielder Ted Page led the offensive attack with a home run and a single. Attendance was not reported.[33]

When the East-West League folded in midseason of 1932, the Negro National League was formed, with Gus Greenlee as president.[34] W. Rollo Wilson in his column "Sports

Shots" reported that Greenlee told him that "last Thanksgiving he was going to try to save baseball in 1933 by organizing a league. He felt that the only way to stimulate interest in the game was by having a real competition. He was not unmindful of the fate of the East-West loop of 1932 and he had hoped to surround himself with men of financial strength who would be willing to count any losses as an investment, an investment which would pay dividends in the years to follow."[35]

Greenlee had written a letter to Rollo outlining his new hope for league stability: "The purpose of this meeting is to sound out club owners, officials and fans on the subject of baseball in general and a baseball league in particular. I do not know who is going to be there, but I suppose that all of the owners East and West have been invited to attend." Greenlee continued: "If there is to be league or an association or more than one of them then it must be constructed on a sane foundation and not reared on such a sandy bottom as that which could not support the weight of the East-West loop of 1932. . . . Negro baseball is at a low ebb and both owners and players must make sacrifices and more sacrifices to maintain it until such a time that the fans are again in funds and able to storm the ballyard ramparts."[36]

The members of the newly formed league lost the first-half title to the Chicago American Giants by one game. The American Giants also claimed the second-half title. However, the validity of some league games played by the American Giants was questioned. After considerable debate, league president Greenlee wielded his power by taking away unofficial league wins from the Giants and declaring his own team the National League champions.

Without a doubt, the East-West All-Star Game held annually at Comiskey Park was Greenlee's biggest contribution to the national pastime. The event became the most visible competition in black sports in America. Greenlee's influence was obvious in the inaugural contest, in which 7 of the 14 Eastern players were Crawfords. However, despite the presence of Cool Papa Bell, Oscar Charleston, Josh Gibson, Judy Johnson, John Henry Russell, Sam Streeter, and Bert Hunter, the team lost to Willie Foster and his Western mates, 11–7.

The 1934 season was a year of peaks and valleys for Greenlee. In July, three armed men at the 28th Street Bridge and Brereton Avenue robbed Gus and his brother Frank, forcing their car to the curb and taking a reported $600, presumably receipts from the Crawford Grill.[37] The apex of Greenlee's ownership career came on the Fourth of July of the same year, when Satchel Paige pitched a 2–0 no-hitter against the crosstown rival Homestead Grays. This victory gave the Crawfords bragging rights in Pittsburgh over the traditionally tough Grays. W. P. "Pimp" Young, who umpired the game, recalled, "As I remember the best that the Grays did all day was to hit a few feeble grounders."[38] Meanwhile, the Crawfords fell to third place and labored to a won-lost record of 29–17.

The glory year in Crawford history came the following season, 1935. Showcasing five future Hall of Famers in Oscar Charleston, Satchel Paige, Josh Gibson, Cool Papa Bell, and Judy Johnson (and Sam Bankhead, who should be in the Hall of Fame), they ran away from the competition, winning 39 of 54 games for an astonishing .722 winning percentage. This team is called by several baseball historians the greatest Negro league team ever assembled and is often compared to the 1927 New York Yankees.[39] The powerful Crawfords repeated as Negro National League Champions in 1936, winning 36 games and losing 24 before disaster struck.

During spring training of 1937, the tables were turned on Greenlee when Dominican Republic dictator Rafael Trujillo raided his team. Trujillo enticed eight Crawfords (center fielder Cool Papa Bell; left fielder Sam Bankhead; first baseman Harry Williams; catchers

Bill Perkins and Josh Gibson; pitchers Leroy Matlock, Satchel Paige, and Ernest "Spoon" Carter) with suitcases of money to join his politically motivated team, the Ciudad Trujillos. Greenlee's Crawfords never recovered from the 1937 assault. The Crawfords finished the first half of the season in next-to-last place. That year, only three Crawford players made the all-star team (Lloyd "Pepper" Bassett, Barney Morris, and Ches Williams) and two more in 1938 (Sam Bankhead and Johnny "Schoolboy" Taylor). In previous years, the Crawfords had seven (in 1933); eight (1934); six (1935); and nine players (1936) in the East-West classics. With losing records in 1937 and 1938, the less-talented Crawfords proved to be a financial handicap for Greenlee, forcing the team to disband.

Philadelphian Eddie Gottlieb, a white booking agent for the league, made a futile attempt to save the Crawford franchise in an April 4, 1939, letter to each owner. Earlier in 1933, Gottlieb became co-owner of the Philadelphia Stars team with Ed Bolden from Darby, Pennsylvania. He later coached and managed the Philadelphia Warriors basketball team in the NBA. But like most white owners of the period, "Fast Eddie" did not allow black players on his basketball team. His 10 percent booking fee for permissions to play in Yankee Stadium, Shibe Park, and other parks was hailed by some black owners and damned by others.

In his letter, Gottlieb devised a plan for every owner to advance Gus Greenlee $200, for a total of $1,000, which would provide some working capital. The loan would be paid back when the Crawfords made their first appearance at the respective park. If the gate receipts did not cover the first visit, then the second visit would surely satisfy the note. With the season soon to start, none of the owners tendered Gottlieb's proposed loan, forcing Greenlee into an unwelcome retirement. The New York Cubans, owned by Alex Pompez, took over for the once-famous Crawfords in the league standings.

On December 10, 1938, the acclaimed Greenlee Field on Bedford Avenue was demolished, becoming the Bedford Dwellings housing project. Writer John L. Clark wrote, "Greenlee Field joins the list of banks, industries and other enterprises, which should not be again attempted in this city for the next 100 years."[40] In February 1939, Greenlee sold the team to some white Toledo (Ohio) businessmen and soon after resigned as league president with a letter to the *Pittsburgh Courier* stating:

> After a careful study of the baseball outlook, and in a review of my experience and losses of the past seven years, I have concluded that my resignation from office as president will serve the best interest of all concerned.
>
> Greenlee Field has passed into history, and we have no home grounds that we can control. We can no longer plan for the day when improved industrial conditions will appear and make more profitable athletics in this section. The Pittsburgh Crawfords baseball club had developed a warm friendship and enthusiastic following east of Pittsburgh. I had planned to be active this year if a major league park could be secured in New York or Brooklyn. Since this is impossible, I can see no good judgment in moving the club to a city west of Pittsburgh. . . . Perhaps new blood will bring new ideas and new weapons.[41]

Although their tenure in the Negro Leagues was short, the Pittsburgh Crawfords can proudly claim three league titles: 1933, 1935, and 1936. Over the years, their all-star lineups included such unheralded stars as Jimmie Crutchfield, Sam Bankhead, and Ted Page and such unsung pitchers as Spoon Carter, Sam Streeter, Bert Hunter, and Johnny "Schoolboy" Taylor. Furthermore, the Crawfords could profess to featuring Hall of Famers

Cool Papa Bell, Oscar Charleston, Josh Gibson, Judy Johnson, and Satchel Paige in their lineups.

In addition to Greenlee's three baseball championships, his expertise extended to the boxing arena. On October 31, 1935, African-American John Henry Lewis became the undisputed, light-heavyweight champion by defeating Bob Olin in St. Louis. The fight was thought to be the first racially mixed championship bout in Missouri history. At the time, Lewis was the only U.S. boxing champion managed by an African-American.

By 1937, Greenlee's stable of fighters included—besides Lewis at 182 pounds—heavyweight Big Jim Thompson; middleweights Red Bruce and Freddie Wilson; welterweight Holman Williams; and featherweight "Silent" Stafford, a deaf fighter from Savannah, Georgia.[42] In the previous two years, from 1935 to 1937, Greenlee's prize fighter Lewis defended his title successfully fifteen times, forcing Greenlee to seek tougher talent at the higher weight class.

In February of 1937, Greenlee accused Joe Louis's managers of ducking his fighter John Henry. He asserted, "[John] Roxborough and [Julian] Black are my personal friends, but I can't agree with them in this thing. They—or Mike Jacobs—draw the color line whenever a good boy is mentioned as a better opponent for Joe than the Eddie Simms or Natie Browns." After two years of fighting rejects, Lewis secured a date to fight the "Brown Bomber." On January 27, 1939, at the famous Madison Square Garden in New York, heavyweight champion Louis made his fifth title defense, this time against John Henry Lewis, some 20 pounds lighter and a 7–1 underdog. The much-hyped fight failed to survive the first round. After three knockdowns, referee Art Donovan stopped the fight. The Brown Bomber had sent Lewis and Greenlee packing to career-ending corners.

On February 17, 1942, Greenlee was released from Montefiore Hospital for an unknown illness and was greeted with some disturbing news. *Pittsburgh Courier* writer John Clark informed him that Abe and Effa Manley were contemplating selling the Newark Eagles. On February 21, Greenlee wrote a letter to Abe, which in part read:

I would rather not be a member [of the league] if you are going to withdraw. As much as we disagreed, I will admire you for sticking to what you believe to be right. After seven years you have a better idea of what it is all about and I am quite sure that our opinion would not differ so widely now.

I am told that you were sponsoring [Joseph] Rainey for [league] President against Tom Wilson.[43] That was a bad move. You should have been the candidate and put every member who opposed you right on the spot. There are too many alibis against an outsider.

I am writing each club owner, explaining what I think of the "probation" period they have given me. Just like any new and unanswered member, they have gone on record as saying that I could not assemble a team, and if I thought I could, I must prove it to them first. After proving this, then they would accept me as an associate member—no voice in the affairs of the league, no dependable place on the schedule, [and] never counted in the standings.

Now, you know me too well to believe that I will accept any part of this. In fact, I consider the whole proceeding a gross insult. They must have forgotten that I once operated the Negro National League, that my own cash money was used for operations, and that many of the clubs received help in different ways from me.

I might have to remind them of these things in a hard way. While I don't want it advertised, I might get a team together and go independent. If I take this step, you know just how far I will raid. But I am not sure yet.

If I was in your place, I would go to the meeting next Saturday, and get placed in the schedule. I will be there, and we can talk things over.

Yours very truly,

W. A. Greenlee

The Manleys did not sell the Eagles. After losing excellent players like Larry Doby and Monte Irvin to the major leagues (in 1948), the Newark club was sold soon after to a group of Houston businessmen. Greenlee, former league president, sought to put another team in the National League for the 1943 season. His only competition for the vacancy was George Mitchell, manager of the St. Louis Stars. The Stars had last played in the Negro American League in 1941 under the banner of the St. Louis–New Orleans Stars. Mitchell had worked with Jim Semler, owner of the New York Black Yankees. Mitchell announced that he and Semler were dissolving their relationship and was asking for a franchise in another city.[44]

Mitchell was granted a franchise in Harrisburg, Pennsylvania, while Greenlee's application was rejected. "If the Negro National League executives had been wise they would have ordered Mitchell to get together with Greenlee and revived the franchise Gus holds here in Pittsburgh," wrote Wendell Smith in his "Sports Spurts" column.[45] Greenlee responded: "I think they gave me a raw deal. I at least had a city to play in, but they turned me down. Mitchell is a grand fellow and I would be the last one to wish him any bad luck, but I'll be hanged if I can see how he is going to make a go of it in Harrisburg. The town is too small. You've gotta get in big towns to make any money in baseball these days. If he had been permitted to team up with me, the National League would have had another good team—and it would have been in a major league city."[46]

Mitchell's team split home games between Harrisburg and Mitchell's old homestead of St. Louis. After winning five of nine games, the Harrisburg–St. Louis Stars withdrew from the league and went on a barnstorming tour with the Dizzy Dean All-Stars.

Greenlee and the Crawfords finally reemerged in 1945 as members of Branch Rickey's experimental all-black United States League (USL). Former player and Cleveland attorney John G. Shackelford was named president and Greenlee vice president. Writer Wendell Smith of the *Courier* hailed Greenlee's new venture: "Greenlee stands today as the great builder in Negro sports. He's a carpenter who knows how to use his tools and where to start nailing a house together. He was the man who brought Satchel Paige into the 'big time.' He was the first president of the present NNL. Through sheer nerve and a gambling spirit, he broke the back of Nat Strong's once famous booking empire, a company that had Negro baseball in the palm of its all-powerful hand. That is, until Mr. Greenlee decided he wouldn't let his Crawfords play for any agency for a mere pittance. When he took this firm, defiant stand, the bookers had to back down and for the first time Negro baseball tasted the pleasantness of 'big money.' He introduced Negro baseball in the big league parks of New York at a time when no one would share the gamble with him. After reviewing Greenlee's sensational record and his ability to get things done, no one can look at his new league and laugh it off with ease."[47]

Besides Pittsburgh, franchises were granted to the Brooklyn Brown Dodgers, Chicago Brown Bombers, Detroit Motor City Giants, Philadelphia Hilldales, Toledo Cubs, and Boston Blues. The league ran into difficulties securing ballparks to meet their schedules. As a result, Brooklyn, Philadelphia, and Toledo failed to finish the season. Soon after, Rickey signed Robinson to a Montreal contract, with Rickey assuring USL owners of the league's continuance. Interestingly, the USL opened the 1946 campaign with a team in Montreal (the Crawfords), the Cleveland Clippers, the Boston Blues, and a revamped Brooklyn Brown Dodgers team, which occupied Rickey's Ebbets Field on occasion. Greenlee remained associated with the Crawford club despite offers from the Negro National League to rejoin the fold.[48]

With the success of Jackie Robinson, Larry Doby, Don Newcombe, Roy Campanella, Hank Thompson, Joe Black, and other African-Americans integrating the major leagues, new leagues and established black teams like the Pittsburgh Crawfords were dismantled in 1938.

During the winter of 1950, Greenlee became ill and was admitted to the Veterans Hospital in Aspinwall, Pennsylvania. During his six-month stay in 1951, the Crawford Grill was destroyed by fire, while the U.S. government sued Greenlee for unpaid income taxes. Today the parking lot of the Pittsburgh Civic Center lies atop the original Grill.

During his lifetime, Greenlee cataloged a unique résumé of achievements. His potpourri of professions included cab driver, politician, nightclub owner, restaurant owner, bootlegger, gambler, numbers baron, card shark, boxing promoter, league official, baseball club owner, and humanitarian.

In 1952, Greenlee died on Satchel Paige's 46th birthday, in his suburban home at 10900 Frankstown Road, where he kept 300 prized white Leghorn chickens. Last rites were given at Gaines Funeral Home on 220 Auburn Street with hundreds in attendance. Regretfully, Gus never got to see Paige, his prize pitcher, become the oldest major league player to appear in an all-star game, at Cincinnati's Crosley Field the following year.

1933

President Franklin D. Roosevelt appoints African-American advisors in forming the first unofficial "Black Cabinet." Prominent individuals include educator Mary McLeod Bethune, political scientist Ralph J. Bunche, economist Robert Weaver, and attorney William H. Hastie, a future candidate for Negro League commissioner.

In his first movie role, former Rutgers football player Paul Robeson plays the role of Brutus Jones in the film *Emperor Jones*—the first Hollywood production starring an African-American with whites in supporting roles. Bill "Bojangles" Robinson, future co-owner of the New York Black Yankees, stars in *Harlem Is Heaven,* the first all-black talking movie.

The New York Rens beat the Original Celtics seven out of eight games.

The cost of a half-gallon of milk is 21 cents and 10 pounds of potatoes costs 23 cents. A three-bedroom home costs about $6,000. A brand-new Chrysler Roadster sells for $695, a four-piece bedroom suite sells for $99, all-steel refrigerators sell for $19.95, tri-ply single or double-breasted suits sell for $21, and the price of a man's topcoat peaks at $25.75.

The first Major League All-Star Game is played in Chicago. Much like his Negro League counterpart Mule Suttles, Babe Ruth hits a two-run homer in the third inning off the Cardinals' Wild Bill Hallahan, leading the American League to a 4–2 victory over the Nationals in the first Major League All-Star Game, which was also played in Chicago. Both clean-up hitters Suttles and Ruth hit home runs in the first all-star game in either league.

In the City of Brotherly Love, Philadelphia, Chuck Klein of the Phillies and Jimmie Foxx of the A's post triple crown seasons, the only time the trifecta happened in both leagues in the same season.

GAME HISTORY

At times, the Negro Leagues lacked the choreography of Cotton Club line dancers. With sketchy statistics, unbalanced schedules, erroneous newspaper accounts, players breaking contracts, and star players loaned out to help a club meet a payroll, organizing an annual event was seemingly an impossible task.

The East-West All-Star Game was the brainchild of writers Roy Sparrow, of the *Pittsburgh Sun-Telegraph,* and Bill Nunn, of the *Pittsburgh Courier.*[1] In July 1933, Nunn and Sparrow met with Cum Posey at the Loendi Club to discuss the possibility of having two black all-star teams perform at the annual New York Milk Fund Day at Yankee Stadium.[2] At Sparrow's suggestion, the all-star game was to be called the North-South Game.[3] After a lengthy discussion of various fund-raising ideas, support for the Milk Fund and other events was defeated. However, the three men still wanted to stage an all-star contest in New York City. They agreed to contact Bill "Bojangles" Robinson, co-owner of the New York Black Yankees, about arrangements to secure Yankee Stadium.

Later that evening, Nunn and Sparrow met with Gus Greenlee at his Crawford's Grill for dinner. When briefed on the idea for an all-star game, Greenlee suggested that Nunn and Sparrow, the Craws' traveling secretary, contact Robert Cole, owner of the Chicago American Giants, about leasing Comiskey Park and instead call the game the East-West Classic.[4] Soon after, Sparrow traveled to Chicago to meet with Cole, and the deal was consummated with the first contest hosted on September 10.

Initially, the game receipts were divided between the benefactors of the game: Greenlee, Cole, and Tom Wilson, owner of the Elite Giants the first three years.[5] Greenlee's rival for the Pittsburgh sports dollar, Cumberland Posey, was left out of the agreement. Starting in 1936, all teams from the Negro National and American Leagues equally shared the profits. Gasoline Gus's share was eliminated in 1938 when he failed to field a league team. Sparrow's efforts to organize the game lasted only a couple of years, while Bill Nunn continued his unselfish campaign of promoting the game with numerous editorials in the *Courier.*

It is indisputable that the East-West classic was the highlight of any season. Many veterans of the Negro Leagues emphasized the all-star game as the pinnacle of their careers. Seldom do you hear a modern major leaguer voice similar praise over selection to an all-star game. As Lester Lockett, who appeared in the four games, said: "If you were picked to play it was a big thrill because you were chosen over a lot of other guys. . . . It really became a big deal."[6] The game became the showcase for the best black stars during baseball's segregated era. It was the mecca of black baseball. It was the ultimate thrill for the fans, who witnessed the best players from around the league in one ballpark, in contrast to the league's world series, which featured only two teams.

Despite a history of uncoordinated scheduling, Negro League officials got in step and kicked off an event that invigorated fan appeal for years to come. Both the major leagues and the Negro Leagues introduced all-star games in Chicago's Comiskey Park during the 1933 season. The major league game, inspired by *Chicago Tribune* sports editor Arch Ward, was announced on May 18 and was played on July 6. After watching an exhibition game at Chicago's World Fair the previous year, Ward thought a game between the best stars from the two leagues would be an attraction. He won the support of each league president and Commissioner Kenesaw Mountain Landis with his suggestion of donating the proceeds to charity.

Similar to the major league contest, players for the East-West All-Star Game were selected by the fans, with prominent black newspapers like the *Pittsburgh Courier,* the *Baltimore Afro-American,* the *Kansas City Call,* and the *Chicago Defender* providing their readers with ballots to choose their favorite players.[7]

Unlike today's major league event, in which the game is an exhibition of talent, the Negro Leaguers played to win at all costs. This competitive approach, along with the showcasing of the country's best black baseball talent, made the black all-star game a more popular event than the league's own world series.

During the early years of the East-West games, America was coming to grips with the Great Depression. The early 1930s found African-Americans, particularly southern blacks, suffering more than other groups in terms of real income and economic opportunity. In 1930, more than 1 million blacks were employed as agricultural laborers, with approximately two-thirds of them located in the South.

Since World War I, southern blacks had been migrating to northern cities in hope of a freer and better life. The Great Migration of 1915 had crested in the early 1930s as northern whites were fighting for the same unskilled and service-oriented jobs normally performed by African-Americans. The city of Chicago, in particular, became a major recipient of the migration movement, as many pawned their hopes for the American dream, or "Dreams Deferred" as poet Langston Hughes would later write.

On a more positive side, the *New York Times,* on June 7, 1930, began to treat black people with respect by capitalizing the word *Negro,* proclaiming the action to be "in recognition of racial self-respect for those who have been for generations in the lowercase."[8] The term *colored* held negative connotations, as it was becoming a code word to include anyone who was not a white Anglo-Saxon American.

With the buying power of African-Americans drastically reduced by a food-line and temporary labor mentality, the future of any economic effort to support the national pastime appeared to shuffle along.

Prior to the first East-West game, most black Americans traditionally voted Republican, the party of Abraham Lincoln and abolitionist Frederick Douglas. In 1932, however, Democratic president Franklin D. Roosevelt presented the "New Deal," promising to cure the ills of the Great Depression. This new sign of hope caused many African-Americans to shift their political allegiance to the Democratic platform. Other blacks discovered the Communist Party, as it elected African-American James W. Ford as its first vice president. Through several New York newspapers, particularly the *New York Daily Worker* and the *People's Voice,* the Communist Party would become a major component in pressuring major league owners to integrate their ball clubs in the 1930s and early 1940s.

With the New Deal came new hope as President Roosevelt created the "Black Cabinet," an advisory group of African-Americans with Dr. Mary McLeod Bethune its most visible member.[9] African-Americans gained an additional ally when first lady Eleanor Roosevelt publicly advocated fair employment and a review of segregated public accommodations in this country. Now, with a new friend in the White House, many black Americans would vote the Democratic ticket for many years to come.

The year 1932 was the beginning of a new sports era for African-Americans. The black New York Rens defeated the powerful all-white Original Celtics to claim the first world basketball championship. In the Los Angeles Olympics of 1932, black Americans began to show dominance in track-and-field events when Eddie Tolan won a gold medal in the 100- and 200-meter runs and Ed Gordon won the gold medal in the broad jump, now called the long jump.

Despite success in the sports arena, black baseball still had its critics. Harvey J. Boyle, in his column "Mirrors of Sport," wrote of "The Colored Man in Baseball," saying:

Like the philosophical old colored mammy organized baseball says to the colored boy:
   Go out and play just as much as they,
   But stay in your own backyard.

The song, if some of you don't remember, had to do with a forlorn pickaninny, who had come back crying to his mammy over a situation which saw white children giving him the well known air — and not a microphone. She gathered him up in her arms and crooned:

Now Honey you stay in your own backyard,
Don't mind what the white folks do.
What show do you suppose they're going to give
A little black coon like you
So stay on this side of the highboard fence
And, honey don't you cry so hard

Just go out and play as much as they
But stay in your own backyard.

Boyle continued:

While there are evidences on every hand that the colored man is generally self-sufficient
I pass up the yawning opportunity to play upon a them that has intrigued Shakespeare,
among the old timers, and Eugene O'Neill among the moderns, to stick closely to the
sport terrain to show that, out of organized baseball, the colored man has formed his
own baseball league and year by year is increasing his stature.[10]

The 1933 season presented new challenges. On February 1, the *New York Daily News*
in an editorial on the race relations of our national pastime called "What's Wrong with
Baseball?" reported: "Another trouble with Major League ball certainly would seem to
be the color line drawn in the big leagues. There have been good baseball players who
were Indians or part Indians, Mexicans, Cubans, etc. A Chinese Hawaiian tried out for the
Giants a few years ago, and would have made the team if he had been able to play a little
better ball. But good Colored ball players aren't eligible and so there must be a lot of possible fans in Harlem who don't stop over to the Stadium of the Polo Grounds to baseball
games."

Alvin Moses, a writer for the *Pittsburgh Courier,* responded on February 11 with his comments: "This symposium comes as water to the parched lips of a traveler who has sought it
in vain for many days. Year after year we've virtually screamed for this sort of recognition
in the columns of the Associated Negro Press, and whatever publication we've labored for.
Yes, that's big part of rottenest with baseball, tennis, golf, cricket, polo, racquets, squash-
tennis . . . and what-have-you. The uncrowned and unsung Babe Ruths, Cochranes, Foxxes,
Gehrigs, Gomezs, Groves, et al, whose skins happen to be of swarthy hue, cry out from the
shadows of 'yesteryear' against this unholy and Un-American idea of fair play to all citizens. If President-elect Roosevelt would perform a service that would renown his name to
posterity, he has only to 'read-out' the unwritten laws of Negrophobes in sportdom at least,
giving our well behaved athletes a rightful place in Major League baseball. The members
of the editorial staff of the 'Daily News' are to be congratulated."

Another challenge came from the inability the previous year to establish a sanctioned
league. Two new leagues, the Negro Southern League and the East-West League, failed to
maintain major league quality status for an entire season. Now a fresh league with an old
name, the Negro National League, was being developed. The league originally consisted of
the Chicago American Giants, Pittsburgh Crawfords, Nashville Elite Giants, Detroit Stars,
Baltimore Black Sox, Akron Black Tyrites, Columbus Blue Birds, and Homestead Grays.
The Cleveland Giants replaced the Blue Birds in August.

The Homestead Grays were banned from the league in June, after compiling an 11-9
won-lost record. A special league meeting was held at Pittsburgh's Greenlee Field on June
23 to schedule games for the second half of the 1933 season. Present at the meeting were
Robert A. Cole and Dave Malarcher, representing Chicago; Arthur J. Peebles from Columbus; Tom Wilson, Nashville; Bill Mosely, Detroit; Bill Gibson, Baltimore; writer William G.
Nunn from the *Pittsburgh Courier;* and Gus Greenlee serving as chairman. The main topic
of discussion was charges of player tampering brought by the Detroit club against the
Homestead Grays. The Grays had contacted third baseman Jimmy Binder and outfielder
John "Big Boy" Williams without the knowledge of Detroit officials. A notice to return
the players or accept suspension was ignored by Grays' owner Cum Posey. When no Grays

7. The sly, smiling Bill Byrd, shown here as a Baltimore Elite Giant, would be allowed to throw his spitball for the remainder of his career. Byrd pitched in seven all-star games, compiling an ERA of 2.25 in 16 innings. Courtesy of NoirTech Research, Inc.

representatives appeared at the board meeting, their absence was assumed to be an admission of guilt. By unanimous vote, the Homestead Grays were discharged from the league. League clubs were forbidden to play the Grays, while Binder and Williams had until July 10 to report back to the Detroit Stars.[11]

Meanwhile, one of the country's most popular teams, the Kansas City Monarchs, continued barnstorming, focusing their play in Nebraska, Iowa, Kansas, and other midwestern states. With marquee players like Newt Allen, Newt Joseph, George Giles, and Frank Duncan, and with top pitchers like Chet Brewer, Andy Cooper, and Wilber "Bullet" Rogan, they provided a major treat for fans living in minor league cities. Playing to entertainment-starved small towns had proved financially beneficial to the Monarchs. In fact, the Chicago American Giants were playing most of their home games this season in Indianapolis at Perry Stadium because of increased fan interest in the Hoosier city and the conversion of the Giants' original Chicago park, at 39th and Wentworth Avenue, to a dog track.[12]

Other league news involved more on-the-field action. Bill Byrd of the Baltimore Elite Giants and John "Neck" Stanley of the New York Black Yankees were officially identified as spitball pitchers. When the new Negro National League was organized in 1933, officials "grandfathered" Byrd and Stanley, giving them lifetime permission to throw their "spitters." However, the league prohibited any other pitchers from adding the wet one to their repertoires.[13] In the major leagues, the spitball had been ruled illegal following the 1919 season.

While the new league was being established, club owners were suggesting innovative ideas. One such idea was the East-West All-Star Game. Optimistically, the owners hoped for success with this new venture. To everyone's surprise, especially league officials, this event became the biggest annual sporting event in black American history. The East-West Game became the spirit and life of Negro League baseball, serving to entertain, educate, and ultimately provide a forum to integrate our national pastime many years later.

First Negro League All-Star Game

Betting Even on Big Game if Foster and Page [Paige] Start

Source: *Chicago Defender,* 9 September 1933

Very little betting is reported on Sunday's game of games, but what wagers are being put up hold the two teams chances even, providing Satchel Paige and Willie Foster start the game. Out West they are betting Willie Foster will hold the East scoreless during the time he is laboring on the mound. The East is betting Paige will out-pitch Foster if they are matched at the beginning.

The baseball prestige of the East will be gallantly defended by the most brilliant representatives of five major clubs in the mammoth East-West diamond classic at Comiskey Park, in Chicago this Sunday.

Winning their berths in an interesting poll of fans which literally combed the nation,

8. Oscar Charleston (left) and Raleigh "Biz" Mackey (right) were named starters in the 1933 game. Charleston is the only man to play, manage, coach, and umpire in the East-West classics. Mackey is the oldest man to play; he received a ceremonial base-on-balls in the '47 classic, on his 50th birthday. Courtesy of NoirTech Research, Inc.

the galaxy of star players selected will be welded into a mighty team by John Henry [Pop] Lloyd, grand old man of the game, who will manage the Eastern aggregation.

Swept into positions in an avalanche of eleventh-hour votes, star players of the Pittsburgh Crawfords, the Philadelphia Stars, the Homestead Grays, the New York Black Yankees and the Baltimore Black Sox were conceded by fans to be the men to represent the East.

Oscar Charleston of the Crawfords, Dick Lundy of the Philadelphia Stars and [Biz] Mackey also of Philadelphia, all stellar performers of national renown, led the mighty vote parade, which accorded them the first base, shortstop and catching positions, respectively.

FAVOR SCALES

The esteem in which George Scales, manager of the New York Black Yankees, [is held] was clearly shown by the fans' votes. Scales was given the most diversified vote of any man, receiving 28,347 ballots for the second base job, 23,549 votes for the third base post and 2,259 tallies for an outfield position. The volume of markers received for the second base berth earned for him a utility infield berth.

The final week of the voting marked a drastic shift in the status of the pitchers for the East team. [Sam] Streeter of the Craws and [George] Britt of the Grays continued to hold their own, with Satchel Paige, Crawford speedball merchant, showing a decided gain. Paige nosed out [Bert] Hunter, also of the Crawfords, for the third place pitcher's position, with Bill Holland of the New York Black Yanks and Porter Charleston of Philadelphia also making strong bids for fourth and fifth places.

Now that the fans have made their selection it will be up to the East's manager, John Lloyd, as to the men he will use and how he will line them up to the best advantage. Lloyd is admittedly one of the smartest students of the game in the East, and the fans are practically unanimous in their confidence in his judgment. The line-up, which Lloyd uses, of course, will figure materially in the winning of the prizes, as advertised.

Power at the bat, speed on the base paths and color in the field mark the selection of the fans who have participated in the mammoth poll which closed Saturday for popular favorites to represent the West in the brilliant East-West diamond classic with historic Comiskey Park as its setting Sunday afternoon.

With four clubs represented and with as brilliant [an] array of diamond stars as ever sank spiked shoes into the turf of a baseball field selected in the nation-wide poll, fans from the land which each day sees the setting sun, feel that their representative will prove to be foemen worthy of their steel.

With the last minute votes pouring into headquarters in a steady stream the final tabulation showed some surprising upsets with recognized favorites sinking into the limbo of "close seconds," which many a player who was considered to have little more than an outside chance swung into the lead as his work during the last few weeks of the contest won additional votes for him.

CHICAGO RULES

Chicago, mighty team of the West, with five selections, leads the list, while Kansas City has four regulars in the running. Nashville garnered two places in the final count and Cleveland shows a regular outfielder and a utility infielder.

Pitching honors went to Willie Foster, greatest southpaw the West has ever produced, with Chet Brewer, lanky Kay See ace, rating second honors. [Sug] Cornelius of Chicago,

9. Willie Foster, half-brother of league founder Rube Foster, was the winning pitcher in the first East-West contest. Foster pitched all nine innings, the only complete game in all-star history. Courtesy of NoirTech Research, Inc.

the kid who was the "jinx" of Crawfords' title hopes ranks third. [Percy] Bailey, Nashville's great pitcher, also earned a place.

The infield, with "Mule" Suttles at first, ran true to form, with Newt Allen getting the call at second. [Willie] Wells winning out easily at short and [Alex] Radcliffe far ahead of the field at the hot corner.

In the outfield Sterns [Stearnes] had little opposition, being followed by [Nat] Rogers, [Steel Arm] Davis, [Bullet] Rogan and [Sam] Bankhead.

You can also figure on reserve power, placing [Leroy] Morney, the "Honus Wagner" of the West, as first utility, and named Suttles and Rogan, who is now in the twilight of a brilliant career, as his running mates.

Editor's note: The only pregame promotion by the white dailies was by the *Chicago Daily News,* which ran a four-inch spread on September 8 listing the starters of the East squad with no mention of the hometown West squad members. Satchel Paige, who would eventually become a household name in the Negro Leagues, was listed by the *Daily News* as "Snatchell Paige, the possible starting pitcher."

EAST-WEST VOTE WINNERS

The players selected to participate in the first Negro all-star game in history are listed below. Each squad had one player at each field position, two catchers, four pitchers and three utility players on their 17-man squads. The respective lineups for each club is:

	EAST	WEST
P	Satchel Paige, Pittsburgh Crawfords	Willie Foster, Chicago American Giants
P	Sam Streeter, Pittsburgh Crawfords	Sug Cornelius, Chicago American Giants
P	George Britt, Homestead Grays	Jim Willis, Nashville Elite Giants
P	Bert Hunter, Pittsburgh Crawfords	Percy Bailey, Nashville Elite Giants
P	Biz Mackey, Philadelphia Stars	Jack Marshall, Chicago American Giants
C	Josh Gibson, Pittsburgh Crawfords	Larry Brown, Chicago American Giants
1B	Oscar Charleston, Pittsburgh Crawfords	Mule Suttles, Chicago American Giants
2B	John Russell, Pittsburgh Crawfords	Newt Allen, Kansas City Monarchs
3B	Jud Wilson, Philadelphia Stars	Alex Radcliffe, Chicago American Giants
SS	Judy Johnson, Pittsburgh Crawfords	Willie Wells, Chicago American Giants
LF	Vic Harris, Homestead Grays	Steel Arm Davis, Chicago American Giants
CF	Cool Papa Bell, Pittsburgh Crawfords	Turkey Stearnes, Chicago American Giants
RF	Rap Dixon, Philadelphia Stars	Sam Bankhead, Nashville Elite Giants
U	Leroy Matlock, Pittsburgh Crawfords	T. J. Young, Kansas City Monarchs
U	Ted Page, Pittsburgh Crawfords	Leroy Morney, Cleveland Giants
U	Andy Cooper, Kansas City Monarchs	Tommy Dukes, Nashville Elite Giants
M	Pop Lloyd, former Lincoln Giant	Joe Green, former Chicago Giant

Editor's note: Jim Willis, T. J. Young, Jack Marshall, Ted Page, and Tommy Dukes did not appear in the inaugural contest and never played in an East-West game.

Heavy Hitting Beats East in Classic

Western Team Slugs Way to 11 to 7 Victory in Chicago;

Suttles' Home Run Featured

Mr. Willie Foster, If You Please!

Source: *Kansas City Call,* 15 September 1933

How about the West's hurler—Willie Foster. In trouble in the fourth and fifth and after that he was himself.

"Jawn Henry" sent up his gunners as pinch hitters. Look at that lineup of sluggers to start with: [Rap] Dixon, [Oscar] Charleston, [Biz] Mackey, [Richard] Lundy, Vic Harris and [Branch] Russell. Look at the pinch hitters, men who are capable to run any pitcher off the mound: Josh Gibson, Judy Johnson, famous wit the Hilldale club and later with Atlantic City; Fat Jenkins who can do more with a basketball and a baseball than the men who invented or perfected the game. Now, Willie Foster just had to have something on that pill—and he did.

After the fifth the East wasn't so hot until the ninth although they threw a scare into the West in the eighth. In the last inning they scored two runs on [George] Britt's single. [Leroy] Morney's error of [Cool Papa] Bell's grounder, Dixon's sacrifice fly scoring Britt, an out by [Oscar] Charleston and [Josh] Gibson's long fly that gave Bell a chance to come home after the catch.

The West was laying 'em down and picking 'em up. Having related the fourth it would be well to say how the first West run counted. It came in the third. [Sam] Bankhead beat out a hit to Lundy in deep short. Brown was out on a neat sacrifice, Wilson to Charleston. Foster fanned. [Turkey] Steams [Stearnes] hit to right sending Bankhead home.

In the home (meaning the West) sixth, Well's opened with a single, [Steel Arm] Davis sacrificed him to second. Exit, Mr. Streeter, enter Mr. Hunter. [Alec] Radcliffe and [Mule] Suttles doubled. Morney singled and Suttles came home.

'TWAS CLASS AND MORE CLASS

The West drove Hunter from the slab in the home seventh. Foster singled, Stearnes doubled. Well's sent a long fly to J. Bell and Foster came home after the catch. Davis doubled sending Steams [Stearnes] home. Radcliffe singled scored Davis.

The West wore natty cream colored uniforms, all new with the letters W E S T across the breast. The stockings were black with a red stripe. The East players wore a bluish gray uniform with the words E A S T across the breast. The stockings were black with a red and white strip.

The game was well handled. It was a pity that the rain-laden clouds which caused a drizzle an hour before game time kept so many away from the park. As it is the game is a fixture, either here or in the East next year. This city being so centrally located may get the battle again.

Among the visiting newspapermen here for the game were Ches Washington and William G. Nunn of the Pittsburgh Courier, Johnson of the Indianapolis Recorder, Russell Cowan of the Detroit Tribune, and of course all the local pen pushers whether baseball or sport writers or janitors, all were out.

Gus Greenlee of the Pittsburgh Crawfords was all in after the game. He lost 10 pounds worrying over the possibility that rain might ruin the game—then too the East lost. Robert Cole, better known as "King Cole" smiled and smiled and shook hands. Yes, the West won and didn't have seven of the nine men who played for the West team from his own club, the American Giants, and didn't the West play just nine men without making a substitution? "Well, I could have told you that all along," he told Greenlee when they gathered in Jim Knight's Tavern on Forty-seventh Street to tell how it happened or why it didn't happen.

20,000 See West Beat East in Baseball "Game of Games"

by Al Monroe

Source: *Chicago Defender,* 16 September 1933

The depression didn't stop 'em—the rain couldn't—and so a howling, thundering mob of 20,000 souls braved an early downpour and a threatening storm to see the pick of the East's baseball players battle the pick of the West in a Game of Games at the White Sox ball park in Chicago last Sunday afternoon.

The contest was pre-billed as the Game of Games, and, gents, a baseball-mad throng—20,000 of 'em—will attest to our story that its promise was fulfilled. This folks, is our story, and we'll stick to it even when informing future generations that we were among those reporting the first of what by all manner of reasoning should become an annual event.

THE GAME IS ON

Promptly at 2:30 the umpires moved from beneath the home dugout like groundhogs searching for that proverbial shadow, only braving steady drizzle to yell the usual "Play ball!" that informs you that the game was on. They paused for a moment while Attorney Nathan K. McGill, general counsel of *The Chicago Defender,* pinch pitching [for Abbott] of the same paper, tossed the first ball, and then drew tighter their masks as Willie Foster hitched his belt to start the first pitch in the direction of the home plate, where "Cool Papa" Bell was awaiting its arrival.

From then on, particularly through the first five frames, there was a ball game. Out in the center of the diamond, at intervals called innings, stood Foster for the West and Streeter for the East, both wrong-side tossers. Sending 'em in through the middle and over the corners, with no thought of yielding to defeat.

Batter after batter came to the plate, and, like Pelicans reaching for the spoils of an overnight tide, they sought in vain to "hit 'em where they ain't," but all in vain. Certainly there was a mild outburst in the West's half of the second [inning] when, after Lundy, king of short fielders, played tag with Bankhead's grounder, Stearnes sent a screaming single to right to score him; but all in all it was peck, peck, peck, with nothing resulting but strikeouts or popouts.

MORNEY ERRS

Then in the East's half of the third [fourth] things took a new turn—a temporarily disastrous turn for the West. [Leroy] Morney—great short fielder that he is—proved conclusively that second basing is not his profession. On two occasions he played tag with balls hit or thrown his way—once with a double play in sight. He seemed to have been alone in thinking the balls were covered with moss that should not be plucked. And to add to the worries of the West's fans, as Morney sought moss or whiskers on the ball, Bill Foster became less steady. Once he walked a man and twice hit Charleston in the side, and the net result was a 3-to-1 advantage for the East.

But there was no tag playing in the West's offense. Trailing by one run, Mule Suttles came to bat with a mate aboard and sent one of Streeter's pitches into the upper deck of the left field stands. From then on the West appeared to find use for those big bludgeons that they were carrying to the plate.

There is an aged adage that to the pitcher striking out the first batter to face him comes ultimate defeat and when Streeter sent both Stearnes and Wells back to the dugout, after whiffing the wind, Eastern supporters shook their heads.

They seemed to sense victory for the West, even at this early point. And it came—not brilliantly—but surely. It was wrapped around the bludgeons of those victory thirsty swings of Mule Suttles, Radcliffe, Davis, Brown and Bankhead. It climaxed the most perfect sports setting a dark and dreary afternoon ever presented.

West's Satellites Eclipse Stars of the East in Classic

by William G. Nunn

Source: *Pittsburgh Courier*, 16 September 1933

Fandom is shouting the praises of three new "stars" tonight; men whose brilliance glittered in all its pristine glory out on the diamond of Comiskey Park here this afternoon as the famous All-West baseball team, picked by diamond fans of the nation, rode roughshod over a mighty Eastern aggregation, to win going away, 11–7.

It was a game which produced thrills galore—and tonight, as we look down upon a scene of bustling, laughing, hilarious humanity, we hear the names of "Wee Willie" Foster, "Mule" Suttles and "Steal Arm" Davis on every tongue.

FOSTER WAS "RIGHT"

This afternoon, Willie Foster, who likes to boast and backs his talk with his mighty left arm, humbled the bats of the greatest all-star aggregation he's ever met and allowed but seven hits.

We saw him pitch airtight ball for three innings—with Jud Wilson, mighty mite from the Quaker City, getting the only hit off him—a looping single to left—and then we saw his defense crumble under the strain in the fourth inning to give the East three runs with nary the semblance of a hit.

We saw the East come back in the next inning, after the West had scored three in the third to score two more runs . . .

Then we saw Mr. Foster settle down and pitch three—hit ball the rest of the way. Two of the hits came in the eighth and the other in the ninth. We saw a great southpaw who was "right" this afternoon. He proved to us that he had a "fighting" heart, and our hats are off to him.

"MULE" GIVES 'EM COURAGE

We saw a great exhibition of "do or die" spirit in forth and sixth innings, and "Mule" Suttles was the man who supplied the punch in each inning.

Trailing three to one in the last of the fourth, we heard [Willie] Wells yell, "Let's go get 'em." There they were baseball's great run-making combination. Wells, Davis and Suttles!

Wells came up and doubled to left. "Steel Arm," in the game to the hilt, followed with another screaming double to left center. Only fast fielding saved it from being a triple. Radcliffe fouled to Biz Mackey and up came the Mule.

Two hundred and thirty pounds of solid bone and muscle, with his knock-knees carrying his huge frame along, and with the biggest bat on the field being carried as though it were a toothpick, Mule advanced to the plate. What an ovation he got? Because, Mule, to colored fandom, is what Ruth is to major-league baseball.

Streeter carried one through his letters for a strike. The next ball was to his liking. With hardly any effort he swung. Like a bullet from a rifle, the ball sped out into deep left center. There was power to the drive. "Cool Papa" Bell started to run. Suddenly he stopped. Pandemonium reigned. Straw hats filled the air. The noise reminded one of machine-gunfire which, on occasion, rocked Chicago in its halcyon days. For "The Mule" had tagged one on the nose. Way up in the upper tier, of the left center field stands, the ball landed and bounced along as a hundred fans scrambled madly for the honor of getting the ball. It was the kind of swat which is worth the price of admission any day.

And then, Mule broke the hearts of the East. Trailing by a run in the sixth, with one run in by virtue of Wells' single, a sacrifice by Davis and a double by Radcliffe, Mule "connected" again. This time it was a slashing double to right and sent the West into a tie. It was here that Morney "crashed" the hall o' fame to deliver a timely single. The hit sent his team into the lead and they were never headed again.

"STEEL ARM" RISES TO GLORY

But to "Steel Arm" Davis, aging outer -gardener of the West must go the glory for being tonight baseball's greatest "money player."

After all, fans expected Mule and Willie to deliver. We've seen Davis in many games this year. We've seen him when he was in his diamond glory. But never have we seen a greater "Steel Arm," than the man who played left field this afternoon.

He covered left field like the morning dew, taking Texas leaguers and dangerous drives that looked like extra bases.

But it was at the plate that he covered himself with laurels. Two slashing doubles and a sacrifice in three official times at bat, with his bludgeon driving in three runs, and with he, himself, carrying two more across the plate, represented a mighty fine days work. Without Davis in the game today, 'it would have been mighty close.

And so, we must give "Steel Arm" credit for being a great "money player" and hand to him the honors which he so richly deserves.

West Triumphs Over East in 11–7 Thriller

Negro Stars Could "Answer Prayers" of Big League Club Owners,

Says Chicago Daily News Experts After Witnessing East-West Game

Charleston, Lundy, Suttles Ranked As Major League Timber

Source: *Pittsburgh Courier,* 16 September 1933

With a plentiful supply of occult calcimine, a bunch of major league club owners who are now on their knees might have their prayers answered, wrote Henry L. Farrell in the *Chicago Daily News,* Monday, after witnessing the East-West colored all-star baseball contest Sunday afternoon.

On the field at Comiskey Park Sunday afternoon, continued Farrell, when the West defeated the East 11 to 7 in the first Negro World Series [All-Star game], there were three ball players who are good enough to play in the white major leagues.

Great sums of money have been marked down in red for players such as Jimmy O'Connell, who proved worth not 50 cents of the $50,000 the New York Giants paid for him."

If Lundy, the shortstop, and Charleston, the first baseman for the Eastern team, and Suttles, first baseman for the Western team, were of a lighter shade, they would be worth double that sum.

And, with major league pitching to work behind, the Eastern team, although it lost might well be moved as a unit into Cincinnati or Boston, where the long suffering patrons of the Reds and the Red Sox have been praying for a magic rod to strike a rock and appease their thirst for a team.

The first of the Negro all-star series drew a crowd of 20,000 and for five innings the spectators saw a game of baseball that compared to many games of baseball's greatest classic. The last innings of the game, when the dusky sluggers, swinging from the hips, started a parade on pitchers, provided material for Octavus Roy Cohen. But nearly every game of the 1920 World Series between the daffy dodgers of Brooklyn and the Cleveland Indians gave Ring Lardner material that convulsed the nation.

Those last innings provided some novelties. Rather appropriately, there was a big guy named Costello calling balls and strikes and the umpires with him were very much on the alert. They caught a runner who pulled a Merkle and didn't touch second, and they spotted a big colored player who left third base for home too soon after an outfield fly. But none of the boys ran ahead of the runner or tripled into a triple play in the unique Babe Herman fashion.

A hot one happened, too, in the fifth inning when Brown, the catcher for the West, smacked a terrific fly to centerfield and the colored gentleman under it didn't catch it.

Brown went on around and came into third and was prepared to stay there. He seemed to be out of run. But the coach stirred him up with a whack and sent him in and he was out from here to the Cuban revolution.

The Chicago fans were very much put out about Brown's overzealous larceny and they gave him the berry. But it was the fault of the unknown traffic officer at third.

LIKE HAL CHASE

The boy, Oscar Charleston, who played first base for the Eastern team, is from the Pittsburgh Crawfords, and he could handle the same job on at least ten clubs in the big leagues. He is rated as the greatest of all Negro baseball players, and (really) he handles the base with the grace and agility of Hal Chase. The stunts he pulled in monkey drill were the greatest the writer ever saw. He didn't get a hit. He was hit twice by Foster, the pitcher for the Western team, when he was up in a clutch Foster used methods well knows around here in knocking off a guy when he was in a jam. Three other times Charleston hit the ball hard but the drives were taken.

The fielding features of the game were provided by Charleston and Lundy, the Eastern shortstop

This Lundy is big league stuff. He goes far back and he goes to the left and the right and once he came in almost to the catcher, snared a bunt and threw out the runner. He didn't hit much, either, but very few of them were hitting Foster.

It has been said that Foster is big league stuff. But he isn't. He might be if he had seven men behind him and around him who never made an error and who never could make one. He was a great pitcher with a lot of stuff when he had only the batter to occupy his attention, but when a man reached base on him he seemed to become completely befuddled. Also, he displayed almost as much petulance as Earl Whitehill when the boys kicked them behind him, and they did some kicking.

HE'S CLUTCH HOME

"Mule" Suttles, the huge first baseman for the Western team is good enough to play on a lot of big-time ball clubs-the Cincinnati Reds, for instance. He's big like Ox Alexander, but he has everything in the way of speed and ability that the Ox hasn't.

Editor's note: As early as 1933, the integration issue of Major League Baseball was entertained. As both leagues, black and white, struggle to overcome the effects of the Great Depression, Bill Veeck, then president of the Chicago Cubs, had expressed a desire to revive interest in baseball.

On August 23, 1933, Syd Pollock, president of the Cuban Stars, a barnstorming semi-pro club wrote a response to Veeck's expression of boosting game appeal. In the late forties and early fifties Pollock would become better known as the owner and promoter of the Indianapolis Clowns, featuring the antics of showmen Be-Bop, Nature Boy and ex-basketball player Goose Tatum. Pollock, a white promoter, recommended placement of an entire Negro club to represent cities like Cincinnati in the National League and Boston in the American League, in hopes of initiating the integration process. Pollock's letter in full reads:

Dear Mr. Veeck

Your statement, "Major League baseball must be something drastic in order to revive interest in 1934" and "only one big league club out of 16 made money last year" has come to my attention through the press.

As owner and president of the Cuban Stars, Inc., an independent semi-pro team baseball club, which has played exhibition games throughout 32 states of the Union during the past season, defeating all opposition, including every minor league club played, may I offer one solution and the only one capable of reviving the waning interest, not only in the majors, but baseball in general.

Baseball has come to a point where semi-pro and minor league ball cannot successfully carry on financially. The majors are in the same predicament. Baseball next season will go into an additional slump if something drastic is not done about it.

My solution is simple, yet would meet with plenty of opposition from the league moguls, but only because of social pride. Social pride and prejudice must be overlooked where a business enterprise is at stake, and no one can dispute the fact that major league ball is a business. A business that furnishes sport and entertainment to an American public, and expects to be rewarded at the box office by a substantial return for the investment at stake.

Your problem can be solved by placing an entire Colored club to represent a city like Cincinnati in the National League and Boston in the American League. [That season the Cincinnati Reds finished in last place with a 58–94 record, while the Boston Red Sox finished seventh out of eight teams with a 63–86 record] Instead of these two clubs being lodged in or near a cellar berth, a real Colored aggregation would bring them into the first division and make a first place contender throughout the season.

Imagine the drawing power of a formidable Colored aggregation playing in New York, Pittsburgh, Brooklyn, Chicago, Philadelphia, St. Louis, Detroit, etc. Imagine the interest they would stimulate by their colorful playing and dash around the diamond. Imagine the increase in attendance at their home parks in Cincinnati or Boston, two spots lacking sorely in attendance figures both at home and abroad.

Babe Ruth recently stated, "The colorfulness of Negroes in baseball and their sparkling brilliancy on the field would have a tendency to increase attendance at games."

Hans Wagner, Pirate coach, stated, "the good Colored clubs play just as good baseball as seen anywhere."

Cy Perkins, Yankee coach says, "When I played for Earle Mack's All-Stars against the Homestead Grays; Vic Harris and [Oscar] Charleston would grace the roster of any big league club." He also thought that Johnny Beckwith could hit a ball harder than any man he ever saw.

One of my Cuban Stars in 1931, Tetelo Vargas, at Sioux City, Iowa, broke the world's record for circling the bases, and in either major league circuit would steal more bases during the length of a season than any two present players combined. This same player only a week prior, hit seven consecutive home runs in two days against tough semi-pro competition, yet his feats were entirely ignored by the white press. With a Colored club in either or both circuits, these feats would not go unnoticed and bring greater interest in baseball with the necessary publicity to go with it.

If there is any doubt about the ability of Colored teams, look back over the results in fall exhibitions between the pick of major league talent and the Colored clubs they played. You will find that the Colored teams won 90 per cent of these exhibition games versus all star major league lineups.

Such teams as the Cuban Stars, Inc., Homestead Grays, Pittsburgh Crawfords, Kansas City Monarchs, Chicago American Giants could today defeat either the Washington Senators or the New York Giants in a series of seven games, and yet all of these mentioned Colored clubs could be improved upon, if considered for a major league berth.

Editor's note: The Senators finished in first place with a 99-53 record. Their leading hitter was Heinie Manush, with a .336 average, and Joe Cronin, future American League president, batted .309. The Senators' 20-game winners included General Crowder at 24-15 and Earl Whitehall at 22-8.

The Giants won their league title with a 91–61 record. The Giants were led by first baseman Bill Terry's .322 average and Mel Ott's 23 home runs. Their only twenty game winner was Carl Hubbell with a 23–12 record.

The writer would be only too glad to go further into detail on the above subject, if any of your league officials should be interested. I am in position to place a real select Colored or Cuban club into the weakest spot of your circuit and can secure the foremost Colored talent in the country to play for me.

May I have your personal views on the subject by return mail.

Very truly yours,

SYD POLLOCK, president,

Cubans Stars, Inc.

First East vs. West Game, Chicago, IL

Play by Play provided by Frank A. Young, Chicago Defender

Source: *Kansas City Call,* 14 September 1933

FIRST INNING

EAST

1 Bell flies out to Davis in left field.
2 Dixon pops out to Wells on the outfield grass.
3 Charleston hits a hard liner to Morney, who makes a leaping catch for the out.
   R-0, H-0, LOB-0, E-0

WEST

1 Stearnes strikes out swinging. [First strikeout in the E/W classic]
2 Wells out on strikes, looking.
3 Davis flies out to Bell in center.
   R-0, H-0, LOB-0, E-0

SECOND INNING

EAST

1 Mackey called out on strikes.
   Jud Wilson singles to left field. [First hit of the E/W classic.]
2–3 Lundy hits into a double play, Wells to Morney to Suttles.
   [First double play of the E/W classic]
   R-0, H-1, LOB-0, E-0

SEPTEMBER 10, 1933, CHICAGO, IL

EAST	AB	R	H	D	T	HR	BI	E	TAVG	TSLG
Cool Papa Bell (Pittsburgh Crawfords), cf	5	1	0	0	0	0	0	0		
Rap Dixon (Philadelphia Stars), rf	4	2	1	0	0	0	1	0		
Oscar Charleston (Pittsburgh Crawfords), 1b	3	2	0	0	0	0	1	0		
Biz Mackey (Philadelphia Stars), c	3	0	1	0	0	0	0	0		
Josh Gibson (Pittsburgh Crawfords), c	2	0	1	0	0	0	0	1		
Jud Wilson (Philadelphia Stars), 3b	3	1	2	0	0	0	3	0		
a) Judy Johnson (Pittsburgh Crawfords), ph-3b	1	0	1	0	0	0	0	0		
Dick Lundy (Philadelphia Stars), ss	3	0	0	0	0	0	0	0		
Vic Harris (Homestead Grays), lf	1	0	0	0	0	0	0	1		
b) Fats Jenkins (New York Black Yankees), ph-lf	2	0	0	0	0	0	0	0		
John Henry Russell (Pittsburgh Crawfords), 2b	2	0	0	0	0	0	1	0		
Sam Streeter (Pittsburgh Crawfords), p	3	0	0	0	0	0	0	0		
Bertrum Hunter (Pittsburgh Crawfords), p	0	0	0	0	0	0	0	0		
George Britt (Homestead Grays), p	1	1	1	0	0	0	0	0		
Team Totals, Average & Slugging Pct.	33	7	7	0	0	0	6	2	.212	.212

a) Batted for Wilson in 8th

b) Batted for Harris in 6th

WEST	AB	R	H	D	T	HR	BI	E	TAVG	TSLG
Turkey Stearnes (Chicago American Giants), cf	5	1	2	1	0	0	1	0		
Willie Wells (Chicago American Giants), ss	4	2	2	1	0	0	1	0		
Steel Arm Davis (Chicago American Giants), lf	4	2	2	1	0	0	2	0		
Alec Radcliffe (Chicago American Giants), 3b	4	1	2	1	0	0	1	0		
Mule Suttles (Chicago American Giants), 1b	4	2	2	1	0	1	3	0		
Leroy Morney (Cleveland Giants), 2b	4	0	1	0	0	0	1	3		
Sam Bankhead (Nashville Elite Giants), rf	4	2	2	0	0	0	0	0		
Larry Brown (Chicago American Giants), c	4	0	1	0	1	0	0	0		
Willie Foster (Chicago American Giants), p	4	1	1	0	0	0	0	0		
Team Totals, Average & Slugging Pct.	37	11	15	5	1	1	9	3	.405	.676

East	000	320	002–7
West	001	303	31X–11

PITCHER/TEAM	GS	IP	H	R	ER	K	BB	WP	HB	W	L
Foster/CAG	1	9	7	7	3	4	3	0	2	1	0
Streeter/PC	1	5 1/3	8	6	6	4	0	0	0	0	1
Hunter/PC		2/3	3	2	2	0	0	0	0	0	0
Britt/HG		2	4	3	1	1	0	0	0	0	0

BB—Harris, Dixon, Lundy

DP—Wells to Morney to Suttles; Bankhead to Radcliffe; Suttles (unassisted)

HBP—Charleston (2) by Foster

LOB—West 2, East 5

SAC—Russell (2)

SB—Dixon, Charleston, Bankhead

East—Pop Lloyd (Mgr.); Coaches Nate Harris, (1b)

West—Candy Jim Taylor (Mgr.); Coaches Joe Green, Chicago Giants (1b); Jim Brown, Chicago American Giants (3b)

Umpires—Costello, Cusack, Baldwin and Stack

Attendance—19,568 Time—

Note: 1st pitch by attorney Nathan K. McGill, general counsel for the Chicago Defender, pinch-pitching for R. S. Abbott, owner and publisher of the Chicago Defender (His Rolls Royce failed to start in the rain.). His battery mate was Alderman William L. Dawson.

1 Alex Radcliffe flies out to Dixon in right field.

2 Suttles grounds out to Lundy at shortstop.

3 Morney goes down swinging at strike three.

R-0, H-0, LOB-0, E-0

THIRD INNING

EAST

Vic Harris works Foster for a walk. [First walk of the E/W classic.]

1 John Henry Russell lays down a sacrifice bunt, moving Harris to second.

2 Streeter out on strikes.

3 Bell flies out to Stearnes in center field.

R-0, H-0, LOB-1, E-0

WEST

Bankhead gets the first hit for the West squad, beating out a deep grounder to Lundy at shortstop.

1 Larry Brown bounces out to Wilson at third. Bankhead goes to second on the play.

2 Willie Foster strikes out.

Stearnes hits a single to right field, scoring Bankhead. [First RBI of the E/W classic.]

3 Stearnes out trying to steal second base, Mackey to Russell

R-1, H-2, LOB-0, E-0

Score after three innings, East 0-West 1

FOURTH INNING

EAST

Dixon walks on five pitches

Charleston is hit by pitch. Runners on first and second.

1 Mackey missed a third strike, on a hit and run. Dixon and Charleston stealing third and second, respectively

Wilson hits a grounder to Morney, who hurries his throw to the plate in unsuccessful effort to get Dixon.

Wilson goes to second on Morney's error, with Charleston also scoring.

Lundy is walked.

Cornelius starts warming up in the bullpen

V. Harris hits into a easy double play to Morney at second, but Morney fumbles ball, loading the bases for John Henry Russell.

2 Russell executes a perfect suicide squeeze play with a bunt down the first base line, with Wilson scoring.

Russell is out, Foster to Suttles.

3 Streeter bounces out, Morney to Suttles

R-3, H-0, LOB-2, E-2

WEST

Wells doubles to left field. [First double of the E/W classic]

Davis hits the first pitch to center field, scoring Wells.

1 Radcliffe fouls out to catcher Mackey

Suttles smashes a pitch to the upper deck for a two-run homer.
2 Morney flies out to Harris in left field.
3 Bankhead hits a spitter for an easy grounder to Lundy at shortstop.

R-3, H-3, LOB-0, E-0

Score after three innings, East 3-West 4

FIFTH INNING

EAST

1 Bell hits a nasty hopper to Wells at shortstop for an out.
   Dixon check-swings a slow roller in front of the plate for a single.
   Charleston is hit by a pitch for the second time
   Mackey drops a Texas leaguer into left center, filling the bases.
   Wilson slaps single to left, scoring Dixon and Charleston
2 Lundy hits a high fly to Bankhead in right field, scoring a hustle Mackey
3 Mackey is called for leaving third base too soon, on an appeal play by third baseman
   Alex Radcliffe

R-2, H-3, LOB-0, E-0

WEST

Larry Brown drills a triple over Bell's head. [First triple of the E/W classic]
1 Brown is out when he overruns third base, Bell to Lundy to Mackey.
2 Willie Foster grounds out Lundy to Charleston.
3 Stearnes grounds out Lundy to Charleston.

R-0, H-1, LOB-0, E-0

Score after five innings, East 5-West 4

SIXTH INNING

EAST

1 Harris [Jenkins] pops up to catcher Brown.
2 Russell hits a stinger to Wells for second out.
3 Streeter drives Bankhead to the right field wall for third out.

R-0, H-0, LOB-0, E-0

WEST

Wells hits a single over second.
1 Davis grounds out to Wilson at third base.
   Radcliffe doubles down left field line, scoring Wells.
Hunter into pitch for the East, as its starts to rain again
   Suttles doubles to right field, scoring Radcliffe
   Morney singles, scoring Suttles.
2 Bankhead grounds out, Lundy to Charleston
   L. Brown hits a single to right but
3 Bankhead [Morney] is out, failing to touch second base, Bell to Lundy to Russell.
   [appeal play]
   L. Brown is credited with a fielder's choice by the official scorer.

R-3, H-4, LOB-1, E-0

Score after six innings, East 5-West 7

SEVENTH INNING

EAST

1 Bell out on a third strike foul tip, held on by Brown.
2 Dixon flies out to Davis in left field
3 Charleston lines out to Stearnes in center field

R-0, H-0, LOB-0, E-0

WEST

Gibson replaces Mackey behind the plate
    Foster hits the first pitch to center for a single. [First hit by a pitcher in the E/W classic.]
Conference on mound between Lloyd, Charleston and Lundy
Britt replaces Hunter on the mound.
    Stearnes hits a double to right field, Foster holding at third.
1 Wells hits a sacrifice fly to Bell in center, scoring Foster.
    Davis doubles to right scoring Stearnes.
    Radcliffe singles to left, sending Davis to third.
    Davis scores when Harris misplays the ball.
2 Suttles goes down swinging.
3 Morney pops up to Lundy

R-3, H-4, LOB-1, E-1

Score after seven innings, East 5-West 10

EIGHTH INNING

EAST

Gibson singles over second base.
    Judy Johnson batting for Wilson, singles to center.
1 Lundy lines out to Davis in left field.
Cornelius of Cole's American Giants and Bailey of Nashville Elite Giants, start to warm up in the bull pen.
2 Jenkins grounds out to Suttles at first.
3 Russell pops out to Suttles near the dugout.

R-0, H-2, LOB-2, E-0

WEST

Bankhead hits first pitch to right for a single.
    Bankhead steals second and scores when Gibson's throw escapes Lundy and Russell.
1 Brown flies out to Jenkins in left.
2 Foster grounds to Lundy at shortstop
3 Stearnes pops up to Judy Johnson at third.

R-1, H-1, LOB-0, E-1

Score after eight innings, East 5-West 11

NINTH INNING

EAST

Britt hits a single to left field.
    Bell safe on Morney's error, Britt going to third base.

1 Dixon flies out to Stearnes in right center, scoring Britt
2 Charleston flies out to Davis, Bell scoring after the catch
3 Gibson lines out to Davis in left field for the final out.

R-2, H-1, LOB-0, E-1

Final score East-7, West-11

Editor's Note: In 1933, sacrifice flies were counted as a time "at bat," and the box score reflects this scoring rule.

1933 VOTING RESULTS: 1,039,817

P

Willie Foster	40,637
Sam Streeter	28,989
Chippy Britt	26,716
Satchel Paige	23,089
Bert Hunter	22,965
Chet Brewer	22,218
Sug Cornelius	17,530
Percy Bailey	13,400
Charles Beverly	9,733
Willie Gisentaner	4,374
Ted Trent	3,936

C

Biz Mackey	37,883
Josh Gibson	35,376
Larry Brown	23,730
T. J. Young	16,268
Frank Duncan	11,752
Tommy Dukes	8,213

1B

Oscar Charleston	43,793
Mule Suttles	35,134
George Giles	29,618
Jim West	24,140

2B

Newt Allen	39,092
John Russell	29,846
Jack Marshall	18,230
Dink Mothel	18,160

3B

Alec Radcliffe	36,712
Newt Joseph	23,600
Felton Snow	19,573

3B-1B

Jud Wilson	37,681

SS

Willie Wells	39,136
Leroy Morney	22,238
Sammy T. Hughes	7,314

OF

Turkey Stearnes	39,994
Vic Harris	28,385
Cool Papa Bell	27,934
Rap Dixon	25,715
Nat Rogers	25,194
Ted Page	23,847
Fats Jenkins	23,260
Bullet Rogan	22,488
Sam Bankhead	21,150
Steel Arm Davis	21,134
Wilson Redus	9,640

1934

The National Football League adopts an unofficial policy to ban black players from playing football, another "gentlemen's agreement" intended to secure jobs for whites during the depression. The ban lasts for 12 years.

Joe Louis wins the light-heavyweight crown in St. Louis, Missouri.

Milk costs only 22 cents a half-gallon, 10 pounds of potatoes costs 23 cents, and 29 cents would bring home the bacon. The average annual income for black tenants and laborers in the South is $278, compared to the average of $452 for whites.

Langston Hughes's first collection of short stories, "The Ways of White Folks," is published.

Destined to become a screen classic, the film *Imitation of Life,* starring Louise Beavers and Fredi Washington, debuts.

The Giants' Carl Hubbell fans five of the American League's premier hitters in a row: Babe Ruth, Lou Gehrig, Jimmie Foxx, Al Simmons, and Joe Cronin. The American League rebounds from the embarrassment by winning the all-star contest, 9–7, played at the Polo Grounds in New York.

Baseball teams from New York—the Dodgers, the Giants, and the Yankees—ban radio broadcast of games, fearing that the new technology will reduce fan attendance.

Meanwhile, Lou Gehrig produces a triple crown season with 49 HR, 165 RBI, and a .363 batting average. Dizzy Dean becomes the last man in the National League to win 30 games in a season, and Sunday baseball becomes legal in Philadelphia for the A's and the Phillies.

PAIGE'S PAGE

Despite being selected for the 1933 East-West game, Satchel Paige did not appear in uniform. In the *Pittsburgh Courier,* Paige stated: "I went to sleep on last year's game, but if the public votes me in the Eastern All-Star lineup this year, I'll be there, on time, and ready to work. I believe the East-West game is the best idea ever tried out to improve Negro baseball."[1]

Satchel Paige was the game's most dominant pitcher during the 1934 season. On his 28th birthday, July 7, the *Pittsburgh Courier* flashed the headline "Paige Hurls No-Hit Classic." Pitching against rookie Buck Leonard and the Homestead Grays, he struck out 17 batters and walked 1. Accounts of the Fourth of July game show that the Grays hit only four balls out of the infield, and one of them, a sure hit of a low line drive by Harry Williams, became simply an out with a fine catch by outfielder Vic Harris. Paige struck out the side in the first and third innings, and two batters each in the second, fourth, eighth, and ninth innings.

GREENLEE'S GREEN THUMB

One of the season's highlights was the four-team doubleheader classic between Paige's Crawfords and Stuart "Slim" Jones's Philadelphia Stars and between the Chicago American Giants and the New York Black Yankees on September 14. The league's top two pitchers faced off in what has been called by many former Negro League players the "greatest game ever played."

The four-team doubleheader was organized by all-star promoter Gus Greenlee and drew roughly 20,000 fans to Yankee Stadium. The American Giants prevailed in the first game, winning 4–3 over the Black Yankees when the Giants' Ted Trent struck out Bill Yancey with the tying and winning runs on base in the bottom of the ninth.

In the nightcap, Paige started slowly, giving up a run in the first inning when Jake Stephens walked and later scored on Dewey Creacy's single and Jud Wilson's sacrifice fly. Slim Jones held the Craws hitless until the seventh when Oscar Charleston smashed a single to center field. In the eighth inning, singles by Judy Johnson and Leroy Morney, aided by an error from right fielder Jake Dunn, let the Craws score their first and only run. After nine innings, with the score tied at one apiece, the game was called because of curfew. Jones gave up three hits and no walks, while Paige surrendered five hits and walked three. Paige and Jones entertained the fans with 12 and 9 strikeouts, respectively. The innovative idea of a four-team doubleheader would become one of the biggest attractions in Negro League baseball.

Years later, league commissioner W. Rollo Wilson wrote in his *Philadelphia Tribune* column "Thru The Eyes of . . ." that this game was "the greatest sports thrill I ever had. The opposing teams were the Philadelphia Stars and the Pittsburgh Crawfords. The pitchers were Slim Jones, rookie from Baltimore, and Satchell Paige, even then a veteran of diamond wars. The clubs were in the stretch run to decide the pennant in the N.N. League. Young Jones, skillfully handled by Bizz Mackey, the master catcher, was having one of his best days and the great Paige was also at the park." After giving a detailed account of the game, Wilson concluded, "Nobody scored in the tenth [ninth], the seven o'clock law ended the game and it was a stalemate."[2]

The successful event would be repeated on September 30 at Yankee Stadium with the same four teams. Despite the cloudy weather and threatening rain, another 20,000 fans turned out to see round two of the Paige versus Jones match-up. Famed toe tapper Bill "Bojangles" Robinson presented travel bags to Satchel and Slim before the game. Paige was the winner this time, as his Crawfords defeated Jones's Stars, 3–1. Paige struck out seven, while Jones struck out six and walked two. The Black Yankees beat the American Giants in the nightcap, 3–2.

The third time was the charm for Slim Jones. On October 12 in Washington DC at Griffith Stadium, Jones was victorious over Leroy Matlock and the Crawfords, 6–1, while the Homestead Grays defeated the New York Black Yankees, 5–2. However, less than 5,000 fans attended!

LEAGUE TITLE CONTESTED

The 1934 season ended in controversy. While the Philadelphia Stars and the Chicago American Giants battled for first place, the teams would meet in a seven-game series to determine the Negro National League Champions. The first four games were played in Chicago, with the American Giants winning three of the games. Needing one victory to clinch the title, the Giants felt secure when they traveled to Philadelphia. However, the Philly Stars swept the last three games. The Giants protested two of the wins because the games were played at night and league rules stated that no championship game should be played after dark. After league officials met, the Philadelphia Stars were named the league champions.

SCHOOLBOY ROWE

Meanwhile, in Detroit, black fans called for an apology from Detroit Tigers ace Lynwood "Schoolboy" Rowe. On August 29, Rowe had suffered a loss to the Philadelphia A's at Shibe Park. The biggest crowd of the year (33,718) had its share of black patrons. The fans came to see Rowe's attempt to eclipse the American League record held by Smokey Joe Wood, Walter "Big Train" Johnson, and Lefty Grove of 16 consecutive wins. Nonetheless, Rowe was run off the mound after 11 runs and 12 hits, in seven innings, by the hammering Athletics. Rowe later attributed his loss to "too many colored people in the grandstands. . . . They brought various objects into the park . . . to conjure up a jinx." The Arkansas pitcher later disowned the alleged slurs, saying, "I want the colored people to know that even though I'm from the South I've never made the alleged discrediting statements to any one regarding them and never will."[3]

Rowe finished the season with a 24-8 record, and his Tigers would meet Jerome "Dizzy" Dean and Paul "Daffy" Dean of the St. Louis Cardinals in the world series. Dizzy Jerome won 30 games that season, while Daffy Paul added 19 wins. The Dean brothers would win two games each to capture the world series crown in seven games.

THE DIZZY DEAN ALL-STARS

With the world series over, the Dean brothers organized some St. Louis talent to play the Kansas City Monarchs in a few pickup games for extra cash. The first game was played in Oklahoma City on October 10 but was called after the fifth inning because the fans refused to leave the field. The Dean boys were up, 4–0. The next day they traveled 160 miles to play in Wichita, Kansas, where the Dean brothers defeated the Monarchs, 8–3. Moving eastward 200 miles to Kansas City, the next day, Friday, they played at Muehlebach Field before 14,000 fans. The Monarchs, behind Andy Cooper, won this time, 7–0. Monarch catcher T. J. Young doubled and tripled in two runs off the Cardinals' 30-game winner. Dizzy Dean said, "We, meaning Paul and myself, haven't been able to fool these Monarchs with our fast balls very much. They are, on the whole, better hitters than the Detroit Tigers." Dizzy added, "Don't expect me to strike out the Monarchs. They are really a major league ball club and I might say they are also gentlemen as well as players."[4]

The next day, Saturday, after another 200-mile trip, this time north to Des Moines, Iowa, the Monarchs captured their second victory over the Dean All-Stars, 9–0. The Dean brothers never climbed the mound in the contest, playing instead with Paul in left field and Dizzy in center, before a crowd of 3,000.

After four games in four days in four different cities, they traveled 340 miles to Chicago. Before 20,000 spectators, the Monarchs defeated the Mills team (local Chicago talents) and the Dean brothers, 13–3. Although six of the eight hits came off the Dean brothers in the first four innings, the Monarchs gathered only two hits in the five remaining innings off the regular Mills pitching staff. In five days, the Monarchs and the Dean brothers had traveled 900 miles on single-lane highways in cars without air conditioning.

With six days of rest, they traveled 350 miles, resuming play on October 21 in Cleveland. Satchel Paige faced Dizzy to start the game, and the Monarchs won. Dean allowed one run and four hits in three innings. Paige struck out 13 men in six innings and allowed no hits. The Monarchs easily defeated the Cleveland Rosenblums, 4–1. The *Pittsburgh Courier* reported that 3,000 fans attended and the Deans were paid $1,500 each.

Games scheduled for October 22 in Columbus, Ohio (150 miles) and for October 23 in Pittsburgh (200 miles) were either never played or not published.

Traveling was always a tough chore in the Negro Leagues. Pittsburgh Crawfords outfielder Jimmie Crutchfield, who played in this year's game and games in 1935, 1936, and 1941, recalled the glory days: "It was July 24, 1934. The hottest day on record in Chicago, and we were playing against the Philadelphia Stars. A doubleheader in those flannels? We didn't have a dressing room, but at the end of those two games we were wet like we took a shower. And we drove all the way to Philadelphia like that. We knew that until we got to the top of the mountains that there was a place we could eat; had to send someone round back to get us some sandwiches. We took off our shirts and tied them onto the windows of the bus and drove off. You had to love the game to put up with all that. But it was love, love for the game. And we knew we were good enough to play in the majors."[5]

RACE RELATIONS

In late October, chewing gum magnate Philip K. Wrigley was named president of the Chicago Cubs. As the new executive in baseball circles, perhaps Wrigley shared an attitude unlike his fellow counterparts. Black newspaper reporters looking for a weak link in the chain of racism hoped Wrigley would offer a candid answer to questioning about apartheid in baseball. When confronted about the race issue in baseball by a *Chicago Defender* reporter, Wrigley stated, "The matter has not been brought up to me and I do not know what action I should take if it is but one thing I do know that I would not vote against such a plan." Wrigley added, "I'd perhaps leave the matter up to Landis and Heydler who are supposed to handle such general matters."[6] It seemed that Wrigley had been enlightened to give the politically correct answer for the times.

GAME REVIEWS

The East vs. West Game Is No All Star Contest

by Fay Young

Source: *Kansas City Call,* 13 July 1934

The East vs. West Negro All-Star baseball game of last year was won by the Chicago American Giants with the help of two other players, Bankhead and Morney. The latter from Columbus was guilty of a few errors which helped the East team gain some runs.

Last year all the newspaper "fell" for the East vs. West contest. Negro sport writers hammered out columns on what they believed was something to bring before the white fans as well as the Negro fans, the high caliber of baseball as played by the Negro player. White newspapers devoted some space to the game. The *Chicago Daily News* was very liberal.

After the game was over the Negro baseball writers woke up. The game was purely a commercial venture and up to this time no one has named a charity or anything else which the net proceeds went to.

In the meantime in cities where teams have made names for themselves, fans are asking why Negro players who stood high in the voting did not take part. These fans also are asking why all but two of the players were Chicago men. They are also puzzled as to how the money went to, [and] what part a daily newspaper man in Chicago and one in Pittsburgh received for their efforts to "poke the game on the public."

Fans are asking why Newt Allen, crack second sacker of the Kansas City Monarchs; George Giles, first baseman of the some club; [Charley] Beverly and Chet Brewer, [Bullet] Rogan and [Frank] Duncan, all of the same club, never appeared in the game. [When] Newt Allen's name appeared in the daily papers [it would] annoy the chosen players who would take part in the game while [because] most of the players knew that the Monarch players were not in Chicago but were in Wichita, Kansas, to play as a team.[7]

An All Star East vs. West game will help the public providing the proceeds go to aid a home for a disabled Negro ball players or some worthwhile national Negro charity. But an East vs. West game in which the votes of the public are ignored and a team thrown on the field that will "answer" the purpose, a game that is for the benefit of two promoters and their two dependent sport editors in Pittsburgh and Chicago, [is not] the East vs. West game which the public is not interested in. It becomes a strict commercial adventure, pure and simple and must by treated as such by reputable newspapers.

As a commercial adventure, it will by treated as such. We cannot go along with it in any other manner. It is just an ordinary game.[8]

Crawfords with East in Big Game

Which Means Foster and Paige Will Meet on Slab

Source: *Chicago Defender,* 21 July 1934

The Pittsburgh Crawfords, with their great array of diamond talent, will appear with the Eastern team in baseball's "Dream Game" to be played at Comiskey Park, Chicago, Sunday afternoon, August 26, while the Kansas City Monarchs will be represented with the Western group.

This far-reaching announcement was made late last week from league headquarters following a conference in Chicago between W. A. Greenlee, chairman of the Negro National League; Tom Wilson, owner of the Nashville Elite Giants, and Robert A. Cole, owner of the Chicago American Giants.

These three men from the special committee, named by the league, to arrange details for the game which last year drew thousands to the big league park located in the heart of the Windy City's South Side.

SAME AS LAST YEAR

The change in plans, which came with lighting-like suddenness, divides the strength of the sections competing for honors in the second annual diamond classic more equally, and brings the game this year back to the same basis on which the teams were selected last season.

In explaining the change, Chairman Greenlee made the following statements:

At our meeting, Mr. Cole and Mr. Wilson, who are representing the West in this set-up, claimed that the fans are demanding the appearance of the Monarchs to such an extent that we have deemed it advisable to include them in the Western set-up. Then, too, Kansas City is strictly a Western town and with the wealth of "big time" material and real diamond stars in their lineup, we feel that no East-West game would be a real success, without allowing the fans an opportunity to vote on the Monarchs.

In the East, we feel that with the Crawfords, the Phillies Stars, the Bacharachs, Newark and Baltimore a great team can be assembled.

Diamond fans will remember the comment of Wesley Ferrell after the game last year, in which he stated that several of the big-league clubs could have moved the East team in to their own ball parks with very gratifying results.

YANKS, SOUTHERN CLUBS

Continuing, Mr. Greenlee said: "In addition to the Eastern teams mentioned, fans will also be able to select their stars from the New York Black Yankees, who sent "Fats" Jenkins to the game last year at their own expense and members of the Southern league, who have a working agreement with the Negro National League.

"The Black Yankees with such stars as "Fats" Jenkins, [Bill] Holland, "Showboat" Thomas, George Scales, [Rev] Cannady, Clint Thomas, Bill Yancey and others in their line-up, are a welcome addition."

INTEREST ALREADY HIGH

Interest in the game, which looms as the greatest diamond spectacle ever observed—a spectacle which will prove to the world at large that Negroes would be "crashing" the major leagues today were it not for the color of their skin—and is rapidly mounting.

From every section of the country, inquiries and votes are beginning to pour into league headquarters, where final tabulations will be made.

Who do you think are the greatest players in the game today? Clip and fill out a coupon and mail to your most convenient color paper.

East vs. West Game Gets a Fanning

No Such Animal

by Frank A. Young

Source: *Kansas City Call,* 27 July 1934

The general impression among baseball fans is that the proposed second East vs. West Negro baseball game is not any East vs. West game at all for the simple reason there are no two leagues such as there once was in Negro baseball.

There was a time when there was an Eastern circuit in which there was Atlantic City Bacharach Giants, the Hilldale Club owned by [Ed] Bolden, Baltimore Black Sox and the Lincoln Giants which formed the nucleus of the league. The Cuban Stars and other clubs filled in. Washington [Potomacs] at one time had a berth in the league.

At the time there was a Western circuit called the Negro National League over which the late Andrew Rube Foster presided and over which he was supreme because of his ability to finance clubs and guarantee Negro ball players their salaries when club owners failed.

KANSAS CITY IN LEAGUE

This Western circuit was made up of the [Chicago] American Giants, Kansas City Monarchs, Detroit Stars, St. Louis Stars, Molina's Cuban Stars, Memphis Red Sox, Birmingham Black Barons and an eight club.

Foster "dropped" some change in trying to put a club in Toledo after a venture in Milwaukee and Columbus, Ohio, failed. Then Cincinnati was tried out and finally all were given up.

Fans all over the country panned Foster because he was both president and treasurer of the league as well as booking agent but he always contended that since the league paid him no salary he used the office of booking agency to make up for that.

The very writer who spent years trying to keep people away from Schorling's Park at Thirty-ninth and Wentworth in Chicago and who ridiculed both the leases of the park and Foster's club, at the same time paying particular attention to the White Sox Park five blocks away and the trainer of the Sox, Bill Buckner, now seeks to have the very people, the Chicago baseball fans, change about and go back to the same park.

Yo-ho, yo-ho! How times change. The knocker of Negro baseball now becomes a booster. Negro baseball teams which then drew better crowds than any of the present crowds, even out of Chicago, (with the exception of the Monarchs who are always a drawing card) were not the equal of the white baseball as long as [Charles] Comiskey sent knocker a season pass book.

Negro baseball got the same black eye during Foster's regime that it gets today—the game takes too long to be played and fans are driven away from the park because of arguments. It took five and a half hours to play a twin bill at the Chicago American Giants Park two weeks ago. The Bacharach Giants of Atlantic City were the opposing team.

Foster's league was as near a league as Negroes have been able have despite any one man's version to the contrary.

DIED A MARTYR

Foster died a martyr to Negro baseball. After his death the game deteriorated. The Kansas City Monarchs see no reason why they should be in any Negro League. Barnstorming pays better than any so-called league.

Time and time again Foster tried to get Posey and his Homestead Grays into the league. Posey and his Grays are not in the league today—he has too much brains for that. He is in the business of making money.

That there was an Eastern circuit and a Western circuit was a fact and I can make it no more explicit than when I call your attention to the theft of [Frank] Warfield and [Clint] Thomas from Detroit by an Eastern league club. Other clubs failed to recognize contracts between owners of the players and players jumped for the most cash. Players often borrowed from owners through the advanced salary deals they put over and did so with the intention of quitting the owner in question and never playing back the advance on salary or loan.

But these ball players and owners who were out to win at all cost and the adverse publicity given them in newspapers gradually cooked the goose that laid the golden egg.

Because Nat Strong who then had an office in the World Trade Building in New York wanted to and did dictate Negro and semi-pro ball in and around the confines of the great city of New York. Foster and Strong were at odds. I remember clearly the Eastern and Western magnates joint meeting in Chicago and how the first Negro World Series were formulated.

The ball players made little out of the series although the first game in Philadelphia between the Monarchs and he Hilldale Club drew 8,000 paid admission at the Philly National League park on a Friday afternoon. The commissioner's salary (I believe it was $300 each) and the expenses took up the big end of the net profits. The late Johnny Howe and myself acted as official score keepers and publicity men, he for the Eastern Circuit and I for the West. We got our expenses and that was all.

I remember [Bingo] DeMoss and several other players trudging into Binga State Bank, now closed, at Thirty-fifth and State Streets to cash a check as their proceeds from one of the World Series. Something like $69. I didn't blame the ball players for becoming discouraged. You wouldn't have either.

A REAL GAME NEEDED

Back to the East vs. West game. Let there be an all-star game but let's have it on the level. Since there is but one league, the league could take the leading club and play the stars from off the other clubs such as was done in the American Association last week. But remember, it was plainly stated that the net proceeds of that game would go into two parts, one-half into the coffers of the league treasury, and the other half to the players who staged the game. The players on the all star team were selected by popular votes of not two newspapers but all newspapers in cities where there were teams in the league.

There is any objection to the game. There IS an objection and big how when the game is simply a ball game, staged by a couple of promoters and their men "Fridays" and palmed off on respectable people would like to see more interest in Negro baseball as an all star "East vs. West" contest.

Game to Inspire Players, Plan to Aid League

by John L. Clark

Source: *Pittsburgh Courier*, 28 July 1934

The East—West game this year will follow closely the plan of the initial venture in 1933. Players will be selected by popular vote conducted through weekly and daily newspapers—

or by mailing direct to League headquarters. Several clubs, members of the Negro National League, and the Kansas City Monarchs will be the principal teams from which to select players.

All expense of promoting the game will be borne by three club owners, namely W. A. Greenlee, R. A. Cole and Tom Wilson. The promotion will be handled on the same broad scale as last year. While the chief advertising medium will be confined to weekly newspapers, outdoor, direct-mail and radio services will also be used.

There is a difference of purpose, however, for the second edition of the All-Star Negro Contest. In 1933, these same owners worked faithfully together during the entire season to revive interest in Negro baseball—and at the same time retain a nucleus for a League of baseball cubs. They blazed trails into prospective territory, traveled long distance to introduce their respective clubs and gambled against all forms of odds to extract merits and demerits of the idea and plan.

Results varied in such a degree that nothing definite could be as ascertained from the normal operations of baseball clubs. This fact brought on the East-West experiment, which cost over $5,000 before the park gates were opened on September 10th. And the net profit to each owner amounted to less than $400.

This year, with baseball interest on an upward swing, with eight clubs operating successfully in the National loop (as against three last year) the three owners have decided to again underwrite the promotion and donate ten percent of the gross receipts to the Negro National League.

Each participating player, umpire and coach will be paid a bonus, plus all expenses, and newspapers will receive an allotment of complimentary tickets. Dividing the receipts in this way will place the League in a desirable condition financially, encourage the pastime among youngsters—and give the public an opportunity to see the cream of Negro Baseball in a contest which shows the best man in each position this year and we hope, the years to follow.

All operations are directed from League headquarters in Pittsburgh by league personnel. The East—West idea, plan of promotion, selection of personnel—has the endorsement of the Commissioner. And from responses reported from all quarters, the players have also endorsed the idea.

These statements are made to explain why there had been no promise to add fake charities, as requested by some cities. League officials believe that the baseball public will better appreciate an open, vigorous effort to put Negro baseball on a higher standard then to advertise the event as sponsored by some non-existent cause.

The initial venture of the East-West game was no secret affair. Sports writers of 35 weeklies, 90 dailies were notified and invited to comment and criticism. Owners and managers of every major league club in America were accorded the same courtesy. In all these notices and every other unit of communication or advertising, the purpose of the venture was stated frankly, without falsification or unnecessary color. About 40 per cent of these communications brought replies of mixed opinions. One or two writers on weekly newspapers discouraged the idea saying that the promotion was too large; that it could not be put over without certain individuals. Writers on the daily newspapers commended the idea as the first worthwhile effort to present Negro baseball on a high class basis—which would have the effect of improving the game, generally, throughout the United States.

The promoters accepted these and other opinions as evidence of interest. Just as the are accepting current criticisms as evidences of interest. If the East-West game did not have merit, or loom as something which the public wants, that players enjoyed being a part of, or regarded with unprecedented success in 1934, there would be no occasion for the volumes of degenerated brain efforts labeled as opinions from "authorities".

The Negro National Association holds no ill will towards its critics. They are exercising a right as members of the Fourth Estate. But the League is also exercising its right to anticipate what the public wants and see that they get it. If we guess wrong, there will be no disappointed orphans, suffering families or struggling hospitals, bewailing because they did not receive something which was promised to them. Disappointment will be confined to the men who had the courage to gamble on the ides, the men who are wagering thousands of dollars that they can guess the public's wishes, baseball players' ambitions—and that the weather will be clear on August 26.

Judgment on the right and wrong of the Classic cannot be rendered by any particular writer, disgruntled club owner or opponents in other categories.

The East—West game was a big event last year. It will be a bigger event this year. All indications point to its expansion and growth.

Giants Go Wild with the Flail, Lead in Swatting

Source: *Chicago Defender*, 4 August 1934

They've released the fielding and batting average of the Negro National League for the first half of the race.

This release, the first authentic one of its kind in several years, while not complete, is based upon facts and figures and shows that the organization is functioning this season as a well-rounded unit.

WELLS LEADS HITTERS

And from the facts, as released from the office of the league secretary, some interesting revelations have been disclosed.

Willie Wells, sparkling shortstop of the Chicago club, and lauded as one of the greatest men in his position colored baseball has ever produced, is leading the hitters with a terrific games Wells has been at bat officially 25 times and garnered 13 hits. In addition to this, he sports a perfect fielding average, having accepted 53 chances without the semblance of a slip-up.

Incidentally Wells has been referred to by white sports writers as the nearest thing to Honus Wagner the diamond game has ever produced. Cum Posey rates him the greatest "money player" in the game today and fans, both East and West, who have observed his spectacular work both at bat and afield rate him as a real threat in the coming East-West game, scheduled for Comiskey Park, Chicago, Sunday, August 26.

CHICAGO HITS HARD

In addition to Wells, Chicago has six other regulars in the .400 circle, with [Jack] Marshall batting .478, Joe Lillard clouting 'em at a .455 gait, [Mule] Suttles hitting .435, [Turkey] Stearnes pasting the apple at a .417 pace, Larry Brown tuning in at .412, and [Alec] Radcliffe swinging an even .400. The club's batting average, based on nine games, is .419.

GIBSON LEADS CRAWFORDS

Josh Gibson, home-run hitter for the Pittsburgh Crawfords, and one of the leading entries for the catching berth on the East team, is leading the Crawford's array of sluggers with a mark of .369. He has also clouted six circuit blows to lead the league.

This basis, however, is compiled on 26 games. Two points behind Gibson comes Vic Harris, with a batting mark of .367, which makes him a left field threat.

Other Crawford players in the charmed circle are Judy Johnson .333; Chester Williams .319; Oscar Charleston .318; and "Cool Papa" Bell, baseball's fastest man, .304. Bell has stolen five bases to lead the speed kings.

JUD WILSON STILL AT IT

Out East the Philly Stars, present league leaders, produced only three men who could crash the .300 class. These men being Jud Wilson, who is ahead of the pack with a .384 average in 21 games; George Carr, clouting at a .375 clip; and Chaney White, the veteran, who has compiled a .333 figure.

Philadelphia, however, boasts the greatest double-play combination in the game—Stevens [Stephens] to Seay to Wilson, and all three of these men will figure prominently in the voting.

LUNDY SLOW STARTING

Figures from Newark indicate that [Buddy] Burbage is winging along at a .514 clip, with [Frank] McCoy, [Bert] Johnson [Johnston], [Paul] Arnold and [Ray] Dandridge all hitting better than .300.

[Dick] Lundy and [John] Beckwith are neither one of them in the charmed circle. Lundy is hitting .214.

Nashville's figures reveal that [Sammy T.] Hughes, the South's second base sensation, is hitting at an even .600. However, these figures reveal his work in only six games, and for this reason have not been given the credence that other figures show, in as much as Nashville played 26 games during the first half.

[Felton] Snow and [Sam] Bankhead, the latter last year's right-fielder for the Western contingent, are hitting at .480 and .471, respectively. Others hitting above .300 are [Jim] West, flashiest fielding first baseman in baseball, who is swinging along at .400; [Tommy] Dukes and [Nish] Williams, both of whom are hitting .333. The club average is .376, second only to Chicago.

Cleveland shows [Wilson] Redus, with .333, and [Pat] Patterson, .311, in the select class.

These are the figures. Is your favorite among them? You may be aided in naming your selection for the East-West game.

E-W Game Seen As Economic Boom

by John L. Clark

Source: *Pittsburgh Courier,* 18 August 1934

Much has been spoken and written about the second annual East-West game to be played at Comiskey Park, August 26. Sports critics have praised and condemned high spots and low spots of the game itself—humorously remarked about the 7–11 score and its association to one of the common gambling pastimes. The ladies continue to talk about pretty gowns, good-looking men and the like. Provincial criterion on things beyond their comprehension insist that an affair so stupendous, spectacular or idealistic should never be touched by our brothers of the sepia tint, and behind all of these opinions, one will find somewhere a smallness of character and divided racial spirit as the motivating cause.

But the plan goes on just the same and only rain or some unseen incident or accident will prevent the game from being played as scheduled.

One angle seems to be overlooked entirely. That is the economic contribution which the idea affords. There seems to be a tendency for our group (especially those claiming to have special and thorough training) to concentrate on minor factors of an idea—and totally disregard that great American principle and standard—the dollar.

Hardly a man or woman has reached voting age without realizing that one of the greatest weapons and most loyal of friends is the American dollar. Those fortunate enough to be endowed with vision and faith supported with courage to experiment with these qualities, have discovered that the dollar is the most effective tool to employ in working out these experiments. And, if they have followed this bent, there is no way to prevent them from knowing that expanded ideas require a greater number of tools than normal or contracted ones.

Now the East-West game is no small toy. It is a broad idea which extends from the lowliest baseball fan to the highest. The finished ball players who take part can only do so because thousands of readers have followed them day by day, voted their endorsements—then put away their worries and cares for one day to observe how their idols measure up to the imaginative standard. This is the human interest angle and little or no money is involved.

Approaching this angle is a picture behind the scene which only the promoters know about. The idea must be conveyed to these people. This must be done with words, pictures and other means of communication. Skilled help must be used to do this job—and this help must be paid. At present, no less than ten people are paid each week to devote time and study to the East-West game. Another ten will be added to this list in the next two days. Fifty or one hundred youngsters might be thrown into service for one week in Chicago. Forty ball players will take part in the contest, six coaches, two managers and four umpires will be added to the payroll for two or three days—all these people must be paid.

We will not assume that these people could not earn if the East-West game was not played. But it is certain that the game will increase their income.

The venture last year found over $7,000 turned over before the gates were opened. Over three-fourths of this amount passed through the hands of Negroes. From all indications the game this year will be better supported and it follows that the promotion expenses will be increased.

Seven thousand dollars is only "a drop in the bucket" for some people. But you can count all the Negroes and Negro organizations who will take the same course as the East-West promoters, with only one day, and one chance to recover the investment, on one hand.

Game Facts

by Al Monroe

Source: *Chicago Defender*, 25 August 1934

STARTING TIME—2:00 p.m. Honorary batter (Toss the first ball) Mayor Kelly, pitcher, and Attorney N. K. McGill, catcher. Probable attendance: 30,000. Officials in charge of game: Gus Greenlee, Pittsburgh and R. A. Cole, Chicago. Where played: Chicago American league baseball park, 35th and Shields. Location of park: 35th street, three blocks West of State street

"For the East, Paige and Gibson; for the West, Foster and Brown" is the announcement the umpire will make Sunday afternoon at 2:00 to start the "Baseball Classic of a Century" at Comiskey Park, 35th and Shields avenue, as a result of a nation-wide poll just completed. Paige and Foster ran far ahead of the field in their respective sections and thus become logical choices of the two managers who will direct play in this great diamond classic. A crowd of 30,000 is predicted for the game.

This year's game should be a corker, even outdistancing the battle of last season. First of all it has Satchel Paige to pit against Bill Foster in Sunday's classic and again the choice of players has been done with more care than was true of last season.

There is little choice between the two teams. Perhaps East will be given a shade because of Paige's great right arm but Bill Foster should be able to match that. Then, too, the West's second, third and fourth choices for pitchers rate above the East since [Ted] Trent, [Chet] Brewer and [Andy] Porter were voted next to Foster. To match this cast the East has Paige, [Slim] Jones of Philadelphia and [Bill] Holland of New York.

Where the West will shine will be in its infield. [George] Giles of Kansas City, [Newt] Allen of Kansas City and [Willie] Wells and [Alec] Radcliffe of Chicago form one of the truly great infields of all time. All are great fielders and hit the apple hard.

The West will likewise present a strong outfield with [Turkey] Stearnes, [Mule] Suttles who moves from first to the outer garden, [Red] Parnell and [Sam] Bankhead.

The East will not suffer from lack of player strength, however, and if you think so just read this list.

Youth triumphed over age and experience in the fans' vote for the second base position with Chester Williams, aggressive Pittsburgh Crawford keystone sacker leading Dick Seay of Philly to the tape by a count of 5,394 to 5,287 votes. Both young players are brilliant performers, but again the stickwork of Williams probably accounted for his narrow margin in the voting. [Jose] Perez, hustling Bacharach infield star and George Scales, seasoned manager of the Black Yanks won third and fourth places in the second base vote.

Jud Wilson who holds the distinction of being one of the Phillies' most versatile infielders and hardest hitters, led Judy Johnson of the Crawfords to the finish line in the race for the "hot corner" berth. [Dewey] Creacy of the Philly club was third, polling 5,009 to Wilson's 5,994 and Johnson's 5,107.

LUNDY AT SHORT

The dual race between Dick Lundy, Newark's pilot and peppery Jake Stevens [Stephens] of Philly at shortstop ended up with Lundy polling 5,515 and Stevens [Stephens] receiving, 4,810. Both shortstops have been playing a whale of a game and the letters coming from the fans indicated that Lundy's ability to hit harder than Steve although no more consistently, gave the Newark manager a margin.

Climaxing one of the most significant polls in baseball history, a mighty team of super diamond stars, upon whose sinewy arms and agile legs will rest the ardent hopes of the East, evolved here Saturday as the final tabulation of ballots for the East—West game was completed.

PAIGE GETS HIGHEST VOTE

Leading the parade of ballots after an avalanche of votes following his brilliant pitching which won for the House of David Denver's "Little World Series," Satchel Paige won the distinction of receiving the highest number of markers. The sensational Paige polled 6,948 votes, with "Slim" Jones running second with 4,877. Bill Holland of the Black Yankees, [Harry] Kincannon of the Craws and [Bob] Evans of Newark held third, fourth and fifth positions in the final count.

CATCHER'S RACE CLOSE

Only the batting ability of the hard-hitting Josh Gibson is believed to be the factor which drew a slight margin for Gibson over his two close rivals, [John] Hayes of Newark and [Robert] Clarke of the Yanks. This three-cornered race, which was not definitely settled until the final count, showed Gibson with 5,496, Hayes with 5,301 and Clarke with 5,010.

THOMAS, CHARLESTON CLASH

Opinion was sharply divided on the first-base position with countless Eastern fans pulling for [David] "Showboat" Thomas. A larger number, however sent in votes for Oscar Charleston with the result that the veteran manager of the Crawfords and still one of the greatest batters in the game today was accorded the largest vote for the job. Both Thomas and Charleston are colorful fielders on the initial sack, but is apparent that Charleston's great hitting ability won him the nod of the fans.

Hawkins Picks Argument over East-West Voting

by Dave Hawkins

Source: *Chicago Defender,* 25 August 1934

Pittsburgh, Pa., Aug. 24— Knowing that he who attempts to prophesy the pitching potions of an East-West All-Star game, is without honor in his own country. Down and around all the local thoroughfares here, the curbstone counselors and pavement preachers are slipping me such dubious distinctions as the Punk and Peerless Picker. Such awards as the exclusive fishing rights of the Sahara desert have already been suggested for me. All of it sounds sinister and screwy to yours here and if my analysis serves me right, me thinks they mean I am plain phttt when it comes to knowing who can pitch. Here and there I do find a lone and loyal supporter of my last week's pitching selections but there is now so much anti-Hawkins sentiment permeating here, he does so at great risk of sudden physical obliteration. In the face of this great adversity, I press forward with my typewriter and portable erasure and again herewith send other parts of my team selections, this time the infields.

From the voting of the West team catchers the fans are either voting backwards or my aunt is my she-uncle. The tabulations now show the game's greatest backstop, [T. J.] Young of the K.C. Monarchs, running so far behind he looks like the tall light on caboose. Here goes my tally to a great guy, a marvelous athlete and a lost cause.

Another one I am giving here for which I'll have to beg your permission to stray from the herd, is [George] McAllister of the Cleveland Red Sox, my choice for the All-Star West team's first-base burden. Nothing flashy about him, but the first ball you see him miss bring it to me with a little barbecue sauce and I'll eat it. He is truly the Joe Judge of the Race and plenty good enough for this one vote I am herewith shoving to yes.

Somewhere on any team there has got to be brains in abundance. I always though second sack was the ideal cerebral center. Smart men like Eddie Collins, Nap Lajoie and Bing DeMoss hung around there and directed things. Mothel of the K.C. Monarchs comes as close to those guys as any second baseman of today. If you catch him pulling any boners, come take all of me, but while you are taking, take this marker for Mothel.

Times before I've said, "Willie Wells" is the Shakespeare of the shortstops, and he still is. Wells and Mothel would make more double plays than a crooked wife. His band wagon is already loaded and here goes one more piling on for Wells.

There isn't anything in the West close to Radcliffe for third base. He is running like a hungry horse to a hay rack and his nearest competitor is as lonesome as a capitalist in Soviet. Here, Rad, I am slipping you one.

Here, Mr. Editor, we observe the customary pause to denote a changeover to Eastern teams. This I trust can be accomplished without the annoyance of the usual editorial interruptions.

Of one of the East team catchers it can be said that there are none better (apologies to Mr. Bernie) than the great Gosh Gibson of the Crawfords, nay should those teams feel a bit abashed over this, because Mr. Gibson is also about the best all-around backstopping man on any team anywhere any of these times. At bat he hits with the fury of an avenging hater, a free swinger and when he contacts they fall to earth we know not where. Giving him this vote of mine is like donating Mr. Rockefeller a dime.

Most fans I am sure, disapprove so many stars from the same team getting into the All-Star line-up, but this first base tangle seems inevitably to send at least one more Crawford workman to do toil on Comiskey soil. From the voting, the difference between [Oscar] Charleston of the Crawfords and [David] Thomas of the Yanks is thinner than a late husband's alibi. The thing looks like a toss up, but age comes before beauty and I thus tender this tally to brother Oscar Charleston, a ball player than whom time and tide has seen no greater.

I see a lot of people are picking over George Scales to find a second baseman of the All-Star game. To me this seems contrary to the better judgment, the Constitution and the proposition that all men are created equal and without clothes on. Looking over Scales to go find a second sacker is like leaving the Niagara to go find a drink. Down on second base he will be one man who can hang on to Josh Gibson's lightning fire peg and tag out flying base runners.

Most of the fans are looking for Dick Lundy to be back in shortstop place at Comiskey field when the umpire whisk-brooms home plate a beauty treatment and calls play ball for the All-Star game. Here is the Old Man River of Negro baseball, has played with and against the best and goes on and on. Fearless and fast and they say he could catch a hot rivet. He and Scales ought to work together like words and music. I stop short here to give my shortstop vote to the grand old man.

At third base I'm in stormy weather and can't get my poor self together. Jud Wilson and Judy Johnson are so close together they look like Siamese in Shanghai. I am between opinions but can't figure out how I am going to get an opinion between them, they are that close and that good. In either case which ever lands in the All-Star game, there will be a whole team playing third base. So I am, for lack of a better way, using the old efficient "Eenie, meenie, minie, moe," catch a gentleman by his largest pedal exterior digit or just plain toe, and if he protest, vociferously, release him go" system. I thus find myself voting for Mr. Jud Wilson with apologies to Judy the Johnson, of Gus (The Great Gusto) Greenlee's Crawfords.

In instances here I have dared to differ with opinion of the greatest number, for this unpardonable sin, and others, I will no doubt get the old bird feathers and all-fowl play if you catch my drift. It's fortunate I don't have to be an artist to draw a conclusion. So here it is leaving you 'til next Saturday, the day before the big All-Star game, at which time I will stick back in again with my final selections—those of the outfields.

Editor's note: Unfortunately, Hawkins's scouting report never appeared in subsequent issues of the *Chicago Defender.*

"Satch" Stop "Big Bad Men" of West Team

by William G. Nunn

Source: *Pittsburgh Courier,* 1 September 1934

We saw a baseball epic unfold itself on this historic field this afternoon.

No diamond masterpiece was this game. No baseball classic. Those words are relegated into the limbo of forgotten things in describing the titanic struggle for supremacy which marked the second meeting of the baseball cream of the East won 1–0 and evened up the series.

And Satchel Paige, pitching sensation of the Pittsburgh Crawfords, "stole the show".

NO GREATER EPITAPH

No greater epitaph can ever be written about the man who ambled to the pitching knoll in the sixth inning here this afternoon, with 25,000 wild-eyed fans on the edge of their seats, with a man on second and none out—retired the side while that man fiddled nervously around the keystone station, and then went on to give one of the greatest mound exhibitions modern baseball has ever seen as he twirling three more scoreless innings to enable the East to chalk up their first victory.

Today's game was more than a masterpiece! It was more than a classic! It was really and truly a diamond eye!

SPECTACULAR SETTING

The facts of the game will be covered by others. This article is a paean of praise to the "man who stole the show" and to the marvelous performances of those diamond stars of sun—tan hue, who once again demonstrated to the world at large that they are on a par with major—league performers. For those two teams reeled off a "once—in—a lifetime" performance.

Close your eyes if you can for a moment. Comiskey Park, situated on the Southside is a natural amphitheater. the double—decked grandstand extends to the far reaches of right—center and left—center field. Only in deep center are bleacher seats.

Sunday was one of those perfect baseball days. Not a cloud in the sky to mar the perfect azure—blue of the heavens. The greensward of Comiskey Park, with the basepaths, the infielder's territory and the pitcher's mound bared, made of the playing field a thing of beauty.

And the lower tier, as far as the eye could reach in all directions, packed with thousands and thousands of people, who came to see the game. The official attendance was 20,882. Figures from the gate, however, informed us that more than 25,000 fans were on hand to witness the game. Of that number, more than 4,000 were white. And this was the setting.

JONES AND TRENT

Dick Lundy, one of Negro baseball's immortals was playing manager for the East, while Dave Malarcher, whose American Giants won the first half of the N.N. League pennant race ran the destinies of the Westerners.

The game started with Stewart [Stuart] Jones, 20-year-old southpaw "ace" of the Philly Stars pitted against Trent of the Kay See Monarchs [sic, Chicago American Giants], one of the greatest twirlers the far West has ever developed.

Jones was in trouble in the second inning, with men on second and third and none out, but he fanned Bankhead, forced Suttles [sic, Brown] to hit to Jud Wilson, who threw out Suttles as the latter attempted to score, and Hughes went out, Wilson to Charleston.

CRUTCHFIELD'S GREAT THROW

Again in the fourth inning, when Chet Brewer and Kincannon went to the mound, the East was in the "danger zone". With one out, Suttles hit a high fly into short center field, and got a triple, when Chet Williams somersaulted in trying to catch the ball. Parnell hit a high fly to Crutchfield in right field, who threw a perfect strike across home plate to nip Suttles, trying once again to score. It was a great throw and drew thunderous applause.

GIBSON'S GREAT ARM

Fans received another thrill in the fifth inning, when Bankhead, Nashville speed demon, singled to third base. On the next pitch, Josh Gibson, who is looming as a truly great receiver, fumbled the ball. Bankhead lit out for second. Gibson pounced on the ball, and threw to Lundy for one of the feature plays of the game. No one but a Gibson could have thrown Bankhead out, and no shortstop but a Lundy could have completed the play.

SATCHEL TO THE RESCUE

Kincannon had been in hot water by the fourth and fifth, while Brewer was coasting smoothly along.

Then came the sixth, the exit of Kincannon and the dramatic entrance of the one and only Satchel. It was drama, stark and commanding! It was the perfect entrance for a great twirler. and satchel lived up to his reputation.

Willie Wells, first man up in this inning, stretched his hit to a double by a fine burst of speed. Lundy called for Paige with the West's wrecking crew looking formidable.

Satchel threw away exactly eleven balls as he struck out Radcliffe and forced Stearnes and Suttles to fly out to left field. Vic Harris making a great running catch on the left field foul line of Suttles dangerous looking bid.

In the last four innings, Paige struck out five men as his blinding fast ball cut the center of the plate, flirted with the corners and set the fans in a frenzy. No "playing" Satchel was out there today. There was a prayer behind every pill as it burned through the ozone by the way into the big mitts of Gibson and Perkins who worked be last two innings.

SCORE ON FOSTER

And it was not until the eighth inning that the row of goose-eggs on the electric score-board in right-center was broken.

In that inning, "Cool Papa" Bell, the fastest man in baseball—bar none—walked as Foster temporarily lost control. That was Willie's undoing, Perkins, who had taken Crutch-field's position in the batting order, struck out, while Bell stole second, arriving ahead of the throw.

Charleston lined out to Mule Suttles. Then with two strikes on him, Jud Wilson, one of the game's most dangerous hitters hit a looping angle over second. It was a hit, but Willie Wells and Hughes both went for it. They broke the ball down, but it rolled a few feet away. Before it could be recovered, Bell, who had set full steam ahead crossed home plate with the all—important marker.

"NO GREATER PITCHER"

No greater pitcher ever performed at Comiskey Park than did the Satchel Paige of Sunday.

Old time patrons of this park, who have seen the burning speed of Walter Johnson, Ed Walsh, Smoky Joe Wood, Lefty Grove, Rube Waddell, Schoolboy Rowe, and other American League immortals, and have witnessed the curves and brainy twirling of such unforgettable as Addie Joss, Russell Ford, and Will Bill Sullivan, will readily concede the fact.

Paige today was unbeatable, and listed, as he was, with that brilliant array of baseball's best surrounding him, his domination was all the more impressive.

Trent and Brewer both twirled masterful ball. They rank with the greats, also, and could well grace the payroll of any big league club.

And so, in closing, we repeat the words of John Henry "Pop" Lloyd, who chuckled in his lounging chair at the Grand Hotel this evening, and said; "Remember what I told you last year. You can't beat unbeatable pitching."

Willie Foster Loses Contest to S. Paige

J. Bell Steals Second, then Scores

by Al Monroe

Source: *Chicago Defender,* 1 September 1934

The largest crowd of fans ever to witness a baseball game between Race teams, 30,000, saw the East defeat the West, 1–0, and even the score in games in the annual East-West classic at Comiskey Park last Sunday. All told six pitchers were used, evenly divided, and they allowed just fifteen hits between them, seven for the losers and eight for the East. Contrary to the dope, neither star twirler, Paige for the East or Foster for the West, started the game, the East sending [Slim] Jones of Philadelphia to pitch the first three frames while [Ted] Trent of Chicago was entrusted with the opening burden for the West, and they pitched great ball. Jones was in trouble in the very first frame when after walking [Willie] Wells, the lead-off man, he committed a balk to send the West's short fielder to second with one out. That was merely a signal for better pitching however and the next three men were helpless in their attempt to score the pesky Wells.

KINCANNON IS NEXT

Following Jones on the mound was [Harry] Kincannon, right handed flinger with the Pittsburgh Crawfords. To counter this change, Manager [Dave] Malarcher sent [Chet] Brewer of Kansas City to the mound. And from this point on this pair attempted to carry on for their departed brothers and Brewer succeeded — Kincannon didn't or at least Lundy was afraid he wouldn't. Brewer allowed just two hits while on the mound and was never in real danger during this three frames on the mound. On the other hand, Kincannon had some trouble and in the 6th after Wells opened with a double, Lundy called his ace, Satchel Paige, in. Paige didn't take long to get down to work, fanning Radcliffe and making Stearnes and Suttles fly out to left field.

FOSTER ENTERS

When the seventh inning opened Malarcher sent Willie Foster to the mound and just as many feared it was Bill's inability to match the pitching of Paige that gave the East its victory. Only a great play by Wells saved Bill on the first play and then after two were out, Wilson singled but nothing came of the drive because of Radcliffe's great play on Paige's smash.

When Paige entered the game with the score tied the West held out little hope for victory. They were hoping that Foster would keep the East's hits down, but felt that Paige would keep things in check until either darkness or the Eastern bats arrived. Well, the bats arrived first, and coupled with a walk by Foster, a theft of second by Bell brought the bacon home for the visitors.

The game was outstanding in many respects. There was a colorful crowd on hand, cheering wildly as the players went about their work of performing the near impossible on the field.

As for honors they were about evenly divided. Paige, Jones, Brewer and Trent stood out as flingers. Wells, Lundy and Crutchfield were the fielding demons while slugging honors go to Suttles, Chester Williams and Jud Wilson.

The game drew people from all sections. From the South came officials of the Southern League; from the East the powers that be of Eastern baseball and then there were just fans from all sections. You've never seen anything like the gathering assembled at Sox Park when Trent tossed the first pitch to Bell, opening the game.

AUGUST 26, 1934, CHICAGO, IL

EAST	AB	R	H	D	T	HR	BI	E	TAVG	TSLG
Cool Papa Bell (Pittsburgh Crawfords), cf	3	1	0	0	0	0	0	0		
Jimmie Crutchfield (Pittsburgh Crawfords), rf	3	0	0	0	0	0	0	0		
Cy Perkins (Pittsburgh Crawfords), c	1	0	0	0	0	0	0	0		
Oscar Charleston (Pittsburgh Crawfords), 1b	4	0	0	0	0	0	0	1		
Jud Wilson (Philadelphia Stars), 3b	3	0	1	0	0	0	1	0		
Josh Gibson (Pittsburgh Crawfords), c-lf	4	0	2	1	0	0	0	0		
Vic Harris (Pittsburgh Crawfords), lf	2	0	1	0	0	0	0	0		
Rap Dixon (Pittsburgh Crawfords), lf	2	0	1	0	0	0	0	0		
Dick Lundy (Newark Dodgers), ss	4	0	0	0	0	0	0	0		
Chester Williams (Pittsburgh Crawfords), 2b	4	0	3	1	0	0	0	0		
Slim Jones (Philadelphia Stars), p	1	0	0	0	0	0	0	0		
Harry Kincannon (Pittsburgh Crawfords), p	1	0	0	0	0	0	0	0		
Satchel Paige (Pittsburgh Crawfords), p	2	0	0	0	0	0	0	0		
Team Totals, Average & Slugging Pct.	34	1	8	2	0	0	1	1	.235	.294

WEST	AB	R	H	D	T	HR	BI	E	TAVG	TSLG
Willie Wells (Chicago American Giants), ss	3	0	1	1	0	0	0	0		
Alec Radcliffe (Chicago American Giants), 3b	4	0	0	0	0	0	0	0		
Turkey Stearnes (Chicago American Giants), cf	4	0	0	0	0	0	0	0		
Mule Suttles (Chicago American Giants), 1b	4	0	3	0	1	0	0	1		
a) Malvin Powell (Chicago American Giants), pr	0	0	0	0	0	0	0	0		
Red Parnell (Nashville Elite Giants), lf	4	0	0	0	0	0	0	0		
Sam Bankhead (Nashville Elite Giants), rf	3	0	1	0	0	0	0	0		
Larry Brown (Chicago American Giants), c	3	0	1	0	0	0	0	0		
Sammy T. Hughes (Nashville Elite Giants), 2b	2	0	0	0	0	0	0	0		
Andy Patterson (Cleveland Red Sox), 2b	1	0	0	0	0	0	0	0		
Ted Trent (Chicago American Giants), p	1	0	0	0	0	0	0	0		
Chet Brewer (Kansas City Monarchs), p	1	0	0	0	0	0	0	0		
Willie Foster (Chicago American Giants), p	1	0	1	0	0	0	0	0		
Team Totals, Average & Slugging Pct.	31	0	7	1	1	0	0	1	.226	.323

a) Ran for Suttles in 9th

East	000	000	010-1
West	000	000	000-0

PITCHER/TEAM	GS	IP	H	R	ER	K	BB	WP	HB	W	L
S. Jones/PS	1	3	1	0	0	4	1	1	0	0	0
Kincannon/PC		2	4	0	0	0	0	0	0	0	0
Paige/PC		4	2	0	0	5	0	0	0	1	0
Trent/CAG	1	3	2	0	0	3	0	0	0	0	0
Brewer/KCM		3	2	0	0	2	1	0	0	0	0
Foster/CAG		3	4	1	1	2	1	0	0	0	1

BALK—S. Jones
BB—Wells, Wilson, Bell
DP—Crutchfield to Gibson; Williams to Charleston
LOB—East 8, West 5
SB—Bell

East—Dick Lundy (Mgr.); Coaches
West—Dave Malarcher (Mgr.); Coaches
Umpires—
Attendance—30,000   Time—

1934 VOTING RESULTS: 1,270,773

P		
Willie Foster	48,957	
Chet Brewer	48,356	
Ted Trent	47,870	
Andy Porter	46,908	
Sug Cornelius	45,853	
Malvin Powell	26,980	
Big Jim Reese	15,689	
Satchel Paige	6,948	
Slim Jones	4,877	
Bill Holland	4,101	
Harry Kincannon	3,776	
Chin Evans	3,485	
Chippy Britt	3,216	
Bert Hunter	3,104	
Darltie Cooper	2,903	
William Bell	2,502	
Leroy Matlock	1,937	
Sam Streeter	1,927	
Burnalle Hayes	1,877	
Joe "Baby Face" Strong	1,278	
Lou Dula	1,201	

P-RF

Jesse Hubbard	5,375

C

Larry Brown	43,965
Tommy Dukes	27,324
Frank Duncan	19,785
Josh Gibson	5,496
Johnny Hayes	5,301
Eggie Clarke	5,010
Cy Perkins	4,998
William "Mickey" Casey	3,919
John Beckwith	1,202

1B

Mule Suttles	41,800
George Giles	40,976
Jim West	21,879
George McAllister	15,097
Popeye Harris	8,385
Oscar Charleston	6,334
Showboat Thomas	5,013
Jud Wilson	4,730
C. Harris	3,091
Zack Clayton	2,942
Buck Leonard	2,011

2B

Newt Allen	40,118
Sammy T. Hughes	37,508
Jack Marshall	29,508
Dink Mothel	21,786
Dickie Seay	5,287
Jose Perez	4,128
George Scales	3,079
Subby Byas	2,008

2B-SS

Ches Williams	10,186

3B

Alec Radcliffe	42,876
Felton Snow	31,568
Newt Joseph	22,987
Jud Wilson	5,994
Judy Johnson	5,107
Dewey Creacy	5,009
Ray Dandridge	4,926
Rev Cannady	3,113

SS

Willie Wells	48,546
Hoss Walker	36,789
Jelly Jackson	21,789
Richard Lundy	5,515
Jake Stephens	4,810
Bill Yancey	4,316
Jake Dunn	3,982
Leroy Morney	3,893
Obie Lackey	2,949

OF

Turkey Stearnes	47,367
Red Parnell	47,157
Sam Bankhead	40,795
Bill Wright	33,865
Joe Lillard	31,975
Big Train Parker	27,739
Jake Dunn	13,223
Chaney White	10,291
Cool Papa Bell	5,912
Jimmie Crutchfield	5,871
Rap Dixon	5,795
Vic Harris	5,446
Fats Jenkins	5,402
Buddy Burbage	4,893
Ed Stone	4,719

1935

Educator Mary McLeod Bethune becomes the first president of the National Council of Negro Women. George Gershwin's black folk opera *Porgy and Bess* debuts in New York City at the Alvin Theatre.

Milk costs 23 cents a half-gallon, 10 pounds of potatoes costs 19 cents, and 41 cents would bring home the bacon. A loaf of bread costs 8 cents.

The first Negro Labor Conference, in Harlem, calls for a 30-hour work week.

John Henry Lewis, promoted by Pittsburgh Crawfords owner Gus Greenlee, becomes the first black boxer to win the light-heavyweight title.

The American League wins its third straight all-star contest behind Jimmie Foxx's two-run homer, 4–1.

The bullpen is created to warm up relief pitchers.

The first major league night game is played at Crosley Field in Cincinnati. President Roosevelt pushes a button in the White House to light up the stadium.

LEAGUE BUSINESS

At the January 12 Negro National Association board meeting, Alex Pompez was granted a franchise for his New York Cuban team by commissioner W. Rollo Wilson; the move was approved by team owners. With Pompez's prior experience as one of the founders of the 1923 Eastern Colored League and as an owner of a team in the ill-fated 1929 American Negro League and the 1932 East-West League, his credentials were impressive. The city of New York would now have two black teams, the Brooklyn Eagles, owned by Abe and Effa Manley, playing at Ebbets Field, and Pompez's Cubans, playing at the newly refurbished Dyckman Oval. The Oval, located between Nagle Avenue and Academy Street near the Harlem Ship Canal, featured a new press box and rain protection for grandstand patrons.

However, Kermit Jackson of Philadelphia and Clemmon Mack of Boston were refused franchises. With the presence of the Philly Stars, league officials did not feel the City of Brotherly Love could support two black teams. League officials also thought Boston was "too far removed from the circuit."[1]

On March 14, in Philadelphia, new officers were elected to the National Association of Negro Baseball Clubs. Gus Greenlee was reelected chairman and New Yorker Ferdinand Q. Morton was named commissioner, succeeding Rollo Wilson. The selection of umpires for the upcoming season was a priority on the agenda. Twenty-four applications were received, with the eight umpires gathering the highest votes being hired.[2]

THE NEW YORK CUBANS: AN ALL-STAR TEAM?

After spending the last three years in the Venezuela League, future Hall of Famer Martin Dihigo was encouraged by Pompez to become player-manager. Frank Forbes was named business manager. With Frank Duncan at catcher (one all-star appearance), Dick Lundy at short (two all-star appearances), and the addition of power hitters Cristobal Torrienti, Lazaro "Cuban Peach" Salazar, and Alejandro Oms (one all-star appearance) to the outfield, the New York Cubans presented a powerful offensive lineup. The Cubans signed pitchers Luis "Señor Skinny" Tiant Sr. (three all-star appearances), who had the best pick-off move in the land, and Johnny "Schoolboy" Taylor (one all-star appearance), the high school wonder from Hartford, Connecticut, who later beat Satchel Paige with a no-hitter. Added to the mix was the legendary Dominican catcher Enrique Lantiqua and the superb fielding shortstop Horacio "Rabbit" Martinez.

In essence, Alex Pompez had created his own all-star team. This team had ten players—Ramon Bragana, Dihigo, Rudolfo Fernandez, Manuel Garcia, Lantiqua, Cando Lopez, Martinez, Oms, Salazar, Torrienti, and Tiant—who would later be elected to the Puerto Rican, Cuban, Dominican, Mexican, or Cooperstown Hall of Fames.

The players' rankings in the voting for the all-star game indicated their value. Luis Tiant received more votes than any pitcher in the league, while Alex Oms ranked second behind Fats Jenkins in votes for left fielders. Mr. Versatility, Martin Dihigo, was the top vote getter of all players. Over the years, much ink has been printed about the talented 1935 Pittsburgh Crawfords, and deservingly so. However, recognition is also due the multicultural New York Cubans, who had some of the most talented ballplayers on earth.

The Cubans won the second-half pennant by defeating the Philadelphia Stars in a doubleheader, 5–1 and 8–6. The Cubans would meet the first-half winners, the Pittsburgh Crawfords, for the league championship on Friday the 13th at Dyckman Oval. The Crawfords featured five future Hall of Famers in Oscar Charleston, Satchel Paige, Cool Papa Bell, Josh Gibson, and Judy Johnson. The Craws also had potential Hall of Famers in shortstop Sam Bankhead and outfielder Jimmie Crutchfield.

The Cuban congregation won the first two games behind the strong pitching of Americans Frank Blake and Neck Stanley. The Craws came back to win game three as Leroy Matlock shut out the Cubans. In game four, the Cubans went with their ace Martin Dihigo to capture their third victory. The Crawfords came right back with their second win to stay alive for the crown drive. Game six was played on neutral soil in Philadelphia, with the Craws winning 7–6, tying the series. The deciding seventh game between black baseball's top talents saw Senior Tiant and his Cuban stars leading 7–5 after seven innings. However, Tiant tired in the next inning, allowing back-to-back home runs by Gibson and Charleston. With the game tied seven-all, Cool Papa Bell singled in Sammy Bankhead for the winning run and the title. This year's edition of the Pittsburgh Crawfords has been called by many baseball historians the greatest Negro League team ever and has often been compared to the 1927 Yankees. Regardless, they struggled to beat baseball's all-star contingent of mostly Latin Americans.

Although the "Latins from Manhattan" (as called by the New York press) lost the series, they later hosted a doubleheader at Dyckman Oval against the Babe Ruth All-Stars before a sold-out crowd of roughly 10,000 fans. Playing first base, Ruth touched Luis Tiant for a double in the first inning. But that was it! Tiant shut down the Babe Ruth All-Stars on four hits, as the Cubans won, 6–1. The second game was no contest as the Cubans romped to a 15–5 victory. The recently retired "Bambino," 40 years old at the time of the game, got one hit in five at bats during the series.[3]

10. Twenty years before Jackie Robinson signed a Brooklyn Dodgers contract, interracial teams were not uncommon outside of the major leagues. Repeat winners of the Denver Post Tournament were the Bismarck club from North Dakota. Back row, left to right: Hilton Smith, Red Haley, Barney Morris, Satchel Paige, Moose Johnson, Quincy Trouppe, and Ted "Double Duty" Radcliffe. Front row, left to right: Joe Desiderato, Leary, owner Neil Churchill, Oberholzer, and Hendee. Besides the African-Americans, the rainbow coalition included a Cuban, a Jew, a Lithuanian, an Italian, an Irishman, and a Swede. The all-black Claybrook Tigers from Arkansas finished a distant second. Courtesy of NoirTech Research, Inc.

THE SATCHEL PAIGE SAGA

The year saw the return of Satchel Paige to the Bismarck Tournament in North Dakota, playing for the Jamestown team. Earlier, in 1933, automobile dealer and Bismarck mayor Neil Churchill sought the services of Paige in an effort to secure state bragging rights. He had wired Crawford owner Gus Greenlee to meet him in Chicago and offered him $15,000 for Paige's services.[4] While baseball teams in North Dakota had been integrated for several years, fair housing was still a problem. Paige and his new bride, the former Janet Howard (a waitress at the Crawford Grill), were denied lodgings and had to live in Churchill's abandoned railroad bunk car.

Churchill also added Monarchs catcher Quincy T. Trouppe, an East-West participant in eight games, to complete a very competitive battery. In July, Churchill signed ace pitcher Hilton Smith, who appeared in seven all-star games, and Ted "Double Duty" Radcliffe, who made six all-star appearances. Churchill later added two-time East-West pitcher Chet Brewer for the seven-game National Semi-Professional Tournament, held in Wichita, Kansas. Other ethnic players for Bismarck included a Cuban first baseman, a Jewish second baseman, a Lithuanian shortstop, an Italian third baseman, an Irishman in left field, a Swede in center field, and a German in right field.[5]

Churchill's team won all seven games in the tournament, with Paige capturing four wins. He struck out a tournament record of 64 batters. For his performance, Churchill presented Paige with a new roadster.

After the championship game, the Bismarck team played a hodgepodge of teams around Colorado and Kansas through the Labor Day weekend. Afterward, they traveled to Kansas City to face the Monarchs. With Paige pitching to Radcliffe, the North Dakota team won handily, 8–4, as Paige struck out 15 of his future teammates.

DEAN REMATCH

The game in Kansas City was a rematch of the previous year's Dean and Paige tour of the Midwest. While the Detroit Tigers were losing to the Chicago Cubs in the fifth game of the major league world series, 2,000 shivering baseball fanatics witnessed a return of the Dean brothers to Kansas City. The single-game match was one to remember. Satchel Paige pitched the full nine innings, striking out 11 batters and walking 4. Dizzy Dean hurled one inning, the fourth, while his brother, Paul, pitched the fifth and sixth innings. The Deans had one strikeout between them. St. Louis Cardinals pitcher Mike Ryba held the Monarchs scoreless on three hits in the first three frames.

The one score of the game came in the third inning when Earl Clark led off with a single to left field. Dutch Siebold, former Kansas City Blues catcher, hit a hot hopper to Willard Brown at shortstop. Brown made the stop and released an errant throw to first base, instead of second base, with both men safe. Ralph Michaels's sacrifice bunt put Clark and Siebold on second and third. The great showman himself Dizzy Dean was up next. He delivered a sacrifice fly to left fielder Henry Milton, scoring the lone tally that would win the ball game for the Dean brothers.[6]

These types of exhibition games gave hope to the black community that some day their ebony stars would perform at the major league level. Dean sung the players' praises, raising expectations by saying that if "big leaguers believed that they were better than the best Negro players they had another thought coming." False optimism was at a premium when Dean suggested organizing an "All Star Sepia Club to go barnstorming and show the Nordics something."[7]

ROWE REVISITED

Detroit pitcher Schoolboy Rowe (with a won-lost record of 19-13)—who faced allegations that he claimed that black fans in Philadelphia spooked him during his effort to set a record of 17 consecutive victories—organized an all-star crew, including teammates Tommy "Tiger" Bridges (21-10) and world series MVP Charlie Gehringer, who hit .330 during the season. Rowe also added minor leaguers Morton and Walker Cooper to his club.

On October 13, about 3,000 fans braved the steady drizzle of liquid sunshine at Muehlebach Field in Kansas City to attend the interracial game between Rowe's club and the Monarchs. General admission tickets were 50 cents, with children's fare a quarter. Joe Bowman (7-10), from the Philadelphia Phillies, pitched the first four innings, yielding four runs and seven hits. Schoolboy Rowe entered the game in the fifth inning amid cheers, not boos, and was promptly greeted by Newt Allen with a single to right field. Later, an outfield fly and throwing error by Rowe on Leroy Taylor's tapper to the mound pushed Allen to third base, with Taylor going to second. The Monarchs' T. J. Young hit another slow roller to Rowe, and Allen was caught in a rundown for the second out of the inning. Unaccustomed to the up-tempo style of Negro League play, the Rowe All-Stars began whipping the ball around the field in celebration of the out, giving Taylor the opportunity to steal home for the fifth run.

Rowe pitched one more inning before yielding to Tommy Bridges and his famous curve ball. Bridges gave up one unearned run on two hits in two innings of work. Bridges and Rowe struck out two batters each.

11. The 1935-36 Puerto Rican All-Stars. Getting ready to leave for Puerto Rico are three future Hall of Famers: Leon Day, Ray Dandridge, and Buck Leonard. Top row, left to right: Ed Stone, Slim Jones, Ray Brown, Rufus Lewis, Terris McDuffie, Leonard, and Johnny Hayes. Bottom row, left to right: Dandridge, Dickie Seay, Bill Sadler, Day, Frank Duncan, and Vic Harris. Courtesy of NoirTech Research, Inc.

The Monarchs' Satchel Paige pitched three innings, struck out three, and held the all-stars to one hit. Left-hander Charley Beverly pitched the remaining six innings, giving up four hits, striking out three, and walking two batters. The hometown Kansas City Monarchs defeated Rowe and Company, 6–0.[8]

The Monarchs and the Rowe All-Stars traveled to Omaha, Nebraska, for Wednesday's game. Before 5,500 fans, the Monarchs won again, 8–2, over the Rowe crew. Satchel Paige pitched the first three innings, striking out five batters. He was relieved by Floyd Kranson, who struck out six, including the great Charlie Gehringer. Willard Brown and Henry Milton hit home runs for the Monarchs. Tommy Bridges took the mound in the fifth inning, striking out the side, but gave up two hits the next inning before being relieved by Schoolboy Rowe. Rowe allowed three hits, striking out one.[9]

ANOTHER ALL-STAR TEAM

After the season, New York Cubans catcher Frank Duncan formed an all-star team. Players selected include three future Hall of Famers: Buck Leonard (Homestead Grays, 1b), Leon Day (Brooklyn Eagles, p), and Ray Dandridge (Newark Dodgers, 3b). Other players chosen were the Brooklyn Eagles' Ed Stone (rf), Bill Sadler (ss), and Terris "The Great" McDuffie (p); the Philadelphia Stars' Stuart "Slim" Jones (p) and Dickie Seay (2b); the Homestead Grays' Ray Brown (p-cf) and Vic Harris (lf); Pittsburgh Crawfords rookie Rufus Lewis (p), and the Newark Dodgers' Johnny Hayes (c). They would play in the Puerto Rican Winter League, but official league records were not kept until the 1938–39 season and it is not known how the team fared in Puerto Rico.

Satchel Can Do No Wrong

by Ed Harris

Source: *Philadelphia Tribune*, 11 April 1935

Satchel Paige is causing his bosses out Pittsburgh way no end of trouble by failing to show up and report. By remaining incognito wherever he is, Satchel is only acting in keeping with that quaint and cute way of his of doing what he wants to do. Regardless of inconvenience to others, the Satchel is the Satchel.

His sweet and lovable character makes him respected and admired by his fellow players. You can tell that by the expression of their faces when ol' Satchel starts some more of his antics. And does the team morale perk up when the long-pedaled one starts acting up? Ask the club manager.

Guys like Paige may be interesting as the devil to the fans sitting in the grandstand. But to his teammates, he's usually a pain where you don't want to be kicked. The pet of the club owners is always giving somebody else a lot of trouble and getting away with it.

And they get away with it. Usually because they're good and know it, and the owner of the club knows it. Connie Mack had the same trouble with Rube Waddell, while other owners and managers have had similar trouble with the same type of player. Regardless of how good they might have been, there was always a tremendous sigh of relief when they passed from the picture.

Now, there's Satchel. Highest salaried man on his team and on a good many teams, his own car from the management—he can ride comfortably while the rest of the team goes by bus. Anything he wants is his and he takes it. But does that make stop and appreciate his good fortune and act like a gentleman? It does not. Ol' Satch just goes off and does what Ol' Satch wants to do.

Is he ever wrong? Not that you would know it. Let one of his mates muff or fumble in a game that he is pitching. Did you ever hear the story of the King of France who came out of his palace to board a coach? The vehicle rumbled up just as the King stepped down the stairs. With a frown, he looked at the driver and said: "You almost made me wait." That, my friend, is the attitude Brother Satch takes. Temperament? The umpire who would call a decision on him would defy lightning. Walk off the field? Think nothing of it.

Of course, Satchel is an excellent pitcher. He can get away with that sort of stuff. But if I were manager of a club with him, either he would be boss or I would be the boss. There wouldn't be me or Satchel running the club. The effects of actions like that on the part of a player are far-reaching. The team as a whole suffers. They get that, "What's the use?" attitude.

The fans in the stands like it. It amuses them to see a grown man stamp his foot and rave like a three-year-old child. But it isn't good baseball and in the end, they get tired of it. Witness the case of Dizzy Dean, who figured he could run the Cards there for a while. But when St. Louis Manager Frankie Frisch got through with him, there wasn't any use.

Expect 30,000 at All-Star Game Sunday

Slim Jones and Trent to Twirl First Three Frames

Source: *Chicago Defender,* 10 August 1935

Two of the greatest ball clubs in the history of the national pastime—teams which could enter either the American or National leagues and show their heels to the leaders—will fight for baseball's golden diadem on the clipped grass and bared infield of Comiskey Park, Chicago next Sunday afternoon. August 11.

The third annual Dream Game, which drew 15,000 people in 1933 [actually 19,568]; 22,000 last year [30,000 reported], and is expected to hit a peak of close to 40,000 this year, will see players in action who have been selected by popular vote throughout the East and the Midwest.

Thousands of ballots, which poured into league headquarters in Pittsburgh up to midnight Saturday, resulted in the selection of two teams which promise to give spectators the ultimo in thrills and spectacular moments.

THE WEST TEAM

The final vote completed after hours of work with a large staff of checkers who worked well into Sunday afternoon getting the final results, shows one or two startling changes. Chief among these is the meteoric rise of [Robert] Griffin [Griffith], Columbus pitcher who nabbed himself a coveted position as a hurler for the Eastern [Western] group. This lad whose work during the past few months has marked him with the stamp of greatness, eased out his teammate, [Jim "Cannonball"] Willis to become one of the four pitchers in the game of games.

The final vote shows [Ray] Brown, [Leroy] Matlock, Griffin and [Ted] Trent heading the parade of Western [Eastern] twirlers.

Charleston eased out in first position in one of the most spirited and hectic races for the first base post ever shown, when he defeated Leonard, the spark plug of the Grays' infield, by one vote.

So close was the fight for this position that it was necessary to check and double-check the count.

HUGHES IN AT SECOND

[Sammy T.] Hughes, great Columbus second sacker, won the berth for the keystone position hands down, but in winning created a problem which only manager Charleston will be able to settle.

In winning he presented a problem with [Pat] Patterson of the Crawfords and [Matt] Carlisle of the Grays running a dead-heat.

These men each had the same number of votes. Chester Williams who "stole the picture" last year both in Chicago and in New York, and who ranked at that time as one of the greatest in the game, showed surprising strength in the past week to zoom down the field second to Willie Wells at shortstop.

Commissioner [Ferninard] Morton, faced with the dead-heat for second based decided that there would be but three players needed in the position and gave the West a double-play combination of Wells to Hughes to Charleston or Wells to C. Williams to Leonard.

Either way it goes diamond fans who witness the game Sunday will see a combination which ranks with the best. Wells is the greatest of present-day shortstops. With almost un-

canny ability to field a ball, with a wide coverage and with a rifle arm he is the perfect infielder. In addition to this, he's a threat at the plate at all times and boasts of a healthy batting average.

RADCLIFFE AND SNOW

At third base, [Alec] Radcliffe, who can do everything and do it well, copped the position for the third year without much trouble.

But the man who finished in the runner-up position to him and who will doubtless be seen in action before the end of the game is one of the most improved fielders in the game.

He's [Felton] Snow of Columbus. He's devoid of color and dash and fire. He's cool as a cucumber and never gets excited. He's proven one of the main cogs of Jim Taylor's club this year. Don't look for dash and flash when Snow walks out to third base. You won't find it. But you'll be looking at a spread eagle infielder who makes the hardest chances look easy. You'll be looking at a finished ball player. Snow is colorless, but there is greatness in his very lack of color. Watch him next Sunday. That's our admonition.

SPEED AND POWER TO BURN

But it's in the outfield that the West team shows speed and power to burn. Here's the first line of defense and offense. Mule Suttles in left field; Turkey Stearnes in middle, and Zollie Wright in right field.

What power and bombardment Mule Suttles—the only player in the history of the classic to park a home run in the second tier of the left-center field grandstand![10] Turkey Stearnes is leading the league in hitting and goes far and wide to get 'em. Zollie Wright, husky, chunky outergardener of the Columbus team, whose big black bat is poison to the opposition.

And if there is a change get this combination! Watch their speed: Parnell, Columbus'

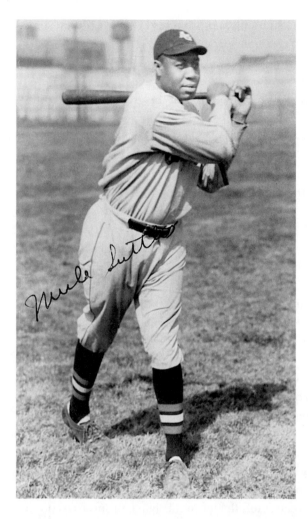

13. The most feared hitter in East-West all-star history was George "Mule" Suttles. Suttles slammed home runs in the 1933 and 1935 games. He injected so much fear in pitchers that he was walked four times in the '35 classic before belting the game-winning homer in the 11th inning with two outs. Courtesy of NoirTech Research, Inc.

great driving fleet-footed left fielder, patrolling the sun field; Cool Papa Bell, fastest man in baseball, the league's leading base pilferer and a turn-around hitter in centerfield, and Crutchfield, 142 pounds of dynamite an speed in right field. It was Crutchfield, whose perfect throw to the plate cut off the tying run in last year's 1–0 epic.

You'll see 'em all come Sunday, and you'll admit that the big leagues can't produce their superiors.

For catching roles, Larry Brown still reigns supreme, with Josh Gibson coming to the front with a rush in the closing days of the voting to ease out his teammate Perkins by a few votes.

LEFTY TIANT IS TOPS

And this year, the Eastern set-up is producing one of the greatest pitchers in the history of the game in Lefty Tiant, ace of the Cuban twirling staff, and admitted to be a pitcher without a weakness.

Tiant has proven to be the sensation of the circuits this year, and the fans have realized it to the extent of naming him above Slim Jones, the elongated Philly twirler, who last year was one of the greatest in the game.

To aid these two stars will be [Leon] Day of Brooklyn and [Bob] Evans, smart hurler of the Newark club.

The catching honors in the East go to big Jim [John] Hayes of Newark this year. Hayes eased Mackey out of first position in the standing and promises to show Chicago some-thing in the way of receiving they haven't seen in years.

SOME INFIELD COMBINATION

The East however will present to the fans just about two of the greatest infield combi-nations ever assembled.

The first four will show [Dewey] Creacy at third, Jake Stevens [Stephens] at short, Dick Seay at second and Jud Wilson at first. That's a combination which has everything! Pecu-liarly enough it's the regular infield combination which has shot the Philly Stars into the lead in the second half campaign of the pennant race and it's one of the greatest of all time.

Nowhere in the country is there a double play combination similar to that of Steven [Stephens] to Seay to Wilson. Both Stevens [Stephens] and Seay are midgets [5'7" & 5'8" respectively]—little fellows. The way they handle the apple is a thing of beauty and joy forever.

And if these men have to be taken out, then envision [Ray] Dandridge of Newark, [Bill] Yancey of Brooklyn, [Dick] Lundy of the Cubans and [George] Giles of Brooklyn. And that's a combination which no one needs to apologize for. There is probably more hitting strength in this combination than the other and their ability to turn in double plays with Dandridge rated with the real comers of the game, and Lundy and Giles to add balance will keep fandom on edge. Yancey has one of the strongest arms in the game and to watch him turn hits into putouts in something to marvel about.

FATS JENKINS IN LEFT

Fats Jenkins gets the call in left field over some high-class competitors. And he right-fully deserves the honor. Rated as the greatest basketball player in the country, this sturdy legged speed demon who is also the greatest left fielder in the game, promises to do the impossible in the way of fielding, hitting and running the bases. A regular greyhound, Jenkins possesses the uncanny faculty of knowing where a ball is going when it leaves the bat, and he gets there in nothing flat!

In centerfield [Paul] Arnold of Newark gets the call. He's tough to pitch to and covers his territory like the morning dew covers the countryside. Another speed demon, he's not as hard a hitter as his teammates, but he hits with disconcerting regularity and punches out his blows when they count for the most.

[Martin] Dihigo is head and shoulders above his competition for the right field berth. He's the greatest in that position in the country. He has the greatest throwing arm in base-ball, and when he hits one on the nose it's headed for distant parts.

Fans' Dream Comes True

Source: *Pittsburgh Courier,* 17 August 1935

The West wins 11 to 8 from the East in a real dream game here this afternoon which ended in true story fashion. Eleven was the lucky number for the West, winning their glori-ous victory in the eleventh inning on the eleventh day of August, with eleven runs and eleven hits.

But it took a Mule to put the "kick" into the game which won it for the West. "Mule" Suttles, bronzed bambino of swat of the Chicago American Giants, clouts the ball deep into the mid-right-field stands for a home run with "C. P." Bell and "Josh" Gibson of the Crawfords, on the base-paths and the score suspended at an 8–8 stalemate. It was a novel-like finish for a thrilling ball game which was chock-full of "its" from start to finish. There were brilliant bits of fielding, terrific hitting and sensational base-running. And the fans got a show which would rival Barnum and Bailey's greatest efforts with the principals including the super stars of the games which they had picked themselves by popular vote and dreamed about to represent the two sections.

Thrills in the game were as numerous as "cowboy" taxis on South Parkway. First "Slim" Jones pitched brilliant ball for the East, holding his opponents to one hit in three innings, then to top off his stellar performance, retaliated with a hit of his own, a terrific home run into the right field grandstand before retiring from the game.

Next in the parade of stars came young Crutchfield, fleet-footed outfielder of the Pittsburgh Crawfords, who made a sensational bare-handed running catch of Biz Mackey's mighty smash into center field. Sox park fans say that it was a greater catch than any big outfielder ever made in the Comiskey ball orchard. Shortly thereafter, Dihigo made a fine catch of Charleston's smash to center. Hughes went way back of second base and made a brilliant catch of speedy "Fats" Jenkins grounder, then tossed him out at first. Then, to climax it all in the eleventh inning, "Mule" Suttles, who had been walked four times during the afternoon, smashed out that screeching home run into the mid-right field stands with Josh Gibson and Chester Williams [Cool Papa Bell] on the basepaths to end the game 11 to 8.

The game this year was not the same type of a 1–0 classic as in 1934, when errors were as scarce as hens' teeth, but the '34 battle of the stars furnished just as many thrills. Fans had a chance of seeing a colorful procession of Negro's baseball diamond satellites, and observed many who turned in performances of big league caliber.

Among the 25,000 in attendance, the list of notables included scores of celebrities of the sports, stage and civic world.

Suttles' Home Run Wins It for the West

Blow Comes in 11th with Score Knotted and 2 On

Too Little Slim; Too Much Suttles

by Al Monroe

Source: *Chicago Defender*, 17 August 1935

The East walked Mule Suttles three times and then they struck him out. The East walked the Mule a fourth time and then when he came up in the last half of the 11th with the score tied and two mates aboard they attempted to strike him out again but this time the Donkey Bludgeon wielder sent 27,000 fans on their way screaming in the wake of an 11 to 8 victory for the Western All-Stars in the third annual intersectional baseball classic at Comiskey Park Sunday afternoon.

Although Suttles' game winning homer was the most decisive and thrilling feature of this weird struggle for baseball supremacy there were numerous other incidents well worth remembering. For the first three innings, Slim Jones, a lanky southpaw, who resembles Pat Carroway, erstwhile American leaguer in everything but color, pitching for the East, and staged an individual demonstration that was not only sensational but had opposing players and fans completely awed with its brilliance. Then in the midst of all this glory,

14. Slim Jones is the only pitcher to hit a home run in the East-West classic. His homer came off of Ray Brown in the 1935 game. Courtesy of NoirTech Research, Inc.

the Slim one registered his second straight hit, a homer into the right field stands, giving his side a four to nothing lead and adding more torture to the hopes of the Western all stars.

With this much of the program completed Jones must have figured his own work was done and immediately after the ball landed in the stands the mighty one strolled leisurely across the diamond to hang up his glove—but the show was just beginning. We need not tell you the West had done absolutely nothing up to this time, for that was what made Jones the hero he was. Only one hard hit had resulted from the bats of the men from the shores of Lake Michigan when Jones left the game, and that one questionable roller that slipped past an unsuspecting infielder. However, here is where things began to happen, though not until after [Leon] Day, who followed Jones on the mound, had proved for two innings that he was a worthy successor. Opposing Jones and Day was R. Brown of the Homestead Grays, who was tolling for the West with indifferent success partly because he had thrown a home run ball to Jones but mainly because of the errant ways of his own team mates. This lad's story should be "You threw me down." Not until the sixth [seventh], the last frame, that Day worked did trouble overtake him and the East have its first cause to worry. This bit of flurry gave the West three runs topped only because of their nasty Jones homer, and made the score board read 4 to 3.

How the West tied the score in its half of the seventh we will let you gather from the play-by-play report on this page and move on to that thrilling tenth when both sides tallied four runs.

CHANGE PITCHERS

Matlock [Griffith] was pitching for the West when both [Jud] Wilson and [Alejandro] Oms singled, and [Biz] Mackey walked to load the Cossacks. With this strange picture before the fans, Wells messed up Jenkins' grounder and one run scored, leaving the bases filled. Then Dandridge hit for [Dickie] Seay and two more runs came home. Day then obliged with a strike out but [Jake] Stevens [Stephens] singled home the fourth run of the inning. When Dandridge crossed the plate, he was met by thousands of spectators who were on their way out, feeling that the game that over. Four runs at this stage of the game appeared to be a cinch but just read on.

The first man up for the West was Chester Williams, now playing short, and he walked. Josh Gibson, who had been a swatting demon all day long hit to right and Chester went to third. Mule Suttles walked, filling the bases and the East started to worry. Snow of Columbus came in to bat for Griffin [Griffith]. Dihigo, a right hander, came in from the outfield to pitch to Snow. [Paul] Arnold of Newark went to center field. Snow swung at a fast one. He looked at another. The next was a ball. Snow singled to center to bring in William's and Gibson. Radcliffe was up there with the folks in a frenzy. He forced Snow at second, Stevens [Stephens] to Dandridge. Suttles scoring. Stearnes drove Dihigo's first pitch through the box into center field, sending Radcliffe to third. McDonald, the East's manager, started warming up, but didn't come in, leaving the burden on the Cuban. Leonard lifted the first ball pitch to Jenkins in left center and Radcliffe came home with the tying run, 8–8. Mackey threw out Stearnes at second. Stevens [Stephens] putting the ball on him for the out.

The eleventh was uneventful for the East but the West got busy. In the eleventh inning Cornelius of Cole's American Giants, was pitching for the West. Wilson walked. Radcliffe threw out Oms. Suttles made a startling dash from deep left field to center to grab Mackey's liner. Hughes nailed Jenkins at first.

This is the wild and wooly ball game that the fans like. They sat down after Suttles catch and decided to stay awhile. Bell walked. Hughes laid down a sacrifice bunt to Dihigo, who threw to Dandridge covering first. Dihigo tried to bean Ches Williams, who grabbed his hand and rolled over on the ground three times (I counted 'em) and raved as though someone had stuck him with a hypodermic syringe. It brought Umpire Turner, Oscar Charleston and McDonald to the plate for a "beefing session." Umpire Harris ordered Williams to bat, the play being ruled a foul. Williams fanned for the second out. Bell was still on second. The Eastern brain trust decided to walk Gibson to get at Suttles. Suttles fouled off two and then broke up the game with a line drive into right center field grandstand to win the game for the West, 11 to 8.

The game was productive of good and indifferent baseball, but it was just what the fans wanted. They wished to see plenty of hits, and hits is what they saw. They saw Willie Wells, ace of shortstops, blow sky high and they saw Josh Gibson stand and permit what should have been a freak double held to a single and they saw plenty of other things. However, many of the fans and players felt that the over-exertion on the part of the gentleman handling the loud speaker kept the players upset.

Dihigo of the East, who twice might have been the hero, unfortunately turned out to be the goat of the game. His tremendous drive in the first that scored two runs, his desperate attempt to catch a drive from the bat of Gibson resulted in his running into the fence were the things that stood out. But his switch from a side arm delivery while pitching to Mule Suttles in the final frame undoubtedly lost the East the game. The Mule is a desperado when thrown certain balls and is weak on certain balls and is weak on certain other pitches. And it so happens that Dihigo gave him one pitch he likes best and the ball game was gone at that instant.[11]

At It Again

Lament on the East-West Game

by Ed Harris

Source: *Philadelphia Tribune,* 29 August 1935

Oh beat the drums, buglers sound taps
While I recite of vile mishaps
   That befell nine young men or more
Whose names you all have heard before.
   The nine young men, baseballers true,
The Western team sought to subdue.
   At Comiskey Park in the Windy City,
25,000 fans, hot and giddy
   Pack the grandstands and the bleachers
To see what was one of the features
   Of all the sports world yearly fare,
There were many more who wished they were there
   Webster MacDonald of the Philly Stars
Headed the East team in the wars
   The Western team was a very tough bunch
They were going to win, they had a hunch
   The umpire screeched, "Come on, play ball,"
Then turned to the fans and said, "How you all?"
   Slim Jones, the great, was at his best
But after the fourth had to take a rest
   Day went in and got a headache
And from the mound, Mac had him to take
   Tiant went in and the Westerners scored
And MacDonald down the bullpen roared
   To warm himself up and make the ball hum,

Cause he knew full well his time was come
>He tossed a few and looked around
And there was Dihigo on the mound
>He called time out but it was too late
Martin had burned one past the plate
>Mac up and yells, "who put you here?"
The fans all said, "It's very queer."
>He started to argue, but what's the use?
The boys had gone and cooked the goose
>Mule Suttles was up, Oh Faithful moved
And Dihigo burned one down the groove
>The bat met ball, the ball passed fence
And with it went the East team's chance
>Turn back, oh time, but the deed is done
Mule Suttles' homer the game had won
>And so my friends, Mac knows full well
That managing, like war, is hell.

AUGUST 11, 1935, CHICAGO, IL

EAST	AB	R	H	D	T	HR	BI	E	TAVG	TSLG
Paul Stephens (Philadelphia Stars), ss	6	1	2	0	0	0	1	1		
George Giles (Brooklyn Eagles), 1b	5	1	0	0	0	0	1	0		
Martin Dihigo (New York Cubans), cf-p	5	1	1	0	0	0	1	2		
Jud Wilson (Philadelphia Stars), 3b	5	1	2	0	0	0	1	0		
Alejandro Oms (New York Cubans), rf	4	1	2	0	0	0	0	0		
Biz Mackey (Philadelphia Stars), c	5	1	0	0	0	0	0	0		
Fats Jenkins (Brooklyn Eagles), lf	5	1	0	0	0	0	0	0		
Dick Seay (Philadelphia Stars), 2b	3	0	1	0	0	0	0	2		
a) Ed Stone (Brooklyn Eagles), ph	1	0	0	0	0	0	0	0		
Slim Jones (Philadelphia Stars), p	2	1	2	0	0	1	1	0		
Leon Day (Brooklyn Eagles), p	1	0	0	0	0	0	0	0		
Ray Dandridge (Newark Dodgers), 2b	1	0	1	0	0	0	2	0		
Luis Tiant (New York Cubans), p	2	0	0	0	0	0	0	0		
Paul Arnold (Newark Dodgers), cf	0	0	0	0	0	0	0	0		
Team Totals, Average & Slugging Pct.	45	8	11	0	0	1	7	5	.244	.311

a) Batted for Seay in 8th

WEST	AB	R	H	D	T	HR	BI	E	TAVG	TSLG
Cool Papa Bell (Pittsburgh Crawfords), cf	4	2	1	0	0	0	0	1		
Sammy T. Hughes (Columbus Elite Giants), 2b	4	0	1	0	0	0	0	0		
Willie Wells (Chicago American Giants), ss	3	0	0	0	0	0	0	1		
Chester Williams (Pittsburgh Crawfords), ss	2	1	0	0	0	0	0	1		
Josh Gibson (Pittsburgh Crawfords), c	5	3	4	2	0	0	1	1		
Mule Suttles (Chicago American Giants), lf	2	3	1	0	0	1	3	0		
Oscar Charleston (Pittsburgh Crawfords), 1b	3	1	0	0	0	0	0	1		
Alec Radcliffe (Chicago American Giants), 3b	5	0	2	0	0	0	3	0		
Jimmie Crutchfield (Pittsburgh Crawfords), rf	2	0	0	0	0	0	0	0		
b) Turkey Stearnes (Chicago American Giants), ph-rf	3	0	1	0	0	0	0	0		
Raymond Brown (Homestead Grays), p	1	0	0	0	0	0	0	0		
Leroy Matlock (Pittsburgh Crawfords), p	1	0	0	0	0	0	0	0		
c) Buck Leonard (Homestead Grays), ph-1b	3	0	0	0	0	0	1	0		
Ted Trent (Chicago American Giants), p	0	0	0	0	0	0	0	0		
d) Bill Wright (Columbus Elite Giants), ph	1	0	0	0	0	0	0	0		
Bob Griffith (Columbus Elite Giants), p	0	0	0	0	0	0	0	0		
e) Felton Snow (Columbus Elite Giants), ph	1	1	1	0	0	0	2	0		
Sug Cornelius (Chicago American Giants), p	0	0	0	0	0	0	0	0		
Team Totals, Average & Slugging Pct.	40	11	11	2	0	1	10	5	.275	.400

b) Batted for Crutchfield in 6th
c) Batted for Matlock in 6th
d) Batted for Trent in 8th
e) Batted for Griffith in 10th

East	200	110	000	40-8
West	000	003	100	43-11

There were two outs in the 11th inning when Mule Suttles hit a home run with two men on base.

PITCHER/TEAM	GS	IP	H	R	ER	K	BB	WP	HB	W	L
S. Jones/PS	1	3	1	0	0	1	2	0	0	0	0
Day/BE		4	6	4	2	3	2	0	0	0	0
Tiant/NYC		2	1	3	3	0	2	0	0	0	0
Dihigo/NYC		1 2/3	3	4	4	1	2	0	0	0	1
R. Brown/HG	1	4	6	3	2	1	0	0	0	0	0
Matlock/PC		2	1	1	0	1	0	0	0	0	0
Trent/CAG		2	0	0	0	1	2	0	0	0	0
Griffith/CEG		2	4	4	3	3	3	0	0	0	0
Cornelius/CAG		1	0	0	0	0	1	0	0	1	0

BB—Oms, Jenkins, Giles, Mackey, Wilson, Dihigo, Suttles (4), Bell (2), Gibson, C. Williams
DP—Wilson (unassisted)
LOB—East 11, West 8
PB—Gibson
SAC—Hughes (2), Oms
SB—Dihigo, Giles
East—Webster McDonald (Mgr.); Coaches Smokey Joe Williams, and Pop Lloyd
West—Oscar Charleston (Mgr.); Coaches Walter Ball and Jim Brown
Umpires—E. C. "Pop" Turner, Johnny Craig, Moe Harris, Jude Gans
Attendance—25,000   Time—3:14

1935 VOTING RESULTS: 554,388

P

Luis Tiant, Sr.	5,937
Slim Jones	5,684
Ray Brown	5,221
Leroy Matlock	4,784
Bob Evans	4,742
Leon Day	3,856
Double Duty Radcliffe	3,650
Will Jackman	3,591
Ted Trent	3,312
Robert Griffith	3,207
William Bell	2,919
Frank Blake	2,814
Jim Willis	2,516
Rocky Ellis	2,392
Sug Cornelius	2,267
Satchel Paige	2,184
Burnalle Hayes	1,855
Willie Foster	1,598

C

Larry Brown	9,475
Josh Gibson	9,189
Cy Perkins	9,083
Johnny Hayes	7,313
Biz Mackey	7,215
Tex Burnett	6,889
Tommy Dukes	6,728
Phil Casey	5,940
Clarence Palm	5,891
Subby Byas	1,751

1B

Jud Wilson	9,863
George Giles	9,750
Oscar Charleston	9,319
Buck Leonard	9,318
Lazaro Salazar	9,144
Leslie Starks	6,787
Steel Arm Davis	6,495
Jim West	5,243

2B

Dickie Seay	13,019
Richard Lundy	12,876
Sammy T. Hughes	11,347
Harry Williams	10,564
Pat Patterson	8,953
Lick Carlisle	8,953
George Scales	7,220
Jack Marshall	5,045

2B-3B

Dewey Creacy	13,019

3B

Alec Radcliffe	13,455
Dewey Creacy	11,883
Ray Dandridge	11,051
Felton Snow	9,872
Dennis Gilchrist	8,967
Judy Johnson	7,480

SS

Willie Wells	16,262
Jake Stephens	14,028
Bill Yancey	13,976
Ches Williams	11,489
Leroy Morney	11,437
Timothy Bond	11,369

OF

Martin Dihigo	15,802
Fats Jenkins	13,480
Zollie Wright	13,246
Mule Suttles	12,460
Alejandro Oms	11,712
Big Jim Williams	11,694
Jimmie Crutchfield	11,053
Wilson Redus	10,979
Chaney White	10,847
Vic Harris	10,825
Red Parnell	10,337
Paul Arnold	10,257
Ed Stone	10,077
Jake Dunn	9,958
Sam Bankhead	9,216
Candy Lopez	8,851
Turkey Stearnes	8,604
Cool Papa Bell	8,578
Jose Perez	8,505
Bill Wright	8,182
Lloyd Davenport	7,842
Jerry Benjamin	7,609
Buddy Burbage	6,528

1936

President Franklin D. Roosevelt establishes the Office of Minority Affairs and names educator Mary McLeod Bethune as administrator.

German boxer Max Schmeling beats Joe Louis in 12 rounds. Olympic sprinter Jesse Owens destroys Hitler's myth of Aryan supremacy by winning four gold medals in track-and-field events.

The movie *The Green Pastures* premieres in New York City's Radio City Music Hall. The movie features Eddie "Rochester" Anderson (of Jack Benny fame), the Hall Johnson Choir, and Rex Ingram as "De Lawd."

Milk costs only 24 cents a half-gallon, 10 pounds of potatoes costs 32 cents, and 41 cents would bring home the bacon. A loaf of bread costs 8 cents. The NAACP files the *Gibbs* v. *Board of Education* lawsuit to eliminate pay differentials between black and white teachers.

At Fenway Park, the National League All-Stars win their first all-star game over the American Leaguers, 4–3, as Dizzy Dean picks up the victory.

RACE RELATIONS

In August, the *Chicago Defender* announced that writers of the *New York Daily Worker* were initiating a full-blown assault of the race issue in Major League Baseball. The campaign was heartily endorsed by James W. Ford, the African-American Communist vice-presidential candidate. Ford decried "the un-American violation of fair play in the big leagues against Negro players, many of whom bring great prestige, skill and advancement to the national game." One plan was to interview prominent white Americans and get their viewpoint on the segregation of minority athletes in baseball.[1]

Dan Parker of the *New York Daily Mirror* agreed: "I see no reason why Negroes should not be admitted to major league baseball. If it weren't for them, where would America be in Hitler's Olympics? There is no place for racial discrimination in the American national game."[2]

Former heavyweight boxing champion Jack Dempsey declared to the *New York Sunday Worker:* "I don't believe there should be any discrimination in athletics. If a Negro has big league qualifications, he should play." On the other side of town, white writer Jimmy Powers of the *New York Daily News* declared: "Negroes belong in big league baseball competition. They have the ability and it is only fair to them as Americans that they be given an equal chance. I believe big league ball would gain added sparkle if the great Negro stars were admitted."[3]

Powers elicited a multitude of responses. One came from Edward (Massa) Brannick,

New York Giants secretary, who telegrammed: "So you want the National League to play in blackface, STOP, Mammy Please STOP."[4]

One person from Washington DC wrote: "Ball players are different. There would be fights in the locker [rooms], cliques and lack of cohesion. In towns like Washington and St. Louis there would be trouble. Didn't you ever hear of the Mason-Dixon line? Or Jim Crow laws? The trouble with you Damyankees is you think New York is the center of the world. You ought to get around the country. This is the silliest idea ever."[5]

Considering the current racial climate, a remarkable answer came from National League president Ford Frick: "Beyond the fundamental requirements that a major league player must have unique ability, good character and habits, I do not recall one instance where baseball has allowed race, creed or color to enter the selection of its players."[6]

LEAGUE BUSINESS

At the January board meeting, the Homestead Grays withdrew from the Negro National League, and Ed Bolden, owner of the Philadelphia Stars, was elected chairman of the league, replacing Gus Greenlee. Greenlee was resigning because of "conflicting business duties."[7] Other elected officials included Ferdinand Q. Morton as commissioner; Abe Manley, vice-chairman; John L. Clark, secretary; and Tom Wilson, treasurer. Cum Posey and Rufus "Sonnyman" Jackson, co-owners of the Homestead Grays, stormed out of the meeting after the treasurer's report was given. "I am through," was Posey's statement to the press. "I cannot stay in a league where there are so many 'miscellaneous' bills for which there is no explanation. The financial report had shown miscellaneous items for $251 and $241. . . . They cannot handle any more money for me."[8]

A New York–based team was denied admission to the league but was granted permission to play any of the franchise clubs. The Chicago American Giants, owned by Horace T. Hall, and Cincinnati were tentatively granted franchises. The former 1924 Olympic long jump champion DeHart Hubbard was owner of the Cincinnati Tigers.[9] But at the March 27 meeting, the applications from Chicago and Cincinnati were denied because of the travel distances from the East Coast clubs to these cities. Both the Chicago club and the Cincinnati club would eventually join the newly created Midwest-based Negro American League the following season. More importantly, the Grays were back in the loop as Posey and Jackson were once again pacified.

The only trade announced at the meeting was the Philadelphia Stars' sending second baseman Dickie Seay (three East-West appearances) to the Crawfords for pitcher Bert Hunter (pitcher for the 1933 Eastern squad) and Curtis "Popeye" Harris, a utility player.[10] Frank Forbes, business manager for Pompez's New York Cubans, announced the signing of Ramon Bragana, Tetelo Vargas (three East-West appearances), and Silvio Garcia (four East-West appearances).[11]

The league meeting agreed to employ three traveling umpires for the season: Pete Cleage of Nashville and Moe Harris and John Craig of Pittsburgh. An umpire employed by the local club owners would assist each umpiring crew.[12]

Although the Black Yankees were denied admission, owner James Semler revealed his club's budget. Semler reported that it cost all eight teams to play five months, from May through September, an estimated $170,000. Each team carried from 16 to 18 men, creating a monthly salary budget of $4,000. Each team paid the league office about $5,000 a year for incidentals and gave the independent booking agents 10 percent of the gate.

Baseball bats were $24 a dozen, with each team carrying 35 to 40 bats at one time.

With the breakage of bats, a team averaged six dozen bats a season. Baseballs were $13 per dozen. Semler estimated that between two and two and one-half dozen baseballs were used per game. Uniforms from Spalding cost from $10 to $12 each, with each player having two uniforms and one jacket.

The teams were responsible for room and board on the road. If there was a rainout, the owner suffered. The owner also paid for gasoline and oil for the team bus. Other expenses included salaries for the bus driver, road secretary, and photographers for publicity purposes.

The players also had expenses. They paid for their shoes, at an average cost of $16.50; their gloves, which ranged from $7.50 to $10; and their sweatshirts, which averaged about $2.50. A player used an average of two pairs of spikes a season.

Semler estimated that there were more than 300,000 black people in New York City. He reported that the Black Yankees averaged about 5,000 fans per game with an admission price of 30 cents a game or 55 cents for a doubleheader. He also revealed that an estimated 5,000 black people attend the white Yankees or Giants games and paid twice as much for tickets compared to Black Yankees games.[13]

On June 18, the Black Yankees were admitted to the league despite objections from Frank Forbes and Roy Sparrow of the New York Cubans. The Cubans protested that Harlem could not support two clubs. The board decided that the Black Yankees would be strictly a traveling club without a home park in order not to conflict with any home dates at Dyckman Oval, home of the Cubans.[14]

On December 6, representatives from six baseball clubs met at the Wabash YMCA in Chicago. Officials from the Detroit Stars, Kansas City Monarchs, Indianapolis Athletics, Cincinnati Tigers, Memphis Red Sox, and Birmingham Black Barons were present. Major Robert Jackson was elected president of the organization. Owners of clubs in Cleveland and Toledo were seeking associate membership in the new league to be called the Negro American League.

Newly elected treasurer J. L. Wilkinson, owner of the Monarchs, expressed a desire for his team to rejoin an organized league but pointed out his traveling concerns: "We would be the farthest club West and it would be necessary for us to have some kind of a stop between here [Chicago] and Kansas City. St. Louis is the logical place but the lack of a suitable baseball park in that city makes this improbable. St. Louis should be a member of such an organization as we plan. It is unfortunate that they are handicapped by the lack of a first rate park. I understand serious attempts are being made to rectify this trouble. If St. Louis comes through with a park, it is almost definite we will become full fledged members. If St. Louis doesn't, we feel an associate membership agreement would be the only thing we could live up to."[15] With Wilkie's comments in mind, the Chicago American Giants and the St. Louis Stars were added to the league for scheduling purposes.

ALL-STAR REVIEW

Tom Wilson, the owner of the Washington Elite Giants, in midseason organized an all-star team to compete in the coveted Denver Post Baseball Tournament, with the grand prize of $5,000 for first place. From the Crawfords, he secured pitchers Satchel Paige and Sam Streeter, catchers Josh Gibson and Paul Hardy, shortstop Ches Williams, third baseman Boisy Marshall, and outfielder Cool Papa Bell. Coming from the Grays were pitcher Ray Brown, first baseman Buck Leonard, and outfielder Vic Harris. The all-around outfielder Burnis "Wild Bill" Wright, second sacker Sammy T. Hughes, third baseman Felton Snow, pitcher Robert Griffith, and manager Candy Jim Taylor came from Wilson's Elite

15. The National League All-Stars were winners of the 1936 Denver Post Tournament. Top row, left to right: Seward Posey (business manager), Sammy T. Hughes, Vic Harris, Bill Wright, and Mr. Mart (masseur). Middle row: Hoody Whitton (trainer), Buck Leonard, Ches Williams, Cool Papa Bell, Felton Snow, Jack Marshall, and Candy Jim Taylor. Bottom row: Paul Hardy, Robert Griffith, Satchel Paige, Ray Brown, Sam Streeter, Josh Gibson, and Horne (Crawfords batboy). Courtesy of Jay Sanford.

Giants. With the exception of Hardy and Marshall, all of the players were East-West performers.

On August 11, the National League All-Stars, as they were called, swept the tournament in seven games, defeating the Enid Oilers 7–0 in the title game. Paige struck out 18 batters, yielding a couple of hits. After filling the sacks in the second inning, Paige struck out the side.[16]

American League Needed Paige to Win All-Star Tilt

Source: *Chicago Defender,* 18 July 1936

When the National league whipped their American loop brothers 4–3 in the All Star game staged at Boston last week the junior loop was suffering its first defeat in the famous classic. Perhaps some will argue that the bats of Medwick, Galan and others spelled doom for the American leaguers but the records will tell another story. Look through the box scores of the game from inning to inning and you will find that superior pitching by Lon Warneke, Dizzy Dean and Carl Hubbell really turned the trick. Further proof that pitching played a big part will be gotten from the fact that Mel Harder, the only American loop pitcher to show any real form, almost saved the day long enough for his side to win out in the end.

With this in mind we just wonder what would have resulted had Satchel Paige started the game instead of Lefty Grove who gave up two runs or Schoolboy Rowe who permitted the final two tallies? Certainly Paige has faced the bulk of the star hitters in both leagues and the records will show that few hits have been recorded off his delivery in the pinches or out.

Really, it is hard to figure why discrimination can remain so powerful and keep Race players out of the league in these day of poor gate receipts. At present, only three or four teams are keeping out of the red and those doing so by keeping on top of the pack. Imagine, if you can, the turnout that would be on hand for a game between the St. Louis Cardinals and the Chicago Cubs with Dizzy Dean twirling against "Satchel" Paige.

Now don't think for a moment that some of the moguls are unaware of this chance to increase their earning power in baseball. The subject has come up many times, but has always tabled for the want of support from the club owners about the country. The first owner to suggest Race player joining major teams was the late John J. McGraw, but John couldn't turn the trick all by himself and the suggestion received little aid from the rest of the loop. In addition to that, Judge Landis, ruler of both leagues, has been flooded with letters of protest at barring Race stars from the leagues. Copies of *The Chicago Defender* and other periodicals making the plea for this just cause have been sent to the judge and all the club owners. Despite this move, however, the majors continue to bar Race players from the leagues. They are even putting prejudice above money.

Promoters in Move to Foil Hit at Game

Split Brings Classic to Comiskey Park

Source: *Chicago Defender,* 22 August 1936

The fourth annual East-West game will staged at Comiskey Park this year because the pioneers of the idea believe that the game belongs in the Windy City.

For three consecutive years it has been supported by Race citizens, and a small profit in some form has resulted.

In 1933, W. A. Greenlee, Thomas T. Wilson and [Robert] R. A. Cole financed the idea which was called a brainstorm by veterans in the game.

Ten per cent of the profits were turned over to the Negro National League in 1934 and last year 50 percent was the league's share. But owners were displeased because the remaining profits were not prorated among them.

Players were dissatisfied because the game had been played under [financial] plans different from the two previous years.

In 1936, the organization passed a rule that all promotions where League finances were used, or where the name of the organization was used for the purposes of advertising, that all such games should be turned over to the league treasurer.

AIMED AT PROMOTIONS

This motion was aimed directly at the East-West game and promotions in major league parks in New York.

But the organization went further and said that the East-West game should be staged in New York. To this Greenlee and Wilson disagreed.

Both owners contended that the game was successful and popular through Harry M. Grabiner, secretary of the White Sox Park—and the citizens of Chicago. And that is why the game remains in Chicago this year.

Umpire Put Race Entry into Major Leagues

Up to J. Louis Comiskey

Source: *Chicago Defender,* 22 August 1936

> August 11, 1936
> Mr. J. Louis Comiskey,
> President Chicago White Sox
> Comiskey Park, Chicago, Ill.

Dear Sir

I am enclosing two clippings, one from the St. Louis *Sporting News* and the other from *The Chicago Defender* and at the same time I would like to ask why the club owners of the major leagues still ignore the drawing power of Negro athletes? They are packing them in whenever they perform, boxing, track, football, etc.

The sensational pitching of Satchel Paige and the catching and hitting of young Josh Gibson, would increase the gate by 150,000 in any major league park. Paige has the praise of such major leaguers as the Waner brothers, the Deans and numerous others who played with him in the winter league on the Pacific Coast.

These two players will be members of the all-stars who play at your park on the 23rd of this month, and whenever the time comes to be the first to sign a Negro player, I am hoping that you will be that man.

There are thousands of loyal Negro White Sox fans to whom this is due and there would be an added 10,000 fans in any major league city visited. We held the highest respect for your late father, and hope that you will carry on and not vote to resort to night games as a stimulus to a dying national pastime.

A manager of the Los Angeles baseball team upon making a tour of the major leagues recently remarked that, "he had never seen so many minor league players in the major leagues."

To avoid the sandlot rule, these two players [Paige and Gibson] could be contracted, sent to say St. Paul on option late this season and watch the result. I hope you will give this consideration.

Sincerely yours,

O. Grady Gregory

Jim West, Gangling First Baseman of the Elites

Fields Like Grimm, Hits Like Gehrig

Washington Star to Shine in the East-West Game

Sources: *Chicago Defender* & *Pittsburgh Courier,* 22 August 1936

A gangling 24 year-old "kid" who has been knocking at the door of the hall o' fame for three years, will have his knock answered Sunday afternoon at Comiskey Park, Chicago, when the fourth edition of the annual East-West diamond classic gets under way.

This youngster, who has developed into the most sensational fielding first baseman in the history of the game, is none other than Jim West of the Washington Elites.

West, who has been fielding this year like a Charlie Grimm and hitting like a Lou Gehrig, sports a batting average of .419 for the first half of the season. Included in his 36 hits out of 86 official times at bat are four doubles, four triples and four circuit clouts.

He's been given a free-ticket to first base seven times.

COMES INTO HIS OWN

West, who has always been the game's most colorful showman, is a close student of the game, if you take the word of his manager, canny 'Candy Jim' Taylor, weighing 216 pounds he studied the styles of major league hitters and finally adopted a loose style at the plate which was a combination of stances of other players.

Immediately he started rattling the fences in the league parks with ringing hits . . . hits which carried distance and force.

And once he started hitting he couldn't be stopped. Batting from both sides of the plate, he proved to a terror alike of right-handers and southpaws.

And strange as it may seem the easiest man for him to hit is Satchel Paige!

GAMES GREATEST SHOWMAN

Race Baseball had has some colorful first basemen including [Dave] Thomas of the Black Yanks, [Oscar] Charleston of the Craws, Ben Taylor of the old ABC's "Highpockets" Hurspeth [Bob Hudspeth] of the Bacharachs and many others.

But West with his floppy old glove, his halting stumbling stride, and his "Houdini" tactics as he spears a high one digs a low one out of the dirt, ranks heads and shoulders above any man modern baseball has produced for color.

He has it in "gobs," and when he starts spilling his color and strutting his stuff around the spot hallowed by such stars as Sisler, Gehrig, Hank Greenberg and others, their shadows will hang their heads in shame over the almost unbelievable feats of Jim West. . . . whose color will always remain black, but who would be a welcome addition to many a major league club!

West's Best No Match for Star Eastern Outfit

by Franklin Penn (a.k.a. Rollo W. Wilson)

Source: *Pittsburgh Courier*, 29 August 1936

Doing everything that a smart ball club ought to do, while their opponents performed like stricken victims of the combined drought and heat spell which had affected the Midwest, the East ball club romped to a 10–2 win over the West at Comiskey Park here on Sunday, before a crowd of 26,400.

The margin of victory was an accurate index of the respective merits of the two clubs. Although the East was recruited from only two teams—the Pittsburgh Crawfords and the Washington Elites—the Charleston-Jim Taylor coached outfit was a perfect machine while the West was but a broken-down fliver, vintage 1919.

Baseball in the West has indeed sunk to a low estate and those who met up with Rube Foster and C. I. Taylor along the banks of the Styx late Sunday afternoon must have shrieked in horror as they fled from the sulfurous "gum beatings" of Baseball's Immortals.

The boys from the sunrise sector lost no time in starting their hit parade. Jim Bell, lead-off man, smacked a brisk single to right field and then stole second base as Cornelius, West hurler, allowed him to get a slight lead. Hughes was walked and Bankhead sacrificed them along.

Biz Mackey, rejuvenated catcher, making his first appearance in three classics, singled over second base and two runs were in, as Crutchfield and William breezed.

Then because they just had to be different, the delayed opening ceremonies were held. Oscar DePriest showing no benefits of the spring training he did not have, tried a one-

16. Gus Greenlee's Crawfords of Pittsburgh were well represented at the 1936 contest with nine players. From left to right: this year's winning pitcher Leroy Matlock, Oscar Charleston (manager of the East squad), light heavyweight boxer John Henry Lewis, and the battery of Satchel Paige and Josh Gibson. Courtesy of NoirTech Research, Inc.

Sammy
Bankhead

Cool Papa
Bell

Jimmy
Crutchfield

17. The speedy all-star Crawfords outfield of Sam Bankhead, Cool Papa Bell, and Jimmie Crutchfield was known as the Raindrop Rangers. Legend has it they were so fast they once kept a field dry by catching raindrops until the storm passed. The trio appeared in a combined 19 all-star games. Courtesy of Jimmie Crutchfield.

pitch strikeout of John Henry Lewis, one of the pundits of pugilism, but it was no soap—John laced a single to right field.

With that event in history the game proceeded with [Eddie] Dwight, first hitter for the West, facing [Leroy] Matlock, headman of 1936 forkhanders. He rapped hard between short and third, but Judy Johnson threw himself to earth grabbed the ball and tossed Dwight out by a distance no greater than the hickness of the ham they were serving in the sandwiches around the ballyard. Newt Allen rolled to [Sammy T.] Hughes and [Wilson] Redus fouled out to West.

Came the fourth inning and the West started again. [Floyd] Kranson walked [Jim] West and Johnson sacrificed him to second. After Byrd had fanned, Bell scored the first baseman with his third hit of the afternoon.

A cascade of basehits in the fifth rolled Kranson from the hill and netted three markers. Hughes doubled, Bankhead grounded to Popsickle Harris and Gibson, batting for Mackey, singled to center. Josh then stole second and scored with Hughes on Zollie Wright's one-base blow. West was hit with a pitched ball and Johnson's single tallied Wright.

Ted Trent went in the seventh but the boys got two runs then and two in the eighth, Bankhead, Gibson, Williams and Snow making the hits and Dial contributing an error which figured in the run-making.

Hits by Radcliffe, Dunlap and Patterson gave the West its first counter in the sixth and the second and final came in the eighth off Satchel, of the Alabama Paiges, after the side should have been retired.

Satchell Paige Is Magnet at E-W Game

Players of Big League Calibre Perform

by William G. Nunn (City Editor)

Source: *Pittsburgh Courier,* 29 August 1936

Press Box, Comiskey Park, Chicago, Aug. 23— There will eventually be "color" in the major leagues and that color will be black.

I sat in this coop, atop the giant stadium which house close to 30,000 people here this afternoon, and saw Negro ball players with the stamp of "major league" qualities written all over them perform in the fourth annual East-West diamond classic.

The fact that the East won, 10–2 . . . and that the game was the worst East-West affair since the inauguration of the event . . . was inconsequential.

Because the East-West game became definitely established this year as an institution and out of the ruins of the West's hopes arose a crop of black athletes who are some day destined to "strut their stuff" on the fields of battle in the "money' parks.

SATCHELL THE MAGNET

There is no disputing the fact that Satchell Paige is the magnet which has drawn thousands of thousands of people through the turnstiles. Long, tall, dark, and with that "color" which sets him apart from the mob, he has proven his worth through the years. Everywhere baseball is talked, they speak of Satchell Paige. In organized baseball . . . in the majors . . . the name of Satchell Paige is no mystery. "Dizzy" Dean admits that the Alabama-born twirler has "everything" and said recently that he knew DiMaggio of the Yanks would make the grade, when he heard that the Italian had secured a hit off Paige.

But long before Satchell strolled onto the mound in the seventh inning here today, the tense drama which had surrounded other East-West games, had faded. The East today . . . a powerhouse on the offense and a blanket spread on defense . . . had safely tucked the game away.

As we watched the game unfold today, we saw "Cool Papa" Bell swing into action, with three hits including a double, in four trips to the plate. We saw Judy Johnson make a circus stop and throw to retire the West's first man in the first inning.

We saw [Sammy T.] Hughes of Nashville [now, Washington] . . . and he ranks heads and shoulders above the other guardians of this section . . . go behind second base to cut off driving, slashing basehits.

We saw speed, dash and class. Oodles of it. We know that Chester Williams as he performed today is better than several major league shortstops.

We know that many a major league would welcome the addition of Bell, either one of the Wright brothers [Bill or Zollie] or [Sam] Bankhead to their roster. . . . We don't believe the majors can produce three outfielders with the all-around ability of "Cool Papa," Bill Wright or Bankhead. They've got speed to burn. Two of the three are turn-around [switch] hitters. And in the outer-garden they really "go places" to get anything which is sent in their general direction.[17]

BYRD AND MATLOCK

In the first three innings, [Leroy] "Lefty" Matlock pitched two-hit ball to shut out the Westerners. Following him on the mound was [Bill] Byrd, who had a world of stuff, but allowed one run in his last inning. Then came Satchell, against whom the last run was

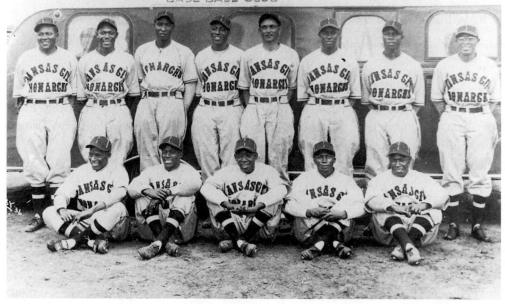

18. *The 1936 Monarchs were not a member of any league but had a record 11 players participate in the all-star game. Back row, left to right: Andy Cooper (p), Pat Patterson (2b), Woody Wilson (p), Chick Harris (1b), Floyd Kranson (p), Bob Madison, Willard Brown (ss), and Leroy Taylor (rf). Front row: Newt Allen (2b, ss), Harry Else (c), Bullet Rogan (lf), Henry Milton, (ph, cf), and Eddie Dwight (cf). Courtesy National Baseball Hall of Fame Library and Archive, Cooperstown, New York.*

scored. The run, however should have been nipped in the bud, but Johnny Washington, playing his first game in the "classic" overran a high fly and a wide-awake Radcliffe . . . who incidentally had three hits . . . scored from second.

The game is an established fact . . . but a word of advice to the promoters is not amiss at this time. Please don't do that usual thing, and expect the game to take care of itself. You failed your public out here today. Where was the amplifying system which would have allowed the people to know who was batting? Where were the broadcasts, which would have assisted in getting white people to the park. Why was it that there was no broadcast of the game as there was last year?

The East-West game is here to stay. Give it protection, please! The people are with the promoters. They realize that all game can't be repetitions of the first three. The East had things their own way this year. But next year is another year, and the same color which will someday dominate the major leagues will be in evidence for another "big day."

30,000 Jam Shows We're Game's Asset

Source: *Chicago Defender,* 29 August 1936

Baseball moguls who continue to bar Race players from the major leagues should certainly pay heed to the 30,000 crowd that watched the East-West game at Comiskey Park Sunday. Hardly any major league park in baseball plays to more than a corporal's guard on week days and even Sunday crowds are correspondingly small in the majority of the parks.

For several seasons club owners and experts have been trying to figure a way to bring fans out to the ball parks but to no avail. In Cincinnati and Boston they are playing night games with fair results but still the fans are remaining away. Thus it is easy to say that one solution would be the admission of Race players into the major leagues.

Let's take that crowd of 30,000 of Sunday and the 25,000 who saw a like game in New York one week ago. Imagine even one-third of them watching the majors in daily play and you have an increase of 10,000 for Sunday games and perhaps 5,000 for week days.

Certainly the appearance of Race players on every major league team in the country would bring the game back to its old drawing power. Not only is this condition apparent to us but the owners know it as well but they continue to hold out. Your *Chicago Defender* has pleaded for the race to get a chance in the majors for years and in recent months one or two of the daily papers have joined the chorus.

The day may come when Judge [Kenesaw Mountain] Landis and others connected with the game will throw open the door but you can do a lot toward speeding this move by writing the club owners in your city.

How would you like to see Satchel Paige and others performing in the majors? You would? Then write the owner of the club in your city and send another letter to Judge Landis at Chicago.

AUGUST 23, 1936, CHICAGO, IL

EAST	AB	R	H	D	T	HR	BI	E	TAVG	TSLG
Cool Papa Bell (Pittsburgh Crawfords), cf	3	1	3	1	0	0	1	0		
Bill Wright (Washington Elite Giants), cf	2	0	0	0	0	0	0	0		
Sammy T. Hughes (Washington Elite Giants), 2b	5	2	1	1	0	0	0	1		
Sam Bankhead (Pittsburgh Crawfords), lf	4	1	2	1	0	0	0	0		
Biz Mackey (Washington Elite Giants), c	2	0	2	1	0	0	2	0		
Josh Gibson (Pittsburgh Crawfords), c	3	2	2	0	0	0	1	0		
Jimmie Crutchfield (Pittsburgh Crawfords), rf	2	0	0	0	0	0	0	0		
Zolley Wright (Washington Elite Giants), rf	1	2	1	1	0	0	2	0		
Chester Williams (Pittsburgh Crawfords), ss	4	0	0	0	0	0	1	1		
Jim West (Washington Elite Giants), 1b	3	1	1	0	0	0	0	1		
Johnny Washington (Pittsburgh Crawfords), 1b	1	0	0	0	0	0	0	1		
Judy Johnson (Pittsburgh Crawfords), 3b	2	0	1	0	0	0	1	0		
Felton Snow (Washington Elite Giants), 3b	2	1	1	0	0	0	0	1		
Leroy Matlock (Pittsburgh Crawfords), p	1	0	0	0	0	0	0	0		
Bill Byrd (Washington Elite Giants), p	3	0	0	0	0	0	0	0		
Satchel Paige (Pittsburgh Crawfords), p	1	0	0	0	0	0	0	0		
Team Totals, Average & Slugging Pct.	39	10	14	5	0	0	8	5	.359	.487

WEST	AB	R	H	D	T	HR	BI	E	TAVG	TSLG
Eddie Dwight (Kansas City Monarchs), cf	2	0	0	0	0	0	0	0		
Newt Allen (Kansas City Monarchs), 2b, ss	5	0	0	0	0	0	0	0		
Wilson Redus (Chicago American Giants), rf	2	0	0	0	0	0	0	0		
Leroy Taylor (Kansas City Monarchs), rf	1	0	0	0	0	0	0	0		
Lou Dials (Chicago American Giants), rf	2	0	0	0	0	0	0	1		
Alec Radcliffe (Chicago American Giants), 3b	4	1	3	0	0	0	0	0		
Bullet Rogan (Kansas City Monarchs), lf	1	0	0	0	0	0	0	0		
Herman Dunlap (Chicago American Giants), lf	2	1	1	0	0	0	0	0		
Harry Else (Kansas City Monarchs), c	1	0	0	0	0	0	0	0		
Subby Byas (Chicago American Giants), c	3	0	1	0	0	0	0	0		
Popsickle Harris (Kansas City Monarchs), 1b	4	0	1	0	0	0	0	0		
Willard Brown (Kansas City Monarchs), ss	1	0	0	0	0	0	0	1		
a) Henry Milton (Kansas City Monarchs), ph-cf	2	0	0	0	0	0	0	0		
Andy Patterson (Kansas City Monarchs), 2b	2	0	2	1	0	0	1	0		
Sug Cornelius (Chicago American Giants), p	1	0	0	0	0	0	0	0		
Floyd Kranson (Kansas City Monarchs), p	0	0	0	0	0	0	0	0		
Andy Cooper (Kansas City Monarchs), p	0	0	0	0	0	0	0	0		
Ted Trent (Chicago American Giants), p	0	0	0	0	0	0	0	0		
Team Totals, Average & Slugging Pct.	33	2	8	1	0	0	1	2	.242	.273

a) Batted for Brown in the fifth

East	200	130	220-10
West	000	001	010-2

PITCHER/TEAM	GS	IP	H	R	ER	K	BB	WP	HB	W	L
Matlock/PC	1	3	2	0	0	0	1	0	0	1	0
Byrd/WEG		3	4	1	0	4	1	0	0	0	0
Paige/PC		3	2	1	0	0	0	0	0	0	0
Cornelius/CAG	1	3	6	2	2	2	1	0	0	0	1
Kranson/KCM		2	4	4	4	1	1	0	1	0	0
Cooper/KCM		1	1	0	0	0	0	0	0	0	0
Trent/CAG		3	3	4	2	1	1	0	0	0	0

BB—Hughes, Z. Wright(2), West, Milton, Else
DP—Cornelius to Allen to Harris
HBP—West by Kranson
LOB—East, West
PB—Gibson
SAC—Bankhead, J. Johnson
SB—Bell, Gibson, Snow
East—Oscar Charleston (Mgr.); Coaches Candy Jim Taylor, and Rube Curry
West—Bingo DeMoss (Mgr.); Coaches Walter Ball, Jim Brown, and Dave Malarcher.
Umpires—T. J. Young, Billy Donaldson, Moe Harris and Johnny Craig
Attendance—26,400   Time—2:28

1936 VOTING RESULTS: 338,433

P

Satchel Paige	18,275
Leroy Matlock	11,106
Ted Trent	10,697
Bill Byrd	9,781
Robert Griffith	9,335
Sug Cornelius	8,786
Martin Dihigo	7,639
Porter Moss	7,531
Andy Cooper	6,017
Willie Foster	4,721
Bert Hunter	4,109
Sam Streeter	3,631
Harry Kincannon	3,519
Floyd Kranson	2,781
Bullet Rogan	2,105

C

Subby Byas	10,177
Harry Else	8,746
Josh Gibson	7,995
Biz Mackey	6,817
Josh Johnson	3,607
Pep Young	3,571
Cy Perkins	2,976
Larry Brown	2,923

1B

Jim West	8,274
Jelly Taylor	6,795
Oscar Charleston	5,979
Popeye Harris	5,871
Mule Suttles	4,227

2B

Sammy T. Hughes	5,902
Dickie Seay	5,195

2B-3B

Pat Patterson	6,478

2B-SS

Newt Allen	7,583

3B

Alec Radcliffe	5,821
Judy Johnson	5,516
Ray Dandridge	2,917
Rainey Bibbs	1,961

SS

Ches Williams	6,674
Willie Wells	6,302
Jake Stephens	2,646
Marlin Carter	2,541

SS-3B

Felton Snow	7,168

OF

Goose Curry	7,220
Cool Papa Bell	6,848
Jimmie Crutchfield	6,457
Bill Wright	6,171
Zollie Wright	5,874
Leroy Taylor	5,621
Wilson Redus	5,127
Henry Milton	4,905
Lou Dials	4,105
Fats Jenkins	3,870
Jud Wilson	3,811
Willard Brown	3,781
Vic Harris	3,364
Eddie Dwight	3,302
Herman Dunlap	3,197

OF-3B

Sam Bankhead	10,085

1937

The Brown Bomber, Joe Louis, knocks out James Braddock to become the world heavy-weight boxing champion. The eight-round bout, before 45,000 fans, has the largest audience to date to witness a boxing match. Louis's reign as champ lasts for 13 years.

The Count Basie Orchestra, with vocalists Billie Holiday and Jimmy Rushing, opens at the Apollo Theatre in Harlem.

Milk costs 25 cents a half-gallon, 10 pounds of potatoes costs 28 cents, and 41 cents would bring home the bacon. A loaf of bread costs 9 cents.

With the beaning of all-star shortstop Willie Wells, Negro League players begin to wear protective head coverings. This is four years before major league teams experiment with wearing hard helmets.

Lou Gehrig leads the American League All-Stars to an 8–3 victory over the Nationals, with a home run and four RBIs.

LEAGUE BUSINESS

In August, Ray Brown of the Homestead Grays beaned all-star shortstop Willie Wells of the Newark Eagles. Wells was rushed to the hospital (or a "rest-awhile" as the press called it), where it was determined he had suffered a concussion. The prognosis for Wells was "out for the season." However, Wells did return to the lineup later in the season, but this time wearing a miner's hardhat without its flashlight. This was the first recorded instance of any player wearing a protective head covering in either the black or the white leagues. Thus, the mother of necessities—a life-threatening headache—caused the invention of the batting helmet.[1]

At the January 28 board meeting, Grays owner Cum Posey offered $2,500 to the Pittsburgh Crawfords for Josh Gibson and third baseman Judy Johnson. Realizing his most productive years were behind him, Johnson, then 37 years old, opted for retirement. Eventually, Gibson was traded for $2,500 plus catcher Lloyd "Pepper" Bassett and Clyde "Big Splo" Spearman. Outfielder Spearman had jumped to Santo Domingo the previous year and played for Aguilas Cibaenas. He batted .352, second in the league to Gibson, but he was no Josh. The deal was the steal of the century, as Gibson led the Grays to nine consecutive league pennants, while Bassett and Spearman had fruitful but less spectacular years than Joltin' Josh.

RACE RELATIONS

The National Association for the Advancement of Colored People (NAACP), founded in 1909, had always been a leader in addressing U.S. race relations. In January 1937, the NAACP sent out letters to the sports editors of white daily newspapers requesting their views of "the use of Negro baseball players in the major leagues." Listed below are some of the responses:

I advocate free and unlimited participation in sports for all the youth of the land regardless of race or creed. (Hugh Bradley, *New York Post*)

If everyone felt about the Negro as I do there would be no question about lifting the ban which now exists against him in organized baseball. Unfortunately, that is not the case. Prejudice is still widespread and it doesn't seem likely that it will be overcome for many years. So long as this situation exists I believe that, for the Negro's own good, he should not seek to break down the bars against him in baseball. So many major league ball players are southerners that a Negro on a major league club would find himself constantly embarrassed and often persecuted. (George R. Edmond, *St. Paul Dispatch* and *St. Paul Pioneer Press*)

I have always contended there could be no absolute claim to any title in sports unless the competition were open to all races. I see no more reason to ban the Negro from organized baseball than from college football, where colored players have earned merit for many years. Yet, organized baseball is peculiarly standardized and is reluctant to set new precedents. I believe the idea is of sufficient importance as to warrant careful study by professional baseball executives in organized baseball. (Ward Burris, *San Antonio Express*)

If the AAU took the stand against colored athletes that organized baseball does, the United States wouldn't have won the last Olympic Games and great athletes like Jesse Owens would have been born to rush unseen and waste their fleetness on the desert air. Boxing would now be dying of stagnation if it took baseball's attitude toward Joe Louis. The Tolans, Metcalfes, Owenses, Johnsons, Threadgills and Peacocks don't seem to have contaminated track and field athletics, and I suspect that baseball would not only survive, but would actually thrive if the bars now set up against colored athletes were let down. (Dan Parker, *New York Mirror*)

Any true sportsman should, and I'm sure does appreciate prowess on the athletic field irrespective of the performer's race. My thought, however, is that what the Negro needs most, for his own good, instead of admission to present organized baseball, is the perfection of a similar organization of his own. As long as we have a North and a South with a Jim Crow law throughout the land below the Mason and Dixon Line, it will be unfair to the Negro to admit him on a basis of equality to our present day baseball. Mixing of the races positively will not be accepted by the South. (George W. White, *Dallas News*)

I am without license to speak in an advisory capacity to the owners of major league baseball franchises. They have big money invested. They are big business men. I would not presume to advise them except in the business of keeping the game honest and presenting it to their public in the most entertaining way. However, in regard to Negro athletes I hold major league baseball no better than the athletics of our colleges where Negroes compete and as a rule do a might good job of it. I presume the major league club owners have their own good reasons as they see them for barring Negro players and I do not presume to go back of them. In fact, I do not know what they are. I do believe, however, that the Negro race has ball players good enough to play major league baseball and my opinion is that they would demean themselves in a manner as sporting and decent as the white players. (C. E. McBride, *Kansas City Star*)

I do not believe that Negroes and major league baseball would ever mix. I say that without any prejudice whatsoever. It is my opinion that white men would never stand for it even in this time of rapid advancement of the Negro athlete. It is a known fact, however, that many of our present day Negro baseball players could play rings around their white brothers in the major leagues. It is not a question in my mind whether the Negro talent should be given a chance in professional baseball, but how the Negro would fare after he crashed into the baseball racket. We can draw on our imagination. The Negro player would be persecuted to death. Professional baseball, I feel certain, would be a living hell for the Negro. (Wilbur Kinsley, *Chattanooga News*)

The probability of Negroes playing major league baseball is so far removed from Oklahoma City that I think it not necessary that I express myself. (Bus Ham, *Daily Oklahoman*)

I can see no reason why Negroes should be barred from participation or elsewhere in baseball. Here in California we find Negroes are participants in football, basketball and track and field competition. They are tennis players and amateur boxers. So far as I have been able to check they not only rate well up athletically with others in competition but they are well behaved and good sportsmen. I cannot see why there should be any dividing line. If there is such an unwritten bar as you state then, by all means, let us have it removed. (Harry B. Smith, *San Francisco Chronicle*)

LEAGUE DEVELOPMENT

In 1937 the popularity of Negro League baseball was at its all-time high. A second league was born, the Negro American League, composed mostly of midwestern teams, such as the Kansas City Monarchs, Chicago American Giants, Detroit Stars, Cincinnati Tigers, Indianapolis Athletics, and St. Louis Stars, and southern teams, such as the Memphis Red Sox and the Birmingham Black Barons. The Monarchs would defeat the American Giants in the playoffs, four games to one with one tie, to capture the new league's first pennant. The tied game, 2–2, was a thrilling 17-inning affair, featuring Willie Foster against Andy Cooper. Foster, who pitched a complete game at the 1933 East-West contest, gave up five hits and two runs over six and two-thirds innings, before being relieved by Sug Cornelius. In 1936 Cooper made his only all-star appearance, at the age of 38. Somewhat like the finesse style of Foster, Cooper was a master at changing speeds with a complete arsenal of breaking pitches like sliders, curve balls, and screwballs. Pitching without the arm stress of throwing a fastball, the ageless Cooper allowed two runs in the first inning and then hurled 16 shutout innings. Cooper gave up 10 hits, 3 of them to Turkey Stearnes, allowed two runs, and struck out seven batters in the marathon game.

ALL-STAR REVIEW

In 1937 Lester Rodney of the *New York Daily Worker* interviewed the great Satchel Paige at the Hotel Olga in Harlem, 15 years before his selection as the oldest player (47 years, 7 days) to the American League all-star team by Casey Stengel. Paige boasted, "Just let them take a vote of the baseball fans as to whether they want us in the game or not. I've been all over the country and I know it would be 100–1 for us." Paige also whistled, "Let the winners of the World Series play us [a Negro All-Star team headed by Paige] just one game at the Yankee Stadium and if we don't beat them before a packed house they don't have to pay us! No all-star team of major leaguers has ever beaten us on the Pacific Coast after the season games. And they had some ball players trying; Joe DiMaggio, Charley Gehringer,

Pepper Martin, Dizzy Dean, Babe Herman and others. There must be something wrong somewhere. The players are OK and the crowds are with us."[2]

Paige was without peer. He stood on his principles and expected rights commensurate with his talent. Author Robert Peterson summed up Paige's plight best: "Paige's appeal transcended race. Bill Veeck, who brought Satchel to the big leagues with the Cleveland Indians in 1948, observed that Paige is interracial and universal. And yet Paige never forgot (nor was allowed to forget) that he was a black man. He was no modern militant, eager to do battle over every slight or insult, whether real or imagined, but in his own way he broke ground toward integration long before the world had ever heard of Jackie Robinson, by refusing to pitch in towns where he could not lodge or get a meal in a restaurant."[3]

MISSING STARS

Over the years, many historians and fans have wondered about the absence of great Negro League players like Satchel Paige and Josh Gibson from 1937's all-star lineup. Several players had signed up to play for Dominican Republic dictator Rafael Trujillo and his Colored All-Stars, with Lazaro Salazar as manager.

Behind the scenes, Martin Dihigo of the New York Cubans had signed to manage Aguilas Cibaenas, taking many of his fellow Cubans with him. Joining Dihigo were pitchers Chet Brewer and Luis Tiant, and position players Clyde Spearman, Raul Alvarez, Cando Lopez, Horacio Martinez, and David "Showboat" Thomas. Now lacking a team, Cuban owner Alex Pompez had to vacate Dyckman Oval, located near the Harlem Ship Canal.

In April, Gus Greenlee, president of the Negro National League, banned Satchel Paige, Cy Perkins, Clarence Palm, Showboat Thomas, Johnny Taylor, Thad Christopher, and Clyde Spearman. The official statement issued by Greenlee read:

> The men who have sacrificed their time and money to develop Negro baseball, will not allow any one player of any group of players to wreck the league. These men must realize that the league is far larger and more powerful than they are. They left without notice, after they had been signed to contracts to play with league clubs. If they fail to report to their clubs by Saturday, May 15, they will be barred from organized baseball for one year and fined. Furthermore no league club will play in any park where outlaw ball players appear.
>
> In addition to the suspension placed against these men, our league is contemplating immediate action Martin Dihigo, former manager of the New York Cubans and [Lazaro] Salazar, to bar them from organized baseball in the States for life.[4]

The Dominicans reportedly offered large sums of money to the banned players. Paige's salary was quoted at $2,500, while his personal catcher, Cy Perkins, got $1,500. Chet Brewer, Leroy Matlock, Cool Papa Bell, Chester Williams, and Sam Bankhead were said to receive $1,000 each. Others, including Spoon Carter, Pat Patterson, and Roy Parnell, got $800 apiece. No salary was reported for Josh Gibson. These salaries were to be paid through the middle of July, when the season ended because of the extremely hot weather in the tropics.

Rumors stirred as to who could afford these huge salaries. Eventually it emerged that the American Sugar Company, which maintained its own fleet of ships, owned property, and operated sugar plantations in South and Central America, was the financier, with the political backing of dictator Rafael Trujillo. The company was said to provide financial support of the league and several teams. The bilingual Dr. Jose Enrique Aybar, dean at the

University of Santo Domingo, was contacted to negotiate the salary terms. Furthermore, to facilitate commerce, persons (or players) traveling on the company's business vessels were not required to have passports.[5]

The greatest aggregation of nonwhite players assembled would be called the Ciudad Trujillo BBC. The club was a rainbow coalition of eight Negro League players, six Cubans, a Dominican, and a Puerto Rican named Perucho "Big Bull" Cepeda, Orlando's father. Acclaimed to be one of the best in the game, the "Big Bull" had refused to play under segregated conditions in America and never came stateside.

Satchel Paige found fame to be dangerous. The trip was no holiday cruise to him and his teammates. Heavily armed troops surrounded the field and ballpark on game days. The day before a game Paige, along with his teammates, was jailed for "protection." Trujillo wanted his players fresh and with no party hangovers.

Their mission to win is best told by Satchel Paige in an article entitled "My Greatest Day in Baseball":

I guess maybe that time down in San Domingo you might say was my biggest day, although I only win the game—that is, my team—by a 6-to-5 score and I had to bear down all the way to get that. But I bet no pitcher ever had more reason to bear down than I did that day.

Sometimes I wonder where ol' Satchel would be if the other team knew what was good for us. "What do you mean we better win?" I asked the manager. He says, "I mean just that. Take my advice and win."

Funny thing, too, we knew we had the umpires on our side in that game and it was a cinch we'd get all the close ones. But then the strain we were playing under was so great sometimes I think we looked like a bunch of scrublotters. We knew all we had to do was get the ball over to first somewheres around the time the batter got there and he was out. Them umpires wasn't no fools.

You see this President Trujillo, who runs the whole show down in San Domingo, wants a team so good it will win the championship, which is a feather in his cap. He's got troops of soldiers around him all the time and he's got power. I never seen a man with such power. He flies us down to Ciudad Trujillo on a big plane and we ain't put out no place to let other passengers on. No sir! We got right of way. And what's more, we don't ever have passports.

Not having passports kinda made me uneasy anyway but that president he fixes it up someways. But I wasn't down there very long until I wished I wasn't. Just to show you, the president he give an order that none of the American ballplayers could be sold any whiskey. And we wasn't either. The guy that done it would have been shot, I guess. We was kept at a hotel and had to be in bed early. No matter what we done—like if we went in swimming—there was soldiers around and nobody could speak to us. The president he didn't want any of his people following us and starting up a conversation.

It was almost like we was in jail. But we was being paid good money. We was President Trujillo's ball club and we got to win that championship because if we don't win maybe the people won't re-elect him again. It's that important.

That's why the manager of the team, Dr. Aybar, says there was only one piece of advice he would give us. We better win. He don't know nothing about baseball hisself but he does know what the winning of this championship game means to President Trujillo.

We was down there to play 15 games and when we come to the championship game we had win seven and lose seven and in some of them we played like we never seen a baseball before. That's because of the strain we was under. Some of them guys the president had watching us sent shivers up and down your spine. They was that tough looking. They packed guns and long knives and I know they could use 'em. We didn't want to give them a chance. I think that's what the manager meant when he said we better win if we know what's good for us. When he said that he looked at them guys carrying them guns. If you think it ain't tough to field a grounder in a situation like that?

It was tough enough, anyway, because the diamond was in a place that looked something like a bull ring only there ain't no bull fights down there. And when we come up to that championship game with Estrellas de Oriente there must have been about 7,000 people in the stands. And all of them had guns, too, and we wondered what would happen if one of them umpires made a decision they didn't like and they started shooting. Boy, my mouth was dry that day!

You see this Estrellas de Oriente team was sponsored by the fellow who was President Trujillo's political rival, only the president was in power and he had the army and so the fans that come to see the game from Estrellas de Oriente didn't say too much. You know how it is: they was outnumbered.

But if we lose that game then the Estrellas de Oriente team is champion and that's a political blow to President Trujillo and maybe when there is an election again the votes go against him. We find that out. "Satchel, old boy," I say to myself, "if you ever pitched, it's now."

But it ain't no cakewalk because that Estrellas de Oriente team is tough because, you see, they loaded up with imported stars, too. We got a flock of colored Americans on our team but they got as many on theirs. How them babies could hit that ball! I don't think I ever threw harder but I wouldn't say I was relaxed. That was one day Paige was not free and easy.

All we could hear from them fans was warnings about we better win. The more they yelled the harder I threw and I bet I never did have a better fast ball only I never see any better hitters than them guys. But in the seventh inning we score two runs and then I managed to shut them out the last two frames and we win, 6 to 5.

No sooner was the game over than we was hustled back to our hotel and the next morning we got up there was a United States ship in the harbor. Sister ship to one which was blown up at Pearl Harbor. There was a plane waiting for us, too, and we were glad to get on board.

I read in a newspaper that Dr. Aybar, our manager, says "baseball in Trujillo City is not commercial. Money makes no difference. Baseball is spiritual in every respect, as indulged in by Latin races."

I am saving the clipping of that paper because I am thinking that if he is right and baseball is spiritual as it is played there ol' Satchel could be a spirit right now if we didn't win that big game. Yep, I guess so far as I'm concerned that was the biggest day of my baseball life although it's one I never wanted to live over again.[6]

After capturing a hard-fought tournament in the tropics, the Trujillo Colored All-Stars returned to the states on Monday, July 19, and were met by Ray Doan, a booking agent. Doan entered his all-stars in the prestigious semipro Denver Post Tournament. The Trujillo All-Stars won the Denver tournament. A check issued by the Denver National Bank awarded $5,179.15 to the winners.[7] The all-stars reached the finals by scores of 17–1, 12–1, 12–0, 10–1, 4–0, and 13–1. But the championship was not won without a hitch. The

19. Burnis "Wild Bill" Wright led the East over the West, 7–2, going three for five, with two RBIS, in the 1937 game. Courtesy of Charles Blockson, Moseley Collection, Temple University.

"Chocolate Whizbangs," as Denver sportswriter Leonard Cahn graced them, won six consecutive games, allowing a total of only four runs. Emery ball specialist Chet Brewer and lefty Leroy Matlock anchored the all-star pitching staff with a young flamethrower named Robert Griffith.

Satchel Paige did not join the all-stars until August 8. Although he was admired by his teammates, they did not want him to pitch the championship game against the Haliburton Cementers from Duncan, Oklahoma. The winning pitcher would receive a bonus of $1,000. Many players felt that the team's ace Leroy Matlock was entitled to the bonus money. The tournament promoters pressured the team to let the walking gate attraction Paige pitch the decisive game. Given the opportunity, Paige pitched marvelously, striking out 17 batters, but his all-stars lost 6–4 in a sloppily played contest. They made four fielding errors: one by first baseman Showboat Thomas, two by center fielder Roy Parnell and one by catcher Clarence Palm, who was also credited with three passed balls. The all-stars made more errors in this game than in the other six games combined.[8]

Roughly 45 years later, an anonymous Trujillo All-Stars infielder told sportswriter Donn Rogosin in his book *Invisible Men* that "we just didn't perform. The ball was hit to you and you just didn't get to it."[9] With each team having six wins and one loss in the double-elimination tournament, the second game of the doubleheader was won 11–1 by the Colored All-Stars with Leroy Matlock on the mound. Matlock struck out seven and gave up seven hits as the Haliburton team made four errors. The second-place Cementers won $3,560.67, while Matlock pocketed a $1,000 bonus.

After the tournament, the Colored All-Stars would entertain the Negro National League All-Stars. However, the *Philadelphia Tribune* and other newspapers called them the "Satchel Paige Outlaws." Besides Paige and Matlock, the outlaw club showcased several East-West participants, including Cool Papa Bell, Chet Brewer, George Scales, Pat Patterson, Roy Parnell, and Sam Bankhead. They would play a three-game series against a team that included many East-West players: Zollie and Bill Wright, Jake Dunn, Jud Wilson, Bill Byrd, Oscar Charleston, Pepper Bassett, Barney Morris, Ches Williams, Ray Dandridge, Mule Suttles, Leon Day, Dick Seay, Willie Wells, Big Jim West, Raleigh "Biz" Mackey, and Johnny "Schoolboy" Taylor.

The Colored All-Stars won the first game, 5–2, in Philadelphia's Parkside Park. History was made in the second game of the trifecta when Taylor faced Paige before 22,500 spectators at the Polo Grounds in New York. To everyone's surprise, the battery of Biz Mackey and 20-year-old, baby-faced Schoolboy Taylor no-hit the talented stars from Santo Domingo. Taylor faced 29 batters, fanned 5, and walked 2. Not a single runner reached second base. Although Paige struck out 8, Big Jim West, from the Philly Stars, connected for a two-run homer off Paige in the eighth inning to nail down the 2–0 victory.

Fans begged for a rematch between the two pitchers. On September 26, before a Sun-

20. Satchel Paige and the schoolboy wonder Johnny Taylor of the New York Cubans. Against all odds, Taylor pitched a no-hitter against Satchel Paige and his all-stars from Trujillo. The Trujillo All-Stars had been touted as the most talented team of tan stars ever assembled. Courtesy of Estelle Taylor.

day crowd of 30,000 fans at Yankee Stadium, Paige and his all-stars beat the handpicked talent this time, 9–4. Paige's teammates belted Taylor out of the box, getting seven runs and eight hits in five innings. In the second game of the doubleheader, the National League All-Stars came back to grab the second contest, a five-inning affair, which was ended by darkness, 1–0.

Besides Paige and Gibson, the 1937 Comiskey all-star contest did not showcase the following Trujillo Colored All-Stars: outfielders Cool Papa Bell, Tetelo Vargas, and Silvio Garcia; infielders Sam Bankhead, Red Parnell, Pat Patterson, Showboat Thomas, George Scales, and Rap Dixon; and pitchers Leroy Matlock, Robert Griffith, Chet Brewer, and Spoon Carter. All of these men had been banned from the East-West classic, making it a less-than-all-star attraction.

Sun Still Rises in East

Source: *Pittsburgh Courier,* 14 August 1937

Again the baseball sun is sinking in the West, another colored East-West game fades into the stalking shadows of memory lane and once more a 7 to 2 score supports the theory that the sun of Diamondom still rises in the East.

The glamorous sport spectacle just unfolded before the widened eyes of twenty thousand developed into a pitched catching prowess as displayed by the West. But the big guns of the East's murderer's row just couldn't be silenced in the ambitious broadsides of the West's mound sharpshooters.

The game was punctuated by some of the most brilliant acts of fielding ever witnessed in addition to thrilling home run smashes, lightning-like double plays and all those other features which have made the East-West clashes the most spectacular contest of each season.

"CAROLINA" SON SHINES

Sparkling among the constellation of stars was Buck Leonard, the peerless product of Rocky Mount in the old North state, who blazed the victory trail for the East by smashing out a home run in the second inning when the score stood at goose eggs for both teams. It was a beautiful wallop, which landed in the second tier of the right field stands, traveling about 360 feet. But more than it was the spark that touched off the East's powder barrel and the big sticks of his teammates did the rest. Leonard's fielding was also of the sensational variety.

Another stellar performer for the East was big Ben [Bill] Wright of Tom Wilson's Washington Elites. Wright led the Orient in batting, getting three hits, one of them a double and turned in the most dazzling catch of the day in snaring Allen's Texas leaguer into short center field. Ben came bounding in like an antelope until he saw that his only chance of catching the ball would be to plunge for it. Then he went into a swan dive, which would be a beautiful sight to behold. With his two hands stretched out far out in front, he skidded along the grass . . . just far enough for his fingers to meet the fast-dropping horsehide. Then he squeezed it robbing Allen of what looked like a sure hit on anybody's ball field. When big Ben [Bill] came back to the dugout, the fans gave him a rousing round of applause.

WEST FINDS STRENGTH IN STRONG

From out of the West, came Ted Strong of Indianapolis to uphold the colors of the Occident. This 21-year-old youth, whose baseball ability probably backs up his family name, proved to be one of the most shining stars of the day, both at bat and afield. Strong smashed out a powerful drive into center field, which would have ordinarily been a triple, but his speed and an instant of mishandling by a fielder allowed him to stretch it into a homer. Ted also turned in an amazing game at fielding ground first base, playing the initial sack for the first time, Strong's regular position is at short for the A.B.C.'s, but he showed worlds of promise as a first baseman in the big show here this afternoon. Off-season, Strong cavorts around the roaring hardwoods as a member of the Harlem Globetrotters basketball team.

The mighty "Turkey" Stearnes also proved a real asset to the West. Turkey strutted around centerfield covering almost as much territory as the state of Texas. He didn't get a clean hit himself, but he took plenty of possible hits away from the big stick fielders from the East.

WELLS, BASSETT, DANDRIDGE ADD THRILLS

While many of the Nordic writers from the dailies looked on in amazement, such super stars as Willie Wells, Pepper Bassett, and Bill [Ray] Dandridge flashed their finest playing form. Wells fielded brilliantly at the shortstop position, drifting balls across to first with the speed of a bullet. His playing today stood out as positive proof that he is one of the greatest infielders ever developed.

Bill [Ray] Dandridge was another Easterner whose handling of the hot corner caught the fancy of the fans. Dandridge handled the liners and grounders in expert fashion and also exhibited one of the best throwing arms seen in many moons.

Pepper Bassett, the big Crawford catcher, who once rocked his way to fame by catching in a rocking chair, also gave the rabble a rare exhibition of swing. Practically sitting on his heels, he swayed as he snatched the fast and slow ones as they came skipping across the plate, and then tossed 'em back without shifting his position.

AUGUST 8, 1937, CHICAGO, IL

EAST	AB	R	H	D	T	HR	BI	E	TAVG	TSLG
Jerry Benjamin (Homestead Grays), rf	5	0	1	0	0	0	0	0		
Willie Wells (Newark Eagles), ss	5	1	1	0	0	0	0	0		
Bill Wright (Washington Elite Giants), cf	5	2	3	1	0	0	2	0		
Buck Leonard (Homestead Grays), 1b	4	2	2	0	0	1	2	1		
Mule Suttles (Newark Eagles), lf	3	0	1	0	0	0	0	0		
Chester Williams (Pittsburgh Crawfords), 2b	3	0	0	0	0	0	1	0		
Jake Dunn (Philadelphia Stars), 2b	1	0	0	0	0	0	0	0		
Ray Dandridge (Newark Eagles), 3b	5	1	2	0	0	0	0	0		
Pepper Bassett (Pittsburgh Crawfords), c	3	0	0	0	0	0	0	0		
Barney Morris (Pittsburgh Crawfords), p	2	0	0	0	0	0	0	0		
Barney Brown (New York Black Yankees), p	1	0	1	0	0	0	0	0		
Leon Day (Newark Eagles), p	1	1	1	1	0	0	0	0		
Team Totals, Average & Slugging Pct.	38	7	12	2	0	1	5	1	.316	.447

WEST	AB	R	H	D	T	HR	BI	E	TAVG	TSLG
Newt Allen (Kansas City Monarchs), 2b-ss	4	0	0	0	0	0	0	0		
Lloyd Davenport (Cincinnati Tigers), rf	4	1	1	1	0	0	0	0		
Wilson Redus (Chicago American Giants), rf	0	0	0	0	0	0	0	0		
Ted Strong (Indianapolis Athletics), 1b	4	1	2	0	0	1	2	2		
Turkey Stearnes (Detroit Stars), cf	4	0	0	0	0	0	0	0		
Willard Brown (Kansas City Monarchs), lf	2	0	0	0	0	0	0	0		
a) Henry Milton (Kansas City Monarchs), ph	1	0	0	0	0	0	0	0		
Alec Radcliffe (Chicago American Giants), 3b	3	0	1	0	0	0	0	0		
Howard Easterling (Cincinnati Tigers), ss	2	0	0	0	0	0	0	0		
Rainey Bibbs (Cincinnati Tigers), 2b	1	0	1	1	0	0	0	0		
Ted Radcliffe (Cincinnati Tigers), c	3	0	0	0	0	0	0	1		
b) Subby Byas (Chicago American Giants), ph	1	0	0	0	0	0	0	0		
Ted Trent (Chicago American Giants), p	0	0	0	0	0	0	0	0		
c) Eldridge Mayweather (Kansas City Monarchs), ph	1	0	0	0	0	0	0	0		
Hilton Smith (Kansas City Monarchs), p	0	0	0	0	0	0	0	1		
Porter Moss (Cincinnati Tigers), p	2	0	0	0	0	0	0	0		
Team Totals, Average & Slugging Pct.	32	2	5	2	0	1	2	4	.156	.313

a) Batted for W. Brown in 9th
b) Batted for T. Radcliffe in 9th
c) Batted for Trent in 3rd

East	010	200	130-7
West	000	101	000-2

PITCHER/TEAM	GS	IP	H	R	ER	K	BB	WP	HB	W	L	SV
Morris/PC	1	3	2	1	1	2	0	0	1	1	0	0
B. Brown/NBY	cell 3	2	1	1	0	2	0	0	0	0	0	
Day/NE	cell 3	1	0	0	4	0	0	0	0	0	1	
Trent/CAG	1	3	2	1	1	0	0	0	0	0	0	0
H. Smith/KCM	cell 0	1	2	1	0	2	1	0	0	1	0	
Moss/CT	cell 6	9	4	1	1	3	0	0	0	0	0	

BB—Suttles (2), Dunn, Bassett, W. Brown, Easterling, Leonard
DP—Moss to T. Radcliffe to Strong; Wells to Dunn to Leonard; Allen to Strong
HBP—A. Radcliffe by Morris
LOB—East 9, West 6
SB—Dandridge, Wright, Suttles
East—Biz Mackey (Mgr.); Coaches Bullet Rogan (1b), Candy Jim Taylor (3b)
West—Candy Jim Taylor (Mgr.)
Umpires—Billy Donaldson, E. C. "Pop" Turner, Virgil Blueitt, Mo Harris
Attendance—25,000   Time—

1937 VOTING RESULTS: 1,398,357

P

Ted Trent	31,809
Porter Moss	30,890
Hilton Smith	29,790
Sug Cornelius	28,782
Andy Cooper	27,659
Charley Justice	24,876
Tommy Johnson	24,786
Ray Brown	21,410
Andy Porter	21,271
Bill Holland	21,143

C

Pepper Bassett	41,463
T. J. Young	21,015
Double Duty Radcliffe	15,879
Frank Duncan	9,672
Subby Byas	4,560

1B

Chili Mayweather	28,765
Luther Gilyard	28,657
Buck Leonard	23,247
Henry McCall	19,546
Jelly Taylor	17,975
Jim West	11,936

1B-SS

Ted Strong	50,636

2B

Sammy T. Hughes	32,467
Newt Allen	29,759
Jack Marshall	27,465
Rainey Bibbs	26,456
Rev Cannady	21,875
Dickie Seay	21,129
Jimmy Ford	19,890

3B

Alec Radcliffe	22,100
Jud Wilson	21,590
Ray Dandridge	21,357
Felton Snow	21,239
Dewey Creacy	21,064

SS

Howard Easterling	22,786
Jelly Jackson	21,873
Jake Stephens	10,982
Willie Wells	9,286

SS-2B

Ches Williams	43,250

OF

Jerry Benjamin	43,436
Turkey Stearnes	29,795
Sam Seagraves	26,809
Herman Dunlap	26,789
Lloyd Davenport	22,896
Vic Harris	22,675
Bill Wright	22,247
Nat Rogers	21,875
Zollie Wright	21,740
Henry Milton	21,736
Fats Jenkins	21,590
Jake Dunn	21,249
Ted Page	21,221
Ed Stone	21,076
Willard Brown	19,800
Wilson Redus	19,689
Bullet Rogan	18,982
Eddie Dwight	18,900
Goose Curry	17,800
Jimmie Crutchfield	11,583
Clint Thomas	11,040

1938

Alabama's Tuskegee Institute sponsors the first intercollegiate golf tournament for black colleges.

Henry Armstrong wins the lightweight championship and becomes the first fighter to hold three titles at one time. Meanwhile, Joe Louis gets revenge and knocks out Max Schmeling in the first round of their rematch.

Milk costs only 25 cents a half-gallon, 10 pounds of potatoes costs 21 cents, and 37 cents would bring home the bacon. A loaf of bread costs 9 cents.

Sister Rosetta Tharpe becomes the first gospel singer to record with a major label when she signs a contract with Decca Records. Benny Goodman refuses to play in a New York club without two black members of his band, vibraphonist Lionel Hampton, an avid Negro League follower, and pianist Teddy Wilson.

After pitching consecutive no-hitters a month earlier, Johnny Vander Meer leads the National League All-Stars to a 4–1 victory, with the aid of four errors by the American League stars. Rapid Bob Feller of the Cleveland Indians strikes out 18 batters in one game to set a major league record.

RACE RELATIONS

In 1938 the Jake Powell incident became a focal point of the season. Powell, a backup outfielder for the New York Yankees, was a guest of Chicago White Sox radio announcer Bob Elson of WGN on July 29. When Elson asked Powell, "How do you keep in trim during the winter months?" Dayton, Ohio, resident Powell blurted, "Oh, that's easy. I'm a policeman and I beat niggers over the head with my blackjack while on my beat."[1] Immediately the station was swamped with angry phone calls. Some of the white press had tried to pass off Powell's racial slur as an innocent joke from a naive southerner, but Powell had been born in Maryland and lived in Ohio.

Elson issued the following statement to the *Chicago Defender* the next day.

An incident occurred on my pre-game broadcast, which was very distasteful to me and, I know, to many of my radio listeners. I regret very much that player Jake Powell of the New York Yankees saw fit to make a remark which was entirely uncalled for and made without being anticipated in any way by me. The remark was strictly Jake Powell's own words, as all of the interviews with players are presented without opportunity for censorship. They are interviews in the strict sense of the word, being wholly unrehearsed and presented without the use of any written copy. I want to repeat that the remark of Mr. Powell was as offensive to me as it was to many of my good friends.[2]

Manager Joe McCarthy defended his player, placing the blame on the radio station. His statement to the *Chicago Defender* read: "The players do not want to engage in these broadcasts. In fact, most of them are afraid of them, but they are pressured until finally one of them gives in. Then in an unguarded moment, something is said, maybe only in a joke, but it's taken the wrong way and then there is trouble."[3]

When the *Defender* asked McCarthy about Powell's remark, McCarthy said he didn't hear the statement because he was on the field at the time but responded meekly, "I don't know what Powell said but whatever it was, I'm pretty sure he meant no harm." McCarthy added, "Perhaps he just meant to get off a wisecrack. So the radio people ran off cold with apologies and I'm out a ball player for 10 days in the thick of the pennant race." McCarthy added he would not permit any of his players to do future radio interviews without a prepared script.[4]

In a prepared statement to the press, Commissioner Landis read, "Although the commissioner believes the remark was carelessly and not purposely made, Powell is suspended for ten days." Powell returned to the lineup on August 16 in the second game of a doubleheader against the Washington Senators at Griffith Stadium. When Powell took his station in left field, he was bombarded with glass bottles. In the seventh inning, he was showered with bottles once again, causing the game to be held up for about 15 minutes. One African-American, Roy Reeves, an employee of the National Park Service, was arrested.[5]

The pop bottle episode caused Senators owner Clark Griffith to declare that beverages would no longer be served to fans in glass containers, leading to a new policy that called for beverages in paper cups only.[6]

Meanwhile, black Americans threatened to boycott the brewery of Yankee owner Jacob Ruppert, and residents of Harlem demanded a public apology. On August 2, Dr. Channing H. Tobias, a prominent black American serving as senior secretary of the national board of the YMCA, sent McCarthy a letter expressing his views of the Powell incident:

> If a member of the Yankee team had publicly stated that he spent his time between seasons "cracking dogs over the heads," that in my judgment would be sufficient warrant for suspension if not expulsion. But for him to show such disrespect for the personality of human beings as to find satisfaction in telling the public that he used his position as guardian of public safety to crack people over the head, seems to put him beyond the defense of even his best friends.
>
> You, yourself as an Irish Catholic belong to a religious group that in the not distant past, even in this country, has been victimized by intolerance and bigotry. Would it not, therefore, be more fitting for you rather than condone such a remark on the part of one of your players, to censure him and apologize to the offended group, particularly when that group happens to be one that is making a desperate effort under terrific handicaps to make itself respectable and respected?
>
> Please understand that I speak in no spirit of bitterness but rather as a citizen of New York and part of a racial community that gives large support to your team. I still hope you may win the pennant, but I would remind you that pennants are won by good ball playing on the part of men who have respect enough for the public that supports them to not offer gratuitous insults to any part of it.[7]

Chicago Daily News writer Lloyd Lewis argued that Powell's suspension was too lenient, "especially in a time when America is looming up, more and more every day, as the one place where racial prejudice is unfashionable."[8]

Due to public pressure, Powell visited Harlem with Yankee executive Col. Hubert ("Black Eagle") Julian at his side and told gatherings at the Mimo Club and Smalls' Grill that he was sorry for the remark. Powell said, "I have not slept any since this thing happened. I want you to believe me. I am on the spot, boys." Powell added that he felt many "colored players" were good enough to play in the white majors and that he was in favor of integration at any time.[9]

Wendell Smith wrote, "Major league baseball will offer the Jake Powell case to us as an example of their deep sincerity. But we know, and they know, that Jake Powell, has never been liked by the fans because of his foul play and unsportsmanlike conduct since he came up to the big leagues. They have used Powell because the Yankees did not need him and because he was on his way back to the minors anyway. He is the modern 'Dreyfus' of big league baseball."[10]

Powell made his last appearance of the season on September 10 at Griffith Stadium, going hitless in four at bats. The press reported no incidents. He finished the season with a .256 batting average. Over the next three seasons, he played in just 12 games for the Yankees before being traded to the Washington Senators in 1943. After the 1944 season, at the age of 37, Jake retired from baseball. He became a police officer in Montgomery County, Maryland.[11] A few years later, on November 11, 1948, Alvin Jacob Powell committed suicide while under arrest in a Washington DC police station on a charge of passing bad checks.[12]

RACE RELATIONS CONTINUED

The issue of integrating Major League Baseball remained a hot topic in the black press. More than seven years before the signing of Jackie Robinson by the Dodgers, Wendell Smith of the *Courier* compared Commissioner Landis to Hitler in his weekly editorial column, "Smitty's Sport Spurts":

Being an American institution, designed to promote fair play democratic ideals and the theory that all men are equal, it will be the duty of this organization [Major League Baseball] to send a protest to Hitler. But they'll feel mighty sheepish about it. They play the same game as Hitler. They discriminate, segregate and hold down a minor race just as he does. While Hitler cripples the Jews, the great leaders of our national pastime refuse to recognize our black ball players.

We must hand it to Adolph [*sic*] for one thing. He comes right out and tells why he objects to Jews. He is wrong, of course, but he doesn't think he is. And, he doesn't hide or refuse to answer when asked about it.

But you take "Hitler" Landis for instance, He, nor any of his sides [sidekicks], have the courage of Adolph. When asked about the inclusion of the black "Jews" into baseball they beat around the bush . . . and then swing out on something else. Of course, they are Americans, men who believe in freedom and all that other bunk Mr. Roosevelt tried to hand Adolph. Incidentally, Mr. Roosevelt would have to scramble some if Adolph asked him why black Americans must ride in Jim Crow cars and the like, in his land of the brave and free![13]

ALL-STAR REVIEW

Meanwhile, the newspaper campaign to integrate Major League Baseball was well under way led by Al Moses, writer for the Associated Negro Press, and a white writer, Jimmy Powers of the *New York Daily News*. On September 5, Powers wrote:

If I could wave a magic wand and break down race prejudice, I'd put this Giant team on the field next spring and guarantee a winner.

Josh Gibson, catcher (Homestead); Hank Danning, catcher (Giants);

Ray Brown, pitcher (Homestead); Barney Brown, pitcher (Black Yanks);

Buck Leonard, first base (Homestead);

Pat Patterson, second base (Philly Stars);

Dick Bartell, shortstop (Giants);

Dick [Ray] Dandridge, third base (Newark Eagles);

Joe Moore, leftfield (Giants);

Mel Ott, rightfield (Giants); and

Sam Bankhead, centerfield (Pittsburgh Crawfords).

In his column, Al Moses added: "All we need now is for the hundred of more leading white writers drawing salaries on large daily newspapers to follow the courageous leadership of New York's Jimmy Powers plus a deal of initiative and fight on the part of our writers and leaders."[14]

SCOUTING REPORTS

Wendell Smith's attack on the segregation issue appeared in the May 14, 1938, edition of his *Courier* column. Smith pleaded with African-Americans to stop supporting Major League Baseball. He explained that by spending their wages on all-white clubs, they only encouraged the lack of cooperation by major league officials. Smith was even more candid, saying that African-Americans did not support their own teams, despite their obvious abilities, suggesting some apathy by fans toward black teams. Smith was not encouraging the segregation of the leagues but insisting that the color line had to be broken. However, Smith could not understand why black fans continued to support an "institution that places a bold 'not welcome' sign over its thriving portal." He added, "Oh, we're an optimistic faithful, prideless lot, we pitiful Black folk."

Smith conducted interviews with 8 major league managers and about 40 white players to determine their positions on race relations in baseball. He published the interviews in a new column called "What Big Leaguers Think of Negro Baseball Players," which ran from July 15, 1939, to September 2, 1939. This tremendous collection of information on such a delicate topic stirred the consciousness of many Americans. The consensus opinion, with the exception of New York Giants manager Bill Terry, was that black players should be allowed into the major leagues.

Smith interviewed the great Jerome "Dizzy" Dean about integration in America. Dean and his team of all-stars had barnstormed against the Satchel Paige All-Stars in 1934. Dean's assessment of Paige and others was very revealing: "If some of the colored players I've played against were given a chance to play in the majors they'd be stars as soon as they joined up. Listen, Satchel Paige could make any team in the majors. I pitched against him in about six exhibition games and came out the loser in four or five of them. He's got everything a pitcher can have. Shucks, only his color holds him back. He could be plenty of help to some of these big league teams—I'm tellin' you. I've seen him fan big league batters just like they were sandlotters. He just stands out there on the mound and blows that ol' fastball by you like nothin' at all. Paige is a big leaguer, if there ever was one."

When Smith asked Dizzy about Josh Gibson, he was equally enthused, saying, "Gibson is one of the best catchers that ever caught a ball. Watch him work this pitcher. He's top at that. And-boy-o-boy, can he hit that ball!"

When Smith told Dean that Walter Johnson had rated Gibson worth $200,000 to any big league team and was a better catcher than Bill Dickey, Dizzy said, "I don't know much about Dickey, but I agree with Walter when he says Gibson is worth $200,000."

"Another guy I think could have made the grade in the majors," said Dean, "was Oscar Charleston. He used to play against us in exhibition games. He could hit a ball a mile. . . . He didn't have a weakness, and when he came up we just hoped he wouldn't get a hold of one. We just threw and hoped like hell he didn't send it out of the park."

Dean added that some of the toughest games he had ever played were against Negro players. He seemed to be proud of the fact that he had pitched against Satchel Paige and one time had struck out Josh Gibson.

"I have played against a Negro all-star team," said Dizzy, "that was so good we didn't think we had a chance. We had a team of big leaguers, too. When we did beat them we thought we had accomplished something."

GAME REVIEWS

Greenlee Says Game Is for the Players, Fans

Profit Angle Was Secondary When Game Was Started, He Says

Source: *Chicago Defender*, 6 August 1938

Gus Greenlee, chairman of the East-West game committee, made his stand clear on what he thinks of the annual East-West classic. The statement came after owners had been haggling over disposition of profits.

Greenlee said: "No owner should nurse the idea that this particular game is promoted for profit alone. We have always tried to be careful in spending so that the men behind the game would not have to dig down in their pockets—and thanks to the good fans in Chicago and surrounding territory, we have always finished with a profit of some kind.

But the profit angle with me, Tom Wilson and R.A. Cole, the men who first gambled with the idea, was secondary. What we set out to do, was to put aside one day of glory for the players who had improved during the year. In presented these players to the public, we replied to demands which loyal fans had been making for a long number of years. The manner in which the classic has been supported each year, bears me out in this claim.

I see no reason to change the purpose of the game, despite what a few owners say to the contrary. At best, colored players are underpaid, and if we are to expect them to continue until a brighter day comes along, one day of glory each year, is certainly a small price to pay for this loyalty.

The East-West game is one for ball players and fans first, and owners second."

West Beats East in Classic Thriller, 5 to 4

30,000 Go Wild When Robinson Drives in Tying Run,

Then Scores Winning Marker on Fluke Homer

Cornelius Driven from Mound; Hilton Smith and Double Duty

Radcliffe Hurl Well; West's Rally and Sparkling Plays Keep Fans on Edge

by Frank A. Young

Source: *Chicago Defender*, 27 August 1938

Thirty thousand fans, bordering on hysteria, all did a "Susie Q" Sunday afternoon at Comiskey Park in the home third of the sixth annual East versus West classic when Neil Robinson (Memphis Red Sox) slammed what should have been a single (or perhaps a double) to center field and Sam Bankhead (Pittsburgh Crawfords) let the ball go through him for a home run inside of the park—and away went the ball game.

It must have been the old urge to see the underdog come from behind that caused women to scream and straw hats to go sailing out on the field. Pandemonium reigned. The great Mister Bankhead had allowed the ball to play him instead of him playing the ball.

Instead of that little round white object taking a hop, it scooted right through the centerfielder's legs. But that's baseball. A rotten error of judgment but you can't mark errors so Robinson got credit for a four-ply smash scoring Alex Radcliffe (Chicago American Giants) and Ted Strong (Indianapolis A.B.C.'s) ahead of him.

Boy, oh boy, what a scene! The West had gone to bat on the short end of a 3 to 1 score.

Lefty Walker of the Homestead Grays walked Henry Milton (Kansas City Monarchs) who promptly stole second. Newt Allen, Kansas City Monarchs second sacker and captain filed out to Vic Harris (Homestead Grays) in leftfield. Alex Radcliffe poked a single to center and Milton scored. When he hit the dirt at the plate and kicked up a cloud of dust, the hopes of the West soared. Ted Strong walked. Both advanced on a passed ball. Quincy Trouppe (Indianapolis) was robbed of a hit by Walter Cannady (New York Black Yankees) who dug the hot grounder out of the dirt, bluffed Trouppe [A. Radcliffe] and Strong back to third and second, respectively and then shot the ball to Buck Leonard [Homestead Grays] at first for the second out. Then Neil Robinson got his hit which scored Trouppe [A. Radcliffe] and Strong and came home himself.

HAMMER WILLIE

The East jumped on Willie Cornelius who had about as much on the ball as the dead Emperor Nero. Those Eastern bats which have knocked out many a victory got busy. Vic Harris doubled to right, the ball bounding back off the wall. Sammy Hughes (Baltimore Elites) singled to left scoring Harris. The West players tricked Hughes and got him out at first. Frank Duncan (Chicago) threw to Newt Allen and Hughes was run down, Strong getting the putout. Willie Wells (Newark) tripled to right. Buck Leonard popped to Strong. Walter Cannady doubled to left and the fans howled for Manager Andy Cooper (Kansas City) to take Cornelius out.

Cooper, however, felt like most of the critics and that was Radcliffe should have knocked down the drive of Cannady's. Wells scored on the hit. Sam Bankhead (Crawfords) singled to right and Cannady scored the third run of the inning. The crowd booed because Cornelius was allowed to stay on the mound. Bill Wright (Baltimore) went out, Newt Allen to Strong. There were five hits and three runs in that inning—a mighty big lead for any team in a game like that.

But the West was not beaten. Milton was hit on the arm and went to first. Allen missed the third strike and since it was a hit and run play, Milton reached second, beating the throw from Bizz Mackey (Baltimore) and got credit for a stolen base. Alex Radcliffe poled a sharp single to right and Professor Milton who came from Wiley College [Marshall, Texas] and who teaches school during the winter months romped home. Strong, heaviest clouter on the West's team went out, Willie Wells to Buck Leonard and Cannady to Leonard disposed of Trouppe.

SMITH STOP 'EM

Big Hilton Smith of Kansas City went to the mound for the West in the second. Mackey was called out on strikes. [Big Edsall] Walker walked [hit by pitch]. [Vic] Harris was safe when Allen elected to play for Walker at second and the throw rolled away from [Byron] Johnson. It was wide and Allen was credited with an error, Walker going to third. Alex Radcliffee made a whale of a play on Hughes' grounder and nipped him at first on a rifle shot to Strong. Wells looked at a fast ball which cut the heart of the plate for the third strike.

The fourth and last East run came in the fifth. Hughes smacked one to left for two bases. Wells beat out one of the most perfectly executed bunts and Hughes pulled up at third. Strong took Wells roller but Willie had beaten Ted to the first base bag. Leonard lifted one to Neil Robinson in center and Hughes scored. Wells hiking to second after the catch. Wells was able to reach second on the throw to the plate. Cannady looked at the third strike go by and the crowd got a treat when Frank Duncan whipped the ball down to Alex Radcliffe getting Wells trying to steal third.

Barney Brown (New York) batted for Walker in the fourth and then took the mound and breezed along fine. Schoolboy Johnny Taylor, 23-year-old youngster from Providence, RI who is the star hurler for the Pittsburgh Crawfords, pitched the seventh and eighth. With two out in the eighth, Larry Brown, in for Duncan, walked. Byron Johnson (Kansas City) singled to right. Wells made a whale of a stop behind second on T. Radcliffe's hot ground, but too late to get anybody and the sacks were loaded. But Taylor wasn't any novice at the game. Milton hit one, which bounded high in front of the plate. Mackey took it and whipped it to first killing the side. The East's catcher saw Larry Brown racing home, too near the plate to get him and his only chance was to get Milton who was going down like War Admiral going under the wire.

DOUBLE DUTY SAVES DAY

For the West, Smith worked until the sixth when the ever-reliable Double Duty Radcliffe, manager of the Memphis Red Sox, took the mound. Barney greeted Radcliffe with a single in the seventh and then superb fielding retired the side. Allen threw out Harris, Alex Radcliffe threw out Hughes and Allen gathered in Wells' fly.

Larry Brown (Memphis) replaced Duncan behind the bat in the seventh.

Leonard opened the eighth a single, Cannady sacrificed, T. Radcliffe to Strong. A. Radcliffe ran close to the box seats for Bankhead's foul fly. Wright went out when Allen raced over in foul territory near the right field boxes for a high foul.

[After Mackey lined out,] Fisher [Jake Dunn] batted for Taylor in the ninth. He singled. Harris forced Fisher [Dunn] at second, Allen to Johnson, but Johnson's throw at first was a trifle late. It hit the ground and then bounded into Strong's hands. Had it been thrown on the line, a double play might have resulted. To make matters worse, the fans, though otherwise peaceful, became irate and one or two lost their heads and tossed a pop bottle or two into the diamond. But the game went on without any interruption. Harris stole second. Robinson came in for Hughes' liner to center for the final out of the game.

Editor's note: The loss by the East squad may have been caused by the absence of key players selected for the game like Josh Gibson (Homestead Grays), Ray Dandridge (Newark Eagles), Mule Suttles (Newark Eagles), and pitcher Ray Brown (Homestead Grays). Eagles owner Effa Manley and Grays owner Cum Posey decided to hold out the players to protect them from injuries. This prompted National League president Tom Wilson to issue a ruling at the next board requiring team owners to send selected players to the East-West game.

How Good Is Negro Baseball?

It's Faster, For One Thing

by Lloyd Lewis

Source: *Chicago Daily News,* 22 August 1938

Negro professional baseball as illustrated by two sets of all-stars in Comiskey Park yesterday, is faster on the bases than the major league ball now being played in the American and National circuits; it is almost as swift and spectacular in the field; it lacks the batting form of the white man's big leagues; it has a shortstop, Willie Wells of Newark, who is as good as a dozen men in that position in the majors today; it has pitchers who could fill places in half the leading teams of the top white leagues.

In the sixth of the annual All-Star matches which are played at Comiskey Park between two Negro leagues, the American circuit, known as the West, and the National, called the East, the West won yesterday, 5–4.

AFIRE WITH SPEED

The game was afire with speed. The bases were run with a swiftness and daring absent from the white man's game for 20 years. Crafty runners kept the pitchers worried, catchers throwing hastily and infielders darting in and out to hold them to the bags. They took chances, ran out every batted ball to the limit and gave the umpires as hectic a day as Comiskey Park hasn't seen since its last world series with the Giants, who under John McGraw, played exactly that kind of baseball.

They stretched singles into doubles, they went down to first so fast that no infield double play succeeded on a ground ball (and those infielders are cats, too), and one of them, antelope-legged [Neal] Robinson from the Memphis Red Sox, made a home run inside the park. The aforementioned Wells dragged and beat out as canny a bunt as Comiskey Park ever saw. "Schoolboy" Taylor, the 23-year-old pitcher from the East's Pittsburgh Crawfords, showed class that was only rivaled by the crafty old "Double Duty" Radcliffe, who slow-balled four shutout innings to protect the West's one-run lead.

A welcome sight in a big-league park was the willingness of Negro outfielders to throw out base runners and of pitchers to whip bunts to second for force plays. Such risks are almost things of the past in the white man's major circuits, particularly in the American League, where hitting was become the criterion of worth for eight positions on a team.

Only in batting are the Negro pros inferior. Lack of scientific training is apparent in their unsmoothness in wielding a bat. Too many of them preserve the hallmark of the amateur, the "foot in the bucket," the shy-away of the front shoe as the pitch comes up.

"SHOWBOATING" WITH GLOVE

A trace of non-professionalism also cropped out here and there yesterday when fielders took throws on lines drives with one hand when two would have been safer. Strong, the tall, magnificently proportioned first baseman from the Indianapolis A.B.C.'s insists upon "showboating" with his glove, a trick of vain glory, which he should forget even if one of his hands is as large as the average man's two. (He is a sensational basketball player in wintertimes.)

But in throwing and base-running the Negro All-Stars will remind you, if you see them a year hence in their "rubber" game, more of the game when it was in its golden age, the days of McGraw and Tinker and Cobb and Chance, than anything around the big-league parks today.

Missed His Date

Source: *Chicago Defender,* 27 August 1938

Mayor Edward J. Kelly came out to the East vs. West game to throw out the first ball and watch two or three innings and then keep several engagements. The game got interesting.

About the time the mayor was ready to reach for his hat, along came the wallop of Neil Robinson, the Memphis boy who was playing in centerfield. It developed into a homer, two runs scored ahead of Robinson. The mayor settled back in his seat and stayed there until the last out.

Editor's note: Mayor Kelly was honored to throw out the ceremonial first pitch. The pitch missed home plate entirely. The mayor claimed he "was a bit off form."

The Stuff Is Here—Past—Present—Future

by Fay Young

Source: REPLY—*Chicago Defender*, 27 August 1938

Concerted action will do much to get the Negro ball players in the major leagues thinks Lloyd Lewis, sports editor of the *Chicago Daily News,* who witnessed the sixth annual East versus West contest Sunday at Comiskey Park.

When the game advanced to the fourth inning, Mr. Lewis believed the two teams as far as they had gone rated above class AA in the minors but a trifle under big league calibre. Understand now, he wasn't judging the individual players, but the two teams as a whole.

Later on he was amazed at the play of Wells, Newark manager and shortstop. When Wells pulled one or two brilliant plays it was only natural for Mr. Lewis to believe the "little wizard," who left the West for the East, was playing over his head. But Wells kept it up. He tried to pull "a fast one" on Larry Brown when Brown overran second.

Wells tagged Brown and the umpire called the runner safe. The crowd, of course, didn't understand. It so happened that when the foxy Mr. Wells tagged Brown, he didn't have the ball in his hand. It was "a slicker play."

After the game was over Mr. Lewis felt free to talk. "What do you think about Mr. Wells now?" I asked Mr. Lewis. He paused a full moment when laughingly said, "I know 16 major league clubs who could use a man like Wells right through now."

Then he went into a long confidential talk on the chances of our boys making the grade. "It is inevitable." went on Mr. Lewis, "Just how soon, no one can tell, but it is sure to come."

He agreed that there isn't a rule in the big leagues against Negroes playing, nor is there anything in the constitution or by-laws of either the National or the American league. The managers always look as though it is an impossible thing to do when confronted with the subject. I told Mr. Lewis, and the owners say it is up to the managers. One owner has come out and said while he could and would vote favorably it would take the majority of the owners to bring about such a change. And right now one owner is game enough to go on record as starting the move. But let the clubs start losing money and the owners will get busy.

Mr. Lewis is of the opinion that more men from colleges and universities need to be injected into the game. He calls attention to the attitude of the white college football players in meeting teams on which there are one or more Negro players. He believes the same thing can be true of big league baseball as has happened in the track and boxing world.

Your boys have made wonderful strides in boxing since Joe Louis became champion. Like the white boy, the Negro boy has his idol. There was a time when the Negro excelled only in the sprints, but now some boys have gone out for the longer distances, and each year brings out a new crop of performers of championship calibre. The have gone in for the shotput, the discus and the high jump and now I find them pole-vaulting about 13 feet. The same will be true of baseball.

You can't keep them out. Just as I say, how soon no one knows, but it is inevitable.

The game is over. The series is tied three and three. There was enough excitement for Mayor Edward J. Kelly to miss two engagements and stay the full nine innings—eight and a half to be exact. Busy men like the mayor don't sit through the entire game unless it is very interesting.

There wasn't any rush for the exits in the first of the ninth. The fans weren't to sure that the one-run lead was enough for the West to bring home the bacon. It was a tribute to Chicago fans. Of the 30,000 folks who watched the game, the vast majority were home folks. And with the Hearst Regatta drawing 200,000 and the Pittsburgh Pirates, league leaders, playing the Chicago Cubs in a double header at Wrigley Field, the attendance was wonderful. As it was, it was the largest in the six-year history of the classic. These 30,000 saw one of the three best games. The first corker was that 1 to 0 contest that East won [in 1934]. The next was in 1934 [1935] when Mule Suttles home run in the eleventh after the East had scored four runs in the 10th, only to have the West come back and score four in their half of the same inning to deadlock the contest again 8 and 8.

The one blot in the picture is the fact that we have no park of our own which can hold such a crowd as was out Sunday. When one stops to think that at least $6,000 was put into the coffers of the White Sox owners for rental, it is time to start figuring with a pencil and paper. The parks are rented on a percentage basis. Then take notice that three games played in the Yankee stadium in New York gave Colonel Ruppert $9,000—out there the flat rental is $3,000.

In other words, four Negro baseball games this year alone have put $15,000 into the pockets of white owners of ball yards. The days isn't far off when some of our businessmen in Chicago will "get hip to themselves" and build a baseball and amusement park. If you don't think it will pay—then something is the matter with your noodle.

AUGUST 21, 1938, CHICAGO, IL

EAST	AB	R	H	D	T	HR	BI	E	TAVG	TSLG
Vic Harris (Homestead Grays), lf	5	1	1	1	0	0	0	0		
Sammy T. Hughes (Baltimore Elite Giants), 2b	5	1	2	1	0	0	1	0		
Willie Wells (Newark Eagles), ss	4	1	2	0	1	0	0	0		
Buck Leonard (Homestead Grays), 1b	4	0	1	0	0	0	1	0		
Rev Cannady (New York Black Yankees), 3b	3	1	1	1	0	0	1	0		
Sam Bankhead (Pittsburgh Crawfords), cf	4	0	2	0	0	0	1	0		
Bill Wright (Baltimore Elite Giants), rf	4	0	0	0	0	0	0	0		
Biz Mackey (Baltimore Elite Giants), c	4	0	0	0	0	0	0	0		
Edsall Walker (Homestead Grays), p	0	0	0	0	0	0	0	0		
a) Barney Brown (New York Black Yankees), ph-p	2	0	1	0	0	0	0	0		
Schoolboy Johnny Taylor (Pittsburgh Crawfords), p	0	0	0	0	0	0	0	0		
b) Jake Dunn (Philadelphia Stars), ph	1	0	1	0	0	0	0	0		
Team Totals, Average & Slugging Pct.	36	4	11	3	1	0	4	0	.306	.444

a) Batted for Walker in 4th
b) Batted for Taylor in 9th

WEST	AB	R	H	D	T	HR	BI	E	TAVG	TSLG
Henry Milton (Kansas City Monarchs), rf	3	2	1	0	0	0	0	0		
Newt Allen (Kansas City Monarchs), 2b	4	0	0	0	0	0	0	1		
Alec Radcliffe (Chicago American Giants), 3b	4	1	2	0	0	0	2	0		
Ted Strong (Indianapolis ABCs), 1b	3	1	0	0	0	0	0	0		
Quincy Trouppe (Indianapolis ABCs), lf	4	0	0	0	0	0	0	0		
Neil Robinson (Memphis Red Sox), cf	4	1	3	0	0	1	3	0		
Frank Duncan (Chicago American Giants), c	1	0	0	0	0	0	0	0		
c) Parnell Woods (Birmingham Black Barons), ph	1	0	0	0	0	0	0	0		
Larry Brown (Memphis Red Sox), c	0	0	0	0	0	0	0	0		
Byron Johnson (Kansas City Monarchs), ss	4	0	1	0	0	0	0	0		
Sug Cornelius (Chicago American Giants), p	0	0	0	0	0	0	0	0		
Hilton Smith (Kansas City Monarchs), p	2	0	1	0	0	0	0	0		
Ted Radcliffe (Memphis Red Sox), p	2	0	1	0	0	0	0	0		
Team Totals, Average & Slugging Pct.	32	5	9	0	0	1	5	1	.281	.375

c) Batted for Duncan in 6th

East	300	010	000-4
West	104	000	00X-5

PITCHER/TEAM	GS	IP	H	R	ER	K	BB	WP	HB	W	L	SV
Walker/HG	1	3	4	5	5	3	3	0	1	0	1	0
B. Brown/NBY		3	2	0	0	1	0	0	0	0	0	0
Taylor/PC		2	3	0	0	2	1	0	0	0	0	0
Cornelius/CAG	1	1	5	3	3	0	0	0	0	0	0	0
H. Smith/KCM		4	3	1	1	3	0	0	1	1	0	0
T. Radcliffe/MRS		4	3	0	0	0	0	0	0	0	0	1

BB—L. Brown, Duncan, Strong, Milton
DP—Duncan to Radcliffe
HBP—Walker by Smith, Milton by Walker
LOB—East 7, West 8
PB—Mackey
SAC—Cannady
SB—Milton (2), Bankhead, Harris
East—Oscar Charleston (Mgr.)
West—Andy Cooper (Mgr.)
Umpires—
Attendance—30,000   Time—2:30

1938 VOTING RESULTS: 2,805,152

P

Schoolboy Taylor	67,124
Sug Cornelius	63,230
Hilton Smith	41,456
Chip McAllister	38,556
Porter Moss	38,468
Andy Porter	37,689
Barney Brown	36,767
Double Duty Radcliffe	36,048
Harry Kincannon	31,532
Andy Cooper	30,948
Slim Jones	30,927
Ted Trent	26,340

C

Frank Duncan	72,122
Larry Brown	52,259
Pepper Bassett	49,899
Biz Mackey	45,728
Quincy Trouppe	43,295
Cy Perkins	42,022
Josh Gibson	33,566
Charlie Ruffin	29,923

1B

Jim West	63,401
Showboat Thomas	59,938
Ted Strong	46,682
Jelly Taylor	40,325
Buck O'Neil	40,211
Buck Leonard	30,678
Mule Suttles	22,536

2B

Sammy T. Hughes	61,592
Rainey Bibbs	42,839
Newt Allen	40,378
Red Longley	37,777
Lick Carlisle	28,544
Pat Patterson	25,390
Dickie Seay	23,933

3B

Jud Wilson	58,409
George Scales	52,599
Dewey Creacy	49,866
Bobby Robinson	43,492
Alec Radcliffe	41,389
Ray Dandridge	31,302
Bus Clarkson	26,389

SS

Ches Williams	62,693
Leroy Morney	59,778
Byron Johnson	50,132
Neil Robinson	30,895
Felton Snow	30,567
Jelly Jackson	28,322
Jake Dunn	25,596
Rev Cannady	24,892
Billy Horne	22,300
Joe Sparks	20,001

OF

Dan Wilson	61,329
Fats Jenkins	61,230
Sam Bankhead	60,456
Zollie Wright	55,735
Speed Whatley	54,672
Ted Christopher	53,580
Bill Wright	51,821
Willard Brown	50,132
Henry Spearman	49,689
Henry Milton	35,682
Vic Harris	34,672
Wilson Redus	30,139
Lloyd Davenport	28,911
Herman Dunlap	27,860
Duke Cleveland	24,638
Bubba Hyde	24,629
Chili Mayweather	14,932
Turkey Stearnes	14,300

1939

Hattie McDaniel, Butterfly McQueen, and other black cast members are barred from attending the premiere of *Gone with the Wind* in Atlanta, Georgia. The Daughters of the American Revolution (DAR) bar Marion Anderson from singing at the Lincoln Memorial.

Historian Dr. Edwin B. Henderson authors *The Negro in Sports,* detailing the plights of African-Americans in various sports. The National Negro Bowling Association is founded in Detroit, Michigan.

Milk costs 24 cents a half-gallon, 10 pounds of potatoes costs 25 cents, and 32 cents would bring home the bacon. A loaf of bread costs 8 cents.

Kenny Washington of UCLA leads the nation's college football players, with 1,370 total yards gained. The NFL does not draft him.

Bob Feller protects the American League All-Stars' 3–1 lead with a flawless performance over the last three and two-thirds innings.

An institution to immortalize baseball's best players is opened in Cooperstown, New York. The first five inductees to the National Baseball Hall of Fame are Ty Cobb, Christy Mathewson, Walter "Big Train" Johnson, George "Babe" Ruth, and Honus Wagner.

NEGRO LEAGUES BUSINESS

The two leagues held a joint board meeting on June 20 in Pittsburgh. Highlights of the board meeting included the following:

- Approval of the East-West All-Star Game to be played in Chicago.
- Clubs will receive a guarantee of $250 for Sunday games and $75 for games played on weekdays and Saturdays.
- If there is a five-game series, the guarantee will be $475, the equivalent guarantee for a four-game series if one of the games were played on a Sunday.
- Rain guarantee is $25 for all games, except the Sunday games, which carry a $50 guarantee.
- Rental paid to ballparks owned by the International and American Associations will be 33 1/3 percent of the gross gate receipts; 30 percent of the gross will be paid to parks owned by the National League or the American League, with the exception of Washington DC's Griffith Stadium, which will be 33 1/3 percent of the gross; and all other park owners will be paid 35 percent of the gross.
- Umpires are to receive $5 for a single game and $7.50 for a doubleheader.
- Salaries are to be paid from May 13 to September 10 inclusive.
- The Wilson ball will be used, except at major league ballparks where the selection of the ball is optional.

- Results of games, won or lost, are to be forwarded to the recording secretary Eddie Gottlieb in Philadelphia.
- All box scores are to be sent to corresponding secretary Cum Posey in Pittsburgh by Thursday of each week.
- Booking agent Eddie Gottlieb will receive 10 percent of the net for all Yankee Stadium promotions.
- Booking agents, including Gottlieb, Bill Leuschner, and Cum Posey, will receive 10 percent of the net for booking nonleague games, with a fourth of their fees to be paid to the league office by the end of the month.
- Playoffs will consist of the first-place team playing the third-place team and the second-place team playing the fourth-place team in a five-game series. The winner of each playoff will meet in a five-game series to determine the league champion.[1]
- Any ballplayer not signed by April 10 will be considered a free agent.
- Any owner, manager, or secretary contacting a player on another team to recruit him will be fined $50 for the first violation and $100 for each subsequent offense.
- Any owner accepting a player under contract from another team will be suspended indefinitely and barred from "organized baseball."[2]
- Any player failing to repay his owner any monies advanced will be suspended from both leagues.[3]

RACE RELATIONS

The last year of the decade proved to be a pivotal year for baseball in America, particularly black baseball. More attention than ever was focused on the integration issue. With the exclusion of the Negro Leagues from the national pastime, the leagues became a symbolic rip in the American flag. More and more press coverage, and more campaigns questioning the "gentlemen's agreement" imposed by major league owners, continued to be front-page news.

One approach was suggested by J. J. McDonald, resident manager of the Hotel Cameron, at 41 West 86th Street in New York City. To break the color barrier, McDonald suggested putting two Negro teams in the major leagues. Noting the futile 1939 attempts by the American League St. Louis Browns and the National League Philadelphia Phillies, McDonald suggested replacing these teams with all-black teams. Both the Browns (43-111, .279, 64 1/2 games back) and the Phillies (45-106, .298, 50 1/2 games back) finished in last place. McDonald's theory was based on the premise that the Browns and Phillies lost money, but the black teams would generate revenue.

He also suggested that if the all-black teams were unable to be affiliated with a particular city, their schedules could be arranged to provide more home games for the remaining teams. Increasing the number of home games would provide the teams with increased gate receipts with only a small increase in park maintenance and the payroll for park personnel. Another advantage, said McDonald, would be the reduced travel expense because of fewer road games. Suggesting that the Negro teams play all their games on the road would increase the other teams' home games to 88 (from the current schedule of 78 home games).

The owners of the Browns and the Phillies would manage the new Negro clubs. McDonald did not state whether the owners of the Negro League teams owning each player's contract would be compensated. Finally, McDonald argued that if neither of the all-black teams won the pennant, the two teams would then play a black world series in two cities to be named at a later date, generating even more revenue for the league.

Obviously, this proposal favored the white teams, financially and competitively. The black teams would be at a distinct disadvantage in winning games because they would never be the home team. As a team always on the road, playing three- and four-game series in various cities, they would become inherently road weary. And never being afforded the comfort of playing 12 to 20 consecutive games in their home park would be an added disadvantage. McDonald's proposal was a start but definitely was not a viable solution for integrating baseball.[4]

BARRIER BREAKER?

Earlier in the season, the New York Giants created a stir in the baseball community with an offer to sign a player with the New York Cubans. Arturo "Polly" Rodriguez, a white Cuban shortstop for Alex Pompez's team, was offered a contract to sign with the Giants' farm club the Chattanooga Lookouts. Giants manager Bill Terry thought Rodriguez, with his silky black hair, pointed nose, and fairly light skin, could easily pass for white. Nonetheless, "high yellow" players were not accustomed to "fooling old Massa."

Rodriguez, speaking through an interpreter, told the *New York Amsterdam News,* "Pompez [is] my friend. He brought me here." He added, "With Pompez I can do a lot of things. I know the offer from the Giants might mean more money and greater fame, but I like playing with my own people and for Pompez."[5]

RACE RELATIONS

As a whole, major league ballparks allowed integrated seating. According to an article in the *New York Amsterdam News,* St. Louis was the only city remaining in the leagues where blacks and whites were segregated in the grandstands.[6] In his book *Lost Ballparks,* Lawrence S. Ritter wrote "in 1944, that Sportsman's Park was the last major league stadium to abolish segregated seating."[7] Until that season, black people were not permitted in the grandstands.

Writers Lester Rodney of the *New York Daily Worker* and Wendell Smith of the *Pittsburgh Courier* started a campaign to interview major league executives for their opinions on the integration of baseball. Some of their responses are listed below:

If the question of admitting colored baseball players into organized baseball becomes an issue I would be heartily in favor of it. I think the Negro people should have an opportunity in baseball just as they have an opportunity in music or anything else. (William E. Benswanger, president of the Pittsburgh Pirates)[8]

Yes, if given permission I would use a Negro player on my team. I have seen at least 25 Negro players who could have made the grade. Offhand, Bullet Joe Rogan, Oscar Charleston, Satchel Paige, Jude Gans, Josh Gibson and countless others. (Deacon Bill McKechnie, Cincinnati Reds manager at the time and later Larry Doby's coach with Cleveland [1947–49])[9]

A few years ago, we played an exhibition game in Oakland, California, against a Negro all-star team. Satchel Paige, the fast ball wizard, pitched against us, and I'm telling you he was great. I said right there that he was as good as Dizzy Dean. When he whipped that fast one in there you could hardly see it. Among the boys he fanned on our team, was Dick Bartell, Billy Jurges, Ernie Pool, Johnny Vergez and myself. (Ernie Lombardi, 1938 National League Most Valuable Player)[10]

Satchel Paige is the greatest pitcher I have ever batted against. (Joe DiMaggio, New York Yankee outfielder and Hall of Famer) [11]

I grew up in Philadelphia which was the hotbed of colored baseball. I saw any number of Negroes who should have made the big leagues. They had some of the best players I have ever seen on those teams. I still remember Cannonball Dick Redding and also [Louis] Santop. They were great players. (Bucky Walters, Cincinnati Reds pitcher and 1939 National League Most Valuable Player) [12]

I certainly wouldn't object to a good Negro ball player on our team. They have some of the best ball players I have ever seen. Although it's none of my business, I don't see why they are barred. (Johnny Vander Meer, Cincinnati Reds pitcher who hurled back-to-back no-hitters in 1938) [13]

Two years ago, I played in some exhibition games out on the Coast. I played in at least five games and I guess I saw at least six colored players whom I thought I could use in the big leagues. I've played against Satchel Paige in at least five games. And I honestly think he is one of the greatest pitchers in baseball. He has a world of stuff and he certainly knows how to use it. His fast ball, I would say is the best I've ever seen. (Doc Thompson Prothro, manager of the last-place Philadelphia Phillies and former Memphis dentist) [14]

I saw two of the greatest ball players that ever lived, Rube Foster and Smokey Joe Williams. They were both pitchers and although I was just a kid, I was convinced that they were certainly good enough for the majors. Smokey Joe was as fast as any pitcher I've ever seen and was a tough man to face in the pinch. He would have been worth plenty to some big league manager when he was in his prime. (Gabby Hartnett, 1935 National League MVP, Chicago Cubs manager at the time, and 1955 Hall of Fame selection) [15]

I'd name this big first baseman from Newark who hits the ball so hard—Mule Suttles— As one Negro player who should be in the big leagues. I've played against him in a number of exhibition games and I think he hit a homer in almost every game. He sure could pound on that ball. He's big and powerful, takes a healthy cut. When he hits one, it goes long and far. (Earl Whitehall, Chicago Cubs pitcher) [16]

I've seen plenty of colored boys who could make the grade in the majors. I have played against some colored boys out on the coast who could play in any big league that ever existed. Paige, Perkins, Suttles and Gibson are good enough to be in the majors right now. All four of them are great players. Listen, there are plenty of colored players around the country who should be in the big leagues. I certainly would use a Negro ball player if the bosses said it was all right. (Leo Durocher, manager of the Brooklyn Dodgers) [17]

I've seen plenty of good colored players and the best ones are just as good as the big leaguers you see out there today. (Dolph Camilli, first baseman whom the Brooklyn Dodgers had just purchased from the Philadelphia Phillies for $45,000) [18]

Yes indeed, I've seen a number of Negro players whom I think were good enough for the majors. I rate Dick Lundy, Satchel Paige, Mule Suttles and [Robert] Clarke among the best players I have ever seen. (Babe Phelps, catcher who hit .367 in 1936) [19]

I've seen a whole gang who could make the grade. Paige, Gibson and Suttles are real big leaguers. (Brooklyn Dodger third baseman Cookie Lavagetto, who would later play with Jackie Robinson in the majors) [20]

[Satchel] Paige, [Turkey] Stearnes, [Mule] Suttles, [Cool Papa] Bell, [Felton] Snow, [Sam] Bankhead, [Jim] West and [Andy] Pullman Porter are as good as any of the players I've seen in the big leagues. All of them are great ball players. Paige had a fire-ball, and Stearnes was one of the best all-around players I've seen. Bell was as fast as greased lightning. And Mule Suttles is one of the best power house hitters I've ever seen. (Tuck Stainback, journeyman outfielder who was once traded with a few other players plus $185,000 for Dizzy Dean) [21]

Most of the great players I've seen are through. However, I'd name [Oscar] Charleston, [Martin] Dihigo and [Carlos] Torrienti. They were good enough for any big league team that ever existed. (Charley Dressen, coach of the Brooklyn Dodgers) [22]

Lester Rodney, a white American who wrote for the Communist newspaper the *New York Daily Worker,* explained his reasons behind his motivation to end racism in baseball:

I belong to an organization which had as part of its party's platform the ending of dis-crimination—as a dream. Even long before I joined that party I had been a red-hot baseball fan and got to know about some of the great players that who were not allowed to play in America's national pastime.

I would go out and see the Kansas City Monarchs and Satchel Paige pitch and all. You couldn't be a real baseball fan without knowing something was wrong there. Especially since my team, the Brooklyn Dodgers of the thirties was pretty pathetic. [23]

Gibson, Suttles and Leonard Held Hitless

Wilson's Homer Gives West Win over East in Classic

40,000 See Thriller

Robinson Stars Rally & West Wins 4 to 2

by Fay Young

Source: *Chicago Defender*, 12 August 1939

In a game packed with thrills and before the most colorful and largest crowd ever to witness any athletic event of our group, the West won the 1939 East versus West annual baseball classic at Comiskey Park, Sunday, August 6. The final score was 4 to 2.

Forty thousands saw a game fighting West team held to two scratch hits, both of them coming in the West first, until the seventh when Neal Robinson, who hit last year's home run to put West out in front, tagged the first offering of [Roy] Lefty Partlow of the Homestead Grays for a homer, 380 feet into the upper deck of the left grandstand.

Right then and there it looked like there was going to be a real ball game. It was! Whatever the West had—it must produce. It did! Not in that inning because Ted Strong of Kansas City popped to Sammy Hughes of Baltimore at second. Horne singled to right field and Mule Suttles, Newark Eagles, saved Partlow by smothering the two balls which Jim Williams of Toledo and Larry Brown, Memphis catcher, lifted into right field.

EAST SCORES FIRST

The East had gone out in front in the second inning. Theo Smith, starting pitcher for the West, had set the East down one, two, three in the first. Ted Strong, playing short, threw to Jelly Taylor, Memphis, at first to dispose of Mule Suttles, Newark's first sacker, who was playing right field and who is the East's home run king, in Mule's first trip to the plate. Then Strong took Buck Leonard's grounder and played with it like a kitten with a rubber ball and the great Homestead Gray's first sacker reached first safely. Pat Patterson, Philadelphia Stars' third sacker, singled to center. Patterson stole second, Leonard holding third. Sammy Hughes, Baltimore, second baseman, singled to center, scoring Leonard and Patterson with the East's only two runs of the game. Alex Radcliffe, Chicago American Giants' third baseman, took the rap Parnell, Philadelphia left fielder, hit near third and forced Hughes at second on a throw to Mourney [Morney], Toledo, but Mourney [Morney] overthrew first. The ball hit the wall in front on the box seats and bounded back far enough for the alert Jelly Taylor to recover it and whip it to Mourney [Morney] to kill Parnell trying to reach second.

WON ON WILSON'S HOMER

The West went out in front in the home eighth. The fans who had been disappointed in not seeing the East's wrecking crew of home run hitters clout out long drives saw another homer from an unexpected source. Ted Radcliffe singled sharply to center. Radcliffe went to second when [Parnell] Woods, Cleveland, third baseman, injected into the game in the visitor's fourth, laid down a perfect sacrifice bunt and was out, Leonard to Hughes who covered first. Dan Wilson looked at two wide ones and then caught one which split the heart of the plate for a homer, 360 feet away, into the lower left grandstand scoring Ted Radcliffe ahead of him and putting the West out in front 3 to 2.

The game was held up until the groundskeepers could clear the field of straw hats and paper. The fans had staged a story book scene. What pent-up enthusiasm had been left in the crowd was turned loose. Manager George Scales of the East waved Partlow to the showers and Scales' New York Black Yankees' teammate, Bill Holland, went to the mound. Alex Radcliffe dumped a single into center field and Suttles then proceeded to lose Neal Robinson's fly in the sun and it went for a two-base hit, putting A. Radcliffe on third. Strong was purposely walked and the bases were full. Bill Horne, Chicago American Giants' second sacker, put into the game at second in the fourth when A. Radcliffe had been shifted to shortstop and Strong on first to relieve Jelly Taylor, was up. Horne and A. Radcliffe worked a squeeze play, Horne pushed the ball to Leonard and A. Radcliffe getting home with the fourth and last run for the West. Leonard had no chance to get A. Radcliffe at the plate, therefore all he could do was to tag Horne out. Willie Wells, Newark, in at shortstop, threw out big Jim Williams, Toledo, right fielder, who substituted for Henry Milton, Kansas City, in the eighth.

DEFENDER WAS RIGHT

What the *Chicago Defender* said three weeks ago and again last week came true. "The West will depend on its hurlers to stop the East's home run kings." The West did that. Josh Gibson, Homestead Grays, catcher, got the ball out of the infield once, that was a fly to Wilson in the first. He walked in the third. Suttles could do nothing in the two times he faced Theo Smith, St. Louis hurler. Strong tossed him out the first time and the second time he hit into a double play—that coming with the bases full in the third.

Hilton Smith, Kansas City Monarchs, relieved Theo Smith in start the East's fourth. He slipped the third strike over on Suttles' who looked sheepishly at the umpire. Ted Radcliffe threw the ball across the plate, past Suttles in the ninth. Suttles missed the first two strikes, looked at a pitch out which Larry Brown, Memphis, who had relieved Pepper Bassett, Chicago American Giant catcher, in the fifth, had called. Then came a roundhouse slow curve which broke under Mule's swing.

Four times Leonard went to the plate for three official times at the bat. He was safe on Strong's error, the only error of the game, in the second. Horne tossed him out in the fourth. He worked Red Radcliffe for a walk to start the seventh but died trying to steal second, Larry Brown to A. Radcliffe who had been shifted to short. In the ninth, Leonard finally got the ball out of the infield. He flied to Jim Williams in right field.

H. SMITH INVINCIBLE

Hilton Smith pitched the fourth, fifth and sixth and allowed nary a hit. Ted Radcliffe, like last year, pitched the seventh, eighth and ninth. He gave up one hit, a double by B. Wright, Baltimore centerfielder, in the eighth after one was out. The two runs were made off Theo Smith in the second off two hits which followed Strong's miscue. B. Wright beat out a hit off Theo Smith in the third and when Mourney [Morney] moved over toward second to take Bassett's throw as B. Wright had started to steal, Willie Wells, Newark shortstop, reached out and spoiled what was meant for a pitch out by singling to right field through Mourney[Morney]'s regular position. Therefore, Theo Smith was charged with four hits.

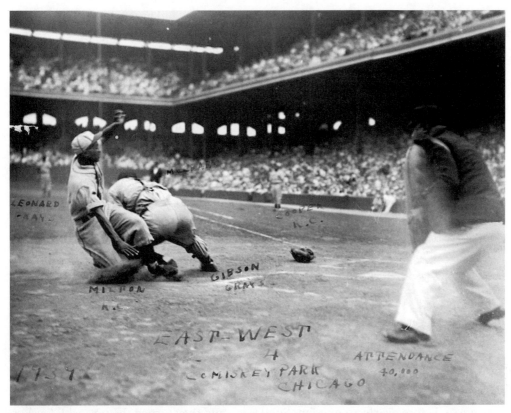

21. On an attempted double steal in the first inning on August 6, 1939, Josh Gibson receives the return throw from Sammy T. Hughes and blocks the plate, preventing Henry Milton from stealing home. Courtesy National Baseball Hall of Fame Library and Archive, Cooperstown, New York.

EAST HAD SOMETHING

Don't think for a minute that the East didn't have anything. It might be truthfully said they had the best team on the field. While the West's pitchers, Hilton Smith hurled three innings without giving up a hit, and Double Duty Radcliffe held them to one safe blow in three, the East had some pitchers.

Wells knocked down Henry Milton's roller to start the second half of the first but couldn't get the Kansas Citian at first. Neal Robinson beat out a hit to Patterson near third after two were gone. That was all of the hits the West could get up to the seventh. An attempted double steal prevented the West from scoring in their first inning, Gibson to Hughes to Gibson, perfect throws by both, gave Gibson time to block Milton three feet from the plate for the third out. Day, Newark, went through the fourth, fifth, and sixth without allowing anything that looked like a hit.

LOUIS PITCHED FIRST BALL

The umpiring was faultless. The game was played in fine time. It started shortly after 3 o'clock when Joe Louis, world heavyweight champion, pitched the first ball, right through the middle of the plate to Gus Greenlee, Pittsburgh, manager of John Henry Lewis, dethroned world light heavyweight champion. Greenlee, with R. A. Cole, then owner of the Chicago American Giants, and Tom Wilson, present president of the Negro National League, originated the East versus West game in 1933. Louis was given a tremendous ovation. In his box was his wife, Mrs. Marva Louis Barrow; Julian A. Mack, co-manager of the champion, and Louis' bodyguard, Sergeant Carl Nelson, Chicago police force.

The win for the West puts them out in front in the series and broke the three and three tie in number of games.

Neal Robinson, Memphis, led the batting. He was up four times and got three hits, including a home run and a double. Ted Radcliffe up once and getting one hit had a perfect batting average. B. Wright up four times got two hits.

Only one double play was made. It came in the East's third with the bases loaded. Suttles hit to Theo Smith, who threw to Bassett forcing B. Wright at the plate and Suttles was out at first, Bassett to Taylor.

Assisting Manager Scales on the East team were Homer Curry, New York Black Yankees, and Willie Wells, Newark Eagles' manager. Assisting manager George Mitchell, manager of the St. Louis Stars, for the West were Andy Cooper, manager of the Kansas City Monarchs, and Alonzo Mitchell, manager of the Cleveland Bears.

"Sez Ches": Sun Rises in the West

by Chester L. Washington Jr.

Source: *Pittsburgh Courier,* 12 August 1939

Chicago, August 6— Maybe it doesn't make sense, but the sun is still rising in the West . . . that is, from a baseball viewpoint.

The stalwart baseball scions of the West beat the highly-touted big bad batsmen of the East, 4 to 2, before nearly 40,000 fans Sunday . . . and they turned the time with flawless pitching.

Playing heroic roles along with the occidental pitchers, T. Smith, H. Smith and Ted Radcliffe—who held the oriental fence-smashers at bay—were two brilliant young swatters who slugged their way into the East-West Hall of Fame. One was 23-year-old Dan Wilson of the St. Louis Stars playing in his first dream game, who poled out the screeching homer into the rightfield stands [leftfield stands] with Double Duty Radcliffe on the basepaths, in the eighth to put the game on ice for the Westerners. And the other was Neal Robinson, the spectacular young Memphis star—by way of Gary, Indiana—who started the fireworks for the West just as he did in last year's game by smashing out a circuit clout in the lucky seventh, which paved the way for the West to win the seventh game of the annual all-star series and make it 4 to 3 for the stars from the wide open spaces.

EAST STARTS OUT A HOUSE FIRE TO TAKE LEAD IN SECOND

Running true to form in so far as the pre-game perceptions were concerned, the East lunged into the lead in their portion of the second inning when Leonard reached first on the shortstop's error, Pat Patterson singled sharply to center, and Leonard raced to third. The alert Patterson stole second just one pitch before Hughes poled out a single to center, on which Buck Leonard and Patterson came sailing across the plate.

At this point the hopes of the thousands of Western rooters hit a new "low", but still the West's pitching continued on a high plane. Eastern base hits were as scarce as hen's teeth and soon the hopes of the West started to roar again.

SEVENTH AND EIGHTH ARE LUCKY FRAMES FOR THE WESTERNERS

The West's assault reached its zenith in the seventh and eighth. It started in the "stretch" inning when center fielder Neal Robinson lifted a fast one into the upper left-field stands for a homer. Came the eighth and a continued batting barrage for the West, with Ted Radcliffe singling sharply to right field and Parnell Woods of Cleveland, laying down a beautiful sacrifice bunt to advance Ted to second.

At this point dangerous Dan Wilson—unknown to the East, but respected for his trusty batting game in the West, walked to the plate. A hush settled over the crowd as if they expected something phenomenal to happen. It was a dramatic moment. Then came Partlow's pitch. It grooved the center of the plate, borne on the wings of speed and skill. Dan's bat connected with a report like the barking of a pistol. The ball soared into the distance like a small white sphere fading into the paling horizon. Lost for a momentous moment, it dropped into sight again with the humanity-packed left-field stands as a background. It made a wide arch and then dropped deep into the lower stands.

Wilson circled the bases, keeping tempo with the roars of the crowd and trailed his teammate, Ted Radcliffe, across the home base. Here half of the Western team had gathered to greet and hail him as a conquering king. They took him on their shoulders like the hero of dear old Truxton, and carried him over to the box occupied by boxing champion of champions. And it was here that Joe Louis personally greeted Dangerous Dan and congratulated him on bringing home the bacon for the West.

BRILLIANT FIELDING, HARD-HITTING AND GOOD PITCHING THRILLS CROWD

Brilliant hits of fielding, good pitching, and that home run hitting gave the mighty throng thrills galore. And the near forty thousand who turned out to see those boys of brown who are battling for an opportunity to break into the big leagues certainly saw everything and eyes more than they had hoped for.

Too sensational playing of such stars as Buck Leonard, Pat Patterson, Neal Robinson, and Dan Wilson, in particular elicited plenty of fine compliments not only from the fans, but from the white and colored baseball experts who filled the press box.

CELEBRITIES ADD COLOR TO THE ANNUAL CLASSIC

In addition to Heavyweight Champion Joe Louis—looking tan and handsome in his white gabardine suit and fresh from a "77" for 18 holes of golf—who threw out the first ball and Gus Greenlee, virtually the father of the East-West game idea—who surprised himself by catching in there were celebrities galore in the boxes and in the stands.

New Orleans Fans Hear Play by Play of East-West Game

Source: *Chicago Defender,* 12 August 1939

New Orleans, August 11 — Fans who attended the double header between the New York Black Yankees and the St. Louis Stars were treated to a play-by-play description of the East-West All-Star game in Chicago, Sunday. Promoter Allen Page, popular hotel owner, and Hayward Jackson, managing editor of the *Sepia Socialite,* sponsored the broadcast via telegrams. The returns were made possible by the cooperation of local Negro business establishments.

Editor's note: Baseball entered the era of media entertainment. On August 26, the first televised major league baseball game was broadcast by W2XBS in New York. Historic Ebbets Field hosted the Brooklyn Dodgers and the Cincinnati Reds in a doubleheader. The tele-

22. A crowd of approximately 40,000 fans saw the West beat the East, 4–2. Courtesy National Baseball Hall of Fame Library and Archive, Cooperstown, New York.

vision station, which was owned by the National Broadcasting Company (NBC) and was located in the Empire State Building, had one camera placed near the visiting team's dugout, or just behind a right-handed batter's position. The other camera was placed on the second level behind the catcher to give the viewers a panoramic view of the field.

The Empire State building, the tallest building in the country at the time, was a logical site to place the antennas. The *New York Times*[24] boastfully reported that the new technology called "radio-camera" carried a signal almost 50 miles away. A reported crowd of 33,000 fans showed up to view the event. At the time, there were estimated 500 black and white television sets in New York City.

This was not the first time a baseball game was televised by NBC. Earlier on May 17, a college game between Columbia and Princeton at Baker Field was telecasted. The latest science had difficulty in following the speed and path of the baseball, sending the technicians back to school. The introduction of televised baseball games had been strongly campaigned against because owners feared it would hurt park attendance. Little did they know that television revenue would become a financial savior for the game some fifty years later.

The Stuff Is Here . . . Past—Present—Future

by Fay Young

Source: *Chicago Defender,* 19 August 1939

After the West defeated the East in the East vs. West classic at Comiskey Park, Sunday, August 6, the owners in the Negro National League were not convinced that the West had a better team, therefore they issued a challenge to the Negro American League for a game to be played in New York on Sunday, August 27, at the Yankee Stadium, home of the New York American league club and the scene of many of Joe Louis' outdoor fights.

The game in New York will not be a second East versus West classic, but will be a game between stars of the two leagues. Many of the same players who took part in the game in Chicago will be in action. In fact the East can hardly produce a better lineup than what was on the field on August 6. True, the home run kings of the Eastern circuit fell down— but don't we all have our off days.

East Meets West Again Sunday

Charleston May Start H. Smith

Source: *Chicago Defender,* 26 August 1939

New York, Aug. 25 — The greatest crowd to ever see two colored teams play ball in the East will be at Yankee Stadium on Sunday, August 27, when the Negro National Leaguers take the field at 3 o'clock.

In this game, like in the seven games played in Chicago, many of the players are far better than many of the major league stars.

Lloyd Lewis, commenting on Wells' play on Sunday, August 6, said the following day in the *Chicago Daily News* that Wells easily covered more ground than Leo Durocher, Brooklyn National League shortstop.

Any of the major league clubs at present could use Gibson, Leonard, Bill Wright, Suttles, Hilton Smith, Ted Strong—oh, why name all of them.

AUGUST 6, 1939, SUNDAY
COMISKEY PARK, CHICAGO (GAME 1 OF 2)

EAST	AB	R	H	D	T	HR	BI	E	TAVG	TSLG
Bill Wright (Baltimore Elite Giants), cf	4	0	2	1	0	0	0	0		
Willie Wells (Newark Eagles), ss	3	0	1	0	0	0	0	0		
Josh Gibson (Homestead Grays), c	3	0	0	0	0	0	0	0		
Mule Suttles (Newark Eagles), rf	4	0	0	0	0	0	0	0		
Buck Leonard (Homestead Grays), 1b	3	1	0	0	0	0	0	0		
Andy Patterson (Philadelphia Stars), 3b	4	1	1	0	0	0	0	0		
Sammy T. Hughes (Baltimore Elite Giants), 2b	3	0	1	0	0	0	2	0		
Red Parnell (Philadelphia Stars), lf	3	0	0	0	0	0	0	0		
Bill Byrd (Baltimore Elite Giants), p	1	0	0	0	0	0	0	0		
Leon Day (Newark Eagles), p	1	0	0	0	0	0	0	0		
Roy Partlow (Homestead Grays), p	1	0	0	0	0	0	0	0		
Bill Holland (New York Black Yankees), p	0	0	0	0	0	0	0	0		
Team Totals, Average & Slugging Pct.	30	2	5	1	0	0	2	0	.167	.200

WEST	AB	R	H	D	T	HR	BI	E	TAVG	TSLG
Henry Milton (Kansas City Monarchs), rf	3	0	1	0	0	0	0	0		
Parnell Woods (Cleveland Bears), 3b	0	0	0	0	0	0	0	0		
Dan Wilson (St. Louis Stars), lf	3	1	1	0	0	1	2	0		
Alec Radcliffe (Chicago American Giants), 3b-ss	4	1	1	0	0	0	0	0		
Neil Robinson (Memphis Red Sox), cf	4	1	3	1	0	1	1	0		
Ted Strong (Kansas City Monarchs), ss-1b	2	0	0	0	0	0	0	1		
Jelly Taylor (Memphis Red Sox), 1b	2	0	0	0	0	0	0	0		
Billy Horne (Chicago American Giants), 2b	2	0	1	0	0	0	1	0		
Leroy Morney (Toledo Crawfords), 2b-ss	1	0	0	0	0	0	0	0		
a) Jim Williams (Toledo Crawfords), rf	2	0	0	0	0	0	0	0		
Pepper Bassett (Chicago American Giants), c	1	0	0	0	0	0	0	0		
Larry Brown (Memphis Red Sox), c	2	0	0	0	0	0	0	0		
Theolic Smith (St. Louis Stars), p	0	0	0	0	0	0	0	0		
Hilton Smith (Kansas City Monarchs), p	1	0	0	0	0	0	0	0		
Ted Radcliffe (Memphis Red Sox), p	1	1	1	0	0	0	0	0		
Team Totals, Average & Slugging Pct.	28	4	8	1	0	2	4	1	.286	.536

a) Batted for Morney in 7th

East	020	000	000-2	
West	000	000	13x-4	

PITCHER/TEAM	GS	IP	H	R	ER	K	BB	WP	HB	W	L
Byrd/BEG	1	3	2	0	0	1	1	0	0	0	0
Day/NE		3	0	0	0	3	2	0	0	0	0
Partlow/HG		1 1/3	4	3	3	0	0	0	0	0	1
Holland/NBY		2/3	2	1	1	0	1	0	0	0	0
T. Smith/SLS	1	3	4	2	1	1	1	0	0	0	0
H. Smith/KCM		3	0	0	0	3	0	0	0	0	0
T. Radcliffe/MRS		3	1	0	0	1	2	0	0	1	0

BB—Wells, Gibson, Leonard, Morney, Strong (2), T. Smith
DP—T. Smith to Bassett to Taylor.
LOB—East, West
SAC—Woods
SB—Patterson, Robinson
East—George Scales (Mgr.); Coaches Homer Curry and, Willie Wells
West—George Mitchell (Mgr); Coaches Andy Cooper and Alonzo Mitchell
Umpires—Virgil Blueitt, Fred McCrary, T. J. Young, E. C. "Pop" Turner
Attendance—40,000   Time—
Note: Joe Louis threw out first pitch to Gus Greenlee.

All-Star East-West Game at Yank Stadium, Aug. 27

Source: *New Jersey Herald News,* 19 August 1939

New York, Aug. 16— For the first time since its conception seven years ago, the East will have the opportunity to witness the Dream Game of Negro baseball, when the All-Star teams of the Negro National and Negro American Leagues clash at the Yankee Stadium Sunday, August 27th.

Defeated by the score of 4 to 2 before over 40,000 spectators, in Comiskey Park, Chicago, Sunday, August 6th the Eastern All-Stars of the Negro National League find themselves with their backs to the wall as they prepare to repel the All-Star Westerners from the Negro American League.

Before the greatest crowd that has ever witnessed a Sepia sporting event, the West, underdogs in the betting, took the lead in the series by coming from behind with a three run rally in the eighth inning faced by a home run of Dan Wilson's of St. Louis Stars. Thus, once again the pre-game favorite East was compelled to taste the bitter dregs of defeat, with their only chance of solace being to reverse the verdict at the Yankee Stadium, Sunday, August 27. This will not be the easiest task in the world when you look over the West's imposing array of diamond satellites. Glance over the West's colorful lineup of superstars and you can visualize the task that confronts the East.

The West will bring as infielders, [Ted] Strong, Kansas City, 1st baseman, and [Newt] Allen, Kansas City, utility. Outfielders, [Neal] Robinson, Memphis, [Henry] Milton, Kansas City, [Jimmy] Williams, Toledo [Crawfords]; [Dan] Wilson, St. Louis and [Smokey] Owens, Cleveland. Catchers, "Pepper" Bassett, Chicago and "Harry" [Larry] Brown, Memphis. Pitchers, Hilton Smith, Kansas City, "Preacher" Henry, Cleveland, "Theo" Smith, St. Louis, "Al" Houston, Chicago, [Porter] Moss and "Double Duty" Radcliffe, Memphis.

The West's pitching staff is their ace in the hole and an idea of its power may be gleamed from the statistics of the Chicago game. Where the West's sharpshooters, Smith, Smith and Radcliffe, handcuffed the vaunted East's sluggers, Gibson, Leonard and Suttles by not allowing them a single hit in eleven times at bat.

The Eastern All-Stars, however, are not daunted by their defeat at Chicago and are determined by their defeat at Chicago and are determined to more than reverse this setback when they face their Western rivals at the Yankee Stadium, Sunday, August 27.

NNL Power Crushes West 10–2

17,000 See Eastern Club Revenge East-West Defeat

by Dan Burley

Source: *New York Amsterdam News,* 2 September 1939

Powerhouse bats of the Negro National League representatives blasted the Negro American Leaguers into submission, 10 to 2, Sunday in the first annual East-West game staged at Yankee Stadium before a crowd of 17,000 fans. The East thus avenged the 4–2 defeat suffered in Chicago in the East-West classic at Comiskey Park. The Eastern outfit made up of players from clubs in the N.N.L. circuit, pounced on the relatively weak Western brand of pitching and took advantage of the breaks to ice away the contest as early as the second inning when the East scored four runs.

The West made one serious threat, that stab coming in the first inning when successive singles by Dan Wilson, St. Louis, Johnny Lyle, Cleveland, Ted Strong, Kansas City, and Neal Robinson, Memphis had the bags jammed. However, Bill Byrd, starting Eastern hurler, got out of the jam with only one run scored.

The second inning was a nightmare to the Western Board of Strategy made up of cagey old Candy Jim Taylor, Chicago, Oscar Charleston, Toledo, and George Mitchell, St. Louis. Leonard walked to start it off. Vic Harris then poked a rifle like single to center and Sammy Hughes walked to choke the hassocks.

Bill Byrd popped to third base, but Bill Wright's smoking single scored Leonard and Harris and the Western Strategies sent in Jimmy Johnson, schoolboy sensation of Toledo. Wells doubled to left and scored Hughes and Wright. E. Stone was an infield out and Johnson purposely walked the "terrible" Josh Gibson. It worked, for Patterson fanned.

SEEING PEOPLE

The East put on a scoring parade again in the eighth when four more trickled across the platter. Wright lashed a double to center. Wells got a bye on a fielder's choice as Radcliffe tried in vain to nip Wright at third. All hands were safe as the crowd went wild. Stone walked to fill the bases and then came Josh Gibson. Denied in other appearances at the plate, the big slugging catcher of the Homestead Grays larruped out a tremendous wallop that bounced off the centerfield wall, 400 feet away for a triple. It cleaned the sacks.

Patterson flied out to center, but Buck Leonard decided it was time to get a piece of that apple, himself, and singled to center to score Gibson. Hughes was an infield out.

The East scored a run in the first inning when Willie Wells was hit by a pitched ball and scored on a single by Stone and a sacrifice fly by Gibson. The other run was picked up in the fifth on a single by Stone; a walk to Gibson and a long fly to center by Patterson on which Gibson was doubled at third on as pretty a throw by Wilson as one would want to see, allowing Stone a chance to scramble across the plate.

The West got its second run in the sixth when Robinson and Radcliffe both singled, Robinson going down to third. Stearnes flied out, Robinson scoring after the catch. Riddle batted for Horne and walked. Johnson fanned to end the forced Radcliffe, but Larry Brown walked. Johnson fanned to end the threat.

Altogether, the game served the purpose of placing two brands of ball played by the Negro leagues on display for the first time in the East. Out West the boys rely on old time strategy; stolen bases, squeeze plays, bunts, and sacrifices. Out here, it is knock it out of the park and be done with it. The power of the East pitted against the smart plays of the West didn't work out in this contest. After the game the Westerners were around Seventh avenue beefing about the fact that Ted Duty Radcliffe, the hurler in the East-West classic in Chicago, being left at home and how Owens, Johnson, and Hilton Smith had undergone the trying experience of facing Josh Gibson, Buck Leonard, Willie Wells, & Co., who had murderous intention, whenever they came to bat.

The crowd was gay and colorful, counting in its number bigwig Elks, politicians, theatrical and nightlife celebrities plus a plentiful sprinkling of Alphas [Alpha Phi Alpha], Deltas [Delta Sigma Theta], and others. Henry Armstrong, welterweight titleholder, threw the first ball, John Henry Lewis, undefeated as light-heavyweight champion, making the attempt to catch it but dropping the ball as it crossed the plate J. Finley Wilson, Grand Exalted Ruler of the Elks, umpired the throw.

East Bats Put West to Rout

by Al Monroe

Source: *Chicago Defender*, 2 September 1939

New York, Sept. 1 — Twenty thousand wild eye fans watched the Negro National League All-Stars combine four errors of commission with a half dozen of omission to induce the Negro American Leaguers to humiliate themselves by a score of 10–2 at Yankee Stadium Sunday afternoon. For one inning Raymond Owens (Cleveland), starting pitcher for the West gave the East and its Byrd (Baltimore) a battle, the scoreboard showing things even-steven at one run each. Then in one-third of the second frame Owens gave them the ball game and after Wells double homed Hughes and Wright, Oscar Charleston (Toledo) gave him the key to the showers. This merciless sock that sent Owens away also sent the margin to 5–1 which later developments proved was more than enough to win.

SOLID SOCKS

Although the Western lads performed yeoman services for the West's cause by almost sloppy play, solid smacking of the old apple had plenty to do with the final result. A base clearing triple by Josh Gibson in the eighth was certainly void of aid from the other side though it must be admitted that an error on a forceout attempt by Radcliffe set the stage. And those of care to do so may criticize Turkey Stearnes for the way he played Gibson. He could have caught the ball but had he played nearer center the drive might have gone for a mere double.

When Gibson added that triple to the humiliation young Jimmy Johnson (Toledo), the only Western twirler to show any class, had gone away in favor of [Hilton] Smith of Kansas City. Johnson, out of respect, perhaps, for the fine pitching exhibition he turned in had been allowed to strike out for himself two frames before, and then taken out at the start of the next frame.

Many thought he would continue to pitch after hitting for himself but the management though differently. Maybe Messrs. Charleston, Taylor and Mitchell of the board of strategy wished to match their own players in errors of omission.

While Johnson was holding the East's sluggers to three hits and one run in 3 1-3 [2/3] frames, the final results indicate a much larger advantage in hits than the recorded 12–7 [13–7] even with the 4–1 [4–0] margin in errors added. But the West answered that in another department, errors of omission. Once the big guns of the opposition started resounding the boys from the lake region blew sky high with slips that cannot be recorded.

Once Radcliffe (Chicago) ran into Lyle's short field territory and after missing the ball allowed himself to be pulled behind a runner who was on second. Then to add to the confusion Lyle was also trapped behind the runner with third base beckoning and un-covered. Another time Strong came in for a bunt and both pitcher Johnson and second sacker Horne became interested spectators while the first baseman played with the fur on the horsehide.

In the eighth with Gibson, a left field hitter up, and a dangerous one Turkey Stearnes in right played near the foul line. With his pretty picture, Gibson who had been robbed by the left and center fielders on long drives twice sent one to the scoreboard in right center. Turkey tore after the ball but by the time he reached it three men had scored and Josh had legged it to third base.

The crown, largest of the season, presented a beautiful spectacle. The boxes were about all filled and the other stand showed little barren place. Among those who saw the game were Henry Armstrong, welterweight champion of the world; John Henry Lewis, undefeated as light heavyweight; Major R. Jackson, head of the Western League; Tom Wilson, president of the Western loop; Ed Barrow, president of the world's champion New York Yanks and many others.

To open the game Henry Armstrong tossed a perfect strike that was missed by [boxer] John Henry Lewis as Finley Wilson, grand exalted of the Elks acted as umpire.

Gibson Leads Attack as East Beats West, 7–2 [10–2]

Big Catcher Triples with Bases Loaded in 8th as 20,000

See Negro All-Star Game at Stadium

Armstrong Throws Out 1st Ball

Source: *New York Daily Worker,* 28 August, 1939

Led by Josh Gibson, whom many big leaguers have called the greatest catcher in the game today, the Eastern All-Stars of the Negro National League pounded out a 10–2 victory over the Western All-Stars before 20,000 fans at the Yankee Stadium yesterday.

That avenged a 4–2 defeat suffered by the East in Chicago a few weeks back.

Gibson tripled with bases loaded in the four-run eight and walloped a 400-foot sacrifice fly that was just short of being a homer to score the first East run in the opening frame.

The West started off nicely getting one run in the first when [John] Lyle, [Ted] Strong and [Neal] Robinson singled. Then the East came back with their tying run and routed West starter [Smoky] Owens with a four-run splash in the second.

The second inning saw West relief hurler [Jimmy "Slim"] Johnson turn in the prettiest hurling of the afternoon when he fanned three of the Eastern sluggers to stop the rally.

Henry Armstrong—they're still disputing his lightweight title loss to Lou Ambers—threw out the first ball to John Henry Lewis, former lightheavy champ uncorked a fast one with a nice hop.

Many more Young Communist League petitions were signed and plenty of the fans said that the way things are breaking now, the end of Jim Crow looks pretty near.

Fay Says

Frank A. Young

Source: *Chicago Defender,* 9 September 1939

New York had an East versus West game. The official paid attendance was a bit over 12,000 [reported 20,000]. That looked like a sack of gooberpeas in the huge Yankee Stadium. There are several reasons for such a small crowd. In the first place, the East has educated New York's baseball fans up to expecting four-team doubleheaders. To have one game on a Sunday afternoon, after several four-team gala bills, naturally left the fans believing they would be paying a price for one-half of what they had been used to getting. The fans, once given a bargain bill, expect bargains to continue.

Mrs. Abe Manley, who owns the Newark Eagles with her husband, usually does a lot of talking. While in Chicago, she opposed and argued against every move that helped put 32,000 paid admissions in Chicago on Sunday, August 6. But the fortunate part of Mrs. Manley's arguments was that the other club owners ignored her. Some of Mrs. Manley's objections, as well as some of her arguments are, as Shakespeare said in The Merchant of Venice, "like two grains of wheat lost in two bushels of chaff, you may seek all day ere you find them—and when you have found them they are not worth their search."

Jimmy Powers, sports editor of the *New York Times,* wrote a nice column the morning of the game on Sunday, August 27, advising baseball fans (and I am presuming he was speaking to the major league fans) to journey out to Yankee Stadium to see the All-Star players in action, many of whom were barred from the major leagues because of their color.

All that was fine on the part of Mr. Powers, but the white people in New York evidently didn't give a tinker's damn about Negro baseball or better yet—the All-Star game—because out of millions of souls, the best the game drew was a few. More too, when Mr. Powers' article appeared on Sunday morning, the folks had already made up their minds where to go and most likely were on their way.

Harlem, with its 275,000 or more of our group, ought to have had a better representation. And where were the folks of our race who live in Brooklyn, Jersey City, Orange, New Jersey, down on Long Island and Philadelphia? Either the game was not publicized right or something is radically wrong.

Mrs. Manley, who strenuously objected to the cost of publicity for the game played in Chicago, probably has a change of heart by now, if that is possible, and will admit that the course pursued in Chicago for six years has brought people through the turnstiles, whereas the miserly methods pursued in the promotion of the New York game left Yankee Stadium three-fourths empty.

The Chicago game taught the promoters a lesson. Of the 32,000, less than 1,500 were white baseball fans paying their way. In other words, the success of the game was made by Negro newspapers and the daily press. Even as liberal as they were here, it didn't put people in the gate. It was the Negro press that carried the percentages, the feats of the various stars all through the year, and it was the readers of the Negro newspapers who had the knowledge of what they were going to see. Folks came from Elkhart, Indiana, Indianapolis, St. Louis, Kansas City, Gary, Indiana, Milwaukee, Detroit and Louisville to see the Chicago classic. Even with these, the greatest part of the crowd where the Chicago fans.

The Negro press has been more than fair with Negro baseball, but some like Mrs. Manley, are not fair with the Negro press.

AUGUST 27, 1939, SUNDAY
YANKEE STADIUM, NEW YORK CITY (GAME 2 OF 2)

WEST	AB	R	H	D	T	HR	BI	E	TAVG	TSLG
Dan Wilson (St. Louis Stars), rf	5	0	1	0	0	0	0	0		
John Lyles (Cleveland Bears), ss	3	1	1	0	0	0	0	1		
Ted Strong (Kansas City Monarchs), 1b	4	0	1	0	0	0	0	0		
Neil Robinson (Memphis Red Sox), cf	3	1	2	0	0	0	1	0		
Alec Radcliffe (Chicago American Giants), 3b	4	0	1	0	0	0	0	1		
Turkey Stearnes (Kansas City Monarchs), rf	3	0	1	0	0	0	1	0		
Billy Horne (Chicago American Giants), 2b	2	0	0	0	0	0	0	0		
a) Marshall Riddle (St. Louis Stars), 2b	2	0	0	0	0	0	0	0		
Pepper Bassett (Chicago American Giants), c	2	0	0	0	0	0	0	1		
Larry Brown (Memphis Red Sox), c	0	0	0	0	0	0	0	0		
b) Lloyd Davenport (Memphis Red Sox), ph	0	0	0	0	0	0	0	0		
Raymond "Smoky" Owens (Cleveland Bears), p	1	0	0	0	0	0	0	0		
Jimmy "Slim" Johnson (Toledo Crawfords), p	2	0	0	0	0	0	0	0		
Hilton Smith (Kansas City Monarchs), p	0	0	0	0	0	0	0	0		
c) Jim Williams (Toledo Crawfords), ph	1	0	0	0	0	0	0	0		
Team Totals, Average & Slugging Pct.	32	2	7	0	0	0	2	3	.219	.219

a) Batted for Horne in 6th
b) Batted for Brown in the 9th
c) Batted for H. Smith in the 9th

EAST	AB	R	H	D	T	HR	BI	E	TAVG	TSLG
Bill Wright (Baltimore Elite Giants), cf	5	2	2	1	0	0	2	0		
Willie Wells (Newark Eagles), ss	4	2	1	1	0	0	2	0		
Ed Stone (Newark Eagles) rf	4	2	3	0	0	0	0	0		
Josh Gibson (Homestead Grays), c	2	1	1	0	1	0	4	0		
Andy Patterson (Philadelphia Stars), 3b	5	0	0	0	0	0	1	0		
Buck Leonard (Homestead Grays), 1b	4	1	2	0	0	0	1	0		
Vic Harris (Homestead Grays), lf	2	1	1	0	0	0	0	0		
d) Cando Lopez (New York Cubans), lf	3	0	1	0	0	0	0	0		
Sammy T. Hughes (Baltimore Elite Giants), 2b	2	1	0	0	0	0	0	0		
Bill Byrd (Baltimore Elite Giants), p	1	0	0	0	0	0	0	0		
Terris McDuffie (New York Black Yankees), p	2	0	0	0	0	0	0	0		
Leon Day (Newark Eagles), p	1	0	0	0	0	0	0	0		
Team Totals, Average & Slugging Pct.	35	10	11	2	1	0	10	0	.314	.429

d) Batted for Harris in 5th

West	100	001	000-2	
East	140	010	04X-10	

PITCHER/TEAM	GS	IP	H	R	ER	K	BB	WP	HB	W	L
Owens/CB	1	1 1/3	3	5	3	0	2	0	1	0	1
J. Johnson/TC		3 2/3	4	1	1	4	3	0	0	0	0
H. Smith/KCM		3	4	4	3	0	1	0	0	0	0
Byrd/BEG	1	3	4	1	1	2	1	0	0	1	0
McDuffie/NYBY		3	3	1	1	3	2	0	0	0	0
Day/NE		3	0	0	0	1	1	0	0	0	0

BB—Hughes, Leonard, Gibson (2), Stone, L. Brown, Stearnes, Lyle, N. Robinson
DP—Wilson to A. Radcliffe
HBP—Wells by Owens
SAC—Gibson, Stearnes
SB—Stone
East—George Scales (Mgr.); Coaches Goose Curry and Willie Wells
West—Oscar Charleston (Mgr.); Coaches George Mitchell and Candy Jim Taylor
Umpires—Virgil Blueitt, T. J. Young, Fred McCray, & E. C. "Pop" Turner
Attendance—20,000   Time—
Note: First pitch by welterweight champion Henry Armstrong to John Henry Lewis, light heavyweight fighter.

1939 VOTING RESULTS: 17,017,518

P		2B	
Hilton Smith	402,631	Billy Horne	401,286
Preacher Henry	308,621	Dan Henderson	387,333
Theo Smith	302,586	Newt Allen	206,120
Porter Moss	300,142	Al Frazier	201,981
Double Duty Radcliffe	298,188	Sammy T. Hughes	116,318
Chip McAllister	296,147	Sam Bankhead	101,138
Andy Cooper	294,444	Dickie Seay	79,402
Bill Harvey	290,896		
Lefty Calhoun	286,509	**3B**	
Bill Byrd	131,302	Alec Radcliffe	501,862
Roy Partlow	126,846	Parnell Woods	496,774
Leon Day	124,791	Fred Bankhead	490,167
Bill Holland	119,642	Bobby Robinson	490,001
Terris McDuffie	101,211	Leroy Morney	486,736
Edsall Walker	99,872	John Lyles	304,102
Jimmy Hill	97,489	Rainey Bibbs	267,243
Ray Brown	82,141	Joe Sparks	203,196
		Pat Patterson	195,419
C		Rev Cannady	172,940
Pepper Bassett	502,394	Felton Snow	160,380
Larry Brown	408,148	Henry Spearman	80,471
Tommy Dukes	396,448	Jud Wilson	79,320
Josh Gibson	112,674		
Jose Fernandez	102,918	**SS**	
Eggie Clarke	62,480	Willie Wells	226,514
Clarence Palm	59,317	Ches Williams	105,547
		Jelly Jackson	89,302
C-1B			
Biz Mackey	189,391	**OF**	
		Jim Williams	486,682
1B		Henry Milton	480,777
Ted Strong	508,327	Neal Robinson	480,682
Jelly Taylor	404,211	Dan Wilson	477,187
Oscar Charleston	380,720	Willard Brown	420,195
Mint Jones	210,401	Lloyd Davenport	360,222
Buck Leonard	204,617	Bill Wright	118,324
Mule Suttles	202,531	Red Parnell	114,871
Jim West	101,114	Goose Curry	103,476
Johnny Washington	88,111	Vic Harris	100,780
Popeye Harris	64,780	Speed Whatley	99,873
Pedro Pages	59,418	Zollie Wright	96,722

1940

Brigadier General Benjamin O. Davis Sr. becomes the first black general in the U.S. Armed Forces. The NAACP protests segregated units in the armed forces.

The United States Postal Service issues the first stamp to honor an African-American, Booker T. Washington.

Richard Wright pens his landmark novel *Native Son*. The literary work becomes the first Book-of-the-Month Club selection written by an African-American author.

The renowned Cotton Club, in Harlem, closes.

Milk costs only 26 cents a half-gallon, 10 pounds of potatoes and a slab of bacon cost about a quarter each. A loaf of bread costs 8 cents.

The first shutout in major league all-star history is achieved when the National Leaguers shut down the American Leaguers, 4–0. Bob Feller of the Cleveland Indians throws an Opening Day no-hitter, six years before Negro Leaguer Leon Day's Opening Day no-hitter in 1946.

RACE RELATIONS

As the Negro National League opened its season in New York City, the state's lieutenant governor, Charles Poletti, threw out the first pitch in a game between the New York Cubans and the New York Black Yankees. Before 10,000 fans, Poletti made a brief speech before the players took the field, stating his wish that the day would soon come when barriers against Negro ballplayers in the big leagues would come down. He added that there was no reason why Negroes could compete in other major sports and still be barred from organized baseball.[1]

MISSING STARS

Although Josh Gibson was the leading vote getter at his position, he did not appear in the all-star game. Gibson was vacationing in Mexico with the Veracruz team. He appeared in only 22 games, in which he hit .467 in 92 at bats. He hit 11 home runs and knocked in 38 runs en route to a .989 slugging percentage. Gibson would remain in Mexico for the 1941 season, missing another East-West classic. He enjoyed another fine season in 1941, leading the Mexican League in homers with 33, RBIs with 124, and slugging with a .754 percentage. His spot at catcher for the 1941 all-star game was taken by a young and upcoming protégé of Biz Mackey named Roy Campanella, from the Baltimore Elite Giants.

One of the league's premier players, Leon Day, was banned from playing in the Negro Leagues and the all-star game. After competing in the Puerto Rican Winter League (1939–40) with Aquadilla, he joined the Vargas team in Venezuela, amassing a 12-1 won-lost record. When the league broke up in August due to Vargas's dominance in league play, Day

23. Although Josh Gibson was the leading vote getter at his position for the 1940 contest, he chose instead to play with Veracruz in the Mexican League to finish out the season. Gibson stayed in Mexico the next season, before returning to the Homestead Grays in 1942. Other top performers missing from the 1940 game were Satchel Paige, Willie Wells, and Ray Dandridge, all future Hall of Famers. Courtesy of Luis Alvelo.

attempted to rejoin a Negro League team. Newark Eagles owner Effa Manley promptly intervened and chastised Art Carter of the *Baltimore Afro-American* for entertaining the notion of letting Day play in league or nonleague games.[2] Day eventually decided not to fight league officials and signed with Veracruz in Mexico, where he added another six victories, against no defeats, to complete a very impressive season. Leon Day returned to play for the Newark Eagles in 1941.

NEGRO LEAGUES BUSINESS

In February the Negro National League's annual meeting became heated over the election of officers. Grays owner Cum Posey and Eagles owner Effa Manley engaged in an argument over selection of the next president. Located in Newark, the Eagles enjoyed the luxury of Yankee Stadium a few miles away. Together with the New York Black Yankees and the New York Cubans, the Eagles sought to oust incumbent president Tom Wilson, owner of the previous year's champion Baltimore Elite Giants. The New York faction nominated Dr. C. P. Powell, a New York publisher, for the presidential post. Meanwhile, Philadelphia Stars owner Ed Bolden, along with booking agent Eddie Gottlieb and Grays owners Rufus Jackson and Posey, voted for the incumbent president, throwing the voting in a three-all deadlock.

Manley sought dismissal of Wilson and his allies because Eddie Gottlieb, as a private booking agent, collected 10 percent on promotion of all games played in Yankee Stadium, the league's most profitable enterprise. She argued that a black league should have a black booking agent. However, Wilson's backers pointed out that the plan to pay Gottlieb for his work had been voted for 5–1 at last year's board meeting to the then complete satisfaction of Mrs. Manley. Effa countered that his rates were too high and should be renegotiated.

The Wilson contingent responded that Gottlieb had saved the league over $3,000 in rental fees the previous season and had obtained a reduction in the guarantee fee for use of Yankee Stadium.[3]

Cum Posey, in his weekly article "Posey's Point" in the *Courier*, vigorously supported Gottlieb, stating that Gottlieb received 10 percent of the net receipts, not the gross, and that Gottlieb put up all the advance monies for park rental and also assumed liability insurance at a cost of $25 for every game. Formerly, the insurance had cost owners $173 for each game. Gottlieb was able to rent Yankee Stadium for each game for $1,000 versus the $3,500 fee the league had paid the previous year. Operating expenses were down to $1,000 per game from the previous year's expenses, which had averaged $2,000 per game. Posey further attacked Effa Manley for attempting to use race as an issue to exonerate Gottlieb, who had been associated with the league since his debut year of 1934. He surmised that it was an embarrassment for all present, inasmuch as such a courtesy would be extended had those present been the lone black member at a white meeting.[4]

Ironically, because of her dark hair and olive complexion, Effa Manley represented herself as an African-American. But Miss Effa was white! In a 1977 interview with historian Bill Marshall, she expressed, "My mother, Bertha Ford Brooks, was a white woman. Her first husband was a Negro by whom she had four children. In the course of her sewing she met my father [John M. Bishop], who was a wealthy white man and I was born as a result."[5] Her mother's husband, Benjamin Brooks, sued Bishop, a stockbroker and won a $10,000 settlement.[6]

The affair prompted the Brooks to divorce, and Effa's mother married another African-American, B. A. Cole. Effa eventually had six black brothers and sisters and was raised her entire life, without regret, in a black world. She often took advantage of her white appearance to secure jobs in New York City and to stay at classy hotels reserved for white patrons only. Before she married Abe in 1933, Effa's first marriage was also to a black man. Throughout her adult life, she campaigned for equal rights for African-Americans, particularly in the clothing industry and financial institutions.[7]

Mysteriously, her marriage license states she was black, while her death certificate lists her as white. Nevertheless, Effa Manley was raised as a black woman and spoke her mind toward promoting the black cause.

Satchel Paige to American League

All Star Game Is Aug. 18

Source: *Chicago Defender,* 29 June 1940

New York— The Negro National league held its annual June meeting at the Woodside Hotel, on Tuesday, June 18, and 19 and a joint night session with the Negro American league representatives on June 18th.

All clubs of the Negro National league were represented. President J. B. Martin, B. B. Martin of Memphis, H. G. Hall of Chicago and George Mitchell of St. Louis, represented the Negro American league at the joint session.

The atmosphere around the Woodside hotel was filled with rumors and counter-rumors prior to the meeting to such an extent that no one could prophesied whether the sun was ready to set on Negro organized baseball or if it was possible to meet the demands of some members and continue the leagues individually and collectively in an amiable manner.

PAIGE CAUSES ROW

The real bone of contention, was once more, that elongated individual, Satchel Paige. Satchel Paige, who was turned over to the Newark Eagles at a previous joint meeting of the two leagues, had refused to play with Newark. Abe Manley claimed the reason Paige had not reported because one of the members of the Negro American league had influenced him not to play with Newark but to play with an independent club in the West bearing his name.

Manley held the Negro American league responsible for this and declared he was going to use any men from the American league on his club until Satchel Paige reported to him in uniform at Newark's baseball park.[8]

To show that he was determined to do this, Manley had played Bus Clarkson and E. [Ernest "Spoon"] Carter, who had been with Toledo Crawfords, of the Negro American League, in a doubleheader at Washington D.C. against Homestead Grays on Sunday June 16, despite the fact that President [Tom] Wilson had telegraphed Umpire Harris to notify Newark not to use these men.

The Grays, officially, protested these games, one of which was lost.

Manley acknowledged that he had used these players despite the ruling of President Wilson but claimed that he had a letter from Rigney of Toledo permitting him to use these men and additionally, he felt he could use any man of the N.A. League until Paige was returned to Newark Eagles.

President J. B. Martin of the American league, stated that he had just attended a meeting of his league in Chicago and they had come to the decision that Paige was not a member of any club in the N.A.L., and they could not force him to go to Newark, but that no club in the N.A. league would play against him or allow him to play in their parks. Dr. Martin then stated that according to the joint agreement, players Clarkson and Carter were members of the N.A.L. and could not be sold or traded to a N.N.L. club until all clubs in the N.A.L. had an opportunity to waive them out of the league.

Manley refused to accept this explanation as final and Dr. Martin called on President Wilson for a decision.

President Wilson ruled that he could not see how the clubs of the Negro American

League could force Paige to go to Newark when he was not a member of their league, players Clarkson and E. Carter belonged to the Negro American League.

Manley stated that he would not send these players back to Toledo or any other N.A.L. club despite the rulings of the two presidents. Then things started to really "jump" at the Woodside [Hotel].

PAIGE COMES WEST

Every league member got into the argument. Dr. B. B. Martin stated that the Negro American league was "sick and tired of having players taken by Negro National league clubs and then threatening to break the agreement between the two leagues in the N.A. league did not allow this."

Negro National league members took exception to these remarks and the "fur flew." It was finally agreed upon that Satchel Paige become the property of the N.A. league and Clarkson and Carter the property of Newark Eagles.

This move was a concession by the N.A. league for the sake of inter-league harmony, although their side of the argument was upheld by various members of the N. N. league.

Presidents Martin and Wilson were voted the power to appoint a committee for the East-West game after a motion by Manley to have a committee of five to handle the game was voted down by 11 to 2 with Cubans not voting.

The East-West game is slated to be at Comiskey Park, Chicago on Sunday, August 18.

The Negro National League voted to play a straight season through to September 8, and then meet the winner of the Negro American league in a world series. The N.A. league plays a split season but assured the N.N. league owners that their pennant-winning club would be known in time to start the World Series on Sunday, September 15.

Editor's note: A world series was not played between the Kansas City Monarchs of the Negro American League and the Homestead Grays of the Negro National League. It would not be until 1942 that the black leagues would host a world series (since 1927). Ironically, the same teams would meet in the 1942 series.

Satchel Paige Not Eligible for 1940 East-West Baseball Classic

by Frank A. Young

Source: *Chicago Defender,* 3 August 1940

Satchel Paige is not going to play in the East vs. West 1940 baseball classic at Comiskey Park if the Negro National and the Negro American leagues are to survive. It would not only set a bad precedent but it would eventually kill both leagues.

The *Chicago Tribune* carried an article last Sunday on its sports pages stating that Paige might be declared eligible to play for this year's game.

The game itself is BIGGER than Paige. The facts confronting the presidents of both leagues, the owners and the managers are such that it would be a calamity to even think of playing Paige and to play him would set Negro baseball back beyond where it was exactly 20 years ago this past winter when Rube Foster and a small group, of whom only a few are yet in baseball, met in the Y.M.C.A. in Kansas City and formed the old Negro National league.

In the first place, the East vs. West game was the brainchild of Gus Greenlee of the Pittsburgh Crawfords and R. A. "King" Cole of the Chicago American Giants. Now the two leagues have taken over the management and all seem to be working fairly well when along comes a so-called publicity expert and bangs anything out on the typewriter without first thinking of what reaction the story might have.

It might seem like it is a great stunt to invite thousands of people to the White Sox park who will expect Paige to play. But the reaction comes when these thousands are disappointed and go away from the park not to be enticed there again.

Paige is NOT a member of the Negro American league although he was voted the property of that league by the Negro National league after Mrs. Abe Manley of the Newark Eagles had threatened to withdraw from the Negro National league if she could not keep Clarkson and another player "loaned her" by Hank Rigney of the Toledo Crawfords, although Rigney had no legal right to do so without getting waivers on the two men from every club in the Western circuit.

Dr. J. B. Martin, Memphis, president of the Negro American league, for the sake of peace and harmony, allowed Newark to retain the two players. Then the Eastern circuit voted Paige to the Negro American league. They knew at the time that Paige was playing with an all-star independent team as he did in 1938, AND that he was billed as the attraction. Newt Joseph, Kansas City, MO., citizen and ex-third sacker manages the team for the Kansas City Monarchs.[9]

J. L. Wilkinson, owner of the Monarchs, has no connection with the independent team. Paige and his All Stars are booked past Labor day. To get him to Chicago would cost much money for transportation and the games scheduled for August 18 as well as the day before would have to be canceled. Some one will have to pay for that loss as the ball club would be idle two days. If Paige can play in the All-star game—THEN ANY PLAYER WHO FAILED to report to his club at the beginning of the season and who decided he would rather play independent ball instead of organized ball is ENTITLED to play in the game. That means that [Sug] Cornelius and [Pepper] Bassett of the Chicago American Giants; Ted Strong of Kansas City; Frank Duncan, who signed up in 1940 with Chicago after playing independent ball in 1939; Willie Wells, Newark shortstop; Josh Gibson, Homestead Grays catcher, and others who walked out on their signed contract have just as much right to ask to be considered as Paige.

Last year Paige did not play and the classic drew its greatest crowd. Why all this excitement about one long-legged pitcher?

The fans support the game. The players along with the fans make the game what it is. The owners must agree that the fans must have confidence in their integrity. When both leagues make rules and declare a suspension or fine the public doesn't expect the rule or suspension will be waived in favor for a publicity buildup. Since Paige is not a member of any team in the Negro American league and hasn't been this season, he is not eligible to play in any East vs. West game between players under contract to the clubs in the two leagues.

We might just as well realize that Negro baseball is more on trial today than it ever was. Negroes who are baseball minded can tell you more about the batting averages of any of the big league players than they can of their players in either Negro league. Negroes who are baseball care and know more about what "ole Diz Dean" does than they do about Satchel Paige or any other Negro pitcher.

There may be a reason for some of this. The radio blares forth with the games in the two major leagues and in Chicago the folks who work can come home and the game is re-broadcast so they can tune in on it during supper.

What publicity is dished out is handed to newspaper offices by the secretaries of the club and the publicity is not false. Parks are kept in excellent condition and money is spent to make money.

Fans in Chicago as well as thousands and thousands outside — can not understand why the East vs. West game should be taken to Comiskey Park at such a tremendous expense when the park at Thirty-ninth Street [Southside Park] should be in such a condition that the game should be played there. Fans here can't understand why the park is allowed to run down. Chicago baseball fans deserve better than what they are getting.

Visiting ball clubs suffer because the attendance is falling off in Chicago.

What both leagues need is a baseball minded commissioner. To date there is no commissioner. True, Major Robert R. Jackson is commissioner of the Negro American League but who ever heard of a commissioner of one league? The late "Brother Woods" who used to sit on the bench along with the late Rube Foster and myself, would turn over in his grave and yelp "Lan' sakes alive," which was his saying when astonished, if he were to see the direction in which we were headed.

The East vs. West game is a great thing for Negro baseball. But the East vs. West game is but one game and we want Negro baseball in Chicago like it was in the days of old Rube Foster, the man whose office door was always open, who met the great and small alike, who had a great ball club, who was known by everybody and whose ball club and his own personality packed them in at Thirty-ninth.

Less that 8,000 saw Sunday's doubleheader between the Kansas City Monarchs and the Chicago American Giants, Sunday. More than that number of Negroes were at the New York Yanks game at the White Sox park. And turning back the pages of the Defender we count the Sundays when the Monarchs played to two and three times the crowd which saw them here on their last trip.

It's not the fans' fault. You can't sell a man vinegar when he wants sorghum.

Lefty Bowe Joins Clowns

East-West Game Meant No Money to Him

by Frank A. Young

Source: *Chicago Defender,* 10 August 1940

Randolph Bowe, crack left hander of the Chicago American Giants, has jumped his contract and joined the Ethiopian Clowns. Ordinarily such news would warrant a two-paragraph story. This time it is big news because if the club owners in the two major Negro leagues do not wake up they will find their best players over in the independent ranks.

BECOMES DISGRUNTLED

Bowe injured his leg last year and was nursed along by the Chicago team. This year, he has been going along fine. Two Sundays ago he turned in a victory over the strong Kansas City Monarchs but right after the game Bowe was disgruntled when, according to his friends, some word or other was passed along to him that he and his mates would have to pay for the new uniforms they were wearing. That and some salary differences plus that fact that he had no assurance of receiving a thing out of the 1940 East vs. West game caused Bowe to take "French leave."

Bowe isn't as much to blame as is Horace G. Hall, president of the Chicago American

Giants, a corporation which the stockholders seem to have little or nothing to say about. Hall went East to the joint meeting of the two leagues in June, talked to Bill Horne who had jumped the Chicago club for the Clowns and took Horne back. Now, you might say that Horne was already the property of the Chicago club. Legally, he was. But neither Hall nor the president of the Negro American league plastered any fine on Horne for jumping the Chicago club. He was welcomed back into the good graces of the Chicago team as if he had only been guilty of walking across the street and buying an ice cream soda between a doubleheader.

Then the Giants and the other league clubs played the Clowns. Syd Pollock is booking agent for the Clowns. There should have been an understanding that as long as Pollock allowed the manager of the Clowns to raid league clubs so long would the Clowns be without attractions in league club parks and against league clubs.

No one can blame Bowe after nothing was done with Horne who ought to have at least been fined then and there.

Now comes the talk about Satchel Paige because Abe Saperstein, booking agent, desires to increase the gate of the 1940 East vs. West game so he can get a big split and isn't bothered about the future of Negro baseball.

Let's do some reckoning. If Paige plays or could play, it will cost something to get him to come here. Two games, the Saturday and Sunday games in which he is booked to play would have to be canceled. Paige's transportation would have to be paid from "way out west" AND Paige would HAVE TO BE PAID to make up what he would lose in money by not being with the independent ball club.

MAY CAUSE STRIKE

Since seven years have gone by and none of the ball players who take part in the East vs. West ball game have received any money or trophy or watch or gold baseball for taking part in the game a word to the wise would be sufficient. The 36 ball players who will take part in the game are not going to sit idly by and see Mr. Paige get paid and they get nothing.

The ball players aren't that dumb. Already there is some talk about the players refusing to take the field IF Paige comes unless some consideration is promised these players for playing. Then, too, the C.I.O. and the A.F. of L. organizers are watching the move. Do the ball players need a union? Some say they do. The entry of Paige in the All-Star game will go a long way to break up the leagues because the East is going to protest—if no one else does. Mrs. Manley will and she has a good right to do so. She has as much right to ask that Willie Wells, who is Newark property, be brought here from Mexico and played after paying Wells expenses.

HANDWRITING ON WALL

Unless I miss my guess, Paige will stay right out West and the game will go on. If I do miss it and Saperstein has his say, the Negro American league will be no more which would be to Saperstein's liking because as long as there is a league he gets no percentage for league games. Weekday and Saturday bookings mean little to him. If the league is BUSTED up, he will get 5 percent for booking Sunday games into Western parks and he can bring all sorts of Eastern teams West. That's what he is aiming at.

Saperstein, who owns the Harlem Globe Trotters basketball team which never saw Harlem, who books the Sir Oliver Bibbs orchestra, who books the Brown Bombers football team, and who is or was the manager of Joe Louis is making his living off Negro activities. The future of them is not his concern—it is the present and what he can get out of it.

Saperstein formed the Tri State league a few years ago in order to tie up ball parks in Indiana, Illinois and Wisconsin—then told the park owners that no Negro clubs could play in these parks unless through his booking. He sent the Columbia Giants down to South Bend [Indiana] to play the Studebaker nine. They were billed as the Cuban Stars. There wasn't a Cuban on the team. The personnel included [George] Harney, Joe Lillard, a couple of Mexican players and a few pickups. The Brown Bombers didn't make room and board out of their football game in New Orleans last fall.

Saperstein put two basketball teams out on the road in an effort to "sew up" the road attractions. One disbanded. One won the so-called world pro championship, luckily, with seven players. The Cleveland Bears were booked for three or four games last week by Saperstein. The "tour" took them 1,500 miles. The Cleveland club made exactly $139.

Why do the Negro American clubs have to be booked into the Chicago Mills and the Spencer Coals Park in Chicago by an outsider? These park owners will either take the league clubs or go idle and since they want attractions they want league clubs and always have wanted them.

GET HALL'S OKAY

And the worst yet is after all this, the American Giants' Hall declares that Saperstein is an asset to the league so much so that he heartily is in accord with Saperstein getting 5 percent of the East vs. West game money, over the objection of President Tom Wilson, Mrs. Abe Manley, Cum Posey, Bill [Jim] Semler and others, while the ball players aren't (or at least haven't been) considered.

Maybe you can figure it out. Why is Saperstein worth more than $1,200 while the ball player gets nothing and the umpires get $10 per man? Why is about $4,000 of the East vs. West money thrown away foolishly and why is Hall paid a salary when he benefits as does the other league clubs out of the profits of the game?

Do you wonder why Bowe jumped and went to the Clowns who are in the Denver tournament and who will, if they finish in the first three, split among the players a nice purse?

Powerful Attack Masterful Mound Work Beats West

by William G. Nunn

Source: *Pittsburgh Courier,* 24 August 1940

Five-hit pitching, as turned in by Henry McHenry, of the Philadelphia Stars; [Silvio] Ruiz, the veteran Cuban; and Ray Brown, of the Grays, coupled by an inner defense which performed brilliantly, silenced the vaunted offensive power of the West's mighty guns here today as the East "slipped in" to an astonishing 11-0 victory, in the eighth annual resumption of the East-West game, to even up the series, 4 to 4.

The West, which took the field this afternoon definitely established as favorites, were beaten before the first inning was over. From that time on, the game was anticlimax to a vast majority of the close to 25,000 fans who braved threatening weather to view this classic, which has become an institution in the second largest city in the country.

24. The August 18, 1940, game would be Hilton Lee Smith's fifth all-star appearance. Smith pitched in seven East-West All-Star Games and has the second-most career strikeouts (15) in the classic. Courtesy of NoirTech Research, Inc.

WEST WAS FAVORED

Pre-game dope favored the Westerners. In the first place they had an edge in pitching, supposedly. Then their "ace" Hilton Smith, had previously pitched six innings of "hitless" ball in two previous East-West games.

The East, by comparison had been raided. Many of the "big names", which had always made the East feared, had been barred because they elected to play somewhere else. There were no "Josh" Gibson, no Willie Wells, and no "Hooks" Dandridge in the line-up.

Mule Suttles had been floored by a recurring illness. Sammy Hughes had been hit on the head by a thrown ball last Wednesday night and was on the shelf.

All in all, it looked bad for the East . . . on paper, at least. But ball games happen to still be played on the diamond, and it was here that he saw an amazing transformation of a group of men with the will to win. They wanted to win—and they had what it took to win.

Defensive honors had to go to the East's infield. That combination of [Howard] Easterling, [Horacio "Rabbit"] Martinez, [Dickie] Searcy [Seay], and [Buck] Leonard performed feats of magic with the ball. Anything hit on the ground was out. Easterling is he fastest fielding thirdsacker we've seen in years. He roams far and wide to get 'em, and can throw with the ease and power of a Dihigo.

Martinez accepted several chances and handled then flawlessly. At second-base, however, Dick Seay did everything that a keystone sacker can be asked. He roamed behind first to knock down hard drives and throw his men out. He turned several potential hits into outs by brilliant defensive work, and his stop and throw of Jelly Taylor's smash in the ninth to start the double play ending the game was a thing of superb diamond artistry. As usual, Leonard was the perfect mechanism at first-base, and his offensive power was never more in evidence.

In comparison with the West's five hits, the East made 14. All of the West's five hits were singles—and one of these of the scratch variety. [Gene] Benson's double and [Alex] Crespo's triple were solid blows with plenty on them.

While the East played errorless ball, the West was charged with six miscues . . . four of these made by Morney, who had a bad day, both at bat and in the field.

After Benson had been retired, Martinez singled to left and took second as Stone bounced out. Buck Leonard drew his first walk of the game. Singles by Easterling and Barker sent in the winning runs.

In the first three innings, the West got one hit—a bouncing single by Milton, the West's first hitter. There were no more hits off Mr. McHenry.

In the fourth, the East scored another run off [Walt "Lefty"] Calhoun. [Cy] Perkins singled, but Seay's attempt to sacrifice failed when he was caught off second on a nice play by Woods. Morney's second error on McHenry's smash enabled Seay to reach second, from where he scored as Benson singled to center.

SCORE AGAIN IN FIFTH

Another run dribbled across in the fifth. After Stone had popped out to the infield, Leonard drove a sharp single to right, stole second, and continued to third as Smith threw wild to center and scored as Barker singled off Woods' glove.

The sixth inning saw the game become a marathon. Here it was that the West made about every mistake in the book, and before the smoke had blown away four runs were in . . . the result of three hits, two error, one hit batsman and a wild pitch. Calhoun had been sent to the showers and Johnson had looked bad on an error of omission, falling to cover first.

Then in the eighth, just to show they had no respect for anyone's feelings, they jumped on MISTER Hilton Smith to score three more runs on four hits. All in all, it was a big day for the East.

AUGUST 18, 1940, CHICAGO, IL

EAST	AB	R	H	D	T	HR	BI	E	TAVG	TSLG
Gene Benson (Philadelphia Stars), cf	6	1	2	1	0	0	2	0		
Rabbit Martinez (New York Cubans), ss	3	1	1	0	0	0	0	0		
a) Bus Clarkson (Newark Eagles), ph-ss	2	1	0	0	0	0	0	0		
Ed Stone (Newark Eagles), rf	3	0	0	0	0	0	0	0		
b) Alejandro Crespo (New York Cubans), ph-lf	2	1	1	0	1	0	1	0		
Buck Leonard (Homestead Grays), 1b	4	1	3	0	0	0	3	0		
Howard Easterling (Homestead Grays), 3b	5	1	2	0	0	0	1	0		
Marvin Barker (New York Black Yankees), cf-rf	5	1	3	0	0	0	1	0		
Cy Perkins (Baltimore Elite Giants), c	5	1	2	0	0	0	1	0		
Robert Clarke (New York Black Yankees), c	0	0	0	0	0	0	0	0		
Dick Seay (New York Black Yankees), 2b	4	2	0	0	0	0	0	0		
Henry McHenry (Philadelphia Stars), p	0	0	0	0	0	0	0	0		
Poppa Ruiz (New York Cubans), p	2	1	0	0	0	0	0	0		
c) Raymond Brown (Homestead Grays), p	2	0	0	0	0	0	1	0		
Team Totals, Average & Slugging Pct.	43	11	14	1	1	0	10	0	.326	.395

a) Batted for Martinez in 6th
b) Batted for Stone in the 6th
c) Batted for Ruiz in 7th

WEST	AB	R	H	D	T	HR	BI	E	TAVG	TSLG
Henry Milton (Kansas City Monarchs), rf	4	0	1	0	0	0	0	0		
Parnell Woods (Birmingham Black Barons), 3b	4	0	1	0	0	0	0	0		
Eldridge Mayweather (New Orleans-St. Louis Stars), 1b	3	0	1	0	0	0	0	0		
Neil Robinson (Memphis Red Sox), cf	2	0	0	0	0	0	0	0		
d) Leslie Green (New Orleans-St. Louis Stars), cf	2	0	1	0	0	0	0	0		
Donald Reeves (Chicago American Giants), lf	4	0	0	0	0	0	0	0		
James Greene (Kansas City Monarchs), c	2	0	0	0	0	0	0	1		
Larry Brown (Memphis Red Sox), c	1	0	1	0	0	0	0	0		
Leroy Morney (Chicago American Giants), ss	2	0	0	0	0	0	0	4		
Curt Henderson (Toledo-Indianapolis Crawfords), ss	1	0	0	0	0	0	0	0		
e) Jelly Taylor (Memphis Red Sox), ph	1	0	0	0	0	0	0	0		
Tommy Sampson (Birmingham Black Barons), 2b	2	0	0	0	0	0	0	0		
Marshall Riddle (New Orleans-St. Louis Stars), 2b	1	0	0	0	0	0	0	1		
Gene Bremer (Memphis Red Sox), p	0	0	0	0	0	0	0	0		
Walt Calhoun (New Orleans-St. Louis Stars), p	1	0	0	0	0	0	0	0		
Connie Johnson (Toledo-Indianapolis Crawfords), p	0	0	0	0	0	0	0	0		
Hilton Smith (Kansas City Monarchs), p	1	0	0	0	0	0	0	0		
Team Totals, Average & Slugging Pct.	31	0	5	0	0	0	0	6	.161	.161

d) Batted for Robinson in 6th

e) Batted for Henderson in 9th

East	200	114	030-11
West	000	000	000-0

PITCHER/TEAM	GS	IP	H	R	ER	K	BB	WP	HB	W	L
McHenry/PS	1	3	1	0	0	1	1	0	0	1	0
Ruiz/NYC		3	2	0	0	0	2	0	0	0	0
R. Brown/HG		3	2	0	0	3	0	0	0	0	0
Bremer/MRS	1	3	3	2	2	4	3	0	0	0	1
Calhoun/SLS		2 1/3	6	6	3	1	1	0	1	0	0
C. Johnson/IC		2/3	1	0	0	1	0	0	0	0	0
H. Smith/KCM		3	4	3	2	3	0	0	1	0	0

BB—Clarkson, Leonard (2), McHenry, Greene, Mayweather, Bremer

DP—Seay to Clarkson to Leonard; Morney to Sampson to Mayweather

HBP—Crespo by Calhoun; Seay by H. Smith

LOB—West 5, East 9

SB—Leonard (2), Benson

East—Felton Snow (Mgr.); Coach Dizzy Dismukes

West—Andy Cooper (Mgr.); Coaches Candy Jim Taylor and George Mitchell

Umpires—Virgil Blueitt, Wilber Rogan, Fred McCrary, Moe Harris

Attendance—25,000   Time—

Note: Each player received an Elgin wrist watch from J. B. Martin, President of the Negro American League

1940 VOTING RESULTS: 3,023,577

P

Hilton Smith	83,773
Bob Bowe	61,180
Ray Brown	59,928
Henry McHenry	59,902
Jimmy Hill	53,482
Schoolboy Taylor	47,826
Chip McAllister	47,772
Johnny Wright	47,708
Lefty Calhoun	34,502
Gene Bremer	32,334
Smokey Sarvis	29,946
Nate Moreland	27,428
Edsall Walker	25,011

C

Biz Mackey	59,455
Cy Perkins	57,992
Larry Brown	56,333
Johnny Hayes	54,355
Roy Campanella	47,678

1B

Buck Leonard	75,578
Buck O'Neil	59,459
Jelly Taylor	58,921
Red Moore	57,890
Chili Mayweather	50,782
Johnny Washington	46,446
Jim West	45,229
Oscar Charleston	42,030
Fran Matthews	39,492

2B

Sammy T. Hughes	61,112
Lick Carlisle	56,445
Rainey Bibbs	48,555
Billy Horne	47,893
Dickie Seay	43,847
Marshall Riddle	38,123
Tommy Sampson	36,773

3B

Howard Easterling	59,992
Felton Snow	57,782
Jake Dunn	47,389
Henry Spearman	46,221
Parnell Woods	44,588
Herb Souell	38,429
Jimmy Ford	32,234

SS

Rabbit Martinez	60,002
Jelly Jackson	57,345
Bus Clarkson	56,723
Leroy Morney	52,358
Pee Wee Butts	42,301
Hickey Redd	38,492
John Lyles	33,674
Jesse Williams	32,422

OF

Donald Reeves	69,968
Henry Milton	58,758
Jerry Benjamin	58,489
Bill Hoskins	52,334
Mule Suttles	52,111
Alex Crespo	48,889
John Ray	48,229
Red Parnell	47,989
Speed Whatley	46,778
Jabo Andrews	37,244
Henry Kimbro	37,239
Gene Benson	35,209
Ed Stone	35,208

1941

Upon pressure by the NAACP, President Franklin D. Roosevelt issues Executive Order 8802, which bans discrimination in war facilities and military training camps. As a result of the order, A. Philip Randolph calls off a planned protest march on the capitol.

Tuskegee University organizes the 99th Pursuit Squadron, an all-black aerial unit. The 99th squadron would later combine with the 332nd Fighter Group. The first all-black-officered regular Army Infantry Regiment, the 366th, is activated.

Milk costs 27 cents a half-gallon, 10 pounds of potatoes costs 24 cents, and 34 cents would bring home the bacon. A loaf of bread costs eight cents.

Japanese aircraft attack Pearl Harbor, initiating World War II.

New York bus companies agree to hire black drivers and mechanics.

Jackie Robinson, halfback for UCLA, is named to the College All-Star Team to play against the world-champion Chicago Bears.

The American League All-Stars are trailing 5–4 when Ted Williams hits a three-run homer in the ninth inning, giving the AL stars a 7–5 victory over the National Leaguers.

Ted Williams ends the season with a .406 batting average, becoming the last major league player to break the .400 barrier. Joltin' Joe DiMaggio of the New York Yankees hits safely in 56 consecutive games. DiMaggio wins the league MVP award.

Lou Gehrig, one of baseball's greatest players, dies of amyotrophic lateral sclerosis. Nicknamed the "Iron Horse" for playing in 2,130 consecutive games, Gehrig dies 17 days before his 38th birthday. The disease is now commonly called Lou Gehrig's disease.

The Brooklyn Dodgers experiment with the first batting helmet made of fiberglass, four years after Negro League players first wore helmets. In 1955, 14 of 16 major league teams would offer protective headgear to their players. By the 1958 season, batting helmets would become mandatory for all teams.

NEGRO LEAGUES BUSINESS

The start of this season found the owners of Negro National League teams placing all of the league's eastern promotions under the direction of Frank Forbes. Forbes was a former player, manager, and umpire. With his baseball experience, Forbes was expected to use his numerous contacts in metropolitan New York to secure parks like Yankee Stadium to showcase Negro League talent.

The recent board meeting also rendered a decision to lift the ban on players who had "jumped" to Mexico, Puerto Rico, and Venezuela. Some of the league's biggest stars, such as Satchel Paige (in Puerto Rico with Guayama) and Josh Gibson (in Mexico with Vera-cruz), were playing south of the border. The suspended players would be required to pay a $100 fine for reentry into homeland black baseball. With the drawing power of Gibson and Paige, teams paid (or waived) the fine to get their stars and others back into their lineups.

In March, Satchel Paige had been fined and banned from the Puerto Rican Baseball League by President Carlos Noceda. Paige, the league's top drawing card as a pitcher for Guayama, was fined for using "dilatory tactics." The wire release from the United Press read:

> UP43—San Juan, Puerto Rico, March 10.—(UP)— Satchel Paige, colored baseball star has been fined $25 and given a year's suspension by Carlos Garcia De Noceda, President of Puerto Rican Semi-Pro League, it was announced today.
>
> Garcia said that he found that Paige, while pitching for Guayama, deliberately used tactics designed to delay the game and cause Ponce to lose. Paige once went so far as to throw the ball far over the outfielder's head.
>
> Fortunately—because Paige has been the league's best drawing card—the suspension does not take effect until the season closes less than two weeks from now. HM544A

Paige returned to the Monarchs, but his stay was temporary. On May 11, Opening Day, the New York Black Yankees hired Paige to pitch one game against the Philadelphia Stars. Each club paid him $100 apiece. With Paige's name on the marquee, 20,000 folks came to Yankee Stadium. Paige won the first game of the doubleheader, 5–3, while Chet Brewer for the Stars captured the nightcap, 4–1. The deal by the Yankees' Jim "Soldier Boy" Semler and the Stars' Eddie Gottlieb to bring in Paige prompted Cum Posey to remind league officials of an earlier ruling on player jumping.

At the February joint meeting in Chicago, the Negro National League and the Negro American League entertained thoughts of dissolving their partnership. The agreement came about because Negro American League officials refused to sign players who had played in Latin American countries, whereby the same players were offered contracts by the Negro National League. The officials resolved to have the players fined, but Posey could not find record of payments by any players. He claimed, "Paige was running Negro organized baseball."[1] Posey was already upset with the American League when it granted permission for the Monarchs to play the Ethiopian Clowns.[2] However, the Monarchs were not the only team to play nonleague clubs. The Baltimore Elite Giants started the season by playing the semipro Dr. Nut Algiers Giants of New Orleans.

In other league news, officials agreed that team rosters would be limited to 18 players. The limit did not include the bus driver, office secretary, traveling secretary, or public relations director. The league would use the Wilson baseball, with an allowance of two dozen balls each game. The teams would estimate expenditures of $65 to provide each player with two uniforms and a traveling jacket. The player would provide his own shoes and sweatshirts.[3]

The total estimated cost to run a club from May through September was $40,000, for salaries, park rental, taxes, equipment, transportation, baseballs, and bats; the figure did not include promotional expenses.[4]

RACE RELATIONS

H. G. Salsinger, a sports editor for the *Detroit News,* expressed his views on the color line after seeing a doubleheader between the Baltimore Elite Giants and the Homestead Grays:

25. *Negro National League executive board meeting on January 11, 1941. Top row, left to right: Charles Brown, Edward Witherspoon, Alex Pompez, Rufus Jackson (standing), Tom Wilson, Art Carter (standing), Mrs. Effa Manley, Jim Semler (standing), Abe Manley, Cum Posey, Jack Waters (standing), and Dr. J. B. Martin. Bottom row: William Laushner, Eddie Gottlieb, Seward Posey, Frank Forbes, Ms. Eary Brown, and Douglas Smith. Courtesy of NoirTech Research, Inc.*

Colored cultural organizations have been trying to beat down the color line and gain admittance for colored ball players to major league rosters. The answer to all their campaigns has been that the colored league lacked players capable of making the big-league grade.

Here was a chance to compare the play of the colored leaguers with that of the major leaguers, and the comparison, made after more than five hours of competition, was in favor of the colored players.

There is one thing that distinguishes the Negro National League ball players from their major league brethren, and that is their whole-hearted enthusiasm and their genuine zest. They look like men who are getting a great deal of fun out of it but who desperately want to win.[5]

The 1941 East-West game hit an all-time high in fan attendance. Ed Harris of the *Philadelphia Tribune* posed the question of when the moguls of major league would realize the potential bonanza of hiring black players in one of his articles:

You read about the 50,000 persons who saw the East-West game and the thousands who were turned away from the classic and you get to wondering what the magnates of the American and National League thought about it when they read the figures. Did any of them feel a faint stir in their hearts; a wish that they could use some of the many stars who saw action to corral some of the coin evidently interested in them? Or did they, hearing the jingling of the turnstiles in this, one of the good seasons baseball has had, just dismiss the motion and reserve the idea of Negro players in the big league until the next time there is a depression and baseball profits began to decline? Fifty thousands people at any baseball game, World Series included, is no small figure. Their All-Star game didn't draw half that number and there will be few games this season which will draw 50,000. But those who don't want to see the colored man playing big league ball don't want to see him because he's colored. He could bring an increase of $25,000 to the team in a season and he still wouldn't be wanted. So 50,000 at the East-West game won't mean much one way or the other.[6]

ALL-STAR REVIEW

In 1941 Monte Irvin was one of the most likely candidates to break Major League's Baseball's color barrier. Only 22 years old at the time, the college-educated Newark shortstop recalled the East-West games in his autobiography:

I played in four (6 games in four years) of these All-Star games and missed four others because of playing in Mexico and serving in World War II. The East-West games were played in Chicago . . . and each one was always a joyful experience. The park would be decorated with red, white, and blue banners that had been put up everywhere, and a jazz band would play between innings. The whole scene was festive and fun. People like Count Basie, Ella Fitzgerald and Billie Holiday would always make it their business to be in town for the East-West game, and we'd be sure to check them out at the jazz clubs. You didn't go to Chicago to sleep.

I remember my first East-West game. When we were selected, we would leave on a Friday and get to Chicago either Friday night or Saturday morning. Count Basie had written a song called, "Goin' to Chicago Blues," and it was a very popular song in 1941. They were playing it on the radio during our train ride and everybody in our car was singing along, "Goin' to Chicago, sorry I can't take you." We finally pulled into Chicago late Friday night and checked into the Grand Hotel.

The game was played on a Sunday afternoon. At the time I think Comiskey Park's capacity was about fifty thousand but sometimes they would have as many as fifty-five thousand in attendance because the promoters could always do business with the fire department and they would let fans sit in the aisles.

People would come from all over the country to be part of the spectacle. They came all the way from Mississippi, New Orleans, Birmingham, Mobile, Kansas City, Detroit, and from all over just to see the big stars. There were a few whites scattered throughout the ballpark, but mostly it was blacks of all backgrounds, all shapes and sizes, men and women and children. Black people used to love baseball.

But the fans really turned out for the East-West game and they always saw a good game and great players. If you picked an All-Star from the two squads, it surely could have rivaled any white major-league all-star of the time. That team would have been a good as any All-Star team that's ever played.

Playing in these games was a way for us to promote the Negro Leagues and to pave the way for the present-day black ball players. But more than anything else, our games gave black Americans hope all across the country. The same thing was true of our regular season games everywhere we traveled. When we would play down South, out West, or here in the East, black people got a chance to come out and see these great players perform on the baseball field and it gave them hope.

They said, "If these ball players can succeed under these very difficult conditions, then maybe we can too." Maybe many of the people who came out to the ballpark caught hell all week. If they had a job, it was usually a menial one, and they were not getting any encouragement at the workplace. But on Saturday or Sunday, they went to a game and saw players the same color performing well on the baseball diamond. They made them feel pretty good and just generally uplifted their spirit.[7]

JACKIE'S JOURNEY

Jackie Robinson was making sports headlines several years before his history-making debut in the major leagues. Fay Young, for the *Chicago Defender,* wrote of Robinson's final collegiate football game:

Jackie Robinson "did his thing" in the All Stars versus the Chicago Bears game at Soldier's Field last Thursday night. The 37–13 score doesn't begin to tell how Robinson did all that was expected of him and more too. He is the first Negro to score a touchdown in the eight games played. The 98,203 paid him a tribute as he left the field.

Robinson represented the University of California at Los Angles [UCLA]. Last year, Kenny Washington of the same school played for the All Stars against the Green Bay Packers. The longest run of a kickoff is down in the books behind Washington's name. He ran one back 88 yards last year.[8]

Realizing Robinson's impact with fans, Young also took the opportunity to promote the integration of the armed forces and sports at the pro level:

The game ought to make the United States Army and Navy wake up. Every time a Negro who is qualified asks to join a particular branch of either service, there is a cry that Negroes and whites can't do this or that together. A great example of what can be done is shown in this College All Star versus pro game for charity. Men from all sections of the country were on the Bears' team. Since professional football draws the color line when it comes to players, no Negro was with the Bears. But the Bears played against Robinson and marveled at his ability. The Green Bay team played against Kenny Washington in 1940 and the New York Giants played against Bernie Jefferson of Northwestern and Horace Bell of Minnesota in 1939.[9]

I Cover the Eastern Front

by Eddie Gant

Source: *Chicago Defender,* 12 July 1941

Washington DC— The halfway mark in the Negro National league was reached last week with the Homestead Grays still out in front. It seems that there is no stopping that hustling gang of Vic Harris' despite the fact that they miss clouting Josh Gibson. Gibson, whose home runs thrilled thousands of fans, isn't missed so much because of his power hitting, as Buck Leonard. Tom [Howard] Easterling and the rest have been swatting the ball at a fine clip, but Gibson's finesse behind the plate has been noticeable since his absence.

Harris has tried several catchers but none seem to have the stuff like Gibson. Jake Gaston, the regular backstop since Gibson's skip to Mexico, was doing a fair job. But the strain of daily work began to tell on Gaston who was forced to toil day and night, with doubleheaders tossed in occasionally for good measure. To relieve the situation, Harris recently signed [Clarence] Palm, formerly of the Philadelphia Stars, which should give the Grays plenty of fortification behind the bat and put them in fine fettle for the long homeward trek in the second half race.

With the catching problem solved, the Grays appear a 5–1 shot to repeat the pennant victory this year, though they are going to catch loads of trouble from their old rivals the Baltimore Elite Giants and the up-and-coming Newark Eagles. The Elites, 1939 champions, and runners-up last year, have been right in the running from the outset this season, but failure to produce winning rallies in several important series kept them out of the top spot. Newark, with the hottest young group of players in the league, seemed to have hit their stride within the last two weeks and things should be pretty hot for the Grays in the second half.

All the teams are going at a rapid rate now with the East-West game just around the corner and every player anxious to gain a place on the coveted East team. The Cubans, Black Yankees and Stars, bring up the lower half of the league but all have strong combinations and at any moment during the remainder of the campaign may surge to the front and upset the dope.

The Cubans, with Dave Barnhill as their ace, are exceptionally favored with good pitching and any day that all the Islanders begin to hit the ball at the same time, the other five league clubs are going to fall victims to them. The Black Yankees are badly off balance, getting only fair hurling, and inconsistent fielding, while the Stars, now bolstered by the addition of Oscar Charleston as manager, may show renewed strength in the second half.

The second half schedule is going to be tough for the clubs have an Inter-league card which will put some teams against Negro American League teams. But we look for a good fight down to the finish with the Grays, Elites and Eagles in a battle for the top position.

Paige to Pitch for East vs. West Game

50,000 Will See Classic in Chicago

Ninth Annual Contest to Feature Battle of Pitchers, Hitters

Source: *Chicago Defender,* 26 July 1941

The ninth annual East versus West baseball classic will be played at Comiskey Park on Sunday afternoon, July 27. The largest crowd in the history of the classic is expected out to watch the 1941 dream game. From the increased interest in the game each year, the 1939 record of 40,000 will be smashed.

Not only from Chicago are fans going but from Detroit, Columbus, Cincinnati and Dayton, Ohio; Kalamazoo, Mich., Battle Creek, Mich., Gary, Ind., Milwaukee, Kansas City, Mo., St. Louis, Springfield, Ill., Rockford, Ill., and thousands of other towns within a radius of 500 miles will be represented. Jackson, Mich., is sending 50 American Legionnaires. Many soldiers at Fort Custer, Mich., where the 184th Field artillery, the old Eighth Illinois National Guard infantry is in camp and others at Savanna, Ill., have asked for "leave of absence" in order that they may witness the game.

A special train is being run from Memphis while other folks from Dixie are coming from Montgomery, Nashville, Louisville and Atlanta. The Memphis fans will come 500 strong thus paying tribute to Dr. J.B. Martin, president of the Negro American league and former resident of Memphis.

What attracts these people will attract any red-blooded American who likes the national pastime. These fans come to see home runs, double plays, bases stolen and lightning-like flashy plays both in the infield and the outfield. These fans come to see players in action whom they have read about.

They are coming out Sunday—and coming early—to see the great Buck Leonard of the Homestead Grays and king of the Negro first sackers vie with Lyman Bostock of the Birmingham Black Barons or Jelly Taylor of the Memphis Red Sox for honors at the initial sack. Leonard topped the voting for the East's team.

Fans will remember that the great Leonard went hitless in the 1939 game although he handled 10 chances at first without a semblance of a bobble. Leonard got three hits last year, scored a run and stole a base.

In that 1939 game, Neal Robinson was credited with three hits, one being a two-bagger and the other being a home run. The Memphis fly chaser will be back in center field this year but on the East's side is the fellow Klien [Pancho] Coimbre, Cuban Stars outfielder who led the batting in the Puerto Rican winter league this past season.

Editor's note: According to the *Enciclopedia Beisbol Ponce Leones* (1938–87) by Rafael Costas, Coimbre did not win the batting crown in 1940–41. The leading batter was Roy Partlow, who hit .443. However, Coimbre did win batting titles during the 1942–43 (.342) and 1944–45 (.425) seasons.

Leroy "Satchel" Paige, the Kansas City Monarch hurler who could win 35 games in either the National or the American league circuits, topped all the voting for both sides. Paige, idol of thousands of fans, will be there hurling for three innings. It isn't likely that Satchel will start the game. Unless the last minute conference decides to the contrary, Candy Jim Taylor, manager of the West for his third time, will start Hilton Smith, Paige's teammate on the Kansas City Monarchs.

26. The scoreboard shows the East leading the West, 8–1, after four innings on July 27, 1941. Courtesy of Robert McNeill.

Taylor is known for his cunning. And it would be a big surprise if Satchel were held to pitching the final three frames for the West. Who the pitcher is that will relieve Hilton Smith, veteran of several East versus West games, is not made known by Taylor or his two coaches, Winfred [Winfield] Welsh [Welch], manager of the Birmingham club, and George Mitchell, manager of the St. Louis Stars.

The manager for the East team is the veteran, Vic Harris, manager of the Homestead Grays.

The East is well fortified with hitters. There is [Bill] Hoskins, Baltimore outfielder; Red Parnell of the Philadelphia Stars, [Lennie] Pearson of the Newark Eagles and others who can clout the ball but they can't clout it any farther than can Dan Wilson of the St. Louis Stars, whose homer in 1939 helped to enliven things and to start the West on the road to the 4 to 2 victory.

Besides Neal Robinson of Memphis, there are heavy stickers in the West's lineup such as Ted Strong of the Kansas City Monarchs who will take care of the right field garden; Parnell Woods, the flashy third sacker of the Jacksonville Red Caps; Lyman Bostick [Bostock] of the Birmingham Black Barons will start the game at first while Jelly Taylor of the Memphis Red Sox is ready to relieve him at any time.

The East will present a fast infield with Felton Snow of Baltimore on third, Manual [Horacio] Martinez of the Cuban Stars at short and Dick Seay of the New York Black Yanks on second. This trio with the ever reliable Buck Leonard on first will be hard to beat.

There has been many a fast double play starting with Seay. He is a past master when it comes to quick thinking. But the East isn't the only pebble on the beach and won't be the only infield at Comiskey Park on Sunday. The West will be there "with the goods." The West will use Parnell Woods of Jacksonville on third, Newt Allen of Kansas City on short, Tommy Sampson of Birmingham on second. Well, just as many double plays can be started with that Sampson to Allen to Bostick [Bostock] or Taylor as the East can bring up—and just as fast.

The two umpires from the West will be Virgil Blueitt of Chicago and "Little Boy" Blueitt of Memphis.

President Tom Wilson of the Negro National league arrived in the city on Tuesday. Dr. J. B. Martin, president of the Negro American league, is already here. These two man are the commissioners and serve with the East vs. West game committee which includes, besides themselves, Horace G. Hall of the Chicago American Giants and William Harrison, manager of the Hotel Grand.

The game ceremonies will get under way at 2:30. The players of each team will be introduced to the fans. The Giles post, American Legion, will take part in the flag raising ceremonies.

The Stuff Is Here: Past—Present—Future

by Fay Young

Source: *Chicago Defender*, 2 August 1941

THE NINTH ANNUAL East versus West classic is history and the East now leads in number of games won, five to four. Sunday, July 27th, was a banner day in Negro sports history. Fifty thousand fans watched the "dream game" at Comiskey Park, Chicago. It was the largest crowd to ever attend a sport event in Negro history.

HOWEVER, IT WAS VERY surprising to see some of our so-called intelligent people become so ignorant of other people's rights. Men and women got in the wrong box seats and because they held box seat tickets for another, refused to move. And some never moved regardless of the pleadings of Andy Frain's ushers who became disgusted and quit trying to straighten out the trouble. The truth of the matter is there were not enough ushers to handle that crowd—and there were not enough policemen.

THE EAST VERSUS WEST game ought to make Chicago fold get busy and have a ballpark of their own. Why is it we have to "rent" the other fellow's belongings? Many get married in a "rented" tuxedo or full dress suit. That suits that individual but it is not at all surprising when people who go to this East vs. West game can't agree with the enormous amount of money paid for the rental of the White Sox park which ought to go into something of our own.

And what makes it all the more sickening is the fact that this year, the Chicago American Giants have played but three games in Chicago and have but one more to play—that for the benefit of Provident Hospital on Sunday, August 31, when Satchel Paige will return here. The Chicago team is unable to build a ball park.

THE PUBLIC WAS fairly well satisfied with the game with the exception of those who wanted the West to win. But even those were satisfied when Satchel Paige finally went to the mound in the eighth inning. There were many who knew that each pitcher could hurl only three innings. They wondered why Paige was not sent in to pitch the seventh. They are still wondering. So are we.

Many in that crowd were attracted by the publicity given Paige. After such a build-up it seemed to be a wise thing to use Paige three full innings. After all, the public must be satisfied. I am still answering phone calls and answering questions as to why Paige was held out. "I don't know!

THE GAME HAD its good points and a lot of bad points. The East, like last year, had too much defense in that infield. Take Dick Seay of the New York Black Yankees off second base and Felton Snow of the Baltimore Elite Giants away from third and yank "Rabbit" Martinez of the New York Cuban Stars out of shortstop and then go hide Buck Leonard, the Homestead Grays first sacker and the West might have scored some runs. Snow and Seay robbed West batters of hits, both pulling down two line drives with one-handed stabs.

The East had an outfield. Oh, forget the ball that [Henry] Kimbro of the New York Black Yanks lost in the sun because even Joe DiMaggio will lose them in that spot in the Sox park. Roy Campenello [Campanella], Baltimore, caught the entire nine innings for the East.

As for the West, there was one serious mistake made. When Hilton Smith left the game, [Dan] Bankhead of the Birmingham club could have gone to the mound. That is second guessing. Ted Radcliffe, called "Double Duty," played in bad luck, although knowing what Leonard is weak on, folks are wondering "how come the home run."

SIX RUNS IN one inning don't look so hot for any all-star combination. It doesn't please the West's followers. Some are criticizing the fact that at one time there were four of the nine West players in Memphis Red Sox uniforms. There was Jelly Taylor at first, Neal Robinson in center, Radcliffe pitching and Larry Brown.

The crowd was appeased when Satchel Paige went to the mound and struck out the first two batters who faced him.

Terris McDuffie, Homestead Grays, who hurled the first two innings, was the winning pitcher. Overcome by heat, he was unable to go to the mound in the third and "Impo" Barnhill relieved him. Hilton Smith, Kansas City Monarchs, was the losing hurler. Newt Allen, Kansas City Monarchs shortstop, was forced from the game by heat.

There was one double play in the game which 90 percent of the fans didn't see. That was Campenello [Campanella] to [Rabbit] Martinez.

FIVE THOUSAND fans were in the Sox park before 11:30 a.m. It was a grand day with the thermometer at 83 [degrees] at 7 a.m. On the field during the game it must have been 112 [degrees]. The players who have been in South America said they had never suffered with the heat to that extent before.

Then to make matters worse, the ceremonies before the game came near spoiling everything. The flag raising, as Miss Juliet Rhea sang "The Star Spangled Banner," was great. Then came a long-winded speech which caused thousands to become restless because these folks came to see a ball game and not hear any race problem address which might have been all right on the street corner two miles away. The folk came to see a ball game, forget what race they belonged to and here it was being dashed into your face like a pail of ice water. Whoever was responsible for it ought to be given one good swift kick in the pants. It's plain damn foolishness and folk don't pay a dollar ten and one sixty-five [cents] to hear it.

And as we sign off, let's hope the West will trot out a victory team next year and not have the East say after the game that the West had a better team on the bench than they had on the field during the game—and *had a team on the bench which might have been able to beat us.*

Buck Leonard's Home Run and Pitching of Paige Feature Game

by John C. Day

Source: *Chicago Defender*, 2 August 1941

Fifty thousand baseball hungry fans jammed their way into Comiskey Park on Sunday, July 27, braving the intense heat which descended upon the city for that afternoon and watched the ninth annual East versus West game go to the East by the score of 8 to 3.

The crowd was the greatest to ever attend a Negro sports event and was the greatest crowd before which Satchel Paige, the greatest Negro pitcher, had ever hurled before in his entire career.

The East started Terris "the Great" McDuffie of the Homestead Grays and Terris was given credit for the victory which gives the East a lead of 5 to 4 in number of games won. Vic Harris took McDuffie out to start the home third because the Easterner was overcome by the intense heat—the sun beaming down on the greensward of the White Sox park and played havoc in right field where even sun glasses failed to prevent fielder's from losing balls in the bright glare.

After a ceremony which was due to start as 2:30 and which was delayed while Edgar G. Brown, president of the United Government Employees Association and publicity director of the Negro CC camps, made a tiresome speech which most of the fans already assembled to the tune of over 40,000 believed would have been given elsewhere—and not at a ball game.

Brown was representing the National Negro Council with headquarters in Washington, the girls collected $6,220.20 for a Negro lobbyist in the nation's capital.

The raising of the American flag with the aid of the detachment from the 184th Field Artillery (the old Eighth Infantry) and the CC enrollees while Miss Julia Rhea sang the national anthem was befitting such an occasion. Then the players of the West were introduced by the announcer who also attempted to introduce the players of the East team but lost his copy and after introducing the starting lineup and the East's pitcher "ran out of gas" and left Red Parnell and several others stranded on the first base line looking like a lot of statues and feeling greatly embarrassed. The officials of the game came in for their bow and the game was on after William E. King, former state senator and now a member of the state industrial commission, tossed the first ball.

The West trotted out Parnell Woods of the Jacksonville Red Caps at third, Newt Allen, manager of the Kansas City Monarchs, at short, and Tommy Sampson of the Birmingham Black Barons on second. Instead of starting Bostick [Bostock] of the Birmingham club at first as he had planned, Candy Jim Taylor, manager of Chicago American Giants ball club and manager of the West's team for the third time, used Jelly Taylor, first sacker of the Memphis Red Sox. The outfield was as the *Chicago Defender* announced last week. Dan Wilson, St. Louis Stars, in left field; Neal Robinson, Memphis Red Sox, in center field, and Ted Strong, Kansas City Monarchs, in right field.

The East's starting lineup was as predicted. Buck Leonard of the Homestead Grays was on first with the ever reliable little Dickey Seay of the New York Black Yankees at second and Rabbit Martinez of Alex Pompez's Cuban Stars at short. Felton Snow, manager of the East's victorious 1940 aggregation and third sacker for the Baltimore Elites, was not on third. The East used Monty Irvin, third sacker for the Newark Eagles, owned by Mr. and Mrs. Abe Manley who were not present at the game this year. The East's manager, Vic Harris, serving his second time as manager of an East team, used a powerful outfield in [Bill] Hoskins of Baltimore in left; Klien [Pancho] Coimbre, Cuban Stars, in center [right], and [Henry] Kimbro, New York Black Yankees' fast running outfielder, in right [center].

And you can take it from the fan who knows inside baseball and from the fans in general, Vic Harris outsmarted the West's manager. In starting McDuffie who went out because of the heat in the third, he crossed up Taylor and crossed him up again in the use of Impo Barnhill, New York Cubans. In fact, most of the fandom assembled looked for Jim Taylor to shoot Satchel Paige in when Barnhill went to the mound. Instead, Taylor used Double Duty Radcliffe of the Memphis Red Sox. Maybe it was sentiment since Dr. J. B. Martin is president of the Negro American league and maybe Taylor was using his best judgment. Anyhow, sometimes the best laid plans of mice and men go wrong—and this time the West's plan went up like a toy balloon which comes in contact with a lighted match. The confounded thing "busted" with a lot of noise.

EAST GETS JUMP

In the meantime, during the hectic fourth inning when the East was salting the game away better than the Gloucester fishermen can put away mackerel in a barrel of brine, all the fans kept wondering *when are they going to send Satchel Paige in.* That's what the folks in the press box also wondered.

The East got the jump on the West in the first inning. Kimbro was safe when Tommy Sampson of Birmingham threw high to Jelly Taylor of Memphis, pulling the Red Sox player off the bag. The New York Black Yankees fleet-footed runner, proceeded to promptly steal second. Klien [Pancho] Coimbre was safe at first when Newt Allen, manager of their Kansas City team, fumbled his roller. Kimbro advanced to third after Allen had pegged too late to get Coimbre at first. Hoskins, Baltimore, fanned. Buck Leonard, Homestead Grays singled sharply to center and Kimbro scored. Coimbre pulled up at third. Monty Irvin, Newark Eagles struck out. Coimbre scored when Pepper Bassett, Chicago, let one of Hilton Smith's pitches get away from him. It was scored as a passed ball, Buck Leonard raced to third. Roy Campenella [Campanella], Baltimore, went out swinging.

The West scored one run in their half of the same frame and it looked like we might see a whale of a ball game. Dan Wilson, St. Louis Stars, was thrown out by McDuffie. Allen hit a high bounder which glanced off McDuffie's glove and looked for a second as though Allen might reach first safely but Rabbit Martinez, Cuban Stars shortstop, raced in and threw Allen out at first to Leonard. Neal Robinson singled to deep short. Ted Strong, Kansas City Monarch outfielder, batting left handed, smashed a two-base hit to left field and Neal Robinson raced home with the first West run. Jelly Taylor, Memphis, scratched a hit off McDuffie's glove and Strong went to third while Taylor reached first safely. Taylor promptly stole second, Campenello [Campanella] preferring not to take any chances of Strong scoring from third and thus failed to try to get Taylor. Parnell Woods, Jacksonville, tapped to McDuffie and was tossed out to Leonard.

With one gone in the second, Dick Seay, New York second sacker, was safe on Allen's second miscue of the game. McDuffie sacrificed Seay to second. Kimbro dumped a short single in short center which Tommy Sampson of Birmingham raced over to get in time to halt any intentions that Seay might have had to score. Woods tossed out Coimbre.

Sampson was hit by a pitched a ball to start the home second. Bassett attempted to sacrifice but Campenello [Campanella], instead of playing for Bassett at first, shot the ball to Martinez and Sampson was deader than a doornail at second. Manager Taylor sent Mathis of the Memphis Red Sox to run for Bassett. Hilton Smith forced Kimbro to back up near the edge of the right field stands for his long fly. Mathis took second after the catch. Dan Wilson lined to Irvin at third. It was a spectacular one-handed catch after Irvin had leaped into the air.

Impo Barnhill, Cuban Stars, went to the mound in the third for the East after McDuffie was overcome by heat in the dugout. Allen popped to Irvin. Neal Robinson was robbed of a hit by Seay's one-handed leaping catch of a drive which was labeled a sure hit. Strong tripled to right center when Coimbre lost his drive in the sun. Martinez came to Barnhill's rescue by tossing out Taylor to end the inning.

The East went into action in the fourth and came mighty near making the game look like an industrial league contest out in Washington Park. Ted "Double Duty" Radcliffe, Memphis Red Sox manager and pitcher, went to the mound for the West. He set Campenello [Campanella] down on strikes. Martinez poked one through Sampson for a single to right. Allen was forced out of the game when suddenly everything went black in front of him. He was assisted off the field. Billy Horne, Chicago American Giants, replaced Allen. Seay walked. Barnhill's single scored Martinez. Kimbro sent a long fly to Neal Robinson and Seay scored after the catch. Dan Wilson raced over to take Coimbre's fly in left center but stumbled as he attempted to catch the ball. He was given a three-base error by the official scorers. Barnhill scored on the play. Hoskins singled to right scoring Coimbre. Buck Leonard poled a home run into the upper deck of the right field stands and Hoskins scored ahead of Leonard. Preacher Henry, Jacksonville, went to the mound and mumbling Double Duty Radcliffe left the game. Henry knocked down Irvin's drive but couldn't retrieve it in time to get the Newark infielder at first and Irvin was given credit for a scratch hit. Irvin stole second and went all the way to third when Larry Brown heaved the ball into center field. Campenello [Campanella], batting the second time, in one inning, struck out. That means Campenello [Campanella] was the tenth man to face the West's hurlers. He started the fourth frame by striking out—and he ended by striking out. That was the East's big inning. The fans who were pulling for the East tossed away straw hats when Leonard poled his homer. As bad as the West's followers felt by having the East cram a victory down their throats, these Western fans gave Leonard a big hand when he crossed home plate after his four-ply swat.

The West couldn't get the ball out of the infield in their half of the fourth frame. Campenello [Campanella] threw out Woods. Ford, St. Louis, batted for Sampson and grounded out to Leonard. Larry Brown fanned.

The West changed two men to the outfield. [Jimmy] Crutchfield of Chicago American Giants took left field in place of Dan Wilson in the East's fifth. [Buddy] Armour, St. Louis, went to centerfield and Neal Robinson came out of the game. Martinez singled. Seay forced Martinez at second. Barnhill beat out a hit to first, Seay halting at second. Kimbro hit to Horne who stepped on second forcing out Barnhill. Coimbre skied to Armour.

Pearson of Newark went to right in Kimbro's place. Cleveland batted for Henry in the home fifth and singled. Crutchfield fouled out to Hoskins off the left field box seats. Horne fanned and Campenello [Campanella] shot the ball to Martinez, nailing Cleveland for the only double play of the game. The West was trying a hit-run play.

Bankhead of Birmingham went to the mound for the West in the sixth. Hoskins flied to Strong. Leonard rapped a hot one which Jelly Taylor fielded and tossed to Bankhead who crossed over to take the out at first. Irvin doubled to left. Campenello [Campanella] ended the inning by flying to Crutchfield.

McHenry, Philadelphia Stars, replaced Impo Barnhill on the mound in the home sixth. Armour rapped a clean single to center. Strong sent a high foul up near the box seats to the east of the screen and Campenello [Campanella] was under it for the first out. Bostock, Birmingham first sacker, batted for Jelly Taylor. He singled to left. Armour stopped at second. Woods flied to Kimbro. Ford rolled to Seay who tossed to Martinez, forcing Bostock for the third out.

In the seventh Bankhead remained on the mound for the West and the fans began wondering if Paige was really going to pitch. Horne threw out Martinez. Manager Taylor sent Paige to the bull pen in left field to warm up. Horne tossed out Dick Seay. McHenry drew a walk. Kimbro lifted one to Bostock. In the home seventh Brown flied to Pearson on centerfield in centerfield. Hudson batted for Bankhead but Martinez to Leonard ended his attempt to start a rally. Seay threw out Crutchfield.

Leroy Satchel Paige was given a hero's welcome when he ambled to the mound. The game was held up while newspaper photographers and a score of others who had Kodaks and no business on the field, took shots of Paige. When they were finally ordered off the playing grass, Paige was ready. He doffed his hat to acknowledge the crowd's cheer. Paige threw two fast ones by Coimbre, who doesn't yet know when it passed the plate and landed in Larry Brown's glove. It split the heart of the plate like a streak of lightning and the Cuban batter was out on strikes. Hoskins also struck out. Leonard popped to Ford near second.

Lefty Hill of Newark took the mound for the East in the eighth. The West scored two runs in the eighth with the help of some errors. Armour missed the third strike and was safe at first when Campenello [Campanella] dropped the ball and Armour legged it to first ahead of the throw. Strong was safe. In the meantime Armour went to third, Bostock hit to Seay and Seay to Martinez killed Strong at second, but Seay threw wild to Leonard allowing Armour to score and Bostock to reach second. Coimbre dropped Woods fly in right, Bostock scoring and Woods going to second. Ford rolled out to Leonard, unassisted.

Paige slipped over two strikes on Irvin and the Newark infielder slammed a long high fly which Crutchfield backed up and pulled in for the first out. Campenello [Campanella] beat out a slow roller. [Larry] Brown to Horne thwarted Campenello's [Campanella] attempt to pilfer second. Horne reinjured his leg which was hurt earlier in the season. Martinez worked Paige for a free ticket to first. Seay flied to Armour for the last East out.

In the last half of the ninth, Byrd of Baltimore went to the mound. Larry Brown was thrown out by Byrd. Paige flied to Pearson. Crutchfield beat out an infield hit. George Mitchell, manager of the St. Louis Stars and one of the West's coaches, batted for Horne. Mitchell didn't get a good chance at Byrd. Crutchfield went out stealing, Campenello [Campanella] to Martinez, ending the 1941 East vs. West contest.

The Women Take to East vs. West Baseball Classic

by Elizabeth Galbreath

Source: *Chicago Defender,* 2 August 1941

Of all the East versus West baseball classics the ninth one, held Sunday, July 27, at Comiskey Park, was perhaps the first of the games where the "spectators" story was as inter-

27. Satchel Paige is pictured here with fiancée Lucy Rodriguez, in Chicago, before the start of the 1941 contest.
Courtesy of Pamela Paige O'Neal.

esting outside the gates as inside. So many persons were refused admittance that a "roving reporter" could make a delightful news story for the society pages about all of the splendid, if somewhat wilted costumes, and disappointed looking faces on the outside. Their pleas for admittance, renewed at each inviting outburst of enthusiasm coming from the thousands within, were met with the assurance from the gatekeepers that there was not even standing room left.

As luck would have it, I could not find the magic words which would open one of the gates myself, but I did see the photographer, Gordon Roger Parks, and followed through on the heels of his effective blitzkrieging methods.

Inside, the beautiful green field did its best to suggest a cool setting. Attractive girls, some of whom represented contestants for this year's title of Miss Bronze America, were busy collecting dimes or "what-have-you." The easy and spectacular pitching of Satchel Paige, the "breaks" which came to whatever side one was for and the knowledge that there were 50,000 other sufferers of the heat out there enjoying the game, all helped to keep one happy, if not cool.

Mrs. Satchel (Lucy Rodriguez) Paige, 2527 Tracy Avenue, Kansas City, Mo., was there to watch her husband's enthusiastic fans cheer him. She wore a rose colored frock.

And the most loyal of all of the East-West classic supporters, Fannie Mae Jones, 3845 South Dearborn was at her usual spot. Says she: "I haven't missed a game."—And hers is a special effort for she has to be brought out in her wheel chair.

Fight Follows East-West Classic

East Wins 8–3

Allen and Ford Are Fined

Source: Chicago Defender, 2 August 1941

Newt Allen, shortstop and manager of the Kansas City Monarchs, and Jim Ford, second baseman of the St. Louis Stars, engaged in a fist fight at the Vincennes Hotel following the East versus West baseball classic at Comiskey Park Sunday.

Allen was charged with two errors in the game before he was forced out when overcome by the heat. Ford supplanted Tommy Sampson of Birmingham at second base.

When the two players got to the Vincennes Hotel, Ford is said to have blamed Allen for causing the defeat of the West team. The East won 8 to 3 staging a six run rally off Double Duty Radcliffe in the visitors' fourth frame, the inning in which Buck Leonard of the Homestead Grays slapped out his home run.

Allen resented the accusation and hot words passed. The two men went to it but were separated by other players.

President J. B. Martin, of the Negro American league of which both clubs to which the two players are now under contract, acted promptly on Monday afternoon after getting the evidence of the fight.

Allen and Ford were fined $25 each and both men were suspended from playing with their teams for two weeks.

JULY 27, 1941, CHICAGO, IL

EAST	AB	R	H	D	T	HR	BI	E	TAVG	TSLG
Henry Kimbro (New York Black Yankees), cf	3	1	1	0	0	0	1	0		
Lennie Pearson (Newark Eagles), cf	2	0	0	0	0	0	0	0		
Pancho Coimbre (New York Cubans), rf	5	2	0	0	0	0	0	1		
Bill Hoskins (Baltimore Elite Giants), lf	5	1	1	0	0	0	1	0		
Buck Leonard (Homestead Grays), 1b	5	1	2	0	0	1	3	0		
Monte Irvin (Newark Eagles), 3b	5	0	2	1	0	0	0	0		
Roy Campanella (Baltimore Elite Giants), c	5	0	1	0	0	0	0	1		
Rabbit Martinez (New York Cubans), ss	4	1	2	0	0	0	0	1		
Dick Seay (New York Black Yankees), 2b	4	1	0	0	0	0	0	1		
Terris McDuffie (Homestead Grays), p	0	0	0	0	0	0	0	0		
Dave Barnhill (New York Cubans), p	2	1	2	0	0	0	1	0		
Henry McHenry (Philadelphia Stars), p	0	0	0	0	0	0	0	0		
Jimmy Hill (Newark Eagles), p	0	0	0	0	0	0	0	0		
Bill Byrd (Baltimore Elite Giants), p	0	0	0	0	0	0	0	0		
Team Totals, Average & Slugging Pct.	40	8	11	1	0	1	6	4	.275	.375

WEST	AB	R	H	D	T	HR	BI	E	TAVG	TSLG
Dan Wilson (St. Louis Stars), lf	2	0	0	0	0	0	0	1		
Jimmie Crutchfield (Chicago American Giants), lf	3	0	1	0	0	0	0	0		
Newt Allen (Kansas City Monarchs), ss	2	0	0	0	0	0	0	2		
Billy Horne (Chicago American Giants), ss	2	0	0	0	0	0	0	0		
a) George Mitchell (St. Louis Stars), ph	0	0	0	0	0	0	0	0		
Neil Robinson (Memphis Red Sox), cf	2	1	1	0	0	0	0	0		
Buddy Armour (St. Louis Stars), cf	2	1	1	0	0	0	0	0		
Ted Strong (Kansas City Monarchs), rf	4	1	2	1	1	0	1	0		
Jelly Taylor (Memphis Red Sox), 1b	2	0	1	0	0	0	0	0		
b) Lyman Bostock (Birmingham Black Barons), 1b	2	0	1	0	0	0	1	0		
Parnell Woods (Jacksonville Red Caps), 3b	4	0	0	0	0	0	1	0		
Tommy Sampson (Birmingham Black Barons) 2b	0	0	0	0	0	0	0	1		
c) Jimmy Ford (St. Louis Stars), 2b	3	0	0	0	0	0	0	0		
Pepper Bassett (Chicago American Giants), c	1	0	0	0	0	0	0	0		
d) Verdell Mathis (Memphis Red Sox), pr	0	0	0	0	0	0	0	0		
Larry Brown (Memphis Red Sox), c	3	0	0	0	0	0	0	1		
Hilton Smith (Kansas City Monarchs), p	1	0	0	0	0	0	0	0		
Ted Radcliffe (Memphis Red Sox), p	0	0	0	0	0	0	0	0		
Preacher Henry (Jacksonville Red Caps), p	0	0	0	0	0	0	0	0		
e) Duke Cleveland (Jacksonville Red Caps), ph	1	0	1	0	0	0	0	0		
Dan Bankhead (Birmingham Black Barons), p	0	0	0	0	0	0	0	0		
f) Willie Henry Hudson (Chicago American Giants), ph	1	0	0	0	0	0	0	0		
Satchel Paige (Kansas City Monarchs), p	1	0	0	0	0	0	0	0		
Team Totals, Average & Slugging Pct.	36	3	8	1	1	0	3	5	.222	.306

a) Announced batting for Horne in 9th

b) Batted for Taylor in 6th

c) Batted for Sampson in 4th

d) Ran for Bassett in 2nd

e) Batted for Henry in 5th

f) Batted for Bankhead in 7th

East	200	600	000-8								
West	100	000	020-3								

PITCHER/TEAM	GS	IP	H	R	ER	K	BB	WP	HB	W	L
McDuffie/HG	1	2	3	1	1	0	0	0	1	1	0
Barnhill/NYC		3	2	0	0	2	0	0	0	0	0
McHenry/PS		2	2	0	0	0	0	0	0	0	0
Hill/NE		1	0	2	0	2	0	0	0	0	0
Byrd/BEG		1	1	0	0	0	0	0	0	0	0
H. Smith/KCM	1	3	2	2	0	3	0	0	0	0	1
T. Radcliffe/MRS		2/3	4	6	2	1	1	0	0	0	0
Henry/JRC		1 1/3	3	0	0	1	0	0	0	0	0
Bankhead/BBB		2	1	0	0	0	1	0	0	0	0
Paige/KCM		2	1	0	0	2	1	0	0	0	0

BB—Seay, Martinez, McHenry
DP—Campanella to Martinez
HBP—Sampson by McDuffie
LOB—East 10, West 7
PB—Bassett
SAC—McDuffie
SB—Kimbro (2), Irvin, Martinez, Taylor
East—Vic Harris (Mgr.)
West—Candy Jim Taylor (Mgr.); Coaches W. S. Welch and George Mitchell
Umpires—Fred McCrary, E. C. "Pop" Turner, Virgil Blueitt, Harry Walker
Attendance—50,256   Time—2:10

P

Satchel Paige	276,418
Hilton Smith	176,311
Preacher Henry	172,906
Dan Bankhead	165,412
Gene Smith	164,619
Double Duty Radcliffe	163,602
Red Ferrell	159,963
Sug Cornelius	151,386
Porter Moss	149,207
Chip McAllister	149,173
Lefty Calhoun	149,173

C

Biz Mackey	209,431
Pepper Bassett	198,305
Larry Brown	191,147
Roy Campanella	183,516
Johnny Hayes	174,042
Clarence Palm	165,803
Carlos Colas	162,177
T. J. Young	154,196
Frank Duncan	130,321

1B

Buck Leonard	227,652
Jelly Taylor	181,322
Fran Matthews	171,420
Buck O'Neil	164,405
Johnny Washington	162,311
Jim West	161,972
Pep Young	153,079
Chili Mayweather	148,725
James Stark	147,053
Lyman Bostock	134,643

2B

Dickie Seay	182,063
Billy Horne	179,621
Clarence Israel,	179,210
Tommy Sampson	177,403
Rainey Bibbs	169,021
Lick Carlisle	168,471
Jimmy Ford	158,638
Harry Blanco	151,312

3B

Parnell Woods	201,435
Howard Easterling	184,078
Felton Snow	181,316
Fred Bankhead	72,502
Harry Williams	169,402
Henry Spearman	164,096

SS

Newt Allen	216,486
Pee Wee Butts	176,393
Rabbit Martinez	172,715
Hickey Redd	162,973
Ches Williams	148,309
Mahlon Duckett	140,702
T. J. Brown	135,454

OF

Dan Wilson	197,503
Willard Brown	188,402
Red Parnell	181,423
Bill Hoskins	178,214
Jimmie Crutchfield	177,311
Ted Strong	176,806
Tetelo Vargas	169,312
Mule Suttles	168,705
Jerry Benjamin	166,334
Pancho Coimbre	154,619
Vic Harris	152,374
William Hudson	148,672
Bubba Hyde	148,672
Speed Whatley	146,503
Donald Reeves	133,518

1942

John H. Johnson publishes the first issue of the *Negro Digest* in Chicago, Illinois. This magazine is the forerunner of *Ebony,* America's most popular black magazine. The U.S. Justice Department threatens 20 editors of black newspapers with sedition charges after several papers feature articles exposing segregation and injustices in the military services.

Billboard creates its first rating chart for black music, the Harlem Hit Parade. "Take It and Git," by Andy Kirk & His Twelve Clouds of Joy, is number one.

Milk costs only 30 cents a half-gallon, 10 pounds of potatoes costs 34 cents, and 39 cents would bring home the bacon. A loaf of bread costs 9 cents.

The newly organized National Basketball League fields two integrated teams: the Toledo Jim White Chevrolets, with Casey Jones, Al Price, and Zano White; and the Chicago Studebaker Champions, with Hillary Brown, Duke Cumberland, Sonny Boswell, Roosie Hudson, Bennie Price, and Ted Strong (former Kansas City Monarchs outfielder).

The first Major League All-Star Game to start at twilight is won by the American League, 3–1. The Polo Grounds becomes the first park to have hosted two Major League All-Star Games.

On July 23, Leon Day of the Newark Eagles strikes out 18 batters in a game, tying Bob Feller's major league record.

At the end of the season, Branch Rickey agrees to be president and general manager of the Brooklyn Dodgers for $80,000 a year.

LEAGUE BUSINESS

In February, as America entered the war years, Major League Baseball was seeking schedule changes.[1] Team owners and Commissioner Landis decided to have 161 night games. The National League would play 84 night games, while the American league would play 77. Responding to a letter from President Franklin D. Roosevelt, the league increased the number of night games so defense workers would be able to attend ball games. The league also removed restrictions on Sunday doubleheaders. Previously, no Sabbath twin bills could be scheduled until after a team's third Sunday at home. League officials asked that players invest 10 percent of their salaries in defense bonds and stamps. This 10-percent defense investment was mandatory for the commissioner, league presidents, and club officials. For other baseball personnel—players, clerks, park employees—the donation would be voluntary.[2] Negro League officials did not suggest any schedule changes or salary reductions.

As the Negro Leagues continued to fight for recognition by the major leagues, they were confronted with the image exhibited by the Ethiopian Clowns baseball team. Wendell Smith, in his weekly editorial column, "Smitty's Sports Spurts," charged the team with "capitalizing on slap-stick comedy and the kind of nonsense which many white people like to believe is typical and characteristic of all Negroes."[3] Smith charged white booking agent and promoter Syd Pollock of Tarrytown, New York, the Clowns' owner, as being responsible for such antics. Such foolery was detrimental as the Negro Leagues attempted to promote a professional image to increase their attraction to the major leagues.

Pollock responded in a letter to Smith's office denying ownership of the team. He claimed the Clowns were owned and operated by Hunter Campbell, an African-American. Pollock claimed he served only as general manager. Smith noted that Pollock's stationery showed that the Clowns played under three names: the Ethiopian Clowns, the Cincinnati Clowns, and the Miami Clowns. Smith noted, "It appears that which ever name is the most convenient is the one used. But more significantly is the fact that the repulsive moniker, 'Clowns' is always attached, no matter where and when they play."[4]

Smith pointed out the tragedy that, if Campbell were the owner, he should realize the social damage in having ballplayers paint their faces and go through minstrel show revues before each ball game.

Smith challenged the mysterious Hunter Campbell to come forward but never received a reply. Smith continued, "I don't know Campbell, but I find it difficult to believe that he, a Negro, advocates and perpetuates an organization which is detrimental in any way to the cause for which we are all fighting—racial advancement." The best evidence shows that Pollock was the sole owner; he continued to promote the Clowns' name and image well into the 1960s.[5]

THE WHITE SOX TRY OUT BLACK PLAYERS

On March 22 Jackie Robinson and Nate Moreland appeared at Brookside Park in Pasadena, California, unannounced.[6] Robinson, then age 23, and Moreland, age 25, requested a tryout from White Sox manager Jimmie Dykes. Dykes allowed them to go through the motions of fielding and pitching, giving words of encouragement, with no guarantees of employment. Dykes claimed, "Personally, I would welcome Negro players on the Sox and I believe every one of the other fifteen big league managers would do likewise. As for the players, they'd all get along too." Dykes added he felt that Robinson would be worth $50,000 to any major league team and suggested they talk with Commissioner Landis and team owners about the possibility of a gainful profession. Dykes claimed: "There is no clause in the baseball constitution, nor is there any one in the by-laws of the major league which prevents Negro baseball players from participating in organized baseball. Rather, it is an unwritten law. The matter is out of the hands of us managers. We are powerless to act and it's strictly up to the club owners and in the first place Judge Landis to start the ball a rolling. Go after them!"[7]

This was not Dykes's first exposure to the talents of Jackie Robinson. During the 1938 White Sox spring training, the Sox played against Pasadena City College, for whom Robinson played shortstop. Robinson got two hits in a 3–2 loss to the White Sox.

Negro League ballplayers met another barrier when Jack Zeller, general manager of the Detroit Tigers, told the press he hadn't seen a Negro player who could make the majors. John R. Williams, editor of the Detroit edition of the *Pittsburgh Courier,* challenged Zeller's statement with an offer to sponsor a benefit game between the Detroit Tigers and an all-star Negro team. In the spirit of the war effort, Williams suggested the proceeds go to the United Service Organizations (USO). Williams fired off an open letter to Zeller in his column, writing:

Mr. Zeller has the right to his opinion. I have the right to mine. No doubt the public too is divided in its opinion. This gives us an excellent opportunity to clarify the matter. The Tigers will scarcely win the pennant in the American League this year, consequently they will be available for a post-season game against a colored club that will produce.

. . . To make the matter interesting to the players, it may be arranged for the white players to be paid, but the Negro players and I as promoter will go all-out for the USO or for any other cause that the Detroit daily newspapers might suggest. There, Mr. Jack Zeller, of Tennessee, is your opportunity.[8]

John Williams later announced he had commitments from various players to form an all-star team to battle the Detroit Tigers in a three-game benefit series scheduled for October 1, 2, and 3. The following players had agreed to compete against the Tigers: Satchel Paige, Leon Day, Willie Wells, Ed Stone, Roy Campanella, Dave "Impo" Barnhill, Josh Gibson, Buck Leonard, and Homer Curry. Williams went public with his challenge in a letter to Leo MacDonell, sports editor of the *Detroit Times*. MacDonell published the letter in his column of August 3. Neither Zeller nor Walter R. Briggs, owner of the Tigers, responded, canceling the game by default.[9]

ALL-STAR GAMES

Thirty thousands fans, reported by the press as the largest crowd of the year, jammed Wrigley Field on May 24 to see Satchel Paige and the Kansas City Monarchs beat a team of former major league ball players on furlough from the armed forces. The major leaguers were led by the former MVP pitcher and future Hall of Famer Dizzy Dean. Arkansas country boy Dean, who was famous for his antics on and off field, often gloated, "It ain't braggin' if you can do it." Paige pitched seven innings, giving up one run and 2 hits, before Hilton Smith came in to hold the Dizzy Dean All-Stars to 1 hit over the last two innings for a 3–1 victory. The Monarchs belted out 10 hits against Dizzy Dean, Johnny Grodzicki of the Cardinals, and Steve Piechota of the Yankees. Other major leaguers included Zeke Bonura, Cecil Travis, Emmet Mueller, Ken Silvesti, and Joe Gallagher. Bob Feller was expected to play but was unable to make travel connections in time to appear in the game. The big league players dressed in their army camp uniforms.[10]

That same day, the Chicago White Sox were hosting the Detroit Tigers in a doubleheader across town, before a crowd of 19,198 fans. Other doubleheaders across the nations reported the following attendance: Cincinnati at St. Louis (NL), 18,074 fans; Chicago at Pittsburgh, 16,746 (NL); Boston at Philadelphia, 10,965 (AL); Philadelphia at Boston, 24,284 (NL); and St. Louis at Cleveland, only 7,386 attendees (AL). However, 29,775 Wrigley Field cheerleaders demonstrated what the fans really wanted.

The next day, several newspapers offered their views of the game. John P. Carmichael of the *Chicago Daily News* wrote: "It was more than just a baseball crowd of 29,775 that saw the legendary Satchel Paige and K.C. Monarchs win 3–1 from Dean & Co. This was more of a picnicking, holiday throng. When shortstop Jesse Williams of the Monarchs made a great play to get Corbitt in the first inning, men threw hats in the air and cheered themselves hoarse."[11]

Wayne K. Otto of the *Chicago Herald American* was inspired to write the following:

To any baseball man the name of Satchel Paige is indelibly interwoven with baseball lore and legend. He is known as the greatest pitcher Negro baseball has ever produced, and you can take it from an old baseball writer that all the things ever said or written about him were, if anything, inaccurate.

Old Satchel, older than a lot of the boys will admit, pitched six [seven] innings against a team of all-major leaguers now in the service of Uncle Sam. He gave them two of the scratchiest kind of hits and they manufactured one unearned run.

In this particular introduction of a Negro topnotch ball club in Wrigley Field, it is only appropriate to say that the Monarchs have plenty on the ball. They play a bang-up, hustling, showmanship kind of game.

Paige, as I have told you, is a wizard and one of the athletic idols of his race. For years this writer has been hearing from major leaguers who batted against him in the off season of his greatness. In fact, even "Diz" Dean who was one of the great pitchers of all time, once said, "That Paige—he's the greatest I've ever seen."

Well, Paige was definitely in the "greatness" class yesterday. The fellow who started somewhere in an environment of obscurity down in the southern cotton picking country, did everything an [Grover] Alexander, [Christy] Mathewson or [Bob] Feller could do.

A word about the Monarch's infield. This Jess Williams has an arm that any major leaguer would give half his life to possess. He as you may know, is the shortstop. Bill Serrell is pretty good at second and Wilbur Cyrus [a.k.a. Herb Souell] at third can do a lot of things well. At first there is Buck O'Neil. He'd fit in any man's club. With Paige pitching, you wouldn't need much more.

In addition, the Monarchs with Willard "Home Run" Brown, Ted Strong and Willie Sims [Simms] in the outfield and Joe Greene catching, the Dean All-Stars were really no match for the Kansas City Monarchs who were on their way to the World Series. With the exception of Sims [Simms] in left field, every Monarch was an East-West game participant.[12]

As first sacker Buck O'Neil recalled: "Yes, we played the Dizzy Dean All-Stars there and we had the Monarchs, and you know they [Dean's team] were really overmatched. You know at that time Dizzy was still pitching, but he had hurt his arm. These men were in the Special Service, and they played in their army baseball uniforms. The army furnished their uniforms. And I do remember Zeke Bonura. He was the first baseman on that team. The next day they wrote that 'Zeke Bonura played first base and you look at Buck O'Neil play first base, it looks like that got the wrong guy on the field.' And don't forget Cecil Travis. He was a darn good ballplayer. You know what happen to Travis was he suffered from frostbite in his feet during the war. He never was the same afterwards. If it hadn't been for that, he would have been a Hall of Famer. A great third baseman and shortstop."[13]

The event was so successful that a rematch was scheduled for Sunday, May 30, in Washington's Griffith Stadium. Before an estimated crowd of 25,000, Paige, on loan to the Homestead Grays, defeated the Dizzy Dean All-Stars, 8–1. The *Washington Post* reported that "fans literally fought their way into the park to get a glimpse of the greatest of all colored pitchers."[14] The Stars really didn't have much of a chance against the likes of East-West performers like Josh Gibson, Jerry Benjamin, Jud Wilson, Howard Easterling, Vic Harris, Sam Bankhead, and knuckleball artist Ray Brown. The 32-year-old Dean pitched one inning in the blowout. Paige pitched five innings, giving up five hits and striking out seven batters, while yielding an unearned run on two fielding errors in the fourth inning. Brown finished the game, permitting three hits and no runs in three innings of work. Bankhead, who would make nine East-West appearances, blasted out three singles and a triple to drive in four runs.

THANK-U-GRAM

To my outstanding friend Jim - Best food in town
Buck O'Neil

28. Satchel Paige suffered his only loss in all-star history at Comiskey Park on August 16, 1942. He gave up five hits and three runs in three innings as the Negro American League team lost, 5–2. Standing from left to right for the National Anthem are W. S. Welch, Art Pennington, Paige, Buck O'Neil, Joe Greene, T. J. Brown, Paul Hardy, Joe Scott, Hilton Smith, batboy, Double Duty Radcliffe, Verdell Mathis, Fred Bankhead, Porter Moss, Fred McDaniel, Sam Jethroe, Ted Strong, Parnell Woods, Ducky Davenport, Willard Brown, Gene Bremer, unknown player, and Marlin Carter. The printed caption is incorrect. Courtesy of Jim Chappell, Chappell's Restaurant.

ROY CAMPANELLA SUSPENDED

Around Labor Day weekend, the Baltimore Elite Giants were fighting for first place against the perennial champion Homestead Grays. Suddenly, Roy Campanella and Sammy T. Hughes were suspended for playing, as Cincinnati Buckeyes, in an exhibition game against a Cleveland all-star sandlot team without permission. Following a dispute with Elite Giants owner Tom Wilson, Campanella abandoned the club for Mexico. Campanella was fined $250 by the league as he joined the Monterrey club for their last 20 games of the season.[15] His manager in Mexico was none other than Lazaro Salazar, who had been banned for life from the Negro Leagues in 1937 for inducing players to join his team in the Dominican Republic during the Trujillo revolt. Campy batted .296 with 2 homers in 81 at bats for Monterrey. Campanella would also spend the 1943 season with Monterrey, compiling a .289 average with 24 doubles, 5 triples, and 12 homers in 342 at bats. Whatever the conflicts were between Wilson and Campanella, they were resolved as Campy rejoined the team in 1944.

RACE RELATIONS: CAN YOU READ?

A campaign called "Can You Read, Judge Landis?" was initiated by the *New York Daily Worker*. With the war effort and national pride foremost in American minds, many socially active groups campaigned for the inclusion of black players in the national pastime. On

March 8, George V. Kelly wrote his views on the subject for the *Catholic Register,* a Denver, Colorado, newspaper:

> The Colored are the only race banned from the organized national pastime and this rank discrimination should end now, so that a badly needed lift can be given to war-ridden baseball. All horsehide officials admit that the national pastime, especially the big league brand, will fall below par this year, because Uncle Sam had dipped deeply into the ranks of the majors. The substitution of Colored stars for the men who have been called to a grimmer game would prevent baseball from losing much of its class, and far more important, would make realities two of the aims cited in the preamble of the Constitution—to "establish justice" and "promote the general welfare."
>
> . . . The Negro, in every field of athletic endeavor has proved that he can measure up to the standards set by his White Brother. Neither his sportsmanship nor his ability has been found wanting.
>
> The conduct of Joe Louis alone should be sufficient to break down the bars of racial discrimination that have prevented the Colored athlete from taking his rightful place in competition beside White men, whether it be in baseball, golf, tennis, or any other field in which the color line is still drawn.
>
> Because the Negro dollar is acceptable to the box office of organized baseball, because the Colored man is expected to pay his just share of the nation's taxes, and because the dusky, soldier is called on to bear arms in his country's defense, the Colored man should be given equality in the athletic world, in baseball, particularly, where democracy is supposed to exist on a far-higher plane than it does in political spheres.
>
> Some liberal-minded sports officials have been waiting "for the right time" in which to unshackle the Negro from the chains that keep him from unlimited competition in athletics. We think the time is now.

Meanwhile, the Greater New York Industrial Union Council, representing over half a million Congress of Industrial Organizations (CIO) trade unionists from more than 250 locals, unanimously passed a resolution to end apartheid in baseball. The resolution was sent to Commissioner Landis with a challenge to other trade unions to follow their example. The council's resolution in part read: "Whereas, in the spirit of national unity, Americans from all sections of the country have united to end the discrimination against race, color or creed. . . . Whereas, President Roosevelt in his address to the nation has stressed the importance of ending discrimination to insure victory. . . . Be it resolved, that we, the Greater New York Industrial Union Council . . . demand that Judge Landis end jim-crow in the big league baseball now."[16]

Another "Can You Read" message was sent by the largest trade union in the United States, Ford Local 600 of the United Automobile Workers (UAW). The Ford factory workers, who were producing tanks and planes to defeat Nazism, sent out telegrams and letters stating their belief that "National Unity embracing all races, colors and creeds is particularly necessary at this point in order to win the war against Fascism." The Ford local claimed to have approximately 15,000 black workers, including board members and union leaders. More than 80,000 workers approved the resolution to Commissioner Landis, which read in part: "Whereas, Ford Local 600 UAW-CIO is opposed at all times to all forms of discrimination anywhere because of race, color or creed, and Whereas, Negroes are barred from playing in Major League baseball and Whereas, such leading baseball players as Joe DiMaggio, Bob Feller, Dizzy Dean and others have claimed that such Negro stars as Satchel Paige, Josh Gibson and others are capable of playing Major League ball, and Therefore be it resolved that Ford Local 600 goes on record against the ban of Negro ball players . . . and petition baseball commissioner Kenesaw Mountain Landis to use his powers to lift this ban."[17]

By the middle of July, more than 1 million signatures had been gathered on a petition to Commissioner Landis to lift the color barrier. *New York Daily Worker* columnist Lester Rodney remembered: "I would say the petition drive was a success when a million signatures landed on Landis's desk. And we didn't have a million Communists. These were people who were going to the ballpark and wanted to see justice. It played a role, but that didn't make the difference. A lot of great people started to join in and make noise."[18]

The "Can You Read" campaign continued at movie houses. The debut of the motion picture *Pride of the Yankees* about Lou Gehrig's career was bombarded with pamphlets titled "In the Spirit of Lou Gehrig," which called for an end to Jim Crow Roughly 20,000 leaflets were distributed to 10 New York theaters. They featured a statement that Gehrig made in 1938: "I have seen and played against many Negro players who could easily be stars in the big leagues. I could name just a few of them like Satchel Paige, Buck Leonard, Josh Gibson and Barney Brown who should be in the Majors. I am all for it, 100%."[19]

The Communist Party was hard at work in a campaign to bring racial equality to the forefront. Nat Low, the sports editor of the *New York Daily Worker,* campaigned for tryouts to include black players. The *Daily Worker* gained momentum by publishing the racial slogans of the Ku Klux Klan, the lynching reports published by the NAACP and the Urban League, and editorials about segregated public places. These tactics shamed and inspired many Americans into raising their consciousness on racial matters. Editorial comments such as "keeping black players out of baseball is like keeping Joe Louis out of the ring or Paul Robeson off the concert slate" were common. The tabloid wars were in vogue as people routinely picketed downtown Manhattan with signs that read "IF WE CAN STOP BULLETS, WHY NOT BALLS?" or, conversely, "[NEW YORK] DAILY NEWS SUPPORTS JIM CROW IN BASEBALL" or "ANTI-NAZI LEAGUE SAYS DAILY NEWS SUPPORTS BIGOTRY."

The day before the highly attended Paige-Dean matchup in Chicago, a May 23 letter written by *Daily Worker* columnist Lester Rodney to Commissioner Landis set the tone for pressuring Landis to react to the apartheid issue in baseball:

> Judge Kenesaw Mountain Landis
> Commissioner of Baseball
> 333 North Michigan Ave.
> Chicago, Illinois
>
> The first casualty lists have been published. Negro soldiers and sailors are among those beloved heroes of the American people who have already died for the preservation of this country and everything this country stands for—yes, including the great game of baseball.
>
> So this letter isn't going to mince words.
>
> You may file this away without comment as you already have done to the petitions of more than a million American baseball fans. You may ignore it as you have ignored the clear statements of the men who play our National Pastime and the men who manage the teams. You may refuse to acknowledge and answer it as you have refused to acknowledge and answer scores of sports columns and editorials in newspapers throughout the country—from Coast to Coast, Philadelphia, New York and down to Louisville and countless smaller cities.

Yes, you may again ignore this. But at least this is going to name the central fact for all to know.

You, the self proclaimed "Czar" of Baseball, are the man responsible for keeping Jim Crow in our National Pastime. You are the one who by your alliance is maintaining a relic of the slave market long repudiated in other American sports. You are the one who is refusing to say the word which would do more to justify baseball's existence in this year of war than any other single thing. You are the one who is blocking the step which would put baseball in line with the rest of the country, with the United States government itself.

There can no longer be any excuse for your silence, Judge Landis. It is a silence that hurts the war effort. You were quick enough to speak up when many Jewish fans asked for the moving back the World Series opening by one day to avoid conflict with the biggest Jewish holiday of the year . . . quick to answer with a sneering refusal. You certainly made it clear then that you were the one with the final authority in baseball. You certainly didn't evade any responsibility then.

America is against discrimination, Judge Landis.

There never was a greater ovation in American's greatest indoor sports arena than that which arose two months ago when Wendell Wilkie, standing in the middle of the Madison Square Garden ring, turned to Joe Louis and said, "How can anyone looking at the wonderful example of this great American think in terms of discrimination for reasons of race, color or creed?"

Dorie Miller, who manned a machine gun at Pearl Harbor when he might have stayed below deck, has been honored by a grateful people. The President of our country has called for an end to discrimination in all jobs [Executive Order 8802].

Your position as big man in our National Pastime carries a much greater responsibility this year than ever before and you can't meet it with your alliance. The temper of the worker who goes to the ball game is not one to tolerate discrimination against 13,000,000 Americans in this year of the grim fight against the biggest Jim Crower of them all—Hitler.

You haven't a leg to stand on. Everybody knows there are many Negro players capable of starring in the big leagues. There was a poll of big league managers and players a couple of years ago and everybody but Bill Terry agreed that Negro players belonged in the big leagues. Terry is not a manager any more and new manager Mel Ott, who hails from Gretna, Louisiana, is one of the players who paid tribute to the great Negro stars.

Bill McKechnie, manager of the Cincinnati Reds, set the tone for all the managers when he said, "I could name at least 20 Negro players who belong in the big leagues and I'd love to have some of them on the Reds if given permission." If given YOUR permission, Judge Landis.

Manager Jimmy Dykes of the Chicago White Sox this spring was forced to tell two fine young Negro applicants [Jackie Robinson and Nate Moreland] for a tryout at the Pasadena training camp, "I know you're good and I'd love to have you. So would the rest of the boys and every other manager in the big leagues I'm sure. But it's not up to me." It's up to YOU, Judge Landis.

Leo Durocher, manager of the Brooklyn Dodgers, who were shut out in Havana this spring by a Negro pitcher, has said, "I wouldn't hesitate a minute to sign up some of those great colored players if I got the OK." YOUR OK, Judge Landis. Get that?

That's the sentiment of player, manager and fan.

The *Louisville Courier Journal* of a month ago, entering the nationwide demand for the end of Jim Crow in our National Pastime said, "Baseball, in this war, should set an example of democracy. What about it, Mr. Landis?"[20] Yes, what about it, Mr. Landis?

The American people are waiting for you. You're holding up the works. And the first casualty lists have been published.

Yours,

Lester Rodney,

Sports Editor, Daily Worker

New York City

Rodney's letter, along with petition campaigns, had prompted Judge Landis into his first official statement on the race issue. On July 17, several newspapers released this statement by the commissioner of baseball, Judge Kenesaw Mountain Landis, on his position of integration:

There is no rule against major clubs hiring Negro baseball players. I have come to the conclusion it is time for me to explain myself on this important issue. Negroes are not barred from organized baseball by the commission and have never been since the 21 years I have served. There is no rule in organized baseball prohibiting their participation to my knowledge.

If [Leo] Durocher, or any other manager, or all of them want to sign one or 25 Negro players, it is all right with me. That is the business of the manager and the club owners. The business of the Commissioner is to interpret the rules and enforce them.[21]

The above statement was provoked by an alleged statement by Durocher, manager of the Brooklyn Dodgers, in which he said, "I would hire Negro players if permitted."[22]

Interviews with several baseball executives were reported in the August 7 issue of the *Kansas City Call*. J. L. Wilkinson, owner of the Kansas City Monarchs, suggested, "I think it would be a fine thing for the game. Although we would lose some of our stars."

An opponent of integration, Larry MacPhail was quoted as follows: "The way they look at it, is that there aren't too many players of major league caliber in the Negro National and American leagues, so, if they should lose their best players to the majors, their own clubs would be hurt at the gate."[23]

New York Giants all-star hurler Carl Hubbell replied to Landis's statement: "Yes, sir, I've seen a lot of colored boys who should have been playing in the majors. First of all I'd name this big guy Josh Gibson for a place. He's one of the greatest backstops in history, I think. Any team in the big leagues could use him right now. Bullet Rogan of Kansas City and Satchel Paige could make any big league team. Paige has the fastest ball I've ever seen."[24]

Alva Bradley, owner of the Cleveland Indians, said, "Cleveland would consider Negro players."[25] His manager Lou Boudreau mentioned that he had played with Negroes in competition and had no objection to having them on his team, but he added, "It's all up to Alva Bradley—he owns the team."[26]

Perhaps with this new attitude toward racial integration in mind, William E. Benswanger, president of the Pittsburgh Pirates, scheduled a tryout for New York Cubans ace Dave Barnhill (actual age 28; reported to be 24), and catcher Roy Campanella (age 20) and second baseman Sammy T. Hughes (actual age 31; reported to be 27), both of the Baltimore Elite Giants. The tryout was originally scheduled for August 4 but was postponed to accommodate the Pirates' return from a road trip that day. "Negroes are American citizens

29. Before Roy Campanella jumped to Mexico in mid-September, he, along with teammate Sammy T. Hughes and Dave "Impo" Barnhill, was promised a tryout with the Pittsburgh Pirates. The tryout never materialized as Pirate owner William Benswanger continued to change the workout dates. Courtesy of Charles Blockson, Moseley Collection, Temple University.

with American rights and deserve all the opportunities given to a white man. They will receive the same trials given to white players," said Benswanger.[27]

Pittsburgh club owner Cum Posey had expressed his skepticism about the tryouts. In an interview with John P. McFarlane, sportswriter for the *Pittsburgh Post-Gazette*, Posey stated: "We've known Bill Benswanger for years. It was through his father-in-law, the late Barney Dreyfuss, that we got into baseball. Bill is sincere and he may go through with this thing, but we imagine that he will not try out colored players until he is sure some of the other teams will do the same, and I hardly think this will be before next spring, if then." [28]

National League president Ford Frick openly declared:

If a contract for a colored player came across my desk today, I would approve it, providing it was otherwise in order. There is nothing in the rules of baseball that I know of that would permit any other action.

I state unequivocally that there is no discrimination against Negroes or anybody else per se, in the National League. And you can quote me on that.

In this exclusive interview with the *Pittsburgh Courier*, Frick pointed out that African-Americans had a false impression of baseball's attitude toward race relations, adding:

This is really a social problem, not a baseball problem. And it would be unfair to call on "organized" baseball to solve it now or any other time.

I don't think that racial or any other kind of discrimination is right. In fact if I thought that the inclusion of Negroes in baseball would end racial discrimination in America, I would start right out today and "crusade for it."

Frick also entertained the issue of equal access to public accommodations for black players, explaining:

> Baseball has nothing to do with discrimination against Negroes in hotels, on trains, in restaurants, training camps and other public places.
>
> A colored player traveling with a white club would be subject to all kinds of embarrassments and humiliations which he would not ordinarily have to face while playing with his own people.
>
> It should also be realized that a ball club is a highly trained group of athletes who live, sleep two in a room, eat, travel and fight their team battles in the ball parks of the nation for eight months a year. They play 154 games in all, 77 at home and 77 on the road. In addition they have to spend from a month to six weeks in the South during a strenuous training period so that the players can quickly develop into a smooth-running athletic machine. Absence of one or more players from training camp might prove an insurmountable problem.
>
> With some of these obstacles in view, however, I still say colored ball players will find no barriers in my office. They are welcome anytime.[29]

After three weeks of excuses and delays, the Pittsburgh Pirates asked Negro League officials, sportswriters, managers, and owners to select four players from the East-West game for tryouts. The short list was narrowed down to Roy Campanella, Sammy T. Hughes, and Dave Barnhill, along with Josh Gibson, Ted Strong, Hilton Smith, Satchel Paige, Willie Wells, Leon Day, Sammy Bankhead, Howard Easterling, Tommy "Pee Wee" Butts, Pat Patterson, and Bill Wright. The tryout was rescheduled for September 1, and Gibson, Wells, Day, and Bankhead were the ones chosen by club owners. The owners also selected eight alternatives, which included the original trio of Campanella, Hughes, and Barnhill, plus Strong, Smith, Easterling, Patterson, and Butts.[30] Paige and Bankhead did not make the cut. With a change in the "game" plan, the black press began to heavily advertise the attributes of the foursome.

Conversely, co-owner of the Grays Cum Posey offered his position on the tryout situation, explaining: "After all, it doesn't make much difference to us in the Negro National League whether, two, three or the frequently mentioned 10 or a dozen players go up to the majors. We're more concerned about the 200 other colored players in this league and with our own investments. I think the colored players themselves feel the same way."[31]

On August 22 the National League standings showed the Pirates in fifth place, four games behind the fourth-place Cincinnati Reds. Catching for the Pirates was 34-year old Al Lopez, batting .250 with 21 RBIs and one home run. Lopez was no competition for Gibson, who was hitting around .375 in his league. At shortstop, the Pirates had Pete Coscarart, a utility player who hit for a .129 average for the Dodgers in 1941. It is doubtful Coscarart would have been a serious challenger to an all-star performer like Wells. Leon Day, who had won 24 games the previous year, could really have helped the Pirates pitching staff. Truett "Rip" Sewell, already 35, had the top Pirates won-lost record, at 12-10. In the Pirates outfield, Van Robays, Vince DiMaggio, and Jimmy Wasdell all batted under .260. Bankhead would have been a welcome addition to this weak outfield, with his all-around power and speed.

The Homestead Grays proceeded to play the Kansas City Monarchs in the 1942 Negro

League world series, as the Pirates finished up their season. Although Gibson would bat less than .200 in the series, he claimed, "I am in good shape for my try out with the Pittsburgh Pirates."[32] After several postponements, the tryouts never materialized. The Pirates management offered no excuses to the press, and the team finished in fifth place (68-81), 38 1/2 games behind the winning St. Louis Cardinals.

The Cleveland Indians announced on September 2 they would try out Cleveland Buckeyes manager and third baseman Parnell Woods (age 30; reported to be 26), outfielder Sam Jethroe (25; reported to be 22), and pitcher Gene Bremer (26) in the near future. John Fuster, sports editor of the *Cleveland Call-Post*, arranged the tryouts. Indians vice president Roger Peckinpaugh would not give a definite date for the workouts. Eventually, like the tryout promised by the Pittsburgh club, the Cleveland organization failed to live up to its word.[33]

New hope reigned during a September 15 meeting at the offices of the Brooklyn Dodgers. William T. Andrews, an assemblyman, and Father Raymond Campion, a Catholic priest, met with Dodger president Larry MacPhail for almost two hours. Others who attended were former Negro League commissioner Ferdinand Q. Morton, Fred Turner of the NAACP, Dan Burley of the *Amsterdam News*, George Hunton of the *Catholic Interracial Review*, and Joe Bostic of the *People's Voice*. When the race issue was presented to MacPhail, he responded: "Plenty of Negro players are ready for the big leagues. In five minutes I could pick half a dozen men who could fit into major league teams." MacPhail added that he thought that "Negroes should have the opportunity not only to play in the leagues, but should have a lot of other opportunities, in employment, housing and other things."

MacPhail also stated he was willing to book his Dodgers team against a winner from the Negro Leagues for a postseason championship if the Dodgers won the National League pennant. He also suggested the use of Ebbets Field, along with a 60–40 split of the gate receipts between the winners and losers. Father Campion and Assemblyman Andrews emphasized that Cleveland and Pittsburgh had failed their commitment to grant players an opportunity to make their teams. MacPhail voiced his criticism of those owners: "It's not necessary to try them out. They're ready and willing to go into the majors [now]." The sports section of the *Daily Worker* boasted in large one-inch type on September 19, "DODGERS MAY PLAY MONARCHS, NEGRO LEAGUE CHAMPS, IN POST SEASON TILTS"[34] Like many promises before, this one failed to materialize as the Dodgers finished two games out of first place.

The 1942 season brought good news and bad news. The campaign started six years earlier by writer Lester Rodney of the *Daily Worker* had finally seen some results. During the course of this season, Rodney became a private in the U.S. Army. Nat Low took over command of the fight and wrote his analysis of the battle: "We DID get the Landis statement, and whereas we DID get the campaign much favorable national publicity and whereas we DID get promises of tryouts from two major league owners—William Benswanger of the Pittsburgh Pirates and Alva Bradley of the Cleveland Indians—we DID NOT succeed in our main objective—to get Negro stars onto major league teams, in uniform."[35]

PAIGE'S THOUGHTS ON INTEGRATION

A rumor floated around the league that Satchel Paige was not interested in a major league contract and that he was against integration of the majors. The rumor claimed Paige had turned down a $10,000 offer to sign with the big leagues. Paige was in Cleveland preparing for the East-West game when he gave an exclusive interview to Sam McKibben of the *Cleveland Call-Post* to set the record straight: "I told a white reporter that I wouldn't sign a $10,000 contract and his eyes widened in surprise. He wanted to know what my present salary amounted to and feeling that was none of his business, and I informed him thusly. The next day I read where I was making $40,000 a year. That started the uncalled revelation that I am going through."

About preparing for the all-star game, Paige said: "Imagine me living at a Negro hotel although I play with a white team. Record my feelings when dishes out of which I eat are broken up in my presence. How could I pitch a decent game with insulting jeers coming from spectators and even some of the players? Just convince me that agitation can be halted and I'll pitch fast balls by Joe DiMaggio."

Paige continued: "If the President hasn't made southern defense plants to hire and use Negro labor in government plants, how can Judge Landis, Connie Mack or anyone make the southern white folk accept the Negro as a ball player? His training camp life in the South would be miserable . . . and the camps won't be moved for one or two Negroes."

Paige added, "What about the tryouts allegedly by the Pittsburgh Pirates? Who will bell the cat [end Jim Crowism]? Will the white trainer work on a Negro, to say nothing to take care of him? Indeed not. I've never been able to get any service out of one."

Paige requested that McKibben "tell the reading public not to believe half of what it reads that I say in the daily papers. I say to others what I am saying to you, but my statements are twisted. Negroes will never get into the major leagues because of Jim Crow. It's a wonderful dream, but it will never come true. With the nation at war not one is going to try to abolish Jim Crow. And even in peacetime, Jim Crowism will flourish. Me, I am going to stick with Wilkie [J. L. Wilkinson, white owner of the Monarchs] and whoever says I am afraid I can't make the grade—is just plain nuts. I experience enough prejudice now. Why court more?"[36]

I Cover the Eastern Front

by Eddie Gant

Source: *Chicago Defender,* 25 July 1942

Washington DC— This question of Negroes in the major leagues has come to a head this week with the announcement by Judge Kenesaw Landis that there is no bar against colored players, either by written law or an understanding, against the hiring of Race players in the leagues. But, from this corner, we think that there is no cause for immediate alarm by players or those who have been campaigning for the admission of Negro players into the leagues. We take this position for two reasons:

> There has never been any law against the admission of Race players and those close to baseball, owners, players, newspapermen and long-time fans, have always known this. (Consequently, Landis' revelation is in effect no revelation at all), and
> Admission of one or two colored players would only serve to take the drawing power from the present colored leagues and probably would not help the situation because of the color bar against Race men in hotels, and other public places where ball players must congregate.

The first player to get such a break in the white leagues would be subject to so much abuse, prejudice practices and discriminatory acts by his fellow players and those he had to come in contact with that the chances are he would be "rode" out of the circuit. He would have to be an exceptionally strong man to stand the gaff.

Take the position of the Cubans and South American players who have been on the Washington Senators. They have been subjected to all sorts of abuses. Rival pitchers have been low enough to try "beaning" them. In other instances, players on their own team have refused to room with them, and in dining cars and other travel facilities discriminated against them.

Such actions aren't calculated to attract many Negro players unless the money offers are very steep.

Anyway it is going to be interesting to watch the "I told you so's" in the event any colored player is hired. We still think it will be a long time, although the big leagues could certainly use some color.

Editor's note: Gant refers to Cuban outfielders Baldomero "Merito" Acosta (1913–18) and Jacinto "Jack" Calvo (1913 and 1920). In 1920, the Cuban battery mate of pitcher Jose Acosta (1920–22) and Ricardo Torres (1920–22) joined the Senators. Other Cuban players to perform in the nation's capital included outfielders Roberto Estallela (1935–36, 1939, and 1942), Roberto Ortiz (1941–42), catcher Fermin "Mike" Guerra (1937), pitcher Rene Monteagudo (1938 and 1940), and utility infielder Gilberto Torres (1940). In 1939 pitcher Alejandro Carrasquel, from Venezuela, joined the Senators and played several years. By the end of 1942, 30 light-skinned Latin American players had integrated major league teams. Cuba had the largest contingent with 25 athletes, followed by Mexico with 3 players and by Puerto Rico and Venezuela with 1 each.

Ethnic roots were sometimes ignored if the player had a fair complexion. Light-skinned Cubans were permitted on major league teams, while their darker-skinned brothers were shunned. For example, former Boston Red Sox pitcher Luis Tiant Jr., a dark-skinned

Cuban, would not have been allowed to play major league ball before 1947. Meanwhile, his Cuban cousin, the fair-complexioned Jose Canseco, would have been perfectly passable.

East Plans to Switch Fielders for Classic

Source: *Chicago Defender,* 1 August 1942

New York— Cumberland Posey, secretary of the Negro National league, stated here Sunday that it may be necessary for officials in charge of the Eastern team for the East-West game in Chicago, Sunday, August 16, to make a number of revisions in the line-up for the team representing the National League.

"Because of the highly contested poll among the players," Posey said, "It may be necessary for us to switch some of the players around. There are a number of players who are not leading in their respective positions, but who are still better in other positions."

Posey pointed out that Leon Day, stocky Newark pitcher, is just as good in the outfield as he is on the mound. While Day is seventh in the pitchers' poll, he is rated on par with the best outfielders in the league and has been playing in the outfield for Newark when not pitching.

"It may develop," Posey said, "that we will have to use Day in the outfield, despite the fact that he is listed in the poll as a pitcher, which is his regular position. The same goes for Sammy Bankhead, Grays' shortstop, who is fifth in the poll for that position, but is also a great outfielder. He has been playing shortstop for the Grays because the team is weak in that spot, but it doesn't mean that we can't use him in the outfield."

He also cited the case of Lonnie [Lennie] Pearson of Newark, who is in the thick of the fight for first base honors. Posey said: "Pearson, [Jim] West and [Buck] Leonard are all good first basemen, but only one of them can win the honor. However, Pearson may be used in the outfield for the East because of his hitting. We will need hitting this year against the West's great pitching staff. Buck Leonard has been out with injuries off-and-on most of the season. We will have to make up for that loss with a man like Lonnie [Lennie], who can really clout ball."

"In selecting the National league team," Posey said, "we are going to try and stick to the results of the poll as much as possible. However, due to circumstances beyond our control, we may have to switch the players around some. We are going all-out to win this ball game on August 16, and if it is necessary to make a few changes we'll make them for the good of the team and league."

Commenting on the nation-wide poll, Posey said: "The votes that are coming in from all over the country are helping us a great deal. We know by them just who the fans want to see in Chicago, and we're going to see to it that those players get in the game. But, as I said before, we may have to place some of the players in positions other than the positions they are playing at present time."

Through the Years ... Past—Present—Future

by Fay Young

Source: *Chicago Defender,* 1 August 1942

While out to the home of the Chicago Cubs, which is Wrigley field, Sunday, I was amused at the hysteria of some of the Negro baseball fans over the statement of High

Commissioner Landis who governs major league and minor league baseball. Landis did tell the truth. There hasn't been any rule in either league against "the brother" playing but we didn't need Landis to tell us that at this late day.

My mind drifts back to more than 25 years ago. At that time a sports writer [Lloyd Thompson] on the *Philadelphia Tribune,* Ira Lewis of the *Courier* and myself were the three Negroes whom Rube Foster said could score anybody's ball game. Between that time and now there have been dozens who should do it as well as that trio mentioned. These dozens include Bill Nunn and Ches Washington, both of Pittsburgh; Russ Cowans, Detroit; Bill Gibson and Art Carter, Baltimore; Rollo Wilson, Philadelphia; Dan Burley, New York, and others. All of these men mentioned and many more have waged a fight against the color barrier in the big leagues—and I wouldn't hesitate to say all of them feel that Landis is starting a buck-passing game.

Since no Negroes are barred, what keeps them out? That's a question that Landis ought to answer. They are out—and they are not in.

Sunday Morning's paper carried a story with a New York dateline. It said that the sixth place Pittsburgh Pirates would "tryout" several Negro players this week.

President Benswanger, of the Pittsburgh National league club, made a fine speech when he said:

"Colored men are American citizens with American rights. I know there are many problems connected with the question, but after all, somebody has to make the first move."

The Pirates club president never came any nearer telling the truth. Then he upset the "apple cart." He said he did not know the names of the players whom the Pirates would try out but that "some paper called me up and asked if I would allow certain members of the Negro National league to try out for my team. I agreed." So far so good, but he added, "I guess the players will come down at their own or the paper's expense."

But before the fans get too far out in the limb painting a rosy picture, let me call your attention to the fact that the major leagues have a player limit and before they can hire a Negro or a white ball player they must let one go. Also, that "trying out" for the team does not mean "being hired" to play with the team.

We Negroes are entirely too careless with the English language. It would pay some of us to consult Webster's Dictionary a little more often. However, Benswanger puts it straight when he says he "wouldn't hire a Negro because he was a Negro."

He said, "Anything I do will be calculated to help our team and our game. If we hire then drop a Negro player who doesn't quite make the grade, I suppose we will be accused of discrimination. But I shall have a clear conscience in the matter and I intend to keep it."

Frank Frisch, manager of the Pirates, said: "I don't believe there is a thing to it."

Out at the Cubs park, it was learned that the Cubs could "try out" Negro players but the management didn't believe in being hypocrites.

President Roosevelt has ordered no discrimination in defense work. That discrimination remains is a certainty. Landis can say there is no rule or law—but the fact remains no Negroes are playing in major league or minor league baseball.

The time may come when they will—but I'd hate to hang by my thumbs until that time came around.

Who knows whether there will be any baseball next year?

Clark Griffith of the Washington Senators advises, and does so rightfully, "build up your own league" but still clings to the Jim Crow attitude of most of the owners. He believes that since Negro baseball has been attracting so much attention that, if properly supervised, the Negro leagues can pay larger salaries and develop stars to such an extent that "someday the top teams (meaning Negro) could play our clubs for the world championship and thus have a chance to really prove their calibre."

Grapevine information is that prior to the All-Star game in New York, the major league owners held a session in which the subject of Negro ball players came up. It was a heated confab and the transcription was ordered destroyed.

The Negro knows Landis is right, but Landis cannot spend a club owner's money. I want to see the black ball player of ability in bigtime baseball. But sentiment won't get him there. And he isn't there. And according to my way of thinking he won't get in the major leagues for sometime.

Yes, the Negro is in the Navy and is being taken in every day without being held down to accept a mess attendant's job. But he isn't an ensign. One is on the medical reserve corps list but the boy won't graduate from Harvard medical school until 1945 and by that time Uncle Sam will have licked Japan, Germany and Italy. The fact is there are NO Negro ensigns yet we are supposed to be "real Americans with American rights."

Benswanger doesn't have to ride South in segregated coaches. He doesn't have to eat in or near the kitchen sink in depot restaurants. He doesn't have to sit in separate sections in auditoriums and the back end of street cars! Yet we are supposed to have full American rights. We are supposed to be able to go as far as our ability can take us. But we are the "supposingest" race on earth.

West Ready to Halt East's Bats

Did It in 1939 and Can Do It Again

Big Classic on Aug. 16

by Frank A. Young

Source: *Chicago Defender,* 8 August 1942

The tenth annual East versus West game ought to be a record breaker—as far as attendance is concerned. On Sunday afternoon, August 16, the West will try to even the score in the series which now stands five games to four in favor of the Atlantic seaboard ball players.

That the West isn't underestimating the strength of the Easterners is shown by the uncanny knowledge the fans have of the defensive and offensive play of the Negro American league players and have chalked their votes in such a way that the game is going to be one which the outcome is hard to predict.

In 1939, the East had this same Sammy Hughes, second sacker of the Baltimore Elites; Buck Leonard, the Homestead Grays' first sacker; Josh Gibson, the Homestead Grays' catcher, and others. Now, let's see what these heavy clouters whom the East must relay on did back in the All-Star classic of 1939. The East lost that year, 4 to 2.

STOPPED EAST'S "BIG 'UNS"

Let us take a look at what the "Big Guns" produced. Buck Leonard got three official trips to the plate, got nary a hit and scored one run. He was free ticketed to first base. Had eight putouts and two assists. He played the entire game at first base.

Bring on Mr. Gibson, the fence buster. Gibson wasn't with the All-Stars of the East last year because both he and Hughes were playing in Old Mexico. Believe it or not, Josh

30. *Grays manager Vic Harris and Buck Leonard visit in the dugout. East Manager Harris managed the most teams (eight) in the East-West classic. Leonard was unable to play in the 1942 East-West game because of a broken left hand. Courtesy of Charles Blockson, Moseley Collection, Temple University.*

Gibson had three official trips to the plate, got a base on balls—and never got a semblance of a hit. He had six putouts and three assists.

Now get your microscope out for Hughes. He did get a single. He, like Gibson, didn't score a run. He had three official times at bat. He had three putouts and one assist. However, the sad Mr. Hughes drove in two runs with his single.

The opposing pitchers were: for the East, William Byrd of Baltimore, who looks as though he will be back again this year; [Leon] Day of the Newark Eagles; [Roy] Partlow of the Homestead Grays and Bill Holland for the New York Black Yanks. For the West: Theo Smith of the St. Louis Stars; Hilton Smith of the Kansas City Monarchs, and Ted "Double Duty" Radcliffe.

Last year, Leonard got two hits, including a home run off Double Duty Radcliffe in the fourth inning, scoring [Bill] Hoskins of Baltimore ahead of him and ending a scoring spree for the East which produced six runs. At the end of the third inning when Hilton Smith left the mound, the East was out in front 2 to 1. After the end of the fourth inning after Ted Radcliffe had been bombarded to such an extent that Manager Candy Taylor finally decided to take him out and send in Preacher Henry, then of the Jacksonville Red Caps but now of the Ethiopian Clowns, to the mound. Henry pitched the balance of the ill fated fourth and fifth. Dan Bankhead, Birmingham, went to the mound for the West. He pitched the sixth and seventh. The great Satchel Paige pitched the eighth and ninth. But the eight runs, six of which were made off of Radcliffe, were more than enough for the East to win the game 8 to 3.

Let's see what Paige did. He was given a great ovation when he went to the mound. He flashed a fast curve across the pan for the third strike on [Pancho] Coimbre of the Cubans. Hoskins of Baltimore missed a fast one for the third strike and an out. Buck Leonard, the hard hitting first sacker of the Homestead Grays, popped to [Jimmy] Ford of St. Louis who was playing second base for the West.

In the ninth, Irvin flied to [Jimmie] Crutchfield in left field. Campanella, catcher for the East, beat out a hit down the third base line to Parnell Woods of Birmingham. Larry Brown pegged Campanella out trying to steal second on a bullet-like throw to Billy Horne of the Chicago American Giants. Dick Seay of the New York Black Yankees flied out to [Buddy] Armour in centerfield after [Horacio] Martinez of the Cubans had walked. What two innings of baseball Satchel Paige did pitch although he had been held out of the game—until it was lost. In the two innings he worked, only Campanella's scratch hit was all that was made off of him. He struck out two and walked one.

Manager W.S. Welch of the West's team realizes the East isn't to be trifled with. [Dave] Barnhill may have had a bad day Sunday in New York against Paige and Hilton Smith but Barnhill is a pitcher. When [Terris] McDuffie was overcome by the heat after the West's second inning, Barnhill went to the pitcher's box in the third. He pitched the third inning, allowing one hit, that coming when Coimbre lost the ball in the sun. He hurled the fourth and allowed nary a hit. The fifth saw [Duke] Cleveland, the Jacksonville outfielder and first man to face him, singled. Crutchfield of Chicago fouled out near the left field line when Hoskins raced over for the out. Horne struck out and Campanella to Martinez nipped Cleveland trying to steal.

But whether they win or not, the fans are going to see the West out there hustling every minute with a firm determination to tie up the series in games won. At present, the East is out in front. It's going to be one grand ball game and all roads will lead to Comiskey Park on Sunday afternoon, August 16.

Let's Get This Straight

by Fay Young

Source: *Chicago Defender,* 15 August 1942

As a bit of gratitude to those who have been trying to elevate the Negro ball player and right at the time when a big controversy over the chances of Negro players getting a tryout in major leagues comes a most disquieting piece of information.

David "Impo" Barnhill, Cuban Stars pitcher; Sammy Hughes, Baltimore second baseman and Roy Campanella, Baltimore catcher showed up in Cleveland Saturday night, Aug. 8 and played with the Buckeyes Sunday, Aug. 9. The three players are members of the Negro National league and were not with the clubs under whom they had signed contracts.

At this writing it has not been learned whether Alex Pompez, the owner of the Cuban Stars, granted Barnhill the right to go. But it has been learned that Tom Wilson, president of the Negro National league and owner of the Baltimore Elites, had complained by long distance telephone to Dr. J. B. Martin, president of the Negro American league that Ernie Wright, of Erie, Pa., owner of the Buckeyes, had been tampering with some of Wilson's players. President Martin then warned Wright.

The players were offered—and said to have been paid—$200 to play in the game Sunday. Now let's get this straight. Nobody has any sympathy for and refuses to deal with men who violate a contract or an agreement, especially a written one. And no ball player white or black is going to stay in organized baseball if that player violates either a contract or playing rules of conduct as laid down by managers—and the Negro fan isn't going to approve of our ball players doing so with Negro managers or owners of Negro clubs.

Let's get it straight once and for all time that there is but one way to conduct operate or carry on anything successfully—that is the right way.

And we aren't going to get anywhere doing it the wrong way and believe it ought to be overlooked because we are Negroes. It isn't that we don't know any better. It is because we think we are a damn sight smarter than the other fellow.

Let's get it straight once and for all. We aren't half as smart as we figure out we are and as a rule we are always doing something to kick ourselves back in the rut than doing something to advance ourselves.

Let's get it straight right now. President Martin: Wright ought to be fined. President Wilson: Barnhill, Hughes and Campanella ought to be fined. The fans are waiting to see what you two men are going to do about this case.

Let's get it straight now—once and for all time.

East Wins before 48,000, 5–2

Eastern Power Team Wins Sixth "Dream Game" in Chicago

by Wendell Smith

Source: *Pittsburgh Courier,* 22 August 1942

Like a legendary king of days long gone "Satchel" Paige, tall, gaunt, and fearless, hero of a thousand conflicts . . . came stalking from distant bullpen in historic Comiskey Park here this afternoon to save the West from impending disaster, and muffle the big bats of the East. It was the fateful seventh and the fireballer from Kansas City, a national hero to the 48,000 cheering fans, was awarded the honor of saving a hardly, courageous band of fighting teammates, who had battled the East for six thrilling innings to a 2–2 standstill in the 10th annual East-West game.

But all great warriors taste the bitter sting of defeat somewhere on the rocky, glittering field of sportsdom. And so it was this afternoon with the mighty Satchel, whose shining armor of invincibility succumbed to the ringing base hits of a merciless, dashing aggregation from the Negro National League.

Not even baseball's immortal Satchel Paige could quell the insurgents from the East, who scored their sixth triumph in 10 years by beating the West, 5 to 2.

TIED IN SIXTH

For six innings the two all-star teams battled on even terms. When Paige made his debut in the seventh it was tie at 2–2. The East broke the ice in the third when Dan Wilson stretched a short hit to center into a double after Gaines had struck out, and Slammin' Sam Bankhead cruised him home with a slashing double to right center.

WEST STRIKES BACK

Undaunted the West came back in the last of the fourth [third] and knotted the count after Hilton Smith was safe on Patterson's over throw and galloped to second when the ball

31. Back in the United States after a sojourn in Mexico, Willie Wells punished the West team by going three for four, including three doubles and two RBIS in a 9-2 win at Municipal Stadium in Cleveland. The following season, after a contract dispute with the Newark Eagles owners, Effa and Abe Manley, Wells returned to Mexico. Courtesy of NoirTech Research, Inc.

rolled almost to the stands. Fred Bankhead of Memphis ran for Smith. When Bell hit to Wells at shortstop, Willie tried to trap Bankhead on the basepaths, but Patterson muffed a perfect throw, enabling Fred to scoot back to safety at second and Bell was safe at first. Woods hit a grounder to Wells, and while the East was trying for a couple killing Bankhead came over with the tying run. Woods was ruled safe on a close play at first, preventing the attempted double play.

The ever-threatening Eastern team took the lead again in the fifth, when Wilson walked stole second and moved to third on Wells long fly to center, Josh Gibson then came through with a whistling single to center, and Wilson came romping home with the East's second run.

WOODS HIT LONGEST

Parnell Woods got credit for the longest hit of the game in the sixth when he led or with a blast over Vargas head in centerfield and pulled up at third. He came home on Green's slow roller to second and the ball game was tied up again.

It was at this point that Satchel Paige entered the game with a tremendous ovation. He was coming in the quell the East and enable the West to push over a winning marker. But the East had different ideas. Manager Vic Harris sent Pearson in to hit for David Barnhill, brilliant pitcher of the New York Cubans and the Newark star dropped a hit into right field when the sun blinded Ted Strong, West rightfielder. With Pearson on second Dan Wilson beat out a perfect bunt and Pearson moved on to third. Pearson scored a moment later when Bankhead filed to center.

That was the ball game. Leon Day held the West in check and the East pushed over two more off Satchel in the ninth, to make it 5–2.

WELLS IS BRILLIANT

While the game itself was far from perfect, it was chock full of sparkling plays. Willie Wells, brilliant shortstop for the East, made three brilliant stops, the last of which brought the crowd to its feet. In the sixth, O'Neil hit what appeared to be perfect hit over second, but the famous Newark pilot raced over behind the sack and scooped up the sizzling grounder and nipped him at first by a step.

Editor's note: Willie Wells was considered the premier fielding shortstop in the league. Buck O'Neil remembered his encounter with "The Devil": "What thrilled me more in the East-West was actually a play made against me. Willie Wells was playing shortstop, and I hit the ball to the right of second base. Just to the right of second base, up the middle. I know I got a base hit. You know that sucker came over and got that ball and threw me out. I looked at him, and he just laughed. That night [when] we were eating dinner, he said, 'You didn't think I was going to catch that ball, did you?' I replied, 'You're the only fellow who could have caught it.'" [37]

EAST TOO POWERFUL

The East was the better all-around ball club this year by a wide margin. With a whole roster of brilliant players, the East was constantly threatening. Although Hilton Smith and Porter Moss, Memphis hurler escaped with only one run charged up against them the East was always threatening and it finally exploded in the later innings on Satchel Paige.

The East pitching, to the surprise of many, was considerably better than that of the West. Barnhill, Day, and Gaines were puzzling throughout. Barney Brown, Philadelphia Stars' ace, was the only East hurler who had to be relieved. Leon Day relieved Barney in the seventh after Paige and Bell both singled with two out. Day pitched two and one-third innings without giving a hit. He struck out five out of seven batters, three of which came in the ninth.

Editor's note: In 1934 Carl Hubbell of the New York Giants fanned five of the American League's premier hitters in a row: Babe Ruth, Lou Gehrig, Jimmie Foxx, Al Simmons, and Joe Cronin. All men were destined for the Hall of Fame. Hubbell's feat is still considered one of the outstanding pitching performances in major league all-star history. However, Hubbell faced a total of 13 men and gave up two hits and two walks during his history-making performance.

In comparison, Day faced only seven batters and struck out five of them, giving up no walks and no hits. Day struck out the side (Buck O'Neil and pinch hitters Art "Superman" Pennington and Lloyd Davenport) in the ninth inning, losing a chance to add to his strikeout string had the game not ended. The previous batters he faced were just as formidable: Monarch power hitters Joe Greene, Willard Brown, and Ted Strong.

Years later, Day gave his scouting report on some of baseball's best hitters: "Buck O'Neil and Willard Brown were pretty tough. I tried to pitch O'Neil outside and he hit the ball, and I tried to go inside on him and he hit the ball. He was little tough on me. Later on I met Brown in the service and we played together. Joe Greene and Ted Strong didn't give me any trouble. Greene had been in our league for awhile before he went to the Monarchs and Strong didn't have a real good eye at the plate, but if he hit it you were in trouble."[38]

48,000 See East All-Stars Beat Paige and West

West Held to Four Hits as National Leaguers Triumph by 5–2 Score

by Frank A. Young

Source: Chicago Defender, 22 August 1942

A crowd of 48,800 of which 45,159 paid to see the game, watched the East All-Stars take the tenth annual game from the West All-Stars and Satchel Paige by the score of 5 to 2 at Comiskey Park Sunday. And fully six thousand, unable to get seats went home — disappointed. Many had come from out of town but had forgotten to send in and get their tickets early.

The East got the breaks of the game—made most of these breaks and the East pitching stopped the batting of such men as Willard Brown of Kansas City, [Sam] Jethroe of the Cincinnati Buckeyes, Ted Strong of the Kansas City Monarchs and [Joe] Greene of the same club.

Perhaps the West may have had an off day. One thing was assured. That was the fans who came looking for those long hitters to clout out home runs saw one of the few East versus West game out of the ten in which no home runs were made. There were several two base hits of the Texas leaguer variety plus one, in the seventh, which Ted Strong lost when it dropped out of the piercing rays of the sun into the darkness of the shadow caused by the grandstand on the West side of the Comiskey Park. At that, and although he wasn't chalked up with an error, there wasn't any excuse for Strong.

Paige got in a hole in the seventh after Lenny Pearson of the Newark Eagles got on through Strong's kindness—or should I say that Dan Wilson's bunt to Paige's left which caught Paige flat-footed and which Wilson by some fast leg-work got to first safely, Pearson went to third on the play. Sammy Bankhead of the Homestead Grays hit a fly to "Cool Papa" Bell of the Chicago American Giants and Pearson romped home after the catch with the run that broke the two and two tie.

Even then Paige was going along all right. Barney Brown, the lefthander of the Philadelphia Stars, started the seventh for the East, but he didn't last longer than a snowball in a fiery furnace. With two out of the way, Paige singled and Bell singled. That was two of the five hits which the West got.

Vic Harris, manager of the Homestead Grays, would take no chances. He held a confab with Tex Burnett of the New York Black Yankees who was coach and Leon Day of the Newark Eagles was brought in from the bullpen in rightfield and Brown sent to the showers. The East seemed to know what it was all about. Day is one of the best pitchers in the business today—white or black. He forced Marlin Carter, Memphis third sacker, to roll out, Wells to Jim West.

Some believed Manager W. S. Welsh [Welch] should have left Parnell Woods of the Cincinnati Buckeyes, who had tripled—the only extra base hit [for the West] in the game—in the sixth, in the game. But those are second guessers.

Then in the ninth, Paige got some bad breaks. Dan Wilson bunted and when O'Neil of Kansas City fielded his roller and threw wide to Paige at first, went to second when the ball rolled near the East dugout. Tommy Sampson of Birmingham came over to cover first when Sammy Bankhead of the Grays attempted to bunt, Sampson proceeded to drop O'Neil's throw, Bankhead being safe and Wilson going to third. Manager Welsh [Welch] ordered Josh Gibson, Grays catcher, to be walked. Then came Bill Wright, the Baltimore outfielder, to the plate. He had hit once into a double play. This time Paige shot a fast one and as it broke Wright slammed a sharp single to right scoring Wilson and Sammy Bankhead and sewing up the game for the East which now leads on the series six games to four and making it three straight for the Negro National leaguers.

With Day pitching there wasn't any question to the outcome. He turned on the steam to strike out all three of the Negro American league batters. They went down in order. O'Neil was the first out and Arthur Pennington, Chicago America Giants, missed the third strike. Floyd [Lloyd] Davenport of the Birmingham Black Barons was called out on strikes, ending the 1942 All-Star game.

The two teams and Paige left Chicago early Tuesday morning for Cleveland where they were scheduled to play a night game in the Municipal Stadium for the benefit of the U.S. Army and U.S. Navy Relief funds.

Through the Years: Past—Present—Future

by Fay Young

Source: *Chicago Defender,* 22 August 1942

Satchel Paige got his first defeat in four East versus West games Sunday at Comiskey Park in Chicago when the East All Stars, made up of Negro National league players, trounced the West All Stars, made up of Negro American leaguers, 5 to 2, in an interesting game before 48,000 fans. To be exact there were 45,179 paid admissions plus about 3,000 who were in on complimentary seats, sailors and soldiers in uniform. Fully seven thousand who wanted to see the game went back home because of their inability to obtain seats.

Next year, you folks who missed the classic will get your tickets early. There wasn't any excuse for the thousands who waited until the last day and until 2 o'clock to stage a blitz on the ticket offices. Nor was there any excuse for the folks acting like a bunch of wild hyenas in a rampage at the turnstiles. Nor is there any excuse for some of our folks going to a ball game with a whiskey bottle in their pocket and staging fights. If anything keeps the Negro ball player out of the major leagues, it will be this rowdy element who seeks to break up everything and build nothing. This sort drives away the decent and peaceful Negro fan and no major league park wants its patronage routed to make room for the once-a-week (on Sunday) fan who insists on seeing his ball game with the help of the whiskey or gin bottle.

Nor is there any plausible excuse for the sudden growth of so-called Negro newspaper cameramen who line the third and first base lines with Kodak and $12.50 cameras. These men who persist in roaming about the field are a disgrace and a humiliation to the real newspaper photographers.

Whenever and wherever there is a bonfire promotion, out of a clean sky comes every person in a newspaper office from the janitor to the president who takes a notion he or she wants to see the game. My hat goes off to the women folk because those who do come out conduct themselves like newspaperwomen should. But every man who has a police reporter's card or even a card with the name of the publication on it believes he has the inherent right to get out on the field or to park in the press room where he interferes with those who are sent to cover the game.

And there are those who for some reason believe they are entitled to working press tickets when they do not write baseball and work on small publications which do not have a sport sheet and which carried no news of the event before it took place. I had a request for a press pass for a man who hasn't been in the news gathering business for three years. I watched men with the uniform of the Illinois Reserve militia get in free because they had on a soldier's uniform. By wearing the uniform of the Illinois National Guard these men saved $1.10. No one kicks on allowing the sailor or the soldier, now in our service, in free. But there must be a line drawn somewhere.

The Sports Bugle

Revolt Almost Wrecked East-West Classic

by Randy Dixon

Source: *Pittsburgh Courier*, 5 September 1942

The grapevine leading from the inner sanctum of big-time Negro baseball tells of a near-revolt among players on the eve of the recent East-West game in Chicago that would have transformed that classic into a rank fiasco.

The money question was the bugaboo that sent the western squad into a huddle from which emanated the ultimatum that unless their ante was raised they refused to play the game.

About the same time, I am told, the Eastern contingent was holding sessions citing their grievances. Vic Harris, manager of the Easterners, got wind of the proceeding and stormed in to berate his underlings for not first bringing their peeves to him.

Vic is known in the sepia baseball firmament as a hombre who fights for the rights of his players. He is highly respected and liked, hence Vic felt that his men were not playing fair with him because they knew he would "go to bat for them" if and when.

After Vic had belched his little woof the Easterners rescinded their plot of revolt, and the Westerners agreed to a compromise.

Pre-game matters among the umpires for the game also went awry. Three of the four arbiters came equipped to work behind the plate, each evidently intent on being the head-man of the extravaganzas.

Don't ask me how this situation was smoothed out. And neither ask me what sophomoric promoting was responsible for all the messeroo.

And when I tell the players of each squad were paid but 50 dollars apiece and the umpires received a puny $15 each for their labors (with an additional $2.50 promised when a protest was made) you'll know why Negro baseballers regard their owners as Shylocks and Chiselers.

Of yes! I forgot to mention that game draw 48,000 spectators with a gross of better than $50,000.

Who said slavery was a thing of the past?

AUGUST 16, 1942, SUNDAY
COMISKEY PARK, CHICAGO (GAME 1 OF 2)

EAST	AB	R	H	D	T	HR	BI	E	TAVG	TSLG
Dan Wilson (New York Black Yankees), lf	4	3	2	1	0	0	0	0		
Sam Bankhead (Homestead Grays), 2b-cf	4	1	2	1	0	0	2	0		
Willie Wells (Newark Eagles), ss	5	0	1	0	0	0	0	0		
Josh Gibson (Homestead Grays), c	3	0	2	0	0	0	1	0		
Bill Wright (Baltimore Elite Giants), rf	5	0	2	0	0	0	2	0		
Jim West (Philadelphia Stars), 1b	5	0	0	0	0	0	0	0		
Andy Patterson (Philadelphia Stars), 3b	3	0	0	0	0	0	0	2		
Tetelo Vargas (New York Cubans), cf	3	0	1	0	0	0	0	0		
a) Herberto Blanco (New York Cubans), pr, 2b	0	0	0	0	0	0	0	0		
Jonas Gaines (Baltimore Elite Giants), p	1	0	0	0	0	0	0	0		
b) Vic Harris (Homestead Grays), ph	1	0	0	0	0	0	0	0		
Dave Barnhill (New York Cubans), p	0	0	0	0	0	0	0	0		
c) Lennie Pearson (Newark Eagles), ph	1	1	1	1	0	0	0	0		
Barney Brown (Philadelphia Stars), p	0	0	0	0	0	0	0	0		
Leon Day (Newark Eagles), p	1	0	0	0	0	0	0	0		
Team Totals, Average & Slugging Pct.	36	5	11	3	0	0	5	2	.306	.389

a) Ran for Vargas in 8th
b) Batted for Gaines in 4th
c) Batted for Barnhill in 7th

WEST	AB	R	H	D	T	HR	BI	E	TAVG	TSLG
Cool Papa Bell (Chicago American Giants), cf	4	0	1	0	0	0	0	0		
Parnell Woods (Cincinnati Buckeyes), 3b	3	1	1	0	1	0	1	0		
d) Marlin Carter (Memphis Red Sox), 3b	1	0	0	0	0	0	0	0		
Ted Strong (Kansas City Monarchs), rf	3	0	1	0	0	0	0	0		
Willard Brown (Kansas City Monarchs), lf	4	0	1	1	0	0	0	0		
Joe Greene (Kansas City Monarchs), c	4	0	0	0	0	0	1	0		
Buck O'Neil (Kansas City Monarchs), 1b	4	0	0	0	0	0	0	1		
Tommy Sampson (Birmingham Black Barons), 2b	3	0	0	0	0	0	0	1		
e) Art "Superman" Pennington (Chicago American Giants), ph	1	0	0	0	0	0	0	0		
T. J. Brown (Memphis Red Sox), ss	3	0	0	0	0	0	0	0		
f) Lloyd Davenport (Birmingham Black Barons), ph	1	0	0	0	0	0	0	0		
Hilton Smith (Kansas City Monarchs), p	1	0	0	0	0	0	0	0		
g) Fred Bankhead (Memphis Red Sox), pr	0	1	0	0	0	0	0	0		
Porter Moss (Memphis Red Sox), p	0	0	0	0	0	0	0	0		
h) Sam Jethroe (Cincinnati Buckeyes), ph	1	0	0	0	0	0	0	0		
Gene Bremer (Cincinnati Buckeyes), p	0	0	0	0	0	0	0	0		
Satchel Paige (Kansas City Monarchs), p	1	0	1	0	0	0	0	0		
Team Totals, Average & Slugging Pct.	34	2	5	1	1	0	2	2	.147	.235

d) Batted for Woods in 7th
e) Batted for Sampson in 9th
f) Batted for T. Brown in 9th
g) Ran for Smith in 3rd
h) Batted for Moss in 5th

East	001	010	102-5
West	001	001	000-2

PITCHER/TEAM	GS	IP	H	R	ER	K	BB	WP	HB	W	L
Gaines/BEG	1	3	1	1	0	0	0	0	0	0	0
Barnhill/NYC		3	2	1	1	4	1	0	0	0	0
B. Brown/PS		2/3	2	0	0	0	0	0	0	0	0
Day/NE		2 1/3	0	0	0	5	0	0	0	1	0
H. Smith/KCM	1	3	4	1	1	3	0	0	0	0	0
Moss/MRS		2	2	1	1	2	3	0	0	0	0
Bremer/CIB		1	0	0	0	1	0	0	0	0	0
Paige/KCM		3	5	3	1	2	2	0	0	0	1

BB—D. Wilson, Gibson (2), Patterson, Vargas, Strong
DP—Sampson to T. Brown to O'Neil (2)
LOB—East 8, West 6
SAC—Wells, S. Bankhead
SB—Patterson, D. Wilson (2), Wells, Vargas
East—Vic Harris (Mgr.); Coach Tex Burnett
West—W. S. Welch (Mgr.)
Umpires—Virgil Blueitt, Greenie Walls, Johnny Craig, Fred McCrary
Attendance—45,179   Paid—44,897   Time—2:58

CLEVELAND GAME REVIEWS

Satch Paige, Josh Gibson at Stadium on August 18

Source: *Cleveland Call-Post*, 15 August 1942

The greatest stars of Negro baseball will trot out into the Cleveland Municipal Stadium diamond on Tuesday night, the 18th, to stage an exhibition game for the Army-Navy Relief Fund. The game will start under the lights at 8:45 p.m.

The same teams which are to play at Chicago on Sunday, August 16th, the all star aggregations chosen from the teams of the Negro American League, and from the Negro National League, and called the East Team and the West Team will remain intact until they oppose each other the second time within two days, to produce the Stadium show next Tuesday.

Looking forward to one of the greatest sports spectacles ever arranged by Negroes in the history of Cleveland, the Army-Navy Benefit game on the 18th managed by Ernie Wright, owner of the Cleveland Buckeyes, Wilbur Hayes, secretary of the Buckeyes, and Cum Posey, generalissimo of the Homestead Grays, is expected to draw at least thirty thousand people to the lake-front amphitheater.

With Josh Gibson, mighty sultan of swat behind the bat, alternating with the sensational young Roy Campanella of the Baltimore Elite Giants, with Willie Wells, of the Newark Eagles at shortstop, with Sammy Hughes of Baltimore at second, with [Howard] Easterling of the Homestead Grays at third, and his team-mate, the hard hitting Buck Leonard, at first, the East's infield, every single one of them, is a hot prospect for the big leagues, if and when the ban on Negroes is actually lifted.

Then on the hill for the East will be Dave Barnhill of the New York Cuban Stars, who with Campanella and Hughes, is once again (this time on September 1st) slated to try-out with the Pittsburgh Pirates. Other hurlers who will appear for the powerful East aggregation are Barney Brown, of the Philly Stars, Ray Brown, of the Homestead Grays, [Jimmy]Hill of the Newark Eagles, and [Eugene] Smith of the New York Black Yankees, [Barney] Morris of the Cuban Stars, and [Jonas] Gaines and [Bill] Byrd of Baltimore.

The East team's outfielders include [Henry] Kimbro and [Bill] Wright of Baltimore, [Jerry] Benjamin of the Grays, [Ed] Stone and [Monte] Irvin of Newark, [Dan] Wilson and [Leslie] Green of the Yanks, [Gene] Benson of Philly, and [Tetelo] Vargas of the Cuban Stars.

Perhaps without so much hitting power but with an infield which ranks with the best combinations (black or white) in the world, the West team hopes to overcome the East's vaunted power at the plate.

Cleveland's own Parnell Woods will cover the hot corner for the West team. Woods is one of the men named by Negro American League president, Dr. Martin, as a player capable of playing big league ball if given a chance in the majors. With [Red] Parnell, either [Fred] Bankhead of Memphis, or Tommy Sampson of Birmingham will play second, Joe [John] O'Neil of Kansas City will be on first, and T. J. Brown of Memphis will camper at shortstop.

[Joe] Greene of the Kansas City Monarchs or "Double Duty" Radcliffe, of the Birmingham Black Barons will start the game behind the plate for the West, and in the outfield will be Willard Brown, Kansas City, Ted Strong, and [Sam] Jethroe, the second Cleveland Buckeye on the starting team the West will put on the field. Other gardeners are Neal Robinson, Memphis; [Lloyd] Davenport, Birmingham; [Art] Pennington, Chicago; [Bubba] Hyde, Memphis; "Cool Papa" Bell and [Jimmy] Crutchfield, Chicago.

In this tenth annual clash of the East and West all star team, W. S. Welch, manager of the Birmingham Black Barons, and tagged the "Black Connie Mack," gets his first shot at the management of a team in the classic, when he is chosen to guide the play for the West. As we go to press the East manager has not been selected, but either Vic Harris, of the Homestead Grays, or Tex Burnett, of the New York Black Yankees seems slated for the post.

All proceeds of the game go the Army-Navy Relief Fund . . . just one more effective bit of evidence that the Negro in sports is doing his bit to aid the war effort of the United States.

Editor's note: Paige did not appear in the Cleveland game because of a sore arm he experienced two days earlier when he pitched the final three innings in a losing effort at the Chicago all-star game. Not having his customary pop to his fastball, Paige had been rocked for five hits, one base-on-balls, and three runs as his West team was defeated, 5–2.

Paige may have been distracted in suffering his only East-West loss. Before he entered the game in the seventh inning, Paige addressed 45,000 fans, with players from both dugouts on the top step, from the public address system. In lieu of the customary "seventh-inning stretch," Paige offered his version of rejecting the major league contract, saying, "Ladies and Gentlemen: I would like to take this opportunity to deny a statement which the daily papers credited to me. I want you to know that I did not say anything against the use of Negro players in the big leagues. A reporter came and asked me what I thought about Negroes playing on major league teams. I told him I thought it was all right. He said, 'Satchel, do you think the white players would play with the colored?' I told him I thought they would, but that if they wouldn't it might be a good idea to put a complete Negro team in the majors."[39]

His epochal defensive speech, between innings, was unprecedented in black baseball. Proceeding to the mound amid cheers, Paige was undoubtedly shaken by the controversy, as he delivered his only subpar performance in all-star history. The year's top vote getter coached third base at the Cleveland all-star game.

East's All-Stars Whip West, 9–2

Controversy over Lights Delays Negro Benefit Game

Source: *Cleveland Plain Dealer,* 19 August 1942

The East romped to a 9-to-2 victory over the West in the Negro All-Star baseball game for the benefit of the Army and Navy Emergency Relief Funds before 10,791 spectators at the stadium last night.

The contest, which ended shortly before midnight, was delayed an hour by pre-game disputes about the lights to be used for the clash.

Under terms of a contract signed by Promoter Wilbur Hayes and the stadium, the game was to have been played under the lights used for football games and other events. Hayes said last night that he did not negotiate with Alva Bradley, Cleveland Indian president, for use of lights used in American league nocturnal games.

When the West team took the field the crowd, largest ever to see a Negro game in the stadium, clamored for the floodlights used at Indian games.

After a 25-minute delay, during which the players left the field, Dick Kroesen, chairman of the Army and Navy Relief Fund of Cuyahoga County, arranged to have the brighter lights turned on and guaranteed to pay the added expense for their usage.

The pre-game ceremonies were topped off by Mayor Frank J. Lausche, who pitched the first ball to Dr. J. B. Martin of Memphis, Tenn., president of the Negro American League.

The East sluggers pounced upon Eugene Bremer, Cleveland Buckeye mound ace, for five runs in the third inning and never were headed.

Sammy Jethroe, Cleveland Buckeye center fielder, and Parnell Woods, third baseman, each failed to get a hit, Jethroe in four times at bat and Woods in two trips to the plate.

Satchel Paige reported with a sore arm and was unable to twirl, but coached at third base for the West for three innings.

10,791 See East All-Stars

Game Score Is 9–2 and Army-Navy Relief Score Is $9,499

by John Fuster, *Call-Post* Sports Editor

Source: *Cleveland Call-Post,* 22 August 1942

Uncle Sam's Army and Navy Relief Fund was enriched by $9,499.04 Tuesday night, when the East all-star team beat the all-star outfit labeled the West 9–2 in nine innings of listless baseball, played under the brilliant lights of the Cleveland Municipal Stadium for the amusement of 10,791 paying spectators, and an undisclosed number who were "franked" through the gates.

The game, all proceeds of which were turned over to the Army and Navy Relief Fund, was arranged by a committee of which Ernie Wright, owner of the Cleveland Buckeyes and "angel" of baseball in Ohio, was chairman, and on which served Wilbur Hayes, business manager of the Buckeyes, and Cum Posey, high muckety-muck of the Homestead Grays, one of the oldest teams in organized baseball.

Pre-game proceedings at the Stadium, on this night of Negro baseball's great contribution to the Army and Navy Relief Fund, included ceremonies in which the local organizations of the Veterans of Foreign Wars, the American Legion, the Elks, Ohio Home Guards, Veterans of the Spanish American War, and Army and Navy figures participated. . . . Under the direction of civic minded Harry Walker, these ceremonies were smoothly conducted.

Probably the highlight of the demonstrations before the game was the superb rendition of the Star Spangled Banner by Mrs. Olive Thompson, soloist for "Wings Over Jordan." Surrounded by representatives of military organizations and city and county officials, as well as by owners of Negro baseball clubs and Negro National and American League officials, Mrs. Thompson thrilled the thousands standing at attention when she raised her glorious voice in the strains of the national anthem.

An interruption of proceedings, of several minutes duration, was brought about when the practice sessions for both the East and the West teams had ended, and the game was scheduled to get under way. From the press box it was evident that the lighting system ordinarily used at all night affairs at the Stadium (except for American League baseball games) was not adequate for the game, and it must have been noticeable out in the grandstands and on the playing field, because the players indicated an unwillingness to go into action under the comparatively dim lights, and the crowd in the stands backed them up.

But the lights used by the Indians in their American League games had never before been used by any other organization, for any purpose what-so-ever, and as far as can be learned, were installed by the Cleveland Baseball Club for the use of the Indians alone

Inspired perhaps by the zeal of the crowd, and himself perhaps convinced that possible injuries to the players might result from a game played without the brilliant lighting system ordinarily reserved for the Indians, Louis Felzer, managing editor of the *Cleveland Press,* "pulled strings" sufficiently hard to switch on the current of the huge, "day-light" electric lighting system which the Indians and only the Indians had hitherused

The crowd gave Felzer a hand when he said, "Surely these stars of the Negro baseball world, playing for the benefit of the Army-Navy Relief, deserve the same lighting facilities for the game which the American League teams have at their disposal when they play here at the Stadium."

Once the lights were on, the game began, and except for the brilliance of the Stadium lights, there was not much brightness in the game put on display at the lakefront amphitheater Tuesday night.

None of the three Cleveland Buckeyes for whom this writer and the *Call-Post* have been trying to get a try-out with the Cleveland Indians covered himself with the proverbial glory, though Parnell Woods, Buckeye and All-Star West team third baseman, and Sammy Jethroe playing centerfield for the same teams, scored the West's only runs.

Eugene Bremer, whom this faithful correspondent has likened to the great Stanley Coveleski, Polish pitcher of the Indians on the World Championship 1920 team, walked four [three] men and allowed four clean hits [in the third inning], on which five runs were scored, before Mathis, of the Memphis Red Sox was sent to his rescue. The barrage came in the first half of the third, and put the game on ice for the East.

Game at Stadium Was Second Loss for West Outfit

Source: *Cleveland Call-Post*, 22 August 1942

In bowing to the East at the Stadium Tuesday night, the West all-star baseball team lost its second fray in two weeks to the powerful aggregation representing the Negro National League. The first game, played at Chicago on Sunday, attracted 48,000 fans, saw the East win out in the latter innings after the aging Satchel Paige had taken over the hurling for the West. The final score was 5–2, but when Paige took over in the 7th, it was tied at 2–2.

Parnell Woods, third baseman of the Cleveland Buckeyes, was the batting hero of the West team in the Chicago game, driving in one run in the first inning, and scoring the other himself, after he had tripled in the sixth. Eugene Bremer, Buckeye pitcher, got by very well in the sixth inning and was allowed to pitch. He struck out two, and Vargas was retired by W. Brown, who made a stirring catch of a drive to left. Sammy Jethroe, the other Buckeye in the West all-star line-up, was inserted into the game in the seventh, to pinch hit for Pennington. [Referring to the Chicago game.]

Uncle Sam's Army and Navy Relief Fund is richer by $9,499.04, a couple of dozen baseball players have another game to their credit, and 10,791 paying spectators, besides an untold number who got by on "franks."

33. The East squad hammered the Western fellows, 9–2. From left to right: George Scales, Big Jim West, Buck Leonard, Felton Snow, Sam Bankhead, Johnny Wright, Jud Wilson, Henry Spearman, Henry Kimbro, Gene Benson, Jerry Benjamin, Pat Patterson, Barney Brown, Bill Byrd, Matt Carlisle, Josh Gibson, and Robert Clarke. Courtesy of the Papers of Art Carter, Moorland-Spingarn Research Center, Howard University.

AUGUST 18, 1942, TUESDAY
MUNICIPAL STADIUM, CLEVELAND (GAME 2 OF 2)

EAST	AB	R	H	D	T	HR	BI	E	TAVG	TSLG
Dan Wilson (New York Black Yankees), lf	6	0	1	1	0	0	0	0		
Sam Bankhead (Homestead Grays), 2b	4	2	2	0	0	0	0	1		
Willie Wells (Newark Eagles), ss	4	1	3	3	0	0	2	1		
Josh Gibson (Homestead Grays), c	4	1	1	0	0	0	1	1		
Bill Wright (Baltimore Elite Giants), rf	4	1	2	1	0	0	1	0		
Jim West (Philadelphia Stars), 1b	4	1	1	0	0	0	0	0		
Andy Patterson (Philadelphia Stars), 3b	4	1	1	0	0	0	1	0		
Tetelo Vargas (New York Cubans), cf	2	0	1	0	0	0	2	0		
a) Lennie Pearson (Newark Eagles), cf	1	0	0	0	0	0	1	0		
Gene Smith (New York Black Yankees), p	3	1	1	0	0	0	0	0		
Jonas Gaines (Baltimore Elite Giants), p	1	0	0	0	0	0	0	0		
Dave Barnhill (New York Cubans), p	0	0	0	0	0	0	0	0		
Herberto Blanco (New York Cubans), 2b	1	1	0	0	0	0	0	0		
Leon Day (Newark Eagles), p	1	0	0	0	0	0	1	0		
Team Totals, Average & Slugging Pct.	39	9	13	5	0	0	9	3	.333	.462

a) Batted for Vargas in 5th

WEST	AB	R	H	D	T	HR	BI	E	TAVG	TSLG
Sam Jethroe (Cincinnati Buckeyes), cf	5	1	1	0	0	0	0	0		
Parnell Woods (Cincinnati Buckeyes), 3b	2	0	0	0	0	0	0	0		
Ted Strong (Kansas City Monarchs), rf	3	0	2	0	0	0	0	1		
Willard Brown (Kansas City Monarchs), lf	4	0	2	0	0	0	2	0		
Joe Greene (Kansas City Monarchs), c	2	0	0	0	0	0	0	1		
Tommy Sampson (Birmingham Black Barons), 2b	3	0	2	0	0	0	0	1		
Buck O'Neil (Kansas City Monarchs), 1b	4	0	0	0	0	0	0	0		
Ralph Wyatt (Chicago American Giants), ss	1	1	1	0	0	0	0	1		
b) James "Cool Papa" Bell (Chicago American Giants), ph-cf	2	0	1	0	0	0	0	0		
Gene Bremer (Cincinnati Buckeyes), p	0	0	0	0	0	0	0	0		
Verdell Mathis (Memphis Red Sox), p	2	0	0	0	0	0	0	0		
Alvin "Bubber" Gipson (Birmingham Black Barons), p	2	0	0	0	0	0	0	0		
Marlin Carter (Memphis Red Sox), 3b	1	0	0	0	0	0	0	1		
Fred Bankhead (Memphis Red Sox), 2b	0	0	0	0	0	0	0	1		
c) "Superman" Pennington (Chicago American Giants), ph-cf	1	0	0	0	0	0	0	0		
Team Totals, Average & Slugging Pct.	32	2	9	0	0	0	2	6	.281	.281

b) Batted for Wyatt in the 7th
c) Batted for Bankhead in the 8th

East	005	011	011-9
West	002	000	000-2

PITCHER/TEAM	GS	IP	H	R	ER	K	BB	WP	HB	W	L
Bremer/CIB	1	2 2/3	6	5	5	1	3	1	1	0	1
Mathis/MRS		3 1/3	4	2	0	2	0	0	0	0	0
Gipson/BBB		3	3	2	1	1	2	1	0	0	0
Smith/NYBY	1	3	3	2	0	2	3	0	0	1	0
Gaines/BEG		2	1	0	0	2	0	0	0	0	0
Barnhill/NYC		2	2	0	0	2	0	0	0	0	0
Day/NE		2	3	0	0	5	2	0	0	0	0

BB—West, Gibson (2), Patterson, Wyatt, Greene, Woods, Blanco, Pennington, Pearson
DP—Blanco to Wells
HBP—Wells by Bremer
LOB—East 10, West 10
SAC—Wright, West
SB—Patterson (2)
East—Vic Harris (Mgr.)
West—Coach Satchel Paige (3b), W. S. Welch (Mgr.)
Umpires—Harry Walker, Johnny Craig, Fred McCrary, Banaham
Attendance—10,791   Time—

MEMPHIS GAME REVIEW

All-Star Baseball Game in Memphis, Oct. 4

Source: *Chicago Defender,* 3 October 1942

Memphis— The All-Star baseball game scheduled for Sunday, Oct. 4 at Russwood Park, will be played between the stars of the Negro National League, managed by Homer "Goose" Curry, and the stars of the Negro American League, managed by Larry Brown of the Memphis Red Sox

Those in the Negro National League outfield are Homer Curry, centerfield; Red Parnell of the Philadelphia Stars, leftfield; and [Ennis] Whatley of the Homestead Grays, rightfield. There will be a contest between the two flashy first basemen, Jelly Taylor of the Memphis Red Sox and Big James West of the Philadelphia Stars.

The starting pitcher for the Negro National League All-Stars will be Gaines of the Baltimore Elite Giants with Verdell Mathis of the Memphis Red Sox on the mound for the Negro American League All-Stars.

Starting line-up for the Negro American League All-Stars is: (Cool) Papa Bell in leftfield; Parnell Woods, third base; Jimmy Crutchfield, rightfield; Neal Robinson, centerfield; Jelly Taylor, first base; T. J. Brown, shortstop; Fred Bankhead, second base; Verdell Mathis, pitching and Larry Brown, caching. Candy Jim Taylor will coach. Thomas T. Wilson, president of the Negro National League, arrived this week and has promised Homer Curry all the cooperation needed to beat the Negro American League All-Stars. Dr. B. B. Martin has selected the cream of the crop from the Negro American League for his manager, Larry Brown.

All of the players of the American League All-Stars have taken part in the annual East-West classic in Chicago. The game will get underway at 3 o'clock.

Editor's note: A third all-star game, in Memphis, was rained out. It was never rescheduled. After a tremendous showing of 45,000 fans in Chicago and a disappointing crowd of 10,000 in Cleveland, league officials were perhaps aspiring to finish the season financially sound with a southern appearance.

1942 VOTING RESULTS: 3,958,874

P

Satchel Paige	236,672
Hilton Smith	157,823
Verdell Mathis	123,657
Gene Bremer	101,902
John Markham	87,328
Dave Barnhill	56,053
Barney Brown	49,538
Ray Brown	46,838
Jimmy Hill	46,002
Gene Smith	45,008
Jonas Gaines	31,265
Leon Day	30,142
Barney Morris	24,050
Bill Byrd	23,112
Terris McDuffie	20,333

C

Double Duty Radcliffe	102,565
Larry Brown	81,825
Josh Gibson	52,822
Roy Campanella	49,376
Johnny Hayes	24,104
Charles Ruffin	20,366
Clarence Palm	20,251

1B

Buck O'Neil	148,390
Jelly Taylor	99,028
Archie Ware	81,274
Jim West	54,351
Buck Leonard	34,122
Lennie Pearson	30,006
Showboat Thomas	21,563
George Scales	16,001
James Starks	11,500

2B

Tommy Sampson	124,506
Fred Bankhead	92,672
Billy Horne	83,829
Sammy T. Hughes	35,026
Dickie Seay	33,459
Lick Carlisle	29,201
Blue Perez	25,904
Harry Williams	24,322

3B

Parnell Woods	106,332
Alec Radcliffe	89,467
Marlin Carter	77,824
Howard Easterling	39,299
Felton Snow	31,607
Henry Spearman	20,858

SS

Willie Wells	55,096
Pee Wee Butts	39,068
Bus Clarkson	38,705
Rabbit Martinez	31,501
Sam Bankhead	30,553

OF

Willard Brown	133,572
Ted Strong	120,997
Sam Jethroe	104,728
Cool Papa Bell	99,203
Lloyd Davenport	87,442
Bubba Hyde	81,924
Art Pennington	81,910
Bill Wright	59,896
Jerry Benjamin	49,201
Dan Wilson	48,308
Tetelo Vargas	45,561
Henry Kimbro	43,289
Ed Stone	43,164

Grand Total of recorded votes, 1933 to 1942: 42,587,886 votes

1943

African-American Dr. Selma Burke is commissioned to sculpt a bust of President Franklin D. Roosevelt. Her profile image would later be used on the Roosevelt Dime.

Delegates at the Professional Golfers Association (PGA) annual meeting vote to limit membership to whites only.

The controversial radio show *Amos 'N Andy* is canceled. George Gershwin's folk story *Porgy and Bess* opens on Broadway.

Milk costs 31 cents a half-gallon, 10 pounds of potatoes costs 46 cents, and 43 cents would bring home the bacon. A loaf of bread costs 9 cents.

The first major league nighttime all-star game is played at Shibe Park in Philadelphia. The American League wins, 5–3, behind Bobby Doerr's three-run homer.

The All-American Girls Professional Baseball League is established with four teams. The league has a "ladies' agreement" prohibiting black women from playing. The league would last until 1954.

LEAGUE DEVELOPMENT

After much controversy over the team's nickname, the Negro American League granted Syd Pollock and his Cincinnati Clowns a franchise. The franchise was granted under the stipulation that there would be no painted faces or "Liza Jane" tap dancing acts on the field. Also, there would be no minstrel acts to follow field play. While celebrating the arrival of a new team to the city, fans expressed no desire to see a Barnum & Bailey sideshow or an "Uncle Tom" tomfoolery show before or during the game. Cincinnati fans requested Pollock to change the team's nickname and suggested a contest with a $25 prize.[1]

Without hesitation, Cum Posey gave his opinion on the subject, saying, "[Abe] Saperstein [co-owner of the Birmingham Black Barons and other black independent teams] and Pollock have less respect for organized colored baseball than Stalin has for Hitler."[2]

The biggest concern at the annual meeting was travel restrictions necessitated by World War II. The Office of Defense Transportation approved unlimited gas rations for bus travel for teams in the major leagues and the Negro Leagues. Now, with an abundance of gas, the owners' only obstacle to fielding a team was a shortage of nondrafted players.

Several former and future East-West players served in the military. The Homestead Grays lost Ray Brown and Vic Harris to employment in defense plants, while the Grays' Bob Thurman (service years, 1942–45), Howard Easterling (1943–45), Wilmer Fields (1944–45), Roy Welmaker (1942–44), and Johnny Wright (1944–45, Navy) were drafted.

The Kansas City Monarchs lost East-West performers Willard Brown (1944–45), Joe Greene (1943–45), Connie Johnson (1943–45), Buck O'Neil (1943–45, Navy), Ted Strong (1943–45, Navy), Hank Thompson (1944–45), and Jesse Williams (1943–45).

The war effort cost the Newark Eagles several East-West stars, including Max Manning (1942–45), Leon Day (1944–45), Larry Doby (1943–45), and Monte Irvin (1943–45).

The Philadelphia Stars saw all-stars James Buster "Bus" Clarkson (1943–45), Jake Dunn (1942–45), and Pat Patterson (1942–45) join the service.

All-Star pitchers Joe Black (1943–45) and Jonas Gaines (1943–45), first baseman Red Moore (1941–45), and second baseman Sammy T. Hughes (1943–46) from the Baltimore Elite Giants joined the war effort.

The Birmingham Black Barons lost Dan Bankhead to the Marines (1943–45), while the Chicago American Giants lost outfielders Jimmie Crutchfield and Lonnie Summers to the Army. Other East-West draftees included Billy Horne (1945) from the Cleveland Buckeyes, pitchers Preacher Henry (1944–45), and Jim "Fireball" Cohen (1942–46) from the Indy Clowns; Olan "Jelly" Taylor (1943–45) from the Memphis Red Sox; Dickie Seay (1944–45) and Eugene Smith (1943–45) from the New York Black Yankees; and Johnny "Schoolboy" Taylor (1942–44) from the New York Cubans.

With the league losing several top-flight players, many teams entertained promotional ideas. For example, the Philadelphia Stars solicited from various local merchants and businesspeople prizes for their Opening Day game. Among the prizes were the following:

First home run—$10 on a suit of clothes
First triple—Pair of pants
First double—Louisville Slugger bat
First single—One box of cigars
First sacrifice—Complete shoe-repair job
First stolen base—One carton of cigarettes
First double play—Cap and slippers
Most strikeouts by a pitcher—Case of soda pop
Most runs batted in—Ten tickets to the Royal Theatre [3]

RACE RELATIONS

Washington Senators owner Clark Griffith, who rented Griffith Stadium to the Homestead Grays, voiced his opinion on the integration issue, saying: "It is my opinion that the Negroes should lend all of their efforts to developing their own National and American leagues. These leagues now have a substantial following and if properly organized and officered, could eventually take their place in the annals of baseball. It is my belief we should have white baseball leagues and colored baseball leagues." [4]

Realizing that Griffith's concerns were more financial than benevolent, the black press questioned his true intentions. Griffith had signed other ethnic players, including Cubans, but had never sought out a black player. With the United States at war, Major League Baseball was in desperate need of players to fill key roster positions. Wendell Smith wrote his views of Griffith's comments, stating: "Griffith is one of the big league owners who prefers to go outside the borders of these United States and bring in players, rather than hire American citizens of color. He has so many foreigners on this team it is necessary to have an interpreter, and if you ever hear this conglomeration of personalities talking to each other in the airport, you'd swear you were sojourning in Madrid, Lisbon, or Havana." [5] The Senators would finish 13 1/2 games behind the American League champion New York Yankees. Arguably, their won-lost record of 84-69 (.549) could have improved with the addition of Homestead players like Josh Gibson, Sam Bankhead, and Buck Leonard.

Toward year's end, at the request of the Negro Newspaper Publishers' Association, major league team owners met at the Roosevelt Hotel in December to discuss the integration issue. The keynote speaker was Ira F. Lewis, president of the *Pittsburgh Courier,* who pleaded his case for admission of Negro Leagues players into major league organizations. Other notables included John Sengstacke, from the *Chicago Defender;* Howard Murphy, secretary of the Negro Publishers' Association (NPA) and business manager for the *Baltimore Afro-American;* and singer, activist, and Rutgers athlete Paul Robeson.

It was reported that 44 major league officials attended the meeting, including Branch Rickey (Brooklyn Dodgers); William Benswanger and Sam Watters (Pittsburgh Pirates); Lou McAvoy, National League vice president; Tom Yawkey (Boston Red Sox); Harry Grabiner (Chicago White Sox); Alva Bradley and Roger Peckinpaugh (Cleveland Indians); George Weiss (New York Yankees); Jack Zeller (Detroit Tigers); Connie Mack (Philadelphia A's); Bill DeWitt and Don Barnes (St. Louis Browns); Clark Griffith (Washington Senators); Leo Bondy (New York Giants); Phil Wrigley (Chicago Cubs); Bob Carpenter and Herb Pennock (Philadelphia Phillies); Warren Giles (Cincinnati Reds); and Bob Quinn (Boston Braves).

Commissioner Landis opened the meeting by restating his position on the integration issue that "clearly understood that there is no rule, nor to my knowledge, has there ever been, formal or informal, or any understanding, written or unwritten, subterranean or sub-anything, against the hiring of Negroes in the major leagues." [6]

He concluded his speech, passing the buck to the owners, by saying, "I can't speak for the owners at all. Really there is absolutely nothing I can tell you." Having stated his position, or nonposition, on the issue, he introduced actor-singer-activist Paul Robeson, who had earned All-American football honors and was Phi Beta Kappa at Rutgers University. Robeson challenged baseball to change its apartheid policy and beseeched the owners to hire Negro players. [7]

Sengstacke, the next speaker, said that the color line was "neither wise nor practical." The so-called "gentlemen's agreement" was a slap in the face of democracy. The next speaker, Lewis, was not shy in voicing his opinions. He downplayed the excuses used by team owners that major league players would refuse to play against Negro Leaguers. In the Wendell Smith interviews conducted in 1939, players and club officials had clearly shown an open-minded attitude toward race relations and had welcomed the talented black player into their competitive environment. Lewis reminded the owners that blacks had been competing with and against whites on the college level with few racial incidents. Lewis also addressed the dire issue of travel and public accommodations, stating that black singers and musicians often traveled with white supporting casts without intervention from Jim Crow authorities. He also addressed fears of having blacks on the ball club during the journey south for spring training. Lewis suggested that training could be held in Cuba and other Latin American countries, such as the Brooklyn Dodgers did in 1941 and 1942 with practices in Havana. [8]

Lewis concluded by saying that Landis's comments about no barriers against blacks was completely untrue and that there indeed existed the unwritten principle against hiring black players. Landis responded forthwith to the accusation and repeated his opening remark that "no rule, formal or informal, existed against the hiring of Negroes." Lewis graciously bowed at the waist and responded diplomatically: "But Judge Landis, we believe that there is a tacit understanding, there is a gentlemen's agreement that no Negroes players be hired." [9]

As the room fell silent, Lewis continued his presentations by expressing his personal feelings: "I feel the bitter pangs of sorrow and disappointment over the unfair and unjust attitude of organized baseball toward Americans of color." Lewis challenged team owners to "allow the National Pastime to become a game for all the boys in America." [10]

Following Lewis, Howard Murphy from the *Baltimore Afro-American* issued a four-point request to the owners:

1. That immediate steps be taken to accept qualified colored players in the framework of organized baseball.
2. That the process by which players are graduated from c, b, a, aa, and aaa teams to the majors be applied, without prejudice or discrimination, to colored players.
3. That the same system by which players are selected from schools, sandlots, semi-pro, and other clubs be used in selected colored players.
4. That a joint statement be issued by this body declaring colored eligible for trials and permanent places on your respective teams. [11]

After Murphy's edict, Landis called for a question-and-answer session. Not one of the 44 officials responded. When the meeting was adjourned, team owners in unison offered the same sympathetic retort as before: "Each club is entirely free to employ Negro players to any and all extent it pleases. The matter is solely for each club's decision, without restriction whatsoever." [12]

Ford Frick, National League president, offered his opinion: "I really think they [the owners] were impressed by the presentation. But I can't say what will happen. The men who came here to present the problem to us did an excellent job." [13]

In rebuttal arguments, Landis emphasized what action, if any, his office would take: "It will be taken under consideration." [14]

However, a few months later, Grays owner Cum Posey offered his view of the meeting: "A group of men [Negro Newspaper Publishers' Association] without consulting one person who had their life savings invested in colored baseball, asked for a meeting presided over by Judge Landis and attended by the owners of the sixteen Major Leagues clubs, and at this meeting asked for the privilege of giving away all the stars of the various Negro baseball clubs, backing up their argument by stating if the white major leagues do this they will draw all of the colored fans who now attend Negro games, citing the annual East-West game as an example of crowds who attend Negro games. If that is not offering a whole Negro enterprise to white businessmen, then what is it? That would automatically put organized Negro baseball out of business." [15]

Yet, Posey wanted to make it clear he was not against the integration of baseball: "If an owner of any Major League club would write to the Homestead Grays for an option on any player on the Grays' team we would be glad to give the players an opportunity to improve themselves financially, but no man wants someone else giving his property away." [16]

ALL-STAR REVIEW

In an attempt to capitalize on Satchel Paige's fame, a four-team doubleheader was scheduled at Wrigley Field in Chicago on July 18. The four teams — the Birmingham Black Barons, the Cincinnati Clowns, the Memphis Red Sox, and the New York Cubans — would celebrate "Satchel Paige Day." The second game would feature the Black Barons, winners of the first half, against the league's newest entry, the Cincinnati Clowns, who were managed by Fred Wilson.

It was indeed Paige's day. Before roughly 20,000 fans, Paige hurled five hitless innings, fanning seven and walking two, while not allowing a ball to be hit out of the infield. His

Red Sox team beat the Cubans, 1–0, as Memphis's Porter "Ankleball" Moss gave up only two hits over the last four frames.

Once again, Satchel Paige's talent was used by a team with whom he did not have a contract. As the property of the Kansas City Monarchs, Paige was allowed to pitch this promotional event in a neutral setting. Additionally, neither the Red Sox nor the Cubans claimed Wrigley Field as their home field. Billed as "Satchel Paige Day," the event was a financial boost for the Red Sox. The office of the league president, J. B. Martin, was based in Chicago, and Martin's brothers, W. S. and B. B., were owners of the Memphis Red Sox. The event was also a precursor to the East-West all-star game; Paige and Dave Barnhill, who pitched for the Cubans, were currently the leading vote getters for starting pitchers.

Later, in September, in the Eastern Negro National League, the Newark Eagles and the Philadelphia Stars combined talents to play the league champion Homestead Grays in a three-game series in Philadelphia. In the first game, Leon Day of the Stars-Eagles team beat himself when he walked in the winning run in the seventh inning. Day had only given up four hits in suffering a 2–1 defeat by the Grays.

The next day, Sunday, the Grays swept a doubleheader, winning the first game, 7–6, behind the pitching of Big Edsall Walker. The second game was dominated by Ray Brown, who gave up three hits in shutting out the all-star team, 9–0.

GAME REVIEWS

Wyatt, Martinez, Starting Shortstops in 11th East vs. West Game on Aug. 1

Source: *Chicago Defender,* 24 July 1943

Davy Wyatt, the Chicago American Giants' shortstop, and little Horacio Martinez, the Cuban infielder, led the poll for shortstop in the 1943 East versus West game classic to be played at Comiskey Park, Chicago, on Sunday afternoon, August 1.

Chicago fans got a taste of what they may expect in the East versus West game on last Sunday, when 25,000 saw Satchel Paige and the Memphis Red Sox turn back the New York Cubans, 1 to 0, in one of the greatest games ever played in Chicago.

And these 25,000 saw Paige stop the Cubans cold for five innings, allowing no hits and striking out seven. They also watched Martinez play a whale of a game at short and watched Dave "Impo" Barnhill lose a tough game after holding the Sox to three hits, none after the third inning. Barnhill, mentioned last year as worthy a tryout with major league clubs, fanned seven.

Last year Barnhill pitched three innings against the West. Paige has seen service in several East versus West games, sometimes as a member of the East team and in 1942 as a hurler for the West although each time he was sent in the East was so far out in front he couldn't overtake them.

Pitchers Star as West Beats East in Thriller

51,000 Present as Westerners Win at Comiskey Park, 2–1

by Wendell Smith

Source: *Pittsburgh Courier,* 7 August 1943

Once again the sun shines brilliantly on the baseball front in the rugged Golden West! And . . . there is no joy in the staid old East as its tattered banner is ripped and lowered from the mast of baseball supremacy. Here today in historic Comiskey Park a great team from the Wild and Wooly West rode high and mighty over a power team from the East in the 11th annual East-West classic. A roaring throng 51,723 saw the West come back again after losing three straight years, and defeat the East, 2 to 1.

It was a great ball game. One packed with thrills and surprises. One cast in a setting as colorful and picturesque as any movie saga. One that will go down in history in brilliant lettering and stand out in bold relief until the pages upon which it is written wither in the dust of time.

Overloaded with power hitters . . . mighty men of swat who were expected to blast the East to victory with towering drives to the distant regions of this spacious ball park the satellites of the National league lacked their vaunted punch today.

LEONARD HOMERS

Only one of these clouting giants, Buck Leonard, famed first-sacker of the Homestead Grays, lived up to expectations. With two out in the ninth and most of the record-breaking throng, wending its way toward the exits. Leonard poled a terrific drive into the right-field stands for the East's only run.

Up until the time Leonard's tremendous smash went screaming into the stands, the East had made but one hit. A single by little Horacio Martinez, Cuban shortstop in the sixth, was the only other hit [there were also hits by Gibson and Easterling].

SENSATIONAL HURLING

For eight and two-thirds innings the courageous moundsmen of the West had the Indian sign on the Easterners. The combined pitching talents of Leroy (Satchel) Paige, Gready McKinnis and Theolic Smith were too much for the East. And . . . but for that mighty blow in the ninth, the East would have been held scoreless all the way.

PAIGE TOPS

During the three innings the worked, Paige was great. He simply reared back and fired that binding fast ball at the big sluggers from the East and sent them back in order. He held them scoreless and hitless. A walk to Josh Gibson was all he gave the East, and four went down via the strikeout route. He fanned Kimbro, Leonard, Bankhead and Bell. Pearson's short fly to right field was the only ball hit out of the infield.

Satchel was too good . . . and the National league sluggers were glad when he walked off the field amid the thunderous ovation of fifty-one thousand fans. After he had doubled to left in the third for the West's only extra base hit of the game, he left as he came—proud and cocky—still the most colorful player in baseball—still the "Great One."

MCKINNIS TOUGH

In the East thought they were going to fare any better with Birmingham's Gready McKinnis, who took up where sadly mistaken. The big left-hander pitched right in Satchel's footsteps as he mowed 'em down effectively with a good hook and blasting fast ball. He pitched the fourth, fifth and sixth. A sharp single to centerfield by Martinis [Martinez] was all the East could accomplish.

WEST SCORES

Meantime, while Paige and McKinnis were baffling the Eastern sluggers, the West scored twice. The first run came in the second inning. Neal Robinson walked on four of Dave (Impo) Barnhill's pitches. O'Neil sacrificed him to second, and plucky Tommy Sampson, Birmingham's sensational second-baseman, brought Robinson home with a single in short right field. Sammy Bankhead and Len Pearson, second baseman and right fielder, respectively, each made a gallant try, but the ball fell between them.

Willard Brown, great centerfielder of Kansas City scored the winning run in the fourth. He stole second after punching a single to center and went to third on an infield out. O'Neil then hit one back to the box and Brown came romping home on the putout at first base. Buck Leonard tried to nail the fleet-footed Brown at the plate, but Willard beat the throw.

And that was the ball game right here. With the exception of a dramatic moment in the ninth, the West was never in danger. Theolic Smith of Cleveland took over the hurling chores in the seventh and did as well as his predecessors until two were out in the ninth. After Smith had set down Bell and Benjamin and only had one hitter to face, the fireworks started.

Buck Leonard smashed a two and two pitch 352 feet into the right-field stands. Then came Josh Gibson, the home run king himself . . . and the crowd of 51,000 settled back in their seats . . . for anything could happen now. Gibson didn't hit for the circuit, but he did rattle a whistling drive off a Jess Williams' shine at shortstop. If Josh's smash had been in the air, it would have still been going yet.

Then came Howard Easterling. He singled to right, sending Gibson to second and for the first time the East was really in the ball game. Smith was weakening on the mound, and the vaunted power of the East was about to explode.

At this point Manager Frank Duncan gave Smith the heave-ho sign and called in the veteran pitcher of Memphis, Porter Moss.

Vic Harris, manager of the East, then pinched hit for Leonard Pearson of Newark. The stage was set for the East with Gibson on second, Easterling on first, and a record-breaking throng expecting anything to happen.

But Valiant Victor wasn't able to come through. He fled to center and the ball game was over. And once again the sun is shining brilliantly on the baseball front in the rugged, Golden West!

Through the Years: Past—Present—Future

by Fay Young

Source: *Chicago Defender,* 7 August 1943

For the first time, the working newspapermen were forced to pay a tax on tickets Sunday at the eleventh annual East versus West game. Nobody should have to pay tax on working press tickets—and no one should have forgotten to have working press tickets printed.

As we have stated for several years we strenuously object to people holding press tickets who aren't working newspapermen or newspaperwomen. That still goes! Complimentary seats should not have the word "press" on them. Furthermore, everybody suddenly becomes a "sport writer" and every one who hold a press ticket demands to get in the press box. And how can you get 900 people in a place built to seat 46?

Many people working for the newspapers, other than in the sport department, had press tickets and they felt they had as much right to sit down in the coolest and airiest spot in hot Comiskey Park Sunday as those who were there to write about the game.

The press coop was so jammed in 1942 that $250 worth of glass was broken and other damages occurred.

This year, the Comiskey Park management didn't want that to happen. The result was people holding press tickets and who were "scoring the game" didn't get in the coop and lots of folks are still cussing us out because we were placed in charge up there.

More too, real newspapermen don't lug their sons, daughters, in-laws, woman friends into a press box or row. They just don't belong there. They keep up a constant chatter and interfere with those writing telegraph copy.

A few weeks ago we decided it was about time to call attention to the uniforms of the Chicago American Giants who appeared on the field on the game against Cleveland with three different kinds of dirty uniforms. Later we had to say that one Alex Radcliffe got unruly and took a dozen pokes at Umpire Virgil Blueitt who is about the most even-tempered man we ever knew.

For all this we got "kicked in the pants." We were against the Chicago American Giants, the Negro American league in particular and the owner of the club. But when Kansas City Monarchs played here on Sunday, July 25, the Chicago American Giants trotted out on the field all dressed up in new uniforms and looking like a real ball club. In fact, the club took two games from Kansas City, which ran the home streak of Chicago wins to five. We then said the Giants looked nice. If we were wrong why were the new suits bought?

And since we took a poke at Mister Alex, in these columns, Mister Alex is behaving like a gentleman and is playing better baseball. All of which goes to show that sometimes it is good for folks to know that sports columnists are the public's watchdogs. And they are not always going to something honeylike about a club when that club isn't playing major league ball and at the same time charging major league prices.

They had a swell ball game Sunday in the West 2 to 1 win over the East. And since they had a swell ball game, we write it that way. But Lord help them if they had played a bad game because 52,000 would have been expecting us to say right where the trouble was and nothing else. And we don't propose to "let our public down."

We felt Jess Williams of the Kansas City Monarchs was about the best shortstop in the Negro American league and that Sampson of Birmingham was best to start at second. We knew Alex Radcliffe would start at third because, Parnell Woods, Cleveland third sacker and manager, had been bothered with a bad shoulder. Then it came to first base. We openly said John O'Neil of Kansas City was a better fielder on ground balls than Pep Young of Chicago by that we had nothing against Chicago's Ralph Wyatt or Young either.

We wanted a winning West team out there for the sole reason that the game is played in Chicago, supported by Chicago fans and these Chicago fans didn't relish "their dog" being kicked around three years in a row by the East team.

Manager Duncan agreed with us. Willard Brown, Kansas City outfielder, was a fixture in centerfield. Davenport, Chicago, was switched from centerfield to rightfield and Neal Robinson, Memphis, was in left. Even then, with Paige pitching and Ted Radcliffe, the Chicago manager, catching, the East looked stronger on paper.

It was a great game, well played, well officiated. The promotion was colossal.

Satchel Paige and West Take East into Camp

2 to 1, as 51,000 Watch

Buck Leonard's Homer in Ninth is Game's Feature

by Frank Young

Source: *Chicago Defender,* 7 August 1943

Satchel Paige was in his glory Sunday. The ace hurler of the Kansas City Monarchs toed the mound for the West in the eleventh annual East versus West All-Star game and was the winning pitcher.

And the 51,723 fans who came out on the perfect afternoon for baseball—the largest crowd ever to attend one of the annual East-West classic—more than got their money's worth. They saw the West triumph over a strong East team 2 to 1. They saw the East's heavy hitters held three innings by Paige without a hit; held two more innings by Gready McKinnis of the Birmingham Black Barons without a hit; later one lone hit off McKinnis—a single by Horacio Martinez—in the fifth [sixth]; held to no hits off [Theolic] Fireball Smith of the Cleveland Buckeyes for two and two-thirds innings and then they got busy.

With two out in the ninth Smith blew up like the Titanic. The East's bats swung into action. Trailing 2 to 0 with what looked like the last ebb of life leaving them, those Negro National leaguers threw a scare into the West, gave the fans a thrill of their lives and drove Smith to the showers.

THAT NINTH INNING

That ninth inning will go down in history as a most determined effort, on the part of the East, falling short. It was a jam-packed inning, which saw Buck Leonard, the Homestead Gray's first sacker, golfball one of Smith's offerings into the right field deck of Comiskey Park for the only home run of the 1943 game. The West elected to pitch to Josh Gibson, the .550 batter of the Homestead Grays. Gibson smashed one—it was really tagged—at Jess Williams, Kansas City Monarch shortstop. Williams tried to field the ball and almost got his hand torn off. Howard Easterling, Homestead Grays' second sacker, who was playing third for the East, singled sharply to right and Manager Frank Duncan waved for Porter Moss to come to Smith's rescue.

Moss couldn't locate the plate on his first two efforts, then, he brought up that under-hand offering for a strike on Vic Harris, manager, who batted for Leonard Pearson of Mrs. Effa Manley's Newark Eagles. You couldn't say the East went down swinging because they went down trying to hammer the ball out of the lot. Harris ended the game by skying out to Willard Brown, the Kansas City Monarchs centerfielder.

That jam-packed session was a humdinger. That ninth started with James "Cool Papa" Bell being robbed of a hit by Lloyd "Ducky" Davenport, the Chicago American Giants centerfielder, who was playing right field. Jerry Benjamin, Homestead Grays batted for Juan Vargas of the Cuban Stars. Tommy Sampson dug Benjamin's roller out of the dirt and whipped the ball to John O'Neil, Kansas City Monarchs, at first to beat Benjamin by a step. Then all hell broke loose and the East scored its only run, had the tying run on second and the winning run on first. Those runs were the ones the East needed and didn't get—they were still on the bases when the last out was made.

Satchel Paige started the game for the West against David "Impo" Barnhill of the New York Cubans who took the mound for the East. Paige allowed nary a hit in the three innings he worked. He threw the third strike past Henry Kimbro of the Baltimore Elites in the first inning for the second out and caused the Western fans to stand up and yell with glee when he fanned Buck Leonard of the Grays for the third out.

Gibson got on first via a walk to start the second. Josh went to second on a passed ball after Easterling of the Grays and Pearson of the Eagles had been easy outs. Sammy Bankhead, another Grays player, fanned. Paige fanned Bell of the Grays for the third out in the third.

In the home third, Paige was allowed to bat although his pitching duties were over for the day. Those who looked for Frank Duncan, West manager and also manager of the 1943 Kansas City Monarchs, to send in a pinch hitter were never so fooled in their lives. Paige repaid his debt of gratitude to Duncan by lacing out a neat double to left after missing the first two of Barnhill's offerings for strikes. [Cowan] Hyde, Memphis, ran for Paige and got caught off third, Bankhead to Gibson to Easterling after Bankhead had gathered in Davenport's drive to right.

PAIGE IS WINNING PITCHER

The West gave Paige a 1 to 0 lead in the home second. Neal Robinson, Memphis Red Sox centerfielder who was playing in left for the West, walked. O'Neil, the Monarch first sacker, went out Barnhill to Leonard. Tommy Sampson, Birmingham, poled a clean single to right and Robinson scored the first run of the game. Ted Radcliffe, Giants, lined to Sammy Bankhead and Sampson was doubled up before he could get back to the initial sack, Bankhead to Leonard.

34. *A quartet of all-stars as they prepare to play in the California winter league as the Kansas City Royals. From left to right: Archie Ware, who played in the 1944, 1945, and 1946 games; Jesse Williams, 1943, 1945, and 1951; Ray Neil, 1941, 1951, and 1953; and Barney Serrell, 1944. Courtesy of Ray Neil and Dick Clark.*

So with the score 1 to 0, Paige became the winning pitcher when that ninth inning barrage failed to produce enough runs to give the East a victory. And Paige had all the more reason to feel proud because he had the only extra base hit of the game until Leonard blasted his homer in the ninth.

Hard luck David Barnhill got credited with the loss of the game. John Wright of the Homestead Grays who relieved Barnhill in the fourth took the mound with the score against him.

The West got their second run on the home fourth, and the way the game turned out they needed it. Willard Brown singled to center and stole second. Neal Robinson went out, Wright to Leonard and Brown went to third. John O'Neil rolled out, Wright to Leonard, but Brown went home and scored on the play. Gibson dropped Leonard's throw to get Brown but wasn't charged with an error as Brown already had the throw beaten. He was sliding across the plate when the ball hit Gibson's glove. Gibson would have had to turn to tag Brown and the only way he could have put Brown out was for Brown to have missed the plate altogether.

That seemed to be all the runs that were in the West's system Sunday and it so happened they were enough.

The game went without a fielding error although the official scorers admit that Easterling had committed a glaring error of judgment on Hyde in the home third. Hyde was on second, running for Paige who had opened the stanza with a double. Jesse Williams, the Kansas City Monarch shortstop, laid down a pretty sacrifice and Barnhill elected to throw to Easterling in an effort to get Hyde on what would have been a fielder's choice. Easterling took the throw in plenty of time but must have thought he had a forceout at third. He failed to tag Hyde who slid into the bag safely as Easterling held the ball and stood glued to the bag.

WELL-PLAYED GAME

The game was well played. Two double plays were made during the afternoon. [Jesse] Williams theft of second in the third and Brown's theft of second in the fourth were the two stolen bases for the day.

There wasn't any squabbling about umpires' decisions either on balls or strikes or on the bases. Virgil Blueitt of Chicago, worked the first four innings behind the plate. Fred McCreary [McCrary] of Philadelphia went behind the plate in the fifth and finished the game there. In the bases were Frank Forbes of New York City and Harry Walker of Cleveland. The quartet handled the game well.

George Scales, Baltimore, assisted Vic Harris with the handling of the East team. Frank Duncan had as his coach, W.S. Welch, manager of the Birmingham Black Barons, winners of the first half of the split Negro American league race.

The national anthem was sung by Mrs. Mabel Malarcher, wife of David Malarcher, former manager of the Chicago American Giants. Oscar DePriest, former United States congressman and now alderman for the third ward, pitched the first ball.

The victory Sunday broke up the East's win streak at three and the East now leads in the series by one game. The East has won six and lost five.

And the writer will have to agree with the majority of the real baseball fans and that is: "It sure was one L of a ball game."

The East-West Classic, Top Sports Event

by Joe Bostic

Source: (New York) *The People's Voice*, 14 August 1943

As we've intimated on a half-dozen occasions in these dispatches, the pilot of this space is a sports enthusiast of the first color and in an incurable fan, not to mention our being a charter member of the Grandstand Managers' Association. In other words, we are a thoroughly impressionable young man — definitely of the gee whiz crowd.

Knowing this about me, it shouldn't be too hard for you to understand my being overwhelmed by the magnitude and the potentialities of the annual East-West classic held annually at Comiskey Park, Chicago, as I consider the game in retrospect from my journalistic cubbyhole back here in New York.

These are some of the thoughts that run through my mind as I reflect on the Chicago Classic: This is not only the biggest Negro sports event, but the largest proposition in the nation from the point of view of patron interest to the extent of paying an admission price . . . No other event begins to draw anything like this one . . . 51,723 paid admissions . . . The nearest that we've come to it in New York is the 29,000 at the Satchel Paige game at Yankee Stadium last summer [two years ago, 1941] and the slightly better than 20,000 who tried to get into Madison Square Garden for the Freedom rally a couple of months ago, and that's not even close . . . The "take" is close to $60,000, which comes under the head of high finance in any league . . . Pleasant to report that the spectacle is singularly free of rowdyism in the stands. Maybe we should import the Chicago fans here in order that they'd give some of the ruffians who attend Yankee Stadium games, a lesson or two in behavior.

We got a terrific thrill when given the honor of introducing the Eastern standard bearers over the public address system to that throng that packed and jammed every available inch of the huge sports amphitheater. . . . Biggest ovation went to Josh Gibson, power hitter. . . . He didn't get a homer, but came through in the ninth inning clutch with a sizzler through short that all but tore off Jesse Williams' arm.

Quite an argument in the press box on the play in which Howard Easterling had an easy out of a base runner coming into third on an infield tap. Thinking that there was a force play at the base, Easterling merely touched the bag with his foot and make no attempt to tag the runner, who, of course, was safe. This writer, along with Art Carter and several others, insisted that the third baseman should have been charged with an error. The opposition, led by Bill Nunn of *The Pittsburgh Courier,* who steadfastly contented that the base runner had gained the base by virtue of a steal, credited him with a stolen base and let Easterling off without an error. . . . But Section 9 of Rule 70 says in part: "An error shall be given for each misplay that prolongs the time at bat of the batsman or prolongs the life of the base-runner or allows a base-runner to make one or more bases when a perfect play would have insured his being put out." Our contention was and still is that the third baseman should be charged with an error because he certainly failed to make a perfect play . . . What do you think?

The game is a monument to the imagination and creativeness of the late Roy Sparrow, who along with Gus Greenlee, conceived the game. . . An outsider is appalled by the fact that the owners, booking agents, and others, who share in the money, haven't seen fit to declare Greenlee in on the proposition. Either it has been overlooked or else there are some unusually ungrateful people associated with baseball. I prefer to think that it is the former, and I fervently hope that the dereliction will be amended before another East-West game is played. . . . It is patently clear that the Negro interests are gradually losing control of the promotion—if indeed they haven't done so already. . . .Seeing the boys operating at the game or least some of them—it wasn't too hard to understand.

The officiating of the game was strictly big league. . . . So good in fact, that you were hardly aware of the presence of the umpires on the field, and that, in the final analysis, is the acid test . . . The East team was actually an augmented Homestead Grays' club . . . such an arrangement seems to this column to miss the whole purpose of the game: to increase fan and player interest in organized baseball as represented by the two leagues. . . Maybe we're dumb, but we can't see why it wouldn't do more good all around if each club was permitted at least three players to help make up the squads . . . As a case in point, certainly if the West squad included Goose Tatum, whose sole job was to entertain the fans with his pre-game antics at first base, then the East surely should have included Jim West and Showboat Thomas to name two. It is a great thing this classic, and I, for one, am proud to be a part of it.

AUGUST 1, 1943, CHICAGO, IL

EAST	AB	R	H	D	T	HR	BI	E	TAVG	TSLG
Cool Papa Bell (Homestead Grays), lf	4	0	0	0	0	0	0	0		
Henry Kimbro (Baltimore Elite Giants), cf	1	0	0	0	0	0	0	0		
Jose "Tetelo" Vargas (New York Cubans), cf	2	0	0	0	0	0	0	0		
a) Jerry Benjamin (Homestead Grays), ph	1	0	0	0	0	0	0	0		
Buck Leonard (Homestead Grays), 1b	4	1	1	0	0	1	1	0		
Josh Gibson (Homestead Grays), c	3	0	1	0	0	0	0	0		
Howard Easterling (Homestead Grays), 3b	4	0	1	0	0	0	0	0		
Lennie Pearson (Newark Eagles), rf	3	0	0	0	0	0	0	0		
b) Vic Harris (Homestead Grays), ph	1	0	0	0	0	0	0	0		
Sam Bankhead (Homestead Grays), 2b	3	0	0	0	0	0	0	0		
Rabbit Martinez (New York Cubans), ss	2	0	1	0	0	0	0	0		
Dave Barnhill (New York Cubans), p	1	0	0	0	0	0	0	0		
Johnny Wright (Homestead Grays), p	0	0	0	0	0	0	0	0		
c) George Scales (Baltimore Elite Giants), ph	1	0	0	0	0	0	0	0		
Bill Harvey (Baltimore Elite Giants), p	0	0	0	0	0	0	0	0		
Leon Day (Newark Eagles), p	1	0	0	0	0	0	0	0		
Team Totals, Average & Slugging Pct.	31	1	4	0	0	1	1	0	.129	.226

a) Batted for Vargas in 9th
b) Batted for Pearson in 9th
c) Batted for Wright in 6th

WEST	AB	R	H	D	T	HR	BI	E	TAVG	TSLG
Jesse Williams (Kansas City Monarchs), ss	3	0	2	0	0	0	0	0		
Lloyd Davenport (Chicago American Giants), rf	2	0	0	0	0	0	0	0		
Alec Radcliffe (Chicago American Giants), 3b	4	0	1	0	0	0	0	0		
Willard Brown (Kansas City Monarchs), cf	3	1	1	0	0	0	0	0		
Neil Robinson (Memphis Red Sox), lf	2	1	0	0	0	0	0	0		
d) Fred Wilson (Cincinnati Clowns), ph	1	0	0	0	0	0	0	0		
Lester Lockett (Birmingham Black Barons), lf	0	0	0	0	0	0	0	0		
Buck O'Neil (Kansas City Monarchs), 1b	2	0	0	0	0	0	1	0		
Tommy Sampson (Birmingham Black Barons), 2b	3	0	1	0	0	0	1	0		
Ted Radcliffe (Chicago American Giants), c	3	0	0	0	0	0	0	0		
Satchel Paige (Kansas City Monarchs), p	1	0	1	1	0	0	0	0		
e) Bubba Hyde (Memphis Red Sox), pr	0	0	0	0	0	0	0	0		
Gread McKinnis (Birmingham Black Barons), p	1	0	0	0	0	0	0	0		
Theolic Smith (Cleveland Buckeyes), p	1	0	0	0	0	0	0	0		
Porter Moss (Memphis Red Sox), p	0	0	0	0	0	0	0	0		
Team Totals, Average & Slugging Pct.	26	2	6	1	0	0	2	0	.231	.269

d) Batted for Robinson in 8th
e) Ran for Paige in 3rd

East	000	000	001-1
West	010	100	00X-2

PITCHER/TEAM	GS	IP	H	R	ER	K	BB	WP	HB	W	L	SV
Barnhill/NYC	1	3	2	1	1	0	1	0	0	0	1	0
Wright/HG		2	2	1	1	2	0	0	0	0	0	0
Harvey/BEG		1	1	0	0	0	0	0	0	0	0	0
Day/NE		2	1	0	0	0	1	0	0	0	0	0
Paige/KCM	1	3	0	0	0	4	1	0	0	1	0	0
McKinnis/BBB		3	1	0	0	1	0	0	0	0	0	0
T. Smith/CLB		2 2/3	3	1	1	2	1	0	0	0	0	0
Moss/MRS		1/3	0	0	0	0	0	0	0	0	0	1

BB—Gibson, N. Robinson

DP—Bankhead to Leonard, Pearson to Gibson to Easterling

LOB—East 5, West 6

PB—T. Radcliffe

SAC—Williams, Davenport, O'Neil

SB—Brown, Williams

East—Vic Harris (Mgr.); Coaches George Scales

West—Frank Duncan (Mgr.); Coaches W. S. Welch and Ted Radcliffe

Umpires—Virgil Blueitt, Fred McCrary, Frank Forbes, Harry Walker

Attendance—51,723   Paid—46,871   Time—2:12

Note: National Anthem sung by Mabel Malarcher, wife of Dave Malarcher;
    Councilman Oscar Depriest threw out the first pitch.

1944

Adam Clayton Powell Jr. of Harlem becomes the first African-American U.S. congressman from a northeastern city. The U.S. Supreme Court rules in *Smith* v. *Allwright* that African-Americans cannot be denied the right to vote in primary elections.

Running back Bill Willis of Ohio State University is the first African-American to start in the college football all-star game.

Milk costs 31 cents a half-gallon, 10 pounds of potatoes costs 47 cents, and 41 cents would bring home the bacon. A loaf of bread costs 9 cents.

The National League All-Stars ride to an easy 7–1 win as Cardinal Whitey Kurowski and Cub Phil Cavaretta lead the offensive attack.

Major league commissioner Judge Kenesaw Mountain Landis dies, after a reign that lasted a quarter of a century.

LEAGUE BUSINESS

Willie Wells was risking missing his fourth all-star game of the 1940s. Earlier, in 1940 and 1941, he had played with Vera Cruz, of the Mexican League. While recording batting averages of .345 and .347, he earned the nickname "El Diablo," translating to "The Devil." He returned to the states in 1942 and played one season with the Newark Eagles as player-manager, for $315 a month. Wells had had a sensational season, hitting .361 for the Eagles. However, after a contract dispute with owner Effa Manley, he returned to Mexico to play with Tampico. In an interview with Wendell Smith of the *Pittsburgh Courier,* Wells expressed his reasons for leaving his homeland:

> I came back here to play ball for Vera Cruz because I have a better future in Mexico than in the States. I wanted to stay and play with Newark because I consider Mr. and Mrs. Manley, the owners of the Newark team, fine people. But they couldn't offer me anything like I can get playing for Vera Cruz. Not only do I get more money playing here, but I live like a king.
>
> Some people look at my situation simply from the standpoint of money. But there's more to it than that. In the first place, I am not faced with the racial problem in Mexico. When I travel with the Vera Cruz team, we live in the best hotels, we eat in the best restaurants and can go any place we care to. You know as well as all other Negroes that we don't enjoy such privileges in the United States. We stay in any kind of hotels far from the best, and eat only where we now we will be accepted. Until recently, Negro players had to go all over the country in buses, while in Mexico, we've always traveled in trains.
>
> Players on teams in the Mexican league live just like big leagues. We have every-

thing first class, plus the fact that the people here are much more considerate than the American baseball fan. I mean that we are heroes here, and not just ballplayers.

I've found freedom and democracy here, something I never found in the United States. I was branded a Negro in the States and had to act accordingly. Every thing I did, including playing ball, was regulated by my color. They wouldn't even give me a chance in the big leagues because I was a Negro, yet they accepted every other nationality under the sun.

Well, here in Mexico I am a man. I can go as far in baseball as I am capable of going. I can live where I please and will encounter no restrictions of any kind because of my race.[1]

Wells did return stateside in 1944 to play for the Memphis Red Sox with his son, Willie Brooks Wells Jr.

This year, the St. Louis Stars had been banned from the league. The restriction was imposed after they played nine games in 1943 and then went on a barnstorming tour with the Dizzy Dean All-Stars.[2]

For the third straight year, the Negro National League was operating without a commissioner. Attorney Ferdinand Q. Morton had served as commissioner from 1935 to 1937. Described as a laid-back official with little power, he was succeeded by Major Jackson of Chicago. Dr. J. B. Martin, a close friend of Jackson, followed with an appointment in 1939 and remained commissioner until 1941.

One major reason a Negro Leagues commissioner was needed was that Negro American League teams continued to play games against the suspended St. Louis Stars. Also, the Homestead Grays and the Chicago American Giants were using ineligible players, with no one willing to confront powerful owners Cum Posey and J. B. Martin.

Other league business involved the hiring of the J. Munro Elias Company, in business since 1876, to compile league statistics. The firm, later known as the Elias Bureau, was paid $25 a week for four months, or $425 for the season. The Elias Bureau was required to furnish all stationery and stamps and to send out releases to 30 black-owned newspapers and more than 50 white daily papers each week.[3]

Some objections were raised by team owners about the hiring of the white-owned company. It was pointed out that some league teams were owned by whites, particularly the Kansas City Monarchs, owned by J. L. Wilkinson and Tom Baird; the Birmingham Black Barons, partly owned by Abe Saperstein (with African-American Tom Hayes); the Cincinnati Clowns, owned by Syd Pollock; and the Philadelphia Stars, partly owned by Ed Gottlieb (with African-American Ed Bolden).

Cum Posey, though not a fan of Pollock or Saperstein, expressed his view on white ownership: "These men put their money into Negro Baseball when it was at its lowest ebb and should not be constantly faced by racial antagonism by some members of the Negro Press." Posey added, "The Negro press constantly preaches to support all Negro enterprises. Negro baseball is second only to the Negro-owned life insurance companies in money handled during a year and salaried paid employees."[4]

Ric Roberts, one of the top black sportswriters in the country, wrote that "Negro Baseball is operated by the six franchises in each the Negro American and National Leagues and is a $2,000,000 business." Roberts added, "Not only that, but the highest paid baseball star in the world is the tall, taciturn Leroy 'Satchel' Paige of the Kansas City Monarchs and Satchel Paige, Inc. That Negro professional baseball has taken its place in the sun is best attested by the fact that Paige earns about $40,000 per season—more than Joe McCarthy of the New York Yankees or any other white major leaguer. Paige has enjoyed this distinction since 1942, when the Selective Service took Hank Greenberg from the Detroit Tigers to nullify his $50,000 per year salary." [5]

RACE RELATIONS

By the end of the year, the king was dead! Former judge Kenesaw Mountain Landis, who had ruled baseball with nearly the authoritative power of a Third World dictator, had died. During Landis's reign as commissioner, he never budged on the issue of admission for black players into Major League Baseball. Writer Lester Rodney gave his view of the powerful Landis:

If you ask any honest sportswriter, he will tell you Landis was a racist. He was a cold man! He could at any time as Commissioner said, "Something is wrong with this game. As Commissioner I am going to change it."

So people say we have wishy-washy commissioners now and wish we had a Judge Landis and someone who can make decisions. But he was not a good man. Happy Chandler was a better man than him. By the time Chandler became commissioner anybody who was commissioner would have done what he did. The tide was in full flow then. The fight was already won. [6]

In his weekly column, Wendell Smith tendered his backhanded praise of Landis:

For 25 years Negroes tried to influence Mr. Landis to take as firm a step on the question of Negroes in the majors as he did on everything else associated with the game. Landis freed baseball "slaves." Landis cracked down on gamblers. Landis barred respectable men, Bing Crosby, for instance, from becoming owners of big league clubs if they were associated with horse racing. He held himself up as a symbol of honesty and courage before the entire sports world. He was against anything that even tended to cast a bad reflection on baseball. Perhaps he was exactly what he appeared to be—a Gibraltar of Honesty. But I cannot help feel that Mr. Landis never set his teeth into the question of Negroes in the majors with the same zest that he did other problems which came under his jurisdiction. True, he did give a representative group of Negroes an opportunity to formally appeal to the owners at a meeting in New York one year ago this month. And he always insisted that there was no rule, "written or otherwise," against Negroes in the majors. But the fact remains he never used his wide and unquestionable powers to do anything about the problem.

Landis played a subtle "fence game" on this question. It was the one problem he preferred to let ride. It was the one problem he never faced with the courage and exactness that he faced others. He created the impression in many quarters that he did not favor the ban against Negro players. But he didn't create that impression in all circles. I have yet to meet a newspaperman, white or Negro, who believed Landis meant what he said on that question. And, in reviewing his great career, it is the one big flaw I find. Perhaps I have misjudged Mr. Landis. Perhaps he did mean what he said.

However, deeds, not just mere words, prove the things a man stands for. Mr. Landis had 25 years to prove that he wanted to see Negroes in the majors. Yet, they buried him this week and we are still fighting for Negroes in the majors. [7]

ALL-STAR REVIEW

In June the Kansas City Monarchs staged a doubleheader against the Chicago Firemen at Wrigley Field. The Firemen had gotten former Chicago Cub pitchers Roy Henshaw and Leroy "Tarzan" Parmalee to face Satchel Paige. Between games, Olympic champion Jesse Owens raced against players to entertain the fans. It was also announced that Owens would attempt to break the world record for circling the bases, but no results were published. Kathryn Dunham, a nationally known dancer who was currently starring in the *Tropical Revue* at Chicago's Blackstone Theater, threw out the first ball in the opener. Boxing champion Henry Armstrong had the honor in the second game. Before approximately 15,000 fans, the Monarchs defeated the Chicago congregation, 4–3, in 10 innings of play. Paige pitched six innings, yielding two hits and one walk, while striking out 11.

A STRIKE?

A strike threatened this year's all-star game. About 20 players on the East team met with league president Tom Wilson at the Grand Hotel and demanded $200 each. Wilson promised to honor their demands, but the distrustful players wanted payments in advance. Wilson paid. The players also asked Wilson and American League president J. B. Martin for a guarantee that they would not later be fined or suspended for threatening to strike.

The West team of roughly 26 players met with Dr. J. B. Martin on Saturday, August 12, and asked for $100 each. Martin honored their request and also raised the umpiring fees from $25 plus expenses to $100 plus expenses.

In the past, squad members had been paid $50 per man, with an allowance for food and incidental expenses not to exceed $15.[8]

Satchel Paige was not granted his request to have the $10,000 proceeds from the game donated to the wounded soldiers of World War II.[9] Paige, a man of his word, did not play in the '44 contest. Financial reports for the 1944 all-star game have never been found.

ALL-STAR VOTING

The *Chicago Defender* and the *Pittsburgh Courier* published their last voting results in 1942. Public sentiment had allowed the more popular players to earn near-automatic spots on the all-star team. Later, the major leagues also suspended voting by the fans in the mid-1950s, only to return the electoral privilege for the 1969 all-star game in Washington DC.

SMITTY'S Sports Spurts

East-West Star Dust

by Wendell Smith

Source: *Pittsburgh Courier,* 19 August 1944

Chicago— The players from the East threatened to strike unless they were paid $100 each to play in the classic. Saturday night, everyone was worried, the Eastern magnates in particular, because the National league aces, including Josh Gibson, Ray Dandridge, Sammy Bankhead and others vowed they wouldn't play unless the owners came across. President Wilson quickly called a peace conference, and the players agreed to go through with the game. They agreed they wouldn't disappoint 50,000 fans. American league players were given $100 and caused no worries. Sunday night, none of the Eastern stars could say whether they were going to get the money they demanded. Insiders claimed that Gus Greenlee, originator of the East-West classic and former president of the Negro National league, inspired the Eastern players to threaten a strike. Greenlee, it is alleged, met with a number of the leading Eastern players on Saturday afternoon and advised them to demand the money. Angry because, he says, the NNL has been giving him the "brush-off," and refused him another franchise in the league, Greenlee came all the way from Pittsburgh to warn Owners [Cum] Posey, [Rufus] Jackson, [Tom] Wilson, [Effa] Manley, [Alex] Pompez, [Ed] Bolden and [James] Semler that he's declared a one-man war on them.[10]

Busiest man here for the past two weeks has been Dr. J. B. Martin, president of the Negro American league. Everyone of any importance—and many more so important— were begging him for tickets. Box seats were sold out five days before the game. Venders [vendors] at the park made small fortunes. Duke Ellington, Bill (Bojangles) Robinson and Lena Horne's father (Teddy Horne) whooped it up for both teams. The Press box was loaded with writers from out-of-town. Among them were Dan (N.Y. Amsterdam News) Burley, Joe (People's Voice) Bostic, Willie (Kansas City Call) Harmon, Harold (Afro) Jackson, Butts (Newark Herald) Brown, Bill Nunn and John R. Williams of the [Pittsburgh] Courier, Frank (Cleveland Call-Post) Young Jr., whose father, Frank (Defender) Young, did a job handling the writers in the Press box.

Ted Radcliffe, the "Birmingham Bomber," proved he's a great catcher. He was hurt while catching in the seventh, and had to be revived. . . . Manager Winfield Welch wanted to take him out, but "Double Duty" said they'd have to call the police before he'd retire from the game. He went back in and finished. . . . Josh Gibson's 440-foot double left everyone in the park gasping. . . . When the ball headed for those centerfield bleachers, it was obvious no one could catch it. . . . Consequently, everyone in the park, except the Western players, of course, hoped that he'd get a home run out of it. . . . It missed a circuit by two feet, landed on top of the public address system and bounced back on the field. . . . He got a terrific hand when he pulled up at second.

Sammy Jethroe pulled a boner early in the game when he misjudged [Buck] Leonard's drive, but came back later with a beautiful throw to nail Gibson at the plate. . . . Everyone agreed that classy, little Art Wilson of Birmingham has "it" plus. . . . He played shortstop like a 15-year veteran. . . . Dr. B. B. Martin, owner of Memphis, was all decked up in a spiffy blue sports jacket and white pants, while his brother, Dr. J. B., wore solid white, as usual. . . . Gus Greenlee and William Harris, owner of the Grand Hotel, which was bulging with visitors and ballplayers, sat together in a box near the West dugout. . . . Everyone looked twice at such beauties as Marva (Mrs. Joe) Louis, Mrs. Ernest Wright, whose husband bosses the Cleveland Buckeyes, and Miss Elizabeth Brammer of Detroit and West Virginia.

"They didn't send me here to pitch," Terris McDuffie, Newark ace, warned American League players before the game. "They sent me here to hit. I'm a slugger, I am." Then "Terrible Terry" lived up to his boasting by socking a triple his first time up. . . . He died on third, however, as Mathis pitched brilliantly with the able advice of Ted Radcliffe. . . . Tom Wilson of the Baltimore Elite Giants learned, much to his surprise, that two of his best players—[Robert] Clark and [David] Harvey, catcher and pitcher, respectively, had quit his team and joined Gus Greenlee's barnstorming Pittsburgh Crawfords . . . Harry Williams, manager of the New York Black Yanks, was one of the classiest dressers among the ballplayers, in his uniform in street clothes.

Conspicuous by his absence was Leroy (Satchel) Paige. . . . He refused to play, and no one knew where he was. . . . Celebrity-struck "goils" hounded the star players wherever they went. . . . The game outdrew all games played in the majors Sunday. . . . Mrs. Effa Manley, who runs the Newark Eagles, gave Terris McDuffie and Ray Dandridge a tongue lashing for threatening to strike. "What the hell could I do?" McDuffie asked later. "I wasn't gonna be branded a strike-breaker. I had to be a union man. Suppose I had refused? The same guys I would be quitting were gonna play behind me in the game." . . . For the first time in many years, Alex Pompez didn't make the trip. He was in New York, where his Cuban Giants played at the Polo Grounds. . . . Trains and buses were loaded. . . . Wilbur Hayes won the prize for speed. He left Chicago early Sunday morning for Cleveland, where the Bucks played, and was back in Chicago by the time the classic was over. He hit the air lanes. . . . Cum Posey, Gray's official, who has been seriously ill (recently lose 40 pounds) for the past two months, flew from Pittsburgh. Sunnyman Jackson, Posey's partner in baseball, did an oration in the Grand Hotel lobby on the sins of booking agents and what he would do to some of them if he had a good strong rope. . . . Bessie Holloway of The Courier staff and now of Uncle Sam's WAC, arrived in time to see the game. . . . Photographers were every place giving people the "flash-it is."

Everyone in Chicago, it seemed, tried to get in the Rhumboogie, Chicago nitery, on Saturday night. . . . Hot spots were all loaded, and so were most of the patrons. . . . Umpires Blueitt, McCrary, Moore and Cockrell worked like big leaguers. . . . John Wright, pitcher for the Grays before he joined the Navy, was getting handshakes from all the ballplayers. . . . He's a star pitcher now for the Great Lakes (Jim Crow) team. . . . Duke Cumberland, Harlem Globetrotters' basketball star, sat on the best Western bench. . . . Floyd Meadows, ex-All American at West Virginia and now a "G.I.," saw the game. . . . Whispers of a new league [United States League by Branch Rickey] being organized for next year were all over the place. . . . As was DeHart Hubbard, former Olympic board jump champion, ex-University of Michigan track star, and now extremely baseball conscious . . . Elk officials were booming their big game here for next Wednesday night between Chicago and Memphis. . . . Allen Page, regarded as the South's greatest baseball promoter, and the sports dean of New Orleans, was cornering owners for games and mapping plans for his annual North-South game in the Crescent City.

Editor's note: Earlier in the season, the Negro National League voted to reject Greenlee's application for a franchise. Cum Posey (league secretary) and Rufus "Sonnyman" Jackson, owners of the Homestead Grays, felt that another team at Forbes Field would infringe on the marketing territory of the Grays. Although the Grays played the majority of their games at Griffith Stadium in Washington DC, Posey and Jackson conveniently called Pittsburgh home.

Paige Threatens Not to Hurl in All Star Game

Veteran Pitcher Puts Owners "On the Spot"

As Classic Game Nears

by Fay Young

Source: *Chicago Defender*, 5 August 1944

Leroy Satchel Paige, the best known pitcher in baseball today, threw a bombshell into the East vs. West game scheduled for Comiskey Park on Sunday, August 13. Or perhaps Paige thought he did.

The Alabama born flinger had a few things to say before he took his turn on the mound against Memphis Red Sox at Wrigley Field Sunday and lost a 3 to 2 eight inning game to Lefty Verdell Mathis. Both Paige and Mathis had been picked to hurl for the West in the 1944 classic.

Paige earnestly told the *Chicago Defender* that he would not pitch in the 1944 game unless the club owners in the East and those in the West met his demands.

He declared that the promotion made money and by his working in it, he deprived himself of pitching that Sunday and making his usual fee. He also declared that it wasn't the question of money for himself as he is willing to give what he makes out of the classic to any Army or Navy charity.

Paige pointed out that the Negro American league had voted to take $10,000 off the top and give it to some service organization but that the Negro National League in a meeting held later turned thumbs down on the proposal. To date no East vs. West game has given anything to any Army or Navy relief organization, to any USO or the like.

Last year, the *Defender* learned, Paige pitched the first three innings and left the game with the West out in front and thereby was officially credited with the victory. The East refused to meet his demands for extra pay as a drawing card. The West paid Paige something in the neighborhood of $800. Other players on the West team made less than $100 each.[11]

The East is of the opinion that the game is bigger than Satchel Paige and even if Paige doesn't want to pitch, he doesn't have to; that the game will come "natural" and the crowd will come Paige or no Paige. They—the Negro National League—stick to their blunt refusal to pay Paige on the grounds that Paige is no better drawing card than Neal Robinson of the Memphis club who has two homers to his credit in the classics, or Buck Leonard or Josh Gibson, the two Washington Homestead Grays fence busters, or to any other player. The East points out that each club uses players and that Paige, the property of Kansas City, if used would be Kansas City's contribution to the game.

The consensus of opinion of the fans is that Paige, while a star hurler, should pitch for the same money other players on his team receive. The fans who were interviewed by the *Defender* this week, also are of the opinion that, since Paige has lost his last two starts in Chicago, that he should give the fans a chance to see him in action in the 1944 classic and not penalize these 50,000 who have supported him whenever he pitched and in whatever town he pitched in.

These same fans are miffed—and to no small degree—because the Negro National League stoutly refuses to do anything for any war relief while the sons, fathers, brothers and some daughters of these fans are in the service—man in the South Pacific, Guam, Australia, Hawaii, England, India, Burma, Italy and Normandy. They point out that they are doing their bit on the home front, working in defense plants, buying Victory Bonds until it pinches their pocketbooks, and now the Negro National League dodges a patriotic move and muffs a chance to show its bigness.

The fans also point out that the Negro National League would not be giving anything out of its pocket in donating to a war relief but would be taking the $10,000 proposed by the Negro American League from the money that the fans paid to see the 1944 classic.

West Depends on Hitters to Whip East Nine Sunday

Paige Gets Himself Fired from Role as Pitcher in East vs. West Classic

by Fay Young, *Defender* Sports Editor

Source: *Chicago Defender,* 12 August 1944

The twelfth annual East vs. West baseball classic at Comiskey Park on Sunday August 13, will be played without the services of the colorful and much publicized Leroy Satchel Paige, the internationally know mound artist. Paige will not work the first three innings or any part of the game because of his threats to "take a walk" and his insinuations that owners of Negro ball clubs are unpatriotic.

Paige will not pitch because Dr. J. B. Martin, president of the Negro American league, says he won't hurl and has notified W. S. Welch, manager of the 1944 West team not to include Paige in the West lineup under any consideration.

Paige told the *Chicago Defender* on Sunday before the second game with the Memphis Red Sox that he would not pitch in the East-West classic this year unless both leagues paid him an extra amount of money for so doing and that he would "give this money to an Army or Navy relief organization."

Paige carried this same news to two Chicago afternoon papers in Monday and the story as printed left him—but momentarily so in the role of a "hero." Paige claimed the East versus West game had never donated any part of the funds collected from the fans to any Army or Navy relief. That part was true. However, Paige forgot that two years ago the players who took part in the tenth annual East-West game moved on to Cleveland [in 1939] for a service men's organization benefit game.

The majority of the fans didn't take so kindly to Paige's so-called great patriotic role. These fans, like the owners in both the Negro National and the Negro American league, are against Paige demanding any specified sum off the top in the East-West game. The fans point out that Paige will only pitch three innings because of a rule that no pitcher can hurl over three innings—this same rule being in vogue in the white major league all-star contest. The fans believe the owners ought to pay all of the players in the game more money and not so much to any one player whether it is Paige or Luke McGluke.

Two years ago, Paige went into the classic near the end. Many fans blamed Candy Jim Taylor, then manager of the West team, for not starting Paige or for not sending him to the mound sooner in the game.

THE TRUTH was that Paige refused to pitch in that game unless his demand for a certain "percentage off the top" of the gate receipts were paid him and it was not until the game was well under way that Paige was pacified by J. L. Wilkinson, owner of the Kansas City Monarchs of which Paige is a member. The Monarch owner told Paige that he would see that Paige was paid if it had to come out of his (Wilkinson's) end.

THE TRUTH is that last year, the East turned thumbs down on Paige's demand for an extra fee for pitching three innings in the 1943 classic but rather than disappoint the public which had been told in advance that Paige would start the game, the West's owners agreed to pay Paige.

THE TRUTH is that other players, including the great Josh Gibson, who was once a battery mate of Paige's and Buck Leonard, first sacker, both of the Washington Homestead Grays and other players each drew less than one-eighth of what Paige was paid.

When Paige made his demands again this year, they were met with a deaf ear by the Negro National leaguers. The Negro American leaguers hadn't parsed any ruling as to what Paige would receive extra—if anything.

It was then that "Mr. Paige went to town." Sunday was an opportune time. He stated plainly "he wouldn't pitch unless the money from the game was given to some war relief." But Paige added, in another breath, that he would pitch the three innings if the East-West game would pay him his demands and then he would turn this money over to a war relief agency of organization.

THE TRUTH is who is Paige trying to fool and when did he suddenly become so patriotic?

THE TRUTH is the fans believe that Paige is hiding behind somebody. Who? Why ask me!

THE TRUTH is that Pearl Harbor was attacked on December 7, 1941. Since that date Paige has pitched in any number of games—some league contests and some exhibition games, while others have been in the East vs. West classics and at NO TIME has Paige decided that he would donate any of these various big sums earned to any Army or Navy relief. Of course, that was his business. He has donated to some charities.

THE TRUTH is that Paige, pitcher for the Kansas City Monarchs against the Chicago American Giants in Briggs stadium on a September afternoon in 1942 received $4,000 for pitching while the best paid player—other than Paige—on the Monarch ball club received less than $500 per month. That was after Pearl Harbor.

SYMPATHETIC MR. PAIGE

THE TRUTH is that Paige was paid $1,200 for pitching nine innings in Chicago in a game for the benefit Provident hospital, according to Mrs. Mary Cole, one of the promoters of the game.

Paige claims that in San Diego this winter, his "heart went out" for the wounded soldiers and sailors in the government hospital who had fought in the South Pacific.

THE TRUTH is that Paige's heart is still OUT for since the day that he gazed on these wounded men, Paige has continued to pitch, continued to draw down handsome sums of money but has NOT contributed one dime to that hospital.

The ball fans who for the past 11 years have supported all of the East-West classics and who will again be present this year point to such star players of the white leagues as Babe Ruth, Ted Williams, Joe DiMaggio, and others, all of whom have played in the all-star classics and who wouldn't have dreamed or dared to have demanded any extra stipend for so doing.

The Negro American league, according to Dr. J. B. Martin, its president, voted to take $10,000 off the top of the 1944 game for an Army Navy relief fund.

The National league, in a later meeting, refused to go along with the proposed move.

However, Tom Wilson, president of the Eastern circuit, said the reason was that the National league club owners had already planned a game for a war relief in the East.

"Plans are in the making, since the National didn't agree to our plans," said Dr. Martin, "to stage a benefit game for some service organization. The players will be from our league."

He added "We don't propose, however, to have Satchel Paige or any other disgruntled ball player dictate to us as to when and how this Army or Navy relief game shall be played."

12th East-West Game May Be Duel of Hurlers

by Fay Young

Source: *Chicago Defender,* 12 August 1944

EAST—CLUB	BATTING
Bell, lf.—Grays	.387
Vargas, cf.—Cubans	.282
Leonard, 1b.—Grays	.287
Gibson, c.—Grays	.330
Dandridge, 3b.—Newark	.354
Pearson, rf.—Newark	.302
S. Bankhead, 2b.—Grays	.264
Martinez, ss.—Cubans	.236

Ray Brown, p; Grays; [Victor] Greenridge [Greenidge], p, Cubans; [Barney] Morris, p, Cubans; Barney Brown, p, Philadelphia Stars; [Tom] Glover, p, Baltimore Elites; [Terris] McDuffie, p, Newark Eagles.

WEST—CLUB	BATTING
Horne, ss.—Cleveland	.235
A Radcliffe, 3b.—Ind.	.263
Davenport, cf.—Chicago	.303
Robinson, lf.—Memphis	.310
Jethroe, rf.—Cleveland	.358
Ware, 1b.—Cleveland	.269
Sampson, 2b.—B'ham	.228
T Radcliffe, c.—B'ham	.301

[Verdell] Mathis, p, Memphis; [Leroy] Sutton, p., Chicago; [Gread] McKinnis, p., Chicago; [Alvin] Gipson, p., Birmingham.

The East will throw all of its batting strength against the West in the twelfth annual East-West game at Comiskey Park on Sunday afternoon, August 13. The Negro National leaguers will send seven of the eight players who were in last year's contest to their respective positions to start the game. The West cannot do that.

The Negro American leaguers will face good hitting and good pitching but these Westerners also have some good hitters and some good pitchers. Manager Welch and his two coaches, Frank Duncan of Kansas City, and Rueben Jones of Memphis, won't be caught napping.

For the East, James Bell, Homestead Grays outfielder; Josh Gibson, Gray's backstop; [Lennie] Pearson, Newark outfielder, and Ray Dandridge, Newark third sacker, all are batting over .300 in league games. They will be out there Sunday trying to break up the game with their bats.

The West will have their fence busters on the job also. Although the East's Bell tops the batting of players in Sunday's game with a percentage of .387. Sam Jethroe, the Cleveland Buckeyes' outfielder, heads the West clouters in Sunday game with a league batting average of .358. Neal Robinson, the Memphis outfielder, is batting .310; Manager Lloyd Davenport of Chicago, .303; and Ted Radcliffe, Birmingham catcher, .301.

A last-minute change has been made in catchers. In place of Larry Brown of Memphis, Red Longeley [Longley] of Memphis will join the West squad here.

Horne, Cleveland shortstop; Alec Radcliffe and Ted Radcliffe; Robinson and Davenport, Jethroe and Sampson have seen service against the East.

With Paige definitely out of the game Sunday, a left-hander may start for the West. Either Lefty Verdell Mathis of Memphis or Lefty Gready McKinnis of Chicago will most likely be the starters against the East.

Whatever the East has go to chuck in against the West, manager Welch says "Fetch it along."

All box seats have been sold. The fans are warned to go early and avoid the rush. Grandstand seats are now on sale at the Hotel Grand and will be at the Comiskey Park office Saturday afternoon and Sunday. The gates will open at 12 o'clock.

Police will put all drunks out of the park. The East-West game committee is determined not to have the rowdy element break up the game.

West Bombs East in "Dream Game" 7 to 4

Radcliffe Brothers Star before 50,000 Fans as West Triumphs

by Wendell Smith, Sports Editor

Source: *Pittsburgh Courier,* 19 August 1944

Press Box, Comiskey Park, Chicago, Ill— Baseball's colorful banner of supremacy still flies brilliantly in the rugged Golden West! Here today (Sunday) in spacious Comiskey Park before another record-breaking, sweltering throng of 50,000 hilarious baseball fanatics, a rough-riding crew from the West beat a mighty band of diamond satellites from the East in the 12th annual "Dream Game," 7 to 4. Fifty thousand cheering fans from every section of the United States saw a powerful, dashing, fighting team from the West, representing the Negro American league, explode in the fifth inning and blast five runs across the plate to win the biggest game and put on the greatest spectacle in Negro baseball— the East-West Classic!

Up to the time the West opened the floodgates and poured over those five big markers, it was a nip and tuck tussle with the teams tied at 2–2, and 50,000 jittery fans sitting on the edges of the seats waiting for something to happen.

BROTHERS HEROES

And now . . . as a colorful, happy throng wends its way out of this picturesque park . . . the names of two men are on everyone's lips. These two men are brothers. . . . and they grew up in baseball. They were famous before today. . . . but now, a fiery sun slowly sinks in the after-glow of a beautiful cloudless day. . . . they're more famous than ever. Right now . . . 50,000 fans are drinking a toast to Ted (Double Duty) Radcliffe and Alex Radcliffe, catcher and third baseman of the victorious Western team, and members of Birmingham and Cincinnati, respectively. Of all the stars who performed here today the sparkle of these brothers surpasses all others, glitters with a brilliance seldom equaled in baseball history.

For it was these two men—Ted and Alex—who led that fighting bands from the West into the fray. They carried the Western banner high and defiantly, hauled the ammunition and fired it. Their aim was unerring and they struck with such dynamic accuracy they blasted the hopes and ambitions of the East to Smithereens.

TED HITS HOMER

It was tough and durable "Double Duty," great catcher of the Birmingham Black Barons, who sewed up the ball game in the fifth inning. The West had pounded Caranza [Carrenza] (Schoolboy) Howard for three runs when he came to the plate with Archie Ware of Cleveland, who had doubled to center, on second base. At this point, Manager Jim Taylor of the East called a halt to hostilities and called in Barney Morris, veteran knuckle ball pitcher. Morris is one of the cagiest pitchers in baseball, a good man for such a spot, owner of the most baffling knuckle ball in the game. Morris made the long jaunt from the right field bullpen and went through the customary warm-up exercises while Ted Radcliffe, defiant and determined, waited to greet him. Umpire Virgil Bluitt [Blueitt] roared "play ball" and Radcliffe stepped into the batter's box. Morris took a look at Ware on second, wheeled and fired on plateward. There was a resounding crash as the horsehide met the willow. Like a lethal missile hurled from the mouth of a "Big Bertha," the ball literally whined and screeched as it soared skyward. James (Cool Papa) Bell, brilliant left fielder of the East, bucked up against the narrow barrier of the stands, hoping the ball would descend and land in his big glove. But that ball wasn't slugged for the convenience of Mr. Bell.

It sailed high and far over his head, landed like a bomb dropped from a "B-29" into the mass of people jammed like sardines in the left field stands. It was a mighty smash and it spelled destruction in capital letters as the grinning, proud and happy Radcliffe jogged around the bases with Archie Ware leading him home, and the crowd of 50,000 gave ol' "Double Duty" a deafening, roaring salute . . . the echo of which must have drown in the choppy waters of nearby Lake Michigan.

That was the ball game. That one mighty blast from the big bat of a guy who lives right here in Chicago during the winter months, and thereby a star right in his own backyard today, was too much for the East to overcome. Not even the big guns of Josh Gibson, Buck Leonard or Roy Campanella could make up for that "Good-bye, East" swat by Ted (Double Duty) Radcliffe.

Meantime, Alex Radcliffe, who was participating in his ninth classic, was starring in the field. He made two brilliant stops, was the sparkplug of the West on defense and walloped a mighty triple to drive Buddy Armour home in the third inning for the West's second run. Later, in the fifth, he hit a ball to centerfield which was caught after a long run by Jim [John] Davis of Newark, enabling Lloyd Davenport to score the first marking of a five-run rally.

And so . . . as I write this high above the thousands now leaving this big ball park . . . the names of Ted and Alex Radcliffe are becoming household words and their exploits will be told and retold here in Chicago and across the Nation by the baseball fanatics who came from the four corners today and it was a great ball game played by two great teams.

Although the stars of the West are now graciously taking their bows—the privilege of the victors—it goes without saying that the East also rates a bit of the glory

GIBSON CLOUTS ONE

The East scored once in the second, again in the fourth and twice in the seventh for their four runs. Josh Gibson, great catcher of the Homestead Grays, hit the longest double ever seen in this park in the seventh, a blast that journeyed 440 feet and hit on top of the public address system in centerfield. It was the longest drive of the day—longer even than Ted Radcliffe's blow into the stands—and yet it only went for a double, because the ball bounded back on the playing field and Josh had to drop anchor at second. It was Gibson who scored the first run for the East in the second. He tripled and come home on Davis's single to center. Later he tried to score from second on another single by Davis, but was nailed at the plate when Sammy Jethroe heaved a prefect strike to Ted Radcliffe from centerfield. Buck Leonard, Gibson's teammate, scored the second run in the fourth after blasting a long triple to right center. Sam Bankhead and Roy Campanella, a pinch hitter, scored the other two in the seventh. Campanella drove Bankhead home from second with a single and scored himself a moment later on Ray Dandridge's single to center.

WEST SCORES FIRST

Art Wilson scored the first West run in the initial inning when he singled, went to second on an infield out and scored when Bankhead and Leonard both committed fielding sins on Armour's easy roller to second. The second run was produced when Alex Radcliffe tripled Buddy Armour home. Then the West came back in the fifth with that five-run splurge on singles by Davenport, Armour, Sorrell [Serrell], a double by Archie Ware and a home run by Ted Radcliffe.

Verdell Mathis, Memphis, Gentry Jessup, Gready McKinnis and Gene Bremmer [Bremer] handled the pitching for the West and they did a good job. McKinnis found the going a bit rough in the seventh, but other than that the West moundsmen were tops. Carranza [Carrenza] Howard, of the New York Cubans, couldn't hold the West and was blasted from the mound in the fifth. However, the other Easterners, Terris McDuffie, Bill Byrd and Barney Morris lived up to expectation.

Ray Dandridge was the fielding star for the East. He made three outstanding plays and was the key man in the infield. He also topped the hitters with two singles and a double.

Willie Simms, an outfielder for the Monarchs remembers the Dandridge's performance, "Ray Dandridge threw out Ducky Davenport without looking at first base on a slow roller. Being that is was the last out of the inning, he left the field of play before the play was completed."[12]

It's all over now, this classic of classics . . . but what transpired here today will live forever. Fifty thousand fans—a total of 46,247 paid—are taking 50 thousand different versions of the game home with them as the West hauls its banner skyward again. Everyone agrees, however that it was a great ball game . . . and that the barrier against Negroes in the major leagues stands out more than ever as an incurable disease that only democratic tolerance and Americanism can master.

Editor's note: Despite Gibson's fine offensive performance, he had been bothered with health problems earlier in the year. In June, Gibson spent a couple of weeks in Gallinger Hospital in Washington DC for observation. He had suffered a nervous breakdown and had sought escape from his undiagnosed mental condition through heavy drinking.

In May, Gibson was suspended for two weeks by Rufus "Sonnyman" Jackson, president of the Grays, for drinking in the clubhouse at Bugle Field in Baltimore. He was sent back to Pittsburgh, where a few days later he was arrested for disorderly conduct and referred to Gallinger for treatment.[13]

This was not the first time Gibson had experienced health problems. During the 1942 world series, when the Grays met the Kansas City Monarchs at Shibe Park, Gibson collapsed in the dugout. A doctor was summoned from the grandstands to revive him. After the series, he recuperated in Hot Springs, Arkansas.[14]

At the 1942 series the Grays were swept in four straight by the Monarchs. Gibson, with two fielding errors, was held to a paltry .154 average with two singles in 13 at bats against the pitching of Satchel Paige, Jack Matchett, and Hilton Smith.

In this year's world series Gibson batted .400 with six hits in 15 at bats, including one home run and no errors in the field. The Grays swept the Birmingham Black Barons in four games.

Sportorial: Was Paige Missed?

by Willie Bea Harmon

Source: *Kansas City Call,* 18 August 1944

The dream classic, the East-West all-star game of 1944 is a part of history now, but the fans are still wondering if Satchel Paige was missed. That was the question on every lip. They wanted to know if Satchel would be missed and when the game was over was he missed? Many would say that he was not missed and point to the 7 to 4 score racked up by the West's heavy hitters. But we say he was missed. Not a single player on either team has the color or should we say the glamour which envelops Paige. He is, as they would say in Hollywood, a "Star."

There were other stars on the field Sunday in Comiskey Park, but not even the heavy-hitting Josh Gibson attracted the attention that Paige would have attracted even if he had been on the bench. Yes, there was Lloyd "Ducky" Davenport, a dream fielder if there ever was one. There was Alec Radcliffe picking the pellet out of the dust at third, making tremendous heaves to first. There was Ted "Double Duty" Radcliffe the only one to clout a homer. There was Buck Leonard, but these [men] were not Satchel Paige.

East-West Game Highlights

by *Amsterdam News* Staff Correspondent

Source: *New York Amsterdam News,* 19 August 1944

Chicago— All tickets for the annual East-West classic were sold as early as Saturday afternoon, the East-West game committee announced adding that a "few" might be had at the Grand Hotel, headquarters for Negro baseball affairs, and at Comiskey Park where the tilt was played Sunday.

Fans came to Chicago from points in Michigan, Ohio, Missouri, Iowa, Texas, Mississippi, Alabama, Louisiana, Arkansas and Tennessee. A few straggled in from New York City, including Louis (Pete's Creole Restaurant) Henry and from as far West as Los Angeles.

Scalpers were as busy as bees in the sidewalks in front of Comiskey Park as early as 11:30 a.m., Sunday selling $1.20 tickets in the grandstands for $5.80 with plenty of buyers. Box seats went for as high as $14 and were gobbled up as soon as seen. Out here folks have so much money, they spend all their off time buying something.

W. A. (Gus) Greenlee of Pittsburgh, resplendent in cream-colored gabardine with black shirt and tie with yellow tie sat in a box behind the West dugout with W. P. Harrison, nationally known manager of the Grand Hotel. Photographers swarmed all about them. Greenlee and Harrison were the original sponsors of the game. In another box not far away sat rotund, greying Robert A. (King) Cole, boss of the famed Metropolitan funeral system here and one time owner of the Chicago American Giants and also a figure in the East-West classic in other seasons.

R. S. Simmons, statistical expert of the Negro American League, took over the microphone to let the world and the fans in the stands know, that this was the 12th annual East-West game, then turned it over to Joe (People's Voice) Bostic as the official announcer for the game although Joe didn't get much to say. Simmons got everybody up to bow their heads in memory of the late Porter Moss, right-hander of the Memphis Red Sox, killed several weeks ago in an episode aboard a train in the deep south.[15]

The press box was filled with a bunch of scribes from all over. Butts Brown was in from the *Newark Herald*. Harold Jackson was there representing the *Washington Afro*. Bill Nunn, Wendell Smith and Henry Lindsay of the *Pittsburgh Courier;* Frank A. (Fay) Young of the *Chicago Defender;* Joe Bostic, *People's Voice,* Harlem; Willie Bea Harmon, *Kansas City Call,* the only gal sport editor about, John R. Williams of the Detroit [version of the] *Pittsburgh Courier;* Bob Turner, *Nashville Globe-Independent;* Wesley O. Jackson, *Indianapolis Recorder;* Sam R. Brown, *Memphis World;* Frank Marshall Davis, *Associated Negro Press,* Dizzy Dismukes, Kansas City Monarchs' statistical giant and many others were there drinking up the free cokes Fay Young paid for out of his own pocket.

A coterie of Chicago good-lookers wearing spic-and-span uniforms of the Joe Louis Service Guild, sold programs in the stands. The famed Memphis brothers—all doctors— J. B., W. S. and B. B. Martin had a box behind the West dugout. J. B. is president of the Negro American League, B. B. owns the Memphis Red Sox.

Through the Years: Time to Call a Halt

by Fay Young

Source: *Chicago Defender,* 28 August 1944

Last week we had the occasion to back the ball player in his demand for what we thought was a reasonable amount of money for playing in the twelfth annual East-West classic in Chicago. We offered a solution to the owners and the game committee. They may not take kindly to our suggestion but that won't change us one wee bit.

Now we, this week, go gunning for the unscrupulous, conniving, downright ornery ball player. There are a number of gentlemen in players uniforms—and there are a number of skunks.

Those on the East team who demanded and received $200 each for playing in the classic and those on the West who received $100 each want to take stock of themselves because some on the East team didn't look like any $200-a-day players to us and some on the West weren't all that they, themselves, would have us believe they are.

Now let's go over a little plain bit of matter which the public ought to know. Lloyd Davenport and several others are in debt to Dr. J. B. Martin, president of the Chicago

American Giants, for monies advanced before payday. In fact, according to the books, the week before the East-West game, Davenport not only owed the club $500 but had quit his club in Detroit and came to Chicago without permission of the owner or the traveling secretary.

Immediately after the East-West game, Davenport signed to play with Gus Greenlee's Pittsburgh Crawfords although he was under contract with the American Giants and had not been traded or released to any other club.

Grady McKinnis, the "worrisome lefthander" not only to opposing batters but to the owners of the Giants, also signed and collected a sum, said to be $200, from Greenlee, jumped the Chicago team and went East but reported back to Chicago and was at Comiskey Park Sunday, but was not in uniform.

Arthur Pennington, Chicago first sacker, also deep in debt to owner Martin, also signed with Greenlee, took some money and showed up with Davenport, Sunday in an American Giants uniform.

As a warning to these men who believe they can "do as they please" let us inform them that the public "refuses to be suckers." The play of the Chicago team Sunday was not what the fans expected. Not because they lost a double-header to the Memphis Red Sox but because the team didn't seem to have any pep. How could they with a leader like Davenport who sets such a bad example.

Pennington, who has been batting well all this season, suddenly took a slump, went to the plate eight time and got one hit. The Chicago team, in the first game, got four hits in two innings and couldn't score.

According to Greenlee, Robert Smith, Chicago catcher, also signed and received money.

AUGUST 13, 1944, CHICAGO, IL

EAST	AB	R	H	D	T	HR	BI	E	TAVG	TSLG
Cool Papa Bell (Homestead Grays), lf	5	0	0	0	0	0	0	0		
Ray Dandridge (Newark Eagles), 3b-2b	5	0	3	1	0	0	1	0		
Pancho Coimbre (New York Cubans), rf	5	0	0	0	0	0	0	0		
Buck Leonard (Homestead Grays), 1b	3	1	1	0	1	0	0	1		
Josh Gibson (Homestead Grays), c	3	1	2	1	0	0	0	0		
John Davis (Newark Eagles), cf	3	0	2	0	0	0	1	0		
Sam Bankhead (Homestead Grays), 2b-ss	3	1	1	0	0	0	1	1		
Pee Wee Butts (Baltimore Elite Giants), ss	2	0	0	0	0	0	0	0		
a) Marvin "Tex" Williams (Philadelphia Stars), ph	1	0	0	0	0	0	0	0		
Rabbit Martinez (New York Cubans), ss	0	0	0	0	0	0	0	0		
b) Roy Campanella (Baltimore Elite Giants), ph, 3b	2	1	1	0	0	0	1	0		
Terris McDuffie (Newark Eagles), p	1	0	1	0	1	0	0	0		
Carrenza Howard (New York Cubans), p	1	0	0	0	0	0	0	0		
Barney Morris (New York Cubans), p	0	0	0	0	0	0	0	0		
c) Henry Kimbro (Baltimore Elite Giants), ph-rf	1	0	0	0	0	0	0	0		
Bill Byrd (Baltimore Elite Giants), p	1	0	0	0	0	0	0	0		
Team Totals, Average & Slugging Pct.	36	4	11	2	2	0	4	2	.306	.472

a) Batted for Butts in 7th
b) Batted for Martinez in 8th
c) Batted for Morris in 7th

WEST	AB	R	H	D	T	HR	BI	E	TAVG	TSLG
Sam Jethroe (Cleveland Buckeyes), cf	3	0	0	0	0	0	0	0		
Neil Robinson (Memphis Red Sox), cf	2	0	0	0	0	0	0	0		
Artie Wilson (Birmingham Black Barons), ss	4	1	2	0	0	0	0	0		
Lloyd Davenport (Chicago American Giants), rf	4	1	1	0	0	0	0	0		
Buddy Armour (Cleveland Buckeyes), lf	4	2	2	0	0	0	0	0		
Alec Radcliffe (Cincinnati Clowns), 3b	4	0	2	0	1	0	2	0		
Bonnie Serrell (Kansas City Monarchs), 2b	3	1	2	0	0	0	1	0		
Archie Ware (Cleveland Buckeyes), 1b	4	1	1	1	0	0	1	0		
Ted Radcliffe (Birmingham Black Barons), c	4	1	3	0	0	1	2	0		
Verdell Mathis (Memphis Red Sox), p	1	0	1	0	0	0	0	0		
Gentry Jessup (Chicago American Giants), p	2	0	0	0	0	0	0	0		
Gread McKinnis (Chicago American Giants), p	0	0	0	0	0	0	0	0		
Gene Bremer (Cleveland Buckeyes), p	0	0	0	0	0	0	0	0		
Team Totals, Average & Slugging Pct.	35	7	14	1	1	1	6	0	.400	.571

East	010	100	200-4
West	101	050	00X-7

PITCHER/TEAM	GS	IP	H	R	ER	K	BB	WP	HB	W	L	SV
McDuffie/NE	1	3	5	2	1	2	1	0	0	0	0	0
Howard/NYC		1 2/3	4	4	4	0	0	0	0	0	1	0
Morris/NYC		1 1/3	2	1	1	1	0	0	0	0	0	0
Byrd/BEG		2	3	0	0	0	0	0	0	0	0	0
Mathis/MRS	1	3	3	1	1	0	0	0	0	0	0	0
Jessup/CAG		3	3	1	1	0	2	0	0	1	0	0
McKinnis/CAG		1 1/3	4	2	2	1	1	0	0	0	0	0
Bremer/CEB		1 2/3	1	0	0	2	0	0	0	0	0	1

BB—Serrell, Gibson, Leonard, J. Davis

SAC—A. Radcliffe, Bremer

SB—Armour

DP—Jethroe to T. Radcliffe; Wilson to Serrell to Ware

LOB—East 8, West 7

PB—T. Radcliffe

East—Candy Jim Taylor, (Mgr.); Coaches Goose Curry and Harry Williams

West—W. S. Welch (Mgr.); Coaches Frank Duncan and Reuben Jones

Umpires—Virgil Blueitt, Fred McCrary, W. Moore, Phil Cockrell

Attendance—46,247   Time—2:35

1945

John Johnson of Chicago, Illinois, begins publication of *Ebony,* an African-American news-magazine.

Milk costs 31 cents a half-gallon, 10 pounds of potatoes costs 49 cents, and 41 cents would bring home the bacon. A loaf of bread costs 9 cents.

No all-star game between the major leagues' American and National Leagues is played due to travel restrictions imposed by the war effort. Albert "Happy" Chandler becomes Major League Baseball's new commissioner.

New York becomes the first state to pass the Fair Employment Practices Commission law.

Richard Wright's autobiography, *Black Boy,* is published and becomes a bestseller.

Army veteran Bert Shepard, who lost a leg in the war, pitches 5 1/3 innings and allows only one run in his only major league appearance. A one-armed outfielder named Pete Gray joins the St. Louis Browns for 77 games. There are still no black players in Major League Baseball.

THE WAR EFFORT

With America still at war with Germany and Japan, African-Americans were serving in all branches of the armed services, albeit in segregated units. Of the approximately 775 generals in the U.S. Army, Benjamin O. Davis Sr. served as the lone African-American general. Back at home, black Americans were protesting segregation in the workplace and picketing stores where they could not shop and factories where they could not work. One sign proclaimed: "Jim Crow versus Baseball: Black Men & White Men are fighting and dying together for democracy. Black Men and White Men should work and play together for posterity." Another picket sign asserted: "If Negro Men Can Carry Guns for Uncle Sam, Surely They Can Drive Milk Wagons for Bowman Dairy." Moreover, if they could stop bullets on the battlefield, they could surely stop baseballs on the playing field. Major League Baseball's supply of white talent had been depleted by the war effort, causing major league owners to notice more of the black talent performing in the other league.

Across the United States, a "Double-V" campaign was launched by the National Association for the Advancement of Colored People (NAACP), promoting victory at home and abroad. The NAACP and the Urban League actively advised all U.S. citizens that the United States should not crusade and fight against Nazi racism in Europe while condoning racism and oppression at home. Their efforts, assisted by the black press, precipitated the establishment of the Fair Employment Practices Commission (FEPC), which initiated passage of the Fair Employment Practices laws in several states. Approval of the New Yor FEPC law in 1945 prompted the creation of the End Jim Crow in Baseball Committee.

"The war tended to help the movement. Although it was two years later before Truman ever announced the end of segregation in the United States Army. It was not a magic bullet. You could still join the Navy and be [only] a mess boy," said writer Lester Rodney, recalling the social attitudes of the time. Rodney claimed, "Guys came back from the war and ran into trouble. They came back wearing the uniform of their country, and in some parts of the country they got a bad reception. So everything wasn't settled then."[1]

MAJOR LEAGUE TRYOUTS?

The highlight of the year was the signing of Kansas City Monarchs infielder Jackie Robinson. Earlier in the year, Robinson, along with Sam Jethroe and Marvin "Tex" Williams, were given tryouts with the Boston Red Sox. The tryouts were the result of pressure by *Pittsburgh Courier* writer Wendell Smith and Boston councilman Isadore Muchnick.

Muchnick, a white politician representing a predominantly black district, pressured the local teams, the Braves and the Red Sox, to sign black ballplayers. Muchnick threatened to revoke licenses permitting the Braves and the Red Sox to play on Sundays, each club's biggest payday. Muchnick wrote letters to owner Tom Yawkey of the Red Sox and general manager Paul Quinn of the Braves stating: "It is my understanding that despite an aroused public opinion and pending legislation for fair employment practices, the practice of discrimination against Negro ball players will prevail. I cannot understand how baseball, which claims to be the national sport, and which in my opinion receives special favors and dispensations from the federal government because of the alleged morale value, can continue a pre–Civil War attitude toward fellow American citizens because of the color of their skin."[2] Facing the threat of having their permits to play Sunday baseball withdrawn, the Red Sox were the first to respond with an invitation.

Muchnick received support from Roger Treat of the *New York Daily News,* who wrote, "The Homestead Grays would beat the Washington Senators six days a week and twice on Sunday." Treat added, "In my opinion Josh Gibson is the best catcher of any race that I have ever seen, and that includes [Mickey] Cochrane and [Bill] Dickey."[3]

Treat hit a home run in support of Muchnick when he wrote: "Baseball's bigoted, prejudiced, intolerance is strange, especially now. We have, and have had, in the past, players of Chinese, Indian and other varying racial origins, and no catastrophe has occurred. We have had a mixture of Scandinavian, and Irish and Anglo-Saxons, and Italians and Slavs, and Germans, and French; baseball liked that. But baseball still flies Jim Crow's flag on the mast-pole in each park where it is an insult to true Americans, and is a banner of shame, blemishing a sport we like to call our national pastime. For baseball mentality and spirit of human relations are still those of a hundred years ago. There is no color line, no race line, on sportsmanship, and hard fighting ability. Until baseball moves over into Democracy's team, there will be few tears shed if it prefers to stab itself with the poisonous knife of hypocrisy."[4]

Dean Newman, a sports editor for the *Anderson Independent-Tribune* in South Carolina, disagreed with Treat, countering:

Any effort to organize Negro players into organized baseball in the South would create a bitter animosity which would certainly not do the Negroes any good. Such an effort would lead to all sorts of racial troubles.

Why can't the Yankees leave the South and it's [sic] race problems alone? We have worked out through experience of many years a working arrangement between the two races which is satisfactory to both.

Newman added, "The Negro has millions of friends among the whites of the South, but interference by outsiders puts off to another day the better things we have planned for our Negroes' education and economic equality."[5]

The tryouts were originally scheduled for April 14 and 15, only to be postponed for unknown reasons. Dave Egan, a writer for the *Boston Daily Record* and an ally for Muchnick's plan to integrate baseball, chastised Red Sox general manager Eddie Collins in an editorial. Egan simply reminded Collins that he was "living in anno domini 1945 and not the dust-covered year 1865, and residing in the city of Boston, Massachusetts and not in the city of Mobile, Alabama."[6] Noting the high qualifications of each candidate, Egan added that if the black players failed to make the first squad, surely there was room in the low minors for their future development.[7]

During the negotiations to schedule a tryout date, Jackie Robinson was making his professional baseball debut with the Kansas City Monarchs. In San Antonio, Texas, on April Fools' Day, he appeared at shortstop against the white Charley Engle's All-Stars. Playing behind his mentor, pitcher Hilton Smith, Robinson accepted eight of nine chances and turned three double plays. His seventh-inning error allowed Engle's team to tie the score. Robinson had one hit in seven at bats, batting in the number six slot. The game ended in a 4–4 tie after 14 innings, when it was called to allow the Monarchs to catch a bus to Houston.[8]

The tryout was eventually held on April 16, a Monday, with neither Joe Cronin nor Eddie Collins in attendance. Coaches Hugh Duffy and Larry Woodall orchestrated the workout. After shagging a few fly balls in the outfield and taking batting practice, the trio was sent home with the message that they would be contacted within 10 days.

When the 10 days passed without news, Wendell Smith wrote Collins for an explanation. Collins gave the evasive answer that he expressed fears of tampering with players who were under contract with Negro League teams.

Earlier, Smith had written: "Why we continue to flock to major league ball parks, spending our hard earned dough, screaming and hollering, stamping our feet and clapping our hands, begging and pleading for some white batter to knock some white pitcher's ears off, almost having fits if the home team loses and crying for joy when they win, is a question that probably never will be answered satisfactorily. What in the world are we thinking about anyhow."

Smith added: "The fact that major league baseball refuses to admit Negro players within its folds makes the question just that much more perplexing. Surely it's sufficient reason for us to quit spending our money and time in their ballparks. Major League baseball does not want us. It never has. Still, we continue to help support this institution that places a bold 'Not Welcome' sign over its thriving portal and refuse to patronize the very place that has shown that it is more than welcome to have us. We black folks are a strange tribe!"[9]

BEAR MOUNTAIN

Smith was not alone in his battle to integrate the major leagues. Earlier, on Friday, April 6, sportswriters Joe Bostic (*People's Voice*) and Nat Low (New York *Daily Worker*) showed up unannounced with Negro League players Dave "Showboat" Thomas, 40 years old, and Terris "The Great" McDuffie, 34, at the Brooklyn Dodgers training camp in Bear Mountain, New York. According to Al Laney, writer for the *Herald-Tribune,* a startled Branch Rickey reluctantly offered an "official" tryout the next day.[10]

Writer Lester Rodney also confirmed Rickey's resistance to the tryout: "Some players went up to spring training at Bear Mountain. Of course, during the war [because of travel restrictions] they weren't traveling down to Florida. Nat Low, the sports editor who followed me [at the time, Rodney was a private in the service] and Joe Bostic of the *People's Voice* and two black players, Rickey greeted them with a cold fury, as if they were putting pressure on him."

Rodney added: "He undoubtedly in his mind had played with the idea [of integrating baseball], and he was going to be the 'great' man. But there was still pressure from the left wing. However, our role was mainly to bring it to the consciousness of a lot of people that had not thought about it before."[11]

On Saturday morning, the group returned at 11 A.M. for a press conference with Rickey, manager Leo Durocher, and coaches Charlie Dressen and Clyde Sukeforth. At about 1:30 P.M., Thomas and McDuffie emerged from the dressing room of the West Point Field House, located at the United States Military Academy, to perform on Durocher Field wearing Dodger uniforms. Bostic formally introduced the men to Durocher, and they were advised by Rickey to jog around the field and loosen up for about 10 minutes.[12]

Joe Bostic wrote the following in his weekly column: "Rickey called Sukeforth to take his place behind the plate and called McDuffie to start pitching. After he had thrown a half dozen or so pitches, Rickey started calling for the kind of pitches he wanted thrown. McDuffie was sharp as a whip and was splitting the plate on pitch after pitch. Once he was underway and the tension eased off, he worked as smoothly as a newly oiled diesel engine. Now, Rickey was shuttling back and forth from the mound to behind the plate and audibly marveling at the control Mac was exhibiting." Bostic added, "When it came to McDuffie's turn to bat, he strode to the plate with that consummate self-assurance, which is his hallmark. He slammed several to distant points, thus making good his boast to Rickey of the day before that 'I'm a hitting pitcher.'"[13]

Another New York paper reported Rickey's assessment of Terris the Great: "His control is not bad; in fact, I would say it is very good. His fastball is good and his curve is also good. He throws what he calls a change. It has too much speed. I believe he can get a better change."[14]

Bostic saw Showboat Thomas's tryout and gave this evaluation: "Thomas was called to bat against a speedy lefthander, which put him at a distinct disadvantage since he is a lefty himself. But he still belted plenty of them for what would have been long safeties in any outfield."[15]

Rickey's evaluation of Thomas was less flattering: "On what you showed me I could not be interested in first baseman Dave Thomas if he were 24 years old instead of 34." Manager Leo Durocher added his comments: "I would not be interested in a 32 year old player who has never played in professional [*sic;* the Negro Leagues were professional] baseball."[16]

Why Bostic and Low took mediocre players to the Dodger training camp may never be known. But with their efforts and those of Wendell Smith, Lester Rodney, and other writers, the pressure to integrate the national pastime was mounting.

"The Communist party played a very important role [in the integration of baseball]. Other forces took over, like Mrs. Roosevelt and some of the better sportswriters. By 1945, we [the *New York Daily Worker*] were only a minor part of the movement," said Lester Rodney.[17]

LEAGUE BUSINESS

Since 1933, coincidentally the debut year of the East-West All-Star Game, Wendell Smith had led a campaign against apartheid baseball. Over the years, Smith, along with fellow black sportswriters like Sam Lacy, Ches Washington, Alvin Moses, Joe Bostic, Lester

Rodney, and Rollo Wilson, had waged a campaign against Commissioner Landis, the team owners, and their club managers to get black players to compete on the level playing field of equality. Their assertive articles and editorials appeared in major black weeklies like the *Pittsburgh Courier, Chicago Defender, Baltimore Afro-American, New York Age, Kansas City Call,* and *New York Amsterdam News,* as well as the *New York Daily Worker.*

A new black league called the United States League was formed this year. Founded by Branch Rickey and East-West game originator Gus Greenlee, the venture immediately sent a signal to the old guard that a new era was coming. Cleveland lawyer John G. Shackelford was named president. Shackelford, an African-American, was a graduate of Wiley College (Marshall, Texas) and the University of Michigan Law School. A former infielder, he had played with the Cleveland Browns, the Chicago American Giants, and the Birmingham Black Barons in the late 1920s. Gus Greenlee served as the league's vice president.

The new league's teams were Greenlee's revamped Pittsburgh Crawfords along with the Toledo Cubs, the Brooklyn Brown Dodgers, the Chicago Brown Bombers, the Detroit Motor City Giants, and the Philadelphia Hilldales. Rickey announced that he had leased Ebbets Field to Joe Hall of the Brooklyn Brown Dodgers for five home dates. The league would debut on May 20 with the Brown Dodgers hosting the Philadelphia Hilldales. The other scheduled dates included a May 27 meeting with Greenlee's Crawfords, May 30 against Detroit, a night game on June 6 against Hilldale, and a June 17 contest with the Chicago Brown Bombers.[18]

Often called "The Mahatma," Rickey, who is credited with starting baseball's minor league system, secured other ballparks for team owners. The Pittsburgh Crawfords played at Forbes Field, Philadelphia at Harrisburg Field, Detroit at Motor City Field, Chicago at Wrigley Field, and Toledo at American Association Park.[19] The shrewd, bow-tied, cigar-chewing Rickey was known for his priestly manner and flowery speech, which sometimes gave him the mannerisms of a con man playing Daddy Grace. He repeatedly charged that the Negro National and Negro American Leagues were unsound and not part of "organized" baseball. The Methodist teetotaler Rickey claimed the black leagues were in "the zone of a racket."[20] However, all-star Grays first baseman Buck Leonard countered, "We were organized, just not recognized."[21]

Remarkably, sentiment against the new league and its owners appeared to be nonexistent among Negro League club owners. Some critics suggested that Rickey's new venture was somehow a delaying act to maintain the Jim Crow status quo in the major leagues. When Chicago sportswriter Luther A. Townsley confronted Dr. J. B. Martin at the East-West All-Star Game about the new competition for black talent, Martin responded with an ambivalent remark: "Negro baseball has had an uphill fight and you may rest assured we endorse any move that will bring Negro players the just recognition they deserve."[22]

Meanwhile, Rickey made no promises that the new league would serve to integrate Negro players into the major leagues. He emphasized that the new league would be *a sound structure and, in time, be accepted by the National Association of Professional Baseball Clubs.*[23] At a press conference, Rickey refused to answer questions about whether the acceptance of the United States League by the Association would make Negro players eligible for signing with major league clubs. Quietly, club owners like Dr. Martin and Effa Manley encouraged a wait-and-see attitude toward Rickey's objectives in establishing this new all-black league. Ironically, Rickey postulated that an all-black league owned by a white American would be accepted by Major League Baseball over an all-black league with African-American ownership.

In April, Wendell Smith met with Branch Rickey to discuss several sensitive issues. At the April 17 meeting, Rickey presented the schedule of the new United States League to Smith for publication. Rickey announced the league would be a developmental vehicle for black players, giving them the opportunity to hone their skills at a "professional" level. At this meeting, Smith recommended a new talent from the Kansas City Monarchs, a college lad named Jackie Robinson, as a player to be considered for breaking the color barrier — if Rickey ever considered such an idea.[24]

However, Robinson was not a cinch to make the big league ball club. In the *Negro Baseball Pictorial Yearbook,* Sam Lacy assessed the young Robinson's abilities: "Having played football with an otherwise all-white team at UCLA, the Kansas City shortstop would be well versed in diplomacy. He would have neither the inferiority complex we must avoid nor the cocky bulldozing attitude we likewise should abandon. All his life has been spent in an interracial setting, a fact that is bound to be a distinct help to the trailblazer."[25]

After shocking the baseball world with the announcement that the Brooklyn Dodgers had signed African-American Jackie Robinson to a Montreal Royals contract, Smith wrote Rickey a letter suggesting another candidate. His December 19 letter reads in part;

> I am writing relative to the spring training situation, which we discussed in your office and over the telephone. I am making definite plans to go to Daytona Beach to cover the training camp sessions of the Montreal Royals.
>
> I would like to know when they start training at Daytona Beach and what, if any, provisions have been made with respect to where Jackie Robinson will stay.
>
> Incidentally, if you are still considering another Negro team-mate for Robinson, I am suggesting that you consider very seriously the possibility of Kenny Washington, who was Jackie's team-mate at UCLA I understand that he is a much better ball player than Robinson and that he plays in the outfield and infield.[26] He is very intelligent person and, I understand, has a wonderful personality. He has been playing baseball and football on the West Coast and is free to be signed without encountering contract technicalities with the Negro leagues.
>
> Sincerely yours, Wendell Smith, Sports Editor, The Pittsburgh Courier[27]

In Robinson's junior year at UCLA, he averaged 11 yards a carry and teamed with All-American Kenny Washington in the backfield. In collegiate football, black players were common. However, no pro football team had featured a black player since Joe Lillard had played for the 1932 Chicago Cardinals. In March 1946 the Los Angeles Rams announced the signing of Kenny Washington, rebreaking professional football's color barrier.

On January 8, 1946, Branch Rickey responded to Wendell Smith's request in a "Personal and Confidential" letter on Brooklyn Dodger letterhead, stating:

> Dear Wendell
>
> The Montreal Club will begin its training season at Daytona Beach on the first of March. There will be two colored boys on the Montreal Club, — Robinson one of them, and the other yet to be selected, probably pitcher [Johnny] Wright. I hope very much that you can arrange to be in Daytona Beach ahead of time to see to it that satisfactory living accommodations are arranged for these boys. It is my understanding that you will be able to stay in Daytona Beach during the training period of about four weeks.
>
> This whole program was more or less your suggestion, as you will recall, and I think it had good point[s] because much harm could come if either of these boys were to do or say something or other out of turn. You might be able to make housing arrangements

without going down, but most certainly I don't want to find ourselves embarrassed on March 1st because of Robinson's not having a place to stay.

Sincerely yours, Branch Rickey, president.[28]

SCOUTING REPORT

After the signing of Jackie Robinson, Cleveland pitcher Bob Feller offered his scouting report on the new ebony star, declaring, "He's tied up in the shoulders and can't hit an inside pitch to save his neck. If he were a white man, I doubt they would even consider him big league material." Little did Feller realize that, in 1962, he and Robinson would go into the Cooperstown National Baseball Hall of Fame together.

After reading of Feller's comments in a Wendell Smith article, Robinson responded with a personal letter to Smith on October 31:

Dear Wendell,

Just read the *Courier* I must say you write very well (smile). The one article by Bob Feller interested me very much inasmuch as I was worried more about my fielding than about my hitting. I value what Feller says because I faced him a couple of times and he is a very good pitcher and when I read where he is one of the best, if not the best pitcher in major league ball, I feel confident that if it is left to my hitting I believe I will do all right. The few times I faced Feller has made me confident that the pitching I have faced in the Negro American League was as tough as any I will have to face if I stick with Montreal. There is one thing I would like to have made clear, just what does Feller really mean when he says I have "football shoulders"?

I want to thank you and the paper for all you have done and are doing in my behalf. As you know I am not worried about what the white press or people think as long as I continue to get the best wishes of my people.

I am leaving it up to your discretion as to what you will print if anything out of this letter. I can only do my best when the time comes. I can't personally discuss whether I can make the grade or not. As I said before I will always be out there doing my best.

Give my regards to Mr. [William] Nunn [staff writer] and all the others that I had the pleasure of meeting.

Sincerely yours,

Jack[29]

Questions persist as to why Jackie Robinson, son of a Georgia sharecropper and grandson of a slave, was the chosen one to integrate the white majors. He had forced the Monarchs' top infielder, Bonnie Serrell, to seek alternative employment.[30]

At the time, the Negro Leagues had several impact players ready for any major league team. However, some of the Negro Leagues' most visible stars were not available. Premier hitter Josh Gibson was emotionally unstable. At the time, some club owners thought Gibson had problems with drugs and alcohol. Only later was it discovered that he suffered from the pains of a brain tumor. Meanwhile, ageless wonder Satchel Paige, the most prolific pitcher of his time, had suspicious arm trouble. And speedster James "Cool Papa" Bell, at age 42, was past his prime as an outfielder and high-average hitter. Power-hitting first baseman Buck Leonard (born in 1907) just told major league officials he was too old for the big leagues.

The league's most popular players, Gibson and Paige, were often cited as the premier candidates to break the color barrier. Their abilities were expressed by writer Sam Lacy of the *Afro-American,* who wrote: "Satchel Paige, judged on his ability as a moundsman, undoubtedly would have covered himself with glory in anybody's league in his heyday. But Satchel soon learned that he could make more money as a showman than he could ever hope to draw as a brilliant flinger. The result was that the redoubtable Kansas City Monarch ace turned his slab assignments into a combination vaudeville act and pitching performance."

Lacy's assessment of Gibson was somewhat unflattering, but truthful:

Josh Gibson . . . is one of the greatest natural hitters the game has ever known, and my observations date back through the eras of Ty Cobb, Babe Ruth, Joe DiMaggio . . . Lou Gehrig and a host of others. I don't think that the man ever lived who possessed a keener batting eye or boasted a more finely developed competitive spirit than the home-run champion of colored baseball.

Gibson, however, measures up as a major leaguer only in this department [batting]. He, like Roy Campanella, is far below the standards set by the average big leaguer as a defensive catcher. He neither receives well, is adept at handling pitchers, nor throws to bases with any passable degree of accuracy and consistency.

Yet, even at 34, Josh is one of my "potentials." Why? Simply because there have been many catchers in the big time who were developed into first-class receivers after they moved up. Given the same careful schooling that is meted out to a prospect from the International League, Gibson has every reason to believe he would master the receiving art and be able to hold his own for a few years in big time company.

Mr. Lacy proudly added, "I haven't the slightest doubt that several Negro players are potentially big league material."[31]

Across the nation, the black press expressed the impact of Jackie Robinson's signing a major league contract. The *New York Amsterdam News* wrote: "just the drop of water in the drought that keeps faith alive in American institutions." They added that Negroes "fought a war for four years to rid the world of vicious racial theories, racial and religious discrimination and segregation. Yet, the fact that Jackie Robinson, a young Negro who is intellectually, culturally and physically superior to most white baseball players, has signed a contract to play in a minor league has caused a national sensation."[32]

The *Michigan Chronicle* reported: "The clubs which insist on drawing the color line have been pushed out on a limb. Sooner or later they will meet the censure of the American public which, despite the popularity of color prejudice, has an ingrained sense of true sportsmanship. Joe Louis would never have won the hearts of Americans if this were not so."[33]

The *Pittsburgh Courier* emphasized that Robinson carried "the hopes, aspirations and ambitions of thirteen million black Americans heaped on his broad, sturdy shoulders."[34]

Earlier, the *Courier* had reported that Rickey had signed Robinson because he was an outstanding prospect and because "his [Rickey's] conscience would not permit him to wallow in the mire of racial discrimination."[35]

Robinson was the ideal candidate to create a legacy greater than the sport itself. He was college educated and articulate, had high morals, and was an army officer and an excellent all-around athlete with no social vices. Coming from UCLA, he possessed the interpersonal communication skills to socialize effectively with white Americans. The bottom line was that Jackie had table manners.

Not everyone was elated over the signing of Jackie Robinson, however. Effa Manley expressed some concerns, stating: "I definitely feel that Negro baseball has a vested right in Jackie Robinson. It isn't fair to take our players without compensation. Negro base-ball has just come through ten lean years. The wealthy white organizations haven't had to share our struggles to develop players. After all, if the major leagues completely raid our leagues and wrecked them, it would help only about 20 Negro players and injure irrepar-ably the 400 or more who are members of Negro organizations. Baseball is a hobby with most major league owners. With we Negroes it is a business, a hard, tough one. Kansas City will present its case to Commissioner Chandler with the full backing of all organized baseball. However, I'm very happy to see our boys make the grade. This is a pretty good example of democracy in action. Robinson is a college fellow and Montreal is a good town because the races mix there on an equal basis." [36]

Judge Jonah J. Goldstein, a candidate for mayor of New York, commented on the sign-ing of Robinson, saying: "Four weeks ago at Yankee Stadium when I threw out the first ball on which I wrote 'discrimination' and said to the batter, 'Sock it.' I was well aware that the end of the color barrier would eventually come, but I must admit it came more sud-denly than most of us expected. New York will continue to lead in showing the way to real democracy." [37]

All-Star Classic Sunday, July 29

Both Sides Boast of Pitchers and Hitters

Source: *Chicago Defender,* 14 July 1945

The thirteenth annual East versus West classic will be played at Comiskey Park, Sunday, July 29 at 3 o'clock. The score in number of games now stands six each. Both sides boast of hitting and pitching strength this year.

The prices of tickets are $3 for box seats, $2 for grandstand and $1 for bleachers. This includes tax.

Seats are on sale at the Rosetta Frock shop, 4719 S. Parkway, The Hotel Grand lobby, 51st and South Parkway, Taylor's Men store, 444 East 47th street and Little's Taylor shop, 3450 S. State street.

The *Chicago Defender* office has no tickets.

Advice is to purchase your tickets early. Go early and avoid the rush. The park is located at 35th and Shields Avenue, one block West of Wentworth Avenue and 35th streetcar lines. There is plenty of parking space. The North and Southbound elevated trains stop at 35th street station near State Street.

The fans will get a preview of the West team on Sunday at Comiskey Park when the 1943 and 1944 Negro American league champion Birmingham Black Barons bob up for a double-header with the Chicago American Giants, now in second place of the split league season.

Americans Too Good for Spiritless East

31,714 See Classic

Davis, Robinson, Radcliffe and Ware Star

As West Pours It on East in Annual All-Star Games

by Wendell Smith

Source: *Pittsburgh Courier,* 4 August 1945

Baseball's flag of supremacy still flies majestically in the rugged, Golden West! Here this afternoon (Sunday) before a throng of 31,714 [reported attendance was 33,088], a fighting band of star-studded diamond gems from the Negro American League humbled a confused, ragged aggregation from the Negro National League to win the thirteenth annual East-West classic, 9–6.

There have been many colorful sensational East-West games in the past. Stars have glittered and sparkled on the turf of Comiskey Park, with a blinding brilliance to make the classic the game of games. In fact, their stellar performances have made it possible for sports writers to refer to the contest as the "Dream Game."

But—as far as the East is concerned—it was only a nightmare here Sunday afternoon!

The West had everything, the East nothing. The West had power at the plate, defense in the field and pitching that was good enough to stop the best the East had to offer. The West was so superior in every department of play, in fact, that it really wasn't a contest. Instead it was just another ball game.

SCORED FOUR IN SECOND

If it is at all possible to attribute any one thing to the East's crushing defeat . . . it can be blamed on a pair of sunglasses and Big Bill Wright's lack of foresight. For it was this one very important shortage that set the stage for a four-run avalanche in the second inning and made it possible for the West's to roar into a commanding lead. After that outburst the East was never in the ball game and the West went galloping merrily along to its seventh classic victory and third successive triumph.

WRIGHT BLINDED BY SUN

The roof fell in on the East in the second inning when Neal Robinson of Memphis stared off by beating out an infield hit. He promptly scampered to third when the veteran Alex Radcliffe powered a drive to right field. Big Bill Wright, ace Baltimore outfielder, failed to get a line on the ball, and was unable to track it down because he was blinded by the sun. Had he stared soon enough he could have caught the drive, but for some strange reason he did not have his sunglasses on and the ball got away from him, and rolled into deep right field. Archie Ware, colorful Cleveland first baseman then drove the first two runs of the game in with a lazy slash over second base. Glover of Baltimore was pitching and the willowy left-hander was never able to get out of this hole. He had a brief respite, however, when Roy Campanella heaved a perfect throw to Willie Wells to nail Ware in an attempted steal.

WILLIAMS' DRIVE MISSED

Quincy Troupe of Cleveland was then given a free pass and Verdell Mathis, Memphis hurler, and starting from the West, slashed a single to left, sending Troupe to third. Jesse Williams of Kansas City, who was injected into the West's lineup at the last minute, was the next hitter. At this point, Manager Vic Harris sent Glover to the showers and called in Bill Ricks, slim Philadelphia right-hander. Williams took a strike across the outside corner and then on the next pitch blasted a drive into right . . . in the direction of Bill Wright, the man without glasses. Again blinded by the sun, Wright was unable to judge the hit and it went for a rousing triple. Two more runs came in and the West held a commanding four run lead. That was really the ball game. The East was never able to recover from that outburst and they simply went through with the act because "the show must go on."

The West really sewed it up in the third when they scored four more runs and Bill Ricks finally had to give in to Martin Dihigo, Cuban right-hander. [Neal] Robinson started the trouble again after Davenport had been thrown out, Ricks to Leonard when he singled to left. Radcliffe got his second hit with a drive over second and Robinson hustled to third. Robinson scored when Steele [no, Lockett] was thrown out, short to first, and Radcliffe came home from second a moment later on Ware's second hit, a sizzling drive into right center. Troupe got his second of three free passes and Mathis filled the bases with a slow roller to second. Jesse Williams then sewed the game up with a single to left, scoring Ware and Troupe.

GAME SEWED UP

That was the ball game right there. The West held an 8 to 0 lead and the East was immediately transformed into a dejected and beaten club. They were never able to overtake the hustling American Leaguers, who did everything they could to pour it on and win their third straight ball game.

Meantime, Verdell Mathis, lean southpaw of Memphis, was doing a masterful job in the box for the West. His blazing fast ball, tricky curve and change-of-pace was too much for the East. He pitched the first three innings and blanked the East. He walked one, struck out three [four], and in general was just too good for the National Leaguers. Chicago's Gentry Jessup followed Mathis and he was equally as successful. He gave up three hits, three walks [one walk] and struck out one. McDaniels of Kansas City followed Jessup, and while he was not as effective as his predecessors, he was still good enough to keep the East from catching up. He was relieved in the ninth with two out after the East had powered four runs across the plate by Eugene Bremer of Cleveland, who eventually put the fire out.

The East's first run was made in the seventh by [Rogelio "Ice Cream"] Linares of the Cubans, who got a free ticket to first, went to second on Watkins single and third on an infield out. He came home on Martinez hit to center.

The only time the East looked anything like a ball club was in the ninth when they scored five times and McDaniel's finally had to leave the ball game. Bill Byrd, Benjamin, Benson, Leonard, and Campanella crossed the plate for the biggest rally the East enjoyed. Willie Wells clouted the only extra base hit during this opening when he doubled home Benson and Benjamin.

In the main, however it really wasn't much of a ball game. The West simply had too much of everything while the East lacked power at the plate, effectiveness on the mound, and even that very important little item they call spirit. They were a beaten ball club before they ever walked out on the field.

Neither Josh Gibson nor Satchel Paige, the kingpins of Negro baseball appeared on the scene. Both stayed in their respective hometowns, which also had a tendency to take some of the color of the game. Paige refused to pitch because of a financial disagreement with the officials and Gibson was suspended two days before the game by Manager Vic Harris for breaking training rules.

West Takes All-Star Classic 9 to 6

Humble East in 13th Game

Mathis and Jessup Give Up No Runs

Source: *Chicago Defender,* 4 August 1945

Good pitching helped the West win the 13th annual East vs. West classic at Comiskey Park Sunday July 29, by the score of 9 to 6. This good hurling by "Lefty" Mathis of the Memphis Red Sox, who allowed no hits and no runs in three innings and was given credit for the victory, and that of Gentry Jessup, Chicago American Giants right hander, who also allowed no runs in three innings, was backed up by the West's bats.

A crowd of 33,088 paid customers saw the game. The greater part of the crowd was from the Chicago area.

The East looked powerfully weak up to the seventh when they nicked Booker McDaniels of the Kansas City Monarchs for one run. The Negro National leaguers refused to go down without a fight and they drove McDaniels from the mound in the ninth, five runs being charged against him.

As it stands now the West is one up on the East and lead in games won seven to six. It was the third in a row for the Negro American leaguers.

The West scored four runs in the second. Neal Robinson of Memphis beat out a hit to [Frank] Austin. Alex Radcliffe doubled. [Marv] Barker tossed out [Lester] Lockett. Ware singled, scoring Robinson and Radcliffe. Ware was caught attempting to steal. Trouppe walked. Mathis singled to center. Tom Glover, Baltimore Elites, starting pitcher for the East, left the game and Bill Ricks of the Philadelphia Stars took the mound. Jesse Williams, Kansas City Monarchs, clouted a triple to right, scoring Trouppe and Mathis. The runs were charged against Glover. Jackie Robinson popped to Willie Wells.[38]

Four more were added in the third. Ricks tossed out Davenport. Neal Robinson singled to left. Radcliffe singled to center. Barker threw out Lockett, but Neal Robinson scored on the play. Ware singled to center and Radcliffe scored. Trouppe walked. Mathis beat out a slow roller to Wells and the bases were full. Williams singled to the right, scoring Ware and Trouppe. Exit Mr. Ricks. Martin Dihigo, New York Cuban pitcher, took the mound. Jackie Robinson popped to Austin for the third out.

In the fourth the West added another to lead 9 to 0. Davenport doubled down the right field foul line. Neal Robinson sacrificed. Dihigo to Leonard, Radcliffe was thrown out by Austin, Davenport scoring the last West run.

The East filled the bases in the sixth on two walks and an infield hit off Jessup. Two were out at the time. J. Williams then threw out Wells.

In the seventh, Rogelio Linares, Cuban outfielder who replaced Bill Wright in the East outfield, walked. Watkins singled to center. Leonard Pearson, Newark, batted for Dihigo, and forced Watkins at second, Linares moving up to third. Jerry Benjamin forced Pearson at second, J. Robinson to Williams, Linares scoring. Horacio Martinez of the New York

Cubans, who had replaced Austin in short, singled to center. J. Robinson threw out Benson, who had replaced Johnny Davis in the East's outfield.

The East woke up in the ninth. Singles by Campanella, Watkins, Benjamin and Martinez and a double by Wells produced four runs after Leonard walked. Eugene Bremmer [Bremer], Cleveland Buckeyes southpaw, relieved McDaniels and Jackie Robinson's fielding of Linares' grounder behind second to nail him at first ended the game.

Roy Welmaker of the world champion Homestead Grays pitched the seventh and the eighth against the West. Tom Glover was charged with the East's defeat.

Scalpers Take Good Beating

East vs. West Game Ducats Scandal

Source: *Chicago Defender,* 4 August 1945

The West All-Star team, made up of Negro American leaguers, made it three in a row in a 9 to 6 triumph over the East All-Stars, Sunday, July 29, at Comiskey Park. The Negro National leaguers, although they staged a ninth-inning rally to score five runs off Booker McDaniels, Kansas City Monarch hurler, took a drubbing.

But there were some things going on that the 33,088 paid customers didn't know about. The scalpers also took a severe beating. Blocks of grandstand tickets were still in the hands of those who sought outlandish prices. The word was passed around that no tickets were available at the park, yet there was plenty of room. Last year's crowd was reported at 46,000 [actual attendance was 46,247].

Police made eight arrests outside the park. Some of the men hauled to the police station were accused of scalping tickets without turning in any federal tax. Others were charged with selling counterfeit tickets.

As late as Sunday afternoon, box seats could be purchased if anyone would come up with $7.50 for a ticket. Some were asking $10 for a box seat ticket. Grandstand $2 tickets sold for $4 each.

A federal representative at Comiskey Park told Dr. J. B. Martin, President of the Negro American league and chairman of the East-West game committee, and Tom Wilson, President of the Negro National league and a member of the committee, the place were most of the ticket scalping originated. Both officials of the game have ordered am investigation.

Those who bought tickets above the purchase price stated on the tickets are asked to write to the *Chicago Defender* sports department or to Dr. Martin, 412 E. 47th street, stating the amount paid over the purchase price printed on the ticket and where the ticket or tickets were bought. The authors of the letters will be protected. Their names will not be made public. However, the letter must be signed and the street address given.

The crowd was orderly and well handled. Five minor disturbances broke out. One woman and man were ejected from the box seats for fighting. The ball players conducted themselves like major leaguers.

The 13th annual classic is now history. The West now leads in games seven to six. Although down on the list to play, Leroy Satchel Paige remained in Kansas City, Mo. Last year, when it was announced that Paige would not play, the crowd was larger by 15 thousand.

Players on both squads in uniform, whether or not they got into the game or not, received $100 each and their traveling expenses, plus expenses while here. Managers and coaches received $300 each. A sum of $300 went to each club to be divided among players who were not selected for the classic.

Gread McKinnis, left-hand ace of the Chicago American Giants, was not called upon to pitch by Manager W. S. Welsh [Welch] of the West team because of an injured forearm.

Alex Radcliffe, Cincinnati Clowns third baseman, was playing his 10th time in the annual classic. He played with an injured ankle.

Cong. William L. Dawson curved over the first ball to start the game. Edward "Mike" Sneed, county commissioner, caught it.

Through the Years: Past—Present—Future

by Fay Young

Source: *Chicago Defender*, 4 August 1945

The West did it again Sunday at Comiskey Park. The East dropped the third East-West classic game in a row. The score of the 13th annual contest was 9 to 6. The West now leads in games seven to six.

The East took a drubbing—so did the scalpers who were left holding blocks of tickets held for outlandish prices. Word passed around early as Monday of last week that the box seats had been sold out. They finally were, with few exceptions, Sunday about noon. But the grandstand seats, reported sold out early Saturday night, just weren't. The expected crowd of between 40 and 50 thousand turned out to be 31,714 paid, with oodles of vacant seats in both the lower and upper decks in left field and right field and some space in the bleacher seats.

More about that later. Next year it will be different. The tickets most likely will be put on sale at one place—an official headquarters.

There weren't any stolen bases in the game. Neal Robinson of Memphis contributed the only sacrifice hit. Jesse Williams, Kansas City, the surprise second baseman for the West because his name didn't appear on any of the lists given to the press, poled the only triple of the game. It came in the second. The West's other extra base hits were by Lloyd Davenport, Cleveland Buckeyes outfielder, in the fourth, and Alex Radcliffe in the second. The East's extra base clout was by the veteran, Willie Wells, now manager of the New York Black Yankees. That came in the ninth.

There weren't any home runs this year.

Only nine men faced Verdell Mathis, Memphis southpaw, who hurled the first three innings for the West. He walked Frank Austin, of Philadelphia, second man up in the first inning, but picked him off first a moment later on a quick throw to Archie Ware of Cleveland who, in turn, pegged to Jackie Robinson of Kansas City at second to kill Austin.

Mathis fanned Johnny Davis of Newark in the first, Buck Leonard of the Grays and Roy Campanella of Baltimore in the second, and Bill Ricks of Philadelphia in the third. Mathis had a perfect day at the bat, getting two hits in two times up.

Quincy Trouppe, Cleveland catcher, also had a perfect day, with one hit in one official time up. He walked three times. Murray Watkins, Newark third sacker, was the only easterner in the charmed circle. He was up twice and got two hits.

Orchids to Alex Radcliffe of the Cincinnati Clowns and Jackie Robinson of Kansas City. Radcliffe knocked down Campanella's smash in the third and after it had rolled a few feet away, retrieved it and dived head first to touch third, forcing Johnny Davis for the third out of the inning and thwarting an East rally.

Robinson hustled over behind second in the ninth inning blitz by the East, dug a nasty hard grounder off the bat of Rogelio Linares of the New York Cuban Stars, out of the dirt and rifled it over to Ware for the final out of the 1945 game.

The umpire, Harry Ward, was none other than the great "Wufang" Ward of Wilberforce football fame in 1924 and 1925.

Jim Taylor, coach of the West, was the East's manager last year. W. S. Welsh [Welch], manager of the West for the second straight year, is the Birmingham Black Barons' manager. Frank Duncan, manager of the Kansas City Monarchs, was coach off first. Vic Harris, manager of the Homestead Grays, was the East's manager.

Archie Ware pulled one for the books. He took Linares' grounder towards first in the eighth and outran Willie Wells, who was trying to make second, to tag Wells before he reached the keystone sack. Now you can look over your score books but you won't find a first baseman making a putout at second, unassisted, on any such play as that.

The Sports Beat

East-West Game Star Dust

by Wendell Smith

Source: *Pittsburgh Courier,* 4 August 1945

Chicago—The two biggest stars in Negro baseball, Josh Gibson and Satchel Paige, were conspicuous by their absence here Sunday. Gibson has been suspended by the Homestead Grays for flagrant and consistent training violations and Paige refused to pitch because he could not reach an agreement with the East-West promoters financially. Although the game was a success from the attendance standpoint, it did not come up to expectations. Instead of the anticipated 50,000 the crowd was counted at 31,714. This shortage caused the officials of the two leagues considerable concern. General consensus was that the switching of the customary date from the first week in August to the last Sunday in July caught a lot of people off guard and they could not make the trip. The recent ODT [Office of Defense Transportation] ban on traveling also had its effect.[39]

Exclusive: Josh Gibson has been suspended and probably has seen his last season with the Homestead Grays. Larry Brown is on his way out as manager of the Memphis Red Sox and Verdell Mathis, brilliant southpaw hurler, is on his way in. Dissatisfaction is running rampant through the Birmingham Black Barons. Captain Art Wilson is in the "doghouse" and as a result was not permitted to play in the classic here. Anything can happen within the Barons' camp and the only one who is sitting safely is Manager Winfield S. Welch, who piloted the West Sunday and has the distinction of piloting three East-West winners against no losses (sic, Welch and his West squad lost both games in 1942 before winning their first game under Welch in 1944).

The goat of the game was Bill Wright, veteran outfielder of Baltimore, who misjudged two drives that might have been caught if he had used his sunglasses. Right field in Comiskey Park is one of the sunniest in the majors. Best looking performer was Jesse Williams, Kansas City second sacker, who was added to the West lineup at the last minute.

JULY 29, 1945, CHICAGO, IL

EAST	AB	R	H	D	T	HR	BI	E	TAVG	TSLG
Jerry Benjamin (Homestead Grays), cf	5	1	1	0	0	0	1	0		
Frank Austin (Philadelphia Stars), ss	2	0	0	0	0	0	0	1		
Rabbit Martinez (New York Cubans), ss	2	0	2	0	0	0	3	0		
John Davis (Newark Eagles), lf	2	0	0	0	0	0	0	0		
Gene Benson (Philadelphia Stars), lf	2	1	0	0	0	0	0	0		
Buck Leonard (Homestead Grays), 1b	3	1	1	0	0	0	0	0		
Roy Campanella (Baltimore Elite Giants), c	5	1	2	0	0	0	0	0		
Willie Wells (Newark Eagles), 2b	5	0	1	1	0	0	2	0		
Bill Wright (Baltimore Elite Giants), rf	1	0	0	0	0	0	0	0		
Rogelio Linares (New York Cubans), rf	3	1	0	0	0	0	0	0		
Marvin Barker (New York Black Yankees), 3b	2	0	1	0	0	0	0	0		
Murray Watkins (Newark Eagles), 3b	2	0	2	0	0	0	0	0		
Tom Glover (Baltimore Elite Giants), p	0	0	0	0	0	0	0	0		
Bill Ricks (Philadelphia Stars), p	0	0	0	0	0	0	0	0		
Martin Dihigo (New York Cubans), p	1	0	0	0	0	0	0	0		
a) Lennie Pearson (Newark Eagles), ph	1	0	0	0	0	0	0	0		
Roy Welmaker (Homestead Grays), p	0	0	0	0	0	0	0	0		
b) Bill Byrd (Baltimore Elite Giants), ph	1	1	0	0	0	0	0	0		
Team Totals, Average & Slugging Pct.	37	6	10	1	0	0	6	1	.270	.297

a) Batted for Dihigo in 7th
b) Batted for Welmaker in 9th

WEST	AB	R	H	D	T	HR	BI	E	TAVG	TSLG
Jesse Williams (Kansas City Monarchs), 2b	5	0	2	0	1	0	4	0		
Jackie Robinson (Kansas City Monarchs), ss	5	0	0	0	0	0	0	0		
Lloyd Davenport (Cleveland Buckeyes), rf	4	1	1	1	0	0	0	0		
Neil Robinson (Memphis Red Sox), cf	2	2	2	0	0	0	0	0		
Alec Radcliffe (Cincinnati-Ind. Clowns), 3b	4	2	2	1	0	0	1	1		
Lester Lockett (Birmingham Black Barons), lf	4	0	0	0	0	0	1	0		
Archie Ware (Cleveland Buckeyes), 1b	4	1	2	0	0	0	3	0		
Quincy Trouppe (Cleveland Buckeyes), c	1	2	1	0	0	0	0	0		
Verdell Mathis (Memphis Red Sox), p	2	1	2	0	0	0	0	0		
Gentry Jessup (Chicago American Giants), p	1	0	0	0	0	0	0	0		
Booker McDaniels (Kansas City Monarchs), p	1	0	0	0	0	0	0	0		
Gene Bremer (Cleveland Buckeyes), p	0	0	0	0	0	0	0	0		
Team Totals, Average & Slugging Pct.	33	9	12	2	1	0	9	1	.364	.485

East	000	000	105-6
West	044	100	00x-9

PITCHER/TEAM	GS	IP	H	R	ER	K	BB	WP	HB	W	L	SV
Glover/BEG	1	1 2/3	5	4	4	0	1	0	0	0	1	0
Ricks/PS		1	5	4	4	0	1	0	0	0	0	0
Dihigo/NYC		3 1/3	2	1	1	0	0	0	0	0	0	0
Welmaker/HG		2	0	0	0	0	1	0	0	0	0	0
Mathis/MRS	1	3	0	0	0	4	1	0	0	1	0	0
Jessup/CAG		3	3	0	0	1	2	0	0	0	0	0
McDaniels/KCM		2 2/3	6	6	6	1	2	0	0	0	0	0
Bremer/CEB		1/3	1	0	0	0	0	0	0	0	0	1

BB—Trouppe (3), Linares, Leonard, Watkins, Austin
LOB—West 5, East 10
SAC—N. Robinson
East—Vic Harris (Mgr.)
West—W. S. Welch (Mgr.); Coaches Frank Duncan and Candy Jim Taylor
Umpires—Virgil Blueitt, Fred McCrary, Harry "Wu Fang" Ward, Moe Harris
Attendance—33,088   Paid—32,762   Time—2:32
Note: Campanella voted MVP by committee of newspapermen. He was awarded the Olde Tymer A. C. Trophy.

1946

The U.S. Supreme Court bans segregation on interstate buses.

Judge William Hastie becomes the first African-American governor of the Virgin Islands. Hastie had previously been considered for commissioner of the Negro Leagues.

The first U.S. commemorative coin is issued honoring an African-American, Booker T. Washington.

Milk costs 35 cents a half-gallon, 10 pounds of potatoes costs 47 cents, while a Franklin half and three wheat pennies would bring home the bacon. A loaf of bread costs 10 cents.

The All-American Football Conference is created and, unlike the National Football League, signs black players.

The United States League, created by Branch Rickey as a developmental league for black players, folds.

Ted Williams hits two homers and two singles with five RBIs to lead the American League to a 12–0 win in the first Major League All-Star Game played at Fenway Park.

The first televised game between two black professional teams, the Newark Eagles and the New York Black Yankees, is broadcast from Ebbets Field in Brooklyn, New York.

THE WAR IS OVER!

This pivotal year saw many social and economic changes in the lives of Americans. World War II ended, and the United States was invaded with the return of GIs from combat. Americans had unwillingly become comfortable with the rationing of food and gasoline during the previous few years. The gasoline shortage and travel restrictions had caused the 1945 major league all-star contest to be canceled. With the economy spurting to renew its old stability, Americans were confronted with the arrival of new products, such as television sets (some predicted the demise of the radio, the "poor man's phonograph"), refrigerators (iceboxes were the norm), automatic washing machines (causing some washhouses to close), and a boom in the music recording industry.

It was also the beginning of the "baby boom" as population growth exceeded all government projections. In the next 10 years, more than 30 million American babies would scream for parental attention. This trend prompted Benjamin Spock to publish his bestselling *Common Sense Book of Baby and Child Care*. Among the baby boomers born in 1946 was Reggie "Mr. October" Jackson, son of Negro Leaguer Martinez Jackson. Reggie Jackson would later become an advocate for the recognition of Negro League history.

In 1945 New York City mayor Fiorello La Guardia created a Mayor's Committee of Unity to examine the racial and religious relations in his city. One of the questions La Guardia was investigating was the integration of Major League Baseball. La Guardia assigned aid Dan W. Dodson to address this racial issue. Realizing his clandestine plan to integrate baseball with Kansas City Monarchs rookie Jackie Robinson might be foiled, Branch Rickey asked for a meeting with Dodson. Rickey asked Dodson not to pressure Major League Baseball to sign black players until he had time to implement his own plan.

Dodson also talked with Larry MacPhail, president of the New York Yankees. MacPhail's point of view was different. He stated that the mayor's office knew nothing about baseball, that the Negro League clubs had a substantial investment in their players, and that white clubs would also lose money under integration because they relied on renting their parks to black teams.[1]

LEAGUE BUSINESS

After Robinson's signing and before the start of a new season, Negro League officials met with new commissioner Albert "Happy" Chandler in Cincinnati. The January meeting between Chandler, Dr. J. B. Martin, Negro American League president, and Thomas Wilson, owner of the Baltimore Elite Giants, was to discuss the possibility of Chandler becoming commissioner of both leagues. Chandler commented to the press: "There have been conferences between myself, [Will] Harridge, and [Ford] Frick, with the presidents of the American and National Negro Leagues. These conferences at the request of the Negro League presidents were with a view toward organizing the Negro Leagues on a strong basis. I was asked if I would also be commissioner for those leagues. I told them to get their house in order then come to baseball with a petition for recognition."[2]

MACPHAIL REPORT

Soon after the January meeting, a new major league steering committee named Mac-Phail chairman to study marketing, advertising, and race relations with fans and Negro League clubs. The committee included league presidents Will Harridge and Ford Frick, along with owners Phil Wrigley (Cubs), Tom Yawkey (Red Sox), and Sam Breadon (Cardinals). Under MacPhail's leadership, the committee was scheduled to meet seven times in July and August of 1946 with a final report to the owners on August 27, 1946.

With race an essential issue in the discussions, Major League Baseball took great pains to keep the committee's findings confidential. Despite orders to destroy all records, a final draft copy issued to Commissioner Chandler survived. Excerpts appeared for the first time in the October 24, 1951, issue of *The Sporting News*.

The findings recognized that the tremendous growth in black attendance for the International League games that Jackie Robinson had played might be a factor in enhancing fan attendance at major league parks, particularly in New York. MacPhail stated: "The Negro leagues rent their parks in many cities from clubs in Organized Baseball. Many major and minor league clubs derive substantial revenue from these rentals. (The Yankee organization, for instance, nets nearly $100,000 a year from rentals and concessions in connection with Negro league games at the Yankee Stadium in New York—and in Newark, Kansas City and Norfolk). Club owners in the major leagues are reluctant to give up revenues amounting to hundreds of thousands of dollars every year. They naturally want the Negro leagues to continue."[3] Other arguments and factors defending the imaginary but very real color line included the following:

Baseball is being pressured by meddling publicity hounds who don't care about blacks: Certain groups in this country including political and social-minded drum beaters, are conducting pressure campaigns in an attempt to force major league clubs to sign Negro players. Members of these groups are not primarily interested in Professional Baseball.

They are not campaigning to provide a better opportunity for thousands of Negro boys who want to play baseball. . . . They know little about baseball—and nothing about the business end of its operation. They single out Professional Baseball for attack because it offers a good publicity medium.

. . .

Signing a few black players won't solve anything because most Negro Leaguers aren't qualified for the majors: Jobs for half a dozen good Negro players now employed in the Negro Leagues are relatively unimportant. Signing new Negro players for the major leagues would be a gesture—but it would contribute little or nothing towards a solution of the real problem.

. . .

Negro Leaguers can't play in the majors because they haven't played in the minors: A major league player must have something besides great natural ability. He must possess the technique, the coordination, the competitive attitude, and the discipline, which is usually acquired only after years of seasoning in the minor leagues. The minor league experience of players on the major league rosters, for instance, averages seven years. The young Negro player never has had a good chance in baseball. Comparatively few good young Negro players are being developed. This is the reason there are not more players who meet major league standards in the Negro Leagues.

. . .

Club owners had to respect Negro League contracts: They do not sign, and cannot properly sign, players under contract to Negro clubs. This is not racial discrimination. It's simply respecting the contractual relationship between the Negro leagues and their players.

. . .

Black players would attract black fans, whose presence might drive away more desirable white patrons. A situation might be presented, if Negroes participate in Major League games, in which the preponderance of Negro attendance in parks such as Yankee Stadium, the Polo Grounds, and Comiskey Park could conceivably threaten the value of Major League franchises owned by these clubs.[4]

The race section of MacPhail's report closed with the following: "There are many factors in this problem and many difficulties which will have to be solved before any generally satisfactory solution can be worked out. The individual action of any one Club may exert tremendous pressures upon the whole structure of Professional Baseball, and could conceivably result in lessening the value of several major league franchises."[5]

JACKIE'S FAN CLUB

Jackie Robinson was completing his first season with the Montreal Royals when a fan wrote a letter to the editors of the *Montreal Herald* in a rebuttal to remarks made by future Hall of Fame pitcher Bob Feller after Robinson signed a Montreal contract.

> Robert Feller,
> c/o Cleveland Indians,
> Cleveland, Ohio

Dear Bobby

Last October you were quoted as saying that "you just couldn't foresee any future for Robinson in big league baseball." You also said something about Robinson not being able to hit inside pitches to save his neck.

Well, I'm sure you'll like to know that Jackie Robinson is the batting champion of the International Baseball League. And in his first year, too. By now you are well aware of his popularity as well as his ability. He finished off the season with an average of .349 and led the league in runs scored with 113. The pace-setting Robinson is the first Montreal batter to win the league's batting championship since 1908. The highest previous average of a Royal was that of Snake Henry, who set a Royal record of .345 in 1930, thus it makes Jackie the best batter to wear a Montreal uniform.

Robbie smashed 155 hits in 444 times at bat, five points ahead of Bobby Brown of the Newark Bears, his nearest rival. Among his 155 hits were 25 two-baggers, nine less than that of leader Eddie Joost of Rochester; eight triples, five less than Marvin Rackley's top of 13. The star second-sacker also batted in 65 runs and stole 40 bases, and though official figures are not out on this department, he probably walked more times than any other batter in the loop.

As a pitcher, you must realize that your fellow hurlers must have tried various offerings on the gifted Robinson including inside pitches. Seldom has Jackie failed to comment in some way. His strikeout record is one of the lowest in the league. He has them all.

You have one consolation, Bobby, you weren't the only one to call the Robinson shot wrong. In fact, very few were right. Those who knew the material Jackie is off, never doubted that he would be right up there.

One of these is Clyde Sukeforth, Brooklyn's No. 1 coach and former manager of the Montreal Royals. When Jackie didn't look too promising during spring training especially at the plate, a "Sukey" was writing to friends that Robbie will come through. And that he did!

There were many skeptics who also talked and wrote about his football shoulders. Then Jackie started hitting. At least he was getting down to first base. The same soothsayers said that it was not his ability at the plate but his fast running pace that was earning those hits for Jackie. The latter never said a word about that, never a complaint. Suddenly he became a power hitter, slamming out needed doubles, triples and a couple of times a homer.

You know about his fielding, Bob. How he changed from his natural shortstop spot into that of second baseman. They just told him that his throw was a bit short, and then there was Stan Beard, Montreal's own shortstop, who the previous season copped the all-star spot. Jackie went to second and within a short time became the sensation of the league on the middle sack.

Of the first ten ballots received in the International League offices on all-star selections, Robinson had nine votes as second sacker. The other named him for third, a position he has tackled only four times.

You know of his attraction at the gate. He's the Ted Williams and Bobby Feller (You see, we recognize talent) of the International League. You know, because you asked him to join your barnstorming troupe of baseballers. He declined because he will be touring with two Royals, Al Campanis and Marvin Rackley [as part of the Jackie Robinson All-Stars]. Jackie helped Montreal set an attendance record at home and on the road. The turnstiles business upped to 412,758 paid, not including Ladies' Day, children or passes, at home, and as many on the road. With the playoffs, the Royals should hit the million mark. Not bad for a minor club.

We in Montreal are very proud of him. The fans and sportswriters, even those who

36. *The Satchel Paige All-Stars played the Bob Feller All-Stars in a 14-game series in various cities. Feller's team was no match for the Paige All-Stars, losing a dozen games. Every member of Paige's team was an East-West participant. Paige is standing in the doorway with an unknown valet and Dizzy Dismukes a few steps lower. On the ground, from left to right, are all-stars Hilton Smith, Howard Easterling, Barney Brown, Sam Jethroe, Gentry Jessup, Hank Thompson, Max Manning, Chico Renfroe, Rufus Lewis, Gene Benson, Buck O'Neil, Frank Duncan, Artie Wilson, and Quincy Trouppe. Courtesy of Quincy Trouppe.*

thought he wouldn't make good, are sure he'll make the grade in the majors. And if he doesn't, a record crowd would be on hand at the ballpark to welcome him back here.

Robinson is the best bunter in the game today, some even go as far as rating him above the immortal Ty Cobb. According to Bruno Bretzel, who managed the Royals last summer, and now handles the same job with the Jersey City "Little" Giants, told Taylor Spink of the St. Louis *Sporting News* that Jackie is the best bunter in any league and also added his voice to the argument that he's better than Cobb. Spink reports Bretzel, a Southerner, as saying "I would like having nine Robinsons. If I had one Jackie I'd room with him myself and put him to bed nights to make sure nothing happened to him."

(Signed) Sam Martin

Writer Lester Rodney best described the transition of Jackie's journey during this post-war era:

Racists was not the majority, but a healthy minority. You didn't have tens of thousands fans screaming epithets at Jackie. You had many hundreds, you know. That's an awful lot, though. Particularly, if somebody can throw a dead black cat out on the field like they did in Philadelphia and get away with it.

At the same time it aroused indignation from other people to accept the discrimination, but a studying of feelings like Eddie Stanky for instance. He was from Mobile,

Alabama. He was on that Dodger team. That why Jackie Robinson had to play first base the first year, because they had Eddie Stanky at second in 1947.

Now Stanky was not part of the Dixie Walker gang although he signed the first petition and all, but he wasn't a bigot. He didn't have those strong feelings. And one day in Philadelphia, when Ben Chapman and his gang was yelling all the stuff at Jackie and knowing that he couldn't fight back, nor even glare back at you, something happen to Stanky! He jumped in front of the dugout steps and he yelled, "You yellow-belly SOB, why don't you pick on somebody who can fight back." As he told me later, he was surprised he did that.

He [Stanky] didn't turn overnight into a fighter for discrimination. As a teammate, he said, "Nobody should have to take that stuff." After a while the racists found they were no longer a healthy minority. They got a little confused. I can't remember exactly when the change started. But by 1949, two years later, that open shouting in the stands was not heard anymore. They began to see those feelings were out of place. That doesn't mean there were no more racists. In terms of Dixie Walker, he never changed, but he stopped doing anything to stop Jackie's progress.

Branch Rickey really laid down the law. At the time they had the reverse clause. There was no such change as free agency. Rickey said you guys play ball or you're off the Dodgers. That was their livelihood. It was a different cultural situation back then.[6]

ALL-STAR REVIEW

After Jackie Robinson completed his first season with Montreal, he organized his own team of all-stars. His pitching staff consisted of Negro Leaguers Johnny Wright and Ross "Satchel" Davis, and Mike Nozinski, a white pitcher for Nashua in the New England League. For offensive support, they had catchers Roy Campanella, from Nashua, and Kansas City Monarch Earl Taborn plus Larry Doby, Monte Irvin, Lennie Pearson, and several other Newark Eagles players gracing the lineup. On October 13, they played Hans Wagner's All-Stars, a conglomeration of players from the Pittsburgh Pirates and the Cincinnati Redlegs. Playing in Chicago, the Robinson All-Stars easily defeated Wagner's major leaguers, 10–5.

BARRIER BREAKER

There had been several fair-complexioned Cubans who played in the major leagues over the years. Conversely, 1946 was the first year that a known Caucasian athlete performed on the field for a Negro League team. His name was Edward Joseph Klep, and he was a Pole from Erie, Pennsylvania. Ernie Wright, owner of the 1945 Negro World Champion Cleveland Buckeyes, had signed Eddie Klep, a stocky left-handed pitcher.

After Klep showed promise in spring training in Oklahoma, Buckeyes general manager Wilbur Hayes signed him to a contract. Unlike the historic signing of Jackie Robinson, there was no press conference to announce this barrier breaker. The news broke in the March 14 issue of the *Erie Herald-Dispatch* with the headline "Eddie Klep, Erie Sandlot Hurler, Joins Negro Nine." The article read: "Branch Rickey, who signed the first Negro player to a contract in organized baseball, has nothing on Ernie Wright, Erie man who owns the Cleveland Buckeyes of the Negro American League. Wright is taking Eddie Klep, white boy, to the Buckeye training camp for a tryout this spring."

Rickey applauded the signing, saying, "Since the white majors are giving Negro talent a chance, the Negro majors should give white players a chance."[7]

On a Buckeyes trip to play the Birmingham Black Barons in Rickwood Field, Jim Crow

37. Eddie Klep, standing on the right, was the first openly known white American to play in the Negro Leagues. Klep played briefly for the Cleveland Buckeyes. Here he is pictured in his Rockview Prison uniform from his 1951 stay. Courtesy of Ethel M. Klep and Dr. Alice Carter.

took the field. Two city police officers cited a city ordinance that prevented any contest between white and black athletes. The "Bullies in Blue," as writer Jimmie N. Jones of the *Cleveland Call-Post* called them, were against race mixing.[8]

Jones, who also served as the Buckeyes' press agent, claimed two officers approached him and asked, "Do you'all have a white boy on yo' team?" Jones responded with an affirmative. "Git him out of here . . . and quick!" the officers demanded. "We don't have no mixin' down here!" When Jones asked if Klep could remain in the dugout, the deputies answered gruffly, "No! He can't set in the dugout or any place else with you. If you want the game to go on, git him off the field and out of them ball clothes or there won't be any game."

Klep, without confrontation, returned to the hotel and changed into his civilian clothes. When he returned to the ballpark, he took a seat behind the Buckeyes' dugout. Once again, the cops demanded he move over to the "Whites Only" section of the grandstand or the Buckeyes would forfeit the game.[9]

On the first Sunday in June, Klep was given his unconditional release from the Buckeyes. Manager Quincy Trouppe said, "Although Klep showed promise in spring training, he failed to measure up to the fast Negro American League standards and needed additional experience."[10] After his release, Klep returned to Erie, where he played with the all-black Pontiac Automen, managed by Claude "Strategy" Harris. Soon after, in September, Klep was convicted of burglary and receiving stolen goods and was sent to Western State Penitentiary in Pittsburgh, Pennsylvania. On January 29, 1948, he was transferred to Rockview State Prison, in Bellefonte, where he played on their ball team.[11] Klep would never return to professional baseball, but his career will remain a footnote in black baseball history.

Klep, the first acknowledged white in the black leagues, had a strange precursor in a white player who "passed" as an African-American ballplayer in the 1920s. Fred "Chick" Meade, alias Dr. Leslie Marshall and Chick Fleming, had played from 1914 to 1922 with several Negro teams, including the Philadelphia Hilldales, the Pittsburgh Colored Stars, the Baltimore Black Sox, the Indianapolis ABCs, and the Harrisburg Giants. A habitual criminal, he sought refuge as a light-skinned Negro to avoid discovery by the authorities. Meade's true identity was not revealed until May 1931, when he wrote a $705 check as payment for an automobile using the account of Dr. Marshall, a Harrisburg physician. When the bogus check bounced, officials at the Ashley Automobile Company contacted the doctor, who notified the local authorities.

Meade was arrested at 436 North Fremont Avenue in Baltimore, where he had been living with a black family. In a background check of Meade, a native of Smithfield, Maryland, the police found his true heritage. According to police records, Meade had been released on May 7 from Atlanta Federal Penitentiary, where he had been serving a two-year sentence for forging money orders. Four days later, he attempted to fleece a car and was arrested on May 16, just nine days after gaining freedom. Meade was sentenced to 18 months in federal prison.[12]

Meade's first arrest had been in 1920 in Atlantic City, New Jersey, for forging checks. He served six months in the Atlantic City jail. In 1925 he was given a three-year sentence for passing bad checks in Pittsburgh. After serving a year and half, he was paroled. He served another six months at the Baltimore House of Corrections in 1927 for passing bad checks. Later in the year, he was caught cashing counterfeit money orders and was sentenced to two years in the Atlantic City jail system.[13]

WASHINGTON DC GAME REVIEWS

The Sports Beat: There's Only One!

by Wendell Smith

Source: *Pittsburgh Courier,* 17 August 1946

> You can take Ziegfield's Follies and Barnum's
>   Great shows and roll 'em all into one.
> You can have the World Series or a Joe Louis fight,
>   With their action, drama and fun.
> But for me—my dear friends—there's only one show
>   And it's greater than all of the rest.
> It's that stupendous, gigantic, colossal attraction
>   When the East locks horns with the West!
>   I'll give you the Derby with its colorful crowds,
>   And the jockeys who ride with such skill.
> Or the great grid classics in the Fall of the year.
>   When they punt and pass for a thrill.
> But for me—my dear friends—there's only one game
>   That passes the crucial test,
> And that's the one in Chicago each year
>   When the East locks horns with the West
>   There's the National Open with its golfers so great,
>   Swinging from the tee to the green.
> And the auto races at Indianapolis,
>   The likes of which few have seen.
> But for me—my dear friends—there's only one show
>   That I watch with interest and zest,
> It's that sensational, colorful, action-packed clash
>   When the East locks horns with the West!
>   Yes! You can have all the others, I give you them free,
>   And hope that you have a good time,
> For there's nothing so great as a good sports event
>   Whether it cost you a dollar or dime.
> But for me—my dear friends—there's only one day
>   I treasure above all the rest,
> And that's the one-Oh! That historic one
>   When the East locks horns with the West!

What a Difference a Year Makes!

by Wendell Smith

Source: *Pittsburgh Courier,* 17 August 1946

Two of the stars who were in last year's classic will be missing Sunday. Their success in a new domain, however, indicates that the gems of Negro baseball have the ability to sparkle in the higher realm of organized baseball. Last year at this time Jackie Robinson and Roy Campanella were named on the East-West roster. Jackie played with the West and

Roy with the East. Robinson's batting average at that time with the Kansas City Monarchs was .333 and Campanella was slugging away at a .345 clip. The West came out of last year's fray the victor by a 9 to 6 score. Campanella banged out two lusty hits in five trips to the plate for the East. Robinson played shortstop for the West. Although he failed to get a safe hit in five trips, he did a great job in the field and was the key man in the American league infield.

Now these two ex-East-West stars are sparkling elsewhere. Robinson is the sensation of the International League. Playing second base for Montreal, he's hitting .375 and doing a great job at the keystone corner. Campanella is hitting .292 for Nashua in the New England league and is considered the best catcher in the circuit.

Last year this time, both Robinson and Campanella were just two real good Negro ball players. They played in the East-West game and then returned to their respective teams in the Negro National and American Leagues. No one in that crowd of 35,000 fans who saw them play at Comiskey Park in the 1945 "Dream Game" ever thought Jackie or Roy would ever be in organized baseball and have a chance to crash the major leagues. Nor did the players themselves.

But today they're playing on crack teams in two good leagues and going great.

WILL THERE BE OTHERS?

Jackie Robinson and Roy Campanella will not be in Sunday's big East-West game. They have moved upstairs and have their sights set on the Brooklyn Dodgers and the major leagues.

Who knows how Fate will treat the stars in this year's "Dream Game?" Will others— like Robinson and Campanella—emerge from the classic and be signed by a major league organization? Will one or more of them have to miss next year's East-West game because they'll be performing in the big leagues?

No one knows . . . it could happen.

The case of Robinson and Campanella proves what can happen in the span of a year. Last year they played in the East-West game. Today they are both knocking on the door of the majors.

Who will it be after Sunday's big game in Chicago?

Dan Burley's Confidentially Yours'

Source: *New York Amsterdam News,* 24 August 1946

To begin with the ball game itself was strictly big league stuff with all the trimmings . . . Josh Gibson, Dan Bankhead, Larry Doby, Chin Evans, Art Wilson, Sammy Jethroe, Buck Leonard, Piper Davis, Barney Brown and the other lads put on a spectacular show, even though the East went down, 4–1.

But the "commercials" almost ruined the day for the folks who came out to enjoy a ball game. A "commercial" in a ballpark is when somebody is paged over the microphone or has his name and address mentioned. Before 45,474 folks that should be worth something. A few samples of what we had to listen to, cutting in as they did on announcements pertaining to the game itself were: "Will Mr. Sweet Potato Jenkins of Whichaway, Alabama, please go to the box-office—It's urgent!" . . . "Mr. J. Picket N. Runn, who operates the swank Greasy Pig Barbecue and Pool Room at 2700 South State Street, will give the player who hits six home runs in a row a free pigs foot plus potato salad and a bottle of beer." . . . "Dr. Ican Cutyou Williams of Lynchtree, Arkansas, will you stand and scratch your head so the folks can see you?" . . . "Profession Jimson Weed, whose remedies for hydrophobia,

39. *The dynamic duo of Monte Irvin and Larry Doby played in both East-West games of 1946, before leading the Newark Eagles to a Negro League world series championship over the Kansas City Monarchs. In the twin bills of 1946, the duo went 5 for 14 (.357), with no extra base hits. Courtesy of NoirTech Research, Inc.*

corns and nappy hair are so well known, is sitting behind the third base line up near the top of the stands. Stand up professor and let the folks look at you." or "Next Wednesday night, the Royal Sisters of the Frying Pan Club will hold a parlor social at the Shooting Gallery, admission is only $1" . . . "Come out and support this worthy cause, all monies are guaranteed to go to pay the members' rent." Many cynics who listened to these "commercials" were sure that they weren't being made "on the house." But I guess the fact that no fights were reported, no throwing of whiskey bottles, etc., gave them license to give the "commercials" the right of way.

The ballplayers struck before the game demanding more than the $50 the owners had planned to give them for bringing in all those players. I heard they finally wangled $100 a man out of the deal. A lot of things are surprising about his famed event, mainly that the rental for Comiskey Park is around $12,000 for that one date. $1,500 goes to the all-white park staff of ushers, etc., who make up Andy Frain's Ushers Union, and the left over gold after Tom [Wilson] and J. B. [Martin] get their cut, is distributed among the club owners, that is, after a lot of "heavy expenses" have been tacked on here and there. And, of course, Wilson and J. B. get their "expenses" on top of the percentage. The poor players get around $6 a day of which they must pay hotel rent, buy their meals, pay for their laundry and pressing bills. And of course, the players get their transportation "free!"

While the participating players get the $10 or whatever it was, their teammates who didn't get the call split up around $300 among them, which means that on most of the clubs which carry around 18 or 20 men, each gets about $10. Dr. J. B. Martin, being on the scene, is also said to get a league president's share; a team owner's share; controls the allotment of tickets, and is said to be the owner of a souvenir program journal chockfull of advertisements that is sold at the park. Which adds up to a pretty good insight of why major league baseball has thus far declined to give recognition to Negro Baseball in any form aside from the brief contacts established by Rickey in acquiring Jackie Robinson, Roy Campanella, Donald Newcombe, Roy Partlow and Lone John Wright.

Well, next year is another year and maybe they'll change the "commercials" or at least make them interesting.

All-Star Classic Delayed by West's Pay Demands

by Sam Lacy

Source: *Baltimore Afro-American*, 24 August 1946

Washington— Players of the West squad representing the Negro American League, held up the all-star game for 15 minutes here Thursday night in a baseball version of the sit-down strike.[14]

The group left the field en masse at the conclusion of the pre-game practice and refused to go through with the contest until an understanding was reached, whereby they would get more money.

DEMAND $100 EACH

According to Dr. J. B. Martin, president of the Negro American League, the players had been guaranteed $50 each for their participation. The men, however, demanded that they be paid $100 apiece.

While approximately 25,000 fans awaiting the first Eastern version of the East-West game clamored for its start, the members of the American League clubs wrangled with President Martin in the dressing room.

Sitting in on the conference were S. H. (See) Posey of the Homestead Grays, Vernon Greene, [Alex] Pompez of the New York Cubans. None of their players however were involved.

Spokesman for the striking players was Joe [Willie] Grace, outfielder of the Cleveland Buckeyes. Grace took the floor when Quincy Trouppe, acting manager of the West, said he knew nothing about the move.

Grace said, "You folks asked us to take $50 because you didn't know how it was going to draw here the first time. You've got a park full of people [the capacity of Griffith Stadium was 29,613], and we thinking we are entitled to $100."

Pompez retaliated with; "This sort of thing every time we have an all-star game has got to stop. You're doing nothing but sending your own baseball to ruin." Grace did not reply.

When Martin agreed to terms, the players filed out and resumed their places in the visiting dugout. None would comment. Grace told the AFRO, "We've already straightened it out; there's nothing to say."

The incident was similar to the strike staged by the East players before the 1944 game in Chicago. At the time the men demanded and got $200 each for participation, returning to the field only after assurances that there would be no later reprisals from the owners.

Editor's note: In an interview, Willie Grace gave a slightly different version of the event:

What the whole thing about was this. We were in Washington DC playing the first all-star game there. So we came out and we were taking infield practice and it was obvious that no one came to play ball. And my owner, Ernie Wright, was sitting right there and knew I didn't cause no strike.

So asked I [Othello] Renfroe what was happening. What are we doing here? Pompez, who owned the Cubans, said the same thing. Won't somebody say something? Why don't somebody get together and tell us what's going on. Nobody knew anything, so I said, "It must be money angle or something like that?" And that's what it was. That broke the ice, and the players started talking.

So that's why they thought I started the strike. What the deal was they was only offering $50 in Washington, while we always got $100 once we got to Chicago for expenses to have fun with and everything. So they agreed to give us the $100. Each player who made the all-star team got a $100 bill from his club owner to be around there a couple, or two, days to have some spending money. In three minutes, this damn thing was settled. Shucks, Happy Chandler, commissioner of baseball, was at the ball game at the time. The next day in the paper they said I caused the strike. I knew nothing about no strike.[15]

At the 1956 East-West All-Star Game, there was another strike. All-star Jim Robinson of the Kansas City Monarchs recalled, "A number of players refused to play in the all-star game after taking part in the pre-game work out. We thought it was an opportune time to pressure the owners for some extra money. Unfortunately, it didn't work because there were still enough players who decided to go ahead and play the game. Those of us who refused to play were docked a half-month's pay. It was quite a mess."[16]

62,000 See East, West Baseball Classic

Baltimore Elites' Bill Byrd Credited With 6–3 Win before 16,268 in Capital

First Eastern Version of Annual Game Offers Exciting Moments for D.C. Fans

by Sam Lacy, AFRO Sports Editor

Source: *Baltimore Afro-American,* 24 August 1946

Washington— Negro National League All-Stars combined clever pitcher with timely hitting to defeat a picked team from the Negro American League, 6–3, here, Thursday night as 16,268 partisan spectators viewed the proceedings.

It was the first time to put on an Eastern version of the East-West extravaganza, held annually in Chicago, and the hordes came from far and near to be on hand.

From shortly after 6 p.m. when for the occasion the gates were opened, until well past 8:30, scheduled game time, the throngs formed a steady stream from nearby Florida Ave., up Georgia Ave., and into the various entrances of the ball park.

BEAU JACK TOSSES BALL

Beau Jack, former lightweight champion of the world, tossed out the first ball, which was speared by Homestead Grays catcher, Josh Gibson. Gibson started behind the plate for the NNL with Barney Brown, southpaw ace of the Philadelphia Stars, on the mound.

The splintery portsider was in superior form and proved to be complete master of the Westerners during his 3-inning stint on the hill.

The National Leaguers lost no time getting to the front with two runs on as many hits in the opening frame.

KIMBRO STARTS TROUBLE

Henry Kimbro of Baltimore started things by working Memphis pitcher Dan Bankhead for a base on balls. Larry Doby, Newark second sacker, singled to center, sending Kimbro to third.

Howard Easterling, Homestead Grays, rapped a one-baser to right to score Kimbro, but when Birmingham's Art Wilson cut off the throw to third, Easterling was caught trying to advance to second and retired in the rundown.

Doby tallied from third with the second run as the Grays' Buck Leonard grounded out to Archie Ware, Cleveland, at first unassisted.

The American League bats were woefully impotent before the offerings of Brown, but things took on a brighter hue when the Cubans' Pat Scantlebury assumed the pitching duties in the fourth.

BANKHEAD ERRS

The West Indian left-hander probably would have fared better if an error by Shortstop Sam Bankhead of the Grays had not been sandwiched between two Western hits.

Wilson started the inning by smashing one off Easterling's glove. Sammy Jethroe, Cleveland centerfielder, then rolled a double-play ball to Bankhead, but the Grays' shortfielder came up with one of his rare bobbles and all hands were safe.

Birmingham's Piper Davis then shot a sizzler down the leftfield foul-line which Monty Irvin of Newark held to a single by some fast fielding. The blow scored Wilson and sent Jethroe to second.

40. *The 1946 East all-star team. Standing, left to right: Felton Snow, Josh Gibson, Monte Irvin, Buck Leonard, Biz Mackey, Pat Scantlebury, Lennie Pearson, Larry Doby, Fernando Pedroso, Silvio Garcia, and Vic Harris. Kneeling: Henry Kimbro, Jonas Gaines, Murray Watkins, Bill Ricks, Gene Benson, Leon Day, Sam Bankhead, and Howard Easterling. Courtesy of NoirTech Research, Inc.*

BYRD TO RESCUE

The latter counted when Cleveland's Joe [Willie] Grace lifted a single to right.

Bill Byrd, Elite righthander, replaced Scantlebury and watched Davis cross the plate as he was vainly trying to throw out Cowan Hyde, Memphis, at first.

Alex Radcliffe, Cincinnati Clown third baseman, brought an abrupt end to the rally by bouncing into a double-play, Bankhead to Leonard.

The East came right back in their half of the fourth, jumping on Vibert Clarke, Cleveland pitcher, for four hits and two scores. The margin was held to the end, giving Byrd credit for the victory.

Easterling beat out a beautiful bunt inside third base and advanced to second as Leonard sacrificed. Irvin singled sharply to center to register Easterling, then went on to third base himself as Josh Gibson poked a one-baser to right.

UNORTHODOX SLIDE

Murray Watkins, Philly Stars, ran for Josh and Newark's Lennie Pearson, batted for Gene Benson, also of the Stars, against the West's third flinger, orthodox Gentry Jessup of Chicago. Pearson tapped to right to get Irvin home with the NNL's second run of the frame.

41. The 1946 West all-star team. Standing, left to right: Hornsby Howell (trainer), Gentry Jessup, John Williams, Clyde Nelson, Ed Steele, Dan Bankhead, Piper Davis, Chin Evans, Willie Grace, Quincy Trouppe, Joe Greene, and Alec Radcliffe. Kneeling: unknown trainer, Candy Jim Taylor, Bubba Hyde, Archie Ware, Larry Brown, Artie Wilson, Chico Renfroe, Jesse Williams, Vibert Clarke, Sam Jethroe, Frank Duncan, and Jim LaMarque. Unidentified batboy in front row. Courtesy of NoirTech Research, Inc.

The scoring ended after the National League fifth. Kimbro got on the virtue of shiftiness afoot and alert headwork.

The speedy Elite gardener dropped a swinging bunt down the first base line, which he barely failed to outrun.

Archie Ware rushed in, fielded the ball and appeared ready to tag Kimbro for the putout. Just as he was about to do so, however, the runner dived on his stomach and eluded Ware's outstretched hand. At the finish of his slide, Kimbro was resting on first base while Ware was looking around with unbelieving eyes.

SCORE AGAIN

A fielder's choice gave Doby a life but choked off Kimbro at second. The Newark star immediately stole second and then went to third as Wilson was unable to make a play on Easterling's hot smash near second.

Doby tallied and Easterling went to third as Jessup uncorked a wild pitch past the Clowns' Buster Haywood, catcher. Easterling made the final run as Leonard was being retired, Davis to Ware.

Sharing the pitching spotlight with Barney Brown were two Baltimore flingers, Bill Byrd and Jonas Gaines, neither of whom gave up a clean hit in the 3 2/3 innings they toiled between them.

Fielding gems were turned in by Doby and Silvio Garcia, Cuban shortstop, for the East, while a sensational bit of teamwork by Davis and Wilson killed another would be NNL run.

Davis snagged a scorcher off the bat of Lenny Pearson over second base in the seventh. Falling as he retrieved the ball, he tossed backhand to Wilson who wheeled around and pegged home to barely nip Cuban Pedro Diaz as he was trying to score.

AUGUST 15, 1946, THURSDAY
GRIFFITH STADIUM, WASHINGTON, D.C. (GAME 1 OF 2)

WEST	AB	R	H	D	T	HR	BI	E	TAVG	TSLG
Artie Wilson (Birmingham Black Barons), ss	3	1	1	0	0	0	0	0		
Othello Renfroe (Kansas City Monarchs), ss	1	0	0	0	0	0	0	0		
Archie Ware (Cleveland Buckeyes), 1b	4	0	0	0	0	0	0	0		
Sam Jethroe (Cleveland Buckeyes), cf	4	1	0	0	0	0	0	0		
Piper Davis (Birmingham Black Barons), 2b	4	1	2	0	0	0	1	0		
Willie Grace (Cleveland Buckeyes), rf	4	0	1	0	0	0	1	0		
Bubba Hyde (Memphis Red Sox), lf	3	0	1	0	0	0	1	0		
John Scott (Kansas City Monarchs), lf	2	0	1	0	0	0	0	0		
Alec Radcliffe (Memphis Red Sox), 3b	3	0	0	0	0	0	0	0		
Quincy Trouppe (Cleveland Buckeyes), c	1	0	0	0	0	0	0	0		
Buster Haywood (Indianapolis Clowns), c	1	0	0	0	0	0	0	0		
a) John Brown (Cleveland Buckeyes), ph	1	0	0	0	0	0	0	0		
Dan Bankhead (Memphis Red Sox), p	1	0	0	0	0	0	0	0		
Vibert Clarke (Cleveland Buckeyes), p	0	0	0	0	0	0	0	0		
Gentry Jessup (Chicago American Giants), p	1	0	0	0	0	0	0	0		
Clyde Nelson (Chicago American Giants), 3b	1	0	0	0	0	0	0	0		
Johnny "Nature Boy" Williams (Indianapolis Clowns), p	0	0	0	0	0	0	0	0		
Team Totals, Average & Slugging Pct.	34	3	6	0	0	0	3	0	.176	.176

a) Batted for Williams in 9th

EAST	AB	R	H	D	T	HR	BI	E	TAVG	TSLG
Henry Kimbro (Baltimore Elite Giants), cf	2	1	1	0	0	0	0	0		
Larry Doby (Newark Eagles), 2b	4	2	2	0	0	0	0	0		
Howard Easterling (Homestead Grays), 3b	4	2	3	0	0	0	1	0		
Buck Leonard (Homestead Grays), 1b	3	0	0	0	0	0	2	0		
Monte Irvin (Newark Eagles), lf	3	1	1	0	0	0	1	0		
Josh Gibson (Homestead Grays), c	2	0	1	0	0	0	0	0		
b) Murray Watkins (Philadelphia Stars), pr	0	0	0	0	0	0	0	0		
Leon Ruffin (Newark Eagles), c	1	0	0	0	0	0	0	0		
Louis Louden (New York Cubans), c	1	0	0	0	0	0	0	0		
Gene Benson (Philadelphia Stars), rf	1	0	1	0	0	0	0	0		
c) Lennie Pearson (Newark Eagles), rf	3	0	1	0	0	0	1	0		
Sam Bankhead (Homestead Grays), ss	2	0	0	0	0	0	0	1		
Silvio Garcia (New York Cubans), ss	2	0	0	0	0	0	0	0		
Barney Brown (Philadelphia Stars), p	1	0	0	0	0	0	0	0		
d) Frank Austin (Philadelphia Stars), pr	0	0	0	0	0	0	0	0		
Pat Scantlebury (New York Cubans), p	0	0	0	0	0	0	0	0		
Bill Byrd (Baltimore Elite Giants), p	1	0	0	0	0	0	0	0		
e) Pedro "Manny" Diaz (New York Cubans), ph	1	0	0	0	0	0	0	0		
Jonas Gaines (Baltimore Elite Giants), p	0	0	0	0	0	0	0	0		
Leon Day (Newark Eagles), p	0	0	0	0	0	0	0	0		
Team Totals, Average & Slugging Pct.	31	6	10	0	0	0	5	1	.323	.323

b) Ran for Gibson in 4th
c) Batted for Benson in 5th
d) Ran for Brown in 3rd
e) Batted for Byrd in 7th

West	000	300	000-3
East	200	220	00x-6

PITCHER/TEAM	GS	IP	H	R	ER	K	BB	WP	HB	W	L	SV
Bankhead/MRS	1	3	3	2	2	2	1	0	0	0	0	0
Clarke/CEB		1/3	3	2	2	0	0	0	0	0	1	0
Jessup/CAG		2 2/3	3	2	2	1	1	1	0	0	0	0
J. Williams/IC		2	1	0	0	0	0	0	0	0	0	0
B. Brown/PS	1	3	0	0	0	0	0	0	0	0	0	0
Scantlebury/NYC		1/3	3	3	2	0	0	0	0	0	0	0
Byrd/BEG		2 2/3	1	0	0	4	1	0	0	1	0	0
Gaines/BEG		2	1	0	0	0	0	0	0	0	0	0
Day/NE		1	1	0	0	0	0	0	0	0	0	1

BB—Kimbro
DP—Wilson to Ware to Davis; Bankhead to Leonard
PB—Trouppe, Haywood (2)
SB—Doby, Irvin, Kimbro
SAC—Leonard
East—Vic Harris (Mgr.)
West—W. S. Welch (Mgr.)
Umpires—
Attendance—16,268   Time—

Comiskey Park Is Scene of 14th Annual Classic

Source: *Chicago Defender,* 17 August 1946

The East team is fetching along the best hitters in the Negro National League in an effort to tie the score of games won. To date the West leads seven games to six, having annexed last year's win 9 to 6 after the East had thrown a scare into the Western rooters by scoring five runs in the ninth.

BOX SEAT TICKETS are being sold fast. However, the public is advised to buy sets at regular places, the Hotel Grand, 51st and South Parkway the Monarch Taylor's Men's Store 444 East 47th street; the Indiana Inn, 40th and Indiana Ave. and the ball park. It is impossible to keep tickets.

Last year counterfeit tickets were sold and the buyers found that these tickets did not get them into the park. Some of those selling such tickets landed in jail.

The public is asked to cooperate with the promotion and to demand the rightful box seats, which are printed on the tickets. In recent years, holders of seats far out have planted themselves early in choice seats and have, after slipping an usher a dollar or two, refused to move. Don't argue with the usher—call a policeman.

Ace West Hurlers Beat East, 4–1

Colorful Crowd of 45,474 Watch

Heavy Hitters Stopped Cold

by Fay Young

Source: *Chicago Defender,* 24 August 1946

Before the most colorful crowd in the history of the East versus West classic—the pitchers of the West team silenced the big bats and made it four in a row by winning the 14th annual classic at Comiskey Park Sunday, Aug. 18. The 4 to 1 victory gave the West the lead in games won 8 to 6.

Although there were four errors in the game, it was one well worth watching. Also there were some errors of judgment on the part of the coaches and managers of both teams.

Fans are still wondering why the West allowed Evans to go to bat in the last of the third. Officially no pitcher can hurl over three innings in the classic. With Hyde (Memphis) having doubled and Quincy Trouppe (Cleveland manager) walked, the logical thing to do was to send in a pitch hitter for Evans was sent in to lay down a sacrifice. He failed twice when the bunts went foul and on the third try he popped to Barney Brown, East's hurler. The West couldn't score in the frame.

For the East, Buck Leonard opened the second with a corking blow to right center and was out trying to stretch it into a two-base hit. With none out, fans believed Buck should have been stopped at first. Some are also wondering why Harris, manager of the East and manager of the East and manager of the Washington Homestead Grays, didn't yank Benson (Philly Stars) for Pearson (Newark Eagles) in the closing innings of the game.

THERE WERE CLOSE to 46,000 people in the park. Of this number the official paid attendance, as announced by President J. B. Martin of the Negro American league and Tom

Wilson, president of the Negro National league, was 45,474 second largest paid attendance in the history of the classic.

It was raining at 8 a.m. and who'd have believed it that so many would have come out. But old Sol shone and we are like the bugs—come out in the sunshine.

Dan Bankhead, former United States marine and outstanding pitcher in the Negro American league, wearing the uniform of the Memphis Red Sox, was winning pitcher. Bill Byrd, Baltimore Elite Giants, was the losing hurler as all four of the runs, two of them unearned came when Byrd was on the mound. Starting pitcher, Felix "Chin" Evans, Memphis Red Sox, left the game without a run being scored by either team as did the East's starting pitcher, Lefty Barney Brown, Philadelphia Stars.

The West broke the ice to score two runs off Brown in the home fourth. Sam Jethroe (Cleveland) popped to Silvio Garcia (Cuban Stars) at short. Lorenzo "Piper" Davis (Birmingham) walked. Willie Grace (Cleveland) poled a nice single to right and Gene Benson (Philadelphia) played with the ball like a kitten with a mouse long enough to let Davis score the first run of the game. Alex Radcliffe (Memphis) laid down a sacrifice. Brown to Buck Leonard (Homestead Grays first sacker). Cowan "Bubber" Hyde (Memphis), singled over second and Grace scored the second run of the game. Dan Bankhead lined to Larry Doby (Newark) near second.

The West moved on to score two more runs in the fifth although one of these runs was not earned. Art Wilson (Birmingham) beat out a hit which Garcia (Cubans) was barely able to knock down. Archie Ware (Cleveland) sacrificed. Byrd to Leonard. Sammy Jethroe (Cleveland) was safe on Garcia's fumble. Wilson and Jethroe worked a double steal, Wilson scoring (see photo) and Jethroe reaching second. The ball went from Josh Gibson (Grays catcher) to Doby (Newark) to Gibson. Doby had attempted to get Jethroe in a chase between first and second (near second) but seeing Wilson headed for home Doby changed his mind and fired the ball to Gibson, too late. Davis (Birmingham) singled to center sending Jethroe home with the last West run of the game. Jonas Gaines (Baltimore) relieved Byrd. Grace (Cleveland) forced Davis at second, Doby to Garcia. Gibson killed Grace for the second of the three times he was nailed trying to steal second in the game.

The East's lone tally came in the eighth. Johnny Williams (Indianapolis Clowns righthander) got by the seventh with no trouble, thanks to a lightning double play, Davis to Wilson to Ware which disposed of Gibson, who had walked, trying to reach second and Benson. Murray Watkins (Philadelphia) batted for [Silvio] Garcia and was hit by a pitched ball. Patrick Scantlebury (Cuban Stars) batted for Jones Gaines (Baltimore) and singled to center, the third hit made off the West's hurlers. Tommy Butts (Baltimore) ran for Scantlebury. Henry Kimbro (Baltimore) forced Butts at second, Ware to Wilson, Watkins going to third. Doby (Newark) was out when Hyde gathered in his drive and Watkins counted thus saving a white wash but Kimbro was out trying to sneak to second after the catch.

That was all the scoring. A single by Monty Irvin (Newark) in the ninth gave the East four hits, two of them off Williams, and one each off Evans and Bankhead.

The West got two hits off Brown; four hits and four runs off Bill Byrd, and one hit off Leon Day (Newark). The West wasn't able to get a safe blow off Jones Gaines (Baltimore) in the two and two thirds innings he toiled.

Evans fanned Doby and Howard Easterling (Grays third sacker) in the first. Bankhead struck out Irvin (Newark) in the third, Josh Gibson (Grays) in the fourth, Byrd in the fifth on three straight pitches. Williams didn't strike out any. Doby got a walk off Bankhead and Gibson a walk off Williams.

Brown threw one by Wilson for a called strikeout and the first out of the West in the first inning. He fanned Davis and Radcliffe in the second. Gaines fanned Radcliffe in the sixth. Day fanned Radcliffe in the eighth. Alex thus struck out three times. Walks were Trouppe, (by Brown) in the third; Davis and Trouppe (ordered walked) by Byrd in the fourth.

It was a great game!

The Sports Beat

Dream Game Star Dust . . .

by Wendell Smith

Source: *Pittsburgh Courier,* 24 August 1946

Chicago— The East just didn't have it here Sunday afternoon. Only two players Buck Leonard and Monty Irvin, hit the ball on the nose. Leonard, however, kept hitting the pellet right into the hands of the opposition. The West worked that double steal like a clock. Sammy Jethroe broke for second and stopped halfway down the line. Gibson threw to Garcia at second and Wilson came charging home from third. Garcia tried to peg him out, but Art slid in safely and Jethroe took second. Felix Evans started for the West and struck out two men in the first inning. Dan Bankhead came in two innings later and handcuffed the East. He struck out Irvin and Gibson, the power hitters of the National League. Gibson couldn't hit the ball out of the infield. The West outfielders only had three chances all afternoon. As usual, the crowd was big and colorful. They started filing in at one o'clock and by game time the stands were almost filled. Art Wilson proved conclusively that he's the best shortstop in the American loop. He handled nine chances without a miscue.

Frank Young, who will be 52 years old in October, and has been writing sports for 30 years, was in charge of the press box. He did his usual good job and kept all kibitzers out. Willie Grace, the classy Cleveland outfielder, led the West in hitting. He got three bingoes and scored one run. He was on base four times and Gibson threw him out three times trying to steal second base. E.S. Simmons handled the public address system and as usual, resorted to "corny" commercials, advertising everything but parties. That's strictly small-time stuff.

Winfield Welch, manager of the Birmingham Black Barons. When he saw the West lineup Sunday morning, he said: "This is the weakest team the West has ever selected for the classic." After the game, he said: "If the East couldn't beat that team, when will they ever win another East-West game?" No one can answer that. The East has dropped four in a row now. Silvio Garcia apparently had the jitters. He booted two easy ones at shortstop and could have been charged with another, but the scorers gave him a break on that one. Piper Davis played his usual brilliant game at second base and scored the first run for the West after working Byrd for a walk.

In the game at Washington, Thursday, Bill Byrd handcuffed the West. Here Sunday, however, he wasn't any trouble at all. The West scored all four runs off him on four hits and two walks. One of the owners in the American League was scalping complimentary tickets in the lobby of the Grand Hotel [in Chicago] before the game. The scalper did okay this year. They were selling $3 tickets for a nickel note. The East got one hit in the third, one in the sixth, one in the eighth, and one in the ninth. At no time during the entire game did they have more than one man on base. Their attack was weaker than lemonade at a Sunday School picnic. Tom Wilson, president of the National League, arrived on the scene Friday. Before the game in Washington, the American League players went out on strike. They held up the game twenty minutes and demanded $100 a man. President J. B. Martin agreed to the deal and they came out on the field. It was a perfect day in Chicago Sunday. The game was played under a blazing sun and the outfield grass was a vivid green.

AUGUST 18, 1946, SUNDAY
COMISKEY PARK, CHICAGO (GAME 2 OF 2)

EAST	AB	R	H	D	T	HR	BI	E	TAVG	TSLG
Henry Kimbro (Baltimore Elite Giants), cf	4	0	0	0	0	0	0	0		
Larry Doby (Newark Eagles), 2b	3	0	1	0	0	0	1	0		
Howard Easterling (Homestead Grays), 3b	4	0	0	0	0	0	0	0		
Buck Leonard (Homestead Grays), 1b	4	0	1	0	0	0	0	0		
Monte Irvin (Newark Eagles), lf	4	0	1	0	0	0	0	0		
Josh Gibson (Homestead Grays), c	3	0	0	0	0	0	0	0		
Gene Benson (Philadelphia Stars), rf	3	0	0	0	0	0	0	1		
Silvio Garcia (New York Cubans), ss	1	0	0	0	0	0	0	2		
a) Murray Watkins (Philadelphia Stars), ph	0	1	0	0	0	0	0	0		
Barney Brown (Philadelphia Stars), p	1	0	0	0	0	0	0	0		
Bill Byrd (Baltimore Elite Giants), p	1	0	0	0	0	0	0	0		
Jonas Gaines (Baltimore Elite Giants), p	0	0	0	0	0	0	0	0		
b) Pat Scantlebury (New York Cubans), ph	1	0	1	0	0	0	0	0		
c) Pee Wee Butts (Baltimore Elite Giants), pr-ss	0	0	0	0	0	0	0	0		
Leon Day (Newark Eagles), p	0	0	0	0	0	0	0	0		
Team Totals, Average & Slugging Pct.	29	1	4	0	0	0	1	3	.138	.138

a) Batted for Garcia in 8th
b) Batted for Gaines in 8th
c) Ran for Scantlebury in 8th

WEST	AB	R	H	D	T	HR	BI	E	TAVG	TSLG
Artie Wilson (Birmingham Black Barons), ss	4	1	1	0	0	0	0	0		
Archie Ware (Cleveland Buckeyes), 1b	2	0	0	0	0	0	0	0		
Sam Jethroe (Cleveland Buckeyes), cf	3	1	0	0	0	0	0	0		
Piper Davis (Birmingham Black Barons), 2b	3	1	1	0	0	0	1	0		
Willie Grace (Cleveland Buckeyes), rf	4	1	3	0	0	0	0	0		
Alec Radcliffe (Memphis Red Sox), 3b	3	0	0	0	0	0	0	0		
Bubba Hyde (Memphis Red Sox), lf	3	0	2	1	0	0	1	1		
Quincy Trouppe (Cleveland Buckeyes), c	1	0	0	0	0	0	0	0		
Felix Evans (Memphis Red Sox), p	1	0	0	0	0	0	0	0		
Dan Bankhead (Memphis Red Sox), p	1	0	0	0	0	0	0	0		
Johnny "Nature Boy" Williams (Indianapolis Clowns), p	1	0	0	0	0	0	0	0		
Team Totals, Average & Slugging Pct.	26	4	7	1	0	0	2	1	.269	.308

East	000	000	010-1
West	000	220	00x-4

PITCHER/TEAM	GS	IP	H	R	ER	K	BB	WP	HB	W	L	SV
B. Brown/PS	1	3	2	0	0	3	1	0	1	0	0	0
Byrd/BEG		1 1/3	4	4	3	0	2	0	0	0	1	0
Gaines/BEG		2 1/3	0	0	0	1	0	0	0	0	0	0
Day/NE		1	1	0	0	1	0	0	0	0	0	0
Evans/MRS	1	3	1	0	0	2	0	0	0	0	0	0
Bankhead/MRS		3	1	0	0	2	1	0	1	1	0	0
J. Williams/IC		3	2	1	1	0	1	0	1	0	0	1

BB—P. Davis, Trouppe (2), Doby, Gibson
DP—Davis to Wilson to Ware, Hyde to Davis
HBP—Garcia by Bankhead; Watkins by Williams; Jethroe by Brown
LOB—West 5, East 5
SAC—Radcliffe, Ware (2)
SB—Wilson, Jethroe, Hyde
East—Vic Harris (Mgr.), Coaches Biz Mackey and Felton Snow
West—Quincy Trouppe (Mgr.), Coaches Candy Jim Taylor and Frank Duncan
Umpires—Fred McCrary, Virgil Blueitt, Wilber Rogan, Phil Cockrell
Attendance—45,474   Time—2:24

1947

The Congress of Racial Equality (CORE) sends the first group of freedom riders through the South on interstate buses.

Wilberforce University of Ohio defeats Bergen College of New Jersey in the first football game between a predominantly black college and a white college.

Milk costs 39 cents a half-gallon, 10 pounds of potatoes costs 50 cents, while three quarters and three pennies would bring home the bacon. A loaf of bread costs 13 cents.

The American League All-Stars win 2–1 behind the pitching of Hal Newhouser for their Wrigley Field victory. The selection of players for the game, with the exception of the pitchers, was transferred from the managers back to the fans.

Former Kansas City Monarch Jackie Robinson becomes the first African-American to be named Rookie of the Year and play in a major league world series.

Other Negro Leaguers—Larry Doby, Hank Thompson, Willard Brown, and Dan Bankhead—break into Major League Baseball. Ironically, the non-baseball-related movie *Gentlemen's Agreement* wins an Oscar for the best movie of the year.

Commissioner Happy Chandler announces that the Gillette Safety Razor Company and Ford Motors will pay $65,000 for joint sponsorship to promote the first televised major league world series.

BARRIER BREAKTHROUGH

This was the first year that Major League Baseball allowed black players to perform. Jackie Robinson joined the Brooklyn Dodgers, and eleven weeks later Larry Doby joined the Cleveland Indians of the American League. These historic events excited fans to explore the talents of the black players. In preceding years, major league ball clubs had experienced a decline in attendance. In 1947, newspapers reported on October 14 that Major League Baseball drew an all-time record total attendance of 19,954,832 for the year.

With almost 20 million fans in the ballparks, Branch Rickey had hit a financial home run with the signing of Jackie Robinson. Undoubtedly, Robinson in the National League and Doby in the American League contributed to this surge in attendance. In fact, Robinson's Dodgers broke single-game attendance records in every ballpark this year, except Cincinnati's Crosley Field. On May 18 Robinson's first appearance at Wrigley Field before 46,572 fans was a record high for the time. The entertainment value of racism in this country had never become more visible. This swelling of rooters caused sportswriter Wendell Smith to report, "Jackie's Nimble, Jackie's Quick, Jackie Makes The Turnstile Click!"

Later, in July, the St. Louis Browns signed Kansas City Monarchs Willard Brown and Hank Thompson. The Browns were forced to release first baseman Jerry Witte and shortstop Perry Currin to make room on the roster. Manager Muddy Ruel commented on the arrival of new players, saying, "The club believes that something had to be done to strengthen it. It happens there is no acceptable player available in our farm system at this time."[1] Thompson replaced Russ Peters at second base, while Brown was attempting to break into the outfield of Ray Coleman, Jeff Heath, and Paul Lehner, not exactly household names.

On July 17 Thompson became the third Negro League player to play in the major leagues. In his St. Louis debut he went hitless in four at bats, with an error, playing second base against the Philadelphia Athletics. The hapless Browns lost 16–2, after the Athletics scored nine runs in the ninth. Hank spent 37 frustrating days with the Browns, hitting only .256 in 78 at bats in 27 games, mostly at second base.

Willard Brown became the first black player to hit a home run in the American League. On August 13, pinch-hitting for Joe Schultz, Brown drilled an inside-the-park homer off Detroit Tigers pitcher Hal Newhouser. However, the fantasy trip was over after 21 games. Hitting less than his weight, a .179 batting average, Willard Brown was released. The struggling Browns, who two years earlier had signed a one-armed outfielder named Pete Gray before considering a black athlete, were not satisfied with Willard's chilly playing style.

As late as 1939, according to the *New York Daily Worker,* the St. Louis organization was the last club in the majors to have segregated seating. The acquisition of Brown and Thompson was seen by most fans as a gate attraction and was not viewed by serious patrons as a means to help the meagerly talented Browns. On August 23 manager Muddy Ruel released Thompson and Brown, with both men rejoining the Monarchs. The "Gold Dust Twins" remained with the Monarchs through the 1948 season.

Tommy Holmes wrote: "The St. Louis Browns signed a couple of colored ballplayers as they started out on a road trip through the East. Along about the time they got back to St. Louis, a city with more Southern than Northern tradition, they released them. There was always some doubt whether these two players—Thompson and Brown—received a genuine trial. Most people believe they didn't."[2]

Although it was unknown at the time, the leisurely integration of baseball would destroy the fabric of the black business community. Advertising in game-day programs and black newspapers would gradually disappear. Minority-owned businesses in Chicago, New York, and Kansas City like George & Chris Chocolate Bar, Wynn's Bar-B-Q and Chicken Inn, Betty's Golden Brown Chicken Inn, Crispee French Fried Shrimps, Charlie Glenn's New Rhumboodie Cafe, Joe's Deluxe Club, Club Congo Chicken Shack, DuSable Circle Bar, Silver Fox Beer, The Duck Inn, Tony's Tavern, Charlie & Ella Mae Chicken Inn & Tavern, Club Delisa, Brown Bros. Valet Shop, Palm Tavern, Sugar Ray's Cafe, Randolph's Shangri-La Shalimar, Joe Louis' Restaurant & Cafe, Monarch Tailors, American Giants Garages, Monarch Cab Company, Hymie's Tap Room, and the Savoy Ballroom would eventually shut down—never to be opened again.

LEAGUE BUSINESS

League officials met on February 24 at the Appomattox Club, and on February 25 at Hotel Grand, in Chicago, Illinois. Ted "Double Duty" Radcliffe, one of the East-West game's most colorful characters, was banned from Negro League baseball for jumping his contract five days before the 1946 season ended to play in Mexico.

The Negro American League voted a franchise to the Detroit Senators, owned by attorney Joseph A. Brown, a Michigan state senator; track star Jesse Owens; Cecil Rowlette;

and W. S. Welch, former manager of the Cincinnati Crescents. The Senators' ability to secure six Sunday dates in Briggs Stadium, home of the Detroit Tigers, encouraged their selection to the league. The St. Louis Stars were also granted league entry. The Cincinnati Crescents, owned by William Margolis, who employed Abe Saperstein as a booking agent, were denied a franchise.

The Sports Beat: Pompez Heads N.Y. All-Star Game Committee

by Wendell Smith

Source: *Pittsburgh Courier,* 19 July 1947

Two nights after the game in Chicago the same two teams clash in New York City in the National League's second annual All-Star battle. This, too, might just as easily be called a "dream game" because it gives the fans in the East a chance to see the game's top players. The All-Star game was adopted because fans in the East never had the opportunity to see the East-West classics. Last year it was held in Washington and the Nationals took the Americans, 6 to 3, before an estimated 16,000 fans. Larry Doby, then with Newark, and Howard Easterling, ex-Homestead Grays star, led the teams in hitting with two safeties each.

Alex Pompez, the good senor from Havana, and the owner of the colorful Cuban Stars, is in charge of this All-Star game. Senor Pompez is working with vim and vigor in an effort to prove that New York fans are just as loyal and enthusiastic about baseball as those in Chicago. Efforts have been made a number of times to switch the East-West Classic from Chicago to New York. But there was always some question about New Yorkers and their zest for Negro baseball. The good senor claims that New York is a better city than even Chicago is and will try to prove it this year. Whatever he does you can be sure that the owner of the Cubans will do a good job and it will be done in grand style. Along with Ernie Wright of the Cleveland Buckeyes, Sonnyman Jackson of the Homestead Grays and Mr. and Mrs. Abe Manley of the Newark Eagles, the gentleman from Havana, is one of the pillars of Negro baseball. They are the people who insist that the future of Negro baseball depends on smoother operation and a sane and honest policy throughout.

The appointment of Dr. John Johnson as president of the National League was one of the most forward steps the Negro National League has ever made. The Manleys, Pompez and Jackson were the key people in the promotion of New York's All-Star game, with Dr. Johnson playing a major role, too.

That should be a great spectacle in New York on July 29!

Classic Tickets to Go on Sale Saturday

Source: *Chicago Defender,* 19 July 1947

Several major league scouts, the men who put their okays on players who are at once signed by owners in the American and National Leagues, will watch the 15th annual East versus West all star baseball game at Comiskey Park on Sunday, July 27. This annual game finds the cream of the Negro National League players on a team known as the East and the pick of the Negro American League players representing the West.

The players who will be observed with the most critical attention will be Henry "Hank" Thompson, Kansas City Monarch infielder; Sammy Jethroe, outfielder of the Cleveland Buckeyes; Monty Irvin, outfielder and infielder of the Newark Eagles, [Claro] Duany, right-fielder for the New York Cubans; Lorenzo "Piper" Davis, second sacker, and Art Wilson, shortstop, both of the Birmingham Black Barons and several pitchers.

It is possible that these scouts will find that several players are of major league possibilities and warrant a tryout next spring.

Tickets for the classic will go on sale Saturday morning, July 12, at the following places: Monarch Tailoring Co., 3450 S. State St.; Hotel Grand, 51st and South Parkway; Indiana Inn, 40th and Indiana; Henry C. Taylor's Men's Store, 444 East 47th St.; LaRue's Tavern, 3601 S. State St.; A & B Liquor Store, 357 E. 61st St.

West Wallops East, 5 to 2, before 48,112 Fans

National League Helpless in Classic

Colored Capacity Crowd Watches West Roll over East

American League Pitchers Set Eastern Team Down with Three Hits

by Wendell Smith, Sports Editor

Source: *Pittsburgh Courier,* 2 August 1947

Chicago— The "Dream Game" of Negro baseball turned out to be a nightmare for the East here Sunday afternoon at Comiskey Park as the West copped the fifteenth annual East-West Classic, 5 to 2, before a roaring, capacity throng of 48,112 fans. Brandishing big bats that smothered the alleged explosiveness of the National Leaguers, the West bombed the East into complete submission and racked up their ninth win in the long series. It was the fifth straight time the roughriders from the American League had bowled over the satellites from the East.

The East was never in the ball game. It was probably the easiest victory the West has scored in the past five years. Brilliant pitching on the part of Dan Bankhead, Gentry Jessup and Chet Brewer handcuffed the National Leaguers completely. They were only able to solve that trio of mounds men for three hits during the game, two of which came in the eight when the East scored one of its two runs. The other marker was made in the second inning, and the other measly hit was in the third.

EAST TEAM WEAK

There is still some question among Easterners supporters about the selection of the National League combination. It certainly didn't perform with the efficiency of Eastern teams in the past. The hitting was putrid, the pitching spotty and in general it looked like a patched up aggregation of second-stringers, rather than the blue-ribbon boys of the National League.

AN EASY VICTORY

On the other hand, the West put a powerful club on the field. They had pitching, hitting and a stonewall defense. They combed Eastern pitchers Max Manning, Luis Tiant, Henry Miller and Johnny Wright—for five runs and twelve home hits. They scored twice in the first and third innings and pushed over the final marker in the eighth. They were never behind and at no time were in any real danger.

The West wasted no time getting started. They banked across two runs in the very first inning. Max Manning, bespectacled right-hander for the East, got rid of Art Wilson via the strikeout route, but Herb Souell, Kansas City third baseman walloped a lusty triple to right center and scored on Sammy Jethroe's infield out: Lorenzo (Piper) Davis, currently under option to the St. Louis Browns of the major leagues, kept things going by doubling to left. Manning walked Catcher Quincy Trouppe and then Jose Colas of the Memphis Red Sox slashed a single to right and Davis came home with the second run.

The West stretched the lead to 4–1 in the third when Trouppe tripled, sending Jethroe, whom had been hit in the back with a pitch and then stole second, home with the third run. Trouppe scored the fourth run when Colas again singled to right. That lead was all the West needed. But they added another in the eighth when Reece (Goose) Tatum of Cincinnati, Buddy Armour, Chicago, and pitcher Chet Brewer of Cleveland, all singled in succession.

MARQUEZ DOUBLES

The floundering Easterners got one of their two runs in the second thanks to some good base running by Monty Irvin, who went from first to third on an infield out and scored on Duany's fly-to center. Irvin got a ticket to first when he was hit by one of Dan Bankhead's curve balls. The other National League run was made in the eighth when Luis Marquez of the Homestead Grays pinch hit for the Cubans' Claro Duany and doubled down the left field line. He scored a moment later when Louis Louden of the Cubans singled to left. That was the second and final run of the day for the East.

From where we sat it wasn't much of a ball game. The West dominated the whole contest—much to the delight of the partisan throng—while the East played spiritless ball throughout. The entire squad of National Leaguers crashed the lineup. Even Biz Mackey, the paunchy, 52-year-old manager of the East got into the fray. He picked up a bat in the eighth and hit for Miller. Mackey worked Brewer for a walk and then Vic Harris, coach for the East and manager of the Homestead Grays, ran for him. Harris didn't have to gallop, however, because the next hitter, Kimbro, hit an easy roller to the box and Brewer threw him out, ending what might have turned out to be real rally.

The West showed little for the East pitching. They blasted Manning for four runs and five hits in two and one-third innings. Luis Tiant relieved Manning in the third. He didn't give up any runs allowing the West two hits in the two innings he worked. Johnny Wright gave up the fifth run in the eighth when the West solved him for three hits.

Meantime, Bankhead, Jessup and Brewer toyed with the "big guns" of the East. Bankhead moved 'em down with his blazing fast ball. Jessup set 'em down without a hit for three innings with dazzling curves and Brewer kept 'em in the palm of his hand with an assortment of "dinky" curves and slippery fast balls.

The game was dull because the East was so hopelessly outclassed. They singled in the third, a blow to center by Manning, and from then until the eighth never even got a good smell of first base.

So the West goes merrily on its way in the East-West series. They have copped five in a row for a total of nine victories out of fifteen contests. And, if the East can't produce a stronger club in the future than they did here Sunday afternoon, all the West will have to do next year is show up for the game and victory will be theirs.

The Sports Beat: Crowd Was Big and Colorful

by Wendell Smith

Source: *Pittsburgh Courier,* 2 August 1947

As usual, the crowd was big and colorful. People seeking general admission tickets were in line as early as 9 o'clock Sunday morning. Scalpers were getting as much as $10 for box seats. When Johnny Washington, first baseman from Baltimore, strolled to the plate in the first inning and the announcer informed the crowd that his batting average for the year was .403, it was greeted with a volume of "ahs" and "ohs." He promptly grounded to second and was thrown out. He didn't hit in four trips to the plate.

J. B. Martin, president of the Negro American League wore this traditional white suit. Dr. John Johnson, National League prexy, sat in a box near the East dugout. Frank Duncan, manager of the victorious Western team, was obviously proud of the fact that he has managed three of the four Negroes to crash the majors—Jackie Robinson, Henry Thompson and Willard Brown [Larry Doby is the exception]. Thompson and Brown were slated to play in the East-West game, but the St. Louis Browns snatched them up before they got the chance. The West didn't need them anyway. They had enough power and pitching to play the East without an outfield.

Reece "Goose" Tatum proved to be the comedian of the day with his antics at first base and at the plate. It has been rumored that Tatum has been scouted by a number of major league clubs. He apparently thinks he can clown his way into the majors. We don't think it's necessary for such tomfoolery at the East-West classic. Wonder why Presidents Martin and Johnson tolerate such foolishness. It seems to us that the Negro baseball's game of the year should be promoted with strict dignity.

BROWNS WANTS TO FARM DAVIS OUT

For the first time in many years Alex Pompez, owner of the New York Cubans, was absent. He was in New York handling the details for Tuesday night's All-Star game. Rufus "Sonnyman" Jackson, Homestead Grays' boss was crying loud and long about the lack of good replacements for his team. "We have to do something to develop young players," he said. "We've looked every place for some youngsters but can't find them." Souell's triple was a ringing blow to left center. The St. Louis Browns hold a thirty-day option on Piper Davis, Birmingham second baseman. They want to send him to their farm club in Elmira, N.Y., but Tom Hayes, owner of the Birmingham team, is discouraging the move. "I think Davis is ready for the majors right now," he said, explaining his position on the matter. The best fielding play of the game happened in the third inning when Wilson, Davis and Tatum teamed up on a sensational double play getting Manning who had singled and Kimbro who hit the ball by an eye-lash at first. Sammy Jethroe who has swiped twenty-nine bases this season, showed the crowd how he does it in the third. He was hit in the back with a fast ball by Manning. Catcher Hayes called for a pitchout on the next pitch and Jethroe streaked for second and made it safely. Jethroe and Tatum were the only switch hitters in the game. One Cuban got another in the eighth when Colas hauled in Minoso's long drive in deep right center.

There were a number of scouts from major league teams in the stands watching the game. The East lacked power at the plate. They could have used power hitters like Buck Leonard of the Grays and Lenny Pearson of Newark. Reserved and box seats were sold out six days before the game. Players on both teams left Chicago for New York Monday afternoon via train. The crowd paid a standing tribute to the late Tom Wilson, ex-president of the Negro National League and owner of the Baltimore Elite Giants. Many of the out-of-towners stayed over to see Jackie Robinson and Brooklyn play the Cubs on Monday.

Sports Lovers of Nation Converge on Chicago for Baseball Classic

by Marian F. Downer—special correspondent

Source: *Chicago Defender,* 2 August 1947

Under capricious skies, here in grand old Comiskey Park, more than 45,000 baseball spectators watched with bated breath the 15th annual East-West baseball classic become history, with the taunting West chalking up its fifth successive victory with a score of 5–2, and a series score of 9 to 6. As in former years patrician society and spirited sportsmen glamour spot always attendant in large gatherings.

From the time Mayor Martin H. Kennelly threw the first ball until the final out every moment was thrill-packed—every minute seemed to produce another big time baseball star. There was never a dull moment—if one's eyes were not glued to some impetuous ball—King Tut, the Cincinnati Clown kept the less game-minded in convulsions with his beloved antics.

The West got off to a good two-run advantage in the first inning and was never dangerously threatened by the East except in the second and eighth innings when the East attempted to garner some extra runs. "Big" Mackey, cagey old manager from the East, went in as a pinch hitter in eighth fray to give his rugged teammates a hypodermic, only to earn an intentional walk maneuvered by cunning Frank Duncan, West manager. Vic Harris, star of many a ball game ran for Mackey, only to fade into magnificence as the revolting West hung up a final 5–2 victory.

WIDELY ATTENDED

Aside from the sports end of the East-West Classic there is always that colorful, glamorous side which brings prominence from all sections of the United States as well as the local front "biggies". Out-of-owners need by this correspondent were Dr. and Mrs. J. E. Burke, Forrest City, Ark.; Prof. J. A. L. Jordan, father of famed Louis Jordan, Brinkley, Ark.; Ulysses Bond, Madison, Ark.; Miss Doris Grisham, Piney Woods, Miss.; Dr. Lawrence C. Jones, principal Piney Woods School, Miss.; Mrs. Florence Bascomb, Mrs. Ida Riley, Miss Mildred Hunter, all of New York; the E. Clifford Turners, St. Louis; Rev. John H. Johnson, president National League; Edward Bolden, Philadelphia; Dr. Joe Wiggins, Cleveland; Julius J. Adams and Dan Burley, New York; William G. Nunn, Pittsburgh; Master Leon Foster, Pittsburgh;

Mr. and Mrs. Ernie Wright, Cleveland; Tom Baird, Kansas City; Charlie Settles, New York; Mrs. Effa Manley, Newark; Miss Jewell Gentry, Memphis; Miss Ruby Wright, Seattle; Dr. B. M. McIntosh, Holly Springs, Miss.; Dr. and Mrs. W. H. Young, Memphis; Mrs. Irby Fogleman, Dr. W. S. Martin, Memphis; Mrs. Lillian Hooks, Memphis; John C. Claybrook, Forrest City, Ark.; Z. T. Terry, Arkansas; Sherman Wilson, Columbus; Mrs. William Saunders, Bill Tory, Memphis; Edward (tailor) Buffington, Memphis; Dr. A. T. Martin and Dr. B. B. Martin, Memphis; N. A. Eggleston and Ralph Dorsey Richmond, Va.; Marguerite Jackson, Betty Wilson, both Los Angeles; Dr. Bedford N. Riddle; Akron, Ohio;

Mr. and Mrs. Zack Hightower, Memphis; Horace P. Clarke, Los Angeles; the Conrad Guilds, Evanston; Atty. and Mrs. Bennie Wilson, Gary, Ind.; Dr. and Mrs. King Solomon Jones, Michigan City, Ind.; the Andrew Wallaces, Los Angeles (newlyweds); Mrs. Theodore Briggs, New York; the Alfred Pollittes, Louisville; Rachelle Huff, Hot Springs; Roman John, Detroit; Theodore Cott Bond, Forrest City, Ark.; Lois Gladney, New York; Leroy Conan, Percy Harris, George Gallimore, E. J. Walker, all of New York; Fluxen Harvey,

Washington; Finley Hoskins, New York; Mrs. William Ward, Seattle, Wash.; Bob King, Idle-wild, Mich.

Local prominence spied by this writer: Sanitary board member A. F. Maciejewski and his "missus"; Mayor Martin H. Kennelly, Police Sgt. John J. Cronin sat with the J. B. Martins, Mr. and Mrs.; Walter L. Lowe, Atty. and Mrs. Earl B. Dickerson and daughter, Diane, Dr. H. Reginald Smith, Mrs. E. M. McCullouch, the Charles B. McMinns and the Robert A. Coles, Mrs. Lovelyn Evans, Mr. and Mrs. Ernest Morris, Atty. Richard Hill, Charles S. Jackson, Freddy Bolden, Mr. and Mrs. Leon Motts, the Frank Smiths, Chet Brewer Sr., the Lucius C. Harpers, Dr. and Mrs. Charles Runner, Lottie Terrell, George Girtley, Olive M. Diggs, Mrs. George Marshall, Jim Knight, the Jim Martins, Henry and Roxie Harris, Mrs. Robert R. Jackson, Atty. Rufus Sampson, Dr. Spurgeon J. Morris, Mr. and Mrs. James Gentry, Mr. and Mrs. John Chamberlain and their son, Douglass, recently discharged marine; Mrs. Annie Little, Mrs. Beatrice Steele, Mrs. Maud Craig. NAACPers plus Chicago prexy Henry McGee got their second annual public goodwill contribution via taggers. The old political warrior ex-Congressman and Mrs. Oscar DePriest were also present.

Dan Burley's Confidentially Yours' East-West Classic Replay

Source: *New York Amsterdam News,* 2 August 1947

Chicago— There'll have to be some changes made if East-West Classic standards are to be maintained and the Negro National League wants to keeps its prestige. In other words, the East went down to its fifth straight defeat before the West in the last five years, the 5 to 2 finisher being administered last Sunday before a record paid crowd of 48,112 at Comiskey Park. You see these all-star teams, East and West, are supposed to be made up on the cream of the players in both leagues and pitted against each other annually in this money-making extravaganza with the fans getting a chance to compare player vs. player ability. When a team is sent all that distance from the East coast to this middlewestern metropolis and can't get but three hits, while the opposition is pounding enemy pitchers for 12, then there's really a reason for getting worried.

The 5–2 lacing the East took last Sunday left the West ahead in the 15 years of play, 9 to 6. In other words, the game is in danger of slipping into the class of Howard-Lincoln football games of the late 1930's and 1940's when Lincoln was swamping the Bison at will and fans-or that faithful band that stuck it out-mainly attended for the social side of the best thing.

Big league scouts, and there were several in the press box here and in the stands, wouldn't have been impressed by what they saw of the Negro National League representatives. The highly touted Newark Eagles, pitcher, Maxwell Manning, gave up five hits in 2 and 2-3 innings which were productive for the West in the sum of four runs which were enough to win the game.

The alleged heavy hitters—Johnny Washington of Baltimore (.406), Henry Kimbro of Baltimore (.357), Monte Irvin of the Newark Eagles (.345), Silvio Garcia, N.Y. Cubans (.326), didn't hit the side of a barn in nine innings of toil. In fact, they folded up contentedly and accepted without argument the assortment of pitches served them by such Western standouts of the mound as Dan Bankhead of Memphis, who started the game and got the decision over Manning; Gentry Jessup of the Chicago American Giants, and Chet Brewer of the Cleveland Buckeyes.

In the eighth inning, Marquez with one down, promptly lined the first good Brewer pitch into left field for a line double. The inept Minosa [Minoso] popped out to right, but Louden smacked a smoker of a single over third base to score Marquez. And that was all.

The East got its other run in the second inning and it was an unearned [earned, but undeserving, as no hits were made] tally. Bankhead hit Irvin with a pitched ball and he went to third as [Silvio] Garcia bounced out weakly to [Herb] Souell of Kansas City who was playing third base. [Claro] Duany, announced over the loud speaker as "batting .987" causing many to rush out and make some policy and numbers plays, flied out to center, Irvin trotting across. Minosa [Minoso] popped out foul to Otis [Quincy] Trouppe, Cleveland catcher.

There seemed to be a lack of interest on the part of East club and this was shown in the very first inning. After Manning had fanned Birmingham's Art Wilson, Herb Souell tripled to right center. Sammy Jethroe of Cleveland was an infield out, but Lorenzo (Piper) Davis double to the left field scoreboard. Souell scored on the hit. Biz Mackey ordered Otis [Quincy] Trouppe walked by Manning and then Jose Colas, Memphis Red Sox, slashed a vivacious liner to right field which Duany, supposedly a topnotch fielder, allowed to fall in front of him for a freak single Duany could have caught the ball had he made an effort to run in for it, but he started late and then allowed it to fall in front of him, playing it on first bounce. Davis scored on the play.

The scouts who were on hand for the game, which has taken on a point of major interest in Negro sports, got an eyeful of the flashy, colorful Reece (Goose) Tatum, Indianapolis Clowns' first baseman. They had a chance to watch both Art Wilson, brother of the famous Jud [Artie and Jud Wilson were not brothers], at shortstop, and Piper Davis at second. Both are members of the Birmingham Black Barons, Piper being on a 30-day option to the St. Louis Browns, Davis, Colas, Tatum and Buddy Armour hitting two doubles, Souell, Trouppe and Jethroe all hit triples, and the Western speed merchants, Davis and Jethroe, stole a base apiece to add to the discomforting of the visitors.

Some of the East players were complaining after the game that they didn't have their proper bats and that if they had, the result would have been different. An interested observer wanted to know where were their bats last year and the four years before that when they took the same kind of manhandling from the West.

There were some who contend that the wrong players were taken to the East-West game and that a better and possibly a winning combination could have been picked if the owner-manager committee picking the men had "opened up" a bit and let somebody else get in. The latter remark referred to the leaving off of an all-star team such sterling pitchers as the two ace left-handers, Barney Brown of the Philly Stars and Jonas Gaines of the Baltimore Elite Giants; Men like Sammy Bankhead of the Homestead Grays, Lenny Pearson of the Newark Eagles, and Jerry Benjamin of the Grays. Those who were making these observations mainly included persons who had either bet on the wrong team or who suffered deep humiliations from the gleeful Western fans who ranked in quite a lot of coin making bets in recesses and under the grandstands.

Other East-West Classic developments saw the spread of the rumor that somebody had gotten hold of a printing press and had run off enough counterfeit tickets to buy the pressman a brand new Cadillac—which westerners buy as easily as we buy cigarettes-or a new house. On that account, the hefty Dr. J. B. Martin, president of the Negro American League who is chairman of the East-West committee, was reported to have sweated off a minimum of 179 of his odd 360 pounds trying to hurry the police into rounding up the ticket mob. The actual paid attendance, it was revealed by a check with park officials-not East-West folks since they are interested in padding-showed 41,000 or thereabouts instead of the glib 48,112 as announced by the committee. The game brought at least $150,000 worth of business to South Side merchants, businesses, nightclubs, etc. The mammoth crowd started pouring into the Windy City as early as Friday and stayed over until Sunday night and Monday afternoon. They came from everywhere, especially from the deep portions of the middle south and so glad to be in Chicago that they spent their gold like mad.

50,000 and Major League Scouts See West Beat East in Great Game

by Fay Young

Source: *Chicago Defender,* 2 August 1947

Playing the best game in the 15 years of the series, the East and the West nines turned in some major league baseball before 50,000 at Comiskey Park on Sunday. Of this crowd 48,112 were paid customers, many from out-of-town. The final score was 5–2 in favor of the West nine, managed by Frank Duncan, veteran manager of the Kansas City Monarchs. The East was managed by Raleigh "Bizz" Mackey, manager of the Newark Eagles, Negro world champions.

Several major league scouts were on hand. Sammy Jethroe, Cleveland outfielder; Piper Davis, Birmingham infielder on whom the St. Louis Browns have a 30-day option; Reece "Goose" Tatum, whom the Philadelphia Nationals have been looking over, and Dan Bankhead, Memphis hurler sought by two clubs in the majors, were on the West nine of Negro American Leaguers.

John Washington, second in the Negro National League with a batting average of .406 may be signed by the San Francisco Seals of the Pacific Coast League which sorely needs a first sacker. Also on the East nine was the flashy Orestes Minosa [Minoso], third sacker for the New York Cubans and who will be signed by Branch Rickey, president of the Brooklyn Dodgers of the National League and sent to Montreal when Roy Campanella formerly of the Baltimore Elite Giants, comes up for a tryout with the Dodgers next spring. Campanella, who saw service behind the plate in the 1945 East versus West game for the East, is now catching for Montreal.[3]

Sunday's crowd was the best handled and most orderly crowd in the series history. There was much dissatisfaction over the method of ticket sales for the game. Box seat ducats could not be purchased at the regular advertised places who hung up "sold out" signs. But a few doors away from certain places, box seats could be bought at scalpers prices which ranged all the way from 50 cents per ticket to $3 more per ticket than the printed price on the same.

In the Hotel Grand, 51st and South Parkway, the elevator boy was doing a rushing business in the gent's washroom. Box seats, the very choicest and in tiers one and two, could be had at fancy prices.

Wesley Jackson of Indianapolis brought in 300 fans on a special train from the Hoosier City.

Dr. R. B. Jackson, last year's president of the Negro Southern League and popular Nashville physician, was seriously injured in an automobile wreck near Evansville, Ind., en route to the game. He was rushed to the City hospital in the Indiana City.

Mayor Martin H. Kennelly pitched the first ball with the Rev. John Johnson, president of the Negro National League, doing the receiving.[4]

Big Leagues Scout 8 Negro Players

Dan Bankhead, Jessup, Tatum Among Group

Owners Ready to Buy Contracts from Negro Club Owners

by Fay Young

Source: *Chicago Defender,* 2 August 1947

Eight ball players, members of the clubs in the Negro National League will be scouted this weekend by major league representatives of a half dozen clubs in the American and National Leagues. Two of these players have been and will be more closely scouted by the two Chicago clubs.

The eight players are:

Dan Bankhead, Memphis Red Sox pitcher, who was given credit for the West win over the East in 1946 and again this year.
Sammy Jethroe, Cleveland Buckeyes outfielder.
Lorenzo "Piper" Davis, Birmingham infielder on whom the St. Louis Browns have a 30-day option.
Gentry Jessup, Chicago American Giants pitcher, who hurled the second three innings for the West last Sunday and didn't allow a hit.
Reece "Goose" Tatum, Indianapolis' colorful first baseman who got two hits for the West in the 5–2 win over the East in the All-Star classic.
Art Wilson, Birmingham shortstop, hitless in the Chicago game but who got four hits in the game in New York in two nights later as the West won, 8–2.
Luis Marquez, Washington Homestead Grays infielder, who is hitting .411 in the Negro National League.
Oreste[s] Minosa[o], New York Cubans Stars, a third sacker who is batting .336 in the Negro National League.

Bankhead, who had a record of seven wins and two loses up to the East vs. West game, will be watched by scouts from three major league clubs Sunday at League Park, Cleveland, and again on Thursday night, August 7, in Buffalo, NY. He will hurl the first game Sunday against the Cleveland Buckeyes.

Bankhead, considered among the top three hurlers in the Negro American League, fanned two men in the East vs. West classic and allowed one hit, a single by the East's pitcher, Max Manning in the third. He allowed no runs.

Jessup, a tall right-hander, will take the mound for the Chicago American Giants at Comiskey Park against the New York Black Yankees. Several times he has been mentioned as a likely White Sox prospect although the White Sox front office doesn't have anything to say at this time.

Piper Davis is under option by the St. Louis Browns but the Browns want to farm Davis out to their Elmira, NY farm club. This does not meet with the approval of Tom Hayes, Jr., Memphis undertaker and owner of the Birmingham club because Elmira cannot pay Davis the salary he is getting with the Black Barons. Davis can play second or first base. He was in the recent East vs. West game. He scored the first run of the game for the West in the opening West first inning when he doubled to left sending Herb Souell of the Kansas City Monarchs, who had tripled, across the plate.

Davis singled to left in the fifth. He walker in the ninth and stole second. His second time up came in the third and he drove Henry Kimbro back for his long fly. Davis is batting .359 in league games.

Sammy Jethroe, the Cleveland outfielder, got one hit in three times up in the East vs. West game. He tripled, with one gone, in the home seventh. The Chicago Defender learned Thursday that efforts were being made by the San Francisco Seals of the Pacific Coast League to sign Jethroe.

WILL SIGN NEGROES

Owner Graham, who has spent 50 years in baseball, told coast reporters that he would sign any Negro ball players who could really help his club. His representatives in Chicago were trying to contact Ernie Wright, Erie, PA, businessman and owner of the Cleveland Buckeyes.

Goose Tatum is 27. He led the Army basketball scorers while on the Lincoln, Nebr., Army Air Baseball quintet during the last year of the war. Last year he played basketball with the Harlem Globetrotters and made the tours to Havana, Cuba, and to Hawaii.

Tatum, a member of the Indianapolis Clowns, is batting .229

Art Wilson, Birmingham shortstop, is batting .376. A flashy fielder, he captures the fans with his sureness.

Oreste[s] Minosa [Minoso] is a young Cuban whom the Brooklyn scouts' approached on the Island last winter. When owner Alex Pompez of the New York Cubans learned that the Mexican League was offering Oreste[s] a fat contract, he boarded a plane and headed straight for Cuba. Oreste[s] is batting .336.

Luis Marquez, the Washington Homestead Grays player can play both the infield and the outfielder. He is batting .411.

ROBINSON PAVES WAY

Jackie Robinson, formerly of the Kansas City Monarchs of the Negro American League opened the door in the major leagues when he became a regular member of the Brooklyn club after one year in the International League. Robinson topped the International League batters and as second baseman for the Montreal Royals, he was the best defensive second baseman in his league. While with the Monarchs he played shortstop.

Branch Rickey, Sr., president of the Dodgers, sent Robinson to first base at a time when the churchmen and regular fans in Brooklyn were down on Leo Durocher, manager of the Dodgers.

Robinson has made good at first base. His playing ability and his deportment on and off the field has been such that he is a credit to baseball and to his race. He follows in the footsteps of Joe Louis, the world heavyweight champion, as far as popularity goes among both the white and Negro sport lovers and newspapermen. Every time he plays, large crowds turn out. Attendance records have been broken.

Since Robinson, the first Negro to be signed to play in organized white baseball in nearly 50 years, pushed open the door, others have followed. They are:

Larry Doby, Newark Eagles infielder, signed on July 5, by the Cleveland Indians.
Willard J. Brown and Henry Thompson, Kansas City Monarchs outfielder and
    infielder, signed by the St. Louis Browns.[5]
Roy Campanella, Baltimore Elite Giants, signed by the Dodgers and sent to Nashua,
    N.H. of the New England League last year and moved up to the International
    League's Montreal team this season and due to come up for a trial with the

Brooklyn club in the spring. Campanella, a native of Philadelphia, caught the entire 1945 East vs. West game for the East.

Don Newcombe tied for first place in games won and lost as a member of the Nashua, N.H. team in the New England League. Playing his second year as a pitcher for that team.

John Wright, signed by the Dodgers and sent to Montreal last year and after a trial sent to the Three Rivers club of the Canadian-American League. This year Wright was given his release and returned to his old club, the Washington Homestead Grays. He worked the home eight against the East in the all-star game and was nicked for three runs and one run.

Roy Partlow, bought by the Brooklyn club from the Philadelphia Stars. Like Wright, he was sent to Montreal and then to the Three Rivers club. This year he is back with the Philadelphia team.

Sammy Gee, Miller High School star athlete of Detroit. He was signed by Brooklyn and sent to Three Rivers club for schooling.

Nate Moreland, El Centro, Calif., Imperials. He has 13 games won and five lost in the class C league.

Chet Brewer, signed by the coast Class C league but didn't stay there. Brewer is now with the Cleveland Buckeyes.

MARTIN APPROACHED

Dr. J. B. Martin, president of the Negro American League and head of the Chicago American Giants admitted that he had been approached by two major league clubs. He admitted the player in question was pitcher Jessup but would make no further comment at this time.

Negro League club owners are playing higher salaries than the American Association or the International League to most of the players.

SKUNKS STAY AWAY

If the Negro player makes or players make good, they will have to be careful of their conduct both on and off the field. In other words, the major league owners and managers will stand for "no stuff" to be pulled. There is no place on any club for the foul-mouthed, uncouth, liquor drinking, huzzy-chasing player. To them he is a plain "rat" and won't get into the barrel to spoil the rest of the lot. This applies to white as well as Negro players.

The white owners prefer men under 26. Married, decent respectable and home loving citizens. If they don't measure up they won't break through even if they can hit like Babe Ruth or pitch like Buck Newsom or Bob Feller or field like Joe DiMaggio.

JULY 27, 1947, SUNDAY
COMISKEY PARK, CHICAGO (GAME 1 OF 2)

EAST	AB	R	H	D	T	HR	BI	E	TAVG	TSLG
Henry Kimbro (Baltimore Elite Giants), cf	4	0	0	0	0	0	0	0		
Pee Wee Butts (Baltimore Elite Giants), ss	2	0	0	0	0	0	0	0		
Johnny Washington (Baltimore Elite Giants), 1b	4	0	0	0	0	0	0	0		
Monte Irvin (Newark Eagles), lf	3	1	0	0	0	0	0	0		
Silvio Garcia (New York Cubans), 2b	3	0	0	0	0	0	0	0		
Claro Duany (New York Cubans), rf	2	0	0	0	0	0	1	0		
Minnie Minoso (New York Cubans), 3b	3	0	0	0	0	0	0	0		
John Hayes (New York Black Yankees), c	1	0	0	0	0	0	0	0		
a) Bob Romby (Baltimore Elite Giants), ph	1	0	0	0	0	0	0	0		
Max Manning (Newark Eagles), p	2	0	1	0	0	0	0	0		
Luis Tiant (New York Cubans), p	1	0	0	0	0	0	0	0		
Luis Marquez (Homestead Grays), rf	1	1	1	1	0	0	0	0		
Louis Louden (New York Cubans), c	1	0	1	0	0	0	1	0		
Frank Austin (Philadelphia Stars), ss	2	0	0	0	0	0	0	0		
Henry Miller (Philadelphia Stars), p	0	0	0	0	0	0	0	0		
b) Biz Mackey (Newark Eagles), ph	0	0	0	0	0	0	0	0		
c) Vic Harris (Homestead Grays), pr	0	0	0	0	0	0	0	0		
Johnny Wright (Homestead Grays), p	0	0	0	0	0	0	0	0		
Team Totals, Average & Slugging Pct.	30	2	3	1	0	0	2	0	.100	.133

a) Batted for Hayes in 6th
b) Batted for Miller in 8th
c) Ran for Mackey in 8th

WEST	AB	R	H	D	T	HR	BI	E	TAVG	TSLG
ArtieWilson (Birmingham Black Barons), ss	4	0	0	0	0	0	0	0		
Herb Souell (Kansas City Monarchs), 3b	5	1	1	0	1	0	0	0		
Sam Jethroe (Cleveland Buckeyes), rf	3	1	1	0	1	0	1	0		
Piper Davis (Birmingham Black Barons), 2b	3	1	2	1	0	0	0	0		
Quincy Trouppe (Cleveland Buckeyes), c	2	1	1	0	1	0	1	0		
Jose Colas (Memphis Red Sox), lf	4	0	2	0	0	0	2	0		
Goose Tatum (Indianapolis Clowns), 1b	4	1	2	0	0	0	0	0		
Buddy Armour (Chicago American Giants), rf	4	0	2	2	0	0	0	0		
Dan Bankhead (Memphis Red Sox), p	2	0	0	0	0	0	0	0		
Gentry Jessup (Chicago American Giants), p	1	0	0	0	0	0	0	0		
Chet Brewer (Cleveland Buckeyes), p	1	0	1	0	0	0	1	0		
Team Totals, Average & Slugging Pct.	33	5	12	3	3	0	5	0	.364	.636

East	010	000	010-2	
West	202	000	01X-5	

PITCHER/TEAM	GS	IP	H	R	ER	K	BB	WP	HB	W	L	SV
Manning/NE	1	2 1/3	5	4	4	3	2	0	1	0	1	0
Tiant/NYC		2 2/3	2	0	0	0	0	0	0	0	0	0
Miller/PS		2	2	0	0	1	1	0	0	0	0	0
J. Wright/HG		1	3	1	1	0	0	0	0	0	0	0
Bankhead/MRS	1	3	1	1	1	2	0	0	1	1	0	0
Jessup/CAG		3	0	0	0	1	0	0	0	0	0	0
Brewer/CEB		3	2	1	1	1	1	0	0	0	0	1

BB—Mackey, Trouppe
DP—Wilson to Davis to Tatum
HP—Irvin by Bankhead; Jethroe by Manning
LOB—East 2, West 9
PB—Louden
SAC—Trouppe
SB—Jethroe, Davis
East—Biz Mackey (Mgr.); Coaches Vic Harris and Jose Fernandez
West—Frank Duncan (Mgr.); Coaches Candy Jim Taylor and Larry Brown
Umpires—Virgil Blueitt, Mark Van Buren, Fred McCrary, Cugalgio Penalver
Attendance—48,112   Time—2:37
Note: Mayor Martin H. Kennelly threw out 1st pitch to Rev. John Johnson.

NEW YORK GAME REVIEWS

East vs. West Classic July 29

PG All-Stars Battle Is Set on July 29

Ray Brown Reinstated in NNL Baseball Following Confab

Source: *New York Amsterdam News,* 21 June 1947

Plans for the annual East-West game, an All-Star game in the East, and the re-instatement of two players were part of the business of the joint meeting of the Negro American and National League in their joint meeting held at the Hotel Theresa, here, [New York], last week.

With Rev. John H. Johnson, president of the National circuit, presiding over the joint sessions, the solons agreed to permit Gread McKinnis of the Chicago American Giants and Ray Brown of the Homestead Grays to become part of the club roster. Both had been placed under a five-year suspension by the league when they failed to return from Mexico by the deadline date.

ALL STAR PLAY FOR THE EAST

July 27 was the date set for the annual East-West classic which will once more be played at Soldier's Field [Comiskey Park], Chicago. An all-star game, to appease eastern fans, will be played in the Polo Grounds, here July 29.

A matter which may have great bearing upon the future of many Negro ball players was advanced to the joint session by Homer "Goose" Curry, manager of the Philadelphia Stars. His plan was to set up some sort of fund which will aid needy ball players when their ability to "make it" with a team has faded.

Curry's plan called for the playing each year of a benefit which would pit a team composed of the northern half of the NNL against its counterpart from the Philadelphia-

Washington area. Reaction from the owners indicate that the plan may be given action this year.

ENTERTAINMENT FEATURED

Following the business of the day the visiting newsmen were feted at Small's Paradise where Dan Burley, managing editor of the Amsterdam News, trotted forth a bevy of entertainers recruited from Fritz Pollard's Sun Tan Studios.

Included were Vanita Smythe, Doc Rhythm, The Victorians, The Stanley Sisters, Lanny Scott, Teddi Horne [Lena's father], Olivia Page and Nipsy Russell.

Speakers for the occasion included Commissioner Ray Jones of the New York Housing Commission; Commissioner Samuel Battles of the Parole Board; Dr. B. B. Martin, President of the Negro American League; Wendell Smith of the Pittsburgh Courier, and Harry Singer of the Bronx Home News. Rev. Johnson presided.

Joe Bostic, columnist of the *Amsterdam News* announced that he had been informed that the game between the Newark Eagles and the New York Black Yankees at Ebbets Field, June 19, would be televised. This will mark the first time that a game between colored teams has been selected for television.

Negro Star Game to American Loop

38,402 See National Leaguers Fall before 14-Hit Attack,

8–2, at Polo Grounds

by Louis Effrat

Source: *New York Times,* 30 July 1947

The second annual "dream game" between the Negro National and American Leagues all-stars attracted 38,402 fans to the Polo Grounds last night.[6] The largest crowd ever to have witnessed a Negro contest in the East saw the American Leaguers score an 8–2 victory.

At least one major league scout—Ed Holly of the Cubs—was among those in attendance. But he made no comments concerning the possibilities of the Cubs signing any athlete.

The victorious combination in this encounter involving the best of the Negro baseball players hammered four National League pitchers for fourteen hits. The losers got eight safeties against the four who hurled for the winners.

WILSON, JETHROE SET PACE

Art Wilson of the Birmingham Barons and Sammy Jethroe of the Cleveland Buckeyes paced the attack, the former polling out four singles. The latter, in whom the Cleveland Indians are said to have shown an interest, came through with two singles and a triple and batted home four runs.

Jethroe sent the American League off to a 1–0 lead in the first, but the Nationals rebounded immediately for a 2–1 edge on singles by John Washington and Monte Irvin and a two-bagger by Silvio Garcia of the New York Cubans. Ford smith, starting and winning pitcher, however, tightened and stopped the rally.

Thereafter, every National League threat was cut short and Rufus Lewis, who started for that side was charged with the setback. He was followed by Luis Tiant, Joe Black, and Henry Miller. Smith preceded John Williams, Ernest Carter and Vibert Clarke.

TWO RUNS IN THIRD

A two-run outburst in the third and a three-run offensive in the fifth, featured by Jethroe's triple and Ray Neil's double, virtually clinched the decision for the Western group.

The teams met at Chicago last Sunday in an East-West all-star game and on that occasion the outcome was the same, the American Leaguers registering a 5–2 triumph.

86,514 See 2 Negro Baseball Classics

38,402 Crowd in PG Biggest Ever in East

Vast Tuesday Night Throng Sees Western All-Stars Win Dream Game, 8 to 2

by Dan Burley

Source: *New York Amsterdam News*, 2 August 1947

A glittering array of the best talent in organized Negro baseball played before the largest crowd to see a Negro sporting event in the East in history—38,402 paid—in the Polo Grounds Tuesday night as the Negro American League All-Stars blasted out an 8 to 2 victory over the Negro National All-Stars in the second annual "Dream Game" between the two rival loops. The victory evened the series started last year in Griffith Stadium, Washington, D.C., where the National Leaguers won.

BIG LEAGUE SCOUTS ON HAND

An announced attendance of 48,112 at the East-West Classic at Comiskey Park in Chicago last Sunday plus that Tuesday night at the Polo Grounds added up to a grand total of 86,514 persons attending Negro sports events over a two-day span. In Chicago and New York less than 2% of the crowd was white.

As in Chicago, big league scouts were on hand to observe at first hand the players most likely to move into the majors and Tuesday night they saw plenty. The Birmingham Black Baron stars, shortstop Art Wilson, and second baseman Lorenzo (Piper) Davis; Cleveland Buckeyes' Sammy Jethroe, a fleet-footed outfielder; and Ernest (Spoon) Carter, right-handed pitcher from the Memphis Red Sox, all of the American League, were the top stars of the classic.

It was a colorful, gay and happy throng that started the trek to the Polo Grounds as early as 6 o'clock. By 7:30 p.m. every subway train at the 155th street stop was disgorging human cargoes heading into the devouring turnstiles of the Polo Grounds. Buses were packed to the walls moving in and out of a regular parade of taxicabs and private cars up Eighth Street, Nicholas and Seventh Avenues and through the side streets, all racing into a common vertex at 156th Street and Eighth Ave.

Adding to the mob was the fact that Primary Election Day closed all taverns and liquor stores from 3 until 10 p.m. and the thousands who might otherwise have been content to hang around their favorite joints, came out to the ball game in person. It was a well-behaved crowd and not a fight or disturbance was recorded. New York socialites rubbed elbows with politicians, ministers, school teachers, students, barmaids and bartenders, housewives, former athletes, singers, dancers, butchers, barbers, nightclub owners, and all the human flotsam, and that goes to make up the individual collectively known as "Gus Fan."

For the years the East has taken low to the West in the matter of crowds at sports events like baseball. The annual East-West Classic in Chicago has been built to a "natural" capacity affair which is around 49,000 or so at Comiskey Park. Last year Satchel Paige's All-Stars, playing against an All-Star Major League ensemble led by Bobby Feller, attracted 35,000 to Yankee Stadium, but the crowd was at least 15% white. Paige has attracted crowds of 25,000 in the past and some games sponsored by the Negro National League have been seen by 30,000 fans. None have gotten to the 38,000 mark, however, in paid attendance. Tuesday night it was believed that there were actually around 42,000 persons on hand, although the paid attendance was 38,402.

A. L. DID EVERYTHING

The American Leaguers did everything right in fashioning their 8–2 triumph over the Nationals. They fused 14 hits into eight runs while the losers were held to a total of eight hits. In additional the Nationals contributed four errors to their own downfall, two by Henry Kimbro of Baltimore in centerfield and one apiece by Silvio Garcia, Cubans, at second base, and Rufus Lewis, Newark. All this was taking place as Art Wilson and Jethroe unleashed a batting onslaught on National League hurlers that got Wilson four singles and Sammy two singles and a triple. Jethroe batted in four runs.

Ed Holly of the Chicago Cubs, a topflight scout, was on hand to see Jethroe send the American Leaguers off to a 1–0 advantage in the first inning. Wilson drew a pass from Lewis and went to second on Rufus' error. Herb Souell of Kansas City fanned, but Jethroe singled to center to score Wilson. Jethroe promptly stole second but died there when Boyd skied to left. The Nationals bounced back in their half of the first when with two out, Johnny Washington of Baltimore beat out a hit off Souell's glove. Monty Irvin of Newark singled him to third and Garcia's sharp double to left off Ford Smith of Kansas City, starting pitcher for the Americans, scored Washington and Irvin.

SMART MANAGERS

The American Leaguers played smart ball both afield and from the managerial side, the veteran Frank Duncan of the Kansas City Monarchs, 1946 league champions, calling the plays from the sidelines. The Westerners fielded a running team that was responsible for many of the hits the players recorded and for spectacular work afield by Jethroe in center, Wilson and Davis at short and at second and Jose Colas of Memphis in right. With Smith bearing down, the National League cause was stopped cold and airtight support to subsequent pitchers made the Americans well nigh invincible.

The Americans went out in front in the third when Wilson whistled a single to left and took second on Souell's sacrifice bunt, and third on Jethroe's infield out. Davis singled to center to score Wilson and Kimbre [Kimbro] juggled the ball allowing it to roll all the way to the wall as Davis raced around third to score. Boyd laced a terrific double off the left field wall, but Colas fanned to end the rally.

Not satisfied with what they had, the American Leaguers put on another scoring exhibition in the fifth when they chalked up three more runs. Wilson poled a single to right and Leon Kellman of Cleveland came in to bat for Souell. Wilson stole second and Garcia threw out Kellman. Jethroe tripled off the left field wall as Wilson cross the plate. Davis scored him on an infield out. Ralph [Ray] Neil of the Indianapolis Clowns batted for Boyd and looped a double to left, Colas singled to center and Neil scored. Garcia threw out

42. *Monte Irvin is out attempting to score in the '47 classic against catcher Quincy Trouppe from the Cleveland Buckeyes. Trouppe's West squad won the game, 5–2. Courtesy of Quincy Trouppe.*

Abernathy and the Westerners didn't score again until the eighth when they chased two more across the platter.

BASES FILLED BUT COULDN'T SCORE

The dramatic highlight of the game was in the sixth when the National Leaguers filled the bases with none out and couldn't score. Here Duncan's handling of pitchers showed to greater advantage. John Williams of the Crowns was on the hill as Romby, Baltimore Elites, batted for Louis Louden, Cubans catcher, and hit to right for a single. Joe Black, third Eastern pitcher, singled to left. Kimbre [Kimbro] walked and the bases were filled. Duncan marched out and thumbed Williams to the shower, motioning to the left field bullpen for Ernest (Spoon) Carter of the Memphis Red Sox, to come in. Carter made Frank Austin, Philadelphia Stars, hit into a fast double play, Carter rubbing out Romby at the plate via a bullet peg to catcher Quincy Trouppe of Cleveland who rifled the ball to first to nail the flying Austin, Washington hoisted to Jethroe as the big crowd went mad.

Chicken-Feed Pay for Negro Umpires

by Dan Burley

Source: *New York Amsterdam News,* 9 September 1947

What about our Negro baseball umpires? They are cussed, discussed, made the subject of all sorts of fuss. They are reviled and often as not, riled as they go about their highly sensitive calling of calling 'em right, knowing that the fans in the stands are prejudicing them from the start, and that the players are the greatest umpire "riders" in the business. If an umpire isn't good, he is subject to spoil an entire game. He can throw players off-key by the ways he calls the play, he can incur for himself bitter animosities that follow him off the diamond into his social life. All together, the life of the Negro umpire isn't cheese and cherries by any means.

But when an umpire has to take the burdens of the baseball world on his back and then doesn't get enough pay for an honest day's work to pay his rent, buy food and other necessities of life, then something should be done about it, not along by baseball officials, but by the fans who follow the game and want to see Negro baseball advance. That's why the letter printed here from big Fred McCrary, a familiar figure at Yankee Stadium games and rated as one of the best arbiters in baseball, black or white, is so pertinent to the issue and filled with factual slants on a deplorable situation.

Dear Dan

I have often wanted to talk to you, but it seems that every time I have the chance, you are busy or I am leaving town for some other point. I notice your writings in your paper that I read every week about different things that go on in the Negro National League, all of which are true. I have also been reading about what you have to say about the player situation and that is true as well. We, as umpires, never get anything or any consideration from the league; we only go on and work on a basis of "dog, take what we give you." For one thing, I have worked in all the East-West games for the past six years, and up until the last two years, they have only given us umpires $10 to work and three days' expense money. It takes three days to get out of Chicago and to come back. For any other days, we get nothing.

I have argued with the league owners for more money, or at least for $50, and they, or at least some of the owners, have gone so far as to say that the umpires are not important in a ballgame, and not nearly as important as the players. I know that is not true, because the umpires can make the game what it is, good or bad. I was asked by Moore of Birmingham after the game Monday in Chicago and by [Virgil] Blueitt and the two western umpires to go with them to the room where the Western club owners were checking up on their share of the receipts and to see what they were getting for their work. They got $100 plus expenses, and Moore's expenses were $35. Dr. J. B. martin, president of the Negro American League, gave him $135. I saw this with my own eyes.

I have worked for this league and for the benefit of all owners, and after that, I get no credit. I have gone so far as to rent rooms in different towns where I have had a three or a four game series to work, and they charge you $3 or $4 for a room now, take it or leave it. That is despite getting only $3.50 expense in any one town for three days, which only pays for my room for one night. I pay the difference for the two nights out of my own pocket. I also have to feed myself for the three days.

Now Cum Posey, secretary of the Negro National League, who gives me this $3.50, sent that expense slip to Mrs. Effa Manley, the league treasurer, to be charged to me. I have gotten $6 and $8 for expenses from some clubs when I was on the road, and they sent that in to be charged against me. I was down in Virginia with the Black Yankees and the Homestead Grays and Posey gave me money to eat and sleep, and he also sent that in against me.

They pay my railroad fare, and if I would come back to Philadelphia every day or night after the games and go back to those towns the next day, it would cost them twice the money for train fare than it would to give me adequate expense money I pay out of my own pocket. But I help them and that's what I get.

I wish you would write something in the umpire's favor. You can quote me because what I am saying is true.

Yours in Sports, Fred D. McCrary.

P. S. From now on, I am returning to Philadelphia every day, so I'll let them spend that money to send me back. They also voted at the league meeting to give me expense money for the road. F. D. M.

In the 1947 East-West Classic at Comiskey Park, where a crowd of 50,000—47,000 of whom paid to get in the annual affair—the Negro National League sheet showed $62.76 for the transportation of two umpires, $20 for their expenses, and $15 each for salary. The players got only $50 per man. This year, the players went on strike and refused to play until a promoter agreed to pay them $200 each. But, the umpires didn't go on strike at all.

With the umpires of such an important affair getting only $14, Dr. J. B. Martin, American League president, and Thomas T. Wilson, president of the Negro National League and owner of the Baltimore Elite Giants, split a cool $3,099.61 between them. That means while Tom and J. B. were eating steaks at Jim Knight's Palm Tavern on Chicago's 47th Street, McCrary and his associate umpires were scuffling in the chili poster.

Mrs. Effa Manley of the Newark Eagles seems to be about the only owner in the N.N.L. who can see the disparity of pay and the treatment of umpires, especially since Negro baseball is having a banner season in gate receipts. It was she who broke the sorry spectacle of umpires running from club owner to club owner after each game trying to collect their pay, or standing on the sidewalk until late in the night to get their measly salary, while the boys in the back room told tall tales of the days when they were young and otherwise took plenty of time before paying off. Maybe, some day, these things will be straightened out, but only when men like McCrary ask for what is rightfully and morally theirs.

JULY 29, 1947, TUESDAY
POLO GROUNDS, NEW YORK (GAME 2 OF 2)

WEST	AB	R	H	D	T	HR	BI	E	TAVG	TSLG
Artie Wilson (Birmingham Black Barons), ss	4	4	4	0	0	0	1	0		
Herb Souell (Kansas City Monarchs), 3b	1	0	0	0	0	0	0	0		
a) Leon Kellman (Cleveland Buckeyes), ph-2b	2	0	0	0	0	0	0	0		
Sam Jethroe (Cleveland Buckeyes), cf	5	1	3	0	1	0	4	0		
Piper Davis (Birmingham Black Barons), 2b	5	1	1	0	0	0	2	0		
Bob Boyd (Memphis Red Sox), 1b	2	0	1	1	0	0	0	0		
b) Ray Neil (Indianapolis Clowns), ph-2b	3	1	2	1	0	0	0	0		
Jose Colas (Memphis Red Sox), lf-rf	5	0	1	0	0	0	1	0		
Buddy Armour (Chicago American Giants), rf	1	0	0	0	0	0	0	0		
James Abernathy (Indianapolis Clowns), lf	4	0	0	0	0	0	0	0		
Pepper Bassett (Birmingham Black Barons), c	2	0	1	0	0	0	0	0		
Quincy Trouppe (Cleveland Buckeyes), c	2	1	1	0	0	0	0	0		
Ford Smith (Kansas City Monarchs), p	1	0	0	0	0	0	0	0		
Johnny "Nature Boy" Williams (Indianapolis Clowns), p	2	0	0	0	0	0	0	0		
Spoon Carter (Memphis Red Sox), p	1	0	0	0	0	0	0	0		
Vibert Clarke (Cleveland Buckeyes), p	0	0	0	0	0	0	0	0		
Team Totals, Average & Slugging Pct.	40	8	14	2	1	0	8	0	.350	.450

a) Batted for Souell in 5th
b) Batted for Boyd in 5th

EAST	AB	R	H	D	T	HR	BI	E	TAVG	TSLG
Henry Kimbro (Baltimore Elite Giants), cf	2	0	1	0	0	0	0	2		
Pee Wee Butts (Baltimore Elite Giants), ss	1	0	0	0	0	0	0	0		
c) Claro Duany (New York Cubans), ph	1	0	0	0	0	0	0	0		
Johnny Washington (Baltimore Elite Giants), 1b	4	1	2	0	0	0	0	0		
Monte Irvin (Newark Eagles), lf	3	1	1	0	0	0	0	0		
Silvio Garcia (New York Cubans), 2b	4	0	1	1	0	0	2	1		
Luis Marquez (Homestead Grays), rf	3	0	0	0	0	0	0	0		
Minnie Minoso (New York Cubans), 3b	4	0	1	0	0	0	0	0		
Louis Louden (New York Cubans), c	2	0	0	0	0	0	0	0		
d) Bob Romby (Baltimore Elite Giants), ph	1	0	1	0	0	0	0	0		
John Hayes (New York Black Yankees), c	1	0	0	0	0	0	0	0		
Rufus Lewis (Newark Eagles), p	1	0	0	0	0	0	0	1		
Luis Tiant, Sr. (New York Cubans), p	0	0	0	0	0	0	0	0		
Frank Austin (Philadelphia Stars), ss	2	0	0	0	0	0	0	0		
Joe Black (Baltimore Elite Giants), p	2	0	1	0	0	0	0	0		
Henry Miller (Philadelphia Stars), p	0	0	0	0	0	0	0	0		
Team Totals, Average & Slugging Pct.	31	2	8	1	0	0	2	4	.258	.290

c) Batted for Butts in 4th

d) Batted for Louden in 6th

West	102	030	020-8
East	200	000	00X-2

PITCHER/TEAM	GS	IP	H	R	ER	K	BB	WP	HB	W	L
F. Smith/KCM	1	3	4	2	2	2	2	0	0	1	0
J. Williams/IC		2	2	0	0	0	5	0	0	0	0
Carter/MRS		3	2	0	0	2	1	0	0	0	0
Clarke/CEB		1	0	0	0	0	1	0	0	0	0
R. Lewis/NE	1	3	5	3	2	4	1	0	0	0	1
Tiant/NYC		2	4	3	3	0	0	0	0	0	0
Black/BEG		3	5	2	2	2	1	0	0	0	0
Miller/PS		1	0	0	0	0	0	0	0	0	0

BB—Wilson, Kimbro

DP—Carter to Trouppe to P. Davis; Neil to Wilson to P. Davis; Wilson to Neil to P. Davis

LOB—West 3, East 12

SAC—Souell, Butts

SB—Washington, Wilson (2), Jethroe

East—Biz Mackey (Mgr.)

West—Frank Duncan (Mgr.)

Umpires—Fred McCrary, Cugalgio Penalver, Oscar Charleston and ? Bourne

Attendance—38,402   Time—2:46

1948

The U.S. Supreme Court voids a California statute prohibiting interracial marriages.

The Ladies Professional Golf Association is formed and bars blacks from membership, although no specific clause to that effect is written in their constitution. It was, in essence, a "ladies' agreement."

The African Methodist Episcopal Church authorizes the ordination of women.

The Original Harlem Globetrotters defeat George Mikan and the NBL champion Minneapolis Lakers in Chicago Stadium.

Milk costs 44 cents a half-gallon, 10 pounds of potatoes costs 56 cents, and 77 cents would bring home the bacon. A loaf of bread costs 14 cents.

Despite injuries to such stars as Joe DiMaggio, Ted Williams, George Kell, and Hal Newhouser, the American League All-Stars win, 5–2, over the National Leaguers.

At age 42, former Negro League star Satchel Paige enters the American League and pitches a shutout in his first start. The only other Negro League veteran to reach the majors this year is former Baltimore Elite Giants catcher Roy Campanella.

Jackie Robinson pens his autobiography, *My Own Story,* with Wendell Smith.

LEAGUE BUSINESS

With Major League Baseball enjoying record attendance highs the previous year, black baseball in the eastern part of country began a decline. The curtains were slowly drawing closed on black baseball, as the Homestead Grays defeated the Birmingham Black Barons in the last official Negro League world series.

Attendance in the East had never reached the record highs of the Midwest. Back in 1941 Ed Harris of the *Philadelphia Tribune* had expressed his perspective on why his Eastern league would always fail to reach the attendance plateaus attained in Chicago:

> One of the soundest evidences of the community spirit in the Middle West. You could hold the East-West game in the East for the next ten years and you wouldn't have the attendance that the Mid-West will have in five.
>
> Say what you will about Chicago and Detroit and the other big towns out that way being away from the places where "things happen," you'll have to admit the fact that colored people really know how to live.
>
> Blasé New York, with its "Living in Harlem is the only thing" and staid Philadelphia, with its self-satisfaction, won't ever make the progress racially that the new up-and-doing communities of the West are.
>
> There have been all-star games here and in New York, where the Yankee Stadium, one of the finest parks in the country was available. The Stadium and the Polo Grounds

aren't a five-minute car ride from the heart of Harlem but do you think 50,000 people got that far? I won't wait for an answer.

So Chicago can take a bow or a couple of bows. The boys who played ball can bow also, that they have the stuff to attract that many people. The Negro American and National Leagues can take a bow for having thought up the attraction, though they are being paid for their investment. The boys really cut a melon, and not a lemon.[1]

Writer Dan Burley said it best when he wrote, "When Robinson went into big league baseball he took the Negro attendance at all-Negro contests with him."[2]

Recently, Dan Topping had taken over ownership of the New York Yankees from Larry MacPhail. Yankee Stadium had been choice rental property for Negro League teams like the Black Yankees, the Baltimore Elite Giants, the Newark Eagles, the Homestead Grays, and the New York Cubans. Topping reported that attendance figures in 1947 for Negro League games had dropped from 158,155 to 63,402.[3] This was a 60-percent decline in attendance. He estimated that more than 200,000 black fans had attended the games in 1945.

Burley estimated that 50,000 black folks lived near Ebbets Field in Queens, Long Island, Jamaica, and Corona, and attributed the decline to four conditions:

1. Jackie Robinson and the Dodgers
2. Jackie Robinson and Radio broadcasts
3. Jackie Robinson and television portrayals of him in action in thousands of bars and grills, and
4. Failure of Negro baseball operators to meet the Robinson threat with counter attractions or even better baseball.[4]

According to Burley: "Some of the top talent sequestered in Mexico was Ray Dandridge, Leon Day, Terris McDuffie, Theolic Smith, Ray Brown, Bus Clarkson and Parnell Woods, all former East-West participants. Until new players are developed the lack of these box office attractions hinders the gate receipts. Additionally, with the salary limits it guarantees that black baseball will not be able to attract young and outstanding talent."

Dan Burley also wrote:

Can the fans be expected to pay big league prices to see a $75 a week shortstop or first baseman perform when he can see Jackie Robinson, Roy Campanella, Larry Doby and others in action who will be getting from $6,000 up and playing that kind of ball since the man isn't going to pay those prices for so-so performances? How about player morale? Because some players got two and three hundred dollars a week salaries in the past, it cannot be taken as an indication that all players were getting what the boys would call "big money." Indeed, the number of $75 and $60 a week players would appall you.

I was told that the idea was to "cut down so we can make our expenses." Maybe so, but it would seem to me that the player is what it takes to get the money. It's common sense that without players you can't have a team and without teams you can't have a league. And it also adds up that players who figure they are underpaid are not going to play highly paid baseball which is what the fans want to see. To me, the ceiling on payrolls is a step backwards, not forward and while it may put a few extra dollars in the coffers of the promoters and club owners, it will not, definitely not, pay off in results.

The players will recall also how they were paying the players in the East-West Classic in Chicago several years ago about $50 on a full house payoff at Comiskey Park until the players woke up and went on strike just before game time and got their just demands. The same thing occurred when they staged the All-Star game in Washington a couple of years back. Players are emotional and last year's abortive attempts to organize a baseball player union might crystallize under the present retrenchment program adopted by both the NNL and the NAL. I don't think that the league will attract players of the high caliber necessary to meet the Jackie Robinson competition, if they go ahead with the ax on salary limits.[5]

Burley also added that it was time to stop paying the high tariffs at Yankee Stadium, the Polo Grounds, and Ebbets Field on a "fly-by-night" proposition and suggested that teams build their own ballparks.

With attendance at record lows, league officials at their annual meeting came up with an idea—a salary cap. Unanimously adopted, it stipulated a $6,000 monthly ceiling for each team's payroll. Also, the board of directors refused to lift the ban on players who had jumped to the outlaw Mexican leagues.[6]

Other league business involved Black Yankees owner James "Soldier Boy" Semler and his attempt to purchase the contract of Monte Irvin from the Newark Eagles for $1,500. Realizing that Irvin was a prime candidate for major league play, the Manleys turned down Semler's offer. Semler, who had acquired his military moniker as a mess cook for a unit in the south of France in 1917, complained, "They're always hollering about New York being the weak sister in the league, yet none of them will move a finger or do anything to help me build up a representative team for our many followers in New York."

Soldier Boy added, "If they'll sell, we'll buy. We've got a treasury, but our money is getting rusty from disuse." Attempting to reorganize his Black Yankees, Semler was also canceling the booking contract of Frank Forbes, a longtime associate. Taking his position was Frank "Country" Mayers, a member of the Grand Elks Lodge. Semler had recently been appointed grand commissioner of athletics for the Elks and had named Mayers as his aide.[7]

The impact of breaking the color barrier and the attention directed to Jackie Robinson had a major impact on the downfall of New York teams. Alex Pompez and his New York Cubans had virtually abandoned league play. And Semler claimed he had lost $20,000 in 1947 due to fans listening to radio coverage of Robinson's exploits and going to Ebbets Field when the Dodgers played. He cried, "If I had gone another two weeks, I'd have been in the poor house. And they [park owners and bookies] don't come down on [their commissions] what they take out of Negro baseball at these big league parks."[8] Meanwhile, the Newark Eagles across the Hudson River were enjoying modest success at Ruppert Stadium, Newark's top minor league park.

In a move to counter the fall in attendance, Soldier Boy Semler approached the president of the Rochester Redwings of the International League about renting their ballpark. The Redwings offered more playing dates and inclusion in their publicity. Semler had voiced his desire to leave New York to Dan Burley of the *Amsterdam News*, saying, "It hasn't been a good idea at all to have two Negro teams less than a stone's throw from each other playing Sunday ball at Yankee Stadium and the Polo Grounds. Many times the fans have been confused as to who was playing where and playing who."[9] The confusion came about because the Polo Grounds or Yankee Stadium were interchangeable as home parks for either the Cubans or the Black Yankees. Semler added, "If Alex Pompez wants to continue at the Polo Grounds, well and good. In fact, he should play and promote there. It will be the only place in the city to see Negro baseball."[10]

The Black Yankees had been a fixture in Harlem for several years and had a strong following of fans until Jackie Robinson "pied pipered" the fans into going to Brooklyn. Moving to upstate New York allowed the Black Yankees to become the only black team in the Rochester-Buffalo-Syracuse area. While the black populace in upstate New York was sparse and scattered, Semler hoped that the white baseball fans wouldn't care about the complexion of his players as long as they played entertaining baseball. Semler was hoping a team with the New York tag in front of its name would be an attraction in itself to Rochester citizens.

In March, at the Theresa Hotel in New York, the Negro National League approved the transfer of Semler's franchise to Rochester and gave Pompez unlimited power to negotiate lease agreements with Yankee Stadium and the Polo Grounds.[11] With Pompez's New York Cubans winning the previous year's world series, this appeared to be a win-win situation for his Cubans this season.

The Black Yankees played their first game in Rochester on May 23 against the Newark Eagles. To everyone's surprise, the Eagles and Yankees were allowed to register at white hotels in Rochester. The teams had broken the hotel color line in upstate New York![12] Customarily, teams in New York stayed at the Woodside Hotel, a black-owned hotel. Other minority-owned hostelries throughout the league included the Grand Hotel in Chicago, the Hotel York in Baltimore, Jean Clore's Guest House in Washington DC, the Majestic Hotel in Cleveland, and Bailey's in Pittsburgh.

The lack of major league ballparks and the financial resources to build suitable facilities would ultimately kill interest in black baseball. Although black teams had produced quality athletes in the past, the rookie player was now being entertained by Major League Baseball. The young and promising athlete was becoming a rare commodity in black baseball. Perhaps the only resource was for Negro League baseball to become a minor league affiliate of Major League Baseball.

RACE RELATIONS

Lester Rodney recalled Larry Doby's exposure to public accommodations in the nation's capital: "Larry Doby when he came on board [in 1947], I was with him when they went to Washington to the Hotel Shoreham. He claimed the closest person he knew, the first one to stick his hand out [when he joined the club], was Joe Gordon. He said, 'Welcome aboard!' Here they come to the hotel, and everyone knows that there are no blacks allowed in that hotel. So Doby turns to Joe Gordon and says, 'What do I do?' Gordon said, 'You walk up there with me and tell them your name and that you're part of the Cleveland Indians.' And Larry went up to the clerk, and Joe signed in and Larry said, 'I am Larry Doby and I'm with the team.' The clerk was all confused and didn't know what to do. It was like a scene from an old movie. The clerk said, 'Excuse me,' and went back and came back in five minutes. 'Everything is okay, Mr. Doby, sign here.' So Joe Gordon said, 'I told you—you're part of the Cleveland Indians.' Everybody was shocked. Lou Boudreau was shocked. He didn't even think Doby would try [to register]."[13]

A year after the breaking of baseball's color barrier, other sports could now be questioned about their policy on admitting African-Americans on their fields, tennis courts, bowling lanes, golf courses, and in the ring. The Golden Gloves and AAU tournaments accepted fighters from all ethnic backgrounds. On the pro level, boxing was currently promoting African-Americans Joe Louis, Jersey Joe Walcott, Ezzard Charles, and Sugar Ray Robinson.

In football, both collegiate and professional, racial bias was on a downward trend with the admission of Buddy Young, Marion Motley, and Jackie's former teammate at UCLA Kenny Washington making impressions in the pro ranks.

In track and field a host of African-Americans continued to make their presence known, with world-record performances from Harrison Dillard, Bill Mathis, and Barney Ewell. In the other sport that wears short pants, the Renaissance Big Five and the Harlem Globetrotters dominated the pro basketball picture, with black players making appearances on previously all-white high school and college rosters across the country.

There was still a ban on black players by the American Bowling Congress, along with other "gentlemen's agreements" enforced by the various official golfing and tennis associations.

ALL-STAR REVIEW

On October 24 an all-star squad of Negro leaguers played the Bob Lemon All-Stars. One of the highlights of the game was watching 45-year-old Cool Papa Bell score from first on a bunt. After reaching first on a single, the next batter, Satchel Paige, laid down a perfect bunt toward third base. The third baseman, pitcher, first baseman, and catcher converged on the ball. Bell had watched Lemon pitch before and noticed that he would always go to the plate after a hard look. So Bell was already off and running to second on the bunt and proceeded to the uncovered third base. Bell peeked at catcher Roy Partee coming up the line and saw him frantically waving for the ball, so he skipped past him and crossed the plate. Partee tried to call time after Bell flew by him, but the umpire just laughed at the catcher.

JACKIE'S JOURNEY

In January, Jackie Robinson was presented with the newly created Rookie of the Year Award. Before approximately 750 patrons at the Chicago Writers' Banquet, which was called the Diamond Dinner, Branch Rickey commented, "This is the first time a colored man has been honored as you have honored Jackie Robinson. You bestowed this honor upon him not because of his color and not in spite of it, but because of his sheer excellence in a competitive sport." [14]

West Selects Players for Big Game Aug. 22

Source: *Chicago Defender,* 31 July 1948

The Negro American league club owners have decided on the players who will represent them in the 16th annual East vs. West game to be played at Comiskey Park, Sunday afternoon, Aug. 22. In event of rain the game will be played that night.

A second game between the East and West teams, called the "Dream game" will be played in New York that week.

The owners have named the team this year. With the exception of a few years, the players were selected by vote of the fans. The Negro National League voted against this method, preferring to make their own selections.

KING TUT TO CLOWN

Each of the six clubs have named three players with the exception of the Indianapolis Clowns which will have two. The third person from the Clowns will be King Tut, the comedian.

Latest word from Dr. J. B. Martin, president of the Western circuit and president of the Chicago American Giants, is to the effect that three more players will be added to bring the playing list to 20.

Fine Pitching by Western Aces Halts East before 42,099

by Bill Nunn

Source: *Pittsburgh Courier,* 28 August 1948

Chicago— As the sun set in the Golden West here at Comiskey Park Sunday it seemed to take with it into the annals of baseball history the end of an era. The once proud gladiators from the East are no more; and in their wake has stepped a haughty, hustling bunch of ball players from out of the West, intent on showing the baseball world that the Negro American League produces the best that there is to offer as far as the diamond sport is concerned. For the sixth straight time, the Eastern All-Stars were forced to bow in complete submission to the Stars from the West as the American Leaguers walked jauntily off the field with a 3–0 shutout victory tucked tightly under their belts.

As 42,099 rabid fans sat glued to their seats (they must have been glued for they had very little to stand up and cheer about), the Westerners went methodically on and chalked up their tenth win in the sixteen-game series.

The mighty pitching trio of Bill Powell, James LaMarque and Gentry Jessup proved to be too much of an obstacle for the Eastern sluggers to take in one afternoon. For nine innings the National Leaguers could muster only three scattered hits. Two of those were on the scratchy side.

After the second inning when the West scored twice, it was strictly no contest.

Rufus Lewis, who started the game for the East, got into trouble in the second frame when the West bounced three hits and walk, good for two runs.

Willard Brown opened the inning with a single to left and he moved along to second when Robert Boyd blasted another single to the same spot. Brown scored a moment later when Neal Robinson blasted the West's third successive single into left field. The runners went to second and third, respectively, when Lucious Easter threw wild to the plate in an effort to get Brown.

Quincy Troupe was given intentional walk to fill the bases, but when Sam Hill grounded out, second to first, Boyd scampered over with the second run.

DOUBLE PLAY CLICKS

An unusual double play enabled Lewis to escape further damage in this inning. With Troupe on second and Robinson on third, Powell hit a ground ball to James Gilliam on second. Gilliam's throw to the plate was in time to trap Robinson between third and home. He was out when William Cash, the East's catcher, threw to Orestes Minsoa [Minoso] at third and the latter made the putout. Minosa [Minoso] then turned and touched Troupe who was caught off second.

In the eighth, the West tagged portly Robert Griffith for two hits and another run.

DAVIS DOUBLES

Piper Davis opened the inning with a screaming double down the left field line. He moved to third when Brown got his second hit of the day, a blooper single to right field. On the play, Brown tried to stretch the bingle [single] into a double and was out, Monty Irvin to Frank Austin.

Boyd followed with a fly ball to left that enabled Davis to trot over with the final run.

From where we sat in the press box row, it appeared to be a very dull game, as the East was able to get only one man as far as second.

The aging Buck Leonard, veteran of many a past All-Star game, reached the keystone sack in the fourth inning when his smash down the first base line deflected off the glove of Boyd and rolled into short right field.

DREAM GAME ACTION

The best form shown by an Eastern pitcher was that of Wilbur [Wilmer] Fields, the Grays' big right hander, who didn't allow a run in the three innings he worked. He gave up one hit. Chicago's Jessup was the West outstanding mound performer. He pitched the last three hitless innings.

The West also gets credit for the game's top fielding performance. Piper Davis, whose performance around second base was nothing less than sensational, came up with a deuce of beautiful stops. In the fourth he went far to his left, made a one-handed stab of Monty Irvin's bid for a hit and threw him out. Then in the fifth, he went behind second and made a back-handed stab of Louis Louden's drive and threw him out by a hair's breath. Robinson raced back 365 feet into left center field in the ninth and literally climbed the concrete wall as he robbed Minoso of a sure-fire triple . . . Jesse Owens and Wilberforce's "Country" Lewis occupied press-box seats . . . the official attendants was first announced at 37,099 and later changed to 50,000 . . . One disturbing fact about the game was the continued blare of the loud speaking system even when their men were at bat . . . It seemed that more people were talking about the performances of Satchel Paige than the game . . . The crowd was asked to stand and pay a silent tribute to the late Babe Ruth.

Defeats East, 3–0, before 42,099 Fans

16th Annual Classic Draws Less than Satchel Paige Did Here Aug. 13

by Fay Young

Source: *Chicago Defender,* 28 August 1948

The Negro American Leaguers, comprising the West nine, shut the East out, 3–0 at Comiskey Park Sunday, Aug. 22, in the 16th annual East vs. West game classic before 42,099 about 9,000 less than Satchel Paige drew at the same park on Friday night. Paige drew 51,000 and turned away a good 15,000.[15] The East vs. West game turned away nobody.

The Negro National Leaguers were unable to solve the slants of William Powell of the Birmingham Black Barons, James LaMarque of the Kansas City Monarchs and Gentry Jessup of the Chicago American Giants.

HOG TIED EAST

The Easterners, all top batters in their league and clouting the ball over .300, were hogtied. Of the three hits they made, two were lucky ones. The only real hit was James Gilliam's rap to right with one down in the second off Bill Powell. The Baltimore second Baseman was thrown out attempting to steal, Quincy Trouppe to Piper Davis.

Buck Leonard's double in the fourth. Orestes Minoso, New York third sacker, beat out a hit to Art Wilson in deep short in the sixth. Both Leonard, the Gray's first sacker, and Minoso got their blows off James LaMarque, Kansas City Monarchs hurler.

43. Heavyweight boxing champion Joe Louis gives the glad hand to Satchel Paige. Paige had just blanked the Chicago White Sox, 5–0, scattering five hits at Comiskey Park. A crowd of 51,013 was reported, while an estimated 15,000 fans were turned away. Courtesy of Pamela Paige O'Neal.

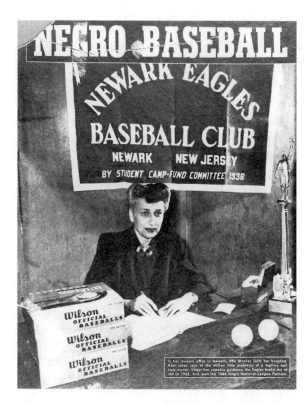

JESSUP IN FORM

Gentry Jessup of the Chicago American Giants hurled the seventh, eighth and ninth for the West and was never in danger. He allowed no hits and struck out one. He walked one.

Not a single East player saw third base. Only two reached second. Lucious Easter, Gray's outfielder, walked and went to second when the fourth ball was a wild pitch in the opening frame. Leonard, also of the Grays doubled in the fourth with two down but Irvin, batting for his teammate, Harvey, of the Newark Eagles, was thrown out by Piper Davis of the Birmingham Black Barons. Minoso drove Neal Robinson of the Memphis Red Sox back against the wall in left-field for his long fly. Robinson was shaken up and the game was delayed a couple of minutes. Lester Lockett of Baltimore walked, but Davis to Wilson to Boyd was a lightning double play which saved Jessup and ended a good ball game.

The East crossed up the West by sending Rufus Lewis of the Newark Eagles to the mound in the place of Robert Romby of Baltimore. Lewis amazed the crowd by striking out Art Wilson, Herb Souell of Kansas City and Piper Davis in the first inning. Davis was called out on strikes.

GET TO LEWIS

The heavy hitters found Lewis in the second. Willard Brown of Kansas City singled to left. Robert Boyd of Memphis dropped a single in left field. Neal Robinson scored Brown with a single, Quincy Trouppe, manager of the West nine and manager of the Chicago American Giants was purposely walked. Sam Hill of Chicago was thrown out by Gilliam, Boyd scoring. Powell hit into a double play, Gilliam to Luis Louden of the Cuban stars at the plate killing Robinson and Louden to Gilliam to Minoso getting Trouppe.

Wilbur [Wilmer] Fields of the Grays got by the fourth, fifth and sixth inning, allowing one scratch hit when Boyd beat out a rap to Minoso with two dead in the sixth. Robert Griffith of the New York Black Yankees hurled the seventh and eighth for the East. With two gone in the eighth, Wilson was safe on an error by Frank Austin of Philadelphia but Griffith forced Herb Souell of Kansas City to foul off two then miss the third strike.

DAVIS SCORES

Piper Davis opened the West's eighth with a corking double way down the far corner of the left field. Willard Brown singled to right putting Davis on third but was out trying to stretch it into a double, Monte Irvin to Austin. Boyd skied out to Lester Lockett in left and Davis romped home after the catch. Robinson walked. Trouppe flied out to Irvin.

Altogether the West nicked the East hurlers for seven safe blows, three off Lewis, one of Fields and three off Griffith.

Piper Davis got the only stolen base. It came in the third.

Scalpers and Politics Mar East-West Game

by Morgan Holsey

Source: *Chicago Defender,* 28 August 1948

Baseball fans and the general public are blaming the slump in the East versus West game attendance to politics and ticket scalping. Last year 48,112 watched the classic. Sunday 42,099 was the attendance announced although it was reported a few minutes before as 37,099.

Leroy "Satchel" Paige drew over 51,000 in the same park on Friday night, August 13. On that night fully 15,000 were unable to get inside the park. Sunday, at the East vs. West game, there weren't any 15,000 on the outside. Sunday the scalpers who had been asking $5 for $3 box seats and $3 for $2 grandstand seats sought to unload the remainder of their block of tickets for regular prices.

Their field of operation which was in the lobby of the Hotel Grand and outside of the Hotel Pershing was suddenly change to in front of Comiskey Park. By the end of the fourth inning there were plenty of empty seats in the left centerfield grandstand and in the right centerfield stands.

Politics played its part in the game ceremonies. U.S. Senator C. Wayland Brooks was escorted to the mound by William E. King, second ward committeeman, and Dr. J. B. Martin, Sanitary District Trustee. All are Republicans. Evidentially the Democratic fans didn't approve because they were booed. Brooks pitched the first ball.

Other Democrats, a few thousand belonging to the organization of William L. Dawson, U.S. Representative from the first congressional district, didn't like the political angle and stayed away from the ball yard. The United States Representative Dawson's Democratic followers from the first Illinois congressional district "took a walk."

Fans believe that politics and baseball don't mix. The East vs. West game, once an East vs. West promotion now seems to be a one-man show.

A third reason for some staying away was the failure of the fans in the past to get box seats which they purchase. Also this year the front rows in the upper deck were sold as box seats.

A second East vs. West game called the "Dream game" in the East, was scheduled to be played in New York's Yankee Stadium on Tuesday night. Same players and all, but there was some talk of offering the players $50 each plus expenses, for the second game.

The money made goes to the 12 club owners in the Negro American League and Negro National Leagues.

AUGUST 22, 1948, SUNDAY
COMISKEY PARK, CHICAGO (GAME 1 OF 2)

EAST	AB	R	H	D	T	HR	BI	E	TAVG	TSLG
Luis Marquez (Homestead Grays), cf	4	0	0	0	0	0	0	0		
Minnie Minoso (New York Cubans), 3b	4	0	1	0	0	0	0	0		
Luke Easter (Homestead Grays), lf	0	0	0	0	0	0	0	1		
Lester Lockett (Baltimore Elite Giants), lf	2	0	0	0	0	0	0	0		
Buck Leonard (Homestead Grays), 1b	4	0	1	1	0	0	0	0		
Bob Harvey (Newark Eagles), rf	1	0	0	0	0	0	0	0		
Monte Irvin (Newark Eagles), rf	2	0	0	0	0	0	0	0		
Junior Gilliam (Baltimore Elite Giants), 2b	3	0	1	0	0	0	0	0		
Louis Louden (New York Cubans), c	3	0	0	0	0	0	0	0		
Bill Cash (Philadelphia Stars), c	0	0	0	0	0	0	0	0		
Pee Wee Butts (Baltimore Elite Giants), ss	2	0	0	0	0	0	0	0		
Frank Austin (Philadelphia Stars), ss	1	0	0	0	0	0	0	1		
Rufus Lewis (Newark Eagles), p	1	0	0	0	0	0	0	0		
Wilmer Fields (Homestead Grays), p	1	0	0	0	0	0	0	0		
Robert Griffith (New York Black Yankees), p	1	0	0	0	0	0	0	0		
Team Totals, Average & Slugging Pct.	29	0	3	1	0	0	0	2	.103	.138

WEST	AB	R	H	D	T	HR	BI	E	TAVG	TSLG
Artie Wilson (Birmingham Black Barons), ss	3	0	0	0	0	0	0	0		
Herb Souell (Kansas City Monarchs), 3b	4	0	0	0	0	0	0	0		
Piper Davis (Birmingham Black Barons), 2b	3	1	1	1	0	0	0	0		
Willard Brown (Kansas City Monarchs), cf	4	1	2	0	0	0	0	0		
Robert Boyd (Memphis Red Sox), 1b	4	1	2	0	0	0	1	1		
Neil Robinson (Memphis Red Sox), lf	3	0	1	0	0	0	1	0		
Quincy Trouppe (Chicago American Giants), c	3	0	0	0	0	0	0	0		
Sam Hill (Chicago American Giants), rf	3	0	0	0	0	0	1	0		
Bill Powell (Birmingham Black Barons), p	1	0	0	0	0	0	0	0		
Jim LaMarque (Kansas City Monarchs), p	1	0	0	0	0	0	0	0		
Gentry Jessup (Chicago American Giants), p	1	0	1	0	0	0	0	0		
Team Totals, Average & Slugging Pct.	30	3	7	1	0	0	3	1	.233	.267

East	000	000	000-0
West	020	000	01X-3

PITCHER/TEAM	GS	IP	H	R	ER	K	BB	WP	HB	W	L	SV
R. Lewis/NE	1	3	3	2	2	4	2	0	0	0	1	0
Fields/HG		3	1	0	0	2	1	0	0	0	0	0
Griffith/NYBY		2	3	1	1	2	1	0	0	0	0	0
Powell/BBB	1	3	1	0	0	2	1	1	0	1	0	0
LaMarque/KCM		3	2	0	0	1	0	0	0	0	0	0
Jessup/CAG		3	0	0	0	1	1	0	0	0	0	1

BB—Trouppe, N. Robinson, Lockett, Easter, S. Hill
DP—Gilliam to Louden to Minoso; Butts to Minoso; Davis to Wilson to Boyd
LOB—East 4, West 6
SB—P. Davis
East—Vic Harris (Mgr.); Coaches Jose Fernandez and Marvin Barker
West—Quincy Trouppe (Mgr.);
Umpires—Virgil Blueitt, Fred McCrary, Walker West, George Suttles
Attendance—42,099   Time—2:19

3rd Annual All-Star Game at Stadium

Cracker Players to Represent East and West—40,000 Cheered Teams

Last Year at the Polo Grounds, West Victor

Source: *New York Amsterdam News,* 14 August 1948

Once in a lifetime we see the unusual; but with the Negro National and American Leagues vying for superiority over each other once a year an extraordinary sports spectacle is in store at the third annual All-Star "Dream Game", to be held at the Yankee Stadium on Tuesday night August 24.

In the two previous meetings each league has won a victory. The Nationals were victorious 6–3 before 25,000 fans at Washington, D.C. in 1946. However, last year the West arose and smoked the Easterners, the National League, 8–2 before 40,000 at the Polo Grounds in New York City, which was the largest crowd ever to witness a Negro sporting event in the East.

Alex Pompez, a New York sportsman and owner of the New York Cubans is chairman of the committee on arrangements for the "Dream Game." He won the honor for heading the committee because he did such a magnificent job last year in handling the affair in such a grand manner. He loves the sporting fan and always endeavors to give them the best.

Performers in this All Star baseball contest extend themselves to the fullest measure as they have no superior in their positions in their respective leagues, which is the reason they were selected.

They also have an eye on cavorting in the Big Leagues. Such a team is a manager's Utopia. Even the fans' curiosity runs high to see who from this year's crop of All Stars will eventually latch on with the majors.

The Westerners team's last year's stars who went up for a trial or to remain in the big league were; Dan Bankhead, pitcher, Sammy Jethroe outfielder, Henry Thompson, infielder and hard hitting Willard Brown.

From the Eastern team Henry Miller and Patricio Scantlebury, both star and crafty hurlers were recently invited to Cleveland for a tryout with the Indians. Although the Indians have delayed their decision about signing them, they are being closely scouted by Cleveland's top talent seekers.

40,000 Expected at Dream Game

Stars to Meet Tuesday under Stadium Lights

Hot Bats of Eastern Sluggers Favored to Cool Off Westerners

by Swig Garlington

Source: *New York Amsterdam News,* 21 August 1948

Approximately 40,000 are expected to gather at Yankee Stadium on Tuesday night, August 24, to witness what is billed as a "Dream Game," between an all-star team of members of the Negro American League and the cream of the crop from the Negro National League.

This all-star classic will mark the third meeting of the best in both leagues, with each team vying to take the lead in this crucial series. The National Leaguers won the first contest in D.C. in 1946, and last year the Westerners were the victors in the Polo Grounds when over 40,000 New Yorkers witnessed the contest.

TO TRANSFER CONTEST

When the "Dream Game" was first announced, it was estimated that about 25,000 would attend the Stadium clash. But, after Dr. John H. Johnson, president of the NNL, announced that he would not allow any one city to "hog" the classic, and that next year's contest will be played in Philly, the rush for tickets jumped and the estimated crowd was upped to "between 40,000 and 50,000."

The all-star clashes between the two leagues started several years ago in the Mid-West, where the same teams will meet on Sunday in Chicago. After this event proved so successful in the West, the Easterners started promoting the affair under a different name. In the West it is called the East-West All-Star Game.

Second East versus West Game Draws 17,928

Source: *Chicago Defender*, 4 September 1948

The second 1948 East vs. West game won by the East here Tuesday night. Aug. 24, before some 17,928 fans. The final score was 6 to 1. The game was played in Yankee Stadium.

The West went ahead in the third when Sam Hill of the Chicago American Giants walked and stole second as Pepper Bassett of the Black Barons fanned on Max Manning's curves. The Newark Eagles pitcher forced Vibert Clark to ground out. Hill taking third. Hill scored when Art Wilson, Birmingham shortstop, singled.

The East bounced right back in the home half. Frank Austin, Philadelphia Stars shortstop singled. Bill Cash, Philadelphia, forced Austin at second. Marvin Barker, New York Black Yankees, went to bat for Manning. He flied to Hill in centerfield. Luis Marquez of the Washington Homestead Grays hit a home run scoring Cash. Orestes Minoso, New York Cubans, who was signed by the Cleveland Indians this week and sent to Dayton, Ohio, of the Central League, doubled. Lester Lockett, Baltimore, singled sending Minoso home.

EAST SCORES AGAIN

The East added one more in the fourth. George Crowe, New York Black Yankees, singled off Jim Cohen of the Indianapolis Clowns. Herb Souell, Kansas City Monarchs, bobbled Frank Austin's rounder and Crowe went to second. Cash singled Crowe to third and Dave "Impo" Barnhill, New York Cuban hurler who wasn't even with the East nine in the Chicago game, was an infield out, Crowe scoring.

Singles by Crowe and Austin in the eighth plus an error by Leon Kellman, Cleveland third sacker, gave the East two more runs in the eighth.

The crowd was asked to stand in silent tribute to the late George Herman "Babe" Ruth [Ruth died August 16, just eight days earlier]. No mention was made of the last Negro baseball men's deaths—namely Josh Gibson, hero of many an East vs. West game; Candy Jim Taylor, manager of the East nine and of the Chicago American Giants; Cum Posey, Homestead Grays and former secretary of the Negro National League. Maybe they didn't amount to much in the eyes of the owners and promoters of the game but the baseball fans wondered why.

Editor's note: The Negro Leagues had lost several personalities the past few years; Candy Jim Taylor died in April 1948, Tom Wilson died in May 1947, Cumberland Posey died in March 1946, and perhaps the greatest slugger in black baseball history, Josh Gibson, died in January 1947.

Negro Nationals Score 6–1 Victory

Beat American League Stars at Stadium

Marquez Homer Highlights 3-Run Third

Source: *New York Times,* 25 August 1948

A three-run out burst in the third inning was the big factor in the 6 to 1 triumph of the Negro National League over the Negro American League at the Yankee Stadium last night in the third annual "Dream Game" between all-star teams representing these rival baseball circuits.

Two of the tallies were the result of a 330-foot homer into the lower right field stands by Luis Marquez, center fielder of the Homestead (Pa.) Grays. Frank Austin, shortstop of the Philadelphia Stars, was on base via a single when Marquez connected.

Later in the same frame, Orestes Minosa [Minoso], third baseman of the New York Cubans, hit the first of his two doubles to right field and scored on a single to left by Lester Lockett, left fielder of the Baltimore Elite Giants.

Vibert Clarke, the American League southpaw starter from the Cleveland Buckeyes was the victim of this attack and charged with the loss. In all, the National Leaguers pounded five [four] rival pitchers for a total of nine [ten] hits.

The victors scored another run in the fourth on two singles and an error and added two unearned tallies to their total in the eighth, when a costly American League misplay followed singles by George Crowe of the New York Black Yankees and Junior Gilliam of the Baltimore Elite Giants.

Maxwell Manning of the Newark Eagles, Dave Barnhill of the New York Cubans and Joe Black of the Baltimore Elite Giants shared the pitching assignment for the National League and among them yielded only five hits.

Negro Club Owners Fail to Deal Fairly with Major Leaguers

Source: *Chicago Defender,* 4 September 1948

Owners in the two Negro leagues are being charged with failure to cooperate with major league baseball which seeks Negro talent. The charge infuriates the Negro fans who want to see their race advanced.

White organized baseball classes the two Negro leagues as Class C.[16] Since the signing of Jackie Robinson by Branch Rickey Sr. pres. of the Brooklyn Dodgers, other Negro players have been signed by white owners.

Robinson went to the Montreal Royals in 1946 and to the Dodgers in 1947 and remains a member of the starting lineup.

Roy Campanella, Brooklyn Dodger Catcher, went to Nashua, N. H., Dodgers in 1946, to Montreal in 1947 and to the Dodgers this year. When the May cut came, Campanella was sent to St. Paul but recalled and is now a Dodger regular.[17]

Dan Bankhead, signed by the Dodgers in 1947 and who got into the World Series against the New York Yankees as a pinch runner, was sent to Nashua this year and last week to St. Paul. Roy [Don] Newcombe, pitcher from the Newark Eagles, spent two years with Nashua and is now with Montreal, second best pitcher in the International League.

Larry Doby, Newark Eagles star was signed by William Veeck, president of the Cleveland Indians last summer and remains as a regular centerfielder. Satchel Paige, signed in July is a regular pitcher for the Cleveland Indians.

Now it remains that only Doby and Paige have jumped out of the Negro leagues into big time company and have had to come up through the minors. Some have failed. Roy Partlow, the Philadelphia Stars pitcher and John Wright hurler for the Washington-Homestead Grays, were tried out by the Montreal club and then sent to the Three Rivers team of the Canadian-American league. They were given their releases and this year are back with their Negro league teams.

Sammy Gee, Detroit shortstop, was signed by Brooklyn and sent to the farm club in the Pony League in upper New York State. This year, after spending the 1947 season with the Dodgers farm system. Gee was released outright and was signed by the New York Cuban Stars.

Sammy Jethroe, Cleveland Buckeyes outfielder, was signed by the Brooklyn Dodgers and sent to the Montreal Royals. Fred Thomas of Canada and Al Smith of the Buckeyes were signed by the Cleveland Indians and sent to Wilkes-Barre, Pa. Young Josh Gibson [Junior], son of the famous catcher, was signed by Youngstown, Ohio.

John Ritchey, catcher in 1947 for the Chicago American Giants, is with the San Diego Padres of the Pacific Coast League.

Monday, Aug. 30, Joe Bankhead, brother of Dan, was signed by Cleveland for the Grand Rapids teams of the Central League in the offices of Abe Saperstein, Cleveland Indian scout of Negro talent.

SIGN MINOSO, SANTIAGO

Orestes Minoso, Cuban Stars third baseman, and Jose Santiago, 19-year-old pitcher for the same club, were signed Friday by the Cleveland Indians. They reported to the Dayton Club on Monday.

All of the above seems to assure the fans that Negro baseball has played an important part in starting these youngsters on their way to success. However, there have been some hitches. Others might have advanced but the Negro club owners are hiking the price when it comes to selling contracts.

There was much publicity given the fact that Jackie Robinson had no signed contract with the Kansas City Monarchs. There was more said when it was found that Ritchie [Ritchey] had no contract with the Chicago American Giants and an exchange of letters between the owner of the San Diego Padres and president of the Negro American League, resulted in a check being sent Martin which the latter said was satisfactory. But the threat made to take the matter up with Commissioner Chandler had its reaction.

The San Francisco club of the Pacific league, which was to try out Gene Richardson, pitcher for the Monarchs and also an infielder, canceled their plans at the last minute. Reason given is they preferred not to get into any controversy over contracts.

Newest angle comes when it was learned that on the week of June 23, Henry Miller, pitcher for the Philadelphia Stars, and Patricio Seantlebury [Scantlebury], pitcher for the Cuban Stars, were tried out by the Cleveland Indians at the same time the Indians signed

45. *1948 West all-star team. Top row, left to right: Neal Robinson, Willard Brown, Spoon Carter, Willie Grace, Gentry Jessup, Sam Hill, Bill Powell, Jim LaMarque, Chet Brewer, Piper Davis, and Quincy Trouppe. Bottom row: Nat Rogers, Leon Kellman, Sam Hairston, Bob Boyd, Ray Neil, Jim Cohen, Verdell Mathis, Herb Souell, Artie Wilson, Roberto Vargas, and unknown trainer. Courtesy of NoirTech Research, Inc.*

Thomas. Both were sent back to their respective clubs and Indian scouts ordered to watch them in Negro National League games.

Although the expenses for the two men were paid, the Cleveland management were surprised to get letters from the Cubans, asking for money to compensate the Negro clubs for the time lost by the two men. When Negro fans learned this they became infuriated, charging the owners with blocking the possible advancement of the two pitchers.

PRICE UNREASONABLE

More recently, to be more specific, the Indians sought, on recommendations of Saperstein, to sign Minoso, who played so well in the 1947 and 1948 East vs. West games as a member of the East team. Bill Killifer and Saperstein watched Santiago hold the Birmingham Black Barons to three hits in a game in New Orleans on Aug. 22.

Although the scouts had tried to get a glimpse of Santiago in action earlier, efforts were balked. It is reported that Alex Pompez, owner, ordered Jose Fernandez not to use Santiago in that particular game. It seems that W. S. Welch, manager of the Cubans, did use him in New Orleans.

When it came to dicker over the price of Minoso and Santiago, it was learned that Santiago was really property of a club in Puerto Rico which allowed Pompez to use him over the summer. Also Santiago was 19 years old and whatever agreement or contract, if any, that Pompez had with Santiago was null and void because Santiago's parents had not signed and in laws of the United States Santiago is still a minor.

However, Pompez is said to have asked $25,000 of the Cleveland Indians for the two men. Now the Indians and their owner Bill Veeck, may be very liberal but they aren't any dummies. If the Negro National League's Cuban Stars had any idea of "taking the fighting Bill Veeck for a ride," they were guessing wrong. Veeck will not have it said that the Indians "took" any player neither will they be brow-beaten into giving more than the player is worth to them. All are of the opinion that Negro league players need more seasoning and the price of minor league players in class C usually is about $5,000.

It has not been learned what was given for Minoso and Santiago—but you can bet your last dollar it wasn't any $25,000.

Another major league club was interested in [Earl] Taborn and Gene Collins, catcher and 22-year-old pitcher for the Kansas City Monarchs. The price asked by the Monarchs was $10,000 for each man. No soap. In other words no sale.

After the East vs. West game, a talent scout phoned the *Chicago Defender* concerning Bill Powell, Birmingham Black Barons owner, Tom Hayes Jr., came nearer to asking the Class C purchase price than any. The Powell case is still in the making.

It was openly stated that, in a meeting prior to the second 1948 East vs. West game in New York, Negro owners, the majority of them going over their losses of the past few years had come to the decision that now is the time to recuperate by getting a big chunk of money for each player the majors would like to try out.

The majors have a stipulated price for Class C players. They refuse to be robbed. They want to do business in a legitimate manner—and if not, no business at all.

The St. Louis Browns signed Willard Brown, centerfielder, and Henry Thompson, outfielder and infielder of the Kansas City Monarchs last season. Both stayed with the club exactly 35 days. They failed to hit as was expected. they failed to pack the St. Louis park principally due to the fact that for years Negroes, until recently, were denied the appearance of Brown and Thompson with the Browns. The St. Louis Negroes retaliated by staying away.

The absence of Brown and Thompson from the Monarchs lineup hurt that club in the Negro American League pennant race. The purchase by the St. Louis Browns, at a price satisfactory to the Monarchs owner, didn't help the St. Louis Browns. The Browns now are not interested in Negro players as box office attraction nor as players.

It is within reason for Negro owners to get all they can for their players but it is also very sensible for these same Negro owners to know you can't get as much for a Ford car

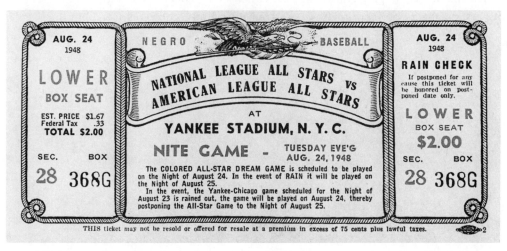

46. An unused ticket for the East-West All-Star Game at Yankee Stadium. Courtesy of Larry Bennett, Colorado.

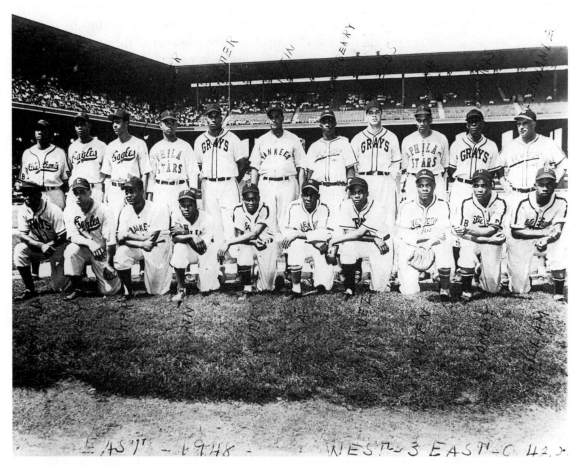

47. *1948 East all-star team. Top row, left to right: Lester Lockett, Monte Irvin, Rufus Lewis, Henry Miller, Luke Easter, Robert Griffith, Pat Scantlebury, Wilmer Fields, Bill Cash, Vic Harris, and Jose Fernandez (manager). Bottom row: Buck Leonard, Bob Harvey, Marvin Barker, Frank Austin, Pee Wee Butts, Minnie Minoso, Luis Marquez, Louis Louden, Bob Romby, and Junior Gilliam. Courtesy of NoirTech Research, Inc.*

as you can for a Cadillac. Regardless as to what these Negro owners may claim or believe, Negro baseball is rated, by the majors as Class C.

The major leagues play a different brand of baseball. The fans know it the major league owners, managers, and scouts know it—in fact everybody seems to know it but the Negro club owners.

AUGUST 24, 1948, TUESDAY
YANKEE STADIUM, NEW YORK CITY (GAME 2 OF 2)

WEST	AB	R	H	D	T	HR	BI	E	TAVG	TSLG
Artis Wilson (Birmingham Black Barons), ss	4	0	3	0	0	0	1	0		
Herb Souell (Kansas City Monarchs), 3b	3	0	0	0	0	0	0	1		
Spoon Carter (Memphis Red Sox), pr	0	0	0	0	0	0	0	0		
Roberto Vargas (Chicago American Giants), p	0	0	0	0	0	0	0	0		
Jim LaMarque (Kansas City Monarchs), p	0	0	0	0	0	0	0	0		
a) Sam Hairston (Indianapolis Clowns), ph	1	0	0	0	0	0	0	0		
Piper Davis (Birmingham Black Barons), 2b	4	0	0	0	0	0	0	0		
Willard Brown (Kansas City Monarchs), cf	3	0	0	0	0	0	0	0		
Bob Boyd (Memphis Red Sox), 1b	3	0	0	0	0	0	0	0		
Willie Grace (Cleveland Buckeyes) lf	3	0	1	0	0	0	0	1		
Sam Hill (Chicago American Giants), rf	2	1	0	0	0	0	0	0		
Pepper Bassett (Birmingham Black Barons), c	2	0	0	0	0	0	0	0		
Quincy Trouppe (Chicago American Giants), c	1	0	0	0	0	0	0	0		
Vibert Clarke (Cleveland Buckeyes), p	1	0	0	0	0	0	0	0		
Jim Cohen (Indianapolis Clowns), p	0	0	0	0	0	0	0	0		
b) Jose Colas (Memphis Red Sox), ph	1	0	1	0	0	0	0	0		
Leon Kellman (Cleveland Buckeyes), 3b	1	0	0	0	0	0	0	1		
Team Totals, Average & Slugging Pct.	29	1	5	0	0	0	1	3	.172	.172

a) Batted for LaMarque in 9th
b) Batted for Cohen in 6th

EAST	AB	R	H	D	T	HR	BI	E	TAVG	TSLG
Luis Marquez (Homestead Grays), cf-rf	5	1	1	0	0	1	2	0		
Minnie Minoso (New York Cubans), 3b	2	1	2	2	0	0	0	0		
Lester Lockett (Baltimore Elite Giants) lf	4	0	1	0	0	0	1	0		
Luke Easter (Homestead Grays), rf	4	0	0	0	0	0	0	0		
Jim Wilkes (Newark Eagles), cf	0	0	0	0	0	0	0	0		
George Crowe (New York Black Yankees), 1b	4	2	2	0	0	0	0	0		
Junior Gilliam (Baltimore Elite Giants), 2b	3	1	1	0	0	0	0	0		
Frank Austin (Philadelphia Stars), ss	3	0	2	0	0	0	0	0		
Bill Cash (Philadelphia Stars), c	3	1	1	0	0	0	0	0		
Louis Louden (New York Cubans), c	1	0	0	0	0	0	0	0		
Max Manning (Newark Eagles), p	0	0	0	0	0	0	0	0		
c) Marvin Barker (New York Black Yankees), ph	1	0	0	0	0	0	0	0		
Dave Barnhill (New York Cubans), p	1	0	0	0	0	0	1	0		
Joe Black (Baltimore Elite Giants), p	1	0	0	0	0	0	0	0		
Team Totals, Average & Slugging Pct.	32	6	10	2	0	1	4	0	.281	.438

c) Batted for Manning in 3rd

West	001	000	000-1
East	003	100	02x-6

PITCHER/TEAM	GS	IP	H	R	ER	K	BB	WP	HB	W	L	SV
Clarke/CEB	1	3	4	3	3	1	1	0	0	0	1	0
Cohen/IC		2	3	1	0	1	0	0	0	0	0	0
Vargas/CAG		1	0	0	0	1	0	0	0	0	0	0
LaMarque/KCM		2	3	2	0	2	0	0	0	0	0	0
Manning/NE	1	3	1	1	1	2	1	0	0	1	0	0
Barnhill/NYC		3	2	0	0	1	0	0	0	0	0	0
Black/BEG		3	2	0	0	0	0	0	0	0	0	1

DB—Wilson to Davis to Boyd; Gilliam to Crowe; Davis to Wilson
LOB—West 2, East 7
SB—Hill, Gilliam
East—Pop Lloyd (Mgr.);
West—Candy Jim Taylor (Mgr.);
Umpires—
Attendance—17,928   Time—2:18

1949

Motown Records in Detroit, Michigan, is founded by several African-American autoworkers, headed by Berry Gordy Jr. The term *rhythm and blues* rather than *race records* becomes the preferred usage to identify recordings by African-Americans. The first wholly black-owned radio station, WERD-AM, airs its programs from Atlanta, Georgia.

The Los Angeles Rams sign Paul "Tank" Younger from Grambling State University. He is the NFL's first player from a predominately black college.

Milk costs 42 cents a half-gallon, 10 pounds of potatoes costs 55 cents, and 67 cents would bring home the bacon. A loaf of bread costs 14 cents.

The Major League All-Star Game features African-American players for the first time: Dodgers Jackie Robinson, Roy Campanella, and Don Newcombe. The National Leaguers lose 11–7 to their American League counterparts.

Earlier in the season, cinder paths called "warning tracks" are placed in front of outfield fences to warn fielders of possible impact.

Minnie Minoso becomes the seventh former Negro Leaguer to make his debut in the majors. Other Negro League veterans Don Newcombe, Monte Irvin, and Luke Easter join him later during the season.

LEAGUE BUSINESS

During the winter of 1948, reelected president J. B. Martin announced that the Homestead Grays, the New York Black Yankees, and the Newark Eagles had withdrawn their membership from the Negro National League. Their departure spelled doom for the six-team eastern-based league. The remaining three teams joined the surviving Negro American League, which would now be composed of Eastern and Western divisions of five teams each. The Western division consisted of the Chicago American Giants, the Kansas City Monarchs, the Memphis Red Sox, the Birmingham Black Barons, and the revamped Newark Eagles, now located in Houston. The Eastern contingent would be the New York Cubans, the Baltimore Elite Giants, the Indianapolis Clowns, the Philadelphia Stars, and the Louisville Buckeyes, formerly of Cleveland.

The eventual demise of the Negro National League was summed up by writer Wendell Smith: "In a grave but tearless ceremony, solemn dignitaries of Negro baseball buried their National League here yesterday when three of its teams were laid to rest amid the debris of last season's financial losses."[1] With the acceptance of black players into the majors, and major league owners offering less than market value (or nothing!) for the players, the Negro Leagues could only be seen as an indentured servant.

Controversy among Negro League owners continued in regard to Branch Rickey's historic move to sign black players. As the major leagues pilfered the black leagues' best players, attendance at ballparks featuring all-black teams declined. Rickey was hailed as the savior of baseball by the press, but silent black owners did not wish to address his methods of securing their top talents because they might be accused of hindering the integration movement.

Fresco Thompson, an official with the Brooklyn Dodgers, assured the Associated Press that despite rumors that the Dodgers were stealing ballplayers, the Dodgers were following normal procedures for signing players. He also said, "It is my impression we also paid the Kansas City Monarchs for the release of Jackie Robinson."

Thomas Younger Baird, who purchased full interest of the club from J. L. Wilkinson in 1948, wrote a seething letter to Thompson:

> I feel that I should advise you that you were definitely under the wrong impression because Mr. Rickey never paid one cent for Jackie Robinson. Rickey was not even gentlemen enough to answer or acknowledge my many letters I wrote him with reference to Jackie Robinson. The owners of the Newark Eagles and the Baltimore Elite Giants state that Rickey never paid one cent for either Don Newcombe or Roy Campanella.
>
> Rickey's acquisition of Negro baseball players reminds me of the fellow who found a rope and when he got home there was a horse on the end of it. I have been informed that Mr. Rickey is a very religious man. If such is true, it appears that his religion runs towards the almighty dollar.
>
> In 1947, Mr. Jack Fournier, scout for the St. Louis Browns, contacted me personally in Kansas and scouted Willard Brown and Henry Thompson of the Kansas City Monarchs. After scouting these players, Mr. Fournier asked my permission to speak with the players which I gladly gave. Mr. Bill DeWitt, Vice President of the St. Louis Browns, called me shortly thereafter and a deal was made for Thompson and Brown. Mr. DeWitt stood by all of his commitments 100%. Mr. Bill Veeck, President of the Cleveland Indians, has acquired several Negro ball players from the Negro Leagues and has paid the Negro Leagues for the player's releases. Why can't the Brooklyn baseball club do business this way?
>
> There is no doubt that Mr. Rickey should be given credit for removing the barriers and allowing Negro ball players to get into Organized baseball. However, it appears that his unethical methods of obtaining Negro players does not meet with the approval of the public.
>
> Very truly yours, Tom Baird, President, Kansas City Monarchs.[2]

This issue of Rickey's theft of Robinson had been addressed at a Negro American League board meeting in March 1948 at the Hotel Grand in Chicago. Wilkinson and Baird admitted that they had no signed contract with Robinson, stating: "We have been in Negro organized baseball since 1920, and had several players whom we did not sign to written contracts because we found that such contracts worked to our detriment. Others players on the Monarchs club became disgruntled when shown contracts calling for more money than they were being paid."

Baird continued in reference to Robinson's stipulation: "Our word was our bond. Telegrams and letters exchanged with Robinson was, as far as we were concerned, a binding contract. We paid what we promised. Robinson admits that we paid him [$400 per month] more than he received as a member of the Montreal Royals."

When Tom Baird was pressured as to why he didn't sue Branch Rickey, he replied: "We welcome Jackie's advancing in baseball and we would have been the last ones to have intimated that we didn't want a Negro player integrated into big time baseball. But we still believe Rickey owes us a moral obligation. Whatever he might have offered would have been okay with us—but to ignore our efforts to obtain something for our great shortstop is preposterous."[3]

Rickey also signed catcher Roy Campanella from the Elite Giants and pitchers Johnny Wright from the Homestead Grays, Dan Bankhead from the Memphis Red Sox, Roy Partlow from the Philadelphia Stars, and Don Newcombe from the Newark Eagles. Rickey also signed Sammy Gee, a highly promising Detroit high school player, who failed to make the majors.

In the interim, all teams in the Negro American and National Leagues were patterning their revised contracts after major league contracts by inserting the word *Negro* where appropriate to give the contracts an authoritative appearance without any loopholes for the convenience of major league officials.

MAJOR LEAGUE SPRING TRAINING

The integration of baseball was now two years old. Just how far had Major League Baseball come in accepting the black athlete within its ranks? One of the great black writers, Sam Lacy, traveled with Larry Doby and Jackie Robinson to Florida and Texas to witness the treatment of Major League Baseball's tan players. On April 2 Lacy wrote for the *Baltimore Afro-American* the following appraisals of race relations outside the white foul lines:

Orlando, Florida— My father would have loved this day. The Old Man Died last spring, still a loyal rooter for the Washington Senators, but adamant in his refusal to attend any of the games at Griffith Stadium in Washington as his own personal protest against President Clark Griffith's attitude toward colored baseball players. . . . Pop had been diehard for the Senators and hadn't missed a game in the 20 years previous to 1947. . . . One of his keepsakes was a letter from Griffith inviting him to the Walter Johnson Day celebration, in which the Senators' president addressed him, "Dear Sam," and signed himself "Clark." . . . But just before the opening of the 1947 season, Pop wrote Griffith and told him he was sorry, but he felt he wouldn't wish to attend any more Washington games, "because of your expressed opposition to integration, not only on your own club, but in the whole of organized baseball." . . . Griffith's reply regretted the action, and said, "It is my sincere hope that someday, you will experience a change of heart." . . . Last week, it was Clark Griffith admitting "a change of heart" and tell the Old Man's son that he is "on the lookout for a good, young colored player" for his Senators.[4]

West Palm Beach, Florida— Colored fandom gave such heavy support to the Philadelphia Athletics' spring training gate for the Brooklyn Dodger games that Connie Mack (who can't see colored players on his team) pulled one of the oldest tricks know to the "hustling" fraternity. . . . For the first game, the "colored" admission was 75 cents. . . . But, when these same patrons arrived at the park for the second contest, they were confronted by signs setting the price of ducats at $1.20, a 45-cent hike on the "suckers." Incidentally, when the Athletics and Washington Senators played their lily-white game the day prior to the Dodgers-A's tilt, a paid "crowd" of 619 was on hand.

Haines City, Florida— This town's colored fans are being admitted to spring training games for the first time in history. In previous years when the Baltimore Orioles— and before them the Kansas City Blues—trained here, only white fans were admitted to the park. When they turned out for the first games played by the Newark Bears, Yale Field workmen had to hurriedly construct a makeshift "colored" stand. This reporter, looking for the "colored restroom" was directed to a tree about 35 yards off from where the rightfield foul line ended.

Beaumont, Texas— The usual "Jim Crow twist" was given reverse English Wednesday when Brooklyn visited here for the first game of the spring exhibition tour. Instead of barring the Dodgers' colored players from the clubhouse, Stuart Stadium officials "suggested" that Jackie Robinson and Roy Campanella use the players' quarters at the park and the rest of the team dress at their hotel. It so happened that the unfinished dressing room floor was covered with mud and water, shower facilities were incomplete and the place was entirely devoid of windows covering.

Undoubtedly, this is the most backward town from a race relations' standpoint the Dodgers have played in their two years of spring barnstorming. Booing, filthy name-calling and insults of varied and sundry degrees have greeted each appearance of Robinson and Campanella on the field and at the plate. In the press coop, the public address man, known as "Tiny," identifies the two players only as "the niggers." The official scorer spends more time picking out one patron after another in the colored section for ridicule, than he puts into watching the game.

Jackie, Campy and I arrived here at 10:35 A.M., after a two-hour train ride from Houston, where we spent last night. We went straight to the ballpark, where we were met by a line two blocks long and four, five and six deep, already standing before the colored ticket booths. Park officials agreed that they have seen nothing like it before. Although the weather was "neither fit for man nor beast," faithfuls fought like mad to cling to their advance positions in the line . . . and late-comers who overran the field, braved ankle-deep mud for nine innings of uninteresting ball . . . and after the game, hundreds stood vigil in a driving rain outside the dressing room, awaiting the Robinson-Campanella autographs.

And finally a stop at San Antonio, Texas— Robbie, conscious of the tremendous partisanship in the stands at Beaumont told teammates: "I'm going to try my best in batting practice to hit one out of the park and watch the colored stands go wild. Then, I'm going to swing like hell on the next pitch and miss. I want to see what the white's reaction will be." He did just that. When his first hit bounced of the fence, the colored patrons broke into a wild demonstration. When he whiffed on the next pitch, the white section became a bedlam of hoots and catcalls. Today, during the game, the typical Dixie attitude prevailed again, and the closeness of the Bums, one to the other, was revealed. Jackie stole second in the fourth and there was unrestricted whooping in one section of the park. A moment later, he was thrown out trying to reach third on a fly to right, and happiness reigned supreme in the other part. Pee Wee Reese, a Southern boy from Kentucky, spoke up: "We can all go home now. Everybody's happy!"

ALL-STAR REVIEW

The Major League All-Star Game featured four black players: Jackie Robinson, Roy Campanella, and Don Newcombe were members of the National League squad, while Larry Doby was the sole representative for the American League team. As of July 8 Robinson was the National League's leading vote getter, second only to Boston slugger Ted Williams, the major league leader. Robinson was currently leading the league in batting with a .367 mark, in hits with 99, and in stolen bases with 15.

In his 11 attempted steals of second base, Robinson had been caught once. He had been thrown out three times trying for third base and once for trying to steal home. He was also the league leader in doubles and runs batted in, while tying for top honors in triples.

Other black players receiving votes were Roy Campanella and Larry Doby. Campy was second in the voting, with 936,463 votes, to Philadelphia Phillies catcher Andy Seminick, who had 1,117,082 votes. Manager Billy Southworth picked Campanella for duty.

Doby finished sixth in the voting, with 847,269 votes compared to Ted Williams's 1,952,876. Doby was batting only .250 in the clean-up spot for the fading Cleveland Indians, but his stellar play in field and good work ethic earned him his first all-star position.

Before 32,577 fans at historic Ebbets Field, four black players crossed the white foul lines to show America their skills.

History was made, as Newcombe became the losing pitcher of record for the Nationals, acquiring the dubious honor of being the first black hurler to lose a Major League All-Star Game. Newcombe pitched 2 2/3 innings, allowing two runs and three hits. He became the losing pitcher when the American League erupted for two runs in the fourth inning.

With Detroit's George Kell on third base and Boston's Ted Williams on second base, Eddie Joost of Philadelphia hit a bad hopper to first baseman Gil Hodges, who could not handle the pellet, while the two runners scored. In all, Big Newk walked one man and struck out no one. At bat, Newcombe failed to get a hit in his only trip to the plate.

Campanella entered the game during the fatal fourth, creating the first black battery in all-star history. Campy also made the team's fifth error, for a new team record. In his two trips to the plate, Campanella failed to get a hit.

Larry Doby became the first black player to play for the American League All-Stars when he entered the game as a pinch runner for Joe DiMaggio in the sixth inning. He later played right and center field, making two put-outs. He was hitless in his only at bat.

Jackie Robinson became the first black player to start a Major League All-Star Game as a second baseman. He played the entire game, getting one hit, a double, in four at bats. The notorious game breaker Robinson scored three times. In the field, he played errorless ball, making one assist and one put-out.

The National League squad fell to the American Leaguers, 11–7.

GAME REVIEWS

Negro Baseball Leagues Starts 1949 Race

Prexy Martin Answer Fans

Source: *New York Amsterdam News,* 30 April 1949

Chicago— In answer to the many recent questions asked about Negro baseball, Dr. J. B. Martin, president of the Negro American league and only Negro member of the Chicago Sanitary Trustee board, came forth last week with the statement that Negro baseball is not on a comeback.

Relating that few people know the inside facts of Negro baseball, he related "actually it has been nowhere to stage a comeback but, without a doubt, 1949 will be its greatest year."

He pointed out that Negro American league operated on a business basis with a margin of profit even during the war when faced with the added burdens of gasoline rationing, and increase in park employees, cost of balls, and operating expenses. These obstacles, plus the rainouts of 1947 and 1948, led to the folding of the Negro National League in 1948.

With four new clubs being added to the six clubs formerly making up the Negro American League, it now has 10 teams. They are the Kansas City Monarchs, Birmingham Black Barons, Memphis Red Sox, Indianapolis Clowns, Louisville Buckeyes (moved from Cleveland), American Giants, Houston Eagles (moved from Newark),[5] New York Cubans, Philadelphia Stars and Baltimore Elite Giants.

MARTIN'S STATEMENT

Sure, Larry Doby of the Newark team, Satchel Paige, of the Kansas City Monarchs, and Orestes Minosa [Minoso] of the New York Cubans are with the Cleveland Indians. Jackie Robinson and Roy Campanella are with the Brooklyn Dodgers. This advancement by players whom Negro club owners started on the road to success may have a tendency to cause concern in some places over attendance when these clubs are playing in cities where Negro league games are booked but this concern should not be alarming.

Our businessmen have invested heavily. Others players have been sold to white major league club owners and have been farmed out for more training. Everyone will have to admit that it was the Negro league club owners who made the sacrifice, and I am positive that the Negro fan is not deserting us when we are continuing our advancement in baseball at large.

ANSWERING SKEPTICS

Skeptical fans have time and again accused our league of not having men who could cope with the play of white organized baseball. This is far from the truth. When Jackie Robinson was taken by Branch Rickey Sr., president of the Brooklyn Dodgers, he was not among the top five in Negro American League batting. Yet, in his first year, as a member of the Montreal Royals of the International League, Robinson topped that league in batting.

Records will show you that Larry Doby hit .300 for the season, his first full year with the Cleveland Indians. Satchel Paige won six and lost one game for the Indians in 1948, his first year. The former Kansas City Monarch hurler was credited by Bill Veeck, president of the Indians, as being responsible for the Indians winning the American League

Pennant. Had any one of the Paige victories been a defeat, the Indians would not have been in the World Series.

Sammy Jethroe brought by Brooklyn from the Cleveland Buckeyes in the middle of the season, topped the International League in stolen bases last year. Orestes Minosa [Minoso], who looms as a fixture with the Indians this year, clouted for a percentage of near .400 for half season with the Dayton team. The Former New York Cuban may be what the Indians need, but he started in Negro baseball.

When our season officially opens on Sunday, May 1, I believe we will be starting the greatest year in Negro baseball. WE will not be starting any comeback. We will be picking up where we left off and in so doing all clubs will be strengthened by players returning from Mexico.

Sports Beat: Baseball Eye's East-West Clash

by Wendell Smith

Source: *Pittsburgh Courier,* 6 August 1949

Chicago — Negro baseball holds its annual "horsehide convention" here next Sunday at Comiskey Park when the stars from the East and West tangle in the big East-West Classic.

The gathering of the stars is a yearly event which grows in importance each year. There was a time when it was merely a contest between the best players in Negro baseball. After it was over everyone packed up and went home, waiting for another year to roll around.

But since Negro players have crashed the once-sturdy door of organized baseball — more than thirty-five are in the fold now — the game is of tremendous significance.

Sunday afternoon, Aug. 14, for instance, there will be scouts from every major league club on hand to witness the fray. They're not coming just to see the ball game either. They're looking for talent and this game gives them a chance to look at the best of the lot on the same field at the same time.

You ask what these scouts are going to see. Well, they'll see some of the best ball players around who have not been signed and sealed by the Rickeys, Veecks and Stonehams.

They'll see a big guy, for instance, by the name of Lenny Pearson who hails from Baltimore and plays first base for the Elite Giants. Some place along the line, the scouts have overlooked Pearson. Just why, no one seems to know. He carries a big bat, hits a long ball and does a right smart fielding job around first base.

IT'S A GAME GLITTERING WITH STARS

Lenny's no kid, as ball players go. He's been around for some time. He's a seasoned veteran in Negro baseball and a household word down in sunny Cuba where he goes each winter to play for the Havana Reds and clout homeruns with his big, explosive bat.

Right now, Lenny's hitting a cool .382. He tops the leagues in doubles with 18, is third in home runs with eight and is up with the leaders in all other departments. Pearson formerly played with Larry Doby, Monty Irvin and Henry Thompson, all of whom have graduated to the majors. He'd like to move up there with them. All he wants is the opportunity. If he plays true to form next Sunday, he may get the long awaited chance. He'll play first base for the East.

But Pearson isn't the only guy who rates major league consideration. There's Birmingham's Lorenzo "Piper" Davis who has "big league" written all over him. Davis is leading both leagues in hitting with a mark of .401. Tall and lean, like Marty Marion of the Cardinals, Davis is the top second baseman in Negro baseball. He'll manage the West and try to lead them to a second straight victory.

Pearson and Davis are veterans, but there's a young fellow from Baltimore who may be snatched up before the game gets under way. His name is Junior Gilliam, a second baseman. Right now Junior is hitting .304 and tops the loop in runs-scored with 54.

BROWN AND THURMAN CLASSY

They've been scouting Gilliam ever since the season started. He can hit, run and field. He's young, aggressive and seems to know exactly what the game is all about. Don't wait to seem him later on, or even next season. Somebody's going to grab him, but quick.

Many of the best players in Negro baseball have already been grabbed by big league clubs. But the game goes on and stars keep developing. The West, for instances, will have Willard Brown in the line-up as an outfielder. Brown plays a lot of baseball for Kansas City. He is currently hitting .354 and leads the league in runs-batted-in with 53.

Two years ago Brown was signed by the St. Louis Browns of the American League. Along with Henry Thompson, now starring for the New York Giants, he had a brief trial and then was released. There were a lot of extenuating circumstances around that release. The real story is yet to be told. Brown is still good enough to play in the majors and he'll try to prove it Sunday before the contingent of scouts on hand.

Another player who seems destined to move up and be slated to play beside Brown in the outfield is Bob Thurman. He is also with Kansas City and many tab him as Josh Gibson's successor when it comes to hitting. Bob is hitting .327 and is a home-run hitter deluxe. Although he's six feet, four, in height and weighs approximately 230 pounds. Thurman's tootsies are lined with mercury. He's leading both leagues in stolen bases with 12. Formerly, a pitcher, he can throw with the best of 'em and is definitely ticketed for the majors.

NEGRO STARS REALLY CLICKING

The history book in which they record past East-West games is packed with drama and color. You'll find stories of such greats as Josh Gibson, Satchel Paige, Jackie Robinson, Mule Settles [Suttles], Neal Robinson, Buck Leonard, Willie Wells, Slim Jones, Roy Campanella and countless others. Down through the years the games have all been colorful and packed with tension. Many of its stars have gone on to greater heights and others have fallen by the wayside.

A quick summary indicates that the brand of ball they play in the Negro American League is better than ordinary. Jackie Robinson, ex-Kansas City Monarchs' star, is leading both major leagues in hitting. Art Wilson, formerly of the Birmingham Black Barons, tops the Pacific Coast League in hitting. Sam Jethroe, ex-Cleveland Buckeyes' ace, threatens to break all base-stealing records in the International League and also has a chance to win the batting crown. Satchel Paige is Cleveland's No. 1 relief hurler and Roy Campanella is regarded as the best all-around catcher in the majors.

They are just a few of the Negro players who have played in East-West games and gone on to become stars in baseball's biggest leagues.

We'll be out there Sunday afternoon to get a preview of the stars of the future when the East battles the West before a crowd at 35,000 or more fans. Why not join us?

Wendell Smith's Sports Beat

Dream Game Is the No. 1 Sports Attraction

Source: *Pittsburgh Courier*, 13 August 1949

It makes no difference if the nation is in the midst of a major depression or riding the wave of prosperity, the East-West game is always a rousing success. It is the biggest sports event ever promoted by Negroes and has been a box office hit from the start. The owners of teams in Negro baseball may have to resort to all kinds of gimmicks to lure the fans to regular games during the season, but when East-West time comes up they have to do is open the gates and the cash customers storm in.

More than a half million fans have turned out for these classics down through the years and paid in the neighborhood of a million to watch the cream of the crop in Negro baseball perform. No other Negro-sponsored affair has ever attracted that many people or made the cash registers sing such a merry tune.

All of which is a tribute to the men who started it and risked so much when it was conceived. The East-West game was originally promoted and fathered by Gus Greenlee, the Pittsburgh restaurant proprietor. Genial Gus surrounded himself with such capable men as King Cole and Fay Young of Chicago and Bill Nunn, Chester Washington, John Clark and Roy Sparrow of Pittsburgh. He was determined to put on the classic, despite opposition on the part of some owners of the clubs involved.

Unfortunately, Greenlee is no longer connected with the game. He stopped out of the sports picture completely. So have the men who assisted him in that first promotion. But the seed they planted as Comiskey Park here in Chicago continues to develop and grow. Fans come from far and near to see the annual battle and it has now become an institution in the world of sports.

GAME HAS COMMISSIONER CHANDLER'S BLESSING

Before the barrier was dropped against Negro players in the majors, the East-West game always was cited as "Exhibit A" when the argument developed concerning the respective abilities of Negro players. After seeing players like the late Josh Gibson, Willie Wells, Mule Settles [Suttles], Oscar Charleston, Buck Leonard, Satchel Paige and other top-ranking Negro players perform, no one in their right mind could deny there were players in the Negro leagues good enough for the majors.

While this ban existed, liberal sports writers of daily papers always attended the East-West game for the express purpose of seeing if there were Negro players good enough for the big leagues. Afterward they have always wrote glowing articles about the stars they saw and at the same time threw printed daggers at the anti-Negro forces within the majors.

If the East-West game served no other purpose, it proved to one and all that the major league ban was absurd. It proved the majors were purposely over-looking a fertile field of players and consequently, the fans of the nation were not seeing the best players by being denied the privileges of seeing the Gibsons, Charlestons, and Paiges and others in their like.

Commissioner Happy Chandler will throw out the first ball Sunday afternoon. His presence merely indicates how this game has grown and developed into a nationally important sports event. By participating in the ceremonies, Chandler is giving the game his unofficial sanction and recognition. It is another step in the campaign to place Negro baseball under the jurisdiction of organized ball.

Eventually that will happen. Some day, if the Negro owners are able to weather the current financial storm, Negro teams will be a part of the organized baseball world and participate in its workings.

When that happens, Moses, Greenlee, Washington, Nunn, Young, and the others who helped make it possible can sit down, satisfied that the contribution they made to the Negro sports world was as important as any made toward advancement in the field of interracial relations.

West Swings Rubber Bats, East Triumphs, 4-0

Victors Launch 10 [11] Hit Attack before 31,000

Happy Chandler Watches

by Russ J. Cowans

Source: *Chicago Defender,* 20 August 1949

They said the big bats of the West would pulverize the weak pitching of the East. At least, they were saying that before last Sunday.

But it would be hard to convince the 31,097 fans who saw the seventeenth annual East West Classic in Comiskey Park Sunday that the West was powerful at the plate. Those fans saw the vaunted West's batting power held to two scattered hits as the East won, 4-0 to hoist their victories to seven against 10 for the West.

The West was helpless against the pitching of burly Bob Griffith, Philadelphia right-hander who started on the mound for the East. Andy Porter, Indianapolis Clowns, was just as effective as Griffith, giving up nary a hit.

Pat Scantlebury took over the burden in the seventh and was touched for the first West hit, a line double to left by Lorenzo (Piper) Davis. Two were out, and Davis died on second when Willard Brown, Kansas City Monarchs, grounded to Tommy Butts, Baltimore Elites, at short.

So brilliant was the hurling of Griffith, Porter and Scantlebury that the West was able to get only six balls to the outfield. The infield smothered the others.

As an indication of what was going on, Junior Gilliam, Baltimore Elite, handled eight assists and two put outs at second.

Not only did the hitting power of the West crumble before the sterling pitching of the East hurlers, but their defense cracked at the seams, one of the errors helping in the manufacture of one of the two runs chased over in the eighth inning.

A. B. Chandler, commissioner of organized baseball, tossed out the first ball to catcher [Lonnie] Summers. Chandler was the guest of J. B. Martin, president of the Negro American League. Martin had invited Chandler to attend the game and pitch the first ball.

Pedro Diaz, New York Cubans, was hitting hero of the day, collecting three hits in four trips to the plate. The West pitchers were unable to get him out until the eighth, when he flied out to center.

The East started out early to prove its superiority. Gene Richardson, Kansas City Monarch southpaw, tossed out eight straight balls as he walked Tommy Butts and Pedro Diaz, New York Cubans. Leon [Lennie] Pearson drove a smashing blow to left center that Willard Brown snared with a one-hand catch after a long run. Bus Clarkson, Philadelphia Stars, with the count two and one, lined a singled to right, Butts racing across the plate.

Another run was added in the second when Howard Easterling, New York Cubans,

48. First sacker Buck O'Neil (without jacket) sits among pitchers Gene Richardson, Satchel Paige, and Hilton Smith, each man a Western all-star during his career. Courtesy of Charles Blockson, Moseley Collection, Temple University.

drilled a single to left, stole second base, and rode home when Griffith punched a single to center.

Two more were added in the seventh when the East took a liking to the balls dished up by Southpaw Gread McKinnis, Chicago American Giants, and rapped out three hits, with a stolen base and an error by Lonnie Summers sandwiched in between, to tally twice. Easterling inserted the hit that sent Sherwood Brewer, Indianapolis Clowns, and Bob Davis, Baltimore Elite, flying over the plate.

Willie Hutchinson, Memphis Red Sox right-hander, replaced McKinnis after Easterling's blow and stifled the rally.

Slumping Crowds at East-West Games Is a Warning Signal

by Luix Virgil Overbea

Source: *Pittsburgh Courier,* 27 August 1949

Chicago—(ANP)— When the East beat the West, 4–0, in the seventeenth annual East-West classic, only 31,097 fans saw the game. Last year more than 42,000 fans paid to see contest, and the year before more than 48,000 viewed the stars.

Is the East-West game a barometer to the waning of the popularity of Negro baseball? Is the game meeting its Dunkirk? Why did the game lose 11,000 fans from last year?

49. Lineup cards are exchanged before the 1949 East-West All-Star Game. Left to right: Buck O'Neil (for the West), umpires Vaughan (first name unknown), Bob Motley, Frank Duncan (former 1937 all-star), and Oscar Charleston (for the East). Courtesy of NoirTech Research, Inc.

No one can claim to know all the answers, but there are a few answers a number of persons are ready to give.

There is a question about whether or not the best players in the league were in the game. For example, how is it that Bob Thurman, recently purchased by the New York Yankees for its Newark Bears [team], was not even a member of the West team at the time of his purchase. His stolen base total still leads the league, and his home run record rates high. Or how about Birmingham's Norman Robinson batting .342 and second on his team to Piper Davis in runs batted in? He would have been a good man in place of either Lloyd (Ducky) Davenport of the Chicago American Giants or Johnny Davis of Houston. How about Pepper Bassett of the Barons behind the plate rather than Lonnie Summers?

Art Pennington of Chicago, batting .349 and leading the league in triples . . . Bob Thurman batting .351, leading the league in stolen bases and high in slugging records . . . Earl Taborn of the Monarchs, probably the best catcher in the circuit, with batting average of .256 . . . Alonzo Perry, Birmingham, 13-3, to rank second in the league in pitching . . . Booker McDaniels, Kansas City, 4-2 . . . What excellent additions to the all-star lineups if only the owners could have waited until 1950 before going up.[6]

Many fans complained about the pegged prices for the game, $3 for box seats, $2 general admission and $1 for bleachers. The bleachers were mighty empty at that East-West game, and so were numerous other sections. Most people felt that the $2, 1.25 and 65 cents, regular major league rates, were high enough.

This brings up the next question—what is the purpose of the game and what happens to the money? What benefits do the ballplayers get out of the game? Does it help then as the major league game does big league players?

And probably the question that should have come first—how about the fans, do they count? Why shouldn't the fans vote for the players to appear in the game? After all, they put down the money that has made the game the success it is today. In fact, why is it the fans know very little about any of the players in the Negro league?

Why can't they find out the results of the games? How about a box score or two?

AUGUST 14, 1949, CHICAGO, IL

EAST	AB	R	H	D	T	HR	BI	E	TAVG	TSLG
Pee Wee Butts (Baltimore Elite Giants), ss	4	1	1	1	0	0	0	0		
Pedro Diaz (New York Cubans), cf	4	0	3	0	0	0	0	0		
Lennie Pearson (Baltimore Elite Giants), 1b	5	0	0	0	0	0	0	0		
Bus Clarkson (Philadelphia Stars), rf	2	0	1	0	0	0	1	0		
Sherwood Brewer (Indianapolis Clowns), rf	2	1	1	0	0	0	0	0		
Butch Davis (Baltimore Elite Giants), lf	4	1	1	0	0	0	0	1		
Junior Gilliam (Baltimore Elite Giants), 2b	4	0	0	0	0	0	0	0		
Howard Easterling (New York Cubans), 3b	4	1	2	0	0	0	2	0		
Bill Cash (Philadelphia Stars), c	4	0	1	1	0	0	0	0		
Bob Griffith (Philadelphia Stars), p	1	0	1	0	0	0	1	0		
a) Dave Hoskins (Cleveland Buckeyes), ph	1	0	0	0	0	0	0	0		
Andy Porter (Indianapolis Clowns), p	0	0	0	0	0	0	0	0		
b) Leon Kellman (Cleveland Buckeyes), ph	1	0	0	0	0	0	0	0		
Pat Scantlebury (New York Cubans), p	1	0	0	0	0	0	0	0		
Team Totals, Average & Slugging Pct.	37	4	11	2	0	0	4	1	.297	.351

a) Batted for Griffith in 4th
b) Batted for Porter in 7th

WEST	AB	R	H	D	T	HR	BI	E	TAVG	TSLG
Jose Burgos (Birmingham Black Barons), ss	2	0	0	0	0	0	0	0		
Orlando Varona (Memphis Red Sox), ss	1	0	0	0	0	0	0	1		
c) Herman Bell (Birmingham Black Barons), ph	1	0	0	0	0	0	0	0		
Bob Boyd (Memphis Red Sox), 1b	4	0	0	0	0	0	0	0		
Pedro Formental (Memphis Red Sox), cf	1	0	0	0	0	0	0	0		
John Davis (Houston Eagles), cf	2	0	0	0	0	0	0	0		
Piper Davis (Birmingham Black Barons), 2b	4	0	1	1	0	0	0	0		
Willard Brown (Kansas City Monarchs), lf-3b	3	0	0	0	0	0	0	0		
Lonnie Summers (Chicago American Giants), c	3	0	1	0	0	0	0	2		
Robert Wilson (Houston Eagles), ss-3b	3	0	0	0	0	0	0	0		
Gene Richardson (Kansas City Monarchs), p	1	0	0	0	0	0	0	0		
Bill Greason (Birmingham Black Barons), p	0	0	0	0	0	0	0	0		
d) Buck O'Neil (Kansas City Monarchs), ph	1	0	0	0	0	0	0	0		
Gread McKinnis (Chicago American Giants), p	0	0	0	0	0	0	0	0		
Willie Hutchinson (Memphis Red Sox), p	1	0	0	0	0	0	0	0		
Jim LaMarque (Kansas City Monarchs), p	1	0	0	0	0	0	0	0		
Team Totals, Average & Slugging Pct.	28	0	2	1	0	0	0	3	.071	.107

c) Batted for Varona in 6th

d) Batted for Greason in 6th

East	110	000	020-4
West	000	000	000-0

PITCHER/TEAM	GS	IP	H	R	ER	K	BB	WP	HB	W	L	SV
Griffith/PS	1	3	0	0	0	1	1	0	0	1	0	0
Porter/IC		3	0	0	0	0	1	0	0	0	0	0
Scantlebury/NYC		3	2	0	0	1	0	0	0	0	0	1
Richardson/KCM	1	3	4	2	1	2	2	0	0	0	1	0
Greason/BBB		3	2	0	0	1	0	0	0	0	0	0
McKinnis/CAG		1 2/3	4	2	1	0	0	0	0	0	0	0
Hutchinson/MRS		1/3	0	0	0	0	0	0	0	0	0	0
LaMarque/KCM		1	1	0	0	0	0	0	0	0	0	0

BB—Butts, Diaz

DP—Boyd to P. Davis; Easterling to Gilliam to Pearson

LOB—East 9, West 2

SB—Easterling, Diaz, R. Davis

East—Hoss Walker (Mgr.); Coaches Buster Haywood

West—Buck O'Neil (Mgr.); Coaches W. S. Welch

Umpires—

Attendance—31, 097   Paid—26,697   Time—

1950

Althea Gibson becomes the first black tennis player to compete in the national championships of the United States Lawn Tennis Association in Forest Hills, New York.

Milk costs only 41 cents a half-gallon, 10 pounds of potatoes costs 46 cents, and 64 cents would bring home the bacon. A loaf of bread costs 14 cents.

Dr. Ralph Bunch becomes the first African-American to receive the Nobel Peace Prize, for his negotiation during the Palestine crisis.

On Halloween, November 1, and November 4, Earl Lloyd, Chuck Cooper, and Nat "Sweetwater" Clifton, respectively, become the first black players in the National Basketball Association (NBA). Clifton later plays in the 1958 East-West All-Star baseball game.

Racial quotas are abolished in the U.S. Army. President Truman authorizes American troops to be sent to Korea.

The National League All-Stars win for the first time in an American League ballpark (Comiskey) and in the first extra-inning (14) game, snapping a four-game losing streak by a score of 4–3, with the aid of Red Schoendienst's home run.

Ted Williams of the Red Sox becomes the highest paid player in major league history, at $125,000 per year. Brooklyn Dodger Jackie Robinson becomes the first African-American to appear on the cover of *Life* magazine.

Sam Jethroe becomes the 12th Negro League veteran in Major League Baseball when he joins the Boston Braves and wins the Rookie of the Year Award.

LEAGUE BUSINESS

The Memphis Red Sox, owned by Dr. W. S. Martin, are sold to Martin's brother Dr. B. B. Martin, with unanimous approval by the Negro American League. Dr. W. S. Martin was also owner of the $300,000 Martin Stadium, where the Red Sox had played their home games since moving from Russwood Park a few years before. Although no longer an owner, W. S. Martin retained ownership of the copyrighted name Memphis Red Sox.[1]

League officials elected were Dr. J. B. Martin of Chicago as president, secretary, and treasurer—boss, scorer, and keeper of the money. Tom Hayes, owner of the Birmingham Black Barons, was elected vice president to replace Ernie Wright, who had leased his Cleveland Buckeyes team to Wilbur Hayes. Dr. W. S. Martin was elected chaplin, and Wilbur Hayes was elected sergeant-at-arms.

Other league officials present at the meeting were Tom Baird and Dizzy Dismukes from the Kansas City Monarchs; Ed Bolden and Ed Gottlieb, Philadelphia Stars; Dick Powell, Baltimore Elite Giants; Alex Pompez, New York Cubans; Tom Hayes, Birmingham Black Barons; Dr. W. H. Young and Hugh Cherry, Houston Eagles; and William Little and Robert S. Simmons, Chicago American Giants.[2]

50. Sam Jethroe played in seven Negro League all-star games. In 1950, as a Boston Braves outfielder, "The Jet" was named National League Rookie of the Year. Courtesy of NoirTech Research, Inc.

The major league career of Satchel Paige appeared to be over as the Cleveland Indians asked for waivers on the former Negro League star. The Indians put Paige on the waiver list for the customary $10,000 asking price, but no team wanted to pay the waiver price plus Paige's reported $25,000 salary. With Paige clearing waivers, any club paying $1 could have the rights to openly negotiate with Paige.

The previous year, 1949, Paige had often been injured and had seldom pitched more than 3 innings in a game. His season totals were four wins and seven losses. In 31 games, he pitched 83 innings, striking out 54 batters and walking 33 men, while compiling a respectable ERA of 3.04.[3]

Shortly after the 1950 season started, fans found Paige pitching for the Philadelphia Stars. But this Paige was not the Paige of old. It was not common to see Negro League teams bomb the 44-year-old legend as he struggled the entire season to an uncharacteristic ERA of 5.19.

ALL-STAR REVIEW

The previous year's Negro League expatriates—Jackie Robinson, Don Newcombe, Roy Campanella, and Larry Doby—returned to this year's all-star game played at Comiskey Park. Before 46,127 fans, this National League squad was victorious over the American Leaguers, 4–3. Robinson collected one hit in four at bats, while his teammates Newcombe and Campanella were hitless in six at bats. Once again, Newcombe performed at less than his standard, giving up two hits and two earned runs in two innings of work. He struck out one batter and walked one in relief of Robin Roberts. Doby had a single and a double in six at bats, while making nine put-outs roaming centerfield.

A future major league all-star that never played in the East-West game was Willie Mays. In June, Mays was playing outfield for the Birmingham Black Barons, who were in the midst of a 13-game winning streak. Scouts from the Boston Braves and the Chicago White Sox were reported at each Black Barons game. Despite this interest, the New York Giants signed one of the Negro Leagues' most exciting players. Mays played 27 games for the Barons before finishing the season with Trenton, a minor league club in the Giants chain. A Black Baron since the late summer of 1948, Mays had compiled some impressive statistics that signaled the start of a great career. His three-season totals were 132 games, 479 at bats, 95 runs, 147 hits, 27 doubles, 6 triples, 10 home runs, 75 RBIs, and 14 stolen bases. The talented Westfield, Alabama, prodigy's career batting average was a modest .307 (with a .451 slugging percentage).

Another tour of stars took place in the South with the Jackie Robinson All-Stars traveling with the Indianapolis Clowns after the season. The reported tour covered 13 states and 35 cities. Syd Pollock, owner of the Indy Clowns, reported grossing more than $200,000 from an estimated total attendance of 125,000 fans. The Robinson All-Stars included Larry Doby, Don Newcombe, and Roy Campanella, while the Clowns featured Henry "Speed" Merchant, Len Williams, Nat Peeples, Ben "Honey" Lott, Willie Cathey, Harry Butts, Ed "Peanuts" Davis, Jim "Fireball" Cohen, Leander Tugerson, Sam "Piggy" Sands, and Jeff Williams.

The Clowns won 7 out of 12 games with one game ending in a 7–7 tie after 12 innings of play. The Jackie Robinson All-Stars and Clowns also combined their talents to play local teams during the tour. This combination of talent won 14 straight games before splitting a doubleheader with a team from Little Rock, Arkansas.[4]

BARRIER BREAKERS

With black players taking aim at the major leagues and attendance rising in major league ballparks, the Negro Leagues took a somewhat different approach to marketing their brand of game to the public. The Chicago American Giants, now owned by William Little, announced the signing of two white Americans, Louis Clarizio, age 18, an outfielder, and Louis Chirban, age 19, a pitcher, both from Crane Tech High School in Chicago. They had played semipro ball with the Chicago Roamers. Clarizio also claimed playing experience with Paducah (Kentucky) in the Class D Mississippi–Ohio Valley League. Press reports also indicated the signing of John Talmo, a pitcher.[5] However, a letter from Talmo reveals he never played: "I had a contract to sign but I had to turn it down because my parents needed me to support our family. So I'm sorry but I wish I would have played with the team, they [the American Giants] were great."[6]

John L. Johnson, in his column "Sport Light," reflected on the signing: "The Chicago American Giants have shown the ideal way for Negro baseball. By hiring players of all races they are at least moving in the democratic pattern. The day has come when both Negro and white fans like the kind of fight that develops when white men and black men compete."[7]

Later, the American Giants also signed a white double play combination of Frank Dyll at shortstop and Stanley Mierko at second. On July 9 Ted "Double Duty" Radcliffe, manager of the Chicago American Giants, started Clarizio and Chirban in the second game of a doubleheader against the Indianapolis Clowns. The Comiskey Park crowd of 8,579 patrons was the largest of the season. Chirban pitched two innings and was nicked for five runs and four hits before being relieved. He walked three batters and struck out two. Clarizio played four innings before being lifted for a pinch hitter. He struck out in his only at bat. The Clowns swept the doubleheader, 7–2 and 11–0.[8]

In August the American Giants entertained the Birmingham Black Barons in Alabama. Jim Crow laws prevented the four white players from taking the field with black players. Sheriff Bull Connor, of civil rights infamy, was also the play-by-play announcer for the Birmingham [White] Barons and was adamantly against race mixing. Connor threatened to cancel the game unless Chirban, Clarizio, Dyll, and Mierko left the stadium. Radcliffe, fearing the loss of a payday, complied with the city ordinance and Bull's demands. The short-handed Giants lost both games, 12–11 and 5–1. Soon afterward, the reverse integration of the black leagues by Chirban and Clarizio, and others, became just a footnote in baseball history as they were released.[9]

Another barrier breaker was Elwood Parsons, a 39-year-old former police court bailiff and chemistry technician from Dayton, Ohio. Parsons became the first full-time African-American scout in baseball when the Brooklyn Dodgers signed him. He was given nationwide access to players and the authority to actually sign players by Branch Rickey. Parsons claimed, "Mr. Rickey placed me under no territory restrictions, but told me to scout only colored players in all stages of development from the sandlot to the Negro League clubs."[10]

Negro Baseball On the Ropes, Needs Support of Negro Fans to Survive

by Luix Virgil Overbea

Source: *Kansas City Call,* 8 August 1950

Chicago—(ANP)— Negro baseball is on the ropes facing a knockout blow unless Negro fans will rally to its support and save it for next year.

Unfortunately, I must write this story of what appears to me a decaying enterprise, Negro baseball. Unless something is done constructively by both the owners and the fans. I fear the next year at this time, I may be forced to write an obituary for organized Negro baseball.

Before going into what I believe are some of the causes of the Negro American League's decline and suggesting a few props for this sagging institution, I first want to tell you why I think there should be Negro baseball.

Racial pride tells me that in the NAL is a Negro enterprise employing Negroes and making money for the race. As a Negro I should support it.

Still, more importantly, I believe is the fact that the Negro league is needed as a training ground or school for Negro players. Nearly every colored player in organized baseball received his early start in a colored league.

Only four major league clubs of 16 have Negro players. From this it is obvious that Negro players in the big leagues are not as widely accepted as one might imagine. Only a small percentage of minor league clubs utilize colored players. It would be almost impossible for a colored player to get to the big leagues if he expected to break in through the minors.

DANGER SIGNALS

What are the danger signs in Negro baseball? In Chicago the danger sign is the weak attendance at the Chicago American Giants baseball games. During the recent Elks convention in Chicago the Giants played a night game at a time when the Elks had nothing scheduled.

The Elks were considered something like sponsors of the game. The attraction was the Memphis Red Sox, at the time leading the league. Yet, in spacious Comiskey Park there were not 5,000 people. Comiskey Park is one of the better big league fields, and it has one of the best lighting systems in the nations.

During the Elks convention round the clock gambling was conducted very successfully and outside taverns were filled all the time money was spent. Yet the American Giants could not get 5,000 persons to spend $1.25 to see them play.

Reports from Baltimore hint that the Elite Giants, 1949 world champions, may be giving up soon. The Philadelphia Stars had to sign up Satchel Paige for $1,000 a game to make money. The Cleveland Buckeyes gave up.

Again fewer people saw the East-West all star game this year than last. New York and the East coast had no repeat performance. An attempt to get a fan vote on stars for this game failed miserably because nobody voted.

Several Negro sports writers have devoted columns to this problem and most of them see red ink for owners.

ROOT OF TROUBLES

What is wrong with Negro baseball to bring on all these troubles? The teams play a very good brand of baseball, better than most minor league clubs. Umpires keep the game moving and prevent those old-time player fist fights. A number of the players are very colorful.

Some of the things wrong are not the fault of the clubs themselves. These include schedules, parks, booking agents, and high costs. An example of park and schedule troubles is the case of the Indianapolis Clowns who did not play a single home game this season because no park was available to them.

The great bugaboo in Negro baseball that clubs can do something about is the lack of fan support. People just do not go out to the parks to see the teams play.

Artificial stimulants are not enough; clubs must build up fan loyalty. The American Giants had a ladies day on opening day and still did not draw 5,000 people to two games. The Giants also hired some white players, but they had not pulled in any crowds either here in Chicago.

The only visiting teams to draw here have been the Indianapolis Clowns and the Kansas City Monarchs. Not very many of these fans come to see the Giants because they are rooting for the home team to win the pennant.

A large percentage still come just to raise the bottle and trouble. In talking to them I have learned that nobody seems to know the players. Some girls come out to see or meet the players. A youngster or two asks for an autograph. Otherwise the players and the game often are ignored.

PLANNED PROGRAM NEEDED

I would like to see in 1951, rosters of every team in the league with biographies on the player and the player's records. These should be published in the newspapers so the fans may learn about them, too.

Even sports writers are ignorant of the teams. They rarely speculate as to the outcomes of the league pennant races and things like that.

Again, I want to see some box scores and results immediately after games are played. Hometown newspapers should know the results of every game the team plays.

All clubs and the league office should get together to map out a year round publicity program on public relations campaign to enroll new fans. This project should include such things as knothole clubs and booster groups.

It also could include a season's pass scheme by which a fan could pay a certain price for the pass, and then bring in his family or friends at reduced prices to any game at home. Financial geniuses of the league could figure out a good plan.

All this sounds like the same things I and many sports writers before me have said. This past year only the Indianapolis Clowns throughout the year maintained a continuous publicity program. The Monarchs kept the Kansas City people posted not only on their own activities but also reminded them of the number of KC men in organized baseball.

The NAL should observe the operation of the big leagues, then utilize some of these ideas in its own activities.

If we want to see Negro players remain in the big leagues, if we want to see a race enterprise succeed, and if we want to maintain our race pride, (particularly in the south) we had better help this NAL out fast.

Now is the time to work and plan for a successful 1951 baseball season or else we may find ourselves preparing for the burial of Negro baseball in 1952.

Editor's note: Despite the plea by Overbea, black fans were more interested in seeing how their black brothers were performing in the major leagues. With former all-star performers like Willard Brown, Hank Thompson, Dan Bankhead, Satchel Paige, Don Newcombe, Larry Doby, and Jackie Robinson now in the white leagues, the curiosity factor of seeing how these players performed with and against their white counterparts was overwhelming. In August 1950 Dodger second baseman Jackie Robinson was in a slump, as he fell to third place in the National League batting race with a steady .330 average. The previous year at this time, Robinson had been leading the league before finishing out of the running with a .342 average, but in 1949 he won the first Most Valuable Player Award awarded to a black player.

United Nations Head to Toss First Ball

40,000 Spectators Expected to Watch Negro Baseball's Biggest Annual Game Sunday, Aug. 20 at Comiskey Park

Source: *Kansas City Call*, 18 August 1950

STARTING LINEUPS

(Tentative)

WEST	EAST
(Probable starters)	(Probable starters)
NcNeal, Chicago, ss .294	Merchant, Clowns, lf .287
Douglas, Chicago, 2b .333	Butts, Baltimore, ss .281
Steele, Birmingham, lf .297	Gilliam, Baltimore, 2b .241
Penningham [Pennington], Chicago, cf .371	Gonzalez, Cubans, 1b .315
Harvey, Houston, 1b .368	Diaz, Cubans, cf .267
Kellman, Memphis, 3b .362	Louden, Cubans, c .277
Washington, Houston, 1b .362	Littles, Philly, rf .252
Jones, Memphis, c .264	Brewer, Clowns, 3b .295
Clarke, Memphis, p 8-7	Wilmore, Baltimore, p 4-4

The 18th annual East-West game will get underway here at 3 p.m., Sunday, Aug. 20, before an expected crowd of 40,000 at Comiskey Park, with Dr. Ralph Bunche, head of the trusteeship division of the United Nations, throwing the first ball of the 1950 classic game of the Negro American League.

This oldest of all-star games, played consecutively is expected to develop into a thrilling clash between the terrific hitting power of the West and the skillful pitching of the East.

Manager Oscar Charleston, pilot of the Eastern division representatives, is confident that his pitching power will be more than enough to halt the vaunted big-stick work of the Western sluggers, who are dominant in the batting averages among the circuit's hitters.

Charleston has five tried and true starting pitchers to hurl at the willow whipping artists from the West.

The East will probably start Al Wilmore (4-4) of Baltimore for the underdog East. Backing up Wilmore may be Jonas Gaines, mainstay of the Philly Stars (5-3). Then there is Raul Galata, (8-6), the Clowns ace, who is second in loop strikeouts with 92; Joe Black (7-1) of the Elite Giants; Harry Butts (6-7) of the Clowns, and the old pro of the East-West games, Pat Scantlebury (4-3) of the N.Y. Cubans.

Against this array of pitching talent the West managed by Ted (Double Duty) Radcliffe, will likely assign its starting honor to Vibert Clarke (8-7) of Memphis. But waiting to take over will be such stars as Cliff Johnson (10-1) Kansas City Monarchs, the leading pitcher of the league; Jehosie Heard (6-8) of the Houston Eagles, and Bill Powell (11-4) of the Birmingham Black Barons.

For the East, the only .300 hitter in the lineup will be first baseman Rene Gonzalez of the N.Y. Cubans, who is hitting .315. The other offensive power will be resting on Pedro Diaz of the Cubans and Sherwood Brewer of the Clowns. Leadoff man Henry (Speed) Merchant of the Clowns will be expected to provide the fans with base running excitement. He has stolen 36 bases this season to lead in the department.

The West will oppose the East pitchers with an array of hitting talent. Among these are: Art Pennington, (.371) of the Chicago American Giants; Robert Harvey, (.368) of the Houston Eagles; Leon Kellman, (.362) Memphis and John Washington, (.362) of the Eagles.

Other dangerous hitters on the West squad are: Jesse Douglas, Chicago, (.333); Clyde McNeal, Chicago, (.294); Ed Steele, Birmingham, (.297); and Casey Jones, Memphis, (.264); all good hitters in the clutch.

For reserve power, Manager Radcliffe will have Herb Souell, the Monarchs, (.325), Curley Williams, Houston, (.299); Pepper Bassett, Birmingham, (.263), and Tommy Cooper, the Monarchs, (.265).

East-West Game Notes

Source: *Kansas City Call,* 18 August 1950

Many coats and a few blankets were in evidence at the 18th annual East-West classic here at Comiskey stadium Sunday afternoon. Many fans gathered as early as 11 a.m. waiting for the gates to open at 12 noon. These had anticipated an SRO crowd and were on hand for a few choice seats, but there was plenty of room for twice the crowd in the huge ball park of the Chicago White Sox.

Dr. Ralph Bunche, U.N. head, sent his telegram of regrets for being unable to toss the first pitch as advertised. He sent a message saying that his young son was seriously ill and that he was standing by.

North Koreans got into action along about the seventh inning in the grandstand between home plate and third base . . . the police were kept busy as some dozen fights broke out one after another . . . but the alert police were able to give the bums rush to most of the battlers . . . prior to the game ticket scalpers were doing big business around the Grand Hotel, near 51st and South Parkway . . . They sold plenty of tickets by implying that the game was a sellout.

Chauncy Downs of Kansas City, fogged in his Elks outfit came in from Boston for the Elks Convention convening here. And Charles Howard of Des Moines, was seen breakfasting at the Grand Hotel cafe, where the service was disgusting slow. Contrary to past years there were few big sleek fishtail Cadillacs with out-of-state tags to be seen, giving evidence that the East-West fans were predominantly local.

Johnny O'Neil, manager of the Monarchs, was busy in the West coaching box. He warmed up the West team in pre-game batting practice. In the press box, where the chilly wind was also felt, there was a significant absentees. Fay Young, long ago the dominant figure among the writers did not show up. Russ Cowan, sports editor of the *Chicago De-*

fender called the official decisions. He was kept busy explaining the action on the field to some of the writers.

Some criticism of the way the classic is handled—scalpers, false tickets—was heard abundantly. But there were no hitches in the manner of play on the field. One had the feeling that nothing should be permitted to kill the East-West game. It is Negro baseball at its best. The annual Negro World Series is a minor affair in comparison with this contest which should be handled wisely each year.

There was a scarcity of Negro writers in the press box, in spite of the free hot dogs and cold beer and pop. As many white scribes and telegraphers were present as there were Negro writers. But no white fans were seen by this scribe, although the game had been widely publicized in the *Chi-Tribune, Sun* and other papers. The consensus was that the 1950 game was an entertaining well-played contest.

West Negro Stars Win 5–3

Source: *Chicago Tribune,* 21 August 1950

The combination of timely hitting and excellent pitching enabled the West to beat the East, 5 to 3, yesterday in Comiskey Park in a game sponsored by the Negro American league. The contest, 18th annual feature of Negro baseball, attracted 24,614, and the triumph was the 11th for the West in the outstanding series.

51. Although primarily known as a singles hitter, Junior Gilliam is the only player in history to hit a home run in both a Negro League All-Star Game and a Major League All-Star Game. Courtesy of Charles Blockson, Moseley Collection, Temple University.

52. Making his last of three East-West appearances in 1950 is Art "Superman" Pennington. In 1943 Pennington hit a blast on the second deck of Comiskey Park, marked on the photo "Home run by Sup. Pennington." This switch hitter had phone booth power that made him a threat to any Negro league pitcher. Courtesy of Art Pennington.

Dr. Ralph J. Bunche, United Nations mediator during the Palestine dispute, threw out the first ball.[11]

James Gilliam, Baltimore Elite Giants' second baseman, put the East in front in the second inning when he drove one of Vibert Clark[e]'s southpaw pitches into the lower deck of the left field stands.

DOUGLAS DRIVES IN TWO

The West went ahead in the third. Curley Williams of the Houston Eagles drew a pass and raced to third when Sherwood Brewer, Indianapolis Clowns third baseman, field Herb Souell's sacrifice bunt and threw the ball into right field, Souell moving to second on the error. Jesse Douglas then drove the two runners home with a single to right.

The West added three runs in the fifth on four hits. A triple by Art Pennington, Chicago American Giants' center fielder, brought in Alonzo Perry, who had singled, and Bob Harvey, who had drawn a pass. Pennington then scored on Ed Steele's single to right.

LITTLE GETS BIG HIT

The East tallied a run in the fourth when Louis Louden singled, was sacrificed to second by Gilliam, and scored when Ben Little rapped a triple off the scoreboard in right field. The final run was scored in the seventh when Tommy Butts walked, moved to third on Rene Gonzalez' second hit, and scored on Pedro Diaz's double.

The East threatened in the ninth when the West committed three errors after two were out, but Bill Powell forced Louden to end the game with a long fly to center.

West Captures 18th Annual East-West Game before 24,614 Fans

Source: *Pittsburgh Courier*, 26 August 1950

A hard-riding crew of diamond stars from the West rolled over the East here, Sunday in the annual classic of Negro baseball before 24,614 fans and triumphed by a score of 5 to 3.

The game was played before a comparatively small crowd and there was little to cheer about during the two hours and forty-six minutes of competing.

The West sewed up the contest in the fifth by breaking a 2–2 tie deadlock and scoring three runs on four hits.

Raul Galata, a small left-hander from the Indianapolis Clowns, was on the hill for the East when the West exploded in the fifth.

With two out, Alonzo Perry singled to center and advanced to second when Jesse Douglas, who stayed the rally by singling to center, was thrown out trying to make third.

FLY BALL LOST

Robert Harvey walked, Art Pennington tripled when Ben Littles of Philadelphia lost his lazy fly ball in the sun, enabling Perry and Harvey to score.

Ed Steele slammed over the third run of the inning and the West's final marker with a ringing single to center scoring Pennington.

That was the ball game right there. The East managed to get one more run off Bill Powell in the seventh but that was all. He held them the rest of the way and except for a threatened rally in the ninth with two outs, was never in any kind of trouble.

The East took the lead in the second inning when pitcher, Vibert Clarke, of Memphis, threw a fast pitch to Junior Gilliam, Baltimore Elite second sacker, and he socked it high and far into the leftfield stands, 353 feet away for a home run.

The West struck back in their half of the third and went ahead on a walk, single and error. Curley Williams, Houston shortstop, worked Pitcher Joe Black of Philadelphia for a walk. Herb Souell, Kansas City third baseman, bunted and when Sherwood Brewer, Indianapolis Clowns' third baseman, committed the first error of the game by throwing wild to first, both runners advanced an extra base.

DOUGLAS HITS

Jesse Douglas then produced the hit that put the West in front by slapping a whistling single to rightfield.

Cliff Johnson, tall right-hander from Kansas City took over the hurtling chores for the West in the fourth inning and immediately ran into trouble. Louis Louden of the New York Cubans singled out to center, went to second on Junior Gilliam's sacrifice and came home a moment later when Ben Littles walloped a double to right center, tying the score at 2–2.

A state of utter confusion was presented in the last of the fifth when Jesse Douglas of Chicago singled sharply to center. He dashed for second on a two and two pitch and over-slide the bag. Junior Gilliam tried to tag him but the Western base stealer got up and headed for third, then changed his mind and scrambled back to second safely.

Alonzo Perry of Birmingham hit an ordinary fly to left and when Diaz and Merchant got their signals mixed, the balls dropped safely. Douglas, however, was nailed for trying to make third.

TROUBLE FOR POWELL

Bill Powell, Birmingham pitcher with a record of eleven victories and four losses, took over the mound job for the West. In the seventh inning and after striking out Henry Merchant, Indianapolis outfielder ran into trouble. Baltimore's Tommy Butts was a hit and went to third on Rene Gonzalez' hit to right—another ball lost in the sun, because right-fielder Robert Harvey did not have the presence of mind to wear sun glasses—Pedro Diaz of the New York Cubans punched a double to right and Butts toted the last run for East home. The rally ended when Powell struck out Louis Louden and Junior Gilliam.

AUGUST 20, 1950, CHICAGO, IL

EAST	AB	R	H	D	T	HR	BI	E	TAVG	TSLG
Henry "Speed" Merchant (Indianapolis Clowns), lf	5	0	0	0	0	0	0	0		
Pee Wee Butts (Baltimore Elite Giants), ss	3	1	0	0	0	0	0	0		
Rene Gonzalez (New York Cubans), 1b	3	0	2	0	0	0	0	0		
Pedro Diaz (New York Cubans), cf	5	0	1	1	0	0	1	0		
Louis Louden (New York Cubans), c	5	1	1	0	0	0	0	0		
Junior Gilliam (Baltimore Elite Giants), 2b	3	1	1	0	0	1	1	0		
Ben Littles (Philadelphia Stars), rf	3	0	2	1	0	0	1	0		
Charles White (Philadelphia Stars), 3b	1	0	0	0	0	0	0	0		
Sherwood Brewer (Indianapolis Clowns), 3b-rf	3	0	0	0	0	0	0	1		
Joe Black (Baltimore Elite Giants), p	1	0	0	0	0	0	0	0		
a) Raul Galata (Indianapolis Clowns), ph-p	2	0	0	0	0	0	0	0		
Jonas Gaines (Philadelphia Stars), p	0	0	0	0	0	0	0	0		
b) Pat Scantlebury (New York Cubans), ph-p	1	0	0	0	0	0	0	0		
Team Totals, Average & Slugging Pct.	35	3	7	2	0	1	3	1	.200	.343

a) Batted Black in the 4th
b) Batted Gaines in the 8th

WEST	AB	R	H	D	T	HR	BI	E	TAVG	TSLG
Curley Williams (Houston Eagles), ss	1	1	0	0	0	0	0	0		
c) Clyde McNeal (Chicago American Giants), ph-ss	3	0	1	0	0	0	0	1		
Herb Souell (Kansas City Monarchs), 3b	1	1	0	0	0	0	0	1		
Leon Kellman (Memphis Red Sox), 3b	2	0	0	0	0	0	0	1		
Jesse Douglas (Chicago American Giants), 3b	4	1	3	0	0	0	2	0		
Alonzo Perry (Birmingham Black Barons), 1b	3	0	2	0	0	0	1	0		
Johnny Washington (Houston Eagles), 1b	2	0	0	0	0	0	0	1		
d) Bob Harvey (Houston Eagles), ph-rf	2	1	0	0	0	0	0	0		
Pepper Bassett (Birmingham Black Barons), c	1	0	1	1	0	0	0	0		
"Superman" Pennington (Chicago American Giants), cf	3	1	1	0	1	0	1	0		
Ed Steele (Birmingham Black Barons), lf	3	0	2	0	0	0	1	1		
Casey Jones (Memphis Red Sox), c	2	0	0	0	0	0	0	0		
e) Tom Cooper (Kansas City Monarchs), ph-c-rf	1	0	0	0	0	0	0	0		
Vibert Clarke (Memphis Red Sox), p	1	0	0	0	0	0	0	0		
Connie Johnson (Kansas City Monarchs), p	2	0	1	0	1	0	0	0		
Bill Powell (Birmingham Black Barons), p	1	0	0	0	0	0	0	0		
Team Totals, Average & Slugging Pct.	32	5	11	1	2	0	5	5	.344	.500

c) Batted for Williams in the 4th
d) Batted for Harvey in the 7th
e) Batted for Jones in the 5th

East	000	200	100-3
West	002	030	000-5

PITCHER/TEAM	GS	IP	H	R	ER	K	BB	WP	HB	W	L	SV
J. Black/BEG	1	3	4	2	1	0	1	oy	0	0	0	0
Galata/NYC		2	5	3	3	1	2	0	1	0	1	0
Gaines/PS		2	2	0	0	3	0	0	0	0	0	0
Scantlebury/NYC		1	0	0	0	1	0	0	0	0	0	0
Clarke/MRS	1	3	2	1	1	3	2	0	0	0	0	0
C. Johnson/KCM		3	3	1	1	3	2	0	0	1	0	0
Powell/BBB		3	2	1	1	4	1	0	0	0	0	1

BB—B. Harvey, C. Williams, S. Brewer, Butts
DP—Gonzales to Steele
HBP—Steele by Galata
SAC—Souell, Gilliam
SB—Douglas (2), Butts
East—Hoss Walker (Mgr.); Coaches Buster Haywood
West—Buck O'Neil (Mgr.); Coaches Winfield Welch
Umpires—Virgil Blueitt, ? Crook, ? Greene, Simon Lewis, ? Livingston, T. H. Jefferson
Attendance—24,614   Time—2:46

1951

The Municipal Appeals Court in Washington outlaws segregation in Washington DC restaurants.

Althea Gibson is the first African-American to play in England's Wimbledon tennis tournament.

Milk costs 46 cents a half-gallon, 10 pounds of potatoes costs 51 cents, and 67 cents would bring home the bacon. African-American chemist Lloyd A. Hall receives a patent for a shorter curing process for bacon.

The National League All-Stars win back-to-back games for the first time, hitting four homers, for an 8–3 win.

Former Negro League stars Luis Marquez, Ray Noble, Artie Wilson, Harry Simpson, Willie Mays, Sam Hairston, Bob Boyd, and Sad Sam Jones break into the majors.

Baseball cards with bubblegum inserts are introduced by the Topps Card Company.

J. Edgar Hoover, FBI director, turns down the position of baseball commissioner. Ford Frick takes the job.

LEAGUE BUSINESS

By 1953 Tom Baird, now sole owner of the Kansas City Monarchs, had sold more players to major league franchises than any other Negro League team owner. Yet not every deal was approved, despite the overall talent of a player. One example of Baird's difficulty in negotiation with club owners was the case of James Harding LaMarque. Pitcher Jimmy "Lefty" LaMarque had led the Negro American League in wins in 1947 and 1948. The left-hander had also appeared in three East-West All-Star Games, two games in 1948 and one in 1949, compiling an ERA of zero. However, when Baird offered LaMarque's contract to the Boston Braves, their frank response indicated an informal racial quota.

"I regret that there has been a delay in answering your letter of February 19, offering the contract of pitcher Jim LaMarque for $3500," wrote Harry Jenkins, the Braves' farm director. "The truth is we now have three colored boys at Milwaukee, and if we can take another, I am fearful that the club would get top-heavy. I am certain you can recognize this is a factor to be considered."[1]

Despite having a league-leading ERA of 1.96 in 1948, LaMarque, now 30 years old, would never sip a "cup of coffee" in the big leagues.

The 1951 season began with 8 teams compared to the 10 clubs of 1950. The Cleveland Buckeyes had folded in the previous July, winning only 3 out of 42 games. Alex Pompez's New York Cubans also did not return this year. The Houston Eagles, who had moved from Newark just one year earlier, were now the New Orleans Eagles. Lacking fan support, the Houston club had moved out of Texas in 1950 to finish the season in Nashville, Tennessee.

On a more positive note, the Indianapolis Clowns would be playing in Bush Stadium, in Indianapolis. For the first time in two years, they would claim a home field. And despite the death of owner Ed Bolden the previous September, the Philadelphia Stars continued in 1951 under the leadership of his daughter, Dr. Hilda Bolden. Eddie Gottlieb continued to do the booking for the Stars.[2]

BARRIER BREAKER

A tiny town 40 miles south of Montreal, boasting 3,000 folks, was the home of the Farnham Pirates. The Pirates played in the Class B Provincial League, composed of eight teams. Two years before, the Farnham entry had offered the manager's job to East-West performer Sam Bankhead, Homestead Grays center fielder and shortstop. Bankhead had declined the position.

This year, Bankhead accepted the position, becoming "organized" baseball's first African-American manager. As player-manager, Bankhead would be responsible for 14 players, including 2 whites. The Canadian-based league consisted of teams from Sherbrooke, Granby, Drummondville, Quebec, St. Hyacinthe, and Three Rivers.

Player-manager Bankhead got into 122 of Farnham's games, batting .274 in 435 at bats, with 119 hits, 46 runs, 51 RBIs, 20 doubles, 2 triples, 2 homers, 12 steals, and 60 walks. He played 118 games at shortstop, leading the league in assists and put-outs, ranking second in fielding with a .948 fielding average.

The Farnham Pirates were rich with Negro League veterans, including Al Pinkston (.301), Joe Taylor (.360), Alonzo Braithwaite (.270), Eudie Napier (.286), Bubba Hyde (.193), Lester Lockett (.217), Archie Ware (.257), and pitchers Bob Trice (7-12) and Cecil Kaiser (14-13). Panamanian Humberto Robinson won 17 games against 13 defeats, accounting for almost a third of their 52 wins. Farnham finished seventh in the eight-team league. Another player was third baseman Josh Gibson Jr., who hit .230, with two homers in 187 at bats, before breaking his leg in midseason.

Sam Bankhead never had a successor. The Pirates switched their Provincial League franchise to St. Jean in 1952, with Farnham and Sherbrooke dropping out of the league due to ballpark fires during the off-season. The Farnham field was never rebuilt. At the time, Farnham was the smallest city in the circuit.[3]

ALL-STAR REVIEW

The quartet of Robinson, Doby, Newcombe, and Campanella made its third straight all-star appearance, this time with former New York Cuban star Minnie Minoso joining the American League squad. Minoso pinch-hit and played a little right field, going zero for two before 52,075 fans at Briggs Stadium. Doby failed to get a hit in his only appearance as a pinch hitter. Meanwhile, Robinson got two hits in 4 at bats, while Campanella was hitless for the third time. Campy was now hitless in 12 all-star at bats. Newcombe had a single in 2 at bats, while pitching a fine game. Big Newk struck out three batters and gave up two hits and no runs in pitching the sixth, seventh, and eighth innings.

Back in the Negro Leagues, the eternal all-star Satchel Paige was now pitching for the Chicago American Giants, who were struggling to meet their payroll. Booking for the Giants was done by Abe Saperstein, a close friend to former Cleveland Indians owner Bill Veeck. There were reports that Veeck was a prospective buyer for the St. Louis Browns and might have rehired Paige if he got the St. Louis club. Sportswriter John Johnson wrote: "The 'Ageless One' is real cute on the hill. He seems to weave a spell over some hitters, as he bends his tall frame forward and backward out there, stretching his arms backward and twiddling this gloved hand and then firing the balls with uncanny control and accuracy." Johnson added: "One of the most colorful players in the history of the game, Paige has the cunning, the know how and the pitching ability to please the fans."[4] By July, Veeck had re-signed the crowd pleaser to a St. Louis Browns contract.

GAME REVIEWS

Sport Light: Let's Boost Baseball

by John L. Johnson

Source: *Kansas City Call,* 29 December 1950

The fate of Negro baseball is still in the hands of the Negro fans. It is theirs to succor or stave. And whether it lives or dies in 1951—admittedly its most crucial year—will be determined by whether its patrons are charitable enough and far-sighted enough to support it for the good it has done, or whether they think it has served its usefulness and is of no further interest to them.

Last season, the circuit staggered to a close. It started out as a 10-club league. But one of the teams was forced to quite early in the season. Another had to change its home city in mid-season because of a lack of fan interest. Most of the others barely were able to hang on to the finish.

Next week, in Chicago, the remaining team owners and league officials will meet to determine whether they should try to go on in 1951, or give up the ghost.

Negro baseball, like the Negro banks, churches, insurance companies and other purely racial institutions, depends for its life on Negro patronage. While it is not the ideal organization in a democratic nation, it serves a purpose which no other organization quite fulfills.

VICTIMS OF ITS GRADUATES

Strangely enough, Negro baseball has been instrumental in bringing about its own predicament. Certainly no one can find fault with the fans who delight in the performances of Robinson, Jethroe, Doby, Easter, Campanella, Newcombe, Thompson, Bankhead and others in the National competition.

Even the most avid owner of a Negro league team can understand the pride and interest his patrons have in the daily play of these boys who measure up with the best on the diamonds.

But even the most ardent worshipper of these big-time stars should remember that they are where they are only through the medium of Negro baseball.

However difficult it may be, the Negroes of this country must, because of necessity, play a dual role in their allegiance. While they may find complete satisfaction in the events of the white world, they yet must remember and aid their own, for unless they do no one else will.

Thus they must consider that as things stand now, there will be no replacements for the Robinsons, the Dobys and the Easters if there is not a source of supply. And only Negro baseball can fill the bill.

The thousands of Negro boys on sandlot diamonds who are ambitious to wear someday a major league uniform will have little opportunity to do so if there is no interest in them and in the only medium which has thus far applied all the Negro players to the major leagues.

PRIDE SHOULD KEEP DOORS OPEN

Whether it is race pride or civic hope, Negro fans should help keep the league game going. To let it die is to close the doors of opportunity to those who will replace the heroes of the hour.

On the whole, Negro league baseball has been pretty fair baseball since the present circuit, or that which remains of it, started back in 1921 [1920]. Generally all the clubs have been staffed with some standout players who have combined to offer the public entertaining play. This is evidenced by the fact that nearly every club has a representative now in either major or minor league play.

Few of the colored players who have been given an opportunity to advance have failed to survive. Playing often under arduous circumstances they have managed to measure up and often to emerge with some of the top honors.

Honorees of the past season were named in the Pacific Coast, International, American Association and other lower class leagues. And they all are graduates of the Negro Leagues.

Until some better medium comes along, the Negro fans should support the Negro league out of pure necessity for the future of the youth if for nothing else. They should encourage it, if only out of a sense of charity. The game serves a need, which no other organization supplies.

So it is with the best wishes of this column that the team owners and officials will meet January 4–5 in Chicago. We hope they can find the means to carry on.

Editor's Note: Indication of the teams' struggle to survive was their many playing dates in minor league cities or small towns. Once critical of the Clowns and their antics, other teams were now resorting to various means to attract fans. One such attraction happened on July 22 at Burnett Field in Dallas, Texas, in a game between the Chicago American Giants and the Kansas City Monarchs. W. S. Welch of the Giants hired clown Ed Hamman to travel with the team.

This was not Hamman's first job as an entertainer. Back in 1948 he had been hired by Bill Veeck to entertain fans at World Series games in Cleveland. That year, Veeck's Indians set a season attendance record of 2,260,627 people.[5] The innovative Veeck was fresh with ideas like free nylons for the ladies, opening a nursery under the stands, flying in orchids from Hawaii, special days to honor "Joe Fan," and of course the signing of ageless rookie Leroy "Satchel" Paige.

Hamman was a white lad from Fostoria, Ohio, and had been associated with the Harlem Globetrotters basketball and baseball teams. It was reported that "Ed is more than a clown, but skilled performer. His feats of fielding a hot grounder around third base and whipping it on a line to first base with a flip around his back has to be seen to be believed. He has no peer in a clever 'pepper' game." The report added: "Making him doubly valuable is the fact that he is also one of the best road secretaries in the business. He doubles in brass in this capacity and as field entertainer for the American Giants."[6]

"His comedy entertains the team as well as the fans," said manager Winfred Welch, "and that's good for the morale of our club."[7] Years later Hamman would go from entertainer to executive, purchasing the Indianapolis Clowns from Syd Pollock.

East-West Vote

Source: *Chicago Defender,* 11 August 1951

The final tabulation of the votes pouring in from all over the country for the 19th annual East-West classic at Comiskey Park on Sunday afternoon, August 12, shows Ed Steele, veteran of many East vs. West games and who is batting .382 in the Negro American League, topping all other players with a total of 10,019. He also leads in votes for members of the

53. Theolic Smith, for the Chicago American Giants, warms up for the West squad at Comiskey Park. Courtesy of NoirTech Research, Inc.

East squad. For the West, Theolic "Fireball" Smith, ace of the Chicago American Giants, leads the West contingent with 9,764. The vote this year has been the largest in recent years, showing an added interest in the classic.

THE FINAL VOTE TABULATION AND WINNERS

East
First base—Wesley Dennis, Baltimore, 9,352
Second base—Ray Neil, Indianapolis, 9,841
Shortstop—Sherwood Brewer, Indianapolis, 9,165
Third base—Milton [Milt Smith], Philadelphia, 8,752
Utility infielder—John Williams, Birmingham, 8,563
Outfielders—Ed Steele, Birmingham, 10,019; Henry Kimbro, Baltimore 9,864; Ben Littles, Philadelphia, 8,214; Norman Robinson, Birmingham, 7,923.
Catchers—John Hayes, Baltimore, 9,671; Buster Haywood, Indianapolis, 7,734
Pitchers—Kelly Searcy, Baltimore, 9,153; Willie Gaines, Philadelphia, 8,667;

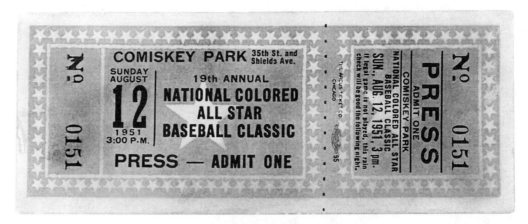

54. A press pass for the 1951 East-West game. Courtesy of Larry Bennett, Colorado.

Leander Tugerson, Indianapolis, 8,312, Roosevelt Lilly, Birmingham, 8,117; Wilmer Harris, Philadelphia, 7,833

West
First base—Gilbert Varona, Memphis, 8,572, Buck O'Neil, Kansas City, 8,127
Second base—Eddie Brooks, New Orleans, 9,522; Henry Baylis, Kansas City, 9,437
Shortstop—Jesse Williams, Kansas City, 9,683; Larry Raines, Chicago, 9,312
Third base—Parnell Woods, Chicago, 9,714; Curley Williams, New Orleans, 9,553
Outfielders—Neal Robinson, Memphis, 9,359; Lonnie Summers, Chicago, 9,320; Larry Guice, New Orleans, 8,868
Catchers—Casey Jones, Memphis, 9,369; Tom Cooper, Kansas City, 9,342
Pitchers—Theolic Smith, Chicago, 9,764; Jehosie Heard, New Orleans, 8,439; George Walker, Kansas City, 7,965; Vibert Clarke, Memphis, 7,649

Two players who were polling votes heavily at the outset have since had their contracts purchased. Satchel Paige went from the Chicago American Giants to the St. Louis Browns and Ben Lott, home run hitting third baseman of the Indianapolis Clowns signed with Colorado Springs in the Chicago White Sox system.

Fay Says: You Telling Me?

by Frank A. Young

Source: *Chicago Defender*, 11 August 1951

Sunday is the big day in Negro baseball. Sunday, the East all-stars meet the West all-stars in the 19th annual East-West baseball classic at Comiskey Park, Chicago. Game time is 3 o'clock but the gates will swing open about noon and at 1:30 Omar Crittenden's K. of P. band will open up with appropriate music and that isn't all. At that time 45 minutes of entertainment for the early customers will get under way.

The teams will take the field for 15 minutes of practice and promptly at 3 o'clock the 1951 dream game gets under way. What will be the outcome? Well, you try and guess it because we are not going out on a limb. Last year's score was 5 to 3 in favor of the West. The West now leads in games won 11 to 7.

The annual baseball classic is more important this year than ever before. The names in

Negro baseball have advanced and are now headliners in either the National or American League. The contribution that Negro league baseball has made to the great America pastime has been tremendous but the Negro club owners have spent many a dollar and suffered many a headache and have gone along practically unnoticed.

Orestes Minoso of the Chicago White Sox, Jackie Robinson of the Brooklyn Dodgers (he played in the 1945 classic) and Roy Campanella, catcher and teammate of Robinson's (he [Campy] was voted the most valuable player in the 1945 game [and the 1939 game]). Larry Doby, centerfielder of the Cleveland Indians, Luis Marquez of the Boston Braves and Sammy Jethroe, also of the Braves, Willie Mays, outfielder; Monte Irvin, first sacker, and Rafael Noble, Cuban catcher, and Hank Thompson, third sacker, all of the New York Giants; Luke Easter of the Indians, Sam Hairston, White Sox backstop; the famous Satchel Paige, now of the St. Louis Browns, and others are graduates of the East versus West games.

In fact, with the exception of Don Newcombe who was pitching for the Newark Eagles and went into the United States Navy at the Great Lakes Naval Training station at the time he would have been a member of the West squad, and Harry Simpson, all of the Negroes in major league baseball today have at one time been a member of either the East or West squad.

No wonder the coming of the 19th annual game will attract such major league owners as Bill Veeck, former president of the Cleveland Indians and now owner of the St. Louis Browns. Hank Greenberg, former Detroit Tiger outfielder star and now owner [general manager] of the Cleveland Indians, scouts from the White Sox, Chicago Cubs, Brooklyn Dodgers, New York Giants, New York Yankees, Cincinnati Reds, Boston Braves, Boston Red Sox and the Pittsburgh Pirates will be on hand for Sunday's diamond classic.

And the Negro fan would do well to support not only the all-star game but the Negro league in general because it is from this organization which virtually has been acting as a training ground for these present day stars (look at the base hitting percentage in both the National and American League, the run getting, the extra base hitters and the base stealers and you'll get a splendid idea). And too don't forget the number of Negro players who are in the American Association, the International, the Pacific Coast, the Canadian-American, the Central and other leagues who have come from our own league.

We will admit that some of the glamour left the East versus West classic when Jackie Robinson, Campanella, [Dan] Bankhead went up and still more when others advanced. Many of us went well overboard for the majors, deserting the very vehicle that made it possible for them to do so. None took into consideration the worries about decreasing attendance that faced Negro league owners nor did it ever occur to some that salaries went on although two or three Sundays the downpour of rain canceled the game with the promotion out considerable money for advanced work done, the transportation of both teams to the scene of the would be game at the same time plus expenses for board and room.

Sidebar: Miss Carolyn Combs, 24, of 6528 St. Lawrence Ave., is crowned Queen of the 19th Annual Negro East-West baseball game, to be played Aug. 12 at Comiskey Park, by Dr. J. B. Martin, president of the sponsoring Negro American League and chairman of the game committee. Miss Combs, a graduate of John Marshall High in St. Paul, Minn., is a senior in the school of liberal arts and sciences at Chicago's Roosevelt College. She is also an administrative clerk in the college's school of music.

East Negro All-Stars Beat West, 3 to 1

Source: *Chicago Tribune,* 13 August 1951

The Eastern All-Stars beat the West, 3 to 1, in the 19th annual Negro American league game yesterday at Comiskey Park. The victory cut the West's edge in the series to 11 to 8.

The crowd of 21,312 saw the East take its first game in three years. Kelly Searcy, of the Baltimore Elite Giants, was the winning pitcher.

The East scored two in the sixth inning to take the lead. Ed Steele of the Birmingham Black Barons tripled, scoring Ray Neil of Indianapolis. Norm Robinson doubled, scoring Steele, but was out trying for third.

Robinson doubled and Ben Littles of the Philadelphia Stars tripled to clinch the game in the ninth.

21,312 See East Beat West, 3–1 in Annual Chicago Classic

Source: *Pittsburgh Courier,* 18 August 1951

Three crafty pitchers muffled the big bats of the West at Comiskey Park Sunday afternoon and a star-studded team from the East won the nineteenth annual East-West classic, 3 to 1, before 21,312 fans.

Leander Tugerson of Indianapolis, Kelly Searcy of Baltimore and Wilmer Harris of Philadelphia did the checking for the East and held the vaunted power of the West is check. They gave up but one run and six scattered hits.

The West was never able to solve any of the East pitchers for more than two hits. They got two blows off each hurler, but they never were able to get successive hits or launch a real rally.

The East sewed up the ball game in the sixth when they pounced on Vibert Clarke of Memphis for two runs on four hits. Ray Neil scored the first run of the game when he singled and Ed Steele blasted him home with a tremendous triple. Norman Robinson powered in the winning run by doubling Steele home. That was enough to win it right there, but just to make sure, the East added another in the ninth.

The West got its lone run in the sixth when Jesse Williams singled, and eventually came home on a foul fly to right field.

The East. meantime, kept pecking away at the Western hurlers Theolic Smith, Vibert Clarke and Jehosie Heard. They got 3 runs and 10 hits, including 2 triples and 2 doubles.

Theolic Smith of the Chicago American Giants slated for the West and gave up but two hits and no runs. Clarke came in the fourth with the score tied at 0–0 and eventually turned out to be the losing pitcher. Heard relieved him with two outs in the sixth and finished the game.

The victory was the eighth for the East in the long series. The West has won eleven. The West won the 1950 game by a 5 to 3 count.

Kelley Searcy, a left-hander from Baltimore got credit for winning the game. He took over in the fourth and was the East hurler when the winning runs were scored.

Smith, veteran right-hander, who specializes in knuckleball offerings started on the mound for the West and had little trouble throttling the East's power. He gave up but two hits, one in the first and another in the second, and held them scoreless.

He was in trouble only once, in the second inning. Wesley Dennis of Baltimore started off with a sharp single to left and advanced to second on an infield out and to third on a wild pitch. After Norman Robinson of Birmingham flied out, Philadelphia's Milton Smith walked and stole second.

With men on third and second, [Theolic] Smith then took care of the situation himself, striking out Judy [Johnny] Hayes of Baltimore.

Manager Buster Haywood started Leander Tugerson of Indianapolis on the mound for the East. He matched Smith's performance by holding the West scoreless and giving up but two singles, but no runs.

Thus the two starting pitchers were on equal terms when they finished at the end of three innings and the teams were deadlocked with a scoreless tie.

Searcy of Baltimore succeeded Tugerson in the fourth and Jose Colas of Memphis promptly greeted the East's left-hander with a single to center, but that was all the West could get off him.

The West had its first big opportunity to score then, because Colas got as far as third on an error and infield out. But the threat died when the East executed a fats double play nailing Andy Anderson, who got on by a fielder's choice, at second, and throwing out the hitter, Tom Cooper, at first.

The East made its first real bold move to break the deadlock to the fifth when Milton Smith bunted safely with one away and streaked to third on Judy [Johnny] Hayes' sharp single left. Henry Kimbro worked Clarke for a walk to fill the bases. But the threat died when Sherwood Brewer hit a bounder to short and Kimbro was forced at second.

The East teed off on Clarke in the sixth, scoring two runs on four hits.

Neil of Indianapolis led off with a single to center and with one out Steele of Birmingham drove him home with the game's first run when he blasted a 415-foot triple over center fielder Colas' head, Robinson then doubled scoring Steele with the winning run. Robinson trying to stretch his hit into a triple was thrown out at third.

Milton Smith kept things going for the East by singling to center. At this point, Manager Winfield Welch of the West decided Clarke needed a shower and called in Heard, a southpaw from New Orleans. In his two and two-third innings of endeavor, Clarke gave up two runs and six hits. Heard put the fire out by striking out Hayes, but the damage had been done.

The West got its first run in the sixth when Jesse Williams of Kansas City led off with an infield hit to short and advanced to second on a wild throw. He moved to third on an infield out and scored a few moments later when Curly Williams hit a long foul to right. Steele made the catch and then Williams streaked home to make the count 2 to 1 in favor of the East.

Wilmer Harris of Philadelphia took over the mound for the East in the seventh. Searcy went out after having given up one run on two hits in three innings.

The East got its third run in the ninth when Robinson doubled and Ben Littles of Philadelphia, batting for Hayes, blasted a triple to center.

AUGUST 12, 1951, CHICAGO, IL

EAST	AB	R	H	D	T	HR	BI	E	TAVG	TSLG
Henry Kimbro (Birmingham Black Barons), cf	4	0	1	0	0	0	0	0		
Sherwood Brewer (Kansas City Monarchs), ss	4	0	0	0	0	0	0	1		
Ray Neil (Indianapolis Clowns), 2b	4	1	1	0	0	0	0	1		
Wesley "Doc" Dennis (Birmingham Black Barons), 1b	4	0	1	0	0	0	0	0		
Ed Steele (Birmingham Black Barons), rf	4	1	1	0	1	0	1	0		
Norman Robinson (Birmingham Black Barons), lf	4	1	2	2	0	0	1	0		
Milt Smith (Philadelphia Stars), 3b	3	0	2	0	0	0	0	1		
Johnny Hayes (Baltimore Elite Giants), c	3	0	1	0	0	0	0	0		
a) Ben Littles (Philadelphia Stars), ph	1	0	1	0	1	0	1	0		
Buster Haywood (Indianapolis Clowns), c	0	0	0	0	0	0	0	0		
Leander Tugerson (Indianapolis Clowns), p	1	0	0	0	0	0	0	0		
Kelly Searcy (Baltimore Elite Giants), p	1	0	0	0	0	0	0	0		
b) Wiley Griggs (New Orleans Eagles), ph	1	0	0	0	0	0	0	0		
Wilmer Harris (Philadelphia Stars), p	1	0	0	0	0	0	0	0		
Team Totals, Average & Slugging Pct.	35	3	10	2	2	0	3	3	.286	.400

a) Batted for Hayes in the 9th

b) Batted for Searcy in 7th

WEST	AB	R	H	D	T	HR	BI	E	TAVG	TSLG
Jesse Williams (Kansas City Monarchs), 2b	4	1	1	0	0	0	0	0		
Parnell Woods (Chicago American Giants), 3b	3	0	0	0	0	0	0	0		
Jose Colas (Memphis Red Sox), cf	3	0	1	0	0	0	0	0		
Curley Williams (New Orleans Eagles) ss	3	0	0	0	0	0	1	0		
Andy Anderson (Chicago American Giants), lf	4	0	1	0	0	0	0	0		
Tom Cooper (Kansas City Monarchs), c-1b	4	0	2	0	0	0	0	0		
Lacey Guice (New Orleans Eagles), rf	3	0	1	0	0	0	0	0		
c) Lonnie Summers (Chicago American Giants), ph	1	0	0	0	0	0	0	0		
Gilbert Varona (Memphis Red Sox), 1b	2	0	0	0	0	0	0	0		
d) Casey Jones (Memphis Red Sox), ph-c	2	0	0	0	0	0	0	0		
Theolic Smith (Kansas City Monarchs), p	1	0	0	0	0	0	0	0		
Vilbert Clarke (Memphis Red Sox), p	1	0	0	0	0	0	0	0		
Jay Heard (New Orleans Eagles), p	1	0	0	0	0	0	0	0		
Team Totals, Average & Slugging Pct.	32	1	6	0	0	0	1	0	.188	.188

c) Batted for Guice in 9th

d) Batted for Varona in 7th

East	000	002	001-3
West	000	001	000-1

PITCHER/TEAM	GS	IP	H	R	ER	K	BB	WP	HB	W	L	SV
Tugerson/IC	1	3	2	0	0	1	0	0	0	0	0	0
Searcy/BEG		3	2	1	0	1	1	0	0	1	0	0
W. Harris/PS		3	2	0	0	4	0	0	0	0	0	1
T. Smith/KCM	1	3	2	0	0	2	1	1	0	0	0	0
Clarke/MRS		2 2/3	6	2	2	1	1	0	0	0	1	0
Heard/NOE		3 1/3	2	1	1	3	0	0	0	0	0	0

BB—Colas, M. Smith, Kimbro, Woods

DP—C. Williams to Varona; Brewer to Neil to Dennis; C. Williams to J. Williams to Varona

LOB—East 7, West 7

PB—Haywood

SAC—C. Williams

SB—P. Woods, M. Smith, Colas

East—Buster Haywood (Mgr.)

West—Winfield S. Welch (Mgr., replaced Buck O'Neil, due to illness)

Umpires—Simon Lewis, T. H. Jefferson, R. W. Garrett, Simmie Gardner, Wallace Williams, Andrew Summers

Attendance—21,312   Paid—14,161   Time—

1952

Tuskegee Institute, which has monitored lynchings since 1882, reports that this is the first year since that date that no African-Americans have been lynched.

Invisible Man, by Ralph Ellison, wins the National Book Award.

Milk costs only 48 cents a half-gallon, 10 pounds of potatoes costs 76 cents, and 65 cents would bring home the bacon. A loaf of bread costs 16 cents.

The National League All-Stars win, 3–2, in the only game ever shortened by rain (five innings), for their third straight victory.

Former Negro League players Hector Rodriguez, George Crowe, Bus Clarkson, Quincy Trouppe, Joe Black, Dave Pope, and Sandy Amoros make their major league debuts.

LEAGUE BUSINESS

Dr. J. B. Martin, president of the Negro American League (NAL), offered his assessment of the plight of black baseball in an editorial: "As far as pure baseball is concerned, the NAL operates on the same rules as does regular organized baseball. The league uses three uniformed umpires in all official games. Players are signed to contracts like those in the big leagues. Every game has an official scorer, and the Howe News Bureau keeps official records of the NAL just as it does for the major leagues and most of the minor leagues."

Martin added an important point that had agitated the league for years:

The NAL fails to meet organized baseball standards on one major count—that is the matter of scheduling its games several months in advance. The chief reason for this discrepancy is that the circuit operates in ballparks owned by clubs in organized baseball. The league must wait until these other home teams already have scheduled their home games, then take what it can get of the open dates.

Because of this difficulty, the league has to make a split season schedule. Our teams usually operate in their home cities on Sunday and holidays and tour other cities during weekdays.

The NAL is recognized by organized baseball as a bona fide loop. Its contracts with players are respected, and club owners of other teams deal with NAL club owners for players just as they did with any league in organized baseball.[1]

Meanwhile, Monte Irvin was inking a 1952 contract with the New York Giants for $25,000.[2] Despite Martin's claim that each league honored the other league's contracts, opportunism was still the norm among league owners.

On September 14 the Negro American League announced an intraleague world series to be held between the divisional winners Indianapolis Clowns and the Birmingham Black

Barons. The Clowns were the defending champions and winners of the first-half title, while the Black Barons had won the second-half crown during Labor Day weekend.

Earlier in the year, the Clowns featured a skinny, cross-handed-hitting youngster from Mobile, Alabama, named Henry Aaron. The Clowns opened their season, on May 11, with Aaron at shortstop. Later that month, Dewey Griggs was scouting the "Funmakers" for the Boston Braves for a doubleheader against the Memphis Red Sox. In his scouting report to Braves executive John Mullen, he wrote:

> Dear John
>
> Henry Aaron the seventeen year old shortstop of the Indianapolis club looked very good. In the first game he had seven chances, two fly balls back of third and five hard hit ground balls. Started one double play from short to second to first, hit three for five, two line drive singles over third and short and a perfect bunt down third base line. His only error was a low throw from deep short. These hits were made off a good looking left-hander.
>
> Altho [sic] the official scorer gave the boy four for five, I gave the third baseman a [sic] error on the play.
>
> In the second game he accepted five chances without an error, started one double play from short to second to first and hit three for four. Off the starting left hander pitcher hit an outside curve ball over the right field fence, three hundred and thirty feet away and dropped down another perfect bunt. In the sixth inning he hit a low inside curve for a single over second base off a right hander with the bases loaded.
>
> At the present time he is hitting around .400 and batting fourth for the club. He made no effort to go either to his right or left as the slippery infield made it impossible to mke [make] these plays.
>
> On June 15th Indianapolis plays two games with Kansas City at Buffalo and at the time I will give you a complete story on the boy. I am satisfied with the boy's hitting. However, I want to see him make plays both to his right and left and slow [slowly] hit balls that he has to come in after. Also another look at his throwing. This boy could be the ANSWER.
>
> Sincerely yours,
> Dewey S. Griggs[3]

Anxious to sell Aaron, Pollock wrote John Mullen two days later outlining the contract purchase price with various stipulations:

> Dear John
>
> Re: our phone conversation, lowest deal I would consider on shortstop HENRY AARON would be $10,000 with $2,500 down payment, balance to be paid after 30-day look, regardless of classification he was started in, and salary of $350 monthly.
>
> On option, to turn him over to your organization at end of this season, would request $1,000 down payment to tie-up to such an agreement, an additional $2,500 if kept 30 days after reporting to your organization starting from first day he reports to spring training or otherwise; an additional $3,500 if at anytime in the future he comes up and remains in Triple-A for 30 days or longer; and an additional $3,000 if he comes up into the Majors and sticks 30 days or longer. Should he skip Triple-A and go right into the Majors from a lower classification, would expect $6,500. In other words I seek to [sic] total sum of $10,000 on this player . . . and am asking other Clubs $15,000.

Pollock also offered his assessment of Aaron, claiming:

I feel this youngster is another Ted Williams in the hitting department and can hit to all fields as well as lay down bunts, and his fielding right now leaves little to be desired, outside of a bit of polishing on getting off his throw.

Cordially,

Syd.[4]

No additional scouting was needed on Hank Aaron. Two days later, Mullen received a telegram confirming the deal, stating:

RE: TEL MAY 28TH THIS WILL CONFIRM MY ACCEPTANCE TERMS AS THEREIN STATED ON PLAYER HENRY AARON. INDIANAPOLIS COWNS [*sic*] BASEBALL CLUB SYD POLLOCK, GEN MGR.[5]

Unknown to Aaron, his contract had already been sold to the Boston Braves. The day before, Mullen had sent the following telegram to George Trautman, league president, outlining the terms of the Aaron minor league contract:

THE FOLLOWING TELEGRAM WAS SENT THIS DATE BY JOHN W. MULLEN, SECRETARY EVANSVILLE BASEBALL CLUB TO SYD POLLACK [*sic*] GENERAL MANAGER INDIANAPOLIS CLOWNS BASEBALL CLUB CARE SHERMAN HOTEL CHICAGO AND ALSO TO 16 PARK AVE BOX 64 TARRYTOWN NY. QUOTE. THIS WILL ACKNOWLEDGE AND ACCEPT THE PROPO-SITION CONTAINED IN YOUR LETTER OF MAY 27 1952, AND CONFIRMED IN OUR TELE-PHONE CONVERSATION OF THIS DATE, WHEREIN YOU AGREED TO RELEASE THE CONTRACT OF PLAYER HENRY AARON TO THE EVANSVILLE BASEBALL CLUB OF THE THREE-I LEAGUE FOR THE SUM OF $2500.00 PAYABLE TO THE INDIANAPOLIS CLOWNS UPON THE PROMULGATION OF THE PLAYERS CONTRACT BY THE NATIONAL ASSOCIA-TION OF PROFESSIONAL BASEBALL LEAGUES AND A FURTHER SUM OF 7500.00 PAY-ABLE TO THE INDIANAPOLIS CLOWNS IF WE RETAIN THE PLAYER UNDER CONTRACT THIRTY OR MORE DAYS AFTER HE REPORTS TO THE CLUB. WE ARE MAILING AN EVANS-VILLE CLUB CONTRACT TO YOU IMMEDIATELY FOR PLAYER HENRY AARON CALLING FOR A SALARY OF $350.00 PER MONTH. PLAYER TO BE DELIVERED JUNE 11, 1952. UNQUOTE. JOHN W. MULLEN SECY, EVANSVILLE BASEBALL CLUB.[6]

Aaron continued to excel for the Clowns. Official league statistics released during June revealed that Aaron was leading the league, hitting .427 with his closest rival, Jose Colas from Memphis, hitting .425. Playing in 26 games, Aaron also led the league in doubles with 8, 5 home runs, 41 hits, and 33 RBIs.[7] Without a doubt, he would be a selection to the East-West all-star classic this year.

Aaron's manager, Buster Haywood, feared that Aaron would not be with the team much longer. Haywood expressed, "Aaron will develop into one of the great shortstops of base-ball within a couple of years." Haywood maintained, "All Aaron needs is to learn more about the little tricks at second base, and these will come while working with Ray Neil."[8]

On June 10 Henry "Hank" Aaron reported to the Eau Claire (Wisconsin) club. Mean-while, former Black Baron outfielder and now Army private Willie Mays reported to Fort Eustis in Virginia, transferring from the induction center at Camp Kilmer in New Jersey.[9] The Clowns struggled without Aaron, winning 18 of 34 games in the second half before meeting Birmingham for the league title.

The dozen-game world series started with whistle stops in Memphis (1), Tennessee; Little Rock (2) and Hot Springs (3), Arkansas; Nashville (4), Tennessee; Welch (5) and Bluefield (6), West Virginia; Newport News (7) and Norfolk (8), Virginia; Columbus (9) and Atlanta (rained-out), Georgia; Mobile (10), Alabama; Biloxi (11), Mississippi; and finally New Orleans (12), Louisiana. The Clowns were triumphant, taking 7 out of 12 games behind the pitching of Frank Carswell and Jim "Fireball" Cohen and the timely hitting of Hank Aaron.

Yes, Hank Aaron! After Aaron finished the season with the Northern League's Eau Claire team, hitting .336, with nine homers in 87 games, he rejoined the Clowns for the world series. Aaron belted five home runs and hit for a .402 average against the Barons. However, Willie Mays did not return to help the Barons challenge for the title. Despite Dr. J. B. Martin's claim that the major leagues were "organized," the big boys were just as fragmented as the Negro Leagues in terms of contractual commitment and obligation.

RACE RELATIONS

The Milwaukee Brewers were in Bartow, Florida, for 1952 spring training with James Buster "Bus" Clarkson. Clarkson had appeared in two East-West games, one in 1940 with the Newark Eagles and later in 1949 with the Philadelphia Stars. The power-hitting right-hander had played with the Brewers of the American Association since 1950. Bus hit .343 in 1951 and became one of Milwaukee's favorite Brewers.

This year, when the team arrived at Municipal Stadium, they found a sign saying "For Whites Only." Manager Jack Tighe of the Buffalo Bison, from the International League, voiced his apologies: "I'm sorry. You white boys can dress here but the Negro must use the National Guard Armory across the street."

In unison, the Brewers shouted, "We dress where Jim dresses. If he goes to the armory, we go too!" And the Brewers did, leaving Tighe scratching his head.

From spring training to the subway series found Joe Black, former East-West pitcher, now with the Brooklyn Dodgers, en route to the Polo Grounds being placed under protection by 20 detectives. The former Morgan State College star, by way of the Baltimore Elite Giants, had received threatening letters in Boston. An anonymous writer threatened to kill Black if he took the mound during the series between the Dodgers and the Giants. Three detectives guarded Black while he dressed, but none were visible when Black warmed up in the bullpen.[10] Black would be voted National League Rookie of the Year this season.

ALL-STAR REVIEW

Just before the pitcher's 46th birthday, Yankee manager Casey Stengel named a rejuvenated Satchel Paige, now with the St. Louis Browns, to his first major league all-star team. Paige earned the honor by pitching for the hapless Browns, who had marinated in last place each year. So far this season, he had won six games and had saved nine more, while pitching brilliantly in several more games. In one night game in Washington DC, he pitched 7 scoreless innings to win the game in the 17th inning. Then he hurled 10 more scoreless relief innings in another game through the 18th in a tie game called due to curfew. And, finally, in a Cleveland game in June, he pitched 10 more scoreless innings in relief and ultimately tired to lose in the 19th in the wee hours of the morning.

Paige did not appear in this year's contest at Philadelphia's Shibe Park. A dampish, rain-soaked crowd of only 32,785 fans saw Jackie Robinson hit his first all-star home run in the first frame. Campanella got the collar once again in his only at bat. Doby played center field but was not credited with an official at bat. Meanwhile, White Sox left fielder Minnie Minoso hit a double in his only time at the plate. Robinson's home run off Yankee hurler Vic Raschi was almost void as the game was canceled after five innings of play, with the National League winning, 3–2.

Chicago Short Fielder Leads in Player Poll

Source: *Chicago Defender,* 9 August 1952

With the deadline for voting at midnight on Wednesday of this week, the East versus West game poll lead is still held by Larry Raines, popular shortstop of the Chicago American Giants who has a total of 24,583 voters.

Several players who had been far up in the voting for positions on either nine have fallen back. However, the consensus is that those currently leading the vote for various positions will be in front after the final tabulation.

The 20th annual all-star game will be played at Comiskey Park here on Sunday afternoon, Aug. 17. Game time is 3 o'clock. In the event of rain, the clubs will play under the lights on Monday, Aug. 18.

Tickets are on sale at the Hotel Grand, 51st and South Parkway, and at the Negro American League headquarters, 412 E. 47th St. Dr. J. B. Martin, president of the league, is chairman of the game committee.

EAST TRAILS WEST

The East trails the West in games won, 11 to 8. Last year, the East came through with a 3 to 1 victory for their first win in three years. Buster Haywood, Indianapolis manager and backstop, will be back again this year as manager of the East team.

Winfield S. Welch, manager of the American Giants last year and who piloted them to both halves of the Western division championship, also manager of the 1951 West nine, has been named manager of the 1952 West team by Dr. J. B. Martin. Welch is at present scout for the St. Louis Browns.

From the present count of votes, Henry Merchant, fleet-footed veteran outfielder of the Indianapolis Clowns; Paul Hardy, Chicago catcher; John Williams, veteran Chicago pitcher; Jimmy Valentine, Memphis infielder; Willie Gaines, Philadelphia hurler; Hiram Gaston, Birmingham pitcher; Jim Tugerson, Indianapolis moundsman; Rube Williams, Indianapolis Clowns third baseman; Frank Russell, Birmingham outfielder; and a few others will not be on either team.

They have been passed in the voting, which seems that the fans have a definite idea as to who will be in the classic this year.

Unless some Kansas Citians get really behind Long Tom Cooper, the all around player the Monarchs who plays every position, the West will have but one man who was in the 1951 lineup. He will be Gilbert Varona of the Memphis Red Sox, but most likely will not start the game. He plays first base.

Editor's note: Players listed in the official scorebook for the 1952 classic, courtesy of former Monarch Duke Henderson, are as follows:

EAST LINE-UP
2, Eddie Brooks, 2b, .278, Birmingham
12, Fate Sims, 3b, .301, Philadelphia
14, Henry Kimbro, cf, .338, Birmingham
15, Jimmy Jones, lf, .359, Philadelphia
20, Jim Wilkes, rf, .325, Indianapolis

55. The Kansas City Monarchs had more participants in the East-West game than any other league team. Some of the Monarchs included (from left to right) Chico Renfroe (selected in 1946 but did not play), Joe Greene (1940–42), Connie Johnson (1940 and 1950), John Scott (1946), and Willard Brown (1936–49). Courtesy of NoirTech Research, Inc.

19, Wesley Dennis, 1b, .306, Birmingham

2, Carl Dent, ss, .247, Philadelphia

27, Al "Buster" Haywood, c, .206, Indianapolis

23 Ted Richardson (12-5), p, .210, Indianapolis, southpaw

Extra Players

8, Otha Bailey (.223), catcher, Birmingham Black Barons

18 Henry [Frank] "Groundhog" Thompson (10-4), pitcher, Birmingham Black Barons

37, Henry Merchant (.281), outfielder, Indianapolis Clowns

30, Jim Cohen (8-5), pitcher, Indianapolis Clowns

14, Wilmer Harris (9-5), pitcher, Philadelphia Stars

16, Joseph Chesnut (6-7), pitcher, Philadelphia Stars

WEST LINE-UP

4, Lawrence Raines, ss, .293, Chicago

10, Henry Baylis, 2b, .250, Kansas City

18, Sherman Watrous, cf, .328 Memphis

25, Duke Henderson, rf, .276, Kansas City

1, Felix McLaurin, lf, .378, Chicago

29, Roy Williams, 3b, .331, Chicago

56. Instrumental in getting Major League Baseball to recognize Negro League talent were writers Sam Lacy (left) and Wendell Smith (right), shown here with former Memphis Red Sox pitcher Dan Bankhead (center) en route to the Brooklyn Dodgers training camp in Florida. Courtesy of Sam Lacy.

19, Willie Patterson, 1b, .272, Chicago
20, Ike "Stonewall" Jackson, c, .291, Kansas City
18, Dick Phillips (8-4), p, .300, Kansas City, Southpaw

Extra Players
24, John Jackson (6-4), pitcher, Kansas City Monarchs
18, William Beverly (7-7), pitcher, Chicago American Giants
8, Gilbert Varona (.220), first base, Memphis Red Sox
10, Manuel Valdez (.240), infielder, Memphis Red Sox
17, Sam "Buddy" Woods (11-7), pitcher, Memphis Red Sox
15, Isiah Harris (6-6), pitcher, Memphis Red Sox

All Baseball Turns Eyes to East-West Tilt

Source: *Chicago Defender,* 16 August 1952

Some 25,000 persons a good number of whom will be major league scouts will crowd Comiskey Park Sunday, to witness the 20th playing of the East-West classic.

Game time is 3 p.m. but between 1:30 and the time the first ball is thrown out, there will be band music, square dancing and the crowning of "Miss East-West" from among a bevy of beauties.

This year's game promises to be one of the most hotly contested, with the Eastern league, who triumphed, 3–1, last year trying to whittle down the 11-8 margin the West holds in victories.

Aside from the color and fast moving baseball the classic provides, it has come to be the "Debut" before many fans of players destined for fans in the major leagues.

Some of the most illustrious graduates of the annual classic are Satchel Paige, Larry Doby and Dan Bankhead, who moved directly from the Negro leagues to the majors. No less outstanding have been the men who went into triple A ball and lower classifications before crashing the big time.

They include Jackie Robinson, Orestes Minoso, Monte Irvin, Sam Jethroe, Roy Campanella, Henry Thompson, Willie Mays, Harry Simpson, George Crowe, Luis Marquez, and Luke Easter.

Scores of others who are making their mark in the minor leagues today are also veterans of the classic.

The first East-West game was played in 1933 at Comiskey Park, as part of the World's Fair fanfare. The idea was originated by the late Gus Greenlee and the classic drew the top stars of the Negro American and Negro National leagues.

Willie Foster, brother of the late Rube Foster, buried the West to an 11–7 victory and set the pattern for future games which have seen laurels seesaw between hurlers such as Paige and Dave Hoskins and Bankhead, and sluggers such as Campanella, Easter and Doby.

West Jars East in Negro Game

Takes 20th All-Star Contest, 7–3

Source: *Chicago Tribune*, 18 August 1952

East met West yesterday in the 20th annual Negro American league all-star game with dire results for the East before 18,279 in Comiskey Park. The West hopped on Frank (Groundhog) Thompson for six runs in the third inning to roll to a 7 to 3 victory, their 12th [13th] in the series. The East won last year, 3 to 1.

The six run blast included doubles by Sherm Watrous and Henry Bayliss [Baylis] and singles by Duke Henderson and Willie Patterson. The damage was heightened by three East errors and a wild pitch by Thompson.

BOBBY, MARANIE REIGN

The pre-game ceremonies were a royal affair, with Miss Bobby Holman, 18, of Melrose High school, Memphis, reigning as queen for the East and Miss Maranie Mitchell, 21 year old Provident hospital nurse of Chicago, ruling for the West.

Alderman Archibald J. Carey of the 3d ward threw out the first ball and Billy Niesen, president of the Chicago Old Timers, presented a plaque of [to] Jack Marshall, coach of the Chicago American Giants and a member of the first West team in 1933.

OLYMPIC STARS PRESENT

Among the guests were Mabel Landry of DePaul University and Barbara Jones of St. Elizabeth High School, members of the United States Olympic track team in the Helsinki games. Also present were Abe Saperstein, Goose Tatum, and Marquis [Marques] Haynes of the Globe Trotters who left last night for the Orient to rejoin the Trotters on their basketball tour. Branch Rickey, Jr. of the Pittsburgh Pirates was on hand, seeking talent.

The East yesterday was managed by Buster Haywood of the Indianapolis Clowns. The West was under the guidance of Winfield Welch, now a scout for the St. Louis Browns. Welch managed the Chicago American Giants last year.

Third Frame Gives West 7–3 Win over East

18,279 See East-West Ball Game

Bad 3rd Inning Gives West 12th Win in 20th Year

by Johnny Johnson, the *Call*'s Sports Editor

Source: *Kansas City Call*, 22 August 1952

Chicago— Disaster struck the East All-Stars Sunday afternoon in the third inning of the 20th annual East-West all-star game and the West Stars piled up six big runs in that frame and went on to win the 20th annual renewal of this Negro American League sponsored contest, 7–3, before a reported 18,279 spectators at Comiskey Park.

WEST LEADS 12-8

The triumph by the West reversed the 1–3 trimming they received here at the same park last year and ran the West's total victories in the series to 12 wins against 8 defeats.

While the crowd was small compared to those of the earlier games, the sponsors were generally elated at the turnout which appeared dwarfed in the big 50,000 capacity stadium. The entire second balcony was as bare as Mother Hubbard's cupboard and there was room for plenty of bones anywhere in the lower grandstand.

Among the celebrities present and announced were Branch Rickey, Jr., of the Pittsburgh Pirates organization; Abe Saperstein, owner of the Harlem Globetrotters and his two star performers, Marques Haynes and Reece "Goose" Tatum, all of whom had delayed their slated Sunday morning flight to the Orient for cage games there to see this 20-year-old clash in which Goose Tatum once played in.

TWO OLYMPIC STARS

Other announced guests included two women Olympic stars Mable Landry and Barbara Jones. Miss Landry, 18, a DePaul University student won honors recently at Helsinki, Finland, by broad jumping 18 feet and 4 3/8 inches to win for the U.S. team. Miss Jones, 15, a student at Chicago's St. Elizabeth High School won Olympic honors as a member of the U.S. 400-meter relay which set a new Olympic record in that event at Helsinki.

Russ Cowans, sports editor of the Chicago Defender set the stage for the afternoon by introducing the personalities that participated in the opening events. Among these were two queens, Miss East and Miss West. The former was Miss Bobbi Holman, 18, a Memphis, Tenn., Melrose High School Senior. The latter Miss West, was Miss Maranie Mitchell, 19, a graduate nurse at Provident hospital, Chicago.

ALDERMAN CAREY PITCHES

Archibald J. Archie Carey, Chicago minister and city Alderman, threw the first ball to get the game underway.

18,279 See Annual Chi Contest

by William G. Nunn

Source: *Pittsburgh Courier*, 23 August 1952

The East's "pony infield" blew wide open here Sunday in the third inning and handed the West a 7–3 Christmas gift, as some 18,279 fans saw the twentieth running of the annual East-West game.

The victory gave the West a 12-8 budge over the series which started back in 1933, when Gus Greenlee, who died last month, first conceived the idea. In the intervening years the classic grew until it became the blue ribbon event of the sports world . . . spawning such all-time greats as Josh Gibson, Turkey Stearns [Stearnes], Oscar Charleston, Satchel Paige, "Mule" Suttles, Roy Campanella, Jackie Robinson, Monte Irvin, George Scales, Martin Dihigo, "Rev" Cannady, Larry Doby, Buck Leonard, "Slim" Jones, Frank Duncan, Willie Wells, Ray Dandridge, "Cool Papa" Bell, "Double Duty" Radcliffe, Larry Brown, Bill Foster and countless others.

In the years, the attraction grew from a spectacle of 7,300 fans in 1933, to the point where more than 52,000 people saw the game in 1944.

Sunday's performance with Dr. J. S. Martin in the driver's seat, saw some of the color and glamour of former years, initiated as the game became once again "the thing."

As to the game itself highlights of the contest was the four-inning no hit pitching stint served up for the East by Ted Richardson former Southern University star, and sterling southpaw now with the Indianapolis Clowns.

But Richardson's work went naught as the East infield "cracked up" in the third inning, in that frame, with Frank Thompson of Birmingham on the mound, three errors, a wild pitch and an attempted sacrifice which saw the ball thrown all over the lot, emptied with singles by Duke Henderson of Kansas City and Willie Patterson of Chicago . . . and doubles by Sherman Watrous of Memphis and Henry Baylis, Kansas City infielder, resulted in six big runs. That was all the scoring for the West . . . but it was enough!

The West scored their first run in the first inning on Henderson's single and McLaurin's [rbi] double.

The East tied up in the second when Otha Bailey's double sent Ted Washington who had singled across the plate.

The East's second run came in the fourth on Dennis' double to left center and Kimbro's sharp single went to third on an error by Raines at short stop, who threw the ball away after making a great stop and scored as Whitting [Whittington] rapped into a double play.

West Defeats East

Winners Mix Hits with Errors to Gain the Verdict

by Fay Young

Source: *Chicago Defender*, 23 August 1952

The West hung up a 7 to 3 victory over the East all-stars in the 20th annual East versus West baseball classic before 18,279 fans, including Branch Rickey, Jr. who was doing some scouting, last Sunday at Chicago's Comiskey Park.

The West, which included players from the Memphis Red Sox, the Chicago American Giants and the Kansas City Monarchs, blasted Frank "Groundhog" Thompson, of the Birmingham Barons, from the mound in the third frame. The Westerners were helped by three errors, a wild pitch and a sacrifice which went astray as far as the defense was concerned.

The West now leads in the series, 12 games to 8. Last year the East won, 3 to 1. Last year Winfield S. Welch, then manager of the Chicago American Giants, managed the West. This year, Welch, who is a scout for the St. Louis Browns, piloted the winning team.

Jack Marshall, member of the 1933 West Squad in the first East versus West game, was presented with a plaque from the Old Time Baseball Players association, William Nelson, president.

Dave Malarcher, real estate dealer and former manager of the American Giants, who managed the West team back in 1933, made the presentation. Another old timer, Oscar Charleston, member of the East teams of 1933 and 1934 and the West nine in 1935 and who has managed several of the East teams in the series, was coach for the East, Charleston, is manager of the Philadelphia Stars.

Pre-game ceremonies, with Russ Cowans, sports editor of the Chicago Defender, acting as toastmaster, included the presentation of Miss Bobbie Holman, Memphis, Tenn., high school student who was the East queen; Miss Maranie Mitchell, charming nurse of Provident hospital, Chicago, who was queen for the West; the Misses Barbara Jones and Mabel Landry, both members of the 1952 United States women's Olympic team and also of the Chicago CYO women's track team which won the junior AAU meet this summer; Abe Saperstein, owner-coach of the famous Harlem Globetrotters basketball team, which left Sunday night for the Orient and the Far East, and his two stars, Captain Marques Haynes and the one and only Reece "Goose" Tatum, and the marching and dancing units from the Chicago fifth district police station, Kenzie Blueitt, acting captain. Music was furnished by Omar Crittenden's K. of P. band.

Manager Welch crossed up the East, made up of players from the Birmingham Black Barons, The Indianapolis Clowns and the Philadelphia Stars, by starting Richard Phillips, the portside flinger of the Monarchs. Three hits, one run was allowed by Phillips in the three innings he worked.

Incidentally, Phillips got credit for the victory because with the score tied, one all, his mates chased "Groundhog" from the mound when the home third was over, with the West out in front, 7 to 1.

However, some fans debated this question—all for naught. John Jackson batted for Phillips in the third of the inning was gone, thus when Phillips left the game, his team was out in front.

The third inning was a blip. Three errors a wild pitch an attempted sacrifice, all were mixed up with singles by Duke Henderson of Kansas City, and Willie Patterson of Chicago, and two-base wallops by Sherman Watrous of the Memphis Red Sox, who has 17 home runs to his credit this season, and by Henry Baylis, the Kansas City infielder.

Before Ted Richardson, left-hander of the Indianapolis Clowns with a 12-5 record this summer could be waved in from the bullpen, six runs were across the plate, and the "Groundhog" on his way out of the game.

Ted had something on the ball. He fanned Ike Jackson, Kansas City catcher, and Manuel Valdez, Memphis second sacker. John Jackson batted for Phillips and walked. Lawrence Raines walked but Duke Henderson tapped to Richardson and was tossed out to Wesley Dennis, Birmingham first sacker.

THAT ENDED THE WEST'S SCORING

The first West run came in the opening frame. Henderson singled with one tucked away. Felix McLaurin of Chicago doubled sending Henderson home with the first run of the game.

The East tied it up in their half of the second. Ted Washington singled and Otha Bailey doubled, sending Ted home. In the fourth, off Kansas City's John Jackson, Dennis hit for two bases and scored on the Birmingham veteran, Henry Kimbro's sharp single to center.

The last East run came in the eighth. Dennis singled to left and went to second when Raines after making a great stop, threw over Gilbert Varona's heat at first. Kimbro walked.

[Don] Whitting [Whittington], the Philadelphia high school rookie from the Philadelphia Stars, hit into a double play, Baylis to Valdez to Varona of the Memphis Red Sox.

AUGUST 17, 1952, CHICAGO, IL

EAST	AB	R	H	D	T	HR	BI	E	TAVG	TSLG
Jimmy Wilkes (Indianapolis Clowns), 1b	3	0	0	0	0	0	0	0		
Henry "Speed" Merchant (Indianapolis Clowns), rf	2	0	0	0	0	0	0	1		
Jimmy Jones (Philadelphia Stars), rf	1	0	0	0	0	0	0	0		
Eddie Brooks (Birmingham Black Barons), 2b	4	0	1	0	0	0	0	0		
Doc Dennis (Birmingham Black Barons), 1b	4	2	2	1	0	0	0	0		
Henry Kimbro (Birmingham Black Barons), cf	3	0	1	0	0	0	1	1		
Don Whittington (Philadelphia Stars), 3b	3	0	0	0	0	0	0	1		
Ted Washington (Philadelphia Stars), ss	4	1	1	0	0	0	0	1		
Otha Bailey (Birmingham Black Barons), c	4	0	1	1	0	0	1	0		
"Groundhog" Thompson (Birmingham Black Barons), p	1	0	0	0	0	0	0	0		
Ted Richardson (Indianapolis Clowns), p	1	0	0	0	0	0	0	0		
a) Wilmer Harris (Philadelphia Stars), ph-p	2	0	1	0	0	0	0	0		
Team Totals, Average & Slugging Pct.	32	3	7	2	0	0	2	4	.219	.281

a) Batting for Richardson in the 7th inning.

WEST	AB	R	H	D	T	HR	BI	E	TAVG	TSLG
Larry Raines (Chicago American Giants), ss	3	1	0	0	0	0	0	1		
Duke Henderson (Kansas City Monarchs), cf	4	2	2	0	0	0	1	0		
Felix McLaurin (Chicago American Giants), lf	1	0	1	1	0	0	2	0		
b) Winn "Pop" Durham (Chicago American Giants), pr-lf	2	1	0	0	0	0	0	0		
Sherman Watrous (Memphis Red Sox), rf	4	1	1	1	0	0	0	0		
Willie Patterson (Chicago American Giants), 1b	4	1	2	0	0	0	2	0		
Gilbert Varona (Memphis Red Sox), 1b	0	0	0	0	0	0	1	0		
Hank Baylis (Kansas City Monarchs), 3b	4	1	1	1	0	0	2	0		
Ike Jackson (Kansas City Monarchs), c	4	0	2	0	0	0	0	0		
Manuel Valdez (Memphis Red Sox), 2b	2	0	0	0	0	0	0	0		
Dick Phillips (Kansas City Monarchs), p	1	0	0	0	0	0	0	0		
John Jackson (Kansas City Monarchs), p	1	0	0	0	0	0	0	0		
Bill "Fireball" Beverly (Chicago American Giants), p	1	0	0	0	0	0	0	0		
Team Totals, Average & Slugging Pct.	31	7	9	3	0	0	8	1	.290	.387

b) Ran for McLaurin in 3rd.

East	010	100	010-3
West	106	000	000-7

PITCHER/TEAM	GS	IP	H	R	ER	K	BB	WP	HB	W	L	SV
Thompson/BBB	1	2	7	7	3	1	2	1	0	0	1	0
Richardson/IC		4	0	0	0	2	2	0	0	0	0	0
Harris/PS		3	2	0	0	0	1	0	0	0	0	0
Phillips/KCM	1	3	3	1	1	1	2	0	0	1	0	0
J. Jackson/KCM		3	2	1	1	2	2	0	0	0	0	0
Beverly/CAG		3	2	1	1	1	1	0	1	0	0	1

BB—Jackson, Raines, Kimbro

DP—Baylis to Valdez to Patterson; Brooks to Dennis

LOB—East 7, West 6

PB—Bailey (2), I. Jackson

SB—Kimbro, Raines

East—Buster Haywood (Mgr.), Coach Oscar Charleston

West—Winfield S. Welch (Mgr.), Coach Jack Marshall

Umpires—Simon Lewis, T. H. Jefferson, R. W. Garrett, Simmie Gardner, Wallace Williams, Andrew Summers.

Attendance—18,279   Paid—14,122   Time—2:15

1953

Willie Mae "Big Mama" Thornton's song "Hound Dog" remains number one on *Billboard*'s R&B charts for seven weeks. Elvis Presley later popularizes her song with his rendition.

James Baldwin writes his signature novel, *Go Tell It On The Mountain*.

Milk now costs about a quarter more, and a 10-pound bag of potatoes and a slab of bacon about 50 cents more than they did in 1933. A loaf of bread is only a nickel plus a dime.

The National Leaguers win their fourth straight all-star game, 5–1, in Cincinnati's Crosley Field.

Ted Williams rejoins the Boston Red Sox following military service in Korea.

A sign of changing times in baseball, the Boston Braves move to Milwaukee. This is the first time in 50 years a Major League Baseball franchise has changed cities. The last time was when the Baltimore Orioles moved to New York and became the Highlanders—later known as the Yankees.

A ballplayers' union—the Major League Players Association—is established.

THE FINAL FRONTIER

A demarcation to decide when to end the history of black baseball's most celebrated event involved much thought. Although Jackie Robinson broke the color barrier in 1947, the Negro Leagues still produced some top-quality athletes in the early 1950s. Unlike the Willard Browns, the Buck Leonards, the Cool Papa Bells, the Willie Wells, and others who were past their productive years when they received their major league invitations, the demise of the black leagues became predictable, as the younger talented blacks were soon signed into the former white leagues. By the mid-1950s, the leagues went from showtime to burlesque. They had become a circus, with the Indianapolis Clowns leading the way.

The span beginning in 1933 and ending in 1953, alpha to omega, Genesis to Revelation, signals the most celebrated period in black baseball history. After 21 years, the East-West games concluded by showcasing the last player to appear first in a Negro League All-Star Game and later a Major League All-Star Game—Ernie Banks. Although destined for the Hall of Fame, Banks was not the only star of the '53 season. Another outstanding player was a middle infielder named Ray Neil, of the Indianapolis Clowns, who hit .397 this year. Another top major league prospect was Ernie "Schoolboy" Johnson, a slender outfielder for the Kansas City Monarchs, who led the league with 11 home runs while hitting a respectable .296. The 24-year-old Johnson starred several years in the minor leagues before hanging up his spikes. Meanwhile Neil, at age 32, was considered by many scouts to be too old and temperamental to accept a new challenge. Before concluding the season with the

Chicago Cubs, Ernie Banks batted .347 in the black leagues, to finish third in the batting race and second in the league, with 16 doubles.

Probably the most curious occurrence of the 1953 season was the debut of a woman named Toni Stone, who played second base, behind Neil, for the Indianapolis Clowns. In 50 games, Stone hit safely 18 times in 74 at bats, for a .243 batting average. Except for one double, all of her hits were singles. She stole one base and drove in three runs. Toni, short for "Tom Boy," played the next year with the Kansas City Monarchs under manager Buck O'Neil before her departure from black baseball.

Besides Banks, and future Hall of Famers Jackie Robinson, Roy Campanella, Larry Doby, Monte Irvin, and Satchel Paige, several East-West all-stars would later grace major league rosters. The list includes the following players:

Winn "Pop" Durham (Baltimore Orioles, debut at age 22)
Pancho Herrera (Philadelphia Phillies, 24)
Willie Smith (Detroit Tigers, 24)
Junior Gilliam (Brooklyn Dodgers, 24)
Sweet Lou Johnson (Chicago Cubs, 25)
Bob Boyd (Chicago White Sox, 25)
Charlie White (Milwaukee Braves, 25)
Minnie Minoso (Cleveland Indians, 26)
Henry "Pistol" Mason (Philadelphia Phillies, 27)
J. C. Hartman (Houston Colt .45s, 28)
Joe Black (Brooklyn Dodgers, 28)
George Crowe (Boston Braves, 29)

Connie Johnson (Chicago White Sox, 30)

Artie Wilson (New York Giants, 30)

John Kennedy (Washington Senators, 30)

Sam Hairston (Chicago White Sox, 31)

Sam Jethroe (Boston Braves, 32)

Jay Heard (Baltimore Orioles, 34)

Willard Brown (St. Louis Browns, 34)

Quincy Trouppe (Cleveland Indians, 39)

Special mention should be given to Memphis Red Sox player and future country and western singer Charlie Pride, who played right field and pitched in the 1956 and 1958 East-West games. Also noteworthy is the 1955 West squad's left fielder Davey Whitney from the Kansas City Monarchs, who has enjoyed tremendous success as a basketball coach at Mississippi's Alcorn State University, earning his 400th career victory in 1997. Whitney had the privilege of playing in 1953 with Satchel Paige, who was returning from a hitch with the St. Louis Browns. Paige pitched three hitless innings and struck out two as the starting hurler. And finally of note is an appearance by the fanciful Harlem Globetrotter Nat "Sweetwater" Clifton, who represented the Detroit Clowns at first base in the 1958 contest. Fans may note that the recently retired Jackie Robinson threw out the first pitch at the 1958 East-West game.

The last league-sanctioned East-West All-Star Game was played in Yankee Stadium on

58. Pictured here are Reece "Goose" Tatum, who appeared in the 1947 all-star contest, and Prince Joe Henry, who played in the 1958 game. Henry, of the Detroit Clowns, an outstanding third baseman, often donned a tailed tuxedo and a raggedy top hat to entertain the fans. Courtesy of Joe Henry.

August 28, 1961, before 7,245 fans. The East started 22-year-old Raleigh Tiger Pete Gilliam, a towering six-foot-five-inch flame thrower, with a reported 10-5 won-lost record. Other Tiger hurlers, James Drummond and Eugene Holmes, also got some game action.

The star performer was none other than 55-year-old Satchel Paige, who gave up only an infield hit to Fred Green, of the Tigers, in three innings of work. Paige was credited with two strikeouts in facing 10 batters. Dick Hemphill and Don Poindexter pitched no-hit ball from the fourth inning. Fittingly, the most recognizable name in black baseball, Satchel Paige, was named MVP of the last official Negro League all-star game.

The impact of Negro League players in the National League was immediate. After the Rookie of the Year Award (now also called the Jackie Robinson Award) was established in 1947, former Negro Leaguers won six of the next seven awards in the National League. Winners included Robinson (from the Kansas City Monarchs), Don Newcombe (Newark Eagles), Sam Jethroe (Cleveland Buckeyes), Willie Mays (Birmingham Black Barons), Joe Black (Baltimore Elite Giants), and Junior Gilliam (Baltimore Elite Giants). Furthermore, 9 of the 11 men voted the National League's Most Valuable Player between 1949 and 1959 were former Negro Leaguers. Award recipients included Robinson in 1949, followed by Roy Campanella in 1951, 1953, and 1955; Willie Mays in 1954; Don Newcombe in 1956 (also the Cy Young winner); Hank Aaron in 1957; and Ernie Banks repeating in 1958 and 1959. It would be 14 years before the American League would crown its first black Most Valuable Player, ex-Monarch outfielder Elston Howard, in 1963. The following year, 1964, the American League would name its first minority Rookie of the Year, Cuban Tony Oliva.

For the next 40 years after the melting pot was set on the stove, nonwhite ballplayers won 18 percent of the Cy Young Awards, 38 percent of the Most Valuable Players, 25 percent of the ERA titles, 39 percent of the home run titles, and 48 percent of the league batting crowns. These percentages are even more impressive when one realizes that nonwhite players comprised less than 25 percent of the baseball population during that period.

JACKIE'S JOURNEY

In 1953, six years after Jackie broke the color barrier, a record 30 black players reported to spring training with major league teams. These trailblazers included Larry Doby, Luke Easter, Harry Simpson, Al Smith, Dave Pope, Sam Jones, Dave Hoskins, and Jose Santiago for the Cleveland Indians; Monte Irvin, Henry Thompson, Ray Noble, Ruben Gomez, and Bill White for the New York Giants; Sam Jethroe, Jim Pendleton, Luis Marquez, George Crowe, and Billy Bruton for the Boston Braves; Angel Scull and Juan Visturer for the Washington Senators; Gene Baker for the Chicago Cubs; Satchel Paige for the St. Louis Browns; and Sandy Amoros, Roy Campanella, Joe Black, Junior Gilliam, and Jackie Robinson for the Brooklyn Dodgers. Latin Americans Scull and Visturer never made a major league club.

In late September FBI agents and local city police were assigned to guard Jackie Robinson while the Dodgers played in St. Louis, Missouri. After receiving several threatening death notices, Robinson was benched for the September 16 game against the Cardinals. One penciled handwritten note read, "Remember what happened to Arnold Schuster in Brooklyn in 1952." (Schuster was fatally shot after he snitched to police where they could find Willie "The Actor" Sutton, a bank robber.) The note continued, "Well Wednesday night, September 16, you die. No use crying for the cops you'll be executed gangland style in Busch Stadium." The letter was signed, "Dodger hater."[1]

Robinson returned to the lineup the next day against the St. Louis Cardinals. If he had any apprehension about playing, it didn't show. Jackie slammed out two hits in four times at bat, leading the Dodgers to a 4–3 victory.

Earlier in the season, the Cardinals had signed their first black ballplayer. Veteran Negro League catcher Quincy Trouppe, scouting for the Cardinals, signed Leonard Tucker from nearby Mounds, Illinois, to a contract with the Cardinals' Fresno farm club. The 23-year-old outfielder was a student at Fresno State College and could only play home games during the school term. Cardinals owner Augie Busch bragged, "Baseball is supposed to be the great American national game and there is no room for discrimination in it."[2] Tucker never made the big league club. The following year, African-Americans Tom Alston, a first baseman, and Brooks Lawrence, a pitcher, would become Cardinals. In 1958, 11 years after Jackie Robinson's debut with the Dodgers, and 5 years after the death threat, perennial gold glove winner Curt Flood would become the Cards' first regular black player. Much like Robinson, Flood was an activist and would later be known for his pioneering efforts in creating free agency contracts.

Another barrier was broken when Don Eaddy, a third baseman for the University of Michigan Wolverines, became the first African-American to play in the college world series. The Wolverines defeated the tourney favorite University of Texas to capture their first collegiate baseball title.[3]

LEAGUE BUSINESS

At the close of the '53 season, Negro American League president Dr. J. B. Martin announced: "For the NAL, 1953 was its best year in the past six years. Although we operated with only four clubs, every club made money." Martin optimistically added, "Several cities are seeking franchises in the NAL, and I predict that we will operate with six teams in 1954."[4] In 1950 the NAL had 10 teams, down to 8 teams from the following year. In 1952 the league had only 6 teams, with only 4 teams scheduled to play during the 1953 season.

The black circuit comprised the champion Kansas City Monarchs, who had winning streaks of 14 and 16 games during the season. They were followed in the standings by the Indianapolis Clowns, the Memphis Red Sox, and the Birmingham Black Barons. Chicago, St. Louis, and Detroit were among several cities seeking franchises for the upcoming year. In 1954 franchises were granted to the Detroit Stars and the Louisville Clippers, with both teams finishing ahead of the cellar-dwelling Monarchs, who had been stripped of their top talent by major league clubs. Ironically, the Monarchs, who finished 20 1/2 games ahead of the competition in 1953, finished an identical 20 1/2 games behind the league champion Indianapolis Clowns in 1954.

ALL-STAR REVIEW

Before a capacity crowd of 30,846 fans at Crosley Field in Cincinnati, the National Leaguers, with Robinson and Campanella, beat the American Leaguers, with Paige, Doby, and Minoso, 5–1. Doby was zero for one, while Minoso collected two hits in two at bats, one a double. The biggest story of the game was the appearance of 47-year old Satchel Paige. The senior hurler was treated harshly as the National Leaguers rocked him for two singles and a double for two earned runs in one inning of pitching. One of the hits was by Campanella, his first hit in 17 all-star attempts. Meanwhile, Robinson failed to deliver a hit in his solo pinch-hitting role.

RACE RELATIONS

Early in the season, with the Cleveland Indians in Daytona Beach, Florida, general manager Hank Greenberg issued a statement saying, "In the future if our Negro boys are not accepted there will be no game."[5] Greenberg's edict was in reference to officials who had barred Billy Harrell and Brooks Lawrence, who were playing for their Reading farm club, from a game on March 28 in Winter Garden, Florida.

Farther west, on April 6, the Cotton States League threatened to discharge the Hot Springs (Arkansas) Bathers from the league for listing two former Indianapolis Clown pitchers, brothers Jim and Leander Tugerson (Leander had pitched a no-hitter in 1951) on their roster. Leander was scheduled to pitch a home game against the Jackson, Mississippi, team, on May 21, when league president Al Haraway (from Helena, Arkansas) declared that Hot Springs had "violated an agreement reached in Greenville, Mississippi, on April 14 banning the use of Negro players." Haraway ordered the league umpires to forfeit every Hot Springs game that the Tugerson names appeared in the lineups.[6] Some 1,500 fans booed as Hot Springs general manager Joe Thomas read Haraway's directive to forfeit the game.

A Mississippi newspaper gave its view of the action taken:

It seems to us that the furor over the possible use of Negro baseball players in the Cotton States League has outgrown the immediate importance of the issue.

These are some of the facts. Negro ball players are on the rosters of major and minor leagues outside of the South and are in the lineups of two southern minor leagues, the South Atlantic and the Texas. Hot Springs in the Cotton States League has signed two Negro ball players. Others of the league members have objected. The Attorney General of Mississippi has ruled in effect that it is against the policy of the state's segregation laws to permit interracial ball teams from playing in the state.[7]

Minor league president George Trautman said the Hot Springs team, currently in last place, could use the African-American players. However, to avoid future incidents, the brothers were optioned to Knoxville of the Class D Mountain States League. Although missing part of the season, Jim Tugerson would lead the league in wins with 29 and 286 strikeouts, as Knoxville finished in second place, eight and a half games behind Maryville-Alcoa.

Cotton States League president Haraway announced the circuit would appeal Trautman's ruling ordering the replay of the May 21 game. The circuit consisted of Meridian, Jackson, and Greenville from Ole Miss and El Dorado, Pine Bluff, and Hot Springs from "The Land of Opportunity." Haraway declared, "Trautman's decision will be appealed to the executive committee of the National Association of Professional Baseball Leagues."[8]

Lewis Goltz, co-owner of the Bathers, resigned from the team and offered his shares in the club for sale. Later in June, at a secret meeting in Jackson, Mississippi, the board of directors approved the transfer of stock from Goltz to H. M. and J. E. Britt. Goltz was giving up his fight to integrate the league. Meanwhile, Haraway announced his strong intentions to keep the league lily white.[9]

Two years later, a 20-year-old Puerto Rican shortstop named Jose Pagan broke the league's color barrier, joining the Eldorado, Arkansas, club. It was the Cotton League's last year of existence.

John L. Johnson's Sport Light

Chicago and the East-West Game

Source: *Kansas City Call,* 26 June 1953

The recent announcement that the Negro American League will stage another East-West game in Comiskey Park, Chicago on August 16, is unadulterated evidence that hope springs eternal in the breasts of baseball men, too.

This annual classic, which once rivaled in great degree many a game of World Series play, is Chicago born. It has been a Windy City institution from the first. Presented by a wealth of publicity the annual classics at one time attracted as many as 50,000 fans from many parts of the nation. An East-West game became an annual holiday for thousands.

But in the last few years the contests have lost some of the appeal they have once had and it appeared for a time that the finale was at hand.

The dwindling of attendance at these classics has not been the result of inferior teams. The truth is that every contest played under the East-West banner has been a demonstration of baseball at its least.

The drop in attendance must be charged to the indifference of the citizens of Chicago. The Negro citizens of the big city have failed to support this athletic institution as they should. And in their lack of support they are guilty of lack of civic pride.

It has been noted that in the latter years it has been the visiting fans who have maintained their interest in and given their support to this biggest annual day in the Negro game.

In view of the diminishing attendance in Chicago some close followers of the East-West game have opened that it would be well if the classics were rotated, say to Birmingham, Memphis, Kansas City or other cities where more appreciative persons might have the opportunity to extend a warmer bit of hospitality to the venture.

THINK CLASSIC SHOULD BE ROTATED

It was their expressed opinions that a change would be good for the game; that by moving them about a greater awareness of the high caliber of the events would be brought to a greater number of fans and thus increase the interest in the classics in particular and in Negro baseball in general.

But as we said at the beginning the club officials have not given up on Chicago as it proved by their announcement of the game in August.

And since they have proved to be pretty wise boys in charting the course of the Negro game through in charting the course of the Negro game through some very rough water the past 30 years, we'll go along with them and contribute as much as we can to make the coming classic a success, although we honestly confess that we believe Kansas City's Blues stadium could attract a larger crowd for the big game than will pay its way into Comiskey stadium on August 16.

Reasons behind the belief that Kaycee would prove a better location for the East-West game, or whatever new name would more properly describe a classic played with only Mid-Western and Southern teams remaining in the loop, is that Kansas City fans have displayed a real genuine civic mindedness.

This spirit of cooperation and helpfulness is distinctly displayed year after year at the Monarchs Home Openers, when some 20,000 fans jam into the stadium.

Such crowds are attracted without the swollen national publicity and countrywide drum beating that has prevailed to draw fans to Comiskey Park.

A very potent reason working in the behalf of Kansas City is that there exists here one of the greatest baseball Boosters clubs in the nation.

It has been proved countless times that whenever this club gets behind a baseball game it insures commendable turnouts.

STARVED AMERICAN GIANTS TO DEATH

But perhaps the most outstanding asset that Kansas City has is a great baseball club in the Kansas City Monarchs.

On the other hand Chicago has no Negro league team; its citizens starved the American Giants to death. They failed to give the club support, and as a result the Giants, a charter member of the league, has folded up.

Several other reasons might be advanced showing why Kansas City would be a better site for the annual classic than Big Windy. But none of these would be effective if the moguls are determined to continue in Chicago.

As we said at the start Chicago it is then and this column will string along with the club owners. They are pretty smart boys and may know the score.

It may be that the Chicago fans will reverse their trend of the past few years and turn out to the coming game. It could be that they have come to the realization that while integrated baseball is grand, that it is democracy in action and that major league play is supposed to be the best baseball in the world; there yet remains cause why the Negro game should be supposed and that most of the tan players they hurry to watch in the uniforms of the Dodgers, Sox, and Tribe got their start in the Negro Classic.

And more to the point, if young Negro players are to replace their current heroes they will most likely come from Negro teams.

See Declining Attendance Figures

What Number of Negro Leaguers Have Gone to the Major Leagues by 1953?

East-West All-Star Game Promises to Rate with Classics of the Past

Source: *Kansas City Call,* August 7 1953

The 21st annual East-West All-Star game which will be played here in Comiskey Park on Sunday, Aug. 16 looms as a classic performance comparable to the old days when giants of the diamond delighted crowds of 40 and 50 thousand spectators.

TOES IN TALENT

Chief reason for the prediction of a gigantic struggle is the extraordinary high caliber of talent that has been concentrated into the four clubs of the Negro American League.

It is doubtful if the rosters of the teams of yesteryear were composed of such highly promising athletes as is presently attracting the attention of astute major league scouts.

The players who will be selected to represent the two divisions in the coming classic will be as modern as a modern motor car. They are rated for speed and future employment by the top clubs in the American pastime.

PROFIT FROM PAST

In contrast to the old timers the kids who will compete in the coming game represent the accumulation of know-how handed down from the oldsters who achieved their ability mainly through trial and error. The present members of the league teams are mostly high school and college graduates. All are ambitious for a baseball future.

Current statistics reveal that each of the four teams has a group of .300 plus hitters and their pitchers possess outstanding ability in getting the ball across the plate.

SCOUTS FOLLOW TEAMS

Indicative of the high performance of the four teams is the fact that major league scouts constantly follow the teams.

Several of the participants in the 21st classic will undoubtedly be playing their final All-Star game for, according to reports, they will be signed up before or by the end of the season

In view of the interest of O. B. in many of the boys it would appear that the rosters are talented and the fans will be treated to outstanding play in the big game.

STANDOUT MANAGERS

Manager Buster Haywood of the Indianapolis Clowns will be skipper to the East team, which trails 8-12 in the series. Homer (Goose) Curry has been selected as coach for the East.

Johnny (Buck) O'Neil, manager of the Kansas City Monarchs, will pilot the West, with Hoss Walker, Black Barons, as coach.

East

Willie James Sheelor, ss, Frank Russell, utility; Fate Simms and Lloyd (Pepper) Bassett, c, Willie Patterson, 1b, Eddie Reed, cf, Raymond Haggins, outfield, and Sam (Buddy) Woods, Isiah Harris and Eddie Hancock pitchers, Memphis Red Sox; and Ray Neil, 2b, Curtis Hardaway, 3b, Verdes Drake, outfield; Julio Toledo, 1b, and Dionisio [Amaro], Ted Richardson and Angel Garcia, pitchers, Indianapolis Clowns.

West

Eddie Brooks, 2b, Wesley Dennis, 1b, Thomas Butts, ss, Henry Kimbro and Carl Long, outfielders, Otha Bailey, c, and Frank Thompson, Danny Wright, Cartledge Minski and Kelly Searcy pitchers, Birmingham Black Barons; Juan Armenteros, c, Ernie Johnson, outfield; Ernie banks, ss; Duke Henderson, outfield; Fran Herrera, 1b, and John Jackson and Berto Nunez, pitchers [from the Kansas City Monarchs].

Heavy Hitters Give West Edge in East-West Classic

by Russ J. Cowans

Source: *Chicago Defender,* 13 August 1953

WEST		EAST
17 Sherwood Brewer (K.C.)	2B	27 Tommy Butts (B'Ham)
12 Eddie Reed (Memphis)	CF	20 Verdes Drake (Clowns)
19 Ernest Johnson (K.C.)	RF	22 Ray Neil (Clowns)
28 Ernie Banks (K.C.)	SS	19 Wesley Dennis (B'Ham)

21 Tom Cooper (K.C.)	C	14 Henry Kimbro (B'Ham)
8 Willie Patterson (Memphis)	1B	32 Curtis Hardaway (Clowns)
4 Don Whittington (Memphis)	3B	11 Carl Long (B'Ham)
22 Lloyd Bassett (Memphis)	C	39 Sam Sands (Clowns)
17 Sam Woods (Memphis)	P	30 Willie Gaines (Clowns)
24 John Jackson [K.C.]	P	

Flourishing a powerful array of batting strength, cushioned on a pitching staff that would be the envy of any manager, the West will be a slight favorite when they square-off against the East in the 21st annual East-West classic in Comiskey Park, Sunday, Aug. 16. The game is slated to start at 3 p.m.

The West triumphed last year, 7–3, to give them a 12-8 lead in the series, and Manager John "Buck" O'Neil has high hopes that his charges will maintain the mastery over the East that started in 1951.

J. B. Martin, president of the Negro American league, sponsors of the game, said he expected a crowd of 25,000 to see the game. This will mark an increase of seven thousand over the 18,000 that saw the 1952 game.

John H. Sengstacke, editor and publisher of The Chicago Defender, will toss the first ball to start play in the classic, and Dr. W. S. Martin, owner of the Memphis Red Sox and stalwart in the Negro American league for 25 years, will be the catcher.

Willie Gaines, crack southpaw with the Indianapolis Clowns will get the star assignment for the East, while Sam "Buddy" Woods, veteran right-hander from the Memphis Red Sox, will start for the West. Both hurlers will go three innings, if not eliminated before his required chore has been done.

The West will present an array of batting strength equivalent to any seen in East-West games of the past. However, the most powerful bat will be wielded by Ray Neil, second baseman of the Indianapolis Clowns. Neil is topping the Negro American league batters with a mark of .425.

While Neil is topping the batters in the Negro American League, the West will have no less than four in the first 10—Ernie Banks, Juan Armenteros, Duke Henderson and Ernest Johnson, all members of the Kansas City Monarchs.

The West also has a strong staff of hurlers, paced by John Jackson, the right-hander of the Monarchs.
Jackson has a record of eighth victories and two defeats in 12 games this year.

Bert Nunez, little Cuban right hander with the Monarchs, has a record of nine wins and three defeats.

On the other side of the ledger, the East has a powerful hitter in Wesley Dennis, big first baseman of the Birmingham Black Barons in 41 games Dennis has collected 50 hits, scored 22 runs, and has driven 41 runs across the plate.

Verdes Drake, recognized as the best defensive outfielder in the league, is another of the East's top hitters. Drake is rapping the ball for .326 and has driven in 35 runs.

The East has one of the top southpaws in the league in Kelly Searcy, who was the top man in the 1951 classic. Searcy, who served a stint in the armed forces, has a record of 1-0.

Last year the West rolled up a 7–3 victory over the East before 18,000 fans. Henderson paced the West batters with two hits in four trips to the plate. The West leads in the series, 12-8.

In a pre-game ceremony, Miss East-West will be crowned by Dr. J. B. Martin, president of the league.

West Defeats East, 5–1

Negro League Battle Attracts 10,000

by Robert Cromie

Source: *Chicago Tribune*, 17 August 1953

The West defeated the East yesterday, 5 to 1, in the Negro American league's annual All-Star game in Comiskey Park before 10,000. It was the West's second straight triumph in the series, and the victory went to Sam (Buddy) Woods of Memphis, who yielded the East's lone run in the opening inning but saw his mates come back in the second to tie the contest and add two more in the third.

Each team made six hits, but the East hurt its cause with four errors, three of them in rapid succession in the third inning, a series which made Willie Gaines of Birmingham the losing hurler. Pitching stars were John Jackson, Kansas City Monarchs' ace who worked the last three innings for the West and held the East hitless, and Minski Cartledge, speedball tosser from Birmingham.

BANKS STARS AFIELD

Ernie Banks, also of the Monarchs, who played the full game at shortstop for the West, went hitless in four times at bat, but lived up to advance notices in the field as he accepted seven chances without error and made of one the game's fielding gems with a spectacular stop of Verdes Drake's smash in the third inning, taking the ball on a short hop and throwing Drake out from deep short.

The East scored in the first inning on successive singles by Ray Neil (Clowns), Wesley Dennis (Barons), and Curtis Hardaway (Barons).

GET TWO ON ERRORS

The West tallied in the second on a double by Willie Patterson [Memphis Red Sox] and a single by Henry Baylis of the Monarchs. They got two more in the third on a single by Eddie Reed of the Memphis Red Sox and three errors by the East infield, and picked up their two final runs in the seventh after loading the bases on singles by Jackson and Sherwood Brewer [Monarchs] and a hit batsman.

Ernie Johnson of the Monarchs, only Chicagoan in the game, singled to right to send Jackson home, and, when Banks fouled out to Eddie Brooks [Indianapolis Clowns], who came over from second to make the catch behind first base, Brewer streaked for home and made it as the surprised Brooks threw high and wide.

Estimated 10,000 See Classic

West Comes from Behind to Win 21st Annual Ball Game

by Johnny Johnson, The Call's Sport Editor

Source: *Kansas City Call*, 21 August 1953

West All-Stars of the Negro American League racked up their 13th victory against eight set-backs when they defeated the East All-Stars, 5–1, in the 21st annual renewal of the classic here at Comiskey Park Sunday afternoon.

FROM BEHIND TO WIN

A crowd estimated at 10,000 turned out to see the selected players of the Birmingham Black Barons and Indianapolis Clowns, representing the East take a one-run lead and then sputtered out before the West stars of the Kansas City Monarchs and the Memphis Red Sox.

Pre-game activities included precision marching by a boys drum and bugle corps, some down-right provocative high stepping by a bevy of teenage girls with educated hips, and an excellent demonstration of acrobatics by the Flying Nesbitts and their extra feature of cop and intruder.

HONORS TO DR. MARTIN

Dr. J. B. Martin, president of the Negro American league and local host of the classic, was honored by being presented with two trophies for his contributions to baseball.

John Sengstacke, publisher of the *Chicago Defender*, threw a perfect knuckle ball to receiver Dr. W. S. Martin of Memphis in the honorary first ball routine. Dr. Martin, muffed the ball after a good try.

Facing the pitching of Sam (Buddy) Woods of Memphis, Tom Butts (Barons) led off by popping up to [Sherwood] Brewer (Monarchs) at second base. Then [Verdes] Drake (Clowns) grounded out pitcher to first.

NEIL FIRST TO SCORE

With two outs, Ray Neil (Clowns) stroked a single past third base [Doc] Dennis (Birmingham) sent Neil to third with a humpback single to center, and Henry Kimbro (Barons) sent Neil across with the first run when he laced a bounder past Patterson at first base.

That was all for the East in the scoring department. They never seriously threatened again. In the third, Neil who proved to be the top hitter of the game with three for three, tripled with two out but he wasted his effort as Woods promptly struck out First Baseman Wesley Dennis on three strikes.

In the fifth the East managed to garner a pair of hits, a single to center by Neil and a safety past short by Minske Cartledge, Barons pitcher who relieved Gaines in the fourth.

STOP EAST HITTERS

The East couldn't buy a hit in the last four innings as Isiah Harris of Memphis and John Jackson of the Monarchs, aided by good fielding and a ripping double play, reeled them away from the plate after Woods had set the pitching pace.

The West Stars failed to get to Willie Gaines. Clowns are hurlers in the first frame. But in the second Willie Patterson, Memphis first sacker teed off for a ringing double to left and came in to score as Henry Baylis, Monarchs followed up with a hit to center to knot the score at 1–1.

ERRORS COST EAST

In the third the West plated a pair of runs and thereby won the ball game. Second Baseman Brewer of the Monarchs got on when First Baseman Wesley Dennis erred on a ground ball at first. Then Eddie Reed, Memphis center fielder, banged a hit to right, driving Brewer to third. At this point a pair of errors, one by Neil the other by Gaines permitted Brewer to score and Reed to take third base.

After one was out, Patterson drove in Reed with the West's second run of the inning by flying out to Kimbro in right and beating the relay.

Minski Cartledge, Barons hurler set the West down in order in the fourth, fifth, and sixth; he gave up no hits and walked only one and struck out only one.

GET TO AMARO

But in the seventh with Reliever Amaro of the Clowns taking over, pitcher Johnny Jackson greeted him with a single to right. This was followed by a base knock to center by Brewer of Kansas City.

Evidently excited Amaro proceeded to hit Reed with a pitched ball, forcing Jackson and Brewer to third and second respectively. At this juncture, Ernie Johnson, Monarchs right fielder ripped a single to right, scoring the two runners making the score, 5–1.

And that's about the way it ended. The hitting power of the West proved the decisive factor.

East-West Game Faces Death in Chicago Park

Scribes Say Game Needs New Climate and a New Doctor

by Johnny Johnson, The *Call*'s Sport Editor

Source: *Kansas City Call,* 21 August 1953

Consensus of the few scribes who took time out to cover the 21st annual Negro game her in Comiskey Park Sunday afternoon was that the annual classic is sick and needs a change of climate and another doctor.

SHE'S DYING FAST

"She is going down hill fast and can't possibly last another two years here in Chicago," they opinionated in almost unison.

They were referring not only to the crowd which has grown steadily smaller each year, but also to the manner in which the contest is directed and managed.

All expressed reluctance to see the game die, for they are aware of the need for such an annual outing if Negro baseball is to continue.

Many of the scribes shook their heads in disbelief when it was guessed that 10,000 fans were in the park. A few set their own estimation at 7,000; some of the less generous ones declared the total was 5,000.

LESS THAN LAST YEAR

The decline in attendance is shown when the estimation last year was set at 18,000 and there were considerable doubts about that figure.

This year they didn't even bother to open the second balcony. No one was up there except the birds, a quartet of park hanger-ons and a quartet of kids who were being paid to recover baseballs. They did a darned good job.

BY PASSED FAY YOUNG

Absent from the press box was the dean of Negro sports writers, the somewhat irascible but efficient Frank (Fay) Young.

Although Frank Young has been on the firing line in behalf of Negro baseball in general and the East-West game in particular for many years, he was absent from the game.

The reason! The officials failed to send him a ticket. How ungrateful can people get?

In the past Young has been the major domo of the press box; he has served as the official scorer, the dispenser of press tickets, final decider of hits and errors.

WORKED FOR GAME

In other words, Frank Young has done as much as some and more than many to keep alive the East-West game during the past 20 years. But this year they threw him away, discarded him, and forgot him.

As we said, Young has a tendency to speak what he thinks. Sure he is a tyrant but he is a benevolent one in the opinion of many who know him.

No single indication of the need for change in the life of the East-West can be found than this seeming slight to Frank Young.

But others exist and the principle one is falling off in attendance. The management shouldn't be allowed to continue the only Negro league classic in a city where it is starving to death.

Several suggestions have been offered to correct this condition. One of them is a method of rotation. The games, these advocates say, should be moved annually to Birmingham, Kansas City, Memphis or other large cities.

WANT ROTATION

The advocates of change point out that the game cannot exist permanently in cities like Chicago where major league games with Negro players are present at the same time.

Sunday Milwaukee was playing at Wrigley field with Bill Bruton, and Jim Pendleton with the Brewers [Braves]. Hundreds of fans, it was estimated attended the major league game.

The confusion from this is that the East-West game is not in position to compete with the O.B. clubs. It has no individual stars, no outstanding players to attract with No Satchel Paiges, Roy Campanellas, and Larry Dobies. All it has to offer is unknown and mostly unarrived youngsters, which excite nobody.

ONLY A FEW SACRIFICES

Chicago with its hundreds of attractions has shown by the falling attendance that it will no longer support this classic.

The scribes in the press box only two of which were from out of town, and only seven present in all, pointed out that the local fans had starved the Chicago American Giants to death and they have less love for the East-West game.

So it looks as if they were on the beam when they said the East-West game needs a new climate and a new doctor if death is to be staved off.

All-Star Tilt Fails to Impress Scouts from Big Leagues

by Wendell Smith

Source: *Pittsburgh Courier*, 22 August 1953

Chicago-Negro baseball, once the happy hunting ground for big league scouts, isn't what it used to be, in the East or West. That was the general consensus here Sunday following the Negro-American League's twenty-first All-Star game in which the West defeated the East, 5 to 1, as Comiskey Park.

A disappointing crowd of 10,000, including a caravan of major league scouts, watched the game under perfect weather conditions and during the two-hour demonstration saw very little talent worthy of serious consideration for future employment in the majors.

The forty best players in the Negro American League—twenty from the East and twenty from the West—were on display for the edification of the critics who purchase talent for Major League clubs, and the faithful fans, who have supported the classic down through the years.

No one apparently was overly impressed despite the fact that the players made a sincere and honest effort to give them a skillful, well-played game.

The Best prospect in the contest was a 22-year-old shortstop owned by the Kansas City Monarchs, Ernie Banks. The flashy youngster failed to hit in four trips to the plate but compensated for his futility there by sparkling in the field, handling six chances flawlessly and was on the starting end of the one double-play completed by the West.[10]

The top performer for the East was Ray Neil, a second baseman from the Indianapolis Clowns, currently the best hitter in Negro baseball. He proved it in this game, pounding out three tries, including a triple in the third inning, best extra-base hit of the game.

Unfortunately, Neil, despite his skill at the plate can't be considered a big league prospect because he has celebrated at least thirty birthdays, which means he is past his peak and in no way attractive to major league scouts.

But he is a good solid ball player. If he were ten years younger, the talent seekers would beat a path to his door and refuse to let him sleep until he signed a contract.

The game itself was only mildly exciting. The West, fortified with good pitching and aided considerably by Eastern infielders, who were stricken with that familiar disease known as "fumble-itis" won the game as early as the third inning.

They broke a 1–1 tie in the third, scoring twice on one hit to take a 3 to 1 lead which was never threatened. The defense of the East cracked wide open in that inning and the West took advantage of three errors.

The East scored its only run in the initial inning, solving starting pitching Sam Woods of the Memphis Red Sox for three hits. Neil got the first hit of the game, a single with two out. The next two hitters, Wesley Dennis and Henry Kimbro, both of Birmingham, also singled and Neil raced home with the East's lone marker.

Woods retired at the end of the third with a record of one run and four hits. Isiah Harris followed and goose-egged the East for the next three stanzas, giving up two hits. Johnny Jackson of Kansas City followed and pitched hitless and scoreless ball through the ninth. Woods, having started, got credit for the win.

Willie Gaines of Indianapolis, started for the East and pitched good ball the first three innings, but errors contributed to his downfall. The West tied it at 1–1 in the second on a double by Willie Patterson, who scored on Ed [Hank] Bayless' [Baylis'] timely single to center.

The West sewed it up in the next inning, scoring twice on one hit: Sherwood Brewer was safe on Hardaway's [Dennis'] error at first base and scooted to third when Eddie Reed singled to right. Successive errors on balls hit by Neil and Gaines enabled Brewer to score and Reed. Those three miscues in one inning set a record for East-West games. They also sealed the East's doom.

The West scored two more in the seventh, after being stopped for three innings by Minski Cartledge of Indianapolis, who succeeded Gaines on the mound.

Dionesio [Dionisio] Amaro, also of Indianapolis, came on to pitch the final three [two] for the East and immediately ran into trouble, Jackson and Brewer singled, and moved up a base when he hit Eddie Reed. Both Jackson and Reed subsequently scored on infield outs. That was the ball game and the thirteenth win of the long series for the West, as against eight for the East. It was also, the second in a row for the West, composed of players from the Kansas City Monarchs and the Memphis Red Sox. The East's roster was made up of players from the Indianapolis Clowns and Birmingham Black Barons.

The pitching for both clubs, incidentally, was acceptable. Each team was held to six hits. The East, however, suffered four miscues and that was fatal.

East-West Game Needs an Overhauling

by William G. Nunn

Source: *Pittsburgh Courier,* 29 August 1953

Chicago— Unless the East-West game is injected with new blood in the form of revolutionary ideas . . . the biggest sports spectacle among Negroes must go the way of all flesh!

This is the conclusion of experts following the miserable showing at Comiskey Park Sunday afternoon a week ago, as the West defeated the East 5 to 1 in the twenty-first annual renewal of the once-famed classic.

Gone . . . in the game, were the tremendous crowds which formally crammed every nook and cranny of the historic South Side Park.

Gone . . . in the game, were the "names" which thrilled the countless thousands as they yelled their defiance to the invisible color barrier that kept their athletes from participation in organized baseball.

Gone . . . was the finesse and promotional skill which had nursed the famous diamond classic from a modest 7,500 start . . . to the acme of entertainment which once saw 51,000 people play to enter the gates, while another 4,000 clamored for admission outside.

The game has lost its pull, color and box-office appeal, because the same methods used to promote it years ago are still in effect.

Granted that the purpose for which the game was originally cast . . . has been met . . . there are still plenty of novel ideas which will once again start the turnstiles to clicking!

That these ideas must be cultivated goes without saying. The affair must take on the form of a mammoth sports spectacle. And this can be done. For instance, this year, Willie Mays and Don Newcombe could both have been guests of the league. A meeting would have been held with Negro coaches, who were present over the weekend, to stress the need for baseball as a major part of the college sports program.

Great Negro baseball players from other years could have been invited as guests of the league . . . and a two-inning "game" been scheduled.

The game could be changed from a Sunday afternoon affair to a night game, with a full program of "events" designed to attract fans scheduled.

There are scores of worthwhile causes and institutions in Chicago who could use funds . . . and these causes and institutions should rightfully receive some of the profits which are a part of the game.

With all due respect to those men who now head the league. . . they have failed to call around them people of prestige and influence to help make of the game, the type of affair it should be.

Twenty-one years of effort going down the drain!

As one of those in at the birth of the idea, we believe that the East-West game can be saved!

We believe that the people of Chicago and the Midwest, will once again rally to make it a sports spectacle without equal in the nation.

But it must be planned carefully . . . and with the co-operation of those who are interested in its perpetuation. It's a challenge . . . and must be met, head-on!

The East-West Game, Should It Be Rotated?

Loop Prexy Wants Opinions

What About East-West Game?

by Dr. J. B. Martin, President, Negro National League

Source: *Kansas City Call,* 4 September 1953

Chicago— For several years now, a number of baseball fans and sports writers have been counting Negro baseball and the East-West Classic out, but each year the Negro American League and the all-star baseball have clicked as scheduled.

SPORTS SCRIBES CRY

During the last couple of years, however, I have noticed that sports editors of several newspapers have complained because the East-West game is played in Chicago every year. They contend that this big game should also be scheduled for other cities.

Because the crowd at this year's dream game was not as large as usual, the howls have been greater than ever. Some other city, the critics say, would have drawn a larger crowd.

Since I know the views of sports writers on the subject, I wonder what do you fans think about the East-West Classic? Where should it be played—in Chicago as it has for 21 previous tilts or in a different city each year?

WHY IN CHICAGO

Maybe you would be interested in knowing why the game happens to be played in the Windy City rather than in some other place. First, the all-star game idea originated in Chicago. In this city we played the first major league all-star game, the first All-Star football game and the first All-Star basketball game. Some other All-Star battles probably were played here first, too, but the above three I remember.

The East-West Classic was first played at Comiskey Park in 1933. As the years rolled by, it grew bigger and bigger and better and better. The fans used to vote for the starting lineups, and some great names performed in this historic series.

FANS INTEREST SWITCHED

In the post–World War II period the game reached its zenith. Crowds of more than 40,000 jammed the ball park for this event. Then the game began to slip because Negro fans were beginning to share a new loyalty—to the Brooklyn Dodgers and Cleveland Indians and other teams that began to feature Negro players in the major leagues.

Little by little, the crowds began to slip in size at the East-West game. In 1951, many predicted the doom of the famed contest, but it attracted more fans in 1952. This year it slipped back once more to the 1951 level.

On the basis of quality, the East-West Classic still is an excellent game. All its stars do not have the luster of the names of old, but they are just about as good.

UP TO THE FANS

In the past, a second East-West game has been played in New York, but this tilt fizzled out because of lack of support. Today, it is up to you fans as to what should be done with the East-West Classic.

I want you to write me, Dr. J. B. Martin, at the Negro American League office, 412 E. 47th Street, Chicago 15, Illinois. The East-West game is THE great spectacle of Negro baseball and it is the fans who keep it alive. Fans and sports writers alike are free to let us, of the NAL, know how they feel and we promise to act according to your wishes.

AUGUST 16, 1953, CHICAGO, IL

EAST	AB	R	H	D	T	HR	BI	E	TAVG	TSLG
Pee Wee Butts (Birmingham Black Barons), ss	3	0	0	0	0	0	0	1		
a) Willie Brown (Indianapolis Clowns), ss	1	0	0	0	0	0	0	0		
Verdes Drake (Indianapolis Clowns), cf	4	0	0	0	0	0	0	0		
Ray Neil (Indianapolis Clowns), 2b	3	1	3	0	1	0	0	1		
b) Eddie Brooks (Birmingham Black Barons), 2b	1	0	0	0	0	0	0	0		
Wesley "Doc" Dennis (Birmingham Black Barons), 1b	4	0	1	0	0	0	0	1		
Henry Kimbro (Birmingham Black Barons), rf	3	0	1	0	0	0	1	0		
Curtis Hardway (Indianapolis Clowns), 3b	2	0	0	0	0	0	0	1		
Irwin Castille (Birmingham Black Barons), 3b	0	0	0	0	0	0	0	0		
Carl Long (Birmingham Black Barons), lf	4	0	0	0	0	0	0	0		
Sam "Piggy" Sands (Indianapolis Clowns), c	3	0	0	0	0	0	0	0		
Otha Bailey (Birmingham Black Barons), c	1	0	0	0	0	0	0	0		
Willy Gaines (Indianapolis Clowns), p	1	0	0	0	0	0	0	1		
Manny Cartledge (Birmingham Black Barons), p	2	0	1	0	0	0	0	0		
Dave Amaro (Indianapolis Clowns), p	1	0	0	0	0	0	0	0		
Buster Haywood (Indianapolis Clowns), ph	1	0	0	0	0	0	0	0		
Team Totals, Average & Slugging Pct.	34	1	6	0	1	0	1	5	.176	.235

a) Ran for Butts in the 5th
b) Ran for Neil in the 5th

WEST	AB	R	H	D	T	HR	BI	E	TAVG	TSLG
Sherwood Brewer (Kansas City Monarchs), 2b	3	2	1	0	0	0	0	0		
Eddie Reed (Memphis Red Sox), cf	3	1	1	0	0	0	0	0		
Billy Ray Haggins (Memphis Red Sox), rf	3	0	0	0	0	0	1	0		
Ernie Johnson (Kansas City Monarchs), rf	1	0	1	0	0	0	2	0		
Ernie Banks (Kansas City Monarchs), ss	4	0	0	0	0	0	0	0		
Tom Cooper (Kansas City Monarchs), lf	3	0	0	0	0	0	0	0		
c) Fate Simms (Memphis Red Sox), lf	1	0	0	0	0	0	0	0		
Willie Patterson (Memphis Red Sox), 1b	3	1	1	1	0	0	1	0		
Pancho Herrera (Kansas City Monarchs), 1b	1	0	0	0	0	0	0	0		
Hank Baylis (Kansas City Monarchs), 3b	4	0	1	0	0	0	1	0		
Pepper Bassett (Memphis Red Sox), c	3	0	0	0	0	0	0	0		
Juan Armenteros (Kansas City Monarchs), c	1	0	0	0	0	0	0	0		
Sam "Buddy" Woods (Memphis Red Sox), p	1	0	0	0	0	0	0	0		
Isiah Harris (Memphis Red Sox), p	0	0	0	0	0	0	0	0		
John "Stony" Jackson (Kansas City Monarchs), p	1	1	1	0	0	0	0	1		
Team Totals, Average & Slugging Pct.	32	5	6	1	0	0	5	1	.188	.219

c) Ran for Cooper in the 6th

East	100	000	000	1
West	012	000	20X	5

PITCHER/TEAM	GS	IP	H	R	ER	K	BB	WP	HB	W	L	SV
Gaines/IC	1	3	3	3	1	1	4	0	0	0	1	0
Cartledge/BBB		3	0	0	0	1	1	0	0	0	0	0
Amaro/IC		2	3	2	2	0	0	0	1	0	0	0
Woods/MRS	1	3	4	1	1	1	0	1	0	1	0	0
Harris/MRS		3	2	0	0	1	2	0	0	0	0	0
J. Jackson/KCM		3	0	0	0	0	1	0	0	0	0	1

DP—Banks to Brewer to Patterson; Hardaway to Neil to Dennis
HBP—Reed by Amaro
LOB—East 10, West 6
SB—Simms
East—Buster Haywood (Mgr.)
West—Buck O'Neil (Mgr.)
Umpires—Bob Motley, T. H. Jefferson, Simon Lewis, Theodore Acklyn
Attendance—10,000   Time—2:00

Respect, Redemption, Recognition

Power, speed, and athleticism were hallmarks of "shadow ball." These were the key elements in an up-tempo style of play that characterized black baseball. With a mixture of folklore, talent, courage, and sometimes a dogmatic attitude, these men combined to create a blend of baseball that was unique to our national pastime.

From town to town, barnstorming players, burdened with the fatigue of travel, were often greeted with expected, but still stunning, reality checks during baseball's apartheid period. One player, Stanley "Doc" Glenn, a Philadelphia Stars catcher, recalled a road sign down South that indirectly spoke to them: "Can't Read, Run Anyway." Much like the "gentlemen's agreement," it was an unwritten rule that it was okay to entertain the white fans by day but not to hang around when the sun went down.

Before 1946 the bases were loaded with racism on first, rejection on second, and ignorance on third. At bat was the "gentlemen's agreement," ready to swing for another racist home run. From the pitcher's mound came three fastballs—respect, redemption, and recognition—striking out Mr. Agreement and ending the game of segregated baseball. These fastballs came in the form of a man named Jackie Robinson.

In 1945, more than three centuries after the first chained and shackled Africans came to America, our national pastime was now ready to accept a black man. Not just any black man, but a man who was educated at a major university, a letterman in four major sports, who was as honest as Diogenes, clean as an alcohol swab, cool as menthol, pure as ivory, perfect as the Hope diamond, with the discipline of a Buckingham Palace guard. A black man with a faultless blend of integrity and character was given the opportunity to play a game.

Will there ever be another Jackie Robinson, a professional athlete with enough pride, character, self-respect, discipline, courage, and depth of knowledge and understanding to risk his well-being for the betterment of African-Americans?

The integration of Major League Baseball predates the civil rights movement in this country. Before the 1954 Supreme Court decision of *Brown* v. *Board of Education*, before Rosa Parks and the 1955 Montgomery Bus Boycott, and before the 1964 Voting Rights Act—Jackie Robinson's monumental efforts initiated more social change than any lawyer, any politician, or any civil rights activist ever generated.

With Robinson and other black stars trickling into the white majors, the Negro Leagues, unexpectedly, embarked on a tin-cup tour, begging for attention. Million-dollar promises became "hundred-dollar" handshakes. The seemingly innocent good-bye party surprised fans and players alike, as their "cookies and cream" stars were now major leaguers. The black teams begin to play before less than a packed house, as fan loyalty shifted to their favorite stars playing now with white-owned teams, white teams that never entertained hiring talented managers, coaches, administrators, or umpires from the darker-skin leagues.

When Jackie joined Brooklyn, the Dodgers became black America's perennial favorite. With the signing of Robinson, Roy Campanella, Don Newcombe, Joe Black, Junior Gilliam, and other minority stars like Sandy Amoros, the Dodgers led the nation in home runs

59. In 1994, at the 65th Major League All-Star Game at Three Rivers Stadium in Pittsburgh, Pennsylvania, Major League Baseball named Phil Rizzuto (American League) and Walter "Buck" Leonard (National League) as honorary captains. "It is with great honor and gratitude that we are able to name Buck Leonard captain of the National League All-Star team," said Leonard Coleman, president of the National League. "Baseball is indeed grateful for the contributions made by the Negro League players to the game. Buck was one of the best and he showcased his talents in Pittsburgh. It is only fitting that we bring him back as captain of the National League All-Star team." This is the first time in baseball history that a former Negro League player had been appointed captain on a major league all-star team. "On behalf of the Negro League players, both past and present, I am honored to serve as honorary captain for the National League All-Star team," said Leonard. Courtesy of Al Gordon with the Pittsburgh Pirates. Text provided by the National League of Professional Baseball Clubs Press Release, July 7, 1994.

of humanity. The new movement caused other Negro Leaguers' passions to become inflamed with hope. As the black players marched into the white leagues, the Negro Leagues soon resembled a eulogy for those men without invitations to The Show.

This was no Cinderella story. By 1960 the midnight hour struck as the major leagues raided the golden goose of black baseball of its best players. The assault left black baseball, a once-prosperous black enterprise and later a farm system, stocked with marginal players, those past their prime or unseasoned. With the absence of a quality product, the black leagues became handicapped and were forced to disband.

By the mid-1950s, the Negro Leagues, and their "shadow ball" act, were now only a shadow of a once-respected and bustling era. With the smell of failure in the air, future Hall of Famer Buck Leonard from the Homestead Grays put it best, "We couldn't draw flies!" The Negro Leagues celebrated their victory of integration only to see their own institution suffer a slow demise. Their ultimate victory gave rise to their death.

The East-West game was only a piece of the socioeconomic puzzle presented by black professional athletes to white America. By 1961 the game that had showcased black baseball's best was only a faded memory. The Negro Leagues now stood as a powerful symbol of the future, evidenced by their successful struggle to overcome adversity. These players, with intense dedication and desire to play a simple game, eventually overcame the hardships of travel, scheduling conflicts, racial attitudes, and unrighteous recognition. Their visions were limited only by a lack of opportunities. Opportunities denied because of their skin color. Moreover, an opportunity denied to all fans to see the best talent, regardless of heritage, on the playing field.

This is only one chapter of the rich Negro League history from which we all can learn. No more myths, no hyperbole, no fantasy baseball, just the plain, simple truth of their fight for acceptance as human beings, athletes, and first-class citizens. In the process, we find this glorious chapter in American history to be saturated with engaging personalities, tremendous athletic accomplishments, testimonials of human spirit, and character that would make founding fathers Rube Foster, C. I. Taylor, and Sol White proud.

Appendixes

Appendixes

Game Summaries

YEAR	RUNNING TALLY	WEST RUNS	WEST MANAGER	EAST RUNS	EAST MANAGER	WINNING PITCHER	LOSING PITCHER	BALLPARK ATTENDANCE
1933	W-1	11	Larry Brown	7	Pop Lloyd	Willie Foster	Sam Streeter	19,568
1934	E-1	0	Dave Malarcher	1	Dick Lundy	Satchel Paige	Willie Foster	30,000
1935*	W-2	11	Oscar Charleston (1)	8	Webster McDonald	Sug Cornelius	Martin Dihigo	25,000
1936	E-2	2	Bingo DeMoss	10	Oscar Charleston (2)	Leroy Matlock	Sug Cornelius	26,400
1937	E-3	2	Candy Jim Taylor (1)	7	Biz Mackey (1)	Barney Morris	Hilton Smith (1)	25,000
1938	W-3	5	Andy Cooper (1)	4	Oscar Charleston (3)	Hilton Smith	Edsall Walker	30,000
1939	W-4	4	George Mitchell	2	George Scales (1)	Ted Radcliffe	Roy Partlow	40,000
1939 NYC	E-4	2	Oscar Charleston (4)	10	George Scales (2)	Bill Byrd	Smoky Owens	20,000
1940	E-5	0	Andy Cooper (2)	11	Felton Snow	Henry McHenry	Gene Bremer (1)	25,000
1941	E-6	3	Candy Jim Taylor (2)	8	Vic Harris (1)	Terris McDuffie	Hilton Smith (2)	50,256
1942	E-7	2	W.S. Welch (1)	5	Vic Harris (2)	Leon Day	Satchel Paige	45,179
1942 Cleve.	E-8	2	W.S. Welch (2)	9	Vic Harris (3)	Gene Smith	Gene Bremer (2)	10,791
1943	W-5	2	Frank Duncan (1)	1	Vic Harris (4)	**Satchel Paige (2)**	Dave Barnhill	**51,723**
1944	W-6	7	W.S. Welch (3)	4	Candy Jim Taylor (3)	Gentry Jessup	Carrenza Howard	46,247
1945	W-7	9	W.S. Welch (4)	6	Vic Harris (5)	Verdell Mathis	Tom Glover	33,088
1946 DC	W-8	4	W.S. Welch (5)	1	Vic Harris (6)	**Bill Byrd (2)**	Vibert Clarke (1)	16,268
1946	E-9	3	Quincy Trouppe	5	Vic Harris (7)	Dan Bankhead	Bill Byrd	45,474
1947	W-9	5	Frank Duncan (2)	2	Biz Mackey (2)	**Dan Bankhead (2)**	Max Manning	48,112
1947 NYC	W-10	8	Frank Duncan (3)	2	Biz Mackey (3)	Ford Smith	Rufus Lewis (1)	38,402
1948	W-11	3	Quincy Trouppe (2)	0	**Vic Harris (8)**	Bill Powell	Rufus Lewis (2)	42,099
1948 NYC	E-10	1	Candy Jim Taylor (4)	6	Pop Lloyd (2)	Max Manning	Vibert Clarke (2)	17,928
1949	E-11	0	Buck O'Neil	4	Hoss Walker (1)	Bob Griffith	Gene Richardson	31,097
1950	W-12	5	Buck O'Neil (2)	3	Oscar Charleston (4)	Connie Johnson	Raul Galata	24,614
1951	E-12	1	W.S. Welch ** (6)	3	Buster Haywood (1)	Kelly Searcy	**Vibert Clarke (3)**	21,312
1952	W-13	7	**W.S. Welch (7)**	3	Buster Haywood (2)	Dick Phillips	Groundhog Thompson	18,279
1953	W-14	5	Buck O'Neil (3)	1	Buster Haywood (3)	Buddy Woods	Willy Gaines	10,000
Totals		104		123				791,837
Avg/Game		4.0		4.7				30,455

Notes: *Eleven innings   ** Replaced Buck O'Neil due to illness
     Boldface indicates leaders in categories
All games played in Comiskey Park, Chicago IL, except were noted.
    Legend: Cleve.—Cleveland OH; NYC—New York City; DC—Washington DC.

West Squad was shut out three (3) times, 1934, 1940 and 1949; East squad was shut out once, 1948.
Highest run total by West teams was 11 runs in 1933, 1935; highest run total by an East team was 11 in 1940.

The West squads won 14 games; while the East squads won 12, although the East scored 19 more runs.
Longest winning streak by the East was from 1939 to 1942 (5 games); and by the West from 1943 to 1946 (4 games).

All-Stars by Team

Listed below are teams and their player representatives for each year. Teams placing players on the all-star teams for more than 10 consecutive years were the Chicago American Giants (20 years), Kansas City Monarchs (18 years) and the Memphis Red Sox (16 years). The American Giants were the only team to have players participate every year until the team's demise in 1952. From 1933 to 1953, the teams with the most representatives were the Monarchs with 78, the American Giants with 74 and the Memphis Red Sox with 61 players. Teams with only one representative were the Detroit Stars, the Cincinnati-Indianapolis Clowns, Cleveland Red Sox, Cleveland Giants and the Indianapolis Athletics. In 1936 the Monarchs, not a member of either league, had a record 11 players make an appearance in the East-West classic. A (2) beside a player's name indicates he played in both games that year.

BALTIMORE ELITE GIANTS — 46 players

1938
Hughes, Samuel Thomas "Sammy T." 2b
Mackey, James Raleigh "Biz" c
Wright, Burnis "Wild Bill" rf

1939
(2) Byrd, William "Bill" p
(2) Hughes, Samuel Thomas "Sammy T." 2b
Suttles, George "Mule" rf
(2) Wright, Burnis "Wild Bill" cf

1940
Perkins, William Gamiel "Cy" c

1941
Byrd, William "Bill" p
Campanella, Roy "Campy" c
Hoskins, William "Bill" lf

1942
(2) Gaines, Jonas Donald "Lefty" p
(2) Wright, Burnis "Wild Bill" rf

1943
Harvey, David William "Bill" p
Kimbro, Henry Allen "Jimbo" cf
Scales, George Walter "Tubby" ph

1944
Butts, Robert Thomas "Pee Wee" ss
Byrd, William "Bill" p
Campanella, Roy "Campy" 3b
Kimbro, Henry Allen "Jimbo" rf

1945
Byrd, William "Bill" ph
Campanella, Roy "Campy" c
Glover, Thomas "Tom" or "Lefty" p
Wright, Burnis "Wild Bill" rf

1946
Butts, Robert Thomas "Pee Wee" ss
(2) Byrd, William "Bill" p
(2) Gaines, Jonas Donald "Lefty" p
(2) Kimbro, Henry Allen "Jimbo" cf

1947
Black, Joseph "Joe" p
(2) Butts, Robert Thomas "Pee Wee" ss
(2) Kimbro, Henry Allen "Jimbo" cf
(2) Romby, Robert L. "Bob" ph
(2) Washington, John G. "Johnny" 1b

1948
Black, Joseph "Joe" p
Butts, Robert Thomas "Pee Wee" ss
(2) Gilliam, James William "Junior" 2b
(2) Lockett, Lester "Buck" rf, lf

1949
Butts, Robert Thomas "Pee Wee" ss
Davis, Robert Lomax "Butch" lf
Gilliam, James William "Junior" 2b
Pearson, Leonard Curtis "Lennie" or "Hoss" 1b

1950
Black, Joseph "Joe" p
Butts, Robert Thomas "Pee Wee" ss
Gilliam, James William "Junior" 2b

1951
Hayes, John William "Johnny" c
Searcy, Kelton "Kelly" or "Lefty" p

BIRMINGHAM BLACK BARONS — 47 Players

1938
Woods, Parnell ph

1940
Sampson Jr., Thomas "Tommy" or "Toots" 2b
Woods, Parnell 3b

1941
Bankhead, Daniel Robert "Dan" p
Bostock Sr., Lyman Wesley 1b
Sampson Jr., Thomas "Tommy" or "Toots" 2b

1942
Davenport, Lloyd "Ducky" ph
Gipson, Alvin "Bubber" p
(2) Sampson Jr., Thomas "Tommy" or "Toots" 2b

1943
Lockett, Lester "Buck" lf
McKinnis, Gread "Lefty" or "Gready" p
Sampson Jr., Thomas "Tommy" or "Toots" 2b

1944
Radcliffe, Theodore Roosevelt "Double Duty" c
Wilson, Arthur Lee "Artie" or "Snoop" ss

1945
Lockett, Lester "Buck" lf

1946
(2) Davis, Lorenzo "Piper" 2b
(2) Wilson, Arthur Lee "Artie" or "Snoop" ss

1947
- Bassett, Lloyd "Pepper" c
- (2) Davis, Lorenzo "Piper" 2b
- (2) Wilson, Arthur Lee "Artie" or "Snoop" ss

1948
- Bassett, Lloyd "Pepper" c
- (2) Davis, Lorenzo "Piper" 2b
- Powell, William Henry "Bill" p
- (2) Wilson, Arthur Lee "Artie" or "Snoop" ss

1949
- Bell, Herman ph
- Burgos, Jose Antonio ss
- Davis, Lorenzo "Piper" 2b
- Greason, Rev. William Henry "Bill" p

1950
- Bassett, Lloyd "Pepper" c
- Perry, Alonzo Thomas 1b
- Powell, William Henry "Bill" p
- Steele, Edward "Ed" or "Stainless" lf

1951
- Dennis, Wesley L. "Doc" 1b
- Kimbro, Henry Allen "Jimbo" cf
- Robinson, Norman Wayne "Bobby" lf
- Steele, Edward "Ed" or "Stainless" rf

1952
- Bailey, Otha William "Bill" c
- Brooks, Eddie 2b
- Dennis, Wesley L. "Doc" 1b
- Kimbro, Henry Allen "Jimbo" cf
- Thompson, Frank "Groundhog" p

1953
- Bailey, Otha William "Bill" c
- Brooks, Eddie 2b
- Butts, Robert Thomas "Pee Wee" ss
- Cartledge, Menske, "Manny" p
- Castille, Irwin 3b
- Dennis, Wesley L. "Doc" 1b
- Hardaway, Curtis 3b
- Kimbro, Henry Allen "Jimbo" rf
- Long, Carl lf

BROOKLYN EAGLES—4 players
1935
- Day, Leon p
- Giles Sr., George Franklin 1b
- Jenkins, Clarence R. "Fats" lf
- Stone, Edward "Ed" or "Ace" ph

CHICAGO AMERICAN GIANTS—74 players
1933
- Brown, Larry "Iron Man" c
- Davis, Walter C. "Steel Arm" lf
- Foster, Willie Hendrick "Bill" p
- Radcliffe, Alexander "Alec" 3b
- Stearnes, Norman Thomas "Turkey" cf

- Suttles, George "Mule" 1b
- Wells, Willie James "Devil" ss

1934
- Brown, Larry "Iron Man" c
- Foster, Willie Hendrick "Bill" p
- Powell, Malvin "Putt" ph
- Radcliffe, Alexander "Alec" 3b
- Stearnes, Norman Thomas "Turkey" cf
- Suttles, George "Mule" 1b
- Trent, Ted "Highpockets" p
- Wells, Willie James "Devil" ss

1935
- Cornelius, William McKinley "Sug" p
- Radcliffe, Alexander "Alec" 3b
- Stearnes, Norman Thomas "Turkey" rf
- Suttles, George "Mule" lf
- Trent, Ted "Highpockets" p
- Wells, Willie James "Devil" ss

1936
- Byas, Richard Thomas "Subby" c
- Cornelius, William McKinley "Sug" p
- Dials, Oland Cecil "Lou" rf
- Dunlap, Herman lf
- Radcliffe, Alexander "Alec" 3b
- Redus, Wilson R. "Frog" rf
- Trent, Ted "Highpockets" p

1937
- Byas, Richard Thomas "Subby" ph
- Radcliffe, Alexander "Alec" 3b
- Redus, Wilson R. "Frog" rf
- Trent, Ted "Highpockets" p

1938
- Cornelius, William McKinley "Sug" p
- Duncan Jr., Frank c
- Radcliffe, Alexander "Alec" 3b

1939
- (2) Bassett, Lloyd "Pepper" c
- (2) Horne, William "Billy" 2b
- (2) Radcliffe, Alexander "Alec" 3b, ss

1940
- Morney, Leroy ss
- Reeves, Donald "Soup" lf

1941
- Bassett, Lloyd "Pepper" c
- Crutchfield, John William "Jimmie" lf
- Horne, William "Billy" ss
- Hudson, William Henry "Lefty" ph

1942
- (2) Bell, James Thomas "Cool Papa" cf, rf
- (2) Pennington, Arthur David "Superman" ph, cf
- Wyatt, Ralph Arthur "Pepper" ss

1943
- Davenport, Lloyd "Ducky" rf
- Radcliffe, Alexander "Alec" 3b
- Radcliffe, Theodore Roosevelt "Double Duty" c

1944

Davenport, Lloyd "Ducky" rf

Jessup, Gentry "Jeep" p

McKinnis, Gread "Lefty" or "Gready" p

1945

Jessup, Gentry "Jeep" p

1946

Jessup, Gentry "Jeep" p

Nelson, Clyde 3b

1947

(2) Armour, Alfred "Buddy" p, rf

Jessup, Gentry "Jeep" p

1948

(2) Hill, Samuel "Sam" rf

Jessup, Gentry "Jeep" p

(2) Trouppe, Quincy Thomas "Big Train" c

Vargas, Roberto Enrique p

1949

McKinnis, Gread "Lefty" or "Gready" p

Summers, Lonnie "Carl" c

1950

Douglas, Jesse Warren 3b

McNeal, Clyde Clifton "Junior" ss

Pennington, Arthur David "Superman" cf

1951

Anderson, Curt "Andy" lf

Woods, Parnell 3b

1952

Beverly, William "Fireball" p

Durham, Joseph Vann "Winn" lf

McLaurin, Felix lf

Patterson Jr., Willie Lee "Pat" 1b

Raines, Lawrence Glenn Hope "Larry" ss

CINCINNATI BUCKEYES—3 players

1942

(2) Bremer Sr., Eugene Joseph "Gene" or "Flash" p

(2) Jethroe, Samuel "Sam" or "The Jet" ph, cf

(2) Woods, Parnell 3b

CINCINNATI CLOWNS—2 players

1943

Wilson, Fred "Sardo" ph

1944

Radcliffe, Alexander "Alec" 3b

CINCINNATI TIGERS—5 players

1937

Bibbs, Junius Alexander "Rainey" 2b

Davenport, Lloyd "Ducky" rf

Easterling, Howard ss

Moss, Porter "Ankleball" p

Radcliffe, Theodore Roosevelt "Double Duty" c

CINCINNATI-INDIANAPOLIS CLOWNS—1 player

1945

Radcliffe, Alexander "Alec" 3b

CLEVELAND BEARS—3 players

1939

Lyles, John ss

Owens, Raymond "Smoky" p

Woods, Parnell 3b

CLEVELAND BUCKEYES—25 players

1943

Smith, Theolic "Fireball" p

1944

Armour, Alfred "Buddy" lf

Bremer Sr., Eugene Joseph "Gene" or "Flash" p

Jethroe, Samuel "Sam" or "The Jet" cf

Ware, Archie Virgil 1b

1945

Bremer Sr., Eugene Joseph "Gene" or "Flash" p

Davenport, Lloyd "Ducky" rf

Trouppe, Quincy Thomas "Big Train" c

Ware, Archie Virgil 1b

1946

Brown, John W. ph

Clarke, Vibert Ernesto "Webbo" p

(2) Grace, Willie "Fireman" rf

(2) Jethroe, Samuel "Sam" or "The Jet" cf

(2) Trouppe, Quincy Thomas "Big Train" c

(2) Ware, Archie Virgil 1b

1947

Brewer, Chester Arthur "Chet" p

Clarke, Vibert Ernesto "Webbo" p

(2) Jethroe, Samuel "Sam" or "The Jet" rf, cf

Kellman, Edric Leon 2b

(2) Trouppe, Quincy Thomas "Big Train" c

1948

Clarke, Vibert Ernesto "Webbo" p

Grace, Willie "Fireman" lf

Kellman, Edric Leon 3b

1949

Hoskins, David Taylor "Dave" ph

Kellman, Edric Leon ph

CLEVELAND GIANTS—1 player

1933

Morney, Leroy 2b

CLEVELAND RED SOX—1 player

1934

Patterson, Andrew Lawrence "Pat" 2b

COLUMBUS ELITE GIANTS—4 players

1935

Griffith, Robert Lee "Schoolboy" p

Hughes, Samuel Thomas "Sammy T." 2b
Snow, Felton "Skipper" ph
Wright, Burnis "Wild Bill" ph

DETROIT STARS — 1 player
1937
Stearnes, Norman Thomas "Turkey" cf

HOMESTEAD GRAYS — 48 players
1933
Britt, George "Chippy" p
Harris, Elander Victor "Vic" lf
1934
Harris, Elander Victor "Vic" lf
1935
Brown, Raymond "Ray" p
Leonard, Walter Fenner "Buck" 1b
1937
Benjamin, Jerry Charles "Ben" rf
Leonard, Walter Fenner "Buck" 1b
1938
Harris, Elander Victor "Vic" lf
Leonard, Walter Fenner "Buck" 1b
Walker, Edsall "Big" p
1939
(2) Gibson, Joshua "Josh" c
Harris, Elander Victor "Vic" lf
(2) Leonard, Walter Fenner "Buck" 1b
Partlow, Roy "Silent Roy" p
1940
Brown, Raymond "Ray" p
Easterling, Howard 3b
Leonard, Walter Fenner "Buck" 1b
1941
Leonard, Walter Fenner "Buck" 1b
McDuffie, Terris "The Great" p
1942
(2) Bankhead, Samuel Howard "Sam" 2b, cf
(2) Gibson, Joshua "Josh" c
Harris, Elander Victor "Vic" ph
1943
Bankhead, Samuel Howard "Sam" 2b
Bell, James Thomas "Cool Papa" lf
Benjamin, Jerry Charles "Ben" ph
Easterling, Howard 3b
Gibson, Joshua "Josh" c
Harris, Elander Victor "Vic" ph
Leonard, Walter Fenner "Buck" 1b
Wright Sr., John Richard "Johnny" p
1944
Bankhead, Samuel Howard "Sam" 2b, ss
Bell, James Thomas "Cool Papa" lf
Gibson, Joshua "Josh" c
Leonard, Walter Fenner "Buck" 1b
1945
Benjamin, Jerry Charles "Ben" cf

Leonard, Walter Fenner "Buck" 1b
Welmaker, Roy Horace "Snook" or "Lefty" p
1946
Bankhead, Samuel Howard "Sam" ss
(2) Easterling, Howard 3b
(2) Gibson, Joshua "Josh" c
(2) Leonard, Walter Fenner "Buck" 1b
1947
Harris, Elander Victor "Vic" pr
(2) Marquez, Luis Angel "Canena" rf
Wright Sr., John Richard "Johnny" p
1948
(2) Easter, Luscious "Luke" rf, lf
Fields, Wilmer Leon "Red" p
Leonard, Walter Fenner "Buck" 1b
(2) Marquez, Luis Angel "Canena" cf, rf

HOUSTON EAGLES — 5 players
1949
Davis, John Howard "Cherokee" cf
Wilson, Robert "Bob" 3b, ss
1950
Harvey, Robert A. "Bob" rf
Washington, John G. "Johnny" 1b
Williams, Willie C. "Curley" ss

INDIANAPOLIS ABCS — 2 players
1938
Strong, Theodore Roosevelt "Ted" or "T. R." 1b
Trouppe, Quincy Thomas "Big Train" lf

INDIANAPOLIS ATHLETICS — 1 player
1937
Strong, Theodore Roosevelt "Ted" or "T. R." 1b

INDIANAPOLIS CLOWNS — 25 players
1946
Haywood, Albert Elliott "Buster" c
(2) Williams, Johnny "Nature Boy" p
1947
Neil, Raymond "Ray" or "Aussa" 2b
Tatum Jr., Reece "Goose" 1b
Williams, Johnny "Nature Boy" p
1948
Cohen, James Clarence "Fireball" p
Hairston, Samuel "Sam" ph
1949
Brewer, Sherwood "Woody" rf
Porter, Andrew "Andy" or "Pullman" p
1950
Brewer, Sherwood "Woody" 3b, rf
Merchant, Henry Lewis "Speed" lf
1951
Haywood, Albert Elliott "Buster" c
Neil, Raymond "Ray" or "Aussa" 2b
Tugerson, Joseph Leander p

1952

Merchant, Henry Lewis "Speed" rf
Richardson, T.W. "Ted" or "Lefty" p
Vazquez, Armando Bernando 2b
Wilkes, James Eugene "Seabiscuit" 1b

1953

Amaro, Dionisio "Dave" p
Brown, William "Willie" ss
Drake, Reynaldo "Verdes" cf
Gaines, Willy "Willie" p
Haywood, Albert Elliott "Buster" ph
Neil, Raymond "Ray" or "Aussa" 2b
Sands, Samuel "Piggy" c

JACKSONVILLE RED CAPS—3 players
1941

Cleveland, Howard "Duke" ph
Henry, Leo "Preacher" p
Woods, Parnell 3b

KANSAS CITY MONARCHS—78 players
1934

Brewer, Chester Arthur "Chet" p

1936 – record 11 players

Allen, Newton Henry "Colt" 2b, ss
Brown, Willard Jesse "Home Run" ss
Cooper, Andrew L. "Andy" p
Dwight, Edward Joseph "Eddie" cf
Else, Harry "Speed" c
Harris, Chick "Popsickle" 1b
Kranson, Floyd Arthur p
Milton, Henry William "Streak" cf
Patterson, Andrew Lawrence "Pat" 2b
Rogan, Wilber "Bullet" lf
Taylor, LeRoy rf

1937

Allen, Newton Henry "Colt" 2b, ss
Brown, Willard Jesse "Home Run" lf
Mayweather, Eldridge E. "Chili" ph
Milton, Henry William "Streak" ph
Smith, Hilton Lee "Smitty" p

1938

Allen, Newton Henry "Colt" 2b
Johnson, Byron "Mex" or "Jew Baby" ss
Milton, Henry William "Streak" rf
Smith, Hilton Lee "Smitty" p

1939

Milton, Henry William "Streak" rf
(2) Smith, Hilton Lee "Smitty" p
Stearnes, Norman Thomas "Turkey" rf
(2) Strong, Theodore Roosevelt "Ted" or "T. R." 1b, ss

1940

Greene, James Elbert "Joe" or "Pea" c
Milton, Henry William "Streak" rf
Smith, Hilton Lee "Smitty" p

1941

Allen, Newton Henry "Colt" ss
Paige, Leroy Robert "Satchel" p
Smith, Hilton Lee "Smitty" p
Strong, Theodore Roosevelt "Ted" or "T. R." rf

1942

(2) Brown, Willard Jesse "Home Run" lf
(2) Greene, James Elbert "Joe" or "Pea" c
(2) O'Neil Jr., John Jordan "Buck" 1b
Paige, Leroy Robert "Satchel" p
Smith, Hilton Lee "Smitty" p
(2) Strong, Theodore Roosevelt "Ted" or "T. R." rf

1943

Brown, Willard Jesse "Home Run" cf
O'Neil Jr., John Jordan "Buck" 1b
Paige, Leroy Robert "Satchel" p
Williams, Jesse Horace "Bill" ss

1944

Serrell, Bonnie Clinton "El Grillo" 2b

1945

McDaniels, Booker Taliaferro "Cannonball" p
Robinson, Jack Roosevelt "Jackie" ss
Williams, Jesse Horace "Bill" 2b

1946

Renfroe Sr., Othello Nelson "Chico" ss
Scott, John lf

1947

Abernathy, Robert William "James" lf
Smith, John Ford "Geronimo" or "Lefty" p
(2) Souell (Cyrus), Herbert "Herb" or "Baldy" 3b

1948

(2) Brown, Willard Jesse "Home Run" cf
(2) LaMarque, James Harding "Lefty" p
(2) Souell (Cyrus), Herbert "Herb" or "Baldy" 3b

1949

Brown, Willard Jesse "Home Run" 3b, lf
LaMarque, James Harding "Lefty" p
O'Neil Jr., John Jordan "Buck" ph
Richardson, Norval Eugene "Gene" or "Britches" p

1950

Cooper, Thomas Roger "Tom" c, rf
Johnson Jr., Clifford "Connie" p
Souell (Cyrus), Herbert "Herb" or "Baldy" 3b

1951

Brewer, Sherwood "Woody" 3b
Cooper, Thomas Roger "Tom" c 1b
Smith, Theolic "Fireball" p
Williams, Jesse Horace "Bill" 2b

1952

Baylis, Henry "Hank" 3b
Henderson, James "Duke" cf
Jackson, Isiah "Ike" c
Jackson Jr., John W. "Stony" p
Phillips Jr., Richard Albaso "Dick" p

1953

Armenteros, Juan c

Banks, Ernest "Ernie" ss
Baylis, Henry "Hank" 3b
Brewer, Sherwood "Woody" 2b
Cooper, Thomas Roger "Tom" lf
Herrera, Juan Francisco "Pancho" 1b
Jackson Jr., John W. "Stony" p
Johnson, Ernest D. "Schooley" rf

MEMPHIS RED SOX— 61 players
1938
Brown, Larry "Iron Man" c
Radcliffe, Theodore Roosevelt "Double Duty" p
Robinson, Cornelius Randall "Neal" or "Shadow" cf
1939
(2) Brown, Larry "Iron Man" c
Davenport, Lloyd "Ducky" ph
Radcliffe, Theodore Roosevelt "Double Duty" p
(2) Robinson, Cornelius Randall "Neal" or
    "Shadow" cf
Taylor, Olan "Jelly" 1b
1940
Bremer Sr., Eugene Joseph "Gene" or "Flash" p
Brown, Larry "Iron Man" c
Robinson, Cornelius Randall "Neal" or "Shadow" cf
Taylor, Olan "Jelly" ph
1941
Brown, Larry "Iron Man" c
Mathis Sr., Verdell "Lefty"
Radcliffe, Theodore Roosevelt "Double Duty" p
Robinson, Cornelius Randall "Neal" or "Shadow" cf
Taylor, Olan "Jelly" 1b
1942
(2) Bankhead, Fred 2b
Brown, Thomas Jefferson "Tom" or "T. J." ss
(2) Carter, Marlin Theodore "Mel" 3b
Mathis Sr., Verdell "Lefty" p
Moss, Porter "Ankleball" p
1943
Hyde, Cowan Fontella "Bubba" pr
Moss, Porter "Ankleball" p
Robinson, Cornelius Randall "Neal" or "Shadow" cf
1944
Mathis Sr., Verdell "Lefty" p
Robinson, Cornelius Randall "Neal" or "Shadow" cf
1945
Mathis Sr., Verdell "Lefty" p
Robinson, Cornelius Randall "Neal" or "Shadow" cf
1946
(2) Bankhead, Daniel Robert "Dan" p
Evans, Felix "Chin" p
(2) Hyde, Cowan Fontella "Bubba" lf
(2) Radcliffe, Alexander "Alec" 3b
1947
Bankhead, Daniel Robert "Dan" p
Boyd, Robert Richard "Bob" 1b
Carter, Ernest C. "Spoon" p

(2) Colas, Jose Luis lf, cf
1948
(2) Boyd, Robert Richard "Bob" 1b
Carter, Ernest C. "Spoon" pr
Colas, Jose Luis ph
Robinson, Cornelius Randall "Neal" or "Shadow" lf
1949
Boyd, Robert Richard "Bob" 1b
Formental, Pedro cf
Hutchinson, Willie "Ace" p
Varona, Orlando Clemente ss
1950
Clarke, Vibert Ernesto "Webbo" p
Jones Jr., Clinton "Casey" c
Kellman, Edric Leon 3b
1951
Clarke, Vibert Ernesto "Webbo" p
Colas, Jose Luis cf
Jones Jr., Clinton "Casey" c
Varona, Gilberto "Gil" 1b
1952
Valdez, Felix "Manuel" 2b
Varona, Gilberto "Gil" 1b
Watrous, Sherman rf
1953
Bassett, Lloyd "Pepper" c
Haggins Jr., Raymond "Billy Ray" rf
Harris, Isiah p
Patterson Jr., Willie Lee "Pat" 1b
Reed, Eddie Lee cf
Sims, Fate lf
Woods, Sam "Buddy" p

NASHVILLE ELITE GIANTS— 4 players
1933
Bankhead, Samuel Howard "Sam" rf
1934
Bankhead, Samuel Howard "Sam" rf
Hughes, Samuel Thomas "Sammy T." 2b
Parnell, Roy "Red" lf

NEWARK DODGERS— 3 players
1934
Lundy, Richard "Dick" or "King Richard" ss
1935
Arnold, Paul cf
Dandridge, Raymond Emmett "Ray" 2b

NEWARK EAGLES— 39 players
1937
Dandridge, Raymond Emmett "Ray" 3b
Day, Leon p
Suttles, George "Mule" lf
Wells, Willie James "Devil" ss
1938
Wells, Willie James "Devil" ss

1939
  (2) Day, Leon p
  Stone, Edward "Ed" or "Ace" rf
  (2) Wells, Willie James "Devil" ss
1940
  Clarkson, James Buster "Bus" ss
  Stone, Edward "Ed" or "Ace" rf
1941
  Hill, Jimmy "Lefty" or "Squab" p
  Irvin, Monford Merrill "Monte" 3b
  Pearson, Leonard Curtis "Lennie" or "Hoss" cf
1942
  (2) Day, Leon p
  (2) Pearson, Leonard Curtis "Lennie" or "Hoss" ph, cf
  (2) Wells, Willie James "Devil" ss
1943
  Day, Leon p
  Pearson, Leonard Curtis "Lennie" or "Hoss" rf
1944
  Dandridge, Raymond Emmett "Ray" 2b, 3b
  Davis, John Howard "Cherokee" cf
  McDuffie, Terris "The Great" p
1945
  Davis, John Howard "Cherokee" lf
  Pearson, Leonard Curtis "Lennie" or "Hoss ph
  Watkins, Murray "Skeeter" 3b
  Wells, Willie James "Devil" 2b
1946
  (2) Day, Leon p
  (2) Doby, Lawrence Eugene "Larry" 2b
  (2) Irvin, Monford Merrill "Monte" lf
  Pearson, Leonard Curtis "Lennie" or "Hoss rf
  Ruffin, Charles Leon "Lassas" c
1947
  (2) Irvin, Monford Merrill "Monte" lf
  Lewis, Rufus "Mississippi" p
  Mackey, James Raleigh "Biz" ph
  Manning, Maxwell "Max" p
1948
  Harvey, Robert A. "Bob" rf
  Irvin, Monford Merrill "Monte" rf
  Lewis, Rufus "Mississippi" p
  Manning, Maxwell "Max" p
  Wilkes, James Eugene "Seabiscuit" cf

NEW ORLEANS EAGLES—4 players
1951
  Griggs, Wiley Lee "Diamond Jim" ph
  Guice, Lacy Kirk "Larry" rf
  Heard, Jehosie "Jay" p
  Williams, Willie C. "Curley" ss

NEW ORLEANS–ST. LOUIS STARS—4 players
1940
  Calhoun, Walter "Lefty" p
  Green Sr., Leslie "Chin" cf

Mayweather, Eldridge E. "Chili" 1b
Riddle, Marshall Lewis "Jit" 2b

NEW YORK BLACK YANKEES—19 players
1933
  Jenkins, Clarence R. "Fats" lf
1937
  Brown, Barney "Brinquitos" p
1938
  Brown, Barney "Brinquitos" p
  Cannady, Walter I. "Rev" 3b
1939
  Holland, Elvis William "Bill" p
  McDuffie, Terris "The Great" p
1940
  Barker, Marvin "Hank" or "Hack" cf, rf
  Clarke, Robert "Eggie" c
  Seay, Richard William "Dickie" 2b
1941
  Kimbro, Henry Allen "Jimbo" cf
  Seay, Richard William "Dickie" 2b
1942
  Smith, Eugene L. "Gene" p
  (2) Wilson, Daniel Richard "Dan" lf
1945
  Barker, Marvin "Hank" or "Hack" 3b
1947
  (2) Hayes, John William "Johnny" c
1948
  Barker, Marvin "Hank" or "Hack" ph
  Crowe, George Daniel "Big George" 1b
  Griffith, Robert Lee "Schoolboy" p

NEW YORK CUBANS—43 PLAYERS
1935
  Dihigo, Martin p cf
  Oms, Alejandro "Walla Walla" rf
  Tiant Sr., Luis Eleuterio "Sir Skinny" p
1939
  Lopez, Candido Justo "Cando" or "Police Car" lf
1940
  Crespo, Alejandro "Alex" lf
  Martinez, Horacio "Rabbit" ss
  Ruiz, Silvino "Poppa" p
1941
  Barnhill, Dave "Impo" p
  Coimbre, Francisco Atiles "Pancho" rf
  Martinez, Horacio "Rabbit" ss
1942
  (2) Barnhill, Dave "Impo" p
  (2) Blanco, Herberto "Harry" 2b, p
  (2) Vargas, Juan Estando "Tetelo" cf
1943
  Barnhill, Dave "Impo" p
  Martinez, Horacio "Rabbit" ss
  Vargas, Juan Estando "Tetelo" cf

1944
Coimbre, Francisco Atiles "Pancho" rf
Howard, Carrenza "Schoolboy" p
Martinez, Horacio "Rabbit" ss
Morris, Barney "Big Ad" p

1945
Dihigo, Martin p
Linares, Rogelio "Ice Cream" rf
Martinez, Horacio "Rabbit" ss

1946
Diaz, Pedro "Manny" ph
Garcia, Silvio ss
Louden, Louis Oliver "Tommy" c
(2) Scantlebury, Patricio Athlestan "Pat" p, ph

1947
(2) Duany, Claro rf, ph
(2) Garcia, Silvio 2b
(2) Louden, Louis Oliver "Tommy" c
(2) Minoso, Saturnino Orestes Arrieta "Minnie" 3b
(2) Tiant Sr., Luis Eleuterio "Sir Skinny" p

1948
Barnhill, Dave "Impo" p
(2) Louden, Louis Oliver "Tommy" c
(2) Minoso, Saturnino Orestes Arrieta "Minnie" 3b

1949
Diaz, Pedro "Manny" cf
Easterling, Howard 3b
Scantlebury, Patricio Athlestan "Pat" p

1950
Diaz, Pedro "Manny" c
Galata, Raul p
Gonzalez, Hiram "Rene" 1b
Louden, Louis Oliver "Tommy" c
Scantlebury, Patricio Athlestan "Pat" p

PHILADELPHIA STARS—46 players
1933
Dixon, Herbert Albert "Rap" rf
Lundy, Richard "Dick" or "King Richard" ss
Mackey, James Raleigh "Biz" c
Wilson, Ernest Judson "Boojum" or "Jud" 3b

1934
Jones, Stuart "Slim" p
Wilson, Ernest Judson "Boojum" or "Jud" 3b

1935
Jones, Stuart "Slim" p
Mackey, James Raleigh "Biz" c
Seay, Richard William "Dickie" 2b
Stephens, Paul Eugene "Jake" ss
Wilson, Ernest Judson "Boojum" or "Jud" 3b

1937
Dunn, Joseph P. "Jake" 2b
1938
Dunn, Joseph P. "Jake" ph
1939
Parnell, Roy "Red" lf

(2) Patterson, Andrew Lawrence "Pat" 3b
1940
Benson, Eugene "Gene" cf
McHenry, Henry "Cream" p
1941
McHenry, Henry "Cream" p
1942
Brown, Barney "Brinquitos" p
(2) Patterson, Andrew Lawrence "Pat" 3b
(2) West, James "Jim" or "Shifty" 1b
1944
Williams, Marvin "Tex" ph
1945
Austin, Frank Samuel "Pee Wee" ss
Benson, Eugene "Gene" lf
Ricks, William "Bill" p
1946
Austin, Frank Samuel "Pee Wee" pr
(2) Benson, Eugene "Gene" rf
(2) Brown, Barney "Brinquitos" p
(2) Watkins, Murray "Skeeter" ph, pr
1947
(2) Austin, Frank Samuel "Pee Wee" ss
(2) Miller, Henry Joseph "Hank" p
1948
(2) Austin, Frank Samuel "Pee Wee" ss
(2) Cash, William Walker "Ready" c
1949
Cash, William Walker "Ready" c
Clarkson, James Buster "Bus" rf
Griffith, Robert Lee "Schoolboy" p
1950
Gaines, Jonas Donald "Lefty" p
Littles, Ben rf
White Jr., Charles "Charlie" 3b
1951
Harris, Wilmer p
Littles, Ben ph
Smith, Milton "Milt" 3b
1952
Harris, Wilmer p
Jones, James "Jimmie" rf
Washington, Ted ss
Whittington, Don 3b

PITTSBURGH CRAWFORDS—35 players
1933
Bell, James Thomas "Cool Papa" cf
Charleston, Oscar McKinley "Charlie" 1b
Gibson, Joshua "Josh" c
Hunter, Bertrum "Nate" or "Buffalo" p
Johnson, William Julius "Judy" 3b
Russell, John Henry "Pistol" 2b
Streeter, Samuel "Lefty" p
1934
Bell, James Thomas "Cool Papa" cf

Charleston, Oscar McKinley "Charlie" 1b
Crutchfield, John William "Jimmie" rf
Gibson, Joshua "Josh" c, lf
Kincannon, Harry "Tin Can" p
Paige, Leroy Robert "Satchel" p
Perkins, William Gamiel "Cy" c
Williams, Chester Arthur "Ches" 2b

1935
Bell, James Thomas "Cool Papa" cf
Charleston, Oscar McKinley "Charlie" 1b
Crutchfield, John William "Jimmie" rf
Gibson, Joshua "Josh" c
Matlock, Leroy p
Williams, Chester Arthur "Ches" ss

1936
Bankhead, Samuel Howard "Sam" lf
Bell, James Thomas "Cool Papa" cf
Crutchfield, John William "Jimmie" rf
Gibson, Joshua "Josh" c
Johnson, William Julius "Judy" 3b
Matlock, Leroy p
Paige, Leroy Robert "Satchel" p
Washington, John G. "Johnny" 1b
Williams, Chester Arthur "Ches" ss

1937
Bassett, Lloyd "Pepper" c
Morris, Barney "Big Ad" p
Williams, Chester Arthur "Ches" 2b

1938
Bankhead, Samuel Howard "Sam" cf
Taylor, Johnny A. "School Boy" p

ST. LOUIS STARS—7 players
1939
Riddle, Marshall Lewis "Jit" 2b
Smith, Theolic "Fireball" p
(2) Wilson, Daniel Richard "Dan" lf, rf
1941
Armour, Alfred "Buddy" cf
Ford, James "Jimmy" 2b
Mitchell, George "Big" ph
Wilson, Daniel Richard "Dan" lf

TOLEDO-INDIANAPOLIS CRAWFORDS—5 players
1939
Johnson, Jimmy "Slim" p
Morney, Leroy 2b, ss
(2) Williams, James "Big Jim" rf, ph
1940
Henderson, Curtis "Dan" ss
Johnson Jr., Clifford "Connie" p

WASHINGTON ELITE GIANTS—8 players
1936
Byrd, William "Bill" p
Hughes, Samuel Thomas "Sammy T." 2b
Mackey, James Raleigh "Biz" c
Snow, Felton "Skipper" 3b
West, James "Jim" or "Shifty" 1b
Wright, Burnis "Wild Bill" cf
Wright, Zollie rf
1937
Wright, Burnis "Wild Bill" cf

Individual Batting Statistics

PLAYER/TEAM	AGE	DATE	AB	R	H	D	T	HR	RBI	W	SAC	SB	E	RAVE	RSLG
Abernathy, Robert William "James" B: 07/12/1918 Columbia, TN D: 09/02/1997 Nashville, TN B/T: R/R 5'9" 175 lbs.
KANSAS CITY MONARCHS	29	29-Jul-47	4	0	0	0	0	0	0	0	0	0	0	.000	.000
Player Totals:		1 Game	4	0	0	0	0	0	0	0	0	0	0	.000	.000
Allen, Newton Henry "Colt" B: 05/19/1902 Austin, TX D: 06/11/1988 Cincinnati, OH B/T: R/R 5'8" 170 lbs.
KANSAS CITY MONARCHS	34	23-Aug-36	5	0	0	0	0	0	0	0	0	0	0	.000	.000
KANSAS CITY MONARCHS	35	08-Aug-37	4	0	0	0	0	0	0	0	0	0	0	.000	.000
KANSAS CITY MONARCHS	36	21-Aug-38	4	0	0	0	0	0	0	0	0	0	1	.000	.000
KANSAS CITY MONARCHS	39	27-Jul-41	2	0	0	0	0	0	0	0	0	0	2	.000	.000
Player Totals:		4 Games	15	0	0	0	0	0	0	0	0	0	3	.000	.000
Amaro, Dionisio "Dave" B: 1930 Havana, Cuba D: — B/T: R/R 6'3" 180 lbs.
INDIANAPOLIS CLOWNS	23	16-Aug-53	1	0	0	0	0	0	0	0	0	0	0	.000	.000
Player Totals:		1 Game	1	0	0	0	0	0	0	0	0	0	0	.000	.000
Anderson, Curt "Andy" B: — D: — B/T: R/R
CHICAGO AMERICAN GIANTS		12-Aug-51	4	0	1	0	0	0	0	0	0	0	0	.250	.250
Player Totals:		1 Game	4	0	1	0	0	0	0	0	0	0	0	.250	.250
Armenteros, Juan Francis B: 06/24/1928 Havana, Cuba Living in Miami, FL B/T: R/R 5'11" 170 lbs.
KANSAS CITY MONARCHS	25	16-Aug-53	1	0	0	0	0	0	0	0	0	0	0	.000	.000
Player Totals:		1 Games	1	0	0	0	0	0	0	0	0	0	0	.000	.000
Armour, Alfred "Buddy" B: 04/27/1915 Jackson, MS D: 04/??/1974 Carbondale, IL B/T: L/L 5'9" 170 lbs.
ST. LOUIS STARS	26	27-Jul-41	2	1	1	0	0	0	0	0	0	0	0	.500	.500
CLEVELAND BUCKEYES	29	13-Aug-44	4	2	2	0	0	0	0	0	0	1	0	.500	.500
CHICAGO AMERICAN GIANTS	32	27-Jul-47	4	0	2	2	0	0	0	0	0	0	0	.500	.700
CHICAGO AMERICAN GIANTS	32	29-Jul-47	1	0	0	0	0	0	0	0	0	0	0	.455	.636
Player Totals:		4 Games	11	3	5	2	0	0	0	0	0	1	0	.455	.636
Arnold, Paul B: 1906 Hopewell, NJ D: — B/T: L/R 5'9" 160 lbs.
NEWARK DODGERS	29	11-Aug-35	0	0	0	0	0	0	0	0	0	0	0	.000	.000
Player Totals:		1 Games	0	0	0	0	0	0	0	0	0	0	0	.000	.000
Austin, Frank Samuel "Pee Wee" B: 05/22/1922 Panama Canal Zone D: 01/15/1960 Panama City, Panama B/T:R/R 5'7" 180 lbs.
PHILADELPHIA STARS	23	29-Jul-45	2	0	0	0	0	0	0	1	0	0	1	.000	.000
PHILADELPHIA STARS	24	15-Aug-46	0	0	0	0	0	0	0	0	0	0	0	.000	.000
PHILADELPHIA STARS	25	27-Jul-47	2	0	0	0	0	0	0	0	0	0	0	.000	.000
PHILADELPHIA STARS	25	29-Jul-47	2	0	0	0	0	0	0	0	0	0	0	.000	.000
PHILADELPHIA STARS	26	22-Aug-48	1	0	0	0	0	0	0	0	0	0	1	.000	.000
PHILADELPHIA STARS	26	24-Aug-48	3	0	2	0	0	0	0	0	0	0	0	.200	.200
Player Totals:		6 Games	10	0	2	0	0	0	0	1	0	0	2	.200	.200
Bailey, Otha William "Bill" B: 06/30/1930 Huntsville, AL Living in Birmingham, AL B/T: R/R 5'6" 150 lbs.
BIRMINGHAM BLACK BARONS	22	17-Aug-52	4	0	1	1	0	0	1	0	0	0	0	.250	.500
BIRMINGHAM BLACK BARONS	23	16-Aug-53	1	0	0	0	0	0	0	0	0	0	0	.200	.400
Player Totals:		2 Games	5	0	1	1	0	0	1	0	0	0	0	.200	.400
Bankhead, Daniel Robert "Dan" B: 05/03/1920 Empire, AL D: 05/02/1976 Houston, TX B/T: R/R 6'1" 185 lbs.
BIRMINGHAM BLACK BARONS	21	27-Jul-41	0	0	0	0	0	0	0	0	0	0	0	.000	.000
MEMPHIS RED SOX	26	15-Aug-46	1	0	0	0	0	0	0	0	0	0	0	.000	.000
MEMPHIS RED SOX	26	18-Aug-46	1	0	0	0	0	0	0	0	0	0	0	.000	.000
MEMPHIS RED SOX	27	27-Jul-47	2	0	0	0	0	0	0	0	0	0	0	.000	.000
Player Totals:		4 Games	4	0	0	0	0	0	0	0	0	0	0	.000	.000

PLAYER/TEAM	AGE	DATE	AB	R	H	D	T	HR	RBI	W	SAC	SB	E	RAVE	RSLG
Bankhead, Fred B: *11/22/1912 Sulligent, AL* D: *12/17/1972 Mississippi* B/T: R/R *5'10"* *165 lbs.*																
MEMPHIS RED SOX	29	16-Aug-42	0	1	0	0	0	0	0	0	0	0	0	.000	.000
MEMPHIS RED SOX	29	18-Aug-42	0	0	0	0	0	0	0	0	0	0	1	.000	.000
Player Totals:	**2 Games**		**0**	**1**	**0**	**0**	**0**	**0**	**0**	**0**	**0**	**0**	**1**	**.000**	**.000**
Bankhead, Samuel Howard "Sam" B: *09/18/1910 Sulligent, AL* D: *07/24/1976 Pittsburgh, PA* B/T: R/R *5'8"* *175 lbs.*																
NASHVILLE ELITE GIANTS	22	10-Sep-33	4	2	2	0	0	0	0	0	0	1	0	.500	.500
NASHVILLE ELITE GIANTS	23	26-Aug-34	3	0	1	0	0	0	0	0	0	0	0	.429	.429
PITTSBURGH CRAWFORDS	25	23-Aug-36	4	1	2	1	0	0	0	0	1	0	0	.455	.545
PITTSBURGH CRAWFORDS	27	21-Aug-38	4	0	2	0	0	0	1	0	0	1	0	.467	.533
HOMESTEAD GRAYS	31	16-Aug-42	4	1	2	1	0	0	2	0	1	0	0	.474	.579
HOMESTEAD GRAYS	31	18-Aug-42	4	2	2	0	0	0	0	0	0	0	1	.478	.565
HOMESTEAD GRAYS	32	01-Aug-43	3	0	0	0	0	0	0	0	0	0	0	.423	.500
HOMESTEAD GRAYS	33	13-Aug-44	3	1	1	0	0	0	1	0	0	0	1	.414	.483
HOMESTEAD GRAYS	35	15-Aug-46	2	0	0	0	0	0	0	0	0	0	1	.387	.452
Player Totals:	**9 Games**		**31**	**7**	**12**	**2**	**0**	**0**	**4**	**0**	**2**	**2**	**3**	**.387**	**.452**
Banks, Ernest "Ernie" B: *01/31/1931 Dallas, TX* *Living in Chicago, IL* B/T: R/R *6'1"* *180 lbs.*																
KANSAS CITY MONARCHS	22	16-Aug-53	4	0	0	0	0	0	0	0	0	0	0	.000	.000
Player Totals:	**1 Game**		**4**	**0**	**0**	**0**	**0**	**0**	**0**	**0**	**0**	**0**	**0**	**.000**	**.000**
Barker, Marvin "Hank" or "Hack" B: — D: — B/T: R/R *5'9"* *175 lbs.*																
NEW YORK BLACK YANKEES		18-Aug-40	5	1	3	0	0	0	1	0	0	0	0	.600	.600
NEW YORK BLACK YANKEES		29-Jul-45	2	0	1	0	0	0	0	0	0	0	0	.571	.571
NEW YORK BLACK YANKEES		24-Aug-48	1	0	0	0	0	0	0	0	0	0	0	.500	.500
Player Totals:	**3 Games**		**8**	**1**	**4**	**0**	**0**	**0**	**1**	**0**	**0**	**0**	**0**	**.500**	**.500**
Barnhill, Dave "Impo" B: *10/30/1913 Greenville, NC* D: *01/08/1983 Miami, FL* B/T: R/R *5'6"* *160 lbs.*																
NEW YORK CUBANS	27	27-Jul-41	2	1	2	0	0	0	1	0	0	0	0	1.000	1.000
NEW YORK CUBANS	28	16-Aug-42	0	0	0	0	0	0	0	0	0	0	0	1.000	1.000
NEW YORK CUBANS	28	18-Aug-42	0	0	0	0	0	0	0	0	0	0	0	1.000	1.000
NEW YORK CUBANS	29	01-Aug-43	1	0	0	0	0	0	0	0	0	0	0	.667	.667
NEW YORK CUBANS	34	24-Aug-48	1	0	0	0	0	0	1	0	0	0	0	.500	.500
Player Totals:	**5 Games**		**4**	**1**	**2**	**0**	**0**	**0**	**2**	**0**	**0**	**0**	**0**	**.500**	**.500**
Bassett, Lloyd "Pepper" B: *08/05/1919 Baton Rouge, LA* D: *02/27/1981 Los Angeles, CA* B/T: S/R *6'3"* *220 lbs.*																
PITTSBURGH CRAWFORDS	18	08-Aug-37	3	0	0	0	0	0	0	1	0	0	0	.000	.000
CHICAGO AMERICAN GIANTS	20	06-Aug-39	1	0	0	0	0	0	0	0	0	0	0	.000	.000
CHICAGO AMERICAN GIANTS	20	27-Aug-39	2	0	0	0	0	0	0	0	0	0	1	.000	.000
CHICAGO AMERICAN GIANTS	21	27-Jul-41	1	0	0	0	0	0	0	0	0	0	0	.000	.000
BIRMINGHAM BLACK BARONS	27	29-Jul-47	2	0	1	0	0	0	0	0	0	0	0	.111	.111
BIRMINGHAM BLACK BARONS	29	24-Aug-48	2	0	0	0	0	0	0	0	0	0	0	.091	.091
BIRMINGHAM BLACK BARONS	31	20-Aug-50	1	0	1	1	0	0	0	0	0	0	0	.167	.250
MEMPHIS RED SOX	34	16-Aug-53	3	0	0	0	0	0	0	0	0	0	0	.133	.200
Player Totals:	**8 Games**		**15**	**0**	**2**	**1**	**0**	**0**	**0**	**1**	**0**	**0**	**1**	**.133**	**.200**
Baylis, Henry "Hank" B: *02/08/1923 Kansas City, MO* D: *12/17/1980 Kansas City, MO* B/T: R/R *5'9"* *175 lbs.*																
KANSAS CITY MONARCHS	29	17-Aug-52	4	1	1	1	0	0	2	0	0	0	0	.250	.500
KANSAS CITY MONARCHS	30	16-Aug-53	4	0	1	0	0	0	1	0	0	0	0	.250	.375
Player Totals:	**2 Games**		**8**	**1**	**2**	**1**	**0**	**0**	**3**	**0**	**0**	**0**	**0**	**.250**	**.375**
Bell, Herman B: — D: — B/T: R/R *5'9"* *195 lbs.*																
BIRMINGHAM BLACK BARONS		14-Aug-49	1	0	0	0	0	0	0	0	0	0	0	.000	.000
Player Totals:	**1 Game**		**1**	**0**	**0**	**0**	**0**	**0**	**0**	**0**	**0**	**0**	**0**	**.000**	**.000**
Bell, James Thomas "Cool Papa" B: *05/17/1903 Starkville, MS* D: *03/07/1991 St. Louis, MO* B/T: S/L *5'11"* *150 lbs.*																
PITTSBURGH CRAWFORDS	30	10-Sep-33	5	1	0	0	0	0	0	0	0	0	0	.000	.000
PITTSBURGH CRAWFORDS	31	26-Aug-34	3	1	0	0	0	0	0	1	0	1	0	.000	.000

PLAYER/TEAM	AGE	DATE	AB	R	H	D	T	HR	RBI	W	SAC	SB	E	RAVE	RSLG
PITTSBURGH CRAWFORDS	32	11-Aug-35	4	2	1	0	0	0	0	2	0	0	1	.083	.083
PITTSBURGH CRAWFORDS	33	23-Aug-36	3	1	3	1	0	0	1	0	0	1	0	.267	.333
CHICAGO AMERICAN GIANTS	39	16-Aug-42	4	0	1	0	0	0	0	0	0	0	0	.263	.316
CHICAGO AMERICAN GIANTS	39	18-Aug-42	2	0	1	0	0	0	0	0	0	0	0	.286	.333
HOMESTEAD GRAYS	40	01-Aug-43	4	0	0	0	0	0	0	0	0	0	0	.240	.280
HOMESTEAD GRAYS	41	13-Aug-44	5	0	0	0	0	0	0	0	0	0	0	.200	.233
Player Totals:	**8 Games**		**30**	**5**	**6**	**1**	**0**	**0**	**1**	**3**	**0**	**2**	**1**	**.200**	**.233**

Benjamin, Jerry Charles "Ben" B: *11/09/1909 Montgomery, AL* D: *11/23/1974 Detroit, MI* B/T: *S/R 5'9" 165 lbs.*

PLAYER/TEAM	AGE	DATE	AB	R	H	D	T	HR	RBI	W	SAC	SB	E	RAVE	RSLG
HOMESTEAD GRAYS	27	08-Aug-37	5	0	1	0	0	0	0	0	0	0	0	.200	.200
HOMESTEAD GRAYS	33	01-Aug-43	1	0	0	0	0	0	0	0	0	0	0	.167	.167
HOMESTEAD GRAYS	35	29-Jul-45	5	1	1	0	0	0	1	0	0	0	0	.182	.182
Player Totals:	**3 Games**		**11**	**1**	**2**	**0**	**0**	**0**	**1**	**0**	**0**	**0**	**0**	**.182**	**.182**

Benson, Eugene "Gene" B: *10/02/1913 Pittsburgh, PA* D: *04/05/1999 Philadelphia, PA* B/T: *L/L 5'8" 180 lbs.*

PLAYER/TEAM	AGE	DATE	AB	R	H	D	T	HR	RBI	W	SAC	SB	E	RAVE	RSLG
PHILADELPHIA STARS	26	18-Aug-40	6	1	2	1	0	0	1	0	0	1	0	.333	.500
PHILADELPHIA STARS	31	29-Jul-45	2	1	0	0	0	0	0	0	0	0	0	.250	.375
PHILADELPHIA STARS	32	15-Aug-46	1	0	1	0	0	0	0	0	0	0	0	.333	.444
PHILADELPHIA STARS	32	18-Aug-46	3	0	0	0	0	0	0	0	0	0	1	.250	.333
Player Totals:	**4 Games**		**12**	**2**	**3**	**1**	**0**	**0**	**1**	**0**	**0**	**1**	**1**	**.250**	**.333**

Beverly, William "Fireball" B: *05/05/1930 Houston, TX* D: *09/11/1996 Houston, TX* B/T: *R/R 6'0" 185 lbs.*

PLAYER/TEAM	AGE	DATE	AB	R	H	D	T	HR	RBI	W	SAC	SB	E	RAVE	RSLG
CHICAGO AMERICAN GIANTS	22	17-Aug-52	1	0	0	0	0	0	0	0	0	0	0	.000	.000
Player Totals:	**1 Game**		**1**	**0**	**0**	**0**	**0**	**0**	**0**	**0**	**0**	**0**	**0**	**.000**	**.000**

Bibbs, Junius Alexander "Rainey" B: *10/31/1910 Henderson, KY* D: *09/11/1980 Indianapolis, IN* B/T: *S/R 5'10" 175 lbs.*

PLAYER/TEAM	AGE	DATE	AB	R	H	D	T	HR	RBI	W	SAC	SB	E	RAVE	RSLG
CINCINNATI TIGERS	26	08-Aug-37	1	0	1	1	0	0	0	0	0	0	0	1.000	2.000
Player Totals:	**1 Game**		**1**	**0**	**1**	**1**	**0**	**0**	**0**	**0**	**0**	**0**	**0**	**1.000**	**2.000**

Black, Joseph "Joe" B: *02/08/1924 Plainfield, NJ Living in Phoenix, AZ* B/T: *R/R 6'2" 210 lbs.*

PLAYER/TEAM	AGE	DATE	AB	R	H	D	T	HR	RBI	W	SAC	SB	E	RAVE	RSLG
BALTIMORE ELITE GIANTS	23	29-Jul-47	2	0	1	0	0	0	0	0	0	0	0	.500	.500
BALTIMORE ELITE GIANTS	24	24-Aug-48	1	0	0	0	0	0	0	0	0	0	0	.333	.333
BALTIMORE ELITE GIANTS	26	20-Aug-50	1	0	0	0	0	0	0	0	0	0	0	.250	.250
Player Totals:	**3 Games**		**4**	**0**	**1**	**0**	**0**	**0**	**0**	**0**	**0**	**0**	**0**	**.250**	**.250**

Blanco, Herberto "Harry" B: *10/07/1920 Bayamo, Cuba Living in Miami, FL* B/T: *R/R 5'7" 165 lbs.*

PLAYER/TEAM	AGE	DATE	AB	R	H	D	T	HR	RBI	W	SAC	SB	E	RAVE	RSLG
NEW YORK CUBANS	21	16-Aug-42	0	0	0	0	0	0	0	0	0	0	0	.000	.000
NEW YORK CUBANS	21	18-Aug-42	1	1	0	0	0	0	0	1	0	0	0	.000	.000
Player Totals:	**2 Games**		**1**	**1**	**0**	**0**	**0**	**0**	**0**	**1**	**0**	**0**	**0**	**.000**	**.000**

Bostock, Lyman Wesley B: *03/11/1918 Birmingham, AL Living in Birmingham, AL* B/T: *L/R 6'3" 215 lbs.*

PLAYER/TEAM	AGE	DATE	AB	R	H	D	T	HR	RBI	W	SAC	SB	E	RAVE	RSLG
BIRMINGHAM BLACK BARONS	23	27-Jul-41	2	0	1	0	0	0	1	0	0	0	0	.500	.500
Player Totals:	**1 Game**		**2**	**0**	**1**	**0**	**0**	**0**	**1**	**0**	**0**	**0**	**0**	**.500**	**.500**

Boyd, Robert Richard "Bob" B: *10/01/1925 Potts Camp, MS Living in Wichita, KS* B/T: *L/L 5'9" 165 lbs.*

PLAYER/TEAM	AGE	DATE	AB	R	H	D	T	HR	RBI	W	SAC	SB	E	RAVE	RSLG
MEMPHIS RED SOX	21	29-Jul-47	2	0	1	1	0	0	0	0	0	0	0	.500	1.000
MEMPHIS RED SOX	22	22-Aug-48	4	1	2	0	0	0	1	0	0	0	1	.500	.667
MEMPHIS RED SOX	22	24-Aug-48	3	0	0	0	0	0	0	0	0	0	0	.333	.444
MEMPHIS RED SOX	23	14-Aug-49	4	0	0	0	0	0	0	0	0	0	0	.231	.308
Player Totals:	**4 Games**		**13**	**1**	**3**	**1**	**0**	**0**	**1**	**0**	**0**	**0**	**1**	**.231**	**.308**

Bremer, Eugene Joseph "Gene" or "Flash" B: *07/18/1916 New Orleans, LA* D: *06/19/1971 Cleveland, OH* B/T: *R/R 5'10" 185 lbs.*

PLAYER/TEAM	AGE	DATE	AB	R	H	D	T	HR	RBI	W	SAC	SB	E	RAVE	RSLG
MEMPHIS RED SOX	24	18-Aug-40	0	0	0	0	0	0	0	1	0	0	0	.000	.000
CINCINNATI BUCKEYES	26	16-Aug-42	0	0	0	0	0	0	0	0	0	0	0	.000	.000
CINCINNATI BUCKEYES	26	18-Aug-42	0	0	0	0	0	0	0	0	0	0	0	.000	.000
CLEVELAND BUCKEYES	28	13-Aug-44	0	0	0	0	0	0	0	0	1	0	0	.000	.000
CLEVELAND BUCKEYES	29	29-Jul-45	0	0	0	0	0	0	0	0	0	0	0	.000	.000
Player Totals:	**5 Games**		**0**	**0**	**0**	**0**	**0**	**0**	**0**	**1**	**1**	**0**	**0**	**.000**	**.000**

PLAYER/TEAM	AGE	DATE	AB	R	H	D	T	HR	RBI	W	SAC	SB	E	RAVE	RSLG
Brewer, Chester Arthur "Chet" B: *01/14/1907 Leavenworth, KS* D: *03/26/1990 Whittier, CA* B/T: S/R 6'4" 185 lbs.															
KANSAS CITY MONARCHS	27	26-Aug-34	1	0	0	0	0	0	0	0	0	0	0	.000	.000
CLEVELAND BUCKEYES	40	27-Jul-47	1	0	1	0	0	0	1	0	0	0	0	.500	.500
Player Totals:	**2 Games**		**2**	**0**	**1**	**0**	**0**	**0**	**1**	**0**	**0**	**0**	**0**	**.500**	**.500**
Brewer, Sherwood "Woody" B: *08/16/1923 Clarksdale, MS Living in Chicago, IL* B/T: R/R 5'8" 165 lbs.															
INDIANAPOLIS CLOWNS	25	14-Aug-49	2	1	1	0	0	0	0	0	0	0	0	.500	.500
INDIANAPOLIS CLOWNS	27	20-Aug-50	3	0	0	0	0	0	0	1	0	0	1	.200	.200
KANSAS CITY MONARCHS	27	12-Aug-51	4	0	0	0	0	0	0	0	0	0	1	.111	.111
KANSAS CITY MONARCHS	30	16-Aug-53	3	2	1	0	0	0	0	0	0	0	0	.167	.167
Player Totals:	**4 Games**		**12**	**3**	**2**	**0**	**0**	**0**	**0**	**1**	**0**	**0**	**2**	**.167**	**.167**
Britt, George "Chippy" B: *06/18/1890 Macon, GA* D: *Jacksonville, FL* B/T: R/R 5'8" 175 lbs.															
HOMESTEAD GRAYS	43	10-Sep-33	1	1	1	0	0	0	0	0	0	0	0	1.000	1.000
Player Totals:	**1 Game**		**1**	**1**	**1**	**0**	**0**	**0**	**0**	**0**	**0**	**0**	**0**	**1.000**	**1.000**
Brooks, Eddie B: — D: — B/T: R/R															
BIRMINGHAM BLACK BARONS		17-Aug-52	4	0	1	0	0	0	0	0	0	0	0	.250	.250
BIRMINGHAM BLACK BARONS		16-Aug-53	1	0	0	0	0	0	0	0	0	0	0	.200	.200
Player Totals:	**2 Games**		**5**	**0**	**1**	**0**	**0**	**0**	**0**	**0**	**0**	**0**	**0**	**.200**	**.200**
Brown, Barney "Brinquitos" B: *10/23/1907 Hartsville, SC* D: *10/??/1985 Philadelphia, PA* B/T: L/L 5'9" 165 lbs.															
NEW YORK BLACK YANKEES	29	08-Aug-37	1	0	1	0	0	0	0	0	0	0	0	1.000	1.000
NEW YORK BLACK YANKEES	30	21-Aug-38	2	0	1	0	0	0	0	0	0	0	0	.667	.667
PHILADELPHIA STARS	34	16-Aug-42	0	0	0	0	0	0	0	0	0	0	0	.667	.667
PHILADELPHIA STARS	38	15-Aug-46	1	0	0	0	0	0	0	0	0	0	0	.500	.500
PHILADELPHIA STARS	38	18-Aug-46	1	0	0	0	0	0	0	0	0	0	0	.400	.400
Player Totals:	**5 Games**		**5**	**0**	**2**	**0**	**0**	**0**	**0**	**0**	**0**	**0**	**0**	**.400**	**.400**
Brown, John W. B: *10/23/1918 Hamburg, AR* D: *03/03/99 Detroit, MI* B/T: R/R 6'0" 155 lbs.															
CLEVELAND BUCKEYES	27	15-Aug-46	1	0	0	0	0	0	0	0	0	0	0	.000	.000
Player Totals:	**1 Game**		**1**	**0**	**0**	**0**	**0**	**0**	**0**	**0**	**0**	**0**	**0**	**.000**	**.000**
Brown, Larry "Iron Man" B: *09/16/1901 Birmingham, AL* D: *04/07/1972 Memphis, TN* B/T: R/R 5'6" 210 lbs.															
CHICAGO AMERICAN GIANTS	31	10-Sep-33	4	0	1	0	1	0	0	0	0	0	0	.250	.750
CHICAGO AMERICAN GIANTS	32	26-Aug-34	3	0	1	0	0	0	0	0	0	0	0	.286	.571
MEMPHIS RED SOX	36	21-Aug-38	0	0	0	0	0	0	0	1	0	0	0	.286	.571
MEMPHIS RED SOX	37	06-Aug-39	2	0	0	0	0	0	0	0	0	0	0	.222	.444
MEMPHIS RED SOX	37	27-Aug-39	0	0	0	0	0	0	0	1	0	0	0	.222	.444
MEMPHIS RED SOX	38	18-Aug-40	1	0	1	0	0	0	0	0	0	0	0	.300	.500
MEMPHIS RED SOX	39	27-Jul-41	3	0	0	0	0	0	0	0	0	0	1	.231	.385
Player Totals:	**7 Games**		**13**	**0**	**3**	**0**	**1**	**0**	**0**	**2**	**0**	**0**	**1**	**.231**	**.385**
Brown, Raymond "Ray" B: *02/23/1908 Ashland Grove, OH* D: *1968 Dayton, OH* B/T: S/R 6'1" 195 lbs.															
HOMESTEAD GRAYS	27	11-Aug-35	1	0	0	0	0	0	0	0	0	0	0	.000	.000
HOMESTEAD GRAYS	32	18-Aug-40	2	0	0	0	0	0	1	0	0	0	0	.000	.000
Player Totals:	**2 Games**		**3**	**0**	**0**	**0**	**0**	**0**	**1**	**0**	**0**	**0**	**0**	**.000**	**.000**
Brown, Thomas Jefferson "Tom" or "T. J." B: *1922* D: — B/T: R/R 5'6" 170 lbs.															
MEMPHIS RED SOX	20	16-Aug-42	3	0	0	0	0	0	0	0	0	0	0	.000	.000
Player Totals:	**1 Game**		**3**	**0**	**0**	**0**	**0**	**0**	**0**	**0**	**0**	**0**	**0**	**.000**	**.000**
Brown, Willard Jessie "Home Run" B: *06/26/1915 Shreveport, LA* D: *08/04/1996 Houston, TX* B/T: R/R 6'0" 195 lbs.															
KANSAS CITY MONARCHS	21	23-Aug-36	1	0	0	0	0	0	0	0	0	0	1	.000	.000
KANSAS CITY MONARCHS	22	08-Aug-37	2	0	0	0	0	0	0	1	0	0	0	.000	.000
KANSAS CITY MONARCHS	27	16-Aug-42	4	0	1	1	0	0	0	0	0	0	0	.143	.286
KANSAS CITY MONARCHS	27	18-Aug-42	4	0	2	0	0	0	2	0	0	0	0	.273	.364
KANSAS CITY MONARCHS	28	01-Aug-43	3	1	1	0	0	0	0	0	0	1	0	.286	.357
KANSAS CITY MONARCHS	33	22-Aug-48	4	1	2	0	0	0	0	0	0	0	0	.333	.389

PLAYER/TEAM	AGE	DATE	AB	R	H	D	T	HR	RBI	W	SAC	SB	E	RAVE	RSLG
KANSAS CITY MONARCHS	33	24-Aug-48	3	0	0	0	0	0	0	0	0	0	0	.286	.333
KANSAS CITY MONARCHS	34	14-Aug-49	3	0	0	0	0	0	0	0	0	0	0	.250	.292
Player Totals:	**8 Games**		**24**	**2**	**6**	**1**	**0**	**0**	**2**	**1**	**0**	**1**	**1**	**.250**	**.292**

Brown, William "Willie" or "Cap" B: 04/04/1927 Fairfield, AL D: 12/30/96 Birmingham, AL B/T: S/R 5'9" 165 lbs.

PLAYER/TEAM	AGE	DATE	AB	R	H	D	T	HR	RBI	W	SAC	SB	E	RAVE	RSLG
INDIANAPOLIS CLOWNS	26	16-Aug-53	1	0	0	0	0	0	0	0	0	0	0	.000	.000
Player Totals:	**1 Game**		**1**	**0**	**0**	**0**	**0**	**0**	**0**	**0**	**0**	**0**	**0**	**.000**	**.000**

Burgos, Jose Antonio B: 01/12/1916 Ponce, Puerto Rico D: — B/T: R/R 5'6" 150 lbs.

PLAYER/TEAM	AGE	DATE	AB	R	H	D	T	HR	RBI	W	SAC	SB	E	RAVE	RSLG
BIRMINGHAM BLACK BARONS	33	14-Aug-49	2	0	0	0	0	0	0	0	0	0	0	.000	.000
Player Totals:	**1 Game**		**2**	**0**	**0**	**0**	**0**	**0**	**0**	**0**	**0**	**0**	**0**	**.000**	**.000**

Butts, Thomas A. "Pee Wee" or "Cool Breeze" B: 08/28/1919 Sparta, GA D: 12/30/1972 Atlanta, GA B/T: R/R 5'7" 140 lbs.

PLAYER/TEAM	AGE	DATE	AB	R	H	D	T	HR	RBI	W	SAC	SB	E	RAVE	RSLG
BALTIMORE ELITE GIANTS	24	13-Aug-44	2	0	0	0	0	0	0	0	0	0	0	.000	.000
BALTIMORE ELITE GIANTS	26	18-Aug-46	0	0	0	0	0	0	0	0	0	0	0	.000	.000
BALTIMORE ELITE GIANTS	27	27-Jul-47	2	0	0	0	0	0	0	0	0	0	0	.000	.000
BALTIMORE ELITE GIANTS	27	29-Jul-47	1	0	0	0	0	0	0	0	1	0	0	.000	.000
BALTIMORE ELITE GIANTS	28	22-Aug-48	2	0	0	0	0	0	0	0	0	0	0	.000	.000
BALTIMORE ELITE GIANTS	29	14-Aug-49	4	1	1	1	0	0	0	1	0	0	0	.091	.182
BALTIMORE ELITE GIANTS	30	20-Aug-50	3	1	0	0	0	0	0	1	0	1	0	.071	.143
BIRMINGHAM BLACK BARONS	33	16-Aug-53	3	0	0	0	0	0	0	0	0	0	1	.059	.118
Player Totals:	**8 Games**		**17**	**2**	**1**	**1**	**0**	**0**	**0**	**2**	**1**	**1**	**1**	**.059**	**.118**

Byas, Richard Thomas "Subby" B: 03/19/1910 Pineland, TX D: 10/02/1985 Chicago, IL B/T: S/R 5'8" 165 lbs.

PLAYER/TEAM	AGE	DATE	AB	R	H	D	T	HR	RBI	W	SAC	SB	E	RAVE	RSLG
CHICAGO AMERICAN GIANTS	26	23-Aug-36	3	0	1	0	0	0	0	0	0	0	0	.333	.333
CHICAGO AMERICAN GIANTS	27	08-Aug-37	1	0	0	0	0	0	0	0	0	0	0	.250	.250
Player Totals:	**2 Games**		**4**	**0**	**1**	**0**	**0**	**0**	**0**	**0**	**0**	**0**	**0**	**.250**	**.250**

Byrd, William "Bill" B: 07/15/1907 Canton, GA D: 01/04/1991 Philadelphia, PA B/T: S/R 6'1" 210 lbs.

PLAYER/TEAM	AGE	DATE	AB	R	H	D	T	HR	RBI	W	SAC	SB	E	RAVE	RSLG
WASHINGTON ELITE GIANTS	29	23-Aug-36	3	0	0	0	0	0	0	0	0	0	0	.000	.000
BALTIMORE ELITE GIANTS	32	06-Aug-39	1	0	0	0	0	0	0	0	0	0	0	.000	.000
BALTIMORE ELITE GIANTS	32	27-Aug-39	1	0	0	0	0	0	0	0	0	0	0	.000	.000
BALTIMORE ELITE GIANTS	34	27-Jul-41	0	0	0	0	0	0	0	0	0	0	0	.000	.000
BALTIMORE ELITE GIANTS	37	13-Aug-44	1	0	0	0	0	0	0	0	0	0	0	.000	.000
BALTIMORE ELITE GIANTS	38	29-Jul-45	1	1	0	0	0	0	0	0	0	0	0	.000	.000
BALTIMORE ELITE GIANTS	39	15-Aug-46	1	0	0	0	0	0	0	0	0	0	0	.000	.000
BALTIMORE ELITE GIANTS	39	18-Aug-46	1	0	0	0	0	0	0	0	0	0	0	.000	.000
Player Totals:	**8 Games**		**9**	**1**	**0**	**0**	**0**	**0**	**0**	**0**	**0**	**0**	**0**	**.000**	**.000**

Calhoun, Walter Allen "Lefty" B: 08/21/1911 Union City, TN D: 10/02/1976 Cleveland, OH B/T: L/L 5'9" 180 lbs.

PLAYER/TEAM	AGE	DATE	AB	R	H	D	T	HR	RBI	W	SAC	SB	E	RAVE	RSLG
NEW ORLEANS-ST. LOUIS STARS	28	18-Aug-40	1	0	0	0	0	0	0	0	0	0	0	.000	.000
Player Totals:	**1 Game**		**1**	**0**	**0**	**0**	**0**	**0**	**0**	**0**	**0**	**0**	**0**	**.000**	**.000**

Campanella, Roy "Campy" B: 11/19/1921 Philadelphia, PA D: 06/26/1993 Woodland Hills, CA B/T: R/R 5'10" 205 lbs.

PLAYER/TEAM	AGE	DATE	AB	R	H	D	T	HR	RBI	W	SAC	SB	E	RAVE	RSLG
BALTIMORE ELITE GIANTS	19	27-Jul-41	5	0	1	0	0	0	0	0	0	0	1	.200	.200
BALTIMORE ELITE GIANTS	22	13-Aug-44	2	1	1	0	0	0	1	0	0	0	0	.286	.286
BALTIMORE ELITE GIANTS	23	29-Jul-45	5	1	2	0	0	0	0	0	0	0	0	.333	.333
Player Totals:	**3 Games**		**12**	**2**	**4**	**0**	**0**	**0**	**1**	**0**	**0**	**0**	**1**	**.333**	**.333**

Cannady, Walter I. "Rev" B: 03/06/1904 Norfolk, VA D: 12/03/1981 Ft. Myers, FL B/T: R/R 6'0" 175 lbs.

PLAYER/TEAM	AGE	DATE	AB	R	H	D	T	HR	RBI	W	SAC	SB	E	RAVE	RSLG
NEW YORK BLACK YANKEES	34	21-Aug-38	3	1	1	1	0	0	1	0	1	0	0	.333	.667
Player Totals:	**1 Game**		**3**	**1**	**1**	**1**	**0**	**0**	**1**	**0**	**1**	**0**	**0**	**.333**	**.667**

Carter, Ernest C. "Spoon" B: 12/08/1902 Harpersville, AL D: 01/23/1974 Birmingham, AL B/T: R/R 5'9" 170 lbs.

PLAYER/TEAM	AGE	DATE	AB	R	H	D	T	HR	RBI	W	SAC	SB	E	RAVE	RSLG
MEMPHIS RED SOX	44	29-Jul-47	1	0	0	0	0	0	0	0	0	0	0	.000	.000
MEMPHIS RED SOX	45	24-Aug-48	0	0	0	0	0	0	0	0	0	0	0	.000	.000
Player Totals:	**2 Games**		**1**	**0**	**0**	**0**	**0**	**0**	**0**	**0**	**0**	**0**	**0**	**.000**	**.000**

PLAYER/TEAM	AGE	DATE	AB	R	H	D	T	HR	RBI	W	SAC	SB	E	RAVE	RSLG
Carter, Marlin Theodore "Mel" B: *12/27/1912 Haslam, TX* D: *12/20/1993 Memphis, TN* B/T: R/R *5'7"* *160 lbs.*															
MEMPHIS RED SOX	29	16-Aug-42	1	0	0	0	0	0	0	0	0	0	0	.000	.000
MEMPHIS RED SOX	29	18-Aug-42	1	0	0	0	0	0	0	0	0	0	1	.000	.000
Player Totals:	2 Games		2	0	0	0	0	0	0	0	0	0	1	**.000**	**.000**
Cartledge, Menske "Manny" or "Robbie" B: *07/20/1925 Umatilla, FL* D: — B/T: R/R *6'4"* 190 lbs.															
BIRMINGHAM BLACK BARONS		16-Aug-53	2	0	1	0	0	0	0	0	0	0	0	.500	.500
Player Totals:	1 Game		2	0	1	0	0	0	0	0	0	0	0	**.500**	**.500**
Cash, William Walker "Ready" B: *02/21/1919 Round Oak, GA* *Living in Philadelphia, PA* B/T: R/R *6'2"* 195 lbs.															
PHILADELPHIA STARS	29	22-Aug-48	0	0	0	0	0	0	0	0	0	0	0	.000	.000
PHILADELPHIA STARS	29	24-Aug-48	3	1	1	0	0	0	0	0	0	0	0	.333	.333
PHILADELPHIA STARS	30	14-Aug-49	4	0	1	1	0	0	0	0	0	0	0	.286	.429
Player Totals:	3 Games		7	1	2	1	0	0	0	0	0	0	0	**.286**	**.429**
Castille, Irwin B: *08/30/1923* D: *06/13/1982 Virginia* B/T: R/R															
BIRMINGHAM BLACK BARONS	19	16-Aug-53	0	0	0	0	0	0	0	0	0	0	0	.000	.000
Player Totals:	1 Game		0	0	0	0	0	0	0	0	0	0	0	**.000**	**.000**
Charleston, Oscar McKinley "Charlie" B: *10/14/1896 Indianapolis, IN* D: *10/05/1954 Philadelphia, PA* B/T: L/L *6'0"* 190 lbs.															
PITTSBURGH CRAWFORDS	36	10-Sep-33	3	2	0	0	0	0	1	0	0	1	0	.000	.000
PITTSBURGH CRAWFORDS	37	26-Aug-34	4	0	0	0	0	0	0	0	0	0	1	.000	.000
PITTSBURGH CRAWFORDS	38	11-Aug-35	3	1	0	0	0	0	0	0	0	0	1	.000	.000
Player Totals:	3 Games		10	3	0	0	0	0	1	0	0	1	2	**.000**	**.000**
Clarke, Robert "Eggie" B: *11/25/1903 Richmond, VA* D: *05/01/1972 Norfolk, VA* B/T: R/R *5'10"* 175 lbs.															
NEW YORK BLACK YANKEES	36	18-Aug-40	0	0	0	0	0	0	0	0	0	0	0	.000	.000
Player Totals:	1 Game		0	0	0	0	0	0	0	0	0	0	0	**.000**	**.000**
Clarke, Vibert Ernesto "Webbo" B: *06/08/1928 Colon, Panama* D: *06/14/1970 Cristobal, Canal Zone* B/T: L/L *6'0"* 170 lbs.															
CLEVELAND BUCKEYES	18	15-Aug-46	0	0	0	0	0	0	0	0	0	0	0	.000	.000
CLEVELAND BUCKEYES	19	29-Jul-47	0	0	0	0	0	0	0	0	0	0	0	.000	.000
CLEVELAND BUCKEYES	20	24-Aug-48	1	0	0	0	0	0	0	0	0	0	0	.000	.000
MEMPHIS RED SOX	22	20-Aug-50	1	0	0	0	0	0	0	0	0	0	0	.000	.000
MEMPHIS RED SOX	23	12-Aug-51	1	0	0	0	0	0	0	0	0	0	0	.000	.000
Player Totals:	5 Games		3	0	0	0	0	0	0	0	0	0	0	**.000**	**.000**
Clarkson, James Buster "Bus" B: *03/13/1915 Hopkins, SC* D: *01/18/1989 Jeanette, PA* B/T: R/R *5'11"* 195 lbs.															
NEWARK EAGLES	25	18-Aug-40	2	1	0	0	0	0	0	1	0	0	0	.000	.000
PHILADELPHIA STARS	34	14-Aug-49	2	0	1	0	0	0	1	0	0	0	0	.250	.250
Player Totals:	2 Games		4	1	1	0	0	0	1	1	0	0	0	**.250**	**.250**
Cleveland, Howard "Duke" B: *West Palm, FL* D: *West Palm, FL* B/T: L/R *6'1"* 190 lbs.															
JACKSONVILLE RED CAPS		27-Jul-41	1	0	1	0	0	0	0	0	0	0	0	1.000	1.000
Player Totals:	1 Game		1	0	1	0	0	0	0	0	0	0	0	**1.000**	**1.000**
Cohen, James Clarence "Fireball" B: *03/26/1918 Evergreen, AL* *Living in Washington, DC* B/T: R/R *5'11"* 190 lbs.															
INDIANAPOLIS CLOWNS	30	24-Aug-48	0	0	0	0	0	0	0	0	0	0	0	.000	.000
Player Totals:	1 Game		0	0	0	0	0	0	0	0	0	0	0	**.000**	**.000**
Coimbre, Francisco Atiles "Pancho" B: *01/29/1909 Coamo, Puerto Rico* D: *11/04/1989 Ponce, Puerto Rico* B/T: R/R *5'8"* 170 lbs.															
NEW YORK CUBANS	32	27-Jul-41	5	2	0	0	0	0	0	0	0	0	1	.000	.000
NEW YORK CUBANS	35	13-Aug-44	5	0	0	0	0	0	0	0	0	0	0	.000	.000
Player Totals:	2 Games		10	2	0	0	0	0	0	0	0	0	1	**.000**	**.000**
Colas, Jose Luis B: *Cuba* D: — B/T: R/R															
MEMPHIS RED SOX		27-Jul-47	4	0	2	0	0	0	2	0	0	0	0	.500	.500

PLAYER/TEAM	AGE	DATE	AB	R	H	D	T	HR	RBI	W	SAC	SB	E	RAVE	RSLG
MEMPHIS RED SOX		29-Jul-47	5	0	1	0	0	0	1	0	0	0	0	.333	.333
MEMPHIS RED SOX		24-Aug-48	1	0	1	0	0	0	0	0	0	0	0	.400	.400
MEMPHIS RED SOX		12-Aug-51	3	0	1	0	0	0	0	1	0	1	0	.385	.385
Player Totals:	**4 Games**		**13**	**0**	**5**	**0**	**0**	**0**	**3**	**1**	**0**	**1**	**0**	**.385**	**.385**

Cooper, Andrew L. "Andy" B: *04/24/1898 Waco, TX* D: *06/03/1941 Waco, TX* B/T: R/L 6'2" 220 lbs.

KANSAS CITY MONARCHS	38	23-Aug-36	0	0	0	0	0	0	0	0	0	0	0	.000	.000
Player Totals:	**1 Game**		**0**	**0**	**0**	**0**	**0**	**0**	**0**	**0**	**0**	**0**	**0**	**.000**	**.000**

Cooper, Thomas Roger "Tom" B: *01/17/1927 Kansas City, Kansas* D: *10/09/1985 Arlington, TX* B/T: R/R 6'2" 180 lbs.

KANSAS CITY MONARCHS	23	20-Aug-50	1	0	0	0	0	0	0	0	0	0	0	.000	.000
KANSAS CITY MONARCHS	24	12-Aug-51	4	0	2	0	0	0	0	0	0	0	0	.400	.400
KANSAS CITY MONARCHS	26	16-Aug-53	3	0	0	0	0	0	0	0	0	0	0	.250	.250
Player Totals:	**3 Games**		**8**	**0**	**2**	**0**	**0**	**0**	**0**	**0**	**0**	**0**	**0**	**.250**	**.250**

Cornelius, William McKinley "Sug" B: *09/03/1906 Atlanta, GA* D: *10/30/1989 Chicago, IL* B/T: R/R 5'8" 180 lbs.

CHICAGO AMERICAN GIANTS	28	11-Aug-35	0	0	0	0	0	0	0	0	0	0	0	.000	.000
CHICAGO AMERICAN GIANTS	29	23-Aug-36	1	0	0	0	0	0	0	0	0	0	0	.000	.000
CHICAGO AMERICAN GIANTS	31	21-Aug-38	0	0	0	0	0	0	0	0	0	0	0	.000	.000
Player Totals:	**3 Games**		**1**	**0**	**0**	**0**	**0**	**0**	**0**	**0**	**0**	**0**	**0**	**.000**	**.000**

Crespo y Quinonez, Alejandro "Alex" B: *02/26/1915 Guira de Melena, Cuba* D: — B/T: R/R 6'1" 205 lbs.

NEW YORK CUBANS	25	18-Aug-40	2	1	1	0	1	0	1	0	0	0	0	.500	1.500
Player Totals:	**1 Game**		**2**	**1**	**1**	**0**	**1**	**0**	**1**	**0**	**0**	**0**	**0**	**.500**	**1.500**

Crowe, George Daniel "Big George" B: *03/22/1921 Whiteland, IN Living in Ocala, FL* B/T: L/L 6'2" 210 lbs.

NEW YORK BLACK YANKEES	27	24-Aug-48	4	2	2	0	0	0	0	0	0	0	0	.500	.500
Player Totals:	**1 Game**		**4**	**2**	**2**	**0**	**0**	**0**	**0**	**0**	**0**	**0**	**0**	**.500**	**.500**

Crutchfield, John William "Jimmie" B: *03/15/1910 Ardmore, MO* D: *03/31/1993 Chicago, IL* B/T: L/R 5'7" 150 lbs.

PITTSBURGH CRAWFORDS	24	26-Aug-34	3	0	0	0	0	0	0	0	0	0	0	.000	.000
PITTSBURGH CRAWFORDS	25	11-Aug-35	2	0	0	0	0	0	0	0	0	0	0	.000	.000
PITTSBURGH CRAWFORDS	26	23-Aug-36	2	0	0	0	0	0	0	0	0	0	0	.000	.000
CHICAGO AMERICAN GIANTS	31	27-Jul-41	3	0	1	0	0	0	0	0	0	0	0	.100	.100
Player Totals:	**4 Games**		**10**	**0**	**1**	**0**	**0**	**0**	**0**	**0**	**0**	**0**	**0**	**.100**	**.100**

Dandridge, Raymond Emmett "Ray" B: *08/31/1913 Richmond, VA* D: *02/12/1994 Palm Bay, FL* B/T: R/R 5'7" 175 lbs.

NEWARK DODGERS	21	11-Aug-35	1	0	1	0	0	0	2	0	0	0	0	1.000	1.000
NEWARK EAGLES	23	08-Aug-37	5	1	2	0	0	0	0	0	0	1	0	.500	.500
NEWARK EAGLES	30	13-Aug-44	5	0	3	1	0	0	1	0	0	0	0	.545	.636
Player Totals:	**3 Games**		**11**	**1**	**6**	**1**	**0**	**0**	**3**	**0**	**0**	**1**	**0**	**.545**	**.636**

Davenport, Lloyd "Ducky" B: *10/28/1911 New Orleans, LA* D: *1988 New Orleans, LA* B/T: L/L 5'4" 150 lbs.

CINCINNATI TIGERS	25	08-Aug-37	4	1	1	1	0	0	0	0	0	0	0	.250	.500
MEMPHIS RED SOX	27	27-Aug-39	0	0	0	0	0	0	0	0	0	0	0	.250	.500
BIRMINGHAM BLACK BARONS	30	16-Aug-42	1	0	0	0	0	0	0	0	0	0	0	.200	.400
CHICAGO AMERICAN GIANTS	31	01-Aug-43	2	0	0	0	0	0	0	1	0	0	0	.143	.286
CHICAGO AMERICAN GIANTS	32	13-Aug-44	4	1	1	0	0	0	0	0	0	0	0	.182	.273
CLEVELAND BUCKEYES	33	29-Jul-45	4	1	1	1	0	0	0	0	0	0	0	.200	.333
Player Totals:	**6 Games**		**15**	**3**	**3**	**2**	**0**	**0**	**0**	**1**	**0**	**0**	**.200**	**.333**

Davis, John Howard "Cherokee" B: *02/06/1917 Ashland, VA* D: *11/17/1982 Fort Lauderdale, FL* B/T: R/R 6'3" 215 lbs.

NEWARK EAGLES	27	13-Aug-44	3	0	2	0	0	0	1	1	0	0	0	.667	.667
NEWARK EAGLES	28	29-Jul-45	2	0	0	0	0	0	0	0	0	0	0	.400	.400
HOUSTON EAGLES	32	14-Aug-49	2	0	0	0	0	0	0	0	0	0	0	.286	.286
Player Totals:	**3 Games**		**7**	**0**	**2**	**0**	**0**	**0**	**1**	**1**	**0**	**0**	**0**	**.286**	**.286**

Davis, Lorenzo "Piper" B: *07/03/1917 Piper, AL* D: *05/21/1997 Birmingham, AL* B/T: R/R 6'2" 180 lbs.

BIRMINGHAM BLACK BARONS	29	15-Aug-46	4	1	2	0	0	0	1	0	0	0	0	.500	.500

PLAYER/TEAM	AGE	DATE	AB	R	H	D	T	HR	RBI	W	SAC	SB	E	RAVE	RSLG
BIRMINGHAM BLACK BARONS	29	18-Aug-46	3	1	1	0	0	0	1	1	0	0	0	.429	.429
BIRMINGHAM BLACK BARONS	30	27-Jul-47	3	1	2	1	0	0	0	0	0	1	0	.500	.600
BIRMINGHAM BLACK BARONS	30	29-Jul-47	5	1	1	0	0	0	2	0	0	0	0	.400	.467
BIRMINGHAM BLACK BARONS	31	22-Aug-48	3	1	1	1	0	0	0	0	0	1	0	.389	.500
BIRMINGHAM BLACK BARONS	31	24-Aug-48	4	0	0	0	0	0	0	0	0	0	0	.318	.409
BIRMINGHAM BLACK BARONS	32	14-Aug-49	4	0	1	1	0	0	0	0	0	0	0	.308	.423
Player Totals:		**7 Games**	**26**	**5**	**8**	**3**	**0**	**0**	**4**	**1**	**0**	**2**	**0**	**.308**	**.423**

Davis, Robert Lomax "Butch" B: — D: 1990 B/T: L/R 6'0" 220 lbs.

PLAYER/TEAM	AGE	DATE	AB	R	H	D	T	HR	RBI	W	SAC	SB	E	RAVE	RSLG
BALTIMORE ELITE GIANTS		14-Aug-49	4	1	1	0	0	0	0	0	0	1	1	.250	.250
Player Totals:		**1 Game**	**4**	**1**	**1**	**0**	**0**	**0**	**0**	**0**	**0**	**1**	**1**	**.250**	**.250**

Davis, Walter C. "Steel Arm" B: 1902 Madison, WS D: 1935 Chicago, IL B/T: L/L 6'1" 175 lbs.

PLAYER/TEAM	AGE	DATE	AB	R	H	D	T	HR	RBI	W	SAC	SB	E	RAVE	RSLG
CHICAGO AMERICAN GIANTS	31	10-Sep-33	4	2	2	1	0	0	2	0	0	0	0	.500	.750
Player Totals:		**1 Game**	**4**	**2**	**2**	**1**	**0**	**0**	**2**	**0**	**0**	**0**	**0**	**.500**	**.750**

Day, Leon B: 10/30/1916 Alexandria, VA D: 03/13/1995 Baltimore, MD B/T: R/R 5'11" 185 lbs.

PLAYER/TEAM	AGE	DATE	AB	R	H	D	T	HR	RBI	W	SAC	SB	E	RAVE	RSLG
BROOKLYN EAGLES	18	11-Aug-35	1	0	0	0	0	0	0	0	0	0	0	.000	.000
NEWARK EAGLES	20	08-Aug-37	1	1	1	1	0	0	0	0	0	0	0	.500	1.000
NEWARK EAGLES	22	06-Aug-39	1	0	0	0	0	0	0	0	0	0	0	.333	.667
NEWARK EAGLES	22	27-Aug-39	1	0	0	0	0	0	0	0	0	0	0	.250	.500
NEWARK EAGLES	25	16-Aug-42	1	0	0	0	0	0	0	0	0	0	0	.200	.400
NEWARK EAGLES	25	18-Aug-42	1	0	0	0	0	0	1	0	0	0	0	.167	.333
NEWARK EAGLES	26	01-Aug-43	1	0	0	0	0	0	0	0	0	0	0	.143	.286
NEWARK EAGLES	29	15-Aug-46	0	0	0	0	0	0	0	0	0	0	0	.143	.286
NEWARK EAGLES	29	18-Aug-46	0	0	0	0	0	0	0	0	0	0	0	.143	.286
Player Totals:		**9 Games**	**7**	**1**	**1**	**1**	**0**	**0**	**1**	**0**	**0**	**0**	**0**	**.143**	**.286**

Dennis, Wesley Lewis "Doc" B: 02/10/1918 Nashville, TN D: 03/06/2001 Nashville, TN B/T: R/R 6'0" 170 lbs.

PLAYER/TEAM	AGE	DATE	AB	R	H	D	T	HR	RBI	W	SAC	SB	E	RAVE	RSLG
BIRMINGHAM BLACK BARONS	33	12-Aug-51	4	0	1	0	0	0	0	0	0	0	0	.250	.250
BIRMINGHAM BLACK BARONS	34	17-Aug-52	4	2	2	1	0	0	0	0	0	0	0	.375	.500
BIRMINGHAM BLACK BARONS	35	16-Aug-53	4	0	1	0	0	0	0	0	0	0	1	.333	.417
Player Totals:		**3 Games**	**12**	**2**	**4**	**1**	**0**	**0**	**0**	**0**	**0**	**0**	**1**	**.333**	**.417**

Dials, Oland Cecil "Lou" B: 01/10/1904 Hot Springs, AR D: 04/05/1994 Modesto, CA B/T: L/L 5'10" 185 lbs.

PLAYER/TEAM	AGE	DATE	AB	R	H	D	T	HR	RBI	W	SAC	SB	E	RAVE	RSLG
CHICAGO AMERICAN GIANTS	32	23-Aug-36	2	0	0	0	0	0	0	0	0	0	1	.000	.000
Player Totals:		**1 Game**	**2**	**0**	**0**	**0**	**0**	**0**	**0**	**0**	**0**	**0**	**1**	**.000**	**.000**

Diaz, Pedro "Manny" B: — D: — B/T: R/R

PLAYER/TEAM	AGE	DATE	AB	R	H	D	T	HR	RBI	W	SAC	SB	E	RAVE	RSLG
NEW YORK CUBANS		15-Aug-46	1	0	0	0	0	0	0	0	0	0	0	.000	.000
NEW YORK CUBANS		14-Aug-49	4	0	3	0	0	0	0	1	0	1	0	.600	.600
NEW YORK CUBANS		20-Aug-50	5	0	1	1	0	0	1	0	0	0	0	.400	.500
EMPlayer Totals:		**3 Games**	**10**	**0**	**4**	**1**	**0**	**0**	**1**	**1**	**0**	**1**	**0**	**.400**	**.500**

Dihigo y Llanos, Martin Magdaleno B: 05/25/1906 Matanzas, Cuba D: 05/20/1971 Cienfuegos, Cuba B/T: R/R 6'2" 215 lbs.

PLAYER/TEAM	AGE	DATE	AB	R	H	D	T	HR	RBI	W	SAC	SB	E	RAVE	RSLG
NEW YORK CUBANS	29	11-Aug-35	5	1	1	0	0	0	1	1	0	1	2	.200	.200
NEW YORK CUBANS	39	29-Jul-45	1	0	0	0	0	0	0	0	0	0	0	.167	.167
Player Totals:		**2 Games**	**6**	**1**	**1**	**0**	**0**	**0**	**1**	**1**	**0**	**1**	**2**	**.167**	**.167**

Dixon, Herbert Albert "Rap" B: 09/02/1902 Kingston, GA D: 07/20/1944 Detroit, MI B/T: R/R 6'2" 185 lbs.

PLAYER/TEAM	AGE	DATE	AB	R	H	D	T	HR	RBI	W	SAC	SB	E	RAVE	RSLG
PHILADELPHIA STARS	31	10-Sep-33	4	2	1	0	0	0	1	1	0	1	0	.250	.250
PITTSBURGH CRAWFORDS	31	26-Aug-34	2	0	1	0	0	0	0	0	0	0	0	.333	.333
Player Totals:		**2 Games**	**6**	**2**	**2**	**0**	**0**	**0**	**1**	**1**	**0**	**1**	**0**	**.333**	**.333**

Doby, Lawrence Eugene "Larry" B: 12/13/1923 Camden, SC Living in Bellwood, NJ B/T: L/R 6'1" 175 lbs.

PLAYER/TEAM	AGE	DATE	AB	R	H	D	T	HR	RBI	W	SAC	SB	E	RAVE	RSLG
NEWARK EAGLES	22	15-Aug-46	4	2	2	0	0	0	0	0	0	1	0	.500	.500
NEWARK EAGLES	22	18-Aug-46	3	0	1	0	0	0	1	1	0	0	0	.429	.429
Player Totals:		**2 Games**	**7**	**2**	**3**	**0**	**0**	**0**	**1**	**1**	**0**	**1**	**0**	**.429**	**.429**

Douglas, Jesse Warren B: *03/27/1916 Longview, TX* D: — B/T: S/R *5'6" 150 lbs.*

PLAYER/TEAM	AGE	DATE	AB	R	H	D	T	HR	RBI	W	SAC	SB	E	RAVE	RSLG
CHICAGO AMERICAN GIANTS	34	20-Aug-50	4	1	3	0	0	0	2	0	0	2	0	.750	.750
Player Totals:	**1 Game**		**4**	**1**	**3**	**0**	**0**	**0**	**2**	**0**	**0**	**2**	**0**	**.750**	**.750**

Drake, Reynaldo "Verdes" B: *1923 Havana, Cuba* D: — B/T: L/L *5'9" 160 lbs.*

PLAYER/TEAM	AGE	DATE	AB	R	H	D	T	HR	RBI	W	SAC	SB	E	RAVE	RSLG
INDIANAPOLIS CLOWNS	30	16-Aug-53	4	0	0	0	0	0	0	0	0	0	0	.000	.000
Player Totals:	**1 Game**		**4**	**0**	**0**	**0**	**0**	**0**	**0**	**0**	**0**	**0**	**0**	**.000**	**.000**

Duany y Hiedra, Claro B: *08/12/1917 Caibarien, Cuba* D: *03/28/1997 Evanston, IL* B/T: L/L *6'2" 210 lbs.*

PLAYER/TEAM	AGE	DATE	AB	R	H	D	T	HR	RBI	W	SAC	SB	E	RAVE	RSLG
NEW YORK CUBANS	29	27-Jul-47	2	0	0	0	0	0	1	0	0	0	0	.000	.000
NEW YORK CUBANS	29	29-Jul-47	1	0	0	0	0	0	0	0	0	0	0	.000	.000
Player Totals:	**2 Games**		**3**	**0**	**0**	**0**	**0**	**0**	**1**	**0**	**0**	**0**	**0**	**.000**	**.000**

Duncan, Frank B: *02/14/1901 Kansas City, MO* D: *12/04/1973 Kansas City, MO* B/T: R/R *6'0" 175 lbs.*

PLAYER/TEAM	AGE	DATE	AB	R	H	D	T	HR	RBI	W	SAC	SB	E	RAVE	RSLG
CHICAGO AMERICAN GIANTS	37	21-Aug-38	1	0	0	0	0	0	0	1	0	0	0	.000	.000
Player Totals:	**1 Game**		**1**	**0**	**0**	**0**	**0**	**0**	**0**	**1**	**0**	**0**	**0**	**.000**	**.000**

Dunlap, Herman B: — D: — B/T: R/R

PLAYER/TEAM	AGE	DATE	AB	R	H	D	T	HR	RBI	W	SAC	SB	E	RAVE	RSLG
CHICAGO AMERICAN GIANTS		23-Aug-36	2	1	1	0	0	0	0	0	0	0	0	.500	.500
Player Totals:	**1 Game**		**2**	**1**	**1**	**0**	**0**	**0**	**0**	**0**	**0**	**0**	**0**	**.500**	**.500**

Dunn, Joseph P. "Jake" B: *11/05/1909 Luther, OK* D: *07/24/1984 Los Angeles, CA* B/T: R/R *5'10" 190 lbs.*

PLAYER/TEAM	AGE	DATE	AB	R	H	D	T	HR	RBI	W	SAC	SB	E	RAVE	RSLG
PHILADELPHIA STARS	27	08-Aug-37	1	0	0	0	0	0	0	1	0	0	0	.000	.000
PHILADELPHIA STARS	28	21-Aug-38	1	0	1	0	0	0	0	0	0	0	0	.500	.500
Player Totals:	**2 Games**		**2**	**0**	**1**	**0**	**0**	**0**	**0**	**1**	**0**	**0**	**0**	**.500**	**.500**

Durham, Joseph Vann "Winn" or "Pop" B: *07/31/1931 Newport News, VA   Living in Randall'sTown, MD* B/T: R/R *6'1" 190 lbs.*

PLAYER/TEAM	AGE	DATE	AB	R	H	D	T	HR	RBI	W	SAC	SB	E	RAVE	RSLG
CHICAGO AMERICAN GIANTS	21	17-Aug-52	2	1	0	0	0	0	0	0	0	0	0	.000	.000
Player Totals:	**1 Game**		**2**	**1**	**0**	**0**	**0**	**0**	**0**	**0**	**0**	**0**	**0**	**.000**	**.000**

Dwight, Edward Joseph "Eddie" B: *02/25/1905 Dalton, GA* D: *11/27/1975 Kansas City, KS* B/T: R/R *5'8" 165 lbs.*

PLAYER/TEAM	AGE	DATE	AB	R	H	D	T	HR	RBI	W	SAC	SB	E	RAVE	RSLG
KANSAS CITY MONARCHS	31	23-Aug-36	2	0	0	0	0	0	0	0	0	0	0	.000	.000
Player Totals:	**1 Game**		**2**	**0**	**0**	**0**	**0**	**0**	**0**	**0**	**0**	**0**	**0**	**.000**	**.000**

Easter, Luscious "Luke" B: *08/04/1915 Jonestown, MS* D: *03/29/1979 Euclid, OH* B/T: L/R *6'5" 240 lbs.*

PLAYER/TEAM	AGE	DATE	AB	R	H	D	T	HR	RBI	W	SAC	SB	E	RAVE	RSLG
HOMESTEAD GRAYS	33	22-Aug-48	0	0	0	0	0	0	0	1	0	1	0	1	.000	.000
HOMESTEAD GRAYS	33	24-Aug-48	4	0	0	0	0	0	0	0	0	0	0	.000	.000
Player Totals:	**2 Games**		**4**	**0**	**0**	**0**	**0**	**0**	**0**	**1**	**0**	**0**	**1**	**.000**	**.000**

Easterling, Howard "Ho" B: *11/26/1911 Mount Olive, MS* D: *09/06/1993 Collins, MS* B/T: S/R *5'10" 175 lbs.*

PLAYER/TEAM	AGE	DATE	AB	R	H	D	T	HR	RBI	W	SAC	SB	E	RAVE	RSLG
CINCINNATI TIGERS	25	08-Aug-37	2	0	0	0	0	0	0	1	0	0	0	.000	.000
HOMESTEAD GRAYS	28	18-Aug-40	5	1	2	0	0	0	1	0	0	0	0	.286	.286
HOMESTEAD GRAYS	31	01-Aug-43	4	0	1	0	0	0	0	0	0	0	0	.273	.273
HOMESTEAD GRAYS	34	15-Aug-46	4	2	3	0	0	0	1	0	0	0	0	.400	.400
HOMESTEAD GRAYS	34	18-Aug-46	4	0	0	0	0	0	0	0	0	0	0	.316	.316
NEW YORK CUBANS	37	14-Aug-49	4	1	2	0	0	0	2	0	0	1	0	.348	.348
Player Totals:	**6 Games**		**23**	**4**	**8**	**0**	**0**	**0**	**4**	**1**	**0**	**1**	**0**	**.348**	**.348**

Else, Harry "Speed" B: *01/09/1904 Kansas City, MO* D: *12/28/1986 San Diego, CA* B/T: R/R *5'11" 170 lbs.*

PLAYER/TEAM	AGE	DATE	AB	R	H	D	T	HR	RBI	W	SAC	SB	E	RAVE	RSLG
KANSAS CITY MONARCHS	32	23-Aug-36	1	0	0	0	0	0	0	1	0	0	0	.000	.000
Player Totals:	**1 Game**		**1**	**0**	**0**	**0**	**0**	**0**	**0**	**1**	**0**	**0**	**0**	**.000**	**.000**

Evans, Felix "Chin" B: *10/03/1910 Atlanta, GA* D: *08/21/1993 Pompano Beach, FL* B/T: R/R *6'2" 180 lbs.*

PLAYER/TEAM	AGE	DATE	AB	R	H	D	T	HR	RBI	W	SAC	SB	E	RAVE	RSLG
MEMPHIS RED SOX	35	18-Aug-46	1	0	0	0	0	0	0	0	0	0	0	.000	.000
Player Totals:	**1 Game**		**1**	**0**	**0**	**0**	**0**	**0**	**0**	**0**	**0**	**0**	**0**	**.000**	**.000**

Fields, Wilmer Leon "Red" B: *08/02/1922 Manassa VA   Living in Manassa, VA* B/T: R/R *6'3" 215 lbs.*

PLAYER/TEAM	AGE	DATE	AB	R	H	D	T	HR	RBI	W	SAC	SB	E	RAVE	RSLG
HOMESTEAD GRAYS	26	22-Aug-48	1	0	0	0	0	0	0	0	0	0	0	.000	.000
Player Totals:	**1 Game**		**1**	**0**	**0**	**0**	**0**	**0**	**0**	**0**	**0**	**0**	**0**	**.000**	**.000**

PLAYER/TEAM	AGE	DATE	AB	R	H	D	T	HR	RBI	W	SAC	SB	E	RAVE	RSLG
Ford, James "Jimmy" B: *10/16/1912 Memphis, TN* D: — B/T: *R/R 5'8" 185 lbs.*															
ST. LOUIS STARS	28	27-Jul-41	3	0	0	0	0	0	0	0	0	0	0	.000	.000
Player Totals:		1 Game	3	0	0	0	0	0	0	0	0	0	0	.000	.000
Formental, Pedro B: *04/19/1915 Baguanos, Cuba* D: *09/15/1992 Cleveland, OH* B/T: *L/L 5'11" 200 lbs.*															
MEMPHIS RED SOX	34	14-Aug-49	1	0	0	0	0	0	0	0	0	0	0	.000	.000
Player Totals:		1 Game	1	0	0	0	0	0	0	0	0	0	0	.000	.000
Foster, Willie Hendrick "Bill" B: *06/12/1904 Calvert, TX* D: *09/16/1978 Lorman, MS* B/T: *S/L 6'1" 195 lbs.*															
CHICAGO AMERICAN GIANTS	29	10-Sep-33	4	1	1	0	0	0	0	0	0	0	0	.250	.250
CHICAGO AMERICAN GIANTS	30	26-Aug-34	1	0	1	0	0	0	0	0	0	0	0	.400	.400
Player Totals:		2 Games	5	1	2	0	0	0	0	0	0	0	0	.400	.400
Gaines, Jonas Donald "Lefty" B: *01/09/1914 New Roads, LA* D: — B/T: *R/L 5'10" 155 lbs.*															
BALTIMORE ELITE GIANTS	28	16-Aug-42	1	0	0	0	0	0	0	0	0	0	0	.000	.000
BALTIMORE ELITE GIANTS	28	18-Aug-42	1	0	0	0	0	0	0	0	0	0	0	.000	.000
BALTIMORE ELITE GIANTS	32	15-Aug-46	0	0	0	0	0	0	0	0	0	0	0	.000	.000
BALTIMORE ELITE GIANTS	32	18-Aug-46	0	0	0	0	0	0	0	0	0	0	0	.000	.000
PHILADELPHIA STARS	36	20-Aug-50	0	0	0	0	0	0	0	0	0	0	0	.000	.000
Player Totals:		5 Games	2	0	0	0	0	0	0	0	0	0	0	.000	.000
Gaines, Willy "Willie" B: *1931 Tuscaloosa, AL* D: — B/T: *R/R 6'1" 190 lbs.*															
INDIANAPOLIS CLOWNS	22	16-Aug-53	1	0	0	0	0	0	0	0	0	0	1	.000	.000
Player Totals:		1 Game	1	0	0	0	0	0	0	0	0	0	1	.000	.000
Galata, Raul B: *10/05/1930 Havana, Cuba* D: — B/T: *L/L 5'9" 170 lbs.*															
NEW YORK CUBANS	19	20-Aug-50	2	0	0	0	0	0	0	0	0	0	0	.000	.000
Player Totals:		1 Game	2	0	0	0	0	0	0	0	0	0	0	.000	.000
Garcia y Rendon, Silvio "Cuban Fredon" B: *10/11/1913 Limonar, Cuba* D: *8/28/1977 Cuba* B/T: *R/R 6'1" 195 lbs.*															
NEW YORK CUBANS	32	15-Aug-46	2	0	0	0	0	0	0	0	0	0	0	.000	.000
NEW YORK CUBANS	32	18-Aug-46	1	0	0	0	0	0	0	0	0	0	2	.000	.000
NEW YORK CUBANS	33	27-Jul-47	3	0	0	0	0	0	0	0	0	0	0	.000	.000
NEW YORK CUBANS	33	29-Jul-47	4	0	1	1	0	0	2	0	0	0	1	.100	.200
Player Totals:		4 Games	10	0	1	1	0	0	2	0	0	0	3	.100	.200
Gibson, Joshua "Josh" B: *12/21/1911 Buena Vista, GA* D: *01/20/1947 Pittsburgh, PA* B/T: *R/R 6'1" 220 lbs.*															
PITTSBURGH CRAWFORDS	21	10-Sep-33	2	0	1	0	0	0	0	0	0	0	1	.500	.500
PITTSBURGH CRAWFORDS	22	26-Aug-34	4	0	2	1	0	0	0	0	0	0	0	.500	.667
PITTSBURGH CRAWFORDS	23	11-Aug-35	5	3	4	2	0	0	1	1	0	0	1	.636	.909
PITTSBURGH CRAWFORDS	24	23-Aug-36	3	2	2	0	0	0	1	0	0	1	0	.643	.857
HOMESTEAD GRAYS	27	06-Aug-39	3	0	0	0	0	0	0	1	0	0	0	.529	.706
HOMESTEAD GRAYS	27	27-Aug-39	2	1	1	0	1	0	4	2	1	0	0	.526	.789
HOMESTEAD GRAYS	30	16-Aug-42	3	0	2	0	0	0	1	2	0	0	0	.545	.773
HOMESTEAD GRAYS	30	18-Aug-42	4	1	1	0	0	0	1	1	0	0	1	.500	.692
HOMESTEAD GRAYS	31	01-Aug-43	3	0	1	0	0	0	0	1	0	0	0	.483	.655
HOMESTEAD GRAYS	32	13-Aug-44	3	1	2	1	0	0	1	0	0	0	0	.500	.688
HOMESTEAD GRAYS	34	15-Aug-46	2	0	1	0	0	0	0	0	0	0	0	.500	.676
HOMESTEAD GRAYS	34	18-Aug-46	3	0	0	0	0	0	0	1	0	0	0	.459	.622
Player Totals:		12 Games	37	8	17	4	1	0	8	10	1	1	3	.459	.622
Giles, George Franklin B: *05/02/1909 Junction City, KS* D: *03/03/1992 Topeka, KS* B/T: *L/R 6'2" 180 lbs.*															
BROOKLYN EAGLES	26	11-Aug-35	5	1	0	0	0	0	1	1	0	1	0	.000	.000
Player Totals:		1 Game	5	1	0	0	0	0	1	1	0	1	0	.000	.000
Gilliam, James William "Junior" B: *10/17/1927 Nashville, TN* D: *10/08/1978 Inglewood, CA* B/T: *S/R 5'10" 170 lbs.*															
BALTIMORE ELITE GIANTS	20	22-Aug-48	3	0	1	0	0	0	0	0	0	0	0	.333	.333
BALTIMORE ELITE GIANTS	20	24-Aug-48	3	1	1	0	0	0	0	0	0	1	0	.333	.333

PLAYER/TEAM	AGE	DATE	AB	R	H	D	T	HR	RBI	W	SAC	SB	E	RAVE	RSLG
BALTIMORE ELITE GIANTS	21	14-Aug-49	4	0	0	0	0	0	0	0	0	0	0	.200	.200
BALTIMORE ELITE GIANTS	22	20-Aug-50	3	1	1	0	0	1	1	0	1	0	0	.231	.462
Player Totals:		**4 Games**	**13**	**2**	**3**	**0**	**0**	**1**	**1**	**0**	**1**	**1**	**0**	**.231**	**.462**

Gipson, Alvin "Bubber" B: 12/11/1913 Shreveport, LA D: 11/21/1992 Shreveport, LA B/T: R/R

PLAYER/TEAM	AGE	DATE	AB	R	H	D	T	HR	RBI	W	SAC	SB	E	RAVE	RSLG
BIRMINGHAM BLACK BARONS	28	18-Aug-42	2	0	0	0	0	0	0	0	0	0	0	.000	.000
Player Totals:		**1 Game**	**2**	**0**	**0**	**0**	**0**	**0**	**0**	**0**	**0**	**0**	**0**	**.000**	**.000**

Glover, Thomas "Tom" or "Lefty" B: — D: — B/T: R/L

PLAYER/TEAM	AGE	DATE	AB	R	H	D	T	HR	RBI	W	SAC	SB	E	RAVE	RSLG
BALTIMORE ELITE GIANTS		29-Jul-45	0	0	0	0	0	0	0	0	0	0	0	.000	.000
Player Totals:		**1 Game**	**0**	**0**	**0**	**0**	**0**	**0**	**0**	**0**	**0**	**0**	**0**	**.000**	**.000**

Gonzalez, Hiram "Rene" B: 10/06/1923 Havana, Cuba Living in Cuba B/T: R/R 6'2" 205 lbs.

PLAYER/TEAM	AGE	DATE	AB	R	H	D	T	HR	RBI	W	SAC	SB	E	RAVE	RSLG
NEW YORK CUBANS	26	20-Aug-50	3	0	2	0	0	0	0	0	0	0	0	.667	.667
Player Totals:		**1 Game**	**3**	**0**	**2**	**0**	**0**	**0**	**0**	**0**	**0**	**0**	**0**	**.667**	**.667**

Grace, Willie "Fireman" B: 06/30/1918 Memphis, TN Living in Erie, PA B/T: S/R 6'0" 170 lbs.

PLAYER/TEAM	AGE	DATE	AB	R	H	D	T	HR	RBI	W	SAC	SB	E	RAVE	RSLG
CLEVELAND BUCKEYES	28	15-Aug-46	4	0	1	0	0	0	1	0	0	0	0	.250	.250
CLEVELAND BUCKEYES	28	18-Aug-46	4	1	3	0	0	0	0	0	0	0	0	.500	.500
CLEVELAND BUCKEYES	30	24-Aug-48	3	0	1	0	0	0	0	0	0	0	1	.455	.455
Player Totals:		**3 Games**	**11**	**1**	**5**	**0**	**0**	**0**	**1**	**0**	**0**	**0**	**1**	**.455**	**.455**

Greason, Rev. William Henry "Bill" B: 09/03/1924 Atlanta, GA Living in Birmingham, AL B/T: R/R 5'10" 170 lbs.

PLAYER/TEAM	AGE	DATE	AB	R	H	D	T	HR	RBI	W	SAC	SB	E	RAVE	RSLG
BIRMINGHAM BLACK BARONS	24	14-Aug-49	0	0	0	0	0	0	0	0	0	0	0	.000	.000
Player Totals:		**1 Game**	**0**	**0**	**0**	**0**	**0**	**0**	**0**	**0**	**0**	**0**	**0**	**.000**	**.000**

Green, Leslie "Chin" B: 02/08/1914 St. Louis, MO D: 03/02/1985 St. Louis, MO B/T: L/R 5'11" 190 lbs.

PLAYER/TEAM	AGE	DATE	AB	R	H	D	T	HR	RBI	W	SAC	SB	E	RAVE	RSLG
NEW ORLEANS-ST. LOUIS STARS	26	18-Aug-40	2	0	1	0	0	0	0	0	0	0	0	.500	.500
Player Totals:		**1 Game**	**2**	**0**	**1**	**0**	**0**	**0**	**0**	**0**	**0**	**0**	**0**	**.500**	**.500**

Greene, James Elbert "Joe" or "Pea" B: 10/17/1911 Stone Mountain, GA D: 07/19/1989 Stone Mountain, GA B/T: R/R 6'1" 200 lbs.

PLAYER/TEAM	AGE	DATE	AB	R	H	D	T	HR	RBI	W	SAC	SB	E	RAVE	RSLG
KANSAS CITY MONARCHS	28	18-Aug-40	2	0	0	0	0	0	0	1	0	0	1	.000	.000
KANSAS CITY MONARCHS	30	16-Aug-42	4	0	0	0	0	0	1	0	0	0	0	.000	.000
KANSAS CITY MONARCHS	30	18-Aug-42	2	0	0	0	0	0	0	2	0	0	1	.000	.000
Player Totals:		**3 Games**	**8**	**0**	**0**	**0**	**0**	**0**	**1**	**3**	**0**	**0**	**2**	**.000**	**.000**

Griffith, Robert Lee "Schoolboy" B: 10/01/1912 Liberty, TN D: 11/08/1977 Indianapolis, IN B/T: L/R 6'2" 215 lbs.

PLAYER/TEAM	AGE	DATE	AB	R	H	D	T	HR	RBI	W	SAC	SB	E	RAVE	RSLG
COLUMBUS ELITE GIANTS	22	11-Aug-35	0	0	0	0	0	0	0	0	0	0	0	.000	.000
NEW YORK BLACK YANKEES	35	22-Aug-48	1	0	0	0	0	0	0	0	0	0	0	.000	.000
PHILADELPHIA STARS	36	14-Aug-49	1	0	1	0	0	0	1	0	0	0	0	.500	.500
Player Totals:		**3 Games**	**2**	**0**	**1**	**0**	**0**	**0**	**1**	**0**	**0**	**0**	**0**	**.500**	**.500**

Griggs, Wiley Lee "Diamond Jim" B: 03/24/1925 Birmingham, AL D: 08/23/1996 Birmingham, AL B/T: R/R 5'11" 160 lbs.

PLAYER/TEAM	AGE	DATE	AB	R	H	D	T	HR	RBI	W	SAC	SB	E	RAVE	RSLG
NEW ORLEANS EAGLES	26	12-Aug-51	1	0	0	0	0	0	0	0	0	0	0	.000	.000
Player Totals:		**1 Game**	**1**	**0**	**0**	**0**	**0**	**0**	**0**	**0**	**0**	**0**	**0**	**.000**	**.000**

Guice, Lacy Kirk "Larry" B: 03/29/1931 D: 07/??/1993 Wichita, KS B/T: R/R

PLAYER/TEAM	AGE	DATE	AB	R	H	D	T	HR	RBI	W	SAC	SB	E	RAVE	RSLG
NEW ORLEANS EAGLES	20	12-Aug-51	3	0	1	0	0	0	0	0	0	0	0	.333	.333
Player Totals:		**1 Game**	**3**	**0**	**1**	**0**	**0**	**0**	**0**	**0**	**0**	**0**	**0**	**.333**	**.333**

Haggins, Raymond "Billy Ray" B: 09/05/1929 Piper, AL Living in Montevallo, AL B/T: L/L 6'1" 195 lbs.

PLAYER/TEAM	AGE	DATE	AB	R	H	D	T	HR	RBI	W	SAC	SB	E	RAVE	RSLG
MEMPHIS RED SOX	23	16-Aug-53	3	0	0	0	0	0	1	0	0	0	0	.000	.000
Player Totals:		**1 Game**	**3**	**0**	**0**	**0**	**0**	**0**	**1**	**0**	**0**	**0**	**0**	**.000**	**.000**

Hairston, Samuel "Sam" B: 01/20/1920 Crawford, MS D: 10/31/1997 Birmingham, AL B/T: R/R 5'10" 185 lbs.

PLAYER/TEAM	AGE	DATE	AB	R	H	D	T	HR	RBI	W	SAC	SB	E	RAVE	RSLG
INDIANAPOLIS CLOWNS	28	24-Aug-48	1	0	0	0	0	0	0	0	0	0	0	.000	.000
Player Totals:		**1 Game**	**1**	**0**	**0**	**0**	**0**	**0**	**0**	**0**	**0**	**0**	**0**	**.000**	**.000**

PLAYER/TEAM	AGE	DATE	AB	R	H	D	T	HR	RBI	W	SAC	SB	E	RAVE	RSLG
Hardaway, Curtis O. B: *1928 Columbus, GA* D: — B/T: R/R 6'0" 185 lbs.															
BIRMINGHAM BLACK BARONS	25	16-Aug-53	2	0	0	0	0	0	0	0	0	0	1	.000	.000
Player Totals:	**1 Game**		**2**	**0**	**0**	**0**	**0**	**0**	**0**	**0**	**0**	**0**	**1**	**.000**	**.000**
Harris, Chick "Popsickle" B: — D: — B/T: R/R															
KANSAS CITY MONARCHS		23-Aug-36	4	0	1	0	0	0	0	0	0	0	0	.250	.250
Player Totals:	**1 Game**		**4**	**0**	**1**	**0**	**0**	**0**	**0**	**0**	**0**	**0**	**0**	**.250**	**.250**
Harris, Elander Victor "Vic" B: *06/10/1905 Pensacola, FL* D: *02/23/1978 San Fernando, CA* B/T: L/R 5'10" 165 lbs.															
HOMESTEAD GRAYS	28	10-Sep-33	1	0	0	0	0	0	0	1	0	0	1	.000	.000
HOMESTEAD GRAYS	29	26-Aug-34	2	0	1	0	0	0	0	0	0	0	0	.333	.333
HOMESTEAD GRAYS	33	21-Aug-38	5	1	1	1	0	0	0	0	0	1	0	.250	.375
HOMESTEAD GRAYS	34	27-Aug-39	2	1	1	0	0	0	0	0	0	0	0	.300	.400
HOMESTEAD GRAYS	37	16-Aug-42	1	0	0	0	0	0	0	0	0	0	0	.273	.364
HOMESTEAD GRAYS	38	01-Aug-43	1	0	0	0	0	0	0	0	0	0	0	.250	.333
HOMESTEAD GRAYS	42	27-Jul-47	0	0	0	0	0	0	0	0	0	0	0	.250	.333
Player Totals:	**7 Games**		**12**	**2**	**3**	**1**	**0**	**0**	**0**	**1**	**0**	**1**	**1**	**.250**	**.333**
Harris, Isiah B: *07/02/1925 Parkin, AR Living in Memphis, TN* B/T: L/L 5'11" 195 lbs.															
MEMPHIS RED SOX	28	16-Aug-53	0	0	0	0	0	0	0	0	0	0	0	.000	.000
Player Totals:	**1 Game**		**0**	**0**	**0**	**0**	**0**	**0**	**0**	**0**	**0**	**0**	**0**	**.000**	**.000**
Harris, Wilmer B: *03/01/1924 Philadelphia, PA Living in Philadelphia, PA* B/T: R/R 6'1" 165 lbs.															
PHILADELPHIA STARS	27	12-Aug-51	1	0	0	0	0	0	0	0	0	0	0	.000	.000
PHILADELPHIA STARS	28	17-Aug-52	2	0	1	0	0	0	0	0	0	0	0	.333	.333
Player Totals:	**2 Games**		**3**	**0**	**1**	**0**	**0**	**0**	**0**	**0**	**0**	**0**	**0**	**.333**	**.333**
Harvey, David William "Bill" B: *03/23/1908 Clarksdale, MS* D: *03/05/1989 Baltimore, MD* B/T: L/L 5'8" 175 lbs.															
BALTIMORE ELITE GIANTS	35	01-Aug-43	0	0	0	0	0	0	0	0	0	0	0	.000	.000
Player Totals:	**1 Game**		**0**	**0**	**0**	**0**	**0**	**0**	**0**	**0**	**0**	**0**	**0**	**.000**	**.000**
Harvey, Robert A. "Bob" B: *05/28/1918 St. Michaels, MD* D: *06/27/1992 Montclair, NJ* B/T: L/R 6'0" 220 lbs.															
NEWARK EAGLES	30	22-Aug-48	1	0	0	0	0	0	0	0	0	0	0	.000	.000
HOUSTON EAGLES	32	20-Aug-50	2	1	0	0	0	0	0	1	0	0	0	.000	.000
Player Totals:	**2 Games**		**3**	**1**	**0**	**0**	**0**	**0**	**0**	**1**	**0**	**0**	**0**	**.000**	**.000**
Hayes, John William "Johnny" B: *04/27/1910 Independence, MO* D: *01/16/1988 Auburn Park, IL* B/T: L/R 5'9" 175 lbs.															
NEW YORK BLACK YANKEES	37	27-Jul-47	1	0	0	0	0	0	0	0	0	0	0	.000	.000
NEW YORK BLACK YANKEES	37	29-Jul-47	1	0	0	0	0	0	0	0	0	0	0	.000	.000
BALTIMORE ELITE GIANTS	41	12-Aug-51	3	0	1	0	0	0	0	0	0	0	0	.200	.200
Player Totals:	**3 Games**		**5**	**0**	**1**	**0**	**0**	**0**	**0**	**0**	**0**	**0**	**0**	**.200**	**.200**
Haywood, Albert Elliott "Buster" B: *01/12/1910 Portsmouth, VA* D: *04/19/2000 Los Angeles, CA* B/T: R/R 5'8" 165 lbs.															
INDIANAPOLIS CLOWNS	36	15-Aug-46	1	0	0	0	0	0	0	0	0	0	0	.000	.000
INDIANAPOLIS CLOWNS	41	12-Aug-51	0	0	0	0	0	0	0	0	0	0	0	.000	.000
INDIANAPOLIS CLOWNS	43	16-Aug-53	1	0	0	0	0	0	0	0	0	0	0	.000	.000
Player Totals:	**3 Games**		**2**	**0**	**0**	**0**	**0**	**0**	**0**	**0**	**0**	**0**	**0**	**.000**	**.000**
Heard, Jehosie "Jay" B: *01/17/1920 Atlanta, GA* D: *11/18/1999 Birmingham, AL* B/T: L/L 5'7" 145 lbs.															
NEW ORLEANS EAGLES	31	12-Aug-51	1	0	0	0	0	0	0	0	0	0	0	.000	.000
Player Totals:	**1 Game**		**1**	**0**	**0**	**0**	**0**	**0**	**0**	**0**	**0**	**0**	**0**	**.000**	**.000**
Henderson, Curtis "Dan" B: *Stambaugh, CT* D: — B/T: R/R															
TOLEDO-INDY CRAWFORDS		18-Aug-40	1	0	0	0	0	0	0	0	0	0	0	.000	.000
Player Totals:	**1 Game**		**1**	**0**	**0**	**0**	**0**	**0**	**0**	**0**	**0**	**0**	**0**	**.000**	**.000**
Henderson, James "Duke" B: *04/15/1924 Dallas, TX* D: *11/04/1984 Los Angeles, CA* B/T: R/R 6'1" 190 lbs.															
KANSAS CITY MONARCHS	28	17-Aug-52	4	2	2	0	0	0	1	0	0	0	0	.500	.500
Player Totals:	**1 Game**		**4**	**2**	**2**	**0**	**0**	**0**	**1**	**0**	**0**	**0**	**0**	**.500**	**.500**

Henry, Leo "Preacher" B: *03/10/1911 Inverness, FL* D: *05/16/1992 Jacksonville, FL* B/T: R/R *5'8"* *155 lbs.*

JACKSONVILLE RED CAPS	30	27-Jul-41	0	0	0	0	0	0	0	0	0	0	0	.000	.000
Player Totals:	**1 Game**		**0**	**0**	**0**	**0**	**0**	**0**	**0**	**0**	**0**	**0**	**0**	**.000**	**.000**

Herrera, Juan Francisco "Pancho" B: *06/16/1934 Santiago de las Vegas, Cuba Living in Miami, FL* B/T: R/R *6'3" 220 lbs.*

KANSAS CITY MONARCHS	19	16-Aug-53	1	0	0	0	0	0	0	0	0	0	0	.000	.000
Player Totals:	**1 Game**		**1**	**0**	**0**	**0**	**0**	**0**	**0**	**0**	**0**	**0**	**0**	**.000**	**.000**

Hill, Jimmy "Lefty" or "Squab" B: *06/06/1918 Plant City, FL* D: *05/31/1993 Sarasota, FL* B/T: L/L *5'5" 145 lbs.*

NEWARK EAGLES	23	27-Jul-41	0	0	0	0	0	0	0	0	0	0	0	.000	.000
Player Totals:	**1 Game**		**0**	**0**	**0**	**0**	**0**	**0**	**0**	**0**	**0**	**0**	**0**	**.000**	**.000**

Hill, Samuel "Sam" B: *11/24/1929* D: *04/23/1992 Dallas, TX* B/T: L/R *6'2" 180 lbs.*

CHICAGO AMERICAN GIANTS	18	22-Aug-48	3	0	0	0	0	0	1	1	0	0	0	.000	.000
CHICAGO AMERICAN GIANTS	18	24-Aug-48	2	1	0	0	0	0	0	0	0	1	0	.000	.000
Player Totals:	**2 Games**		**5**	**1**	**0**	**0**	**0**	**0**	**1**	**1**	**0**	**1**	**0**	**.000**	**.000**

Holland, Elvis William "Bill" B: *02/28/1901 Indianapolis, IN* D: *12/03/1973 Hamilton Grange, NY* B/T: S/R *5'9" 180 lbs.*

NEW YORK BLACK YANKEES	38	06-Aug-39	0	0	0	0	0	0	0	0	0	0	0	.000	.000
Player Totals:	**1 Game**		**0**	**0**	**0**	**0**	**0**	**0**	**0**	**0**	**0**	**0**	**0**	**.000**	**.000**

Horne, William J. "Billy" or "Little Grumbler" B: *New Orleans, LA* D: — B/T: R/R *5'6" 165 lbs.*

CHICAGO AMERICAN GIANTS		06-Aug-39	2	0	1	0	0	0	1	0	0	0	0	.500	.500
CHICAGO AMERICAN GIANTS		27-Aug-39	2	0	0	0	0	0	0	0	0	0	0	.250	.250
CHICAGO AMERICAN GIANTS		27-Jul-41	2	0	0	0	0	0	0	0	0	0	0	.167	.167
Player Totals:	**3 Games**		**6**	**0**	**1**	**0**	**0**	**0**	**1**	**0**	**0**	**0**	**0**	**.167**	**.167**

Hoskins, David Taylor "Dave" B: *08/04/1925 Greenwood, MS* D: *04/02/1970 Flint, MI* B/T: L/R *6'1" 180 lbs.*

CLEVELAND BUCKEYES	24	14-Aug-49	1	0	0	0	0	0	0	0	0	0	0	.000	.000
Player Totals:	**1 Game**		**1**	**0**	**0**	**0**	**0**	**0**	**0**	**0**	**0**	**0**	**0**	**.000**	**.000**

Hoskins, William Charles "Big Bill" B: *03/14/1916 Charleston, MS* D: *03/??/1975* B/T: L/R *6'3" 190 lbs.*

BALTIMORE ELITE GIANTS	25	27-Jul-41	5	1	1	0	0	0	1	0	0	0	0	.200	.200
Player Totals:	**1 Game**		**5**	**1**	**1**	**0**	**0**	**0**	**1**	**0**	**0**	**0**	**0**	**.200**	**.200**

Howard, Candasie Carrenza "Schoolboy" B: *12/16/1920 Daytona Beach, FL* D: *10/16/1993 Clair Mel City, FL* B/T: R/R *6'2" 210 lbs.*

NEW YORK CUBANS	23	13-Aug-44	1	0	0	0	0	0	0	0	0	0	0	.000	.000
Player Totals:	**1 Game**		**1**	**0**	**0**	**0**	**0**	**0**	**0**	**0**	**0**	**0**	**0**	**.000**	**.000**

Hudson, William Henry "Lefty" B: *Cincinnati, OH* D: — B/T: L/L *6'4" 180 lbs.*

CHICAGO AMERICAN GIANTS		27-Jul-41	1	0	0	0	0	0	0	0	0	0	0	.000	.000
Player Totals:	**1 Game**		**1**	**0**	**0**	**0**	**0**	**0**	**0**	**0**	**0**	**0**	**0**	**.000**	**.000**

Hughes, Samuel Thomas "Sammy T." B: *10/20/1910 Louisville, KY* D: *08/09/1981 Los Angeles, CA* B/T: R/R *6'3" 190 lbs.*

NASHVILLE ELITE GIANTS	23	26-Aug-34	2	0	0	0	0	0	0	0	0	0	0	.000	.000
COLUMBUS ELITE GIANTS	24	11-Aug-35	4	0	1	0	0	0	0	0	2	0	0	.167	.167
WASHINGTON ELITE GIANTS	25	23-Aug-36	5	2	1	1	0	0	0	1	0	0	1	.182	.273
BALTIMORE ELITE GIANTS	27	21-Aug-38	5	1	2	1	0	0	1	0	0	0	0	.250	.375
BALTIMORE ELITE GIANTS	28	06-Aug-39	3	0	1	0	0	0	2	0	0	0	0	.263	.368
BALTIMORE ELITE GIANTS	28	27-Aug-39	2	1	0	0	0	0	0	1	0	0	0	.238	.333
Player Totals:	**6 Games**		**21**	**4**	**5**	**2**	**0**	**0**	**3**	**2**	**2**	**0**	**1**	**.238**	**.333**

Hunter, Bertrum "Nate" or "Buffalo" B: *1906* D: — B/T: R/R *5'9" 175 lbs.*

PITTSBURGH CRAWFORDS	27	10-Sep-33	0	0	0	0	0	0	0	0	0	0	0	.000	.000
Player Totals:	**1 Game**		**0**	**0**	**0**	**0**	**0**	**0**	**0**	**0**	**0**	**0**	**0**	**.000**	**.000**

PLAYER/TEAM	AGE	DATE	AB	R	H	D	T	HR	RBI	W	SAC	SB	E	RAVE	RSLG
Hutchinson, Willie "Ace" B: 04/23/1920 D: 10/??/1992 Denver, CO B/T: R/R 5'10" 165 lbs.															
MEMPHIS RED SOX	29	14-Aug-49	1	0	0	0	0	0	0	0	0	0	0	.000	.000
Player Totals:	**1 Game**		**1**	**0**	**0**	**0**	**0**	**0**	**0**	**0**	**0**	**0**	**0**	**.000**	**.000**
Hyde, Cowan Fontella "Bubba" B: 04/10/1908 Pontotoc, MS Living in St. Louis, MO B/T: R/R 5'8" 150 lbs.															
MEMPHIS RED SOX	35	01-Aug-43	0	0	0	0	0	0	0	0	0	0	0	.000	.000
MEMPHIS RED SOX	38	15-Aug-46	3	0	1	0	0	0	1	0	0	0	0	.333	.333
MEMPHIS RED SOX	38	18-Aug-46	3	0	2	1	0	0	1	0	0	1	1	.500	.667
Player Totals:	**3 Games**		**6**	**0**	**3**	**1**	**0**	**0**	**2**	**0**	**0**	**1**	**1**	**.500**	**.667**
Irvin, Monford Merrill "Monte" B: 02/25/1919 Halesburg, AL Living in Homosassa, FL B/T: R/R 6'1" 190 lbs.															
NEWARK EAGLES	22	27-Jul-41	5	0	2	1	0	0	0	0	0	1	0	.400	.600
NEWARK EAGLES	27	15-Aug-46	3	1	1	0	0	0	1	0	0	1	0	.375	.500
NEWARK EAGLES	27	18-Aug-46	4	0	1	0	0	0	0	0	0	0	0	.333	.417
NEWARK EAGLES	28	27-Jul-47	3	1	0	0	0	0	0	1	0	0	0	.267	.333
NEWARK EAGLES	28	29-Jul-47	3	1	1	0	0	0	0	0	0	0	0	.278	.333
NEWARK EAGLES	29	22-Aug-48	2	0	0	0	0	0	0	0	0	0	0	.250	.300
Player Totals:	**6 Games**		**20**	**3**	**5**	**1**	**0**	**0**	**1**	**1**	**0**	**2**	**0**	**.250**	**.300**
Jackson, Isiah "Ike" B: 05/31/1923 Darling, MS D: 04/07/1964 Fresno, CA B/T: R/R 6'1" 210 lbs.															
KANSAS CITY MONARCHS	29	17-Aug-52	4	0	2	0	0	0	0	0	0	0	0	.500	.500
Player Totals:	**1 Game**		**4**	**0**	**2**	**0**	**0**	**0**	**0**	**0**	**0**	**0**	**0**	**.500**	**.500**
Jackson, John W. "Stony" B: 06/01/1928 Lumberton, MS Living in Hodge, LA B/T: R/R 5'10" 180 lbs.															
KANSAS CITY MONARCHS	24	17-Aug-52	1	0	0	0	0	0	0	1	0	0	0	.000	.000
KANSAS CITY MONARCHS	25	16-Aug-53	1	1	1	0	0	0	0	0	0	0	1	.500	.500
Player Totals:	**2 Games**		**2**	**1**	**1**	**0**	**0**	**0**	**0**	**1**	**0**	**0**	**1**	**.500**	**.500**
Jenkins, Clarence R. "Fats" B: 01/19/1898 New York, NY D: 12/06/1968 Philadelphia, PA B/T: L/L 5'7" 180 lbs.															
NEW YORK BLACK YANKEES	35	10-Sep-33	2	0	0	0	0	0	0	0	0	0	0	.000	.000
BROOKLYN EAGLES	37	11-Aug-35	5	1	0	0	0	0	0	1	0	0	0	.000	.000
Player Totals:	**2 Games**		**7**	**1**	**0**	**0**	**0**	**0**	**0**	**1**	**0**	**0**	**0**	**.000**	**.000**
Jessup, Joseph Gentry "Jeep" B: 07/04/1914 Mount Airy, NC D: 03/26/1998 Springfield, MA B/T: R/R 6'0" 180 lbs.															
CHICAGO AMERICAN GIANTS	30	13-Aug-44	2	0	0	0	0	0	0	0	0	0	0	.000	.000
CHICAGO AMERICAN GIANTS	31	29-Jul-45	1	0	0	0	0	0	0	0	0	0	0	.000	.000
CHICAGO AMERICAN GIANTS	32	15-Aug-46	1	0	0	0	0	0	0	0	0	0	0	.000	.000
CHICAGO AMERICAN GIANTS	33	27-Jul-47	1	0	0	0	0	0	0	0	0	0	0	.000	.000
CHICAGO AMERICAN GIANTS	34	22-Aug-48	1	0	1	0	0	0	0	0	0	0	0	.167	.167
Player Totals:	**5 Games**		**6**	**0**	**1**	**0**	**0**	**0**	**0**	**0**	**0**	**0**	**0**	**.167**	**.167**
Jethroe, Samuel "Sam" or "The Jet" B: 01/20/1917 East St. Louis, IL D: 06/16/2001 Erie, PA B/T: S/R 6'1" 175 lbs.															
CINCINNATI BUCKEYES	25	16-Aug-42	1	0	0	0	0	0	0	0	0	0	0	.000	.000
CINCINNATI BUCKEYES	25	18-Aug-42	5	1	1	0	0	0	0	0	0	0	0	.167	.167
CLEVELAND BUCKEYES	27	13-Aug-44	3	0	0	0	0	0	0	0	0	0	0	.111	.111
CLEVELAND BUCKEYES	29	15-Aug-46	4	1	0	0	0	0	0	0	0	0	0	.077	.077
CLEVELAND BUCKEYES	29	18-Aug-46	3	1	0	0	0	0	0	0	0	1	0	.063	.063
CLEVELAND BUCKEYES	30	27-Jul-47	3	1	1	0	1	0	1	1	0	1	0	.105	.211
CLEVELAND BUCKEYES	30	29-Jul-47	5	1	3	0	1	0	4	0	0	1	0	.208	.375
Player Totals:	**7 Games**		**24**	**5**	**5**	**0**	**2**	**0**	**5**	**1**	**0**	**3**	**0**	**0.208**	**.375**
Johnson, Byron "Mex" or "Jew Baby" B: 09/16/1911 Little Rock, AR Living in Denver, CO B/T: R/R 5'8" 160 lbs.															
KANSAS CITY MONARCHS	26	21-Aug-38	4	0	1	0	0	0	0	0	0	0	0	.250	.250
Player Totals:	**1 Game**		**4**	**0**	**1**	**0**	**0**	**0**	**0**	**0**	**0**	**0**	**0**	**.250**	**.250**
Johnson, Clifford "Connie" B: 12/27/1922 Stone Mountain, GA Living in Kansas City, MO B/T: R/R 6'4" 200 lbs.															
TOLEDO-INDY CRAWFORDS	17	18-Aug-40	0	0	0	0	0	0	0	0	0	0	0	.000	.000
KANSAS CITY MONARCHS	27	20-Aug-50	2	0	1	0	1	0	0	0	0	0	0	.500	1.500
Player Totals:	**2 Games**		**2**	**0**	**1**	**0**	**1**	**0**	**0**	**0**	**0**	**0**	**0**	**.500**	**1.500**

PLAYER/TEAM	AGE	DATE	AB	R	H	D	T	HR	RBI	W	SAC	SB	E	RAVE	RSLG
Johnson, Ernest D. "Schooley" B: 11/04/1928 Clinton, MS Living in Des Moines, IA B/T: L/R 6'3" 170 lbs.															
KANSAS CITY MONARCHS	24	16-Aug-53	1	0	1	0	0	0	2	0	0	0	0	1.000	1.000
Player Totals:	**1 Game**		**1**	**0**	**1**	**0**	**0**	**0**	**2**	**0**	**0**	**0**	**0**	**1.000**	**1.000**
Johnson, Jimmy "Slim" B: 1922 D: — B/T: L/L 6'1" 170 lbs.															
TOLEDO-INDY CRAWFORDS	17	27-Aug-39	2	0	0	0	0	0	0	0	0	0	0	.000	.000
Player Totals:	**1 Game**		**2**	**0**	**0**	**0**	**0**	**0**	**0**	**0**	**0**	**0**	**0**	**.000**	**.000**
Johnson, William Julius "Judy" B: 10/26/1899 Snow Hill, MD D: 06/15/1989 Wilmington, DE B/T: R/R 5'11" 150 lbs.															
PITTSBURGH CRAWFORDS	33	10-Sep-33	1	0	1	0	0	0	0	0	0	0	0	1.000	1.000
PITTSBURGH CRAWFORDS	36	23-Aug-36	2	0	1	0	0	0	1	0	1	0	0	.667	.667
Player Totals:	**2 Games**		**3**	**0**	**2**	**0**	**0**	**0**	**1**	**0**	**1**	**0**	**0**	**.667**	**.667**
Jones, Clinton "Casey" B: 07/19/1918 Cohoma County, MS D: 11/17/1998 Memphis, TN B/T: L/R 6'2" 205 lbs.															
MEMPHIS RED SOX	32	20-Aug-50	2	0	0	0	0	0	0	0	0	0	0	.000	.000
MEMPHIS RED SOX	33	12-Aug-51	2	0	0	0	0	0	0	0	0	0	0	.000	.000
Player Totals:	**2 Games**		**4**	**0**	**0**	**0**	**0**	**0**	**0**	**0**	**0**	**0**	**0**	**.000**	**.000**
Jones, James "Jimmie" B: — D: — B/T: R/R															
PHILADELPHIA STARS		17-Aug-52	1	0	0	0	0	0	0	0	0	0	0	.000	.000
Player Totals:	**1 Game**		**1**	**0**	**0**	**0**	**0**	**0**	**0**	**0**	**0**	**0**	**0**	**.000**	**.000**
Jones, Stuart "Slim" B: 05/06/1913 Baltimore, MD D: 12/??/1938 Baltimore, MD B/T: L/L 6'6" 185 lbs.															
PHILADELPHIA STARS	21	26-Aug-34	1	0	0	0	0	0	0	0	0	0	0	.000	.000
PHILADELPHIA STARS	22	11-Aug-35	2	1	2	0	0	1	1	0	0	0	0	.667	1.667
Player Totals:	**2 Games**		**3**	**1**	**2**	**0**	**0**	**1**	**1**	**0**	**0**	**0**	**0**	**.667**	**1.667**
Kellman, Edric Leon B: 07/11/1921 Gatun, Panama Canal Zone D: 09/??/1981 Orlando, FL B/T: R/R 5'10" 175 lbs.															
CLEVELAND BUCKEYES	26	29-Jul-47	2	0	0	0	0	0	0	0	0	0	0	.000	.000
CLEVELAND BUCKEYES	27	24-Aug-48	1	0	0	0	0	0	0	0	0	0	1	.000	.000
CLEVELAND BUCKEYES	28	14-Aug-49	1	0	0	0	0	0	0	0	0	0	0	.000	.000
MEMPHIS RED SOX	29	20-Aug-50	2	0	0	0	0	0	0	0	0	0	1	.000	.000
Player Totals:	**4 Games**		**6**	**0**	**0**	**0**	**0**	**0**	**0**	**0**	**0**	**0**	**2**	**.000**	**.000**
Kimbro, Henry Allen "Jimbo" B: 02/10/1912 Nashville, TN D: 07/11/1999 Nashville, TN B/T: L/R 5'8" 175 lbs.															
NEW YORK BLACK YANKEES	29	27-Jul-41	3	1	1	0	0	0	1	0	0	2	0	.333	.333
BALTIMORE ELITE GIANTS	31	01-Aug-43	1	0	0	0	0	0	0	0	0	0	0	.250	.250
BALTIMORE ELITE GIANTS	32	13-Aug-44	1	0	0	0	0	0	0	0	0	0	0	.200	.200
BALTIMORE ELITE GIANTS	34	15-Aug-46	2	1	1	0	0	0	0	1	0	1	0	.286	.286
BALTIMORE ELITE GIANTS	34	18-Aug-46	4	0	0	0	0	0	0	0	0	0	0	.182	.182
BALTIMORE ELITE GIANTS	35	27-Jul-47	4	0	0	0	0	0	0	0	0	0	0	.133	.133
BALTIMORE ELITE GIANTS	35	29-Jul-47	2	0	1	0	0	0	0	1	0	0	2	.176	.176
BIRMINGHAM BLACK BARONS	39	12-Aug-51	4	0	1	0	0	0	0	1	0	0	0	.190	.190
BIRMINGHAM BLACK BARONS	40	17-Aug-52	3	0	1	0	0	0	1	1	0	1	1	.208	.208
BIRMINGHAM BLACK BARONS	41	16-Aug-53	3	0	1	0	0	0	1	0	0	0	0	.222	.222
Player Totals:	**10 Game**		**27**	**2**	**6**	**0**	**0**	**0**	**3**	**4**	**0**	**4**	**3**	**.222**	**.222**
Kincannon, Harry "Tin Can" B: 07/30/1909 D: 10/??/1965 B/T: R/R 5'10" 190 lbs.															
PITTSBURGH CRAWFORDS	25	26-Aug-34	1	0	0	0	0	0	0	0	0	0	0	.000	.000
Player Totals:	**1 Game**		**1**	**0**	**0**	**0**	**0**	**0**	**0**	**0**	**0**	**0**	**0**	**.000**	**.000**
Kranson, Floyd Arthur B: 07/24/1913 D: 09/??/1967 B/T: R/R 6'1" 180 lbs.															
KANSAS CITY MONARCHS	23	23-Aug-36	0	0	0	0	0	0	0	0	0	0	0	.000	.000
Player Totals:	**1 Game**		**0**	**0**	**0**	**0**	**0**	**0**	**0**	**0**	**0**	**0**	**0**	**.000**	**.000**
LaMarque, James Harding "Lefty" B: 07/29/1921 Potosi, MO D: 01/15/2000 North Kansas City, MO B/T: R/L 6'1" 180 lbs.															
KANSAS CITY MONARCHS	27	22-Aug-48	1	0	0	0	0	0	0	0	0	0	0	.000	.000
KANSAS CITY MONARCHS	27	24-Aug-48	0	0	0	0	0	0	0	0	0	0	0	.000	.000
KANSAS CITY MONARCHS	28	14-Aug-49	1	0	0	0	0	0	0	0	0	0	0	.000	.000
Player Totals:	**3 Games**		**2**	**0**	**0**	**0**	**0**	**0**	**0**	**0**	**0**	**0**	**0**	**.000**	**.000**

PLAYER/TEAM	AGE	DATE	AB	R	H	D	T	HR	RBI	W	SAC	SB	E	RAVE	RSLG
Leonard, Walter Fenner "Buck" B: _09/08/1907 Rocky Mount, NC_ D: _11/27/1997 Rocky Mount, NC_ B/T: L/L _5'10"_ _185 lbs._															
HOMESTEAD GRAYS	27	11-Aug-35	3	0	0	0	0	0	1	0	0	0	0	.000	.000
HOMESTEAD GRAYS	29	08-Aug-37	4	2	2	0	0	1	2	1	0	0	1	.286	.714
HOMESTEAD GRAYS	30	21-Aug-38	4	0	1	0	0	0	1	0	0	0	0	.273	.545
HOMESTEAD GRAYS	31	06-Aug-39	3	1	0	0	0	0	0	1	0	0	0	.214	.429
HOMESTEAD GRAYS	31	27-Aug-39	4	1	2	0	0	0	1	1	0	0	0	.278	.444
HOMESTEAD GRAYS	32	18-Aug-40	4	1	3	0	0	0	3	2	0	2	0	.364	.500
HOMESTEAD GRAYS	33	27-Jul-41	5	1	2	0	0	1	3	0	0	0	0	.370	.593
HOMESTEAD GRAYS	35	01-Aug-43	4	1	1	0	0	1	1	0	0	0	0	.355	.645
HOMESTEAD GRAYS	36	13-Aug-44	3	1	1	0	1	0	0	1	0	0	1	.353	.676
HOMESTEAD GRAYS	37	29-Jul-45	3	1	1	0	0	0	0	1	0	0	0	.351	.649
HOMESTEAD GRAYS	38	15-Aug-46	3	0	0	0	0	0	2	0	1	0	0	.325	.600
HOMESTEAD GRAYS	38	18-Aug-46	4	0	1	0	0	0	0	0	0	0	0	.318	.568
HOMESTEAD GRAYS	40	22-Aug-48	4	0	1	1	0	0	0	0	0	0	0	.313	.563
Player Totals:	**13 Game**		**48**	**9**	**15**	**1**	**1**	**3**	**14**	**7**	**1**	**2**	**2**	**0.313**	**.563**
Lewis, Rufus "Mississippi" B: _12/13/1919 Hattiesburg, MS_ D: _December 17, 1999 Detroit, MI_ B/T: R/R _6'1"_ _190 lbs._															
NEWARK EAGLES	27	29-Jul-47	1	0	0	0	0	0	0	0	0	0	1	.000	.000
NEWARK EAGLES	28	22-Aug-48	1	0	0	0	0	0	0	0	0	0	0	.000	.000
Player Totals:	**2 Games**		**2**	**0**	**0**	**0**	**0**	**0**	**0**	**0**	**0**	**0**	**1**	**.000**	**.000**
Linares, Rogelio "Ice Cream" B: _09/20/1909 Havana, Cuba_ D: — B/T: L/L _5'10"_ _175 lbs._															
NEW YORK CUBANS	35	29-Jul-45	3	1	0	0	0	0	0	1	0	0	0	.000	.000
Player Totals:	**1 Game**		**3**	**1**	**0**	**0**	**0**	**0**	**0**	**1**	**0**	**0**	**0**	**.000**	**.000**
Littles, Ben B: — D: — B/T: R/R															
PHILADELPHIA STARS		20-Aug-50	3	0	2	1	0	0	1	0	0	0	0	.667	1.000
PHILADELPHIA STARS		12-Aug-51	1	0	1	0	1	0	1	0	0	0	0	.750	1.500
Player Totals:	**2 Games**		**4**	**0**	**3**	**1**	**1**	**0**	**2**	**0**	**0**	**0**	**0**	**.750**	**1.500**
Lockett, Lester "Buck" B: _03/26/1912 Princeton, IN_ _Living in Chicago, IL_ B/T: R/R _5'11"_ _185 lbs._															
BIRMINGHAM BLACK BARONS	31	01-Aug-43	0	0	0	0	0	0	0	0	0	0	0	.000	.000
BIRMINGHAM BLACK BARONS	33	29-Jul-45	4	0	0	0	0	0	1	0	0	0	0	.000	.000
BALTIMORE ELITE GIANTS	36	22-Aug-48	2	0	0	0	0	0	0	1	0	0	0	.000	.000
BALTIMORE ELITE GIANTS	36	24-Aug-48	4	0	1	0	0	0	1	0	0	0	0	.100	.100
Player Totals:	**4 Games**		**10**	**0**	**1**	**0**	**0**	**0**	**2**	**1**	**0**	**0**	**0**	**.100**	**.100**
Long, Carl B: _05/09/1935 Rockhill, SC_ _Living in Kinston, NC_ B/T: R/R _6'2"_ _140 lbs._															
BIRMINGHAM BLACK BARONS	18	16-Aug-53	4	0	0	0	0	0	0	0	0	0	0	.000	.000
Player Totals:	**1 Game**		**4**	**0**	**0**	**0**	**0**	**0**	**0**	**0**	**0**	**0**	**0**	**.000**	**.000**
Lopez, Candido Justo "Cando" or "Police Car" B: _10/15/1902 Cuba_ D: _09/??/1979 Puerto Rico_ B/T: R/R															
NEW YORK CUBANS	36	27-Aug-39	3	0	1	0	0	0	0	0	0	0	0	.333	.333
Player Totals:	**1 Game**		**3**	**0**	**1**	**0**	**0**	**0**	**0**	**0**	**0**	**0**	**0**	**.333**	**.333**
Louden, Louis Oliver "Tommy" B: _08/19/1919 West Point, VA_ D: _08/31/1989 Newark, NJ_ B/T: R/R _5'9"_ _175 lbs._															
NEW YORK CUBANS	26	15-Aug-46	1	0	0	0	0	0	0	0	0	0	0	.000	.000
NEW YORK CUBANS	27	27-Jul-47	1	0	1	0	0	0	1	0	0	0	0	.500	.500
NEW YORK CUBANS	27	29-Jul-47	2	0	0	0	0	0	0	0	0	0	0	.250	.250
NEW YORK CUBANS	29	22-Aug-48	3	0	0	0	0	0	0	0	0	0	0	.143	.143
NEW YORK CUBANS	29	24-Aug-48	1	0	0	0	0	0	0	0	0	0	0	.125	.125
NEW YORK CUBANS	31	20-Aug-50	5	1	1	0	0	0	0	0	0	0	0	.154	.154
Player Totals:	**6 Games**		**13**	**1**	**2**	**0**	**0**	**0**	**1**	**0**	**0**	**0**	**0**	**.154**	**.154**
Lundy, Richard "Dick" or "King Richard" B: _07/10/1898 Jacksonville, FL_ D: _01/05/1965 Jacksonville, FL_ B/T: S/R _5'11"_ _170 lbs._															
PHILADELPHIA STARS	35	10-Sep-33	3	0	0	0	0	0	0	1	0	0	0	.000	.000
NEWARK DODGERS	36	26-Aug-34	4	0	0	0	0	0	0	0	0	0	0	.000	.000

PLAYER/TEAM	AGE	DATE	AB	R	H	D	T	HR	RBI	W	SAC	SB	E	RAVE	RSLG
Player Totals:	**2 Games**		7	0	0	0	0	0	0	1	0	0	0	.000	.000

Lyles, John B: *03/18/1912 St. Louis, MO* D: *07/15/1991* B/T: *S/R 5'9" 190 lbs.*

PLAYER/TEAM	AGE	DATE	AB	R	H	D	T	HR	RBI	W	SAC	SB	E	RAVE	RSLG
CLEVELAND BEARS	27	27-Aug-39	3	1	1	0	0	0	0	1	0	0	1	.333	.333
Player Totals:	**1 Game**		3	1	1	0	0	0	0	1	0	0	1	**.333**	**.333**

Mackey, James Raleigh "Biz" B: *07/27/1897 Eagle Pass, TX* D: *09/22/1965 Los Angeles, CA* B/T: *S/R 6'1" 215 lbs.*

PLAYER/TEAM	AGE	DATE	AB	R	H	D	T	HR	RBI	W	SAC	SB	E	RAVE	RSLG
PHILADELPHIA STARS	36	10-Sep-33	3	0	1	0	0	0	0	0	0	0	0	.333	.333
PHILADELPHIA STARS	38	11-Aug-35	5	1	0	0	0	0	0	1	0	0	0	.125	.125
WASHINGTON ELITE GIANTS	39	23-Aug-36	2	0	2	1	0	0	2	0	0	0	0	.300	.400
BALTIMORE ELITE GIANTS	41	21-Aug-38	4	0	0	0	0	0	0	0	0	0	0	.214	.286
NEWARK EAGLES	49	27-Jul-47	0	0	0	0	0	0	0	1	0	0	0	.214	.286
Player Totals:	**5 Games**		14	1	3	1	0	0	2	2	0	0	0	**.214**	**.286**

Manning, Maxwell "Max" B: *11/18/1918 Rome, GA Living in Pleasantville, NJ* B/T: *L/R 6'4" 180 lbs.*

PLAYER/TEAM	AGE	DATE	AB	R	H	D	T	HR	RBI	W	SAC	SB	E	RAVE	RSLG
NEWARK EAGLES	28	27-Jul-47	2	0	1	0	0	0	0	0	0	0	0	.500	.500
NEWARK EAGLES	29	24-Aug-48	0	0	0	0	0	0	0	0	0	0	0	.500	.500
Player Totals:	**2 Games**		2	0	1	0	0	0	0	0	0	0	0	**.500**	**.500**

Marquez, Luis Angel "Canena" B: *10/28/1925 Aguadilla, Puerto Rico* D: *03/??/1988 Aguadilla, Auerto Rico* B/T: *R/R 5'10" 165 lbs.*

PLAYER/TEAM	AGE	DATE	AB	R	H	D	T	HR	RBI	W	SAC	SB	E	RAVE	RSLG
HOMESTEAD GRAYS	21	27-Jul-47	1	1	1	1	0	0	0	0	0	0	0	1.000	2.000
HOMESTEAD GRAYS	21	29-Jul-47	3	0	0	0	0	0	0	0	0	0	0	.250	.500
HOMESTEAD GRAYS	22	22-Aug-48	4	0	0	0	0	0	0	0	0	0	0	.125	.250
HOMESTEAD GRAYS	22	24-Aug-48	5	1	1	0	0	1	2	0	0	0	0	.154	.462
Player Totals:	**4 Games**		13	2	2	1	0	1	2	0	0	0	0	**.154**	**.462**

Martinez, Horacio "Rabbit" B: *10/20/1912 Santiago, Santo Domingo* D: *04/14/1992* B/T: *R/R 5'9" 155 lbs.*

PLAYER/TEAM	AGE	DATE	AB	R	H	D	T	HR	RBI	W	SAC	SB	E	RAVE	RSLG
NEW YORK CUBANS	27	18-Aug-40	3	1	1	0	0	0	0	0	0	0	0	.333	.333
NEW YORK CUBANS	28	27-Jul-41	4	1	2	0	0	0	0	1	0	1	1	.429	.429
NEW YORK CUBANS	30	01-Aug-43	2	0	1	0	0	0	0	0	0	0	0	.444	.444
NEW YORK CUBANS	31	13-Aug-44	0	0	0	0	0	0	0	0	0	0	0	.444	.444
NEW YORK CUBANS	32	29-Jul-45	2	0	2	0	0	0	3	0	0	0	0	.545	.545
Player Totals:	**5 Games**		11	2	6	0	0	0	3	1	0	1	1	**.545**	**.545**

Mathis, Verdell "Lefty" B: *11/18/1914 Crawfordsville, AR* D: *10/30/1998 Memphis, TN* B/T: *L/L 5'10" 150 lbs.*

PLAYER/TEAM	AGE	DATE	AB	R	H	D	T	HR	RBI	W	SAC	SB	E	RAVE	RSLG
MEMPHIS RED SOX	26	27-Jul-41	0	0	0	0	0	0	0	0	0	0	0	.000	.000
MEMPHIS RED SOX	27	18-Aug-42	2	0	0	0	0	0	0	0	0	0	0	.000	.000
MEMPHIS RED SOX	29	13-Aug-44	1	0	1	0	0	0	0	0	0	0	0	.333	.333
MEMPHIS RED SOX	30	29-Jul-45	2	1	2	0	0	0	0	0	0	0	0	.600	.600
Player Totals:	**4 Games**		5	1	3	0	0	0	0	0	0	0	0	**.600**	**.600**

Matlock, Leroy B: *03/12/1907 Moberly, MO* D: *02/06/1968 St. Paul, MN* B/T: *L/L 5'9" 175 lbs.*

PLAYER/TEAM	AGE	DATE	AB	R	H	D	T	HR	RBI	W	SAC	SB	E	RAVE	RSLG
PITTSBURGH CRAWFORDS	28	11-Aug-35	1	0	0	0	0	0	0	0	0		0	.000	.000
PITTSBURGH CRAWFORDS	29	23-Aug-36	1	0	0	0	0	0	0	0	0		0	.000	.000
Player Totals:	**2 Games**		2	0	0	0	0	0	0	0	0	0	0	**.000**	**.000**

Mayweather, Eldridge E. "Chili" B: *02/26/1909 Shreveport, LA* D: *02/19/1966 Kansas City, MO* B/T: *L/L 5'10" 180 lbs.*

PLAYER/TEAM	AGE	DATE	AB	R	H	D	T	HR	RBI	W	SAC	SB	E	RAVE	RSLG
KANSAS CITY MONARCHS	28	08-Aug-37	1	0	0	0	0	0	0	0	0	0	0	.000	.000
NEW ORLEANS-ST. LOUIS STARS	31	18-Aug-40	3	0	1	0	0	0	0	1	0	0	0	.250	.250
Player Totals:	**2 Games**		4	0	1	0	0	0	0	1	0	0	0	**.250**	**.250**

McDaniels, Booker Taliaferro "Cannonball" B: *09/13/1913 Blackwell, AR* D: *12/12/1974 Kansas City, MO* B/T: *R/R 6'2" 195 lbs.*

PLAYER/TEAM	AGE	DATE	AB	R	H	D	T	HR	RBI	W	SAC	SB	E	RAVE	RSLG
KANSAS CITY MONARCHS	31	29-Jul-45	1	0	0	0	0	0	0	0	0	0	0	.000	.000
Player Totals:	**1 Game**		1	0	0	0	0	0	0	0	0	0	0	**.000**	**.000**

McDuffie, Terris Chester "The Great" B: *07/22/1910 Mobile, AL* D: *05/??/1968 New York, NY* B/T: *R/R 6'1" 195 lbs.*

PLAYER/TEAM	AGE	DATE	AB	R	H	D	T	HR	RBI	W	SAC	SB	E	RAVE	RSLG
NEW YORK BLACK YANKEES	29	27-Aug-39	2	0	0	0	0	0	0	0	0	0	0	.000	.000

PLAYER/TEAM	AGE	DATE	AB	R	H	D	T	HR	RBI	W	SAC	SB	E	RAVE	RSLG
HOMESTEAD GRAYS	31	27-Jul-41	0	0	0	0	0	0	0	0	1	0	0	.000	.000
NEWARK EAGLES	34	13-Aug-44	1	0	1	0	1	0	0	0	0	0	0	.333	1.000
Player Totals:	**3 Games**		**3**	**0**	**1**	**0**	**1**	**0**	**0**	**0**	**1**	**0**	**0**	**.333**	**1.000**

McHenry, Henry "Cream" B: 04/03/1910 D: 02/09/1981 Brooklyn, NY B/T: R/R 6'0" 200 lbs.

PLAYER/TEAM	AGE	DATE	AB	R	H	D	T	HR	RBI	W	SAC	SB	E	RAVE	RSLG
PHILADELPHIA STARS	30	18-Aug-40	0	0	0	0	0	0	0	1	0	0	0	.000	.000
PHILADELPHIA STARS	31	27-Jul-41	0	0	0	0	0	0	0	1	0	0	0	.000	.000
Player Totals:	**2 Games**		**0**	**0**	**0**	**0**	**0**	**0**	**0**	**2**	**0**	**0**	**0**	**.000**	**.000**

McKinnis, Gread "Lefty" or "Gready" B: 08/11/1913 Union, AL D: 03/08/1991 Chicago, IL B/T: R/L 6'1" 175 lbs.

PLAYER/TEAM	AGE	DATE	AB	R	H	D	T	HR	RBI	W	SAC	SB	E	RAVE	RSLG
BIRMINGHAM BLACK BARONS	29	01-Aug-43	1	0	0	0	0	0	0	0	0	0	0	.000	.000
CHICAGO AMERICAN GIANTS	31	13-Aug-44	0	0	0	0	0	0	0	0	0	0	0	.000	.000
CHICAGO AMERICAN GIANTS	36	14-Aug-49	0	0	0	0	0	0	0	0	0	0	0	.000	.000
Player Totals:	**3 Games**		**1**	**0**	**0**	**0**	**0**	**0**	**0**	**0**	**0**	**0**	**0**	**.000**	**.000**

McLaurin, Felix B: 09/05/1921 Jacksonville, FL D: 05/??/1972 B/T: L/L 5'9" 185 lbs.

PLAYER/TEAM	AGE	DATE	AB	R	H	D	T	HR	RBI	W	SAC	SB	E	RAVE	RSLG
CHICAGO AMERICAN GIANTS	30	17-Aug-52	1	0	1	1	0	0	2	0	0	0	0	1.000	2.000
Player Totals:	**1 Game**		**1**	**0**	**1**	**1**	**0**	**0**	**2**	**0**	**0**	**0**	**0**	**1.000**	**2.000**

McNeal, Clyde Clifton "Junior" B: 12/15/1928 San Antonio, TX D: 04/13/1996 San Antonio, TX B/T: R/R 6'0" 170 lbs.

PLAYER/TEAM	AGE	DATE	AB	R	H	D	T	HR	RBI	W	SAC	SB	E	RAVE	RSLG
CHICAGO AMERICAN GIANTS	21	20-Aug-50	3	0	1	0	0	0	0	0	0	0	1	.333	.333
Player Totals:	**1 Game**		**3**	**0**	**1**	**0**	**0**	**0**	**0**	**0**	**0**	**0**	**1**	**.333**	**.333**

Merchant, Henry Lewis "Speed" B: 02/17/1918 Birmingham, AL D: 08/23/1982 Cincinnati, OH B/T: L/L 6'3" 180 lbs.

PLAYER/TEAM	AGE	DATE	AB	R	H	D	T	HR	RBI	W	SAC	SB	E	RAVE	RSLG
INDIANAPOLIS CLOWNS	32	20-Aug-50	5	0	0	0	0	0	0	0	0	0	0	.000	.000
INDIANAPOLIS CLOWNS	34	17-Aug-52	2	0	0	0	0	0	0	0	0	0	1	.000	.000
Player Totals:	**2 Games**		**7**	**0**	**0**	**0**	**0**	**0**	**0**	**0**	**0**	**0**	**1**	**.000**	**.000**

Miller, Henry Joseph "Hank" B: 07/17/1917 Glenolden, PA D: 08/30/1972 Philadelphia, PA B/T: R/R 6'1" 180 lbs.

PLAYER/TEAM	AGE	DATE	AB	R	H	D	T	HR	RBI	W	SAC	SB	E	RAVE	RSLG
PHILADELPHIA STARS	30	27-Jul-47	0	0	0	0	0	0	0	0	0	0	0	.000	.000
PHILADELPHIA STARS	30	29-Jul-47	0	0	0	0	0	0	0	0	0	0	0	.000	.000
Player Totals:	**2 Games**		**0**	**0**	**0**	**0**	**0**	**0**	**0**	**0**	**0**	**0**	**0**	**.000**	**.000**

Milton, Henry William "Streak" B: 1910 D: 07/??/1943 B/T: L/L 5'9" 155 lbs.

PLAYER/TEAM	AGE	DATE	AB	R	H	D	T	HR	RBI	W	SAC	SB	E	RAVE	RSLG
KANSAS CITY MONARCHS	26	23-Aug-36	2	0	0	0	0	0	0	1	0	0	0	.000	.000
KANSAS CITY MONARCHS	27	08-Aug-37	1	0	0	0	0	0	0	0	0	0	0	.000	.000
KANSAS CITY MONARCHS	28	21-Aug-38	3	2	1	0	0	0	0	1	0	2	0	.167	.167
KANSAS CITY MONARCHS	29	06-Aug-39	3	0	1	0	0	0	0	0	0	0	0	.222	.222
KANSAS CITY MONARCHS	30	18-Aug-40	4	0	1	0	0	0	0	0	0	0	0	.231	.231
Player Totals:	**5 Games**		**13**	**2**	**3**	**0**	**0**	**0**	**0**	**2**	**0**	**2**	**0**	**.231**	**.231**

Minoso, Saturnino Orestes Arrieta "Minnie" B: 11/29/1922 Perico, Cuba Living in Chicago, IL B/T: R/R 5'10" 175 lbs.

PLAYER/TEAM	AGE	DATE	AB	R	H	D	T	HR	RBI	W	SAC	SB	E	RAVE	RSLG
NEW YORK CUBANS	24	27-Jul-47	3	0	0	0	0	0	0	0	0	0	0	.000	.000
NEW YORK CUBANS	24	29-Jul-47	4	0	1	0	0	0	0	0	0	0	0	.143	.143
NEW YORK CUBANS	25	22-Aug-48	4	0	1	0	0	0	0	0	0	0	0	.182	.182
NEW YORK CUBANS	25	24-Aug-48	2	1	2	2	0	0	0	0	0	0	0	.308	.462
Player Totals:	**4 Games**		**13**	**1**	**4**	**2**	**0**	**0**	**0**	**0**	**0**	**0**	**0**	**.308**	**.462**

Mitchell, George "Big" B: 12/20/1898 Sparta, IL D: 1/??/1964 New Jersey B/T: R/R 6'4" 200 lbs.

PLAYER/TEAM	AGE	DATE	AB	R	H	D	T	HR	RBI	W	SAC	SB	E	RAVE	RSLG
ST. LOUIS STARS	42	27-Jul-41	0	0	0	0	0	0	0	0	0	0	0	.000	.000
Player Totals:	**1 Game**		**0**	**0**	**0**	**0**	**0**	**0**	**0**	**0**	**0**	**0**	**0**	**.000**	**.000**

Morney, Leroy B: 05/13/1909 Columbus, OH D: 11/??/1980 Oak Forest, IL B/T: L/R 5'10" 170 lbs.

PLAYER/TEAM	AGE	DATE	AB	R	H	D	T	HR	RBI	W	SAC	SB	E	RAVE	RSLG
CLEVELAND GIANTS	24	10-Sep-33	4	0	1	0	0	0	1	0	0	0	3	.250	.250
TOLEDO-INDY CRAWFORDS	30	06-Aug-39	1	0	0	0	0	0	0	1	0	0	0	.200	.200
CHICAGO AMERICAN GIANTS	31	18-Aug-40	2	0	0	0	0	0	0	0	0	0	4	.143	.143
Player Totals:	**3 Games**		**7**	**0**	**1**	**0**	**0**	**0**	**1**	**1**	**0**	**0**	**7**	**.143**	**.143**

PLAYER/TEAM	AGE	DATE	AB	R	H	D	T	HR	RBI	W	SAC	SB	E	RAVE	RSLG
Morris, Barney "Big Ad" B: *06/03/1913 Shreveport, LA* D: — B/T: *L/R 6'1" 170 lbs.*															
PITTSBURGH CRAWFORDS	24	08-Aug-37	2	0	0	0	0	0	0	0	0	0	0	.000	.000
NEW YORK CUBANS	31	13-Aug-44	0	0	0	0	0	0	0	0	0	0	0	.000	.000
Player Totals:	**2 Games**		**2**	**0**	**0**	**0**	**0**	**0**	**0**	**0**	**0**	**0**	**0**	**.000**	**.000**
Moss, Porter "Ankleball" B: *06/19/1910 Cincinnati, OH* D: *07/16/1944 Jackson, TN* B/T: *R/R 5'11" 185 lbs.*															
CINCINNATI TIGERS	27	08-Aug-37	2	0	0	0	0	0	0	0	0	0	0	.000	.000
MEMPHIS RED SOX	32	16-Aug-42	0	0	0	0	0	0	0	0	0	0	0	.000	.000
MEMPHIS RED SOX	33	01-Aug-43	0	0	0	0	0	0	0	0	0	0	0	.000	.000
Player Totals:	**3 Games**		**2**	**0**	**0**	**0**	**0**	**0**	**0**	**0**	**0**	**0**	**0**	**.000**	**.000**
Neil, Raymond "Ray" or "Aussa" B: *10/12/1920 Apoka, FL Living in Benton Harbor, MI* B/T: *R/R 5'9" 165 lbs.*															
INDIANAPOLIS CLOWNS	26	29-Jul-47	3	1	2	1	0	0	0	0	0	0	0	.667	1.000
INDIANAPOLIS CLOWNS	30	12-Aug-51	4	1	1	0	0	0	0	0	0	0	1	.429	.571
INDIANAPOLIS CLOWNS	32	16-Aug-53	3	1	3	0	1	0	0	0	0	0	1	.600	.900
Player Totals:	**3 Games**		**10**	**3**	**6**	**1**	**1**	**0**	**0**	**0**	**0**	**0**	**2**	**.600**	**0.900**
Nelson, Clyde B: *09/01/1921 Bradenton, FL* D: *07/25/1949 Philadelphia, PA* B/T: *R/R*															
CHICAGO AMERICAN GIANTS	24	15-Aug-46	1	0	0	0	0	0	0	0	0	0	0	.000	.000
Player Totals:	**1 Game**		**1**	**0**	**0**	**0**	**0**	**0**	**0**	**0**	**0**	**0**	**0**	**.000**	**.000**
Oms, Alejandro "Walla Walla" B: *05/13/1895 Santa Clara, Cuba* D: *11/05/1946 Havana, Cuba* B/T: *L/L 5'9" 190 lbs.*															
NEW YORK CUBANS	40	11-Aug-35	4	1	2	0	0	0	0	1	1	0	0	.500	.500
Player Totals:	**1 Game**		**4**	**1**	**2**	**0**	**0**	**0**	**0**	**1**	**1**	**0**	**0**	**.500**	**.500**
O'Neil, John Jordan "Buck" B: *11/13/1911 Carabelle, FL Living in Kansas City, MO* B/T: *R/R 6'2" 190 lbs.*															
KANSAS CITY MONARCHS	30	16-Aug-42	4	0	0	0	0	0	0	0	0	0	1	.000	.000
KANSAS CITY MONARCHS	30	18-Aug-42	4	0	0	0	0	0	0	0	0	0	0	.000	.000
KANSAS CITY MONARCHS	31	01-Aug-43	2	0	0	0	0	0	1	0	1	0	0	.000	.000
KANSAS CITY MONARCHS	37	14-Aug-49	1	0	0	0	0	0	0	0	0	0	0	.000	.000
Player Totals:	**4 Games**		**11**	**0**	**0**	**0**	**0**	**0**	**1**	**0**	**1**	**0**	**1**	**.000**	**.000**
Owens, Raymond "Smoky" B: *1912 Alabama* D: *09/07/1942 Geneva, OH* B/T: *L/L*															
CLEVELAND BEARS	27	27-Aug-39	1	0	0	0	0	0	0	0	0	0	0	.000	.000
Player Totals:	**1 Game**		**1**	**0**	**0**	**0**	**0**	**0**	**0**	**0**	**0**	**0**	**0**	**.000**	**.000**
Paige, Leroy Robert "Satchel" B: *07/07/1906 Mobile, AL* D: *06/08/1982 Kansas City, MO* B/T: *R/R 6'3.5" 180 lbs.*															
PITTSBURGH CRAWFORDS	28	26-Aug-34	2	0	0	0	0	0	0	0	0	0	0	.000	.000
PITTSBURGH CRAWFORDS	30	23-Aug-36	1	0	0	0	0	0	0	0	0	0	0	.000	.000
KANSAS CITY MONARCHS	35	27-Jul-41	1	0	0	0	0	0	0	0	0	0	0	.000	.000
KANSAS CITY MONARCHS	36	16-Aug-42	1	0	1	0	0	0	0	0	0	0	0	.200	.200
KANSAS CITY MONARCHS	37	01-Aug-43	1	0	1	1	0	0	0	0	0	0	0	.333	.500
Player Totals:	**5 Games**		**6**	**0**	**2**	**1**	**0**	**0**	**0**	**0**	**0**	**0**	**0**	**.333**	**.500**
Parnell, Roy "Red" B: *09/17/1905 Austin, TX* D: *06/??/1969 Terrell, TX* B/T: *R/R 5'10" 180 lbs.*															
NASHVILLE ELITE GIANTS	28	26-Aug-34	4	0	0	0	0	0	0	0	0	0	0	.000	.000
PHILADELPHIA STARS	33	06-Aug-39	3	0	0	0	0	0	0	0	0	0	0	.000	.000
Player Totals:	**2 Games**		**7**	**0**	**0**	**0**	**0**	**0**	**0**	**0**	**0**	**0**	**0**	**.000**	**.000**
Partlow, Roy "Silent Roy" B: *06/08/1911 Washington, GA* D: *04/19/1987 Cherry Hill, NJ* B/T: *L/L 6'0" 180 lbs.*															
HOMESTEAD GRAYS	28	06-Aug-39	1	0	0	0	0	0	0	0	0	0	0	.000	.000
Player Totals:	**1 Game**		**1**	**0**	**0**	**0**	**0**	**0**	**0**	**0**	**0**	**0**	**0**	**.000**	**.000**
Patterson, Andrew Lawrence "Pat" B: *12/19/1911 Chicago, IL* D: *05/16/1984 Houston, TX* B/T: *S/R 5'11" 185 lbs.*															
CLEVELAND RED SOX	22	26-Aug-34	1	0	0	0	0	0	0	0	0	0	0	.000	.000
KANSAS CITY MONARCHS	24	23-Aug-36	2	0	2	1	0	0	1	0	0	0	0	.667	1.000
PHILADELPHIA STARS	27	06-Aug-39	4	1	1	0	0	0	0	0	0	1	0	.429	.571
PHILADELPHIA STARS	27	27-Aug-39	5	0	0	0	0	0	1	0	0	0	0	.250	.333
PHILADELPHIA STARS	30	16-Aug-42	3	0	0	0	0	0	0	1	0	1	2	.200	.267

PLAYER/TEAM	AGE	DATE	AB	R	H	D	T	HR	RBI	W	SAC	SB	E	RAVE	RSLG
PHILADELPHIA STARS	30	18-Aug-42	4	1	1	0	0	0	1	1	0	2	0	.211	.263
Player Totals:	**6 Games**		**19**	**2**	**4**	**1**	**0**	**0**	**3**	**2**	**0**	**4**	**2**	**.211**	**.263**

Patterson, Willie Lee "Pat" B: *04/01/1919 Americus, GA Living in Birmingham, AL* B/T: R/R *5'11" 170 lbs.*

PLAYER/TEAM	AGE	DATE	AB	R	H	D	T	HR	RBI	W	SAC	SB	E	RAVE	RSLG
CHICAGO AMERICAN GIANTS	33	17-Aug-52	4	1	2	0	0	0	2	0	0	0	0	.500	.500
MEMPHIS RED SOX	34	16-Aug-53	3	1	1	1	0	0	1	0	0	0	0	.429	.571
Player Totals:	**2 Games**		**7**	**2**	**3**	**1**	**0**	**0**	**3**	**0**	**0**	**0**	**0**	**.429**	**.571**

Pearson, Leonard Curtis "Lennie" or "Hoss" B: *05/23/1918 Akron, OH D: 12/07/1980 East Orange, NJ* B/T: R/R *6'1" 195 lbs.*

PLAYER/TEAM	AGE	DATE	AB	R	H	D	T	HR	RBI	W	SAC	SB	E	RAVE	RSLG
NEWARK EAGLES	23	27-Jul-41	2	0	0	0	0	0	0	0	0	0	0	.000	.000
NEWARK EAGLES	24	16-Aug-42	1	1	1	1	0	0	0	0	0	0	0	.333	.667
NEWARK EAGLES	24	18-Aug-42	1	0	0	0	0	0	1	1	0	0	0	.250	.500
NEWARK EAGLES	25	01-Aug-43	3	0	0	0	0	0	0	0	0	0	0	.143	.286
NEWARK EAGLES	27	29-Jul-45	1	0	0	0	0	0	0	0	0	0	0	.125	.250
NEWARK EAGLES	28	15-Aug-46	3	0	1	0	0	0	1	0	0	0	0	.182	.273
BALTIMORE ELITE GIANTS	31	14-Aug-49	5	0	0	0	0	0	0	0	0	0	0	.125	.188
Player Totals:	**7 Games**		**16**	**1**	**2**	**1**	**0**	**0**	**2**	**1**	**0**	**0**	**0**	**.125**	**.188**

Pennington, Arthur David "Superman" B: *05/18/1923 Memphis, TN Living in Cedar Rapid, IA* B/T: L/R *5'11" 195 lbs.*

PLAYER/TEAM	AGE	DATE	AB	R	H	D	T	HR	RBI	W	SAC	SB	E	RAVE	RSLG
CHICAGO AMERICAN GIANTS	19	16-Aug-42	1	0	0	0	0	0	0	0	0	0	0	.000	.000
CHICAGO AMERICAN GIANTS	19	18-Aug-42	1	0	0	0	0	0	0	1	0	0	0	.000	.000
CHICAGO AMERICAN GIANTS	27	20-Aug-50	3	1	1	0	1	0	1	0	0	0	0	.200	.600
Player Totals:	**3 Games**		**5**	**1**	**1**	**0**	**1**	**0**	**1**	**1**	**0**	**0**	**0**	**.200**	**.600**

Perkins, William Gamiel "Cy" B: *Georgia D: —* B/T: R/R *5'11" 195 lbs.*

PLAYER/TEAM	AGE	DATE	AB	R	H	D	T	HR	RBI	W	SAC	SB	E	RAVE	RSLG
PITTSBURGH CRAWFORDS		26-Aug-34	1	0	0	0	0	0	0	0	0	0	0	.000	.000
BALTIMORE ELITE GIANTS		18-Aug-40	5	1	2	0	0	0	1	0	0	0	0	.333	.333
Player Totals:	**2 Games**		**6**	**1**	**2**	**0**	**0**	**0**	**1**	**0**	**0**	**0**	**0**	**.333**	**.333**

Perry, Alonzo Thomas B: *04/14/1923 Birmingham, AL D: 10/13/1982 Birmingham, AL* B/T: L/R *6'3" 190 lbs.*

PLAYER/TEAM	AGE	DATE	AB	R	H	D	T	HR	RBI	W	SAC	SB	E	RAVE	RSLG
BIRMINGHAM BLACK BARONS	27	20-Aug-50	3	0	2	0	0	0	1	0	0	0	0	.667	.667
Player Totals:	**1 Game**		**3**	**0**	**2**	**0**	**0**	**0**	**1**	**0**	**0**	**0**	**0**	**.667**	**.667**

Phillips, Richard Albaso "Dick" B: *— D: —* B/T: R/R

PLAYER/TEAM	AGE	DATE	AB	R	H	D	T	HR	RBI	W	SAC	SB	E	RAVE	RSLG
KANSAS CITY MONARCHS		17-Aug-52	1	0	0	0	0	0	0	0	0	0	0	.000	.000
Player Totals:	**1 Game**		**1**	**0**	**0**	**0**	**0**	**0**	**0**	**0**	**0**	**0**	**0**	**.000**	**.000**

Porter, Andrew "Andy" or "Pullman" B: *03/07/1911 Little Rock, AR Living in Los Angeles, CA* B/T: R/R *6'4" 190 lbs.*

PLAYER/TEAM	AGE	DATE	AB	R	H	D	T	HR	RBI	W	SAC	SB	E	RAVE	RSLG
INDIANAPOLIS CLOWNS	38	14-Aug-49	0	0	0	0	0	0	0	0	0	0	0	.000	.000
Player Totals:	**1 Game**		**0**	**0**	**0**	**0**	**0**	**0**	**0**	**0**	**0**	**0**	**0**	**.000**	**.000**

Powell, Malvin "Putt" B: *05/30/1908 Edwards, MS D: 02/??/1985 Chicago, IL* B/T: R/R *5'6" 150 lbs.*

PLAYER/TEAM	AGE	DATE	AB	R	H	D	T	HR	RBI	W	SAC	SB	E	RAVE	RSLG
CHICAGO AMERICAN GIANTS	26	26-Aug-34	0	0	0	0	0	0	0	0	0	0	0	.000	.000
Player Totals:	**1 Game**		**0**	**0**	**0**	**0**	**0**	**0**	**0**	**0**	**0**	**0**	**0**	**.000**	**.000**

Powell, William Henry "Bill" B: *05/08/1919 Comer, GA Living in Birmingham, AL* B/T: R/R *6'2" 180 lbs.*

PLAYER/TEAM	AGE	DATE	AB	R	H	D	T	HR	RBI	W	SAC	SB	E	RAVE	RSLG
BIRMINGHAM BLACK BARONS	29	22-Aug-48	1	0	0	0	0	0	0	0	0	0	0	.000	.000
BIRMINGHAM BLACK BARONS	31	20-Aug-50	1	0	0	0	0	0	0	0	0	0	0	.000	.000
Player Totals:	**2 Games**		**2**	**0**	**0**	**0**	**0**	**0**	**0**	**0**	**0**	**0**	**0**	**.000**	**.000**

Radcliffe, Alexander "Alec" B: *07/26/1905 Mobile, AL D: 07/18/1983 Chicago, IL* B/T: R/R *6'0" 200 lbs.*

PLAYER/TEAM	AGE	DATE	AB	R	H	D	T	HR	RBI	W	SAC	SB	E	RAVE	RSLG
CHICAGO AMERICAN GIANTS	28	10-Sep-33	4	1	2	1	0	0	1	0	0	0	0	.500	.750
CHICAGO AMERICAN GIANTS	29	26-Aug-34	4	0	0	0	0	0	0	0	0	0	0	.250	.375
CHICAGO AMERICAN GIANTS	30	11-Aug-35	5	0	2	0	0	0	3	0	0	0	0	.308	.385
CHICAGO AMERICAN GIANTS	31	23-Aug-36	4	1	3	0	0	0	0	0	0	0	2	.412	.471
CHICAGO AMERICAN GIANTS	32	08-Aug-37	3	0	1	0	0	0	0	0	0	0	0	.400	.450
CHICAGO AMERICAN GIANTS	33	21-Aug-38	4	1	2	0	0	0	2	0	0	0	0	.417	.458
CHICAGO AMERICAN GIANTS	34	06-Aug-39	4	1	1	0	0	0	0	0	0	0	0	.393	.429

PLAYER/TEAM	AGE	DATE	AB	R	H	D	T	HR	RBI	W	SAC	SB	E	RAVE	RSLG
CHICAGO AMERICAN GIANTS	34	27-Aug-39	4	0	1	0	0	0	0	0	0	0	1	.375	.406
CHICAGO AMERICAN GIANTS	38	01-Aug-43	4	0	1	0	0	0	0	0	0	0	0	.361	.389
CINCINNATI CLOWNS	39	13-Aug-44	4	0	2	0	1	0	2	0	1	0	0	.375	.450
CINCINNATI-INDY CLOWNS	40	29-Jul-45	4	2	2	1	0	0	1	0	0	0	1	.386	.477
MEMPHIS RED SOX	41	15-Aug-46	3	0	0	0	0	0	0	0	0	0	0	.362	.447
MEMPHIS RED SOX	41	18-Aug-46	3	0	0	0	0	0	0	0	1	0	0	.340	.420
Player Totals:	**13 Game**		50	6	17	2	1	0	9	0	2	0	2	.340	.420

Radcliffe, Theodore Roosevelt "Double Duty" B: 07/07/1902 Mobile, AL Living in Chicago, IL B/T: R/R 5'10" 190 lbs.

PLAYER/TEAM	AGE	DATE	AB	R	H	D	T	HR	RBI	W	SAC	SB	E	RAVE	RSLG
CINCINNATI TIGERS	35	08-Aug-37	3	0	0	0	0	0	0	0	0	0	1	.000	.000
MEMPHIS RED SOX	36	21-Aug-38	2	0	1	0	0	0	0	0	0	0	0	.200	.200
MEMPHIS RED SOX	37	06-Aug-39	1	1	1	0	0	0	0	0	0	0	0	.333	.333
MEMPHIS RED SOX	39	27-Jul-41	0	0	0	0	0	0	0	0	0	0	0	.333	.333
CHICAGO AMERICAN GIANTS	41	01-Aug-43	3	0	0	0	0	0	0	0	0	0	0	.222	.222
BIRMINGHAM BLACK BARONS	42	13-Aug-44	4	1	3	0	0	1	2	0	0	0	0	.385	.615
Player Totals:	**6 Games**		13	2	5	0	0	1	2	0	0	0	1	.385	.615

Raines, Lawrence Glenn Hope "Larry" B: 03/09/1930 St. Albans, WV D: 01/28/1978 Lansing, MI B/T: R/R 5'10" 165 lbs.

PLAYER/TEAM	AGE	DATE	AB	R	H	D	T	HR	RBI	W	SAC	SB	E	RAVE	RSLG
CHICAGO AMERICAN GIANTS	22	17-Aug-52	3	1	0	0	0	0	0	1	0	1	1	.000	.000
Player Totals:	**1 Game**		3	1	0	0	0	0	0	1	0	1	1	.000	.000

Redus, Wilson R. "Frog" B: 01/29/1905 Muskogee, OK D: 03/23/1979 Tulsa, OK B/T: R/R 5'5" 160 lbs.

PLAYER/TEAM	AGE	DATE	AB	R	H	D	T	HR	RBI	W	SAC	SB	E	RAVE	RSLG
CHICAGO AMERICAN GIANTS	31	23-Aug-36	2	0	0	0	0	0	0	0	0	0	0	.000	.000
CHICAGO AMERICAN GIANTS	32	08-Aug-37	0	0	0	0	0	0	0	0	0	0	0	.000	.000
Player Totals:	**2 Games**		2	0	0	0	0	0	0	0	0	0	0	.000	.000

Reed, Eddie Lee B: 10/12/1929 Straven, AL D: — B/T: L/R 6'2" 175 lbs.

PLAYER/TEAM	AGE	DATE	AB	R	H	D	T	HR	RBI	W	SAC	SB	E	RAVE	RSLG
MEMPHIS RED SOX	23	16-Aug-53	3	1	1	0	0	0	0	0	0	0	0	.333	.333
Player Totals:	**1 Game**		3	1	1	0	0	0	0	0	0	0	0	.333	.333

Reeves, Donald "Soup" B: — D: — B/T: L/L 6'2" 190 lbs.

PLAYER/TEAM	AGE	DATE	AB	R	H	D	T	HR	RBI	W	SAC	SB	E	RAVE	RSLG
CHICAGO AMERICAN GIANTS		18-Aug-40	4	0	0	0	0	0	0	0	0	0	0	.000	.000
Player Totals:	**1 Game**		4	0	0	0	0	0	0	0	0	0	0	.000	.000

Renfroe, Othello Nelson "Chico" B: 03/01/1923 Newark, NJ D: 09/03/1991 Atlanta, GA B/T: R/R 5'11" 175 lbs.

PLAYER/TEAM	AGE	DATE	AB	R	H	D	T	HR	RBI	W	SAC	SB	E	RAVE	RSLG
KANSAS CITY MONARCHS	23	15-Aug-46	1	0	0	0	0	0	0	0	0	0	0	.000	.000
Player Totals:	**1 Game**		1	0	0	0	0	0	0	0	0	0	0	.000	.000

Richardson, Norval Eugene "Gene" or "Britches" B: 01/26/1928 San Diego, CA D: 08/??/1997 Paradise Hills, CA B/T: L/L 5'10" 170 lbs.

PLAYER/TEAM	AGE	DATE	AB	R	H	D	T	HR	RBI	W	SAC	SB	E	RAVE	RSLG
KANSAS CITY MONARCHS	21	14-Aug-49	1	0	0	0	0	0	0	0	0	0	0	.000	.000
Player Totals:	**1 Game**		1	0	0	0	0	0	0	0	0	0	0	.000	.000

Richardson, T. W. "Ted" or "Lefty" B: 12/15/1928 D: 05/??/1974 Cincinnati, OH B/T: R/L

PLAYER/TEAM	AGE	DATE	AB	R	H	D	T	HR	RBI	W	SAC	SB	E	RAVE	RSLG
INDIANAPOLIS CLOWNS	23	17-Aug-52	1	0	0	0	0	0	0	0	0	0	0	.000	.000
Player Totals:	**1 Game**		1	0	0	0	0	0	0	0	0	0	0	.000	.000

Ricks, William "Bill" B: — D: — B/T: R/R 6'1" 190 lbs.

PLAYER/TEAM	AGE	DATE	AB	R	H	D	T	HR	RBI	W	SAC	SB	E	RAVE	RSLG
PHILADELPHIA STARS		29-Jul-45	0	0	0	0	0	0	0	0	0	0	0	.000	.000
Player Totals:	**1 Game**		0	0	0	0	0	0	0	0	0	0	0	.000	.000

Riddle, Marshall Lewis "Jit" B: 04/22/1918 Warren, AR D: 09/02/1988 St. Louis, MO B/T: L/R 5'8" 155 lbs.

PLAYER/TEAM	AGE	DATE	AB	R	H	D	T	HR	RBI	W	SAC	SB	E	RAVE	RSLG
ST. LOUIS STARS	21	27-Aug-39	2	0	0	0	0	0	0	0	0	0	0	.000	.000
NEW ORLEANS-ST. LOUIS STARS	22	18-Aug-40	1	0	0	0	0	0	0	0	0	0	1	.000	.000
Player Totals:	**2 Games**		3	0	0	0	0	0	0	0	0	0	1	.000	.000

Robinson, Cornelius Randall "Neal" or "Shadow" B: 07/31/1907 Grand Rapids, MI D: 07/23/1983 Cincinnati, OH B/T: R/R 5'11" 190 lbs.

PLAYER/TEAM	AGE	DATE	AB	R	H	D	T	HR	RBI	W	SAC	SB	E	RAVE	RSLG
MEMPHIS RED SOX	31	21-Aug-38	4	1	3	0	0	1	3	0	0	0	0	.750	1.500

PLAYER/TEAM	AGE	DATE	AB	R	H	D	T	HR	RBI	W	SAC	SB	E	RAVE	RSLG
MEMPHIS RED SOX	32	06-Aug-39	4	1	3	1	0	1	1	0	0	1	0	.750	1.625
MEMPHIS RED SOX	32	27-Aug-39	3	1	2	0	0	0	1	1	0	0	0	.727	1.364
MEMPHIS RED SOX	33	18-Aug-40	2	0	0	0	0	0	0	0	0	0	0	.615	1.154
MEMPHIS RED SOX	33	27-Jul-41	2	1	1	0	0	0	0	0	0	0	0	.600	1.067
MEMPHIS RED SOX	36	01-Aug-43	2	1	0	0	0	0	0	1	0	0	0	.529	.941
MEMPHIS RED SOX	37	13-Aug-44	2	0	0	0	0	0	0	0	0	0	0	.474	.842
MEMPHIS RED SOX	37	29-Jul-45	2	2	2	0	0	0	0	0	1	0	0	.524	.857
MEMPHIS RED SOX	41	22-Aug-48	3	0	1	0	0	0	1	1	0	0	0	.500	.792
Player Totals:	**9 Games**		**24**	**7**	**12**	**1**	**0**	**2**	**6**	**3**	**1**	**1**	**0**	**.500**	**.792**

Robinson, Jack Roosevelt "Jackie" B: *01/31/1919 Cairo, GA* D: *10/24/1972 Stamford, CN* B/T: R/R *5'11" 190 lbs.*

PLAYER/TEAM	AGE	DATE	AB	R	H	D	T	HR	RBI	W	SAC	SB	E	RAVE	RSLG
KANSAS CITY MONARCHS	26	29-Jul-45	5	0	0	0	0	0	0	0	0	0	0	.000	.000
Player Totals:	**1 Game**		**5**	**0**	**0**	**0**	**0**	**0**	**0**	**0**	**0**	**0**	**0**	**.000**	**.000**

Robinson, Norman Wayne "Bobby" B: *04/01/1913 Oklahoma City, OK* D: *03/26/1984 Pacoima, CA* B/T: S/R *5'10" 180 lbs.*

PLAYER/TEAM	AGE	DATE	AB	R	H	D	T	HR	RBI	W	SAC	SB	E	RAVE	RSLG
BIRMINGHAM BLACK BARONS	38	12-Aug-51	4	1	2	2	0	0	1	0	0	0	0	.500	1.000
Player Totals:	**1 Game**		**4**	**1**	**2**	**2**	**0**	**0**	**1**	**0**	**0**	**0**	**0**	**.500**	**1.000**

Rogan, Wilber "Bullet" B: *07/28/1889 Oklahoma City, OK* D: *03/04/1967 Kansas City, MO* B/T: R/R *5'7" 170 lbs.*

PLAYER/TEAM	AGE	DATE	AB	R	H	D	T	HR	RBI	W	SAC	SB	E	RAVE	RSLG
KANSAS CITY MONARCHS	47	23-Aug-36	1	0	0	0	0	0	0	0	0	0	0	.000	.000
Player Totals:	**1 Game**		**1**	**0**	**0**	**0**	**0**	**0**	**0**	**0**	**0**	**0**	**0**	**.000**	**.000**

Romby, Robert L. "Bob" B: *12/15/1918 Shreveport, LA Living in Cumberland, VA* B/T: L/L *5'11" 180 lbs.*

PLAYER/TEAM	AGE	DATE	AB	R	H	D	T	HR	RBI	W	SAC	SB	E	RAVE	RSLG
BALTIMORE ELITE GIANTS	28	27-Jul-47	1	0	0	0	0	0	0	0	0	0	0	.000	.000
BALTIMORE ELITE GIANTS	28	29-Jul-47	1	0	1	0	0	0	0	0	0	0	0	.500	.500
Player Totals:	**2 Games**		**2**	**0**	**1**	**0**	**0**	**0**	**0**	**0**	**0**	**0**	**0**	**.500**	**.500**

Ruffin, Charles Leon "Lassas" B: *02/11/1912 Portsmouth, VA* D: *08/14/1970 Portsmouth, VA* B/T: R/R *5'11" 175 lbs.*

PLAYER/TEAM	AGE	DATE	AB	R	H	D	T	HR	RBI	W	SAC	SB	E	RAVE	RSLG
NEWARK EAGLES	34	15-Aug-46	1	0	0	0	0	0	0	0	0	0	0	.000	.000
Player Totals:	**1 Game**		**1**	**0**	**0**	**0**	**0**	**0**	**0**	**0**	**0**	**0**	**0**	**.000**	**.000**

Ruiz, Silvino "Poppa" B: — D: — B/T: R/R

PLAYER/TEAM	AGE	DATE	AB	R	H	D	T	HR	RBI	W	SAC	SB	E	RAVE	RSLG
NEW YORK CUBANS		18-Aug-40	2	1	0	0	0	0	0	0	0	0	0	.000	.000
Player Totals:	**1 Game**		**2**	**1**	**0**	**0**	**0**	**0**	**0**	**0**	**0**	**0**	**0**	**.000**	**.000**

Russell, John Henry "Pistol" B: *02/24/1898 Dolcito, AL* D: *12/04/1972 Cleveland, OH* B/T: R/R *5'10" 155 lbs.*

PLAYER/TEAM	AGE	DATE	AB	R	H	D	T	HR	RBI	W	SAC	SB	E	RAVE	RSLG
PITTSBURGH CRAWFORDS	35	10-Sep-33	2	0	0	0	0	0	1	0	2	0	0	.000	.000
Player Totals:	**1 Game**		**2**	**0**	**0**	**0**	**0**	**0**	**1**	**0**	**2**	**0**	**0**	**.000**	**.000**

Sampson, Thomas "Tommy" or "Toots" B: *08/31/1912 Calhoun, AL Living in Elizabeth City, NC* B/T: R/R *6'1" 180 lbs.*

PLAYER/TEAM	AGE	DATE	AB	R	H	D	T	HR	RBI	W	SAC	SB	E	RAVE	RSLG
BIRMINGHAM BLACK BARONS	27	18-Aug-40	2	0	0	0	0	0	0	0	0	0	0	.000	.000
BIRMINGHAM BLACK BARONS	28	27-Jul-41	0	0	0	0	0	0	0	0	0	0	1	.000	.000
BIRMINGHAM BLACK BARONS	29	16-Aug-42	3	0	0	0	0	0	0	0	0	0	1	.000	.000
BIRMINGHAM BLACK BARONS	29	18-Aug-42	3	0	2	0	0	0	0	0	0	0	1	.250	.250
BIRMINGHAM BLACK BARONS	30	01-Aug-43	3	0	1	0	0	0	1	0	0	0	0	.273	.273
Player Totals:	**5 Games**		**11**	**0**	**3**	**0**	**0**	**0**	**1**	**0**	**0**	**0**	**3**	**.273**	**.273**

Sands, Samuel "Piggy" B: *07/22/1918 Miami, FL* D: *07/??/1978* B/T: R/R *6'2" 195 lbs.*

PLAYER/TEAM	AGE	DATE	AB	R	H	D	T	HR	RBI	W	SAC	SB	E	RAVE	RSLG
INDIANAPOLIS CLOWNS	35	16-Aug-53	3	0	0	0	0	0	0	0	0	0	0	.000	.000
Player Totals:	**1 Game**		**3**	**0**	**0**	**0**	**0**	**0**	**0**	**0**	**0**	**0**	**0**	**.000**	**.000**

Scales, George Walter "Tubby" B: *08/16/1900 Talladega, AL* D: *04/15/1976 Carson, CA* B/T: R/R *6'0" 205 lbs.*

PLAYER/TEAM	AGE	DATE	AB	R	H	D	T	HR	RBI	W	SAC	SB	E	RAVE	RSLG
BALTIMORE ELITE GIANTS	42	01-Aug-43	1	0	0	0	0	0	0	0	0	0	0	.000	.000
Player Totals:	**1 Game**		**1**	**0**	**0**	**0**	**0**	**0**	**0**	**0**	**0**	**0**	**0**	**.000**	**.000**

Scantlebury, Patricio Athlestan "Pat" B: *11/11/1917 Colon, Panama Canal Zone* D: *04/24/1991 Glen Ridge, NJ* B/T: L/L *6'1" 180 lbs.*

PLAYER/TEAM	AGE	DATE	AB	R	H	D	T	HR	RBI	W	SAC	SB	E	RAVE	RSLG
NEW YORK CUBANS	28	15-Aug-46	0	0	0	0	0	0	0	0	0	0	0	.000	.000
NEW YORK CUBANS	28	18-Aug-46	1	0	1	0	0	0	0	0	0	0	0	1.000	1.000

PLAYER/TEAM	AGE	DATE	AB	R	H	D	T	HR	RBI	W	SAC	SB	E	RAVE	RSLG
NEW YORK CUBANS	31	14-Aug-49	1	0	0	0	0	0	0	0	0	0	0	.500	.500
NEW YORK CUBANS	32	20-Aug-50	1	0	0	0	0	0	0	0	0	0	0	.333	.333
Player Totals:	**4 Games**		**3**	**0**	**1**	**0**	**0**	**0**	**0**	**0**	**0**	**0**	**0**	**.333**	**.333**

Scott, John B: *08/28/1913 Magnolia, AR* D: — B/T: L/L *5'10" 165 lbs.*

PLAYER/TEAM	AGE	DATE	AB	R	H	D	T	HR	RBI	W	SAC	SB	E	RAVE	RSLG
KANSAS CITY MONARCHS	32	15-Aug-46	2	0	1	0	0	0	0	0	0	0	0	.500	.500
Player Totals:	**1 Game**		**2**	**0**	**1**	**0**	**0**	**0**	**0**	**0**	**0**	**0**	**0**	**.500**	**.500**

Searcy, Kelton "Kelly" or "Lefty" B: *01/25/1931 Nashville, TN* D: *11/29/1978* B/T: L/L *5'11" 180 lbs.*

PLAYER/TEAM	AGE	DATE	AB	R	H	D	T	HR	RBI	W	SAC	SB	E	RAVE	RSLG
BALTIMORE ELITE GIANTS	20	12-Aug-51	1	0	0	0	0	0	0	0	0	0	0	.000	.000
Player Totals:	**1 Game**		**1**	**0**	**0**	**0**	**0**	**0**	**0**	**0**	**0**	**0**	**0**	**.000**	**.000**

Seay, Richard William "Dickie" B: *11/30/1904 West New York, NJ* D: *04/06/1981 Jersey City, NJ* B/T: R/R *5'8" 155 lbs.*

PLAYER/TEAM	AGE	DATE	AB	R	H	D	T	HR	RBI	W	SAC	SB	E	RAVE	RSLG
PHILADELPHIA STARS	30	11-Aug-35	3	0	1	0	0	0	0	0	0	0	2	.333	.333
NEW YORK BLACK YANKEES	35	18-Aug-40	4	2	0	0	0	0	1	0	0	0	0	.143	.143
NEW YORK BLACK YANKEES	36	27-Jul-41	4	1	0	0	0	0	0	1	0	0	1	.091	.091
Player Totals:	**3 Games**		**11**	**3**	**1**	**0**	**0**	**0**	**1**	**1**	**0**	**0**	**3**	**.091**	**.091**

Serrell, Bonnie Clinton "El Grillo" or "Barney" B: *03/09/1920 Dallas, TX* D: *08/19/1996 East Palo Alto, CA* B/T: L/R *5'10" 160 lbs.*

PLAYER/TEAM	AGE	DATE	AB	R	H	D	T	HR	RBI	W	SAC	SB	E	RAVE	RSLG
KANSAS CITY MONARCHS	24	13-Aug-44	3	1	2	0	0	0	1	1	0	0	0	.667	.667
Player Totals:	**1 Game**		**3**	**1**	**2**	**0**	**0**	**0**	**1**	**1**	**0**	**0**	**0**	**.667**	**.667**

Sims, Fate B: *03/23/1929 Charlotte, NC* D: *06/??/1979 Cleveland, OH* B/T: R/R

PLAYER/TEAM	AGE	DATE	AB	R	H	D	T	HR	RBI	W	SAC	SB	E	RAVE	RSLG
MEMPHIS RED SOX	24	16-Aug-53	1	0	0	0	0	0	0	0	0	1	0	.000	.000
Player Totals:	**1 Game**		**1**	**0**	**0**	**0**	**0**	**0**	**0**	**0**	**0**	**1**	**0**	**.000**	**.000**

Smith, Eugene L. "Gene" B: *04/23/1917 Ansley, LA* *Living in Vinita Park, MO* B/T: S/R *6'1" 185 lbs.*

PLAYER/TEAM	AGE	DATE	AB	R	H	D	T	HR	RBI	W	SAC	SB	E	RAVE	RSLG
NEW YORK BLACK YANKEES	25	18-Aug-42	3	1	1	0	0	0	0	0	0	0	0	.333	.333
Player Totals:	**1 Game**		**3**	**1**	**1**	**0**	**0**	**0**	**0**	**0**	**0**	**0**	**0**	**.333**	**.333**

Smith, Hilton Lee "Smitty" B: *02/27/1907 Giddings, TX* D: *11/18/1983 Kansas City, MO* B/T: R/R *5'11" 185 lbs.*

PLAYER/TEAM	AGE	DATE	AB	R	H	D	T	HR	RBI	W	SAC	SB	E	RAVE	RSLG
KANSAS CITY MONARCHS	30	08-Aug-37	0	0	0	0	0	0	0	0	0	0	1	.000	.000
KANSAS CITY MONARCHS	31	21-Aug-38	2	0	1	0	0	0	0	0	0	0	0	.500	.500
KANSAS CITY MONARCHS	32	06-Aug-39	1	0	0	0	0	0	0	0	0	0	0	.333	.333
KANSAS CITY MONARCHS	32	27-Aug-39	0	0	0	0	0	0	0	0	0	0	0	.333	.333
KANSAS CITY MONARCHS	33	18-Aug-40	1	0	0	0	0	0	0	0	0	0	0	.250	.250
KANSAS CITY MONARCHS	34	27-Jul-41	1	0	0	0	0	0	0	0	0	0	0	.200	.200
KANSAS CITY MONARCHS	35	16-Aug-42	1	0	0	0	0	0	0	0	0	0	0	.167	.167
Player Totals:	**7 Games**		**6**	**0**	**1**	**0**	**0**	**0**	**0**	**0**	**0**	**0**	**1**	**.167**	**.167**

Smith, John Ford "Geronimo" or "Lefty" B: *01/09/1919 Phoenix, AZ* D: *02/26/1983 Phoenix, AZ* B/T: S/L *6'1" 200 lbs.*

PLAYER/TEAM	AGE	DATE	AB	R	H	D	T	HR	RBI	W	SAC	SB	E	RAVE	RSLG
KANSAS CITY MONARCHS	28	29-Jul-47	1	0	0	0	0	0	0	0	0	0	0	.000	.000
Player Totals:	**1 Game**		**1**	**0**	**0**	**0**	**0**	**0**	**0**	**0**	**0**	**0**	**0**	**.000**	**.000**

Smith, Milton "Milt" B: *03/27/1929 Columbus, GA* D: *04/11/1997 San Diego, CA* B/T: R/R *5'10" 165 lbs.*

PLAYER/TEAM	AGE	DATE	AB	R	H	D	T	HR	RBI	W	SAC	SB	E	RAVE	RSLG
PHILADELPHIA STARS	22	12-Aug-51	3	0	2	0	0	0	0	1	0	1	1	.667	.667
Player Totals:	**1 Game**		**3**	**0**	**2**	**0**	**0**	**0**	**0**	**1**	**0**	**1**	**1**	**.667**	**.667**

Smith, Theolic "Fireball" B: *05/19/1913 Wabbesika, AR* D: *11/03/1981 Compton, CA* B/T: S/R *6'0" 175 lbs.*

PLAYER/TEAM	AGE	DATE	AB	R	H	D	T	HR	RBI	W	SAC	SB	E	RAVE	RSLG
ST. LOUIS STARS	26	06-Aug-39	0	0	0	0	0	0	0	1	0	0	0	.000	.000
CLEVELAND BUCKEYES	30	01-Aug-43	1	0	0	0	0	0	0	0	0	0	0	.000	.000
KANSAS CITY MONARCHS	38	12-Aug-51	1	0	0	0	0	0	0	0	0	0	0	.000	.000
Player Totals:	**3 Games**		**2**	**0**	**0**	**0**	**0**	**0**	**0**	**1**	**0**	**0**	**0**	**.000**	**.000**

Snow, Felton "Skipper" B: *10/23/1905 Oxford, AL* D: *03/16/1974 Louisville, KY* B/T: R/R *5'10" 155 lbs.*

PLAYER/TEAM	AGE	DATE	AB	R	H	D	T	HR	RBI	W	SAC	SB	E	RAVE	RSLG
COLUMBUS ELITE GIANTS	29	11-Aug-35	1	1	1	0	0	0	2	0	0	0	0	1.000	1.000
WASHINGTON ELITE GIANTS	30	23-Aug-36	2	1	1	0	0	0	0	0	0	1	1	.667	.667
Player Totals:	**2 Games**		**3**	**2**	**2**	**0**	**0**	**0**	**2**	**0**	**0**	**1**	**1**	**.667**	**.667**

PLAYER/TEAM	AGE	DATE	AB	R	H	D	T	HR	RBI	W	SAC	SB	E	RAVE	RSLG

Souell (Cyrus), Herbert "Herb" or "Baldy" B: 02/05/1913 West Monroe, LA D: 07/12/1978 Los Angeles County, C
B/T: L/R 5'7" 150 lbs.

PLAYER/TEAM	AGE	DATE	AB	R	H	D	T	HR	RBI	W	SAC	SB	E	RAVE	RSLG
KANSAS CITY MONARCHS	34	27-Jul-47	5	1	1	0	1	0	0	0	0	0	0	.200	.600
KANSAS CITY MONARCHS	34	29-Jul-47	1	0	0	0	0	0	0	0	1	0	0	.167	.500
KANSAS CITY MONARCHS	35	22-Aug-48	4	0	0	0	0	0	0	0	0	0	0	.100	.300
KANSAS CITY MONARCHS	35	24-Aug-48	3	0	0	0	0	0	0	0	0	0	1	.077	.231
KANSAS CITY MONARCHS	37	20-Aug-50	1	1	0	0	0	0	0	0	1	0	1	.071	.214
Player Totals:	**5 Games**		**14**	**2**	**1**	**0**	**1**	**0**	**0**	**0**	**2**	**0**	**2**	**.071**	**.214**

Stearnes, Norman Thomas "Turkey" B: 05/08/1901 Nashville, TN D: 09/04/1979 Detroit, MI B/T: L/L 6'0" 175 lbs.

PLAYER/TEAM	AGE	DATE	AB	R	H	D	T	HR	RBI	W	SAC	SB	E	RAVE	RSLG
CHICAGO AMERICAN GIANTS	32	10-Sep-33	5	1	2	1	0	0	1	0	0	0	0	.400	.600
CHICAGO AMERICAN GIANTS	33	26-Aug-34	4	0	0	0	0	0	0	0	0	0	0	.222	.333
CHICAGO AMERICAN GIANTS	34	11-Aug-35	3	0	1	0	0	0	0	0	0	0	0	.250	.333
DETROIT STARS	36	08-Aug-37	4	0	0	0	0	0	0	0	0	0	0	.188	.250
KANSAS CITY MONARCHS	38	27-Aug-39	3	0	1	0	0	0	1	1	1	0	0	.211	.263
Player Totals:	**5 Games**		**19**	**1**	**4**	**1**	**0**	**0**	**2**	**1**	**1**	**0**	**0**	**.211**	**.263**

Steele, Edward "Ed" or "Stainless" B: 08/08/1916 Selma, AL D: 02/??/1974 Birmingham, AL B/T: L/R 5'10" 195 lbs.

PLAYER/TEAM	AGE	DATE	AB	R	H	D	T	HR	RBI	W	SAC	SB	E	RAVE	RSLG
BIRMINGHAM BLACK BARONS	34	20-Aug-50	3	0	2	0	0	0	1	0	0	0	1	.667	.667
BIRMINGHAM BLACK BARONS	35	12-Aug-51	4	1	1	0	1	0	1	0	0	0	0	.429	0.714
Player Totals:	**2 Games**		**7**	**1**	**3**	**0**	**1**	**0**	**2**	**0**	**0**	**0**	**1**	**.429**	**0.714**

Stephens, Paul Eugene "Jake" B: 02/10/1900 Pleasureville, PA D: 02/05/1981 York, PA B/T: R/R 5'7" 150 lbs.

PLAYER/TEAM	AGE	DATE	AB	R	H	D	T	HR	RBI	W	SAC	SB	E	RAVE	RSLG
PHILADELPHIA STARS	35	11-Aug-35	6	1	2	0	0	0	1	0	0	0	1	.333	.333
Player Totals:	**1 Game**		**6**	**1**	**2**	**0**	**0**	**0**	**1**	**0**	**0**	**0**	**1**	**.333**	**.333**

Stone, Edward "Ed" or "Ace" B: 08/21/1909 Black Cat, DE D: 03/20/1983 New York, NY B/T: L/R 6'0" 195 lbs.

PLAYER/TEAM	AGE	DATE	AB	R	H	D	T	HR	RBI	W	SAC	SB	E	RAVE	RSLG
BROOKLYN EAGLES	25	11-Aug-35	1	0	0	0	0	0	0	0	0	0	0	.000	.000
NEWARK EAGLES	30	27-Aug-39	4	2	3	0	0	0	0	1	0	1	0	.600	.600
NEWARK EAGLES	30	18-Aug-40	3	0	0	0	0	0	0	0	0	0	0	.375	.375
Player Totals:	**3 Games**		**8**	**2**	**3**	**0**	**0**	**0**	**0**	**1**	**0**	**1**	**0**	**.375**	**.375**

Streeter, Samuel "Lefty" B: 09/17/1900 New Market, AL D: 08/09/1985 Pittsburgh, PA B/T: R/L 5'7" 170 lbs.

PLAYER/TEAM	AGE	DATE	AB	R	H	D	T	HR	RBI	W	SAC	SB	E	RAVE	RSLG
PITTSBURGH CRAWFORDS	32	10-Sep-33	3	0	0	0	0	0	0	0	0	0	0	.000	.000
Player Totals:	**1 Game**		**3**	**0**	**0**	**0**	**0**	**0**	**0**	**0**	**0**	**0**	**0**	**.000**	**.000**

Strong, Theodore Reginald "Ted" or "T. R." B: 01/02/1914 South Bend, IN D: 03/01/1978 Chicago, IL B/T: S/R 6'6" 210 lbs.

PLAYER/TEAM	AGE	DATE	AB	R	H	D	T	HR	RBI	W	SAC	SB	E	RAVE	RSLG
INDIANAPOLIS ATHLETICS	23	08-Aug-37	4	1	2	0	0	1	2	0	0	0	2	.500	1.250
INDIANAPOLIS ABCS	24	21-Aug-38	3	1	0	0	0	0	0	1	0	0	0	.286	.714
KANSAS CITY MONARCHS	25	06-Aug-39	2	0	0	0	0	0	0	2	0	0	1	.222	.556
KANSAS CITY MONARCHS	25	27-Aug-39	4	0	1	0	0	0	0	0	0	0	0	.231	.462
KANSAS CITY MONARCHS	27	27-Jul-41	4	1	2	1	1	0	1	0	0	0	0	.294	.647
KANSAS CITY MONARCHS	28	16-Aug-42	3	0	1	0	0	0	0	1	0	0	0	.300	.600
KANSAS CITY MONARCHS	28	18-Aug-42	3	0	2	0	0	0	0	0	0	0	1	.348	.609
Player Totals:	**7 Games**		**23**	**3**	**8**	**1**	**1**	**1**	**3**	**4**	**0**	**0**	**4**	**.348**	**.609**

Summers, Lonnie "Carl" B: 08/02/1915 Davis, OK D: 08/24/1999 Inglewood, CA B/T: R/R 6'0" 200 lbs.

PLAYER/TEAM	AGE	DATE	AB	R	H	D	T	HR	RBI	W	SAC	SB	E	RAVE	RSLG
CHICAGO AMERICAN GIANTS	34	14-Aug-49	3	0	1	0	0	0	0	0	0	0	2	.333	.333
CHICAGO AMERICAN GIANTS	36	12-Aug-51	1	0	0	0	0	0	0	0	0	0	0	.250	.250
Player Totals:	**2 Games**		**4**	**0**	**1**	**0**	**0**	**0**	**0**	**0**	**0**	**0**	**2**	**.250**	**.250**

Suttles, George "Mule" B: 03/31/1900 Brockton, AL D: 07/09/1966 Newark, NJ B/T: R/R 6'2" 225 lbs.

PLAYER/TEAM	AGE	DATE	AB	R	H	D	T	HR	RBI	W	SAC	SB	E	RAVE	RSLG
CHICAGO AMERICAN GIANTS	33	10-Sep-33	4	2	2	1	0	1	3	0	0	0	0	.500	1.500
CHICAGO AMERICAN GIANTS	34	26-Aug-34	4	0	3	0	1	0	0	0	0	0	1	.625	1.375
CHICAGO AMERICAN GIANTS	35	11-Aug-35	2	3	1	0	0	1	3	4	0	0	0	.600	1.500
NEWARK EAGLES	37	08-Aug-37	3	0	1	0	0	0	0	2	0	1	0	.538	1.231

PLAYER/TEAM	AGE	DATE	AB	R	H	D	T	HR	RBI	W	SAC	SB	E	RAVE	RSLG
BALTIMORE ELITE GIANTS	39	06-Aug-39	4	0	0	0	0	0	0	0	0	0	0	.412	0.941
Player Totals:	**5 Games**		17	5	7	1	1	2	6	6	0	1	1	**.412**	**0.941**

Tatum, Reece "Goose" B: 05/03/1921 Eldorado, AR D: 01/18/1967 El Paso, TX B/T: R/R 6'3" 195 lbs.

PLAYER/TEAM	AGE	DATE	AB	R	H	D	T	HR	RBI	W	SAC	SB	E	RAVE	RSLG
INDIANAPOLIS CLOWNS	26	27-Jul-47	4	1	2	0	0	0	0	0	0	0	0	.500	.500
Player Totals:	**1 Game**		4	1	2	0	0	0	0	0	0	0	0	**.500**	**.500**

Taylor, Johnny Arthur "School Boy" B: 02/04/1916 Hartford, CN D: 06/15/1987 Hartford, CN B/T: R/R 6'0" 165 lbs.

PLAYER/TEAM	AGE	DATE	AB	R	H	D	T	HR	RBI	W	SAC	SB	E	RAVE	RSLG
PITTSBURGH CRAWFORDS	22	21-Aug-38	0	0	0	0	0	0	0	0	0	0	0	.000	.000
Player Totals:	**1 Game**		0	0	0	0	0	0	0	0	0	0	0	**.000**	**.000**

Taylor, LeRoy "Ben" B: 08/11/1902 Marshall, TX D: 03/07/1968 Los Angeles, CA B/T: R/R 5'11" 175 lbs.

PLAYER/TEAM	AGE	DATE	AB	R	H	D	T	HR	RBI	W	SAC	SB	E	RAVE	RSLG
KANSAS CITY MONARCHS	34	23-Aug-36	1	0	0	0	0	0	0	0	0	0	0	.000	.000
Player Totals:	**1 Game**		1	0	0	0	0	0	0	0	0	0	0	**.000**	**.000**

Taylor, Olan "Jelly" B: 07/07/1910 London, OH D: 10/??/1976 Cleveland, OH B/T: L/L 5'10" 190 lbs.

PLAYER/TEAM	AGE	DATE	AB	R	H	D	T	HR	RBI	W	SAC	SB	E	RAVE	RSLG
MEMPHIS RED SOX	29	06-Aug-39	2	0	0	0	0	0	0	0	0	0	0	.000	.000
MEMPHIS RED SOX	30	18-Aug-40	1	0	0	0	0	0	0	0	0	0	0	.000	.000
MEMPHIS RED SOX	31	27-Jul-41	2	0	1	0	0	0	0	0	0	1	0	.200	.200
Player Totals:	**3 Games**		5	0	1	0	0	0	0	0	0	1	0	**.200**	**.200**

Thompson, Frank "Groundhog" B: 10/23/1918 Maryville, LA Living in Shelbyville, TN B/T: L/L 5'4" 150 lbs.

PLAYER/TEAM	AGE	DATE	AB	R	H	D	T	HR	RBI	W	SAC	SB	E	RAVE	RSLG
BIRMINGHAM BLACK BARONS	33	17-Aug-52	1	0	0	0	0	0	0	0	0	0	0	.000	.000
Player Totals:	**1 Game**		1	0	0	0	0	0	0	0	0	0	0	**.000**	**.000**

Tiant Sr., Luis Eleuterio "Sir Skinny" B: 08/27/1906 Havana, Cuba D: 12/10/1976 Milton, MA B/T: R/L 5'10" 150 lbs.

PLAYER/TEAM	AGE	DATE	AB	R	H	D	T	HR	RBI	W	SAC	SB	E	RAVE	RSLG
NEW YORK CUBANS	28	11-Aug-35	2	0	0	0	0	0	0	0	0	0	0	.000	.000
NEW YORK CUBANS	40	27-Jul-47	1	0	0	0	0	0	0	0	0	0	0	.000	.000
NEW YORK CUBANS	40	29-Jul-47	0	0	0	0	0	0	0	0	0	0	0	.000	.000
Player Totals:	**3 Games**		3	0	0	0	0	0	0	0	0	0	0	**.000**	**.000**

Trent, Ted "Highpockets" B: 12/17/1903 Jacksonville, FL D: 01/10/1944 Chicago, IL B/T: R/R 6'3" 185 lbs.

PLAYER/TEAM	AGE	DATE	AB	R	H	D	T	HR	RBI	W	SAC	SB	E	RAVE	RSLG
CHICAGO AMERICAN GIANTS	30	26-Aug-34	1	0	0	0	0	0	0	0	0	0	0	.000	.000
CHICAGO AMERICAN GIANTS	31	11-Aug-35	0	0	0	0	0	0	0	0	0	0	0	.000	.000
CHICAGO AMERICAN GIANTS	32	23-Aug-36	0	0	0	0	0	0	0	0	0	0	0	.000	.000
CHICAGO AMERICAN GIANTS	33	08-Aug-37	0	0	0	0	0	0	0	0	0	0	0	.000	.000
Player Totals:	**4 Games**		1	0	0	0	0	0	0	0	0	0	0	**.000**	**.000**

Trouppe, Quincy Thomas "Big Train" B: 12/25/1912 Dublin, GA D: 08/10/1993 Creve Coeur, MO B/T: S/R 6'3" 215 lbs.

PLAYER/TEAM	AGE	DATE	AB	R	H	D	T	HR	RBI	W	SAC	SB	E	RAVE	RSLG
INDIANAPOLIS ABCS	25	21-Aug-38	4	0	0	0	0	0	0	0	0	0	0	.000	.000
CLEVELAND BUCKEYES	32	29-Jul-45	1	2	1	0	0	0	0	3	0	0	0	.200	.200
CLEVELAND BUCKEYES	33	15-Aug-46	1	0	0	0	0	0	0	0	0	0	0	.167	.167
CLEVELAND BUCKEYES	33	18-Aug-46	1	0	0	0	0	0	0	2	0	0	0	.143	.143
CLEVELAND BUCKEYES	34	27-Jul-47	2	1	1	0	1	0	1	1	1	0	0	.222	.444
CLEVELAND BUCKEYES	34	29-Jul-47	2	1	1	0	0	0	0	0	0	0	0	.273	.455
CHICAGO AMERICAN GIANTS	35	22-Aug-48	3	0	0	0	0	0	0	1	0	0	0	.214	.357
CHICAGO AMERICAN GIANTS	35	24-Aug-48	1	0	0	0	0	0	0	0	0	0	0	.200	.333
Player Totals:	**8 Games**		15	4	3	0	1	0	1	7	1	0	0	**.200**	**.333**

Tugerson, Joseph Leander B: 06/05/1922 Florence Villa, Florida D: 11/01/1985 Florence Villa, FL B/T: R/R 6'1" 165 lbs.

PLAYER/TEAM	AGE	DATE	AB	R	H	D	T	HR	RBI	W	SAC	SB	E	RAVE	RSLG
INDIANAPOLIS CLOWNS	29	12-Aug-51	1	0	0	0	0	0	0	0	0	0	0	.000	.000
Player Totals:	**1 Game**		1	0	0	0	0	0	0	0	0	0	0	**.000**	**.000**

Valdez, Felix "Manuel" B: Cuba D: — B/T: R/R 5'10" 150 lbs.

PLAYER/TEAM	AGE	DATE	AB	R	H	D	T	HR	RBI	W	SAC	SB	E	RAVE	RSLG
MEMPHIS RED SOX		17-Aug-52	2	0	0	0	0	0	0	0	0	0	0	.000	.000
Player Totals:	**1 Game**		2	0	0	0	0	0	0	0	0	0	0	**.000**	**.000**

Vargas, Juan Estando "Tetelo" B: 04/11/1906 Santo Domingo, DR D: 12/30/1971 Guayama, PR B/T: R/R 5'10" 160 lbs.

PLAYER/TEAM	AGE	DATE	AB	R	H	D	T	HR	RBI	W	SAC	SB	E	RAVE	RSLG
NEW YORK CUBANS	36	16-Aug-42	3	0	1	0	0	0	0	1	0	1	0	.333	.333

PLAYER/TEAM	AGE	DATE	AB	R	H	D	T	HR	RBI	W	SAC	SB	E	RAVE	RSLG
NEW YORK CUBANS	36	18-Aug-42	2	0	1	0	0	0	2	0	0	0	0	.400	.400
NEW YORK CUBANS	37	01-Aug-43	2	0	0	0	0	0	0	0	0	0	0	.286	.286
Player Totals:		**3 Games**	**7**	**0**	**2**	**0**	**0**	**0**	**2**	**1**	**0**	**1**	**0**	**.286**	**.286**

Vargas, Roberto Enrique B: 05/29/1929 Santurce, PR Living in Guaynabo, PR B/T: L/L 5'11" 175 lbs.

CHICAGO AMERICAN GIANTS	19	24-Aug-48	0	0	0	0	0	0	0	0	0	0	0	.000	.000
Player Totals:		**1 Game**	**0**	**0**	**0**	**0**	**0**	**0**	**0**	**0**	**0**	**0**	**0**	**.000**	**.000**

Varona, Gilberto "Gil" B: Cuba D: — B/T: R/R

MEMPHIS RED SOX		12-Aug-51	2	0	0	0	0	0	0	0	0	0	0	.000	.000
MEMPHIS RED SOX		17-Aug-52	0	0	0	0	0	0	1	0	0	0	0	.000	.000
Player Totals:		**2 Games**	**2**	**0**	**0**	**0**	**0**	**0**	**1**	**0**	**0**	**0**	**0**	**.000**	**.000**

Varona y Fleitas, Orlando Clemente B: 12/08/1925 Havana, Cuba D: 03/02/1977 New York, NY B/T: R/R 6'0" 170 lbs.

MEMPHIS RED SOX	23	14-Aug-49	1	0	0	0	0	0	0	0	0	0	1	.000	.000
Player Totals:		**1 Game**	**1**	**0**	**0**	**0**	**0**	**0**	**0**	**0**	**0**	**0**	**1**	**.000**	**.000**

Walker, Edsall Elliott "Big" B: 09/15/1910 Catskill, NY D: 02/19/1997 Catskill, NY B/T: R/L 5'11" 215 lbs.

HOMESTEAD GRAYS	27	21-Aug-38	0	0	0	0	0	0	0	0	0	0	0	.000	.000
Player Totals:		**1 Game**	**0**	**0**	**0**	**0**	**0**	**0**	**0**	**0**	**0**	**0**	**0**	**.000**	**.000**

Ware, Archie Virgil B: 06/19/1918 Greenville, FL D: 12/13/1990 Los Angeles, CA B/T: L/L 5'9" 160 lbs.

CLEVELAND BUCKEYES	26	13-Aug-44	4	1	1	1	0	0	1	0	0	0	0	.250	.500
CLEVELAND BUCKEYES	27	29-Jul-45	4	1	2	0	0	0	3	0	0	0	0	.375	.500
CLEVELAND BUCKEYES	28	15-Aug-46	4	0	0	0	0	0	0	0	0	0	0	.250	.333
CLEVELAND BUCKEYES	28	18-Aug-46	2	0	0	0	0	0	0	2	0	0	0	.214	.286
Player Totals:		**4 Games**	**14**	**2**	**3**	**1**	**0**	**0**	**4**	**0**	**2**	**0**	**0**	**.214**	**.286**

Washington, John G. "Johnny" or "Big Red" B: 01/09/1916 Montgomery, AL D: 07/??/1984 Detroit, MI B/T: L/R 6'2" 180 lbs.

PITTSBURGH CRAWFORDS	20	23-Aug-36	1	0	0	0	0	0	0	0	0	0	1	.000	.000
BALTIMORE ELITE GIANTS	31	27-Jul-47	4	0	0	0	0	0	0	0	0	0	0	.000	.000
BALTIMORE ELITE GIANTS	31	29-Jul-47	4	1	2	0	0	0	0	0	0	1	0	.222	.222
Player Totals:		**1 Game**	**9**	**1**	**2**	**0**	**0**	**0**	**0**	**0**	**0**	**1**	**1**	**.000**	**.000**

Washington, Johnny B: 04/20/1930 Chicago, IL D: — B/T: L/L 5'11" 170 lbs.

HOUSTON EAGLES	20	20-Aug-50	2	0	0	0	0	0	0	0	0	0	1	000	.000
Player Totals:		**1 Game**	**2**	**0**	**0**	**0**	**0**	**0**	**0**	**0**	**0**	**0**	**1**	**.000**	**.000**

Washington, Ted B: — D: — B/T: R/R

PHILADELPHIA STARS		17-Aug-52	4	1	1	0	0	0	0	0	0	0	1	.250	.250
Player Totals:		**1 Game**	**4**	**1**	**1**	**0**	**0**	**0**	**0**	**0**	**0**	**0**	**1**	**.250**	**.250**

Watkins, Murray "Skeeter" B: 10/16/1915 Towson, MD D: 03/26/1987 Bolton Hills, MD B/T: L/R 5'4" 145 lbs.

NEWARK EAGLES	29	29-Jul-45	2	0	2	0	0	0	0	1	0	0	0	1.000	1.000
PHILADELPHIA STARS	30	15-Aug-46	0	0	0	0	0	0	0	0	0	0	0	1.000	1.000
PHILADELPHIA STARS	30	18-Aug-46	0	1	0	0	0	0	0	0	0	0	0	1.000	1.000
Player Totals:		**3 Games**	**2**	**1**	**2**	**0**	**0**	**0**	**0**	**1**	**0**	**0**	**0**	**1.000**	**1.000**

Watrous, Sherman B: 03/07/1925 D: 06/13/1997 Houston, TX B/T: R/R

MEMPHIS RED SOX	27	17-Aug-52	4	1	1	1	0	0	0	0	0	0	0	.250	.500
Player Totals:		**1 Game**	**4**	**1**	**1**	**1**	**0**	**0**	**0**	**0**	**0**	**0**	**0**	**.250**	**.500**

Wells, Willie James "Devil" B: 08/10/1904 Shawnee, OK D: 01/22/1989 Austin, TX B/T: R/R 5'8" 170 lbs.

CHICAGO AMERICAN GIANTS	29	10-Sep-33	4	2	2	1	0	0	1	0	0	0	0	.500	.750
CHICAGO AMERICAN GIANTS	30	26-Aug-34	3	0	1	1	0	0	0	1	0	0	0	.429	.714
CHICAGO AMERICAN GIANTS	31	11-Aug-35	3	0	0	0	0	0	0	0	0	0	1	.300	.500
NEWARK EAGLES	32	08-Aug-37	5	1	1	0	0	0	0	0	0	0	0	.267	.400
NEWARK EAGLES	34	21-Aug-38	4	1	2	0	1	0	0	0	0	0	0	.316	.526
NEWARK EAGLES	34	06-Aug-39	3	0	1	0	0	0	0	1	0	0	0	.318	.500

PLAYER/TEAM	AGE	DATE	AB	R	H	D	T	HR	RBI	W	SAC	SB	E	RAVE	RSLG
NEWARK EAGLES	35	27-Aug-39	4	2	1	1	0	0	2	0	0	0	0	.308	.500
NEWARK EAGLES	38	16-Aug-42	5	0	1	0	0	0	0	0	1	1	0	.290	.452
NEWARK EAGLES	38	18-Aug-42	4	1	3	3	0	0	2	0	0	0	1	.343	.571
NEWARK EAGLES	40	29-Jul-45	5	0	1	1	0	0	2	0	0	0	0	.325	.550
Player Totals:	**1 Game**		**40**	**7**	**13**	**7**	**1**	**0**	**7**	**2**	**1**	**1**	**2**	**.325**	**.550**

Welmaker, Roy Horace "Snook" or "Lefty" B: 12/06/1913 Atlanta, GA D: 02/03/1998 Decatur, GA B/T: S/L
5'9" 165 lbs.

PLAYER/TEAM	AGE	DATE	AB	R	H	D	T	HR	RBI	W	SAC	SB	E	RAVE	RSLG
HOMESTEAD GRAYS	31	29-Jul-45	0	0	0	0	0	0	0	0	0	0	0	.000	.000
Player Totals:	**1 Game**		**0**	**0**	**0**	**0**	**0**	**0**	**0**	**0**	**0**	**0**	**0**	**.000**	**.000**

West, James "Jim" or "Shifty" B: 08/08/1911 Mobile, AL D: 06/??/1970 Philadelphia, PA B/T: S/R 6'2" 220 lbs.

PLAYER/TEAM	AGE	DATE	AB	R	H	D	T	HR	RBI	W	SAC	SB	E	RAVE	RSLG
WASHINGTON ELITE GIANTS	25	23-Aug-36	3	1	1	0	0	0	0	1	0	0	1	.333	.333
PHILADELPHIA STARS	31	16-Aug-42	5	0	0	0	0	0	0	0	0	0	0	.125	.125
PHILADELPHIA STARS	31	18-Aug-42	4	1	1	0	0	0	0	1	1	0	0	.167	.167
Player Totals:	**3 Games**		**12**	**2**	**2**	**0**	**0**	**0**	**0**	**2**	**1**	**0**	**1**	**.167**	**.167**

White, Charles "Charlie" or "Hoss" B: 08/12/1927 Kinston, NC D: 05/26/1998 Sea-Tac, WA B/T: L/R 5'11" 190 lbs.

PLAYER/TEAM	AGE	DATE	AB	R	H	D	T	HR	RBI	W	SAC	SB	E	RAVE	RSLG
PHILADELPHIA STARS	22	20-Aug-50	1	0	0	0	0	0	0	0	0	0	0	.000	.000
Player Totals:	**1 Game**		**1**	**0**	**0**	**0**	**0**	**0**	**0**	**0**	**0**	**0**	**0**	**.000**	**.000**

Whittington, Don B: 12/01/1935 Philadelphia, PA D: 08/??/1986 B/T: R/R

PLAYER/TEAM	AGE	DATE	AB	R	H	D	T	HR	RBI	W	SAC	SB	E	RAVE	RSLG
PHILADELPHIA STARS	16	17-Aug-52	3	0	0	0	0	0	0	0	0	0	1	.000	.000
Player Totals:	**1 Game**		**3**	**0**	**0**	**0**	**0**	**0**	**0**	**0**	**0**	**0**	**1**	**.000**	**.000**

Wilkes, James Eugene "Seabiscuit" B: 10/01/1925 Philadelphia, PA Living in Brantford, ON, Canada B/T: L/L
5'6" 150 lbs.

PLAYER/TEAM	AGE	DATE	AB	R	H	D	T	HR	RBI	W	SAC	SB	E	RAVE	RSLG
NEWARK EAGLES	22	24-Aug-48	0	0	0	0	0	0	0	0	0	0	0	.000	.000
INDIANAPOLIS CLOWNS	26	17-Aug-52	3	0	0	0	0	0	0	0	0	0	0	.000	.000
Player Totals:	**2 Games**		**3**	**0**	**0**	**0**	**0**	**0**	**0**	**0**	**0**	**0**	**0**	**.000**	**.000**

Williams, Chester Arthur "Ches" B: 1908 D: 12/25/1952 Lake Charles, LA B/T: R/R 5'9" 180 lbs.

PLAYER/TEAM	AGE	DATE	AB	R	H	D	T	HR	RBI	W	SAC	SB	E	RAVE	RSLG
PITTSBURGH CRAWFORDS	26	26-Aug-34	4	0	3	1	0	0	0	0	0	0	0	.750	1.000
PITTSBURGH CRAWFORDS	27	11-Aug-35	2	1	0	0	0	0	0	1	0	0	1	.500	.667
PITTSBURGH CRAWFORDS	28	23-Aug-36	4	0	0	0	0	0	1	0	0	0	1	.300	.400
PITTSBURGH CRAWFORDS	29	08-Aug-37	3	0	0	0	0	0	1	0	0	0	0	.231	.308
Player Totals:	**4 Games**		**13**	**1**	**3**	**1**	**0**	**0**	**2**	**1**	**0**	**0**	**2**	**.231**	**.308**

Williams, James "Big Jim" B: — D:— B/T: R/R 6'1" 200 lbs.

PLAYER/TEAM	AGE	DATE	AB	R	H	D	T	HR	RBI	W	SAC	SB	E	RAVE	RSLG
TOLEDO-INDY CRAWFORDS		06-Aug-39	2	0	0	0	0	0	0	0	0	0	0	.000	.000
TOLEDO-INDY CRAWFORDS		27-Aug-39	1	0	0	0	0	0	0	0	0	0	0	.000	.000
Player Totals:	**2 Games**		**3**	**0**	**0**	**0**	**0**	**0**	**0**	**0**	**0**	**0**	**0**	**.000**	**.000**

Williams, Jesse Horace "Bill" B: 06/22/1913 Henderson, TX D: 02/27/1990 Kansas City, MO B/T: R/R 5'11" 160 lbs.

PLAYER/TEAM	AGE	DATE	AB	R	H	D	T	HR	RBI	W	SAC	SB	E	RAVE	RSLG
KANSAS CITY MONARCHS	30	01-Aug-43	3	0	2	0	0	0	0	0	1	1	0	.667	.667
KANSAS CITY MONARCHS	32	29-Jul-45	5	0	2	0	1	0	4	0	0	0	0	.500	.750
KANSAS CITY MONARCHS	38	12-Aug-51	4	1	1	0	0	0	0	0	0	0	0	.417	.583
Player Totals:	**3 Games**		**12**	**1**	**5**	**0**	**1**	**0**	**4**	**0**	**1**	**1**	**0**	**.417**	**.583**

Williams, Johnny "Nature Boy" B: 1916 Shreveport, LA D: — B/T: R/R 6'2" 210 lbs.

PLAYER/TEAM	AGE	DATE	AB	R	H	D	T	HR	RBI	W	SAC	SB	E	RAVE	RSLG
INDIANAPOLIS CLOWNS	30	15-Aug-46	0	0	0	0	0	0	0	0	0	0	0	.000	.000
INDIANAPOLIS CLOWNS	30	18-Aug-46	1	0	0	0	0	0	0	0	0	0	0	.000	.000
INDIANAPOLIS CLOWNS	31	29-Jul-47	2	0	0	0	0	0	0	0	0	0	0	.000	.000
Player Totals:	**3 Games**		**3**	**0**	**0**	**0**	**0**	**0**	**0**	**0**	**0**	**0**	**0**	**.000**	**.000**

Williams, Marvin "Tex" B: 02/12/1923 Houston, TX D: 12/23/2000 Conroe, TX B/T: R/R 6'0" 190 lbs.

PLAYER/TEAM	AGE	DATE	AB	R	H	D	T	HR	RBI	W	SAC	SB	E	RAVE	RSLG
PHILADELPHIA STARS	21	13-Aug-44	1	0	0	0	0	0	0	0	0	0	0	.000	.000
Player Totals:	**1 Game**		**1**	**0**	**0**	**0**	**0**	**0**	**0**	**0**	**0**	**0**	**0**	**.000**	**.000**

PLAYER/TEAM	AGE	DATE	AB	R	H	D	T	HR	RBI	W	SAC	SB	E	RAVE	RSLG

Williams, Willie C. "Curley" B: 05/25/1925 Orangeburg, SC Living in Sarasota, FL B/T: L/R 5'11" 175 lbs.

PLAYER/TEAM	AGE	DATE	AB	R	H	D	T	HR	RBI	W	SAC	SB	E	RAVE	RSLG
HOUSTON EAGLES	25	20-Aug-50	1	1	0	0	0	0	0	1	0	0	0	.000	.000
NEW ORLEANS EAGLES	26	12-Aug-51	3	0	0	0	0	0	1	0	1	0	0	.000	.000
Player Totals:		**2 Games**	**4**	**1**	**0**	**0**	**0**	**0**	**1**	**1**	**1**	**0**	**0**	**.000**	**.000**

Wilson, Arthur Lee "Artie" or "Snoop" B: 10/28/1920 Springville, AL Living in Portland, OR B/T: L/R 5'10" 160 lbs.

PLAYER/TEAM	AGE	DATE	AB	R	H	D	T	HR	RBI	W	SAC	SB	E	RAVE	RSLG
BIRMINGHAM BLACK BARONS	23	13-Aug-44	4	1	2	0	0	0	0	0	0	0	0	.500	.500
BIRMINGHAM BLACK BARONS	25	15-Aug-46	3	1	1	0	0	0	0	0	0	0	0	.429	.429
BIRMINGHAM BLACK BARONS	25	18-Aug-46	4	1	1	0	0	0	0	0	0	1	0	.364	.364
BIRMINGHAM BLACK BARONS	26	27-Jul-47	4	0	0	0	0	0	0	0	0	0	0	.267	.267
BIRMINGHAM BLACK BARONS	26	29-Jul-47	4	4	4	0	0	0	1	1	0	2	0	.421	.421
BIRMINGHAM BLACK BARONS	27	22-Aug-48	3	0	0	0	0	0	0	0	0	0	0	.364	.364
BIRMINGHAM BLACK BARONS	27	24-Aug-48	4	0	3	0	0	0	1	0	0	0	0	.423	.423
Player Totals:		**7 Games**	**26**	**7**	**11**	**0**	**0**	**0**	**2**	**1**	**0**	**3**	**0**	**.423**	**.423**

Wilson, Daniel Richard "Dan" B: 09/13/1913 St. Louis, MO D: 12/23/1986 St. Louis, MO B/T: S/R 6'1" 160 lbs.

PLAYER/TEAM	AGE	DATE	AB	R	H	D	T	HR	RBI	W	SAC	SB	E	RAVE	RSLG
ST. LOUIS STARS	25	06-Aug-39	3	1	1	0	0	1	2	0	0	0	0	.333	1.333
ST. LOUIS STARS	25	27-Aug-39	5	0	1	1	0	0	2	0	0	0	0	.250	.750
ST. LOUIS STARS	27	27-Jul-41	2	0	0	0	0	0	0	0	0	0	1	.200	.600
NEW YORK BLACK YANKEES	28	16-Aug-42	4	3	2	1	0	0	1	0	2	0	.286	.643
NEW YORK BLACK YANKEES	28	18-Aug-42	6	0	1	1	0	0	0	0	0	0	0	.250	.550
Player Totals:		**5 Games**	**20**	**4**	**5**	**3**	**0**	**1**	**4**	**1**	**0**	**2**	**1**	**.250**	**0.550**

Wilson, Ernest Judson "Boojum" or "Jud" B: 02/28/1894 Remington, VA D: 06/26/1963 Washington, DC B/T: L/R 5'8" 195 lbs.

PLAYER/TEAM	AGE	DATE	AB	R	H	D	T	HR	RBI	W	SAC	SB	E	RAVE	RSLG
PHILADELPHIA STARS	39	10-Sep-33	3	1	2	0	0	0	3	0	0	0	0	.667	.667
PHILADELPHIA STARS	40	26-Aug-34	3	0	1	0	0	0	1	1	0	0	0	.500	.500
PHILADELPHIA STARS	41	11-Aug-35	5	1	2	0	0	0	1	1	0	0	0	.455	.455
Player Totals:		**3 Games**	**11**	**2**	**5**	**0**	**0**	**0**	**5**	**2**	**0**	**0**	**0**	**.455**	**.455**

Wilson, Fred "Sardo" B: 1909 Hastings, FL D: — B/T: L/R 6'1" 195 lbs.

PLAYER/TEAM	AGE	DATE	AB	R	H	D	T	HR	RBI	W	SAC	SB	E	RAVE	RSLG
CINCINNATI CLOWNS	34	01-Aug-43	1	0	0	0	0	0	0	0	0	0	0	.000	.000
Player Totals:		**1 Game**	**1**	**0**	**0**	**0**	**0**	**0**	**0**	**0**	**0**	**0**	**0**	**.000**	**.000**

Wilson, Robert "Bob" B: 02/22/1925 Dallas, TX D: 04/23/1985 Dallas, TX B/T: R/R 5'11" 195 lbs.

PLAYER/TEAM	AGE	DATE	AB	R	H	D	T	HR	RBI	W	SAC	SB	E	RAVE	RSLG
HOUSTON EAGLES	24	14-Aug-49	3	0	0	0	0	0	0	0	0	0	0	.000	.000
Player Totals:		**1 Game**	**3**	**0**	**0**	**0**	**0**	**0**	**0**	**0**	**0**	**0**	**0**	**.000**	**.000**

Woods, Parnell L. B: 02/16/1912 Birmingham, AL D: 07/23/1977 Cleveland, OH B/T: R/R 5'9" 170 lbs.

PLAYER/TEAM	AGE	DATE	AB	R	H	D	T	HR	RBI	W	SAC	SB	E	RAVE	RSLG
BIRMINGHAM BLACK BARONS	26	21-Aug-38	1	0	0	0	0	0	0	0	0	0	0	.000	.000
CLEVELAND BEARS	27	06-Aug-39	0	0	0	0	0	0	0	0	1	0	0	.000	.000
BIRMINGHAM BLACK BARONS	28	18-Aug-40	4	0	1	0	0	0	0	0	0	0	0	.200	.200
JACKSONVILLE RED CAPS	29	27-Jul-41	4	0	0	0	0	0	1	0	0	0	0	.111	.111
CINCINNATI BUCKEYES	30	16-Aug-42	3	1	1	0	1	0	1	0	0	0	0	.167	.333
CINCINNATI BUCKEYES	30	18-Aug-42	2	0	0	0	0	0	0	1	0	0	0	.143	.286
CHICAGO AMERICAN GIANTS	39	12-Aug-51	3	0	0	0	0	0	0	1	0	1	0	.118	.235
Player Totals:		**7 Games**	**17**	**1**	**2**	**0**	**1**	**0**	**2**	**2**	**1**	**1**	**0**	**.118**	**.235**

Woods, Sam "Buddy" B: 1922 D: Philadelphia, PA B/T: R/R 6'2" 205 lbs.

PLAYER/TEAM	AGE	DATE	AB	R	H	D	T	HR	RBI	W	SAC	SB	E	RAVE	RSLG
MEMPHIS RED SOX	31	16-Aug-53	1	0	0	0	0	0	0	0	0	0	0	.000	.000
Player Totals:		**1 Game**	**1**	**0**	**0**	**0**	**0**	**0**	**0**	**0**	**0**	**0**	**0**	**.000**	**.000**

Wright, Burnis "Wild Bill" B: 06/06/1914 Milan, TN D: 08/03/1996 Aguascalientes, MX B/T: S/R 6'4" 220 lbs.

PLAYER/TEAM	AGE	DATE	AB	R	H	D	T	HR	RBI	W	SAC	SB	E	RAVE	RSLG
COLUMBUS ELITE GIANTS	21	11-Aug-35	1	0	0	0	0	0	0	0	0	0	0	.000	.000
WASHINGTON ELITE GIANTS	22	23-Aug-36	2	0	0	0	0	0	0	0	0	0	0	.000	.000
WASHINGTON ELITE GIANTS	23	08-Aug-37	5	2	3	1	0	0	2	0	0	1	0	.375	.500
BALTIMORE ELITE GIANTS	24	21-Aug-38	4	0	0	0	0	0	0	0	0	0	0	.250	.333

PLAYER/TEAM	AGE	DATE	AB	R	H	D	T	HR	RBI	W	SAC	SB	E	RAVE	RSLG
BALTIMORE ELITE GIANTS	25	06-Aug-39	4	0	2	1	0	0	0	0	0	0	0	.313	.438
BALTIMORE ELITE GIANTS	25	27-Aug-39	5	2	2	0	0	0	0	0	0	0	0	.333	.429
BALTIMORE ELITE GIANTS	28	16-Aug-42	5	0	2	0	0	0	2	0	0	0	0	.346	.423
BALTIMORE ELITE GIANTS	28	18-Aug-42	4	1	2	1	0	0	1	0	1	0	0	.367	.467
BALTIMORE ELITE GIANTS	31	29-Jul-45	1	0	0	0	0	0	0	0	0	0	0	.355	.452
Player Totals:		**9 Games**	**31**	**5**	**11**	**3**	**0**	**0**	**5**	**0**	**1**	**1**	**0**	**.355**	**.452**

Wright, John Richard "Johnny"   B: *11/28/1916 New Orleans, LA*   D: *05/10/1990 Jackson, MS*   **B/T:** R/R   *5'11"*   *175 lbs.*

PLAYER/TEAM	AGE	DATE	AB	R	H	D	T	HR	RBI	W	SAC	SB	E	RAVE	RSLG
HOMESTEAD GRAYS	26	01-Aug-43	0	0	0	0	0	0	0	0	0	0	0	.000	.000
HOMESTEAD GRAYS	30	27-Jul-47	0	0	0	0	0	0	0	0	0	0	0	.000	.000
Player Totals:		**2 Games**	**0**	**0**	**0**	**0**	**0**	**0**	**0**	**0**	**0**	**0**	**0**	**.000**	**.000**

Wright, Zollie   B: *09/17/1909 Milford, TX*   D: *04/??/1976 Philadelphia, PA*   **B/T:** R/R   *5'9"*   *190 lbs.*

PLAYER/TEAM	AGE	DATE	AB	R	H	D	T	HR	RBI	W	SAC	SB	E	RAVE	RSLG
WASHINGTON ELITE GIANTS	26	23-Aug-36	1	2	1	1	0	0	2	2	0	0	0	1.000	2.000
Player Totals:		**1 Game**	**1**	**2**	**1**	**1**	**0**	**0**	**2**	**2**	**0**	**0**	**0**	**1.000**	**2.000**

Wyatt, Ralph Arthur "Pepper"   B: *09/17/1917 Chicago, IL*   D: *03/??/1990 Auburn Park, IL*   **B/T:** R/R   *5'10"*   *160 lbs.*

PLAYER/TEAM	AGE	DATE	AB	R	H	D	T	HR	RBI	W	SAC	SB	E	RAVE	RSLG
CHICAGO AMERICAN GIANTS	24	18-Aug-42	1	1	1	0	0	0	0	1	0	0	1	1.000	1.000
Player Totals:		**1 Game**	**1**	**1**	**1**	**0**	**0**	**0**	**0**	**1**	**0**	**0**	**1**	**1.000**	**1.000**

Individual Pitching Statistics

PLAYER/TEAM	AGE	DATE	GS	CG	W	L	PCT	IP	H	K	BB	RS	ER	ERA
Amaro, Dionisio "Dave" B: *1930 Havana, Cuba* D: B/T: R/R *6'3" 180 lbs.*														
INDIANAPOLIS CLOWNS	23	16-Aug-53	0	0	0	0		2.00	3	0	0	2	2	9.00
Player Totals:		**1 Game**	**0**	**0**	**0**	**0**	**.000**	**2.00**	**3**	**0**	**0**	**2**	**2**	**9.00**
Bankhead, Daniel Robert "Dan" B: *05/03/1920 Empire, AL* D: *05/02/1976 Houston, TX* B/T: R/R *6'1" 185 lbs.*														
BIRMINGHAM BLACK BARONS	21	27-Jul-41	0	0	0	0		2.00	1	0	1	0	0	0.00
MEMPHIS RED SOX	26	15-Aug-46	1	0	0	0		3.00	3	2	1	2	2	3.60
MEMPHIS RED SOX	26	18-Aug-46	0	0	1	0		3.00	1	2	1	0	0	2.25
MEMPHIS RED SOX	27	27-Jul-47	1	0	1	0		3.00	1	2	0	1	1	2.45
Player Totals:		**4 Games**	**2**	**0**	**2**	**0**	**1.000**	**11.00**	**6**	**6**	**3**	**3**	**3**	**2.45**
Barnhill, Dave "Impo" B: *10/30/1913 Greenville, NC* D: *01/08/1983 Miami, FL* B/T: R/R *5'6" 160 lbs.*														
NEW YORK CUBANS	27	27-Jul-41	0	0	0	0		3.00	2	2	0	0	0	0.00
NEW YORK CUBANS	28	16-Aug-42	0	0	0	0		3.00	2	4	1	1	1	1.50
NEW YORK CUBANS	28	18-Aug-42	0	0	0	0		2.00	2	2	0	0	0	1.13
NEW YORK CUBANS	29	01-Aug-43	1	0	0	1		3.00	2	2	0	1	1	1.64
NEW YORK CUBANS	34	24-Aug-48	0	0	0	0		3.00	2	1	0	0	0	1.29
Player Totals:		**5 Games**	**1**	**0**	**0**	**1**	**.000**	**14.00**	**10**	**11**	**1**	**2**	**2**	**1.29**
Beverly, William "Fireball" B: *05/05/1930 Houston, TX* D: *09/11/1996 Houston, TX* B/T: R/R *6'0" 185 lbs.*														
CHICAGO AMERICAN GIANTS	22	17-Aug-52	0	0	0	0		3.00	2	1	1	1	1	3.00
Player Totals:		**1 Game**	**0**	**0**	**0**	**0**	**.000**	**3.00**	**2**	**1**	**1**	**1**	**1**	**3.00**
Black, Joseph "Joe" B: *02/08/1924 Plainfield, NJ* Living in Phoenix, AZ B/T: R/R *6'2" 210 lbs.*														
BALTIMORE ELITE GIANTS	23	29-Jul-47	0	0	0	0		3.00	5	2	1	2	2	6.00
BALTIMORE ELITE GIANTS	24	24-Aug-48	0	0	0	0		3.00	2	0	0	0	0	3.00
BALTIMORE ELITE GIANTS	26	20-Aug-50	1	0	0	0		3.00	4	0	1	2	1	3.00
Player Totals:		**3 Games**	**1**	**0**	**0**	**0**	**.000**	**9.00**	**11**	**2**	**2**	**4**	**3**	**3.00**
Bremer, Eugene Joseph "Gene" or "Flash" B: *07/18/1916 New Orleans, LA* D: *06/19/1971 Cleveland, OH* B/T: R/R *5'10" 185 lbs.*														
MEMPHIS RED SOX	24	18-Aug-40	1	0	0	1		3.00	3	4	3	2	2	6.00
CINCINNATI BUCKEYES	26	16-Aug-42	0	0	0	0		1.00	0	1	0	0	0	4.50
CINCINNATI BUCKEYES	26	18-Aug-42	1	0	0	1		2.67	6	1	3	5	5	9.45
CLEVELAND BUCKEYES	28	13-Aug-44	0	0	0	0		1.67	1	2	0	0	0	7.55
CLEVELAND BUCKEYES	29	29-Jul-45	0	0	0	0		0.33	1	0	0	0	0	7.27
Player Totals:		**5 Games**	**2**	**0**	**0**	**2**	**.000**	**8.67**	**11**	**8**	**6**	**7**	**7**	**7.27**
Brewer, Chester Arthur "Chet" B: *01/14/1907 Leavenworth, KS* D: *03/26/1990 Whittier, CA* B/T: S/R *6'4" 185 lbs.*														
KANSAS CITY MONARCHS	27	26-Aug-34	0	0	0	0		3.00	2	2	1	0	0	0.00
CLEVELAND BUCKEYES	40	27-Jul-47	0	0	0	0		3.00	2	1	1	1	1	1.50
Player Totals:		**2 Games**	**0**	**0**	**0**	**0**	**.000**	**6.00**	**4**	**3**	**2**	**1**	**1**	**1.50**
Britt, George "Chippy" B: *06/18/1890 Macon, GA* D: *Jacksonville, FL* B/T: R/R *5'8" 175 lbs.*														
HOMESTEAD GRAYS	43	10-Sep-33	0	0	0	0		2.00	4	1	0	3	1	4.50
Player Totals:		**1 Game**	**0**	**0**	**0**	**0**	**.000**	**2.00**	**4**	**1**	**0**	**3**	**1**	**4.50**
Brown, Barney "Brinquitos" B: *10/23/1907 Hartsville, SC* D: *10/01/1985 Philadelphia, PA* B/T: L/L *5'9" 165 lbs.*														
NEW YORK BLACK YANKEES	29	08-Aug-37	0	0	0	0		3.00	2	0	2	1	1	3.00
NEW YORK BLACK YANKEES	30	21-Aug-38	0	0	0	0		3.00	2	1	0	0	0	1.50
PHILADELPHIA STARS	34	16-Aug-42	0	0	0	0		0.67	2	0	0	0	0	1.35
PHILADELPHIA STARS	38	15-Aug-46	1	0	0	0		3.00	0	0	0	0	0	0.93
PHILADELPHIA STARS	38	18-Aug-46	1	0	0	0		3.00	2	3	1	0	0	0.71
Player Totals:		**5 Games**	**2**	**0**	**0**	**0**	**.000**	**12.67**	**8**	**4**	**3**	**1**	**1**	**0.71**
Brown, Raymond "Ray" B: *02/23/1908 Ashland Grove, OH* D: *1968 Dayton, OH* B/T: S/R *6'1" 195 lbs.*														
HOMESTEAD GRAYS	27	11-Aug-35	1	0	0	0		4.00	6	1	0	3	2	4.50

PLAYER/TEAM	AGE	DATE	GS	CG	W	L	PCT	IP	H	K	BB	RS	ER	ERA
HOMESTEAD GRAYS	32	18-Aug-40	0	0	0	0		3.00	2	3	0	0	0	2.57
Player Totals:		**2 Games**	1	0	0	0	.000	7.00	8	4	0	3	2	2.57

Byrd, William "Bill" B: 07/15/1907 Canton, GA D: 01/04/1991 Philadelphia, PA B/T: S/R 6'1" 210 lbs.

PLAYER/TEAM	AGE	DATE	GS	CG	W	L	PCT	IP	H	K	BB	RS	ER	ERA
WASHINGTON ELITE GIANTS	29	23-Aug-36	0	0	0	0		3.00	4	4	1	1	0	0.00
BALTIMORE ELITE GIANTS	32	06-Aug-39	1	0	0	0		3.00	2	1	1	0	0	0.00
BALTIMORE ELITE GIANTS	32	27-Aug-39	1	0	1	0		3.00	4	1	1	1	1	1.00
BALTIMORE ELITE GIANTS	34	27-Jul-41	0	0	0	0		1.00	1	0	0	0	0	0.90
BALTIMORE ELITE GIANTS	37	13-Aug-44	0	0	0	0		2.00	3	0	0	0	0	0.75
BALTIMORE ELITE GIANTS	39	15-Aug-46	0	0	1	0		2.67	1	4	1	0	0	0.61
BALTIMORE ELITE GIANTS	39	18-Aug-46	0	0	0	1		1.33	4	0	2	4	3	2.25
Player Totals:		**7 Games**	2	0	2	1	.667	16.00	19	10	6	6	4	2.25

Calhoun, Walter Allen "Lefty" B: 08/21/1911 Union City, TN D: 10/02/1976 Cleveland, OH B/T: L/L 5'9" 180 lbs.

PLAYER/TEAM	AGE	DATE	GS	CG	W	L	PCT	IP	H	K	BB	RS	ER	ERA
NEW ORLEANS-ST. LOUIS STARS	28	18-Aug-40	0	0	0	0		2.33	6	1	1	6	3	11.59
Player Totals:		**1 Game**	0	0	0	0	.000	2.33	6	1	1	6	3	11.59

Carter, Ernest C. "Spoon" B: 12/08/1902 Harpersville, AL D: 01/23/1974 Birmingham, AL B/T: R/R 5'9" 170 lbs.

PLAYER/TEAM	AGE	DATE	GS	CG	W	L	PCT	IP	H	K	BB	RS	ER	ERA
MEMPHIS RED SOX	44	29-Jul-47	0	0	0	0		3.00	2	2	1	0	0	0.00
Player Totals:		**1 Game**	0	0	0	0	.000	3.00	2	2	1	0	0	0.00

Cartledge, Menske "Manny" or "Robbie" B: 07/20/1925 Umatilla, FL D: — B/T: R/R 6'4" 190 lbs.

PLAYER/TEAM	AGE	DATE	GS	CG	W	L	PCT	IP	H	K	BB	RS	ER	ERA
BIRMINGHAM BLACK BARONS	28	16-Aug-53	0	0	0	0		3.00	0	1	1	0	0	0.00
Player Totals:		**1 Game**	0	0	0	0	.000	3.00	0	1	1	0	0	0.00

Clarke, Vibert Ernesto "Webbo" B: 06/08/1928 Colon, Panama D: 06/14/1970 Cristobal, Canal Zone B/T: L/L 6'0" 170 lbs.

PLAYER/TEAM	AGE	DATE	GS	CG	W	L	PCT	IP	H	K	BB	RS	ER	ERA
CLEVELAND BUCKEYES	18	15-Aug-46	0	0	0	1		0.33	3	0	0	2	2	54.55
CLEVELAND BUCKEYES	19	29-Jul-47	0	0	0	0		1.00	0	0	1	0	0	13.53
CLEVELAND BUCKEYES	20	24-Aug-48	1	0	0	1		3.00	4	1	1	3	3	10.39
MEMPHIS RED SOX	22	20-Aug-50	1	0	0	0		3.00	2	3	2	1	1	7.37
MEMPHIS RED SOX	23	12-Aug-51	0	0	0	1		2.67	6	1	1	2	2	7.20
Player Totals:		**5 Games**	2	0	0	3	.000	10.00	15	5	5	8	8	7.20

Cohen, James Clarence "Fireball" B: 03/26/1918 Evergreen, AL Living in Washington, DC B/T: R/R 5'11" 190 lbs.

PLAYER/TEAM	AGE	DATE	GS	CG	W	L	PCT	IP	H	K	BB	RS	ER	ERA
INDIANAPOLIS CLOWNS	30	24-Aug-48	0	0	0	0		2.00	3	1	1	0	0	0.00
Player Totals:		**1 Game**	0	0	0	0	.000	2.00	3	0	1	1	0	0.00

Cooper, Andrew L. "Andy" B: 04/24/1898 Waco, TX D: 06/03/1941 Waco, TX B/T: R/L 6'2" 220 lbs.

PLAYER/TEAM	AGE	DATE	GS	CG	W	L	PCT	IP	H	K	BB	RS	ER	ERA
KANSAS CITY MONARCHS	38	23-Aug-36	0	0	0	0		1.00	1	0	0	0	0	0.00
Player Totals:		**1 Game**	0	0	0	0	.000	1.00	1	0	0	0	0	0.00

Cornelius, William McKinley "Sug" B: 09/03/1906 Atlanta, GA D: 10/30/1989 Chicago, IL B/T: R/R 5'8" 180 lbs.

PLAYER/TEAM	AGE	DATE	GS	CG	W	L	PCT	IP	H	K	BB	RS	ER	ERA
CHICAGO AMERICAN GIANTS	28	11-Aug-35	0	0	1	0		1.00	0	0	1	0	0	0.00
CHICAGO AMERICAN GIANTS	29	23-Aug-36	1	0	0	1		3.00	6	2	1	2	2	4.50
CHICAGO AMERICAN GIANTS	31	21-Aug-38	1	0	0	0		1.00	5	0	0	3	3	9.00
Player Totals:		**3 Games**	2	0	1	1	.500	5.00	11	2	2	5	5	9.00

Day, Leon B: 10/30/1916 Alexandria, VA D: 03/13/1995 Baltimore, MD B/T: R/R 5'11" 185 lbs.

PLAYER/TEAM	AGE	DATE	GS	CG	W	L	PCT	IP	H	K	BB	RS	ER	ERA
BROOKLYN EAGLES	18	11-Aug-35	0	0	0	0		4.00	6	3	2	4	2	4.50
NEWARK EAGLES	20	08-Aug-37	0	0	0	0		3.00	1	4	0	0	0	2.57
NEWARK EAGLES	22	06-Aug-39	0	0	0	0		3.00	0	3	2	0	0	1.80
NEWARK EAGLES	22	27-Aug-39	0	0	0	0		3.00	0	2	1	0	0	1.38
NEWARK EAGLES	25	16-Aug-42	0	0	1	0		2.33	0	5	0	0	0	1.17
NEWARK EAGLES	25	18-Aug-42	0	0	0	0		2.00	3	0	0	0	0	1.04
NEWARK EAGLES	26	01-Aug-43	0	0	0	0		2.00	1	5	2	0	0	0.93
NEWARK EAGLES	29	15-Aug-46	0	0	0	0		1.00	1	0	0	0	0	0.89
NEWARK EAGLES	29	18-Aug-46	0	0	0	0		1.00	1	1	0	0	0	0.84
Player Totals:		**9 Games**	0	0	1	0	1.000	21.33	13	23	7	4	2	0.84

Dihigo y Llanos, Martin Magdaleno B: 05/25/1906 Matanzas, Cuba D: 05/20/1971 Cienfuegos, Cuba B/T: R/R
6'2" 215 lbs.

PLAYER/TEAM	AGE	DATE	GS	CG	W	L	PCT	IP	H	K	BB	RS	ER	ERA
NEW YORK CUBANS	29	11-Aug-35	0	0	0	1		1.67	3	1	2	4	4	21.56
NEW YORK CUBANS	39	29-Jul-45	0	0	0	0		3.33	2	0	0	1	1	9.00
Player Totals:	2 Games		0	0	0	1	.000	5.00	5	1	2	5	5	9.00

Evans, Felix "Chin" B: 10/03/1910 Atlanta, GA D: 08/21/1993 Pompano Beach, FL B/T: R/R 6'2" 180 lbs.

PLAYER/TEAM	AGE	DATE	GS	CG	W	L	PCT	IP	H	K	BB	RS	ER	ERA
MEMPHIS RED SOX	35	18-Aug-46	1	0	0	0		3.00	1	2	2	0	0	0.00
Player Totals:	1 Game		1	0	0	0	.000	3.00	1	2	2	0	0	0.00

Fields, Wilmer Leon "Red" B: 08/02/1922 Manassa. VA Living in Manassa, VA B/T: R/R 6'3" 215 lbs.

PLAYER/TEAM	AGE	DATE	GS	CG	W	L	PCT	IP	H	K	BB	RS	ER	ERA
HOMESTEAD GRAYS	26	22-Aug-48	0	0	0	0		3.00	1	2	1	0	0	0.00
Player Totals:	1 Game		0	0	0	0	.000	3.00	1	2	1	0	0	0.00

Foster, Willie Hendrick "Bill" B: 06/12/1904 Calvert, TX D: 09/16/1978 Lorman, MS B/T: S/L 6'1" 195 lbs.

PLAYER/TEAM	AGE	DATE	GS	CG	W	L	PCT	IP	H	K	BB	RS	ER	ERA
CHICAGO AMERICAN GIANTS	29	10-Sep-33	1	1	1	0		9.00	7	4	3	7	3	3.00
CHICAGO AMERICAN GIANTS	30	26-Aug-34	0	0	0	1		3.00	4	2	1	1	1	3.00
Player Totals:	2 Games		1	1	1	1	.500	12.00	11	6	4	8	4	3.00

Gaines, Jonas Donald "Lefty" B: 01/09/1914 New Roads, LA D: B/T: R/L 5'10" 155 lbs.

PLAYER/TEAM	AGE	DATE	GS	CG	W	L	PCT	IP	H	K	BB	RS	ER	ERA
BALTIMORE ELITE GIANTS	28	16-Aug-42	1	0	0	0		3.00	1	0	0	1	0	0.00
BALTIMORE ELITE GIANTS	28	18-Aug-42	0	0	0	0		2.00	1	2	0	0	0	0.00
BALTIMORE ELITE GIANTS	32	15-Aug-46	0	0	0	0		2.00	1	0	0	0	0	0.00
BALTIMORE ELITE GIANTS	32	18-Aug-46	0	0	0	0		2.33	0	1	0	0	0	0.00
PHILADELPHIA STARS	36	20-Aug-50	0	0	0	0		2.00	2	3	0	0	0	0.00
Player Totals:	5 Games		1	0	0	0	.000	11.33	5	6	0	1	0	0.00

Gaines, Willy "Willie" B: 1931 Tuscaloosa, AL D: B/T: R/R 6'1" 190 lbs.

PLAYER/TEAM	AGE	DATE	GS	CG	W	L	PCT	IP	H	K	BB	RS	ER	ERA
INDIANAPOLIS CLOWNS	22	16-Aug-53	1	0	0	1		3.00	3	1	4	3	1	3.00
Player Totals:	1 Game		1	0	0	1	.000	3.00	3	1	4	3	1	3.00

Galata, Raul B: 10/05/1930 Havana, Cuba D: B/T: L/L 5'9" 170 lbs.

PLAYER/TEAM	AGE	DATE	GS	CG	W	L	PCT	IP	H	K	BB	RS	ER	ERA
NEW YORK CUBANS	19	20-Aug-50	0	0	0	1		2.00	5	1	2	3	3	13.50
Player Totals:	1 Game		0	0	0	1	.000	2.00	5	1	2	3	3	13.50

Gipson, Alvin "Bubber" B: 12/11/1913 Shreveport, LA D: 11/21/1992 Shreveport, LA B/T: R/R

PLAYER/TEAM	AGE	DATE	GS	CG	W	L	PCT	IP	H	K	BB	RS	ER	ERA
BIRMINGHAM BLACK BARONS	28	18-Aug-42	0	0	0	0		3.00	3	1	2	2	1	3.00
Player Totals:	1 Game		0	0	0	0	.000	3.00	3	1	2	2	1	3.00

Glover, Thomas "Tom" or "Lefty" B: — D:— B/T: R/L

PLAYER/TEAM	AGE	DATE	GS	CG	W	L	PCT	IP	H	K	BB	RS	ER	ERA
BALTIMORE ELITE GIANTS		29-Jul-45	1	0	0	1		1.67	5	0	1	4	4	21.56
Player Totals:	1 Game		1	0	0	1	.000	1.67	5	0	1	4	4	21.56

Greason, Rev. William Henry "Bill" B: 09/03/1924 Atlanta, GA Living in Birmingham, AL B/T: R/R 5'10" 170 lbs.

PLAYER/TEAM	AGE	DATE	GS	CG	W	L	PCT	IP	H	K	BB	RS	ER	ERA
BIRMINGHAM BLACK BARONS	24	14-Aug-49	0	0	0	0		3.00	2	1	0	0	0	0.00
Player Totals:	1 Game		0	0	0	0	.000	3.00	2	1	0	0	0	0.00

Griffith, Robert Lee "Schoolboy" B: 10/01/1912 Liberty, TN D: 11/08/1977 Indianapolis, IN B/T: L/R 6'2" 215 lbs.

PLAYER/TEAM	AGE	DATE	GS	CG	W	L	PCT	IP	H	K	BB	RS	ER	ERA
COLUMBUS ELITE GIANTS	22	11-Aug-35	0	0	0	0		2.00	4	3	3	4	3	13.50
NEW YORK BLACK YANKEES	35	22-Aug-48	0	0	0	0		2.00	3	2	1	1	1	9.00
PHILADELPHIA STARS	36	14-Aug-49	1	0	1	0		3.00	0	1	1	0	0	5.14
Player Totals:	3 Games		1	0	1	0	1.000	7.00	7	6	5	5	4	5.14

Harris, Isiah B: 07/02/1925 Parkin, AR Living in Memphis, TN B/T: L/L 5'11" 195 lbs.

PLAYER/TEAM	AGE	DATE	GS	CG	W	L	PCT	IP	H	K	BB	RS	ER	ERA
MEMPHIS RED SOX	28	16-Aug-53	0	0	0	0		3.00	2	1	2	0	0	0.00
Player Totals:	1 Game		0	0	0	0	.000	3.00	2	1	2	0	0	0.00

Harris, Wilmer B: 03/01/1924 Philadelphia, PA Living in Philadelphia, PA B/T: R/R 6'1" 165 lbs.

PLAYER/TEAM	AGE	DATE	GS	CG	W	L	PCT	IP	H	K	BB	RS	ER	ERA
PHILADELPHIA STARS	27	12-Aug-51	0	0	0	0		3.00	2	4	0	0	0	0.00

PLAYER/TEAM	AGE	DATE	GS	CG	W	L	PCT	IP	H	K	BB	RS	ER	ERA
PHILADELPHIA STARS	28	17-Aug-52	0	0	0	0		3.00	2	0	1	0	0	0.00
Player Totals:		**2 Games**	**0**	**0**	**0**	**0**	**.000**	**6.00**	**4**	**4**	**1**	**0**	**0**	**0.00**

Harvey, David William "Bill" B: 03/23/1908 Clarksdale, MS D: 03/05/1989 Baltimore, MD B/T: L/L 5'8" 1/5 lbs.

BALTIMORE ELITE GIANTS	35	01-Aug-43	0	0	0	0		1.00	1	0	0	0	0	0.00
Player Totals:		**1 Game**	**0**	**0**	**0**	**0**	**.000**	**1.00**	**1**	**0**	**0**	**0**	**0**	**0.00**

Heard, Jehosie "Jay" B: 01/17/1920 Atlanta, GA Living in Birmingham, AL B/T: L/L 5'7" 145 lbs.

NEW ORLEANS EAGLES	31	12-Aug-51	0	0	0	0		3.33	2	3	0	1	1	2.70
Player Totals:		**1 Game**	**0**	**0**	**0**	**0**	**.000**	**3.33**	**2**	**3**	**0**	**1**	**1**	**2.70**

Henry, Leo "Preacher" B: 03/10/1911 Inverness, FL D: 05/16/1992 Jacksonville, FL B/T: R/R 5'8" 155 lbs.

JACKSONVILLE RED CAPS	30	27-Jul-41	0	0	0	0		1.33	3	1	0	0	0	0.00
Player Totals:		**1 Game**	**0**	**0**	**0**	**0**	**.000**	**1.33**	**3**	**1**	**0**	**0**	**0**	**0.00**

Hill, Jimmy "Lefty" or "Squab" B: 06/06/1918 Plant City, FL D: 05/31/1993 Sarasota, FL B/T: L/L 5'5" 145 lbs.

NEWARK EAGLES	23	27-Jul-41	0	0	0	0		1.00	0	2	0	2	0	0.00
Player Totals:		**1 Game**	**0**	**0**	**0**	**0**	**.000**	**1.00**	**0**	**2**	**0**	**2**	**0**	**0.00**

Holland, Elvis William "Bill" B: 02/28/1901 Indianapolis, IN D: 12/03/1973 Hamilton Grange, NY B/T: S/R 5'9" 180 lbs.

NEW YORK BLACK YANKEES	38	06-Aug-39	0	0	0	0		0.67	2	0	1	1	1	13.43
Player Totals:		**1 Game**	**0**	**0**	**0**	**0**	**.000**	**0.67**	**2**	**0**	**1**	**1**	**1**	**13.43**

Howard, Candasie Carrenza "Schoolboy" B: 12/16/1920 Daytona Beach, FL D: 10/16/1993 Clair Mel City, FL B/T: R/R 6'2" 210 lbs.

NEW YORK CUBANS	23	13-Aug-44	0	0	0	1		1.67	4	0	0	4	4	21.56
Player Totals:		**1 Game**	**0**	**0**	**0**	**1**	**.000**	**1.67**	**4**	**0**	**0**	**4**	**4**	**21.56**

Hunter, Bertrum "Nate" or "Buffalo" B: 1906 D: B/T: R/R 5'9" 175 lbs.

PITTSBURGH CRAWFORDS	27	10-Sep-33	0	0	0	0		0.67	3	0	0	2	2	26.87
Player Totals:		**1 Game**	**0**	**0**	**0**	**0**	**.000**	**0.67**	**3**	**0**	**0**	**2**	**2**	**26.87**

Hutchinson, Willie "Ace" B: 04/23/1920 D: 10/01/1992 Denver, CO B/T: R/R 5'10" 165 lbs.

MEMPHIS RED SOX	29	14-Aug-49	0	0	0	0		0.33	0	0	0	0	0	0.00
Player Totals:		**1 Game**	**0**	**0**	**0**	**0**	**.000**	**0.33**	**0**	**0**	**0**	**0**	**0**	**0.00**

Jackson, John W. "Stony" B: 06/01/1928 Lumberton, MS Living in Hodge, LA B/T: R/R 5'10" 180 lbs.

KANSAS CITY MONARCHS	24	17-Aug-52	0	0	0	0		3.00	2	2	2	1	1	3.00
KANSAS CITY MONARCHS	25	16-Aug-53	0	0	0	0		3.00	0	0	1	0	0	1.50
Player Totals:		**2 Games**	**0**	**0**	**0**	**0**	**.000**	**6.00**	**2**	**2**	**3**	**1**	**1**	**1.50**

Jessup, Joseph Gentry "Jeep" B: 07/04/1914 Mount Airy, NC D: 03/26/1998 Springfield, MA B/T: R/R 6'0" 180 lbs.

CHICAGO AMERICAN GIANTS	30	13-Aug-44	0	0	1	0		3.00	3	0	2	1	1	3.00
CHICAGO AMERICAN GIANTS	31	29-Jul-45	0	0	0	0		3.00	3	1	2	0	0	1.50
CHICAGO AMERICAN GIANTS	32	15-Aug-46	0	0	0	0		2.67	3	1	1	2	2	3.11
CHICAGO AMERICAN GIANTS	33	27-Jul-47	0	0	0	0		3.00	0	1	0	0	0	2.31
CHICAGO AMERICAN GIANTS	34	22-Aug-48	0	0	0	0		3.00	0	1	1	0	0	1.84
Player Totals:		**5 Games**	**0**	**0**	**1**	**0**	**1.000**	**14.67**	**9**	**4**	**6**	**3**	**3**	**1.84**

Johnson, Clifford "Connie" B: 12/27/1922 Stone Mountain, GA Living in Kansas City, MO B/T: R/R 6'4" 200 lbs.

TOLEDO-INDY CRAWFORDS	17	18-Aug-40	0	0	0	0		0.67	1	1	0	0	0	0.00
KANSAS CITY MONARCHS	27	20-Aug-50	0	0	1	0		3.00	3	3	2	1	1	2.45
Player Totals:		**2 Games**	**0**	**0**	**1**	**0**	**1.000**	**3.67**	**4**	**4**	**2**	**1**	**1**	**2.45**

Johnson, Jimmy "Slim" B: 1922 D: B/T: L/L 6'1" 170 lbs.

TOLEDO-INDY CRAWFORDS	17	27-Aug-39	0	0	0	0		3.67	4	4	3	1	1	2.45
Player Totals:		**1 Game**	**0**	**0**	**0**	**0**	**.000**	**3.67**	**4**	**4**	**3**	**1**	**1**	**2.45**

Jones, Stuart "Slim" B: 05/06/1913 Baltimore, MD D: 12/01/1938 Baltimore, MD B/T: L/L 6'6" 185 lbs.

PHILADELPHIA STARS	21	26-Aug-34	1	0	0	0		3.00	1	4	1	0	0	0.00

PLAYER/TEAM	AGE	DATE	GS	CG	W	L	PCT	IP	H	K	BB	RS	ER	ERA
PHILADELPHIA STARS	22	11-Aug-35	1	0	0	0		3.00	1	1	2	0	0	0.00
Player Totals:	**2 Games**		**2**	**0**	**0**	**0**	**.000**	**6.00**	**2**	**5**	**3**	**0**	**0**	**0.00**

Kincannon, Harry "Tin Can" B: 07/30/1909 D: 10/01/1965 B/T: R/R 5'10" 190 lbs.

PITTSBURGH CRAWFORDS	25	26-Aug-34	0	0	0	0		2.00	4	0	0	0	0	0.00
Player Totals:	**1 Game**		**0**	**0**	**0**	**0**	**.000**	**2.00**	**4**	**0**	**0**	**0**	**0**	**0.00**

Kranson, Floyd Arthur B: 07/24/1913 D: 09/01/1967 B/T: R/R 6'1" 180 lbs.

KANSAS CITY MONARCHS	23	23-Aug-36	0	0	0	0		2.00	4	1	1	4	4	18.00
Player Totals:	**1 Game**		**0**	**0**	**0**	**0**	**.000**	**2.00**	**4**	**1**	**1**	**4**	**4**	**18.00**

LaMarque, James Harding "Lefty" B: 07/29/1921 Potosi, MO D: 01/15/2000 Kansas City, MO B/T: R/L 6'1" 180 lbs.

KANSAS CITY MONARCHS	27	22-Aug-48	0	0	0	0		3.00	2	1	0	0	0	0.00
KANSAS CITY MONARCHS	27	24-Aug-48	0	0	0	0		2.00	3	0	2	2	0	0.00
KANSAS CITY MONARCHS	28	14-Aug-49	0	0	0	0		1.00	1	0	0	0	0	0.00
Player Totals:	**3 Games**		**0**	**0**	**0**	**0**	**.000**	**6.00**	**6**	**1**	**2**	**2**	**0**	**0.00**

Lewis, Rufus "Lew" B: 12/13/1919 Hattiesburg, MS D: 12/17/1999 Detroit, MI B/T: R/R 6'1" 190 lbs.

NEWARK EAGLES	27	29-Jul-47	1	0	0	1		3.00	5	4	1	3	2	6.00
NEWARK EAGLES	28	22-Aug-48	1	0	0	1		3.00	3	4	2	2	2	6.00
Player Totals:	**2 Games**		**2**	**0**	**0**	**2**	**.000**	**6.00**	**8**	**8**	**3**	**5**	**4**	**6.00**

Manning, Maxwell "Max" B: 11/18/1918 Rome, GA Living in Pleasantville, NJ B/T: L/R 6'4" 180 lbs.

NEWARK EAGLES	28	27-Jul-47	1	0	0	1		2.33	5	3	2	4	4	15.45
NEWARK EAGLES	29	24-Aug-48	1	0	1	0		3.00	1	2	1	1	1	8.44
Player Totals:	**2 Games**		**2**	**0**	**1**	**1**	**.500**	**5.33**	**6**	**5**	**3**	**5**	**5**	**8.44**

Mathis, Verdell "Lefty" B: 11/18/1914 Crawfordsville, AR D: 10/30/1998 Memphis, TN B/T: L/L 5'10" 150 lbs.

MEMPHIS RED SOX	27	18-Aug-42	0	0	0	0		3.33	4	2	0	2	0	0.00
MEMPHIS RED SOX	29	13-Aug-44	1	0	0	0		3.00	3	0	0	1	1	1.42
MEMPHIS RED SOX	30	29-Jul-45	1	0	1	0		3.00	0	4	1	0	0	0.96
Player Totals:	**3 Games**		**2**	**0**	**1**	**0**	**1.000**	**9.33**	**7**	**6**	**1**	**3**	**1**	**0.96**

Matlock, Leroy B: 03/12/1907 Moberly, MO D: 02/06/1968 St. Paul, MN B/T: L/L 5'9" 175 lbs.

PITTSBURGH CRAWFORDS	28	11-Aug-35	0	0	0	0		2.00	1	1	0	1	0	0.00
PITTSBURGH CRAWFORDS	29	23-Aug-36	1	0	1	0		3.00	2	0	1	0	0	0.00
Player Totals:	**2 Games**		**1**	**0**	**1**	**0**	**1.000**	**5.00**	**3**	**1**	**1**	**1**	**0**	**0.00**

McDaniels, Booker Taliaferro "Cannonball" B: 09/13/1913 Blackwell, AR D: 12/12/1974 Kansas City, MO B/T: R/R 6'2" 195 lbs.

KANSAS CITY MONARCHS	31	29-Jul-45	0	0	0	0		2.67	6	1	2	6	6	20.22
Player Totals:	**1 Game**		**0**	**0**	**0**	**0**	**.000**	**2.67**	**6**	**1**	**2**	**6**	**6**	**20.22**

McDuffie, Terris Chester "The Great" B: 07/22/1910 Mobile, AL D: 05/01/1968 New York, NY B/T: R/R 6'1" 195 lbs.

NEW YORK BLACK YANKEES	29	27-Aug-39	0	0	0	0		3.00	3	3	2	1	1	3.00
HOMESTEAD GRAYS	31	27-Jul-41	1	0	1	0		2.00	3	0	0	1	1	3.60
NEWARK EAGLES	34	13-Aug-44	1	0	0	0		3.00	5	2	1	2	1	3.38
Player Totals:	**3 Games**		**2**	**0**	**1**	**0**	**1.000**	**8.00**	**11**	**5**	**3**	**4**	**3**	**3.38**

McHenry, Henry "Cream" B: 04/03/1910 D: 02/09/1981 Brooklyn, NY B/T: R/R 6'0" 200 lbs.

PHILADELPHIA STARS	30	18-Aug-40	1	0	1	0		3.00	1	1	1	0	0	0.00
PHILADELPHIA STARS	31	27-Jul-41	0	0	0	0		2.00	2	0	0	0	0	0.00
Player Totals:	**2 Games**		**1**	**0**	**1**	**0**	**1.000**	**5.00**	**3**	**1**	**1**	**0**	**0**	**0.00**

McKinnis, Gread "Lefty" or "Gready" B: 08/11/1913 Union, AL D: 03/08/1991 Chicago, IL B/T: R/L 6'1" 175 lbs.

BIRMINGHAM BLACK BARONS	29	01-Aug-43	0	0	0	0		3.00	1	1	0	0	0	0.00
CHICAGO AMERICAN GIANTS	31	13-Aug-44	0	0	0	0		1.33	4	1	1	2	2	4.16
CHICAGO AMERICAN GIANTS	36	14-Aug-49	0	0	0	0		3.00	4	0	0	2	1	3.68
Player Totals:	**3 Games**		**0**	**0**	**0**	**0**	**.000**	**7.33**	**9**	**2**	**1**	**4**	**3**	**3.68**

PLAYER/TEAM	AGE	DATE	GS	CG	W	L	PCT	IP	H	K	BB	RS	ER	ERA
Miller, Henry Joseph "Hank" B: *07/17/1917 Glenolden, PA* D: *08/30/1972 Philadelphia, PA* B/T: R/R *6'1" 180 lbs.*														
PHILADELPHIA STARS	30	27-Jul-47	0	0	0	0		2.00	2	1	1	0	0	0.00
PHILADELPHIA STARS	30	29-Jul-47	0	0	0	0		1.00	0	0	0	0	0	0.00
Player Totals:	**2 Games**		0	0	0	0	.000	3.00	2	1	1	0	0	0.00
Morris, Barney "Big Ad" B: *06/03/1913 Shreveport, LA* D: B/T: L/R *6'1" 170 lbs.*														
PITTSBURGH CRAWFORDS	24	08-Aug-37	1	0	1	0		3.00	2	2	0	1	1	3.00
NEW YORK CUBANS	31	13-Aug-44	0	0	0	0		1.33	2	1	0	1	1	4.16
Player Totals:	**2 Games**		1	0	1	0	1.000	4.33	4	3	0	2	2	4.16
Moss, Porter "Ankleball" B: *06/19/1910 Cincinnati, OH* D: *07/16/1944 Jackson, TN* B/T: R/R *5'11" 185 lbs.*														
CINCINNATI TIGERS	27	08-Aug-37	0	0	0	0		6.00	9	1	3	4	1	1.50
MEMPHIS RED SOX	32	16-Aug-42	0	0	0	0		2.00	2	2	3	1	1	2.25
MEMPHIS RED SOX	33	01-Aug-43	0	0	0	0		0.33	0	0	0	0	0	2.16
Player Totals:	**3 Games**		0	0	0	0	.000	8.33	11	3	6	5	2	2.16
Owens, Raymond "Smoky" B: *1912 Alabama* D: *09/07/1942 Geneva, OH* B/T: L/L														
CLEVELAND BEARS	27	27-Aug-39	1	0	0	1		1.33	3	0	2	5	3	20.30
Player Totals:	**1 Game**		1	0	0	1	.000	1.33	3	0	2	5	3	20.30
Paige, Leroy Robert "Satchel" B: *07/07/1906 Mobile, AL* D: *06/08/1982 Kansas City, MO* B/T: R/R *6'3.5" 180 lbs.*														
PITTSBURGH CRAWFORDS	28	26-Aug-34	0	0	1	0		4.00	2	5	0	0	0	0.00
PITTSBURGH CRAWFORDS	30	23-Aug-36	0	0	0	0		3.00	2	0	1	0	0	0.00
KANSAS CITY MONARCHS	35	27-Jul-41	0	0	0	0		2.00	1	2	1	0	0	0.00
KANSAS CITY MONARCHS	36	16-Aug-42	0	0	0	1		3.00	5	2	2	3	1	0.75
KANSAS CITY MONARCHS	37	01-Aug-43	1	0	1	0		3.00	0	4	1	0	0	0.60
Player Totals:	**5 Games**		1	0	2	1	.667	15.00	10	13	4	4	1	0.60
Partlow, Roy "Silent Roy" B: *06/08/1911 Washington, GA* D: *04/19/1987 Cherry Hill, NJ* B/T: L/L *6'0" 180 lbs.*														
HOMESTEAD GRAYS	28	06-Aug-39	0	0	0	1		1.33	4	0	0	3	3	20.30
Player Totals:	**1 Game**		0	0	0	1	.000	1.33	4	0	0	3	3	20.30
Phillips, Richard Albaso "Dick" B: — D: — B/T: R/R														
KANSAS CITY MONARCHS		17-Aug-52	1	0	1	0		3.00	3	1	2	1	1	3.00
Player Totals:	**1 Game**		1	0	1	0	1.000	3.00	3	1	2	1	1	3.00
Porter, Andrew "Andy" or "Pullman" B: *03/07/1911 Little Rock, AR Living in Los Angeles, CA* B/T: R/R *6'4" 190 lbs.*														
INDIANAPOLIS CLOWNS	38	14-Aug-49	0	0	0	0		3.00	0	0	1	0	0	0.00
Player Totals:	**1 Game**		0	0	0	0	.000	3.00	0	0	1	0	0	0.00
Powell, William Henry "Bill" B: *05/08/1919 Comer, GA Living in Birmingham, AL* B/T: R/R *6'2" 180 lbs.*														
BIRMINGHAM BLACK BARONS	29	22-Aug-48	1	0	1	0		3.00	1	2	1	0	0	0.00
BIRMINGHAM BLACK BARONS	31	20-Aug-50	0	0	0	0		3.00	2	4	1	1	1	1.50
Player Totals:	**2 Games**		1	0	1	0	1.000	6.00	3	6	2	1	1	1.50
Radcliffe, Theodore Roosevelt "Double Duty" B: *07/07/1902 Mobile, AL Living in Chicago, IL* B/T: R/R *5'10" 190 lbs.*														
MEMPHIS RED SOX	36	21-Aug-38	0	0	0	0		4.00	3	0	0	0	0	0.00
MEMPHIS RED SOX	37	06-Aug-39	0	0	1	0		3.00	1	1	2	0	0	0.00
MEMPHIS RED SOX	39	27-Jul-41	0	0	0	0		0.67	4	1	1	6	2	2.35
Player Totals:	**3 Games**		0	0	1	0	1.000	7.67	8	2	3	6	2	2.35
Richardson, Norval Eugene "Gene" or "Britches" B: *01/26/1928 San Diego, CA* D: *08/01/1997 Paradise Hills, CA* B/T: L/L *5'10" 170 lbs.*														
KANSAS CITY MONARCHS	21	14-Aug-49	1	0	0	1		3.00	4	2	2	2	1	3.00
Player Totals:	**1 Game**		1	0	0	1	.000	3.00	4	2	2	2	1	3.00
Richardson, T.W. "Ted" or "Lefty" B: *12/15/1928* D: *05/01/1974 Cincinnati, OH* B/T: R/L														
INDIANAPOLIS CLOWNS	23	17-Aug-52	0	0	0	0		4.00	0	2	2	0	0	0.00
Player Totals:	**1 Game**		0	0	0	0	.000	4.00	0	2	2	0	0	0.00

PLAYER/TEAM	AGE	DATE	GS	CG	W	L	PCT	IP	H	K	BB	RS	ER	ERA
Ricks, William "Bill" B: — D:— B/T: R/R 6'1" 190 lbs.														
PHILADELPHIA STARS		29-Jul-45	0	0	0	0		1.00	5	0	1	4	4	36.00
Player Totals:		1 Game	0	0	0	0	.000	1.00	5	0	1	4	4	**36.00**
Ruiz, Silvino "Poppa" B: — D: — B/T: R/R														
NEW YORK CUBANS		18-Aug-40	0	0	0	0		3.00	2	0	2	0	0	0.00
Player Totals:		1 Game	0	0	0	0	.000	3.00	2	0	2	0	0	**0.00**
Scantlebury, Patricio Athlestan "Pat" B: 11/11/1917 Colon, Panama Canal Zo D: 04/24/1991 Glen Ridge, NJ B/T: L/L 6'1" 180 lbs.														
NEW YORK CUBANS	28	15-Aug-46	0	0	0	0		0.33	3	0	0	3	2	54.55
NEW YORK CUBANS	31	14-Aug-49	0	0	0	0		3.00	2	1	0	0	0	5.41
NEW YORK CUBANS	32	20-Aug-50	0	0	0	0		1.00	0	1	0	0	0	4.16
Player Totals:		3 Games	0	0	0	0	.000	4.33	5	2	0	3	2	**4.16**
Searcy, Kelton "Kelly" or "Lefty" B: 04/17/1921 Nashville, TN D: 10/01/1970 B/T: L/L 5'11" 180 lbs.														
BALTIMORE ELITE GIANTS	30	12-Aug-51	0	0	1	0		3.00	2	1	1	1	0	0.00
Player Totals:		1 Game	0	0	1	0	1.000	3.00	2	1	1	1	0	**0.00**
Smith, Eugene L. "Gene" B: 04/23/1917 Ansley, LA Living in Vinita Park, MO B/T: S/R 6'1" 185 lbs.														
NEW YORK BLACK YANKEES	25	18-Aug-42	1	0	1	0		3.00	3	2	3	2	0	0.00
Player Totals:		1 Game	1	0	1	0	1.000	3.00	3	2	3	2	0	**0.00**
Smith, Hilton Lee "Smitty" B: 02/27/1907 Giddings, TX D: 11/18/1983 Kansas City, MO B/T: R/R 5'11" 185 lbs.														
KANSAS CITY MONARCHS	30	08-Aug-37	0	0	0	1		0.00	1	0	2	2	1	0.00
KANSAS CITY MONARCHS	31	21-Aug-38	0	0	1	0		4.00	3	3	0	1	1	4.50
KANSAS CITY MONARCHS	32	06-Aug-39	0	0	0	0		3.00	0	3	0	0	0	2.57
KANSAS CITY MONARCHS	32	27-Aug-39	0	0	0	0		3.00	4	0	1	4	3	4.50
KANSAS CITY MONARCHS	33	18-Aug-40	0	0	0	0		3.00	4	3	0	3	2	4.85
KANSAS CITY MONARCHS	34	27-Jul-41	1	0	0	1		3.00	2	3	0	2	0	3.94
KANSAS CITY MONARCHS	35	16-Aug-42	1	0	0	0		3.00	4	3	0	1	1	3.79
Player Totals:		7 Games	2	0	1	2	.333	19.00	18	15	3	13	8	**3.79**
Smith, John Ford "Geronimo" or "Lefty" B: 01/09/1919 Phoenix, AZ D: 02/26/1983 Phoenix, AZ B/T: S/L 6'1" 200 lbs.														
KANSAS CITY MONARCHS	28	29-Jul-47	1	0	1	0		3.00	4	2	2	2	2	6.00
Player Totals:		1 Game	1	0	1	0	1.000	3.00	4	2	2	2	2	**6.00**
Smith, Theolic "Fireball" B: 05/19/1913 Wabbesika, AR D: 11/03/1981 Compton, CA B/T: S/R 6'0" 175 lbs.														
ST. LOUIS STARS	26	06-Aug-39	1	0	0	0		3.00	4	1	1	2	1	3.00
CLEVELAND BUCKEYES	30	01-Aug-43	0	0	0	0		2.67	3	2	1	1	1	3.17
KANSAS CITY MONARCHS	38	12-Aug-51	1	0	0	0		3.00	2	2	1	0	0	2.08
Player Totals:		3 Games	2	0	0	0	.000	8.67	9	5	3	3	2	**2.08**
Streeter, Samuel "Lefty" B: 09/17/1900 New Market, AL D: 08/09/1985 Pittsburgh, PA B/T: R/L 5'7" 170 lbs.														
PITTSBURGH CRAWFORDS	32	10-Sep-33	1	0	0	1		5.33	8	4	0	6	6	10.13
Player Totals:		1 Game	1	0	0	1	.000	5.33	8	4	0	6	6	**10.13**
Taylor, Johnny Arthur "School Boy" B: 02/04/1916 Hartford, CN D: 06/15/1987 Hartford, CN B/T: R/R 6'0" 165 lbs.														
PITTSBURGH CRAWFORDS	22	21-Aug-38	0	0	0	0		2.00	3	2	1	0	0	0.00
Player Totals:		1 Game	0	0	0	0	.000	2.00	3	2	1	0	0	**0.00**
Thompson, Frank "Groundhog" B: 10/23/1918 Maryville, LA Living in Shelbyville, TN B/T: L/L 5'4" 150 lbs.														
BIRMINGHAM BLACK BARONS	33	17-Aug-52	1	0	0	1		2.00	7	1	2	7	3	13.50
Player Totals:		1 Game	1	0	0	1	.000	2.00	7	1	2	7	3	**13.50**
Tiant Sr., Luis Eleuterio "Sir Skinny" B: 08/27/1906 Havana, Cuba D: 12/10/1976 Milton, MA B/T: R/L 5'10" 150 lbs.														
NEW YORK CUBANS	28	11-Aug-35	0	0	0	0		2.00	1	0	2	3	3	13.50
NEW YORK CUBANS	40	27-Jul-47	0	0	0	0		2.67	2	0	0	0	0	5.78
NEW YORK CUBANS	40	29-Jul-47	0	0	0	0		2.00	4	0	0	3	3	8.10
Player Totals:		3 Games	0	0	0	0	.000	6.67	7	0	2	6	6	**8.10**

PLAYER/TEAM	AGE	DATE	GS	CG	W	L	PCT	IP	H	K	BB	RS	ER	ERA
Trent, Ted "Highpockets" B: *12/17/1903 Jacksonville, FL* D: *01/10/1944 Chicago, IL* B/T: R/R *6'3" 185 lbs.*														
CHICAGO AMERICAN GIANTS	30	26-Aug-34	1	0	0	0		3.00	2	3	0	0	0	0.00
CHICAGO AMERICAN GIANTS	31	11-Aug-35	0	0	0	0		2.00	0	1	2	0	0	0.00
CHICAGO AMERICAN GIANTS	32	23-Aug-36	0	0	0	0		3.00	3	1	1	4	2	2.25
CHICAGO AMERICAN GIANTS	33	08-Aug-37	1	0	0	0		3.00	2	0	0	1	1	2.45
Player Totals:	**4 Games**		**2**	**0**	**0**	**0**	**.000**	**11.00**	**7**	**5**	**3**	**5**	**3**	**2.45**
Tugerson, Joseph Leander B: *06/05/1922 Florence Villa, FL* D: *11/01/1985 Florence Villa, FL* B/T: R/R *6'1" 165 lbs.*														
INDIANAPOLIS CLOWNS	29	12-Aug-51	1	0	0	0		3.00	2	1	0	0	0	0.00
Player Totals:	**1 Game**		**1**	**0**	**0**	**0**	**.000**	**3.00**	**2**	**1**	**0**	**0**	**0**	**0.00**
Vargas, Roberto Enrique B: *05/29/1929 Santurce, PR Living in Guaynabo, PR* B/T: L/L *5'11" 175 lbs.*														
CHICAGO AMERICAN GIANTS	19	24-Aug-48	0	0	0	0		1.00	0	0	1	0	0	0.00
Player Totals:	**1 Game**		**0**	**0**	**0**	**0**	**.000**	**1.00**	**0**	**0**	**1**	**0**	**0**	**0.00**
Walker, Edsall Elliott "Big" B: *09/15/1910 Catskill, NY* D: *02/19/1997 Catskill, NY* B/T: R/L *5'11" 215 lbs.*														
HOMESTEAD GRAYS	27	21-Aug-38	1	0	0	1		3.00	4	3	3	5	5	15.00
Player Totals:	**1 Game**		**1**	**0**	**0**	**1**	**.000**	**3.00**	**4**	**3**	**3**	**5**	**5**	**15.00**
Welmaker, Roy Horace "Snook" or "Lefty" B: *12/06/1913 Atlanta, GA* D: *02/03/1998 Decatur, GA* B/T: S/L *5'9" 165 lbs.*														
HOMESTEAD GRAYS	31	29-Jul-45	0	0	0	0		2.00	0	0	1	0	0	0.00
Player Totals:	**1 Game**		**0**	**0**	**0**	**0**	**.000**	**2.00**	**0**	**0**	**1**	**0**	**0**	**0.00**
Williams, Johnny "Nature Boy" B: *1916 Shreveport, LA* D: B/T: R/R *6'2" 210 lbs.*														
INDIANAPOLIS CLOWNS	30	15-Aug-46	0	0	0	0		2.00	1	0	0	0	0	0.00
INDIANAPOLIS CLOWNS	30	18-Aug-46	0	0	0	0		3.00	2	0	1	1	1	1.80
INDIANAPOLIS CLOWNS	31	29-Jul-47	0	0	0	0		2.00	2	0	5	0	0	1.29
Player Totals:	**3 Games**		**0**	**0**	**0**	**0**	**.000**	**7.00**	**5**	**0**	**6**	**1**	**1**	**1.29**
Woods, Sam "Buddy" B: *1922* D: *Philadelphia, PA* B/T: R/R *6'2" 205 lbs.*														
MEMPHIS RED SOX	31	16-Aug-53	1	0	1	0		3.00	4	1	0	1	1	3.00
Player Totals:	**1 Game**		**1**	**0**	**1**	**0**	**1.000**	**3.00**	**4**	**1**	**0**	**1**	**1**	**3.00**
Wright, John Richard "Johnny" B: *11/28/1916 New Orleans, LA* D: *05/10/1990 Jackson, MS* B/T: R/R *5'11" 175 lbs.*														
HOMESTEAD GRAYS	26	01-Aug-43	0	0	0	0		2.00	2	2	0	1	1	4.50
HOMESTEAD GRAYS	30	27-Jul-47	0	0	0	0		1.00	3	0	0	1	1	6.00
Player Totals:	**2 Games**		**0**	**0**	**0**	**0**	**.000**	**3.00**	**5**	**2**	**0**	**2**	**2**	**6.00**
Grand Total:			**52**	**1**	**26**	**26**	**.500**	**458.2/3**	**446**	**251**	**163**	**228**	**168**	**3.30**

All-Star Leaders, 1933–1953

INDIVIDUAL BATTING

Most Games
13, Buck Leonard, 1935–48
13, Alec Radcliffe, 1933–46
12, Josh Gibson, 1933–46
10, Willie Wells, 1933–45
10, Henry Kimbro, 1941–53

Most At Bats, Career
50, Alec Radcliffe, 13 games
48, Buck Leonard, 13 games
40, Willie Wells, 10 games
37, Josh Gibson, 12 games
32, Bill Wright, 9 games
31, Sam Bankhead, 9 games

Most At Bats, Game
6, Jake Stephens, 8–11–1935
6, Gene Benson, 8–18–1940
6, Dan Wilson, 8–18–1942

Most Runs Scored, Career
9, Buck Leonard, 13 games
8, Josh Gibson, 12 games
7, Artie Wilson, 7 games
7, Neal Robinson, 9 games
7, Sam Bankhead, 9 games
7, Willie Wells, 10 games

Most Runs Scored, Game
4, Artie Wilson, 7–29–1947
3, Josh Gibson, 8–11–1935
3, Mule Suttles, 8–11–1935
3, Dan Wilson, 8–16–1942

Most Hits, Career
17, Josh Gibson, 12 games
17, Alec Radcliffe, 13 games
15, Buck Leonard, 13 games
13, Willie Wells, 10 games
12, Sam Bankhead, 9 games
12, Neal Robinson, 9 games

Most Hits, Game
4, Josh Gibson, 8–11–1935
4, Artie Wilson, 7–29–1947

Most Consecutive Appearances
with a Hit
9, Alec Radcliffe, 1935–45
7, Willie Wells, 1937–45
6, Buck Leonard, 1939–45
6, Josh Gibson, 1939–46

Most Doubles, Career
7, Willie Wells, 10 games
4, Josh Gibson, 12 games
3, Bill Wright, 9 games
3, Piper Davis, 7 games
3, Dan Wilson, 5 games

Most Doubles, Game
3, Willie Wells, 8–18–1942

Most Triples, Career
2, Sam Jethroe, 7 games

Most Triples, Game
Several tied at 1

Most Home Runs, Career
3, Buck Leonard, 13 games
2, Mule Suttles, 5 games
2, Neal Robinson, 9 games

Most Home Runs, Game
Several tied at 1

Most Walks, Career
10, Josh Gibson, 12 games
7, Quincy Trouppe, 8 games
7, Buck Leonard, 13 games
6, Mule Suttles, 5 games

Most Walks, Game
4, Mule Suttles, 8–11–35
3, Quincy Trouppe, 7–29–45

Most RBIs, Career
14, Buck Leonard, 13 games,
48 ab
9, Alec Radcliffe, 13 games, 51 ab
8, Josh Gibson, 12 games, 38 ab
7, Willie Wells, 10 games, 40 ab
6, Mule Suttles 5 games, 17 ab

Most RBIs, Game
4, Josh Gibson, 8–27–1939
4, Jesse Williams, 7–29–1945
4, Sam Jethroe, 7–29–1947
3, Mule Suttles, 9–10–1933
3, Mule Suttles, 8–11–1935
3, Jud Wilson, 9–10–1933
3, Alec Radcliffe, 8–11–1935
3, Neal Robinson, 8–21–1938
3, Buck Leonard, 8–18–1940
3, Buck Leonard, 7–27–1941
3, Rabbit Martinez, 7–29–1945
3, Archie Ware, 7–29–1945

Most Total Bases, Career
27, Buck Leonard, 13 games
23, Josh Gibson, 12 games
22, Willie Wells, 10 games
21, Alec Radcliffe, 13 games
19, Neal Robinson, 9 games

Most Total Bases, Game
7, Neal Robinson, 8–6–1939
6, Neal Robinson, 8–21–1938
6, Mule Suttles, 9–10–1933
6, Josh Gibson, 8–11–1935
6, Willie Wells, 8–18–1942
6, Alec Radcliffe, 8–13–1944

Most Stolen Bases, Career
4, Pat Patterson, 6 games
4, Henry Kimbro, 10 games

3, Artie Wilson, 7 games
3, Sam Jethroe, 7 games

Most Stolen Bases, Game
2, Henry Milton, 8–21–1938
2, Buck Leonard, 8–18–1940
2, Henry Kimbro, 7–27–1941
2, Dan Wilson, 8–16–1942
2, Pat Patterson, 8–18–1942
2, Artie Wilson, 7–29–1942
2, Jesse Douglas, 8–20–1950

Batting Averages over .400
(minimum 15 ABs)
.500, Neal Robinson, 9 games
.459, Josh Gibson, 12 games
.423, Artie Wilson, 7 games
.412, Mule Suttles, 5 games

Slugging Percentage over .500
(minimum 15 ABs)
.941, Mule Suttles, 5 games
.792, Neal Robinson, 9 games
.622, Josh Gibson, 12 games
.609, Ted Strong, 7 games
.563, Buck Leonard, 13 games
.550, Dan Wilson, 5 games
.550, Willie Wells, 10 games

CLUB BATTING

Most Official At-Bats, 9 Inning
Game, One Club
43, East Squad, 8–18–1940

Most Official At-Bats, 9 Inning
Game, Both Clubs
76, East 40, West 36, 7–27–1941

Fewest Official At-Bats, 9 Inning
Game, One Club
26, West Squad, 8–1–1943
26, West Squad, 8–18–1946

Fewest Official At-Bats, 9 Inning
Game, Both Clubs
55, East 29, West 26, 8–18–1946

Most Runs Scored, Game, One Club
11, West, 9–10–1933
11, West, 8–11–1935
11, East, 8–18–1940

Most Runs Scored, 9 Inning Game,
Both Clubs
18, West 11, East 7, 9–10–1933

Most Runs Scored, Inning, One
Club
6, East, 4th inning, 7–27–1941
6, West, 3rd inning, 8–17–1952

Most Runs Scored, Inning, Both
Clubs
8, 10th inning, 8–11–1935

Most Hits, Game, One Club

15, West, 9-10-1933

14, East, 8-18-1940

14, West, 7-29-1947

14, East, 8-23-1936

14, West, 8-13-44

Most Hits, Game, Both Clubs

25, East 11, West 14, 8-13-1944

Fewest Hits, Game, One Club

2, West, 8-14-1949

3, East, 7-27-1947

3, East, 8-22-1948

Fewest Hits, Game, Both Clubs

10, East 4, West 6, 8-1-1943

10, East 3, West 7, 8-22-1948

Most Singles, Game, One Club

12, by East, 8-18-1940

Most Singles, Game, Both Clubs

18, 8-11-1935, East 10, West 8

18, 7-29-1945, East 9, West 9

18, 7-29-1947, West 11, East 7

Most Doubles, Game, One Club

5, West, 9-10-1933

5, East, 8-23-1936

Most Doubles, Game, Both Clubs

6, East 5, West 1, 8-23-1936

Most Triples, Game, One Club

3, West, 7-27-1947

Most Triples, Game, Both Clubs

3, East 2, West 1, 8-13-1944

3, West 3, East 0, 7-27-1947

Most Home Runs, Game, One Club

2, West, 8-6-1939

Most Home Runs, Game, Both Clubs

2, East 1, West 1, 8-11-1935

2, East 1, West 1, 8-8-1937

2, East 0, West 2, 8-6-1939

Most RBIs, Game, One Club

10, West, 8-11-1935

10, East, 8-27-1939

10, East, 8-18-1940

Most RBIs, Game, Both Clubs

17, East 7, West 10, 8-11-1935

Most Total Bases, Game, One Club

26, West, 9-10-1933

Most Total Bases, Game, Both Clubs

37, 8-13-1944

No extra bases by either club

8-15-1946

INDIVIDUAL PITCHING

Most Games Pitched, Career

9, Leon Day, 1935-46

7, Bill Byrd, 1936-46

7, Hilton Smith, 1937-42

Most Complete Games

1, Willie Foster, 1933

Most Games Won

2, Dan Bankhead, 1946, 1947

2, Bill Byrd, 1939, 1946

2, Satchel Paige, 1934, 1943

Most Games Lost

3, Vibert Clarke, 1946, 1948, 1951

2, Hilton Smith, 1937, 1941

2, Rufus Lewis, 1947, 1948

2, Gene Bremer, 1940, 1942

Most Innings Pitched, Career

21 1/3, Leon Day, 9 games

19, Hilton Smith, 7 games

16, Bill Byrd, 7 games

15, Satchel Paige, 5 games

14 2/3, Gentry Jessup, 5 games

14, Dave Barnhill, 5 games

Most Innings Pitched, Game

9, Willie Foster, 9-10-1933

Most Hits Allowed, Career

18, Hilton Smith, 7 games

18, Bill Byrd, 7 games

15, Vibert Clarke, 5 games

13, Leon Day, 9 games

Most Hits Allowed, Game

9, Porter Moss in 6 innings,
8-8-37

7, Willie Foster in 9 innings,
9-10-33

7, Frank Thompson in 2 innings,
8-17-52

Least Hits per Nine Innings, Career

(minimum 9 innings)

4.0, Jonas Gaines, 11 1/3 innings

4.9, Dan Bankhead, 11 innings

5.5, Gentry Jessup, 14 2/3
innings

5.5, Leon Day, 21 1/3 innings

5.7, Barney Brown, 12 2/3
innings

5.7, Ted Trent, 11 innings

Most Strikeouts, Career

23, Leon Day, 21 1/3 innings

15, Hilton Smith, 19 innings

13, Satchel Paige, 15 innings

11, Dave Barnhill, 14 innings

10, Bill Byrd, 16 innings

Most Strikeouts, Game

5, Satchel Paige in 4 innings,
8-26-34

5, Leon Day in 2 1/3 innings,
8-16-42

5, Leon Day in 2 innings,
8-18-42

Most Strikeouts per Nine Innings,
Career

(minimum 9 innings)

9.7, Leon Day, 21 1/3 innings

7.8, Satchel Paige, 15 innings

7.1, Dave Barnhill, 14 innings

7.1, Hilton Smith, 19 innings

Most Walks, Career

7, Hilton Smith, 7 games

6, Bill Byrd, 7 games

6, Porter Moss, 3 games

6, Gentry Jessup, 5 games

6, Johnny Williams, 3 games

Most Walks, Game

5, Johnny Williams in 2 innings,
7-29-47

4, Willy Gaines in 3 innings,
8-16-53

Least Walks per Nine Innings,
Career

(minimum 9 innings)

0.0, Jonas Gaines, 11 1/3 innings

0.6, Dave Barnhill, 14 innings

1.0, Verdell Mathis, 9 1/3 innings

1.4, Hilton Smith, 19 innings

2.0, Joe Black, 9 innings

2.1, Barney Brown, 12 2/3
innings

Lowest ERA, Career

(minimum 9 innings, and less than
2 runs)

0.00, Jonas Gaines, 11 1/3
innings

0.60, Satchel Paige, 15 innings

0.71, Barney Brown, 11 2/3
innings

0.84, Leon Day, 21 1/3 innings

0.96, Verdell Mathis, 9 1/3
innings

1.29, Dave Barnhill, 14 innings

1.84, Gentry Jessup, 14 2/3
innings

Most starts by a pitcher

2, Dan Bankhead, 1946, 1947

2, Gene Bremer, 1940, 1942

2, Barney Brown, 1946 (both
games)

2, Bill Byrd, 1939 (both games)

2, Vibert Clarke, 1948, 1950

2, Sug Cornelius, 1936, 1938

2, Slim Jones, 1934, 1935

2, Rufus Lewis, 1947, 1948

2, Max Manning, 1947, 1948

2, Verdell Mathis, 1944, 1945

2, Terris McDuffie, 1941, 1944

2, Hilton Smith, 1941, 1942

2, Theolic Smith, 1939, 1951
2, Ted Trent, 1934, 1937
Pitchers, 40 years and older
40, Chet Brewer in 1947
40, Luis Tiant Sr. in 1947
43, George Britt in 1933
44, Spoon Carter in 1947

Leading East-West Hitters by Position

Minimum of 9 at bats, batting .300 or More (pitchers only require 5 at bats)

POSITION	NAME	G	AB	R	H	D	T	HR	RBI	AVG	SLG
Pitchers	Verdell Mathis	3	5	1	3	0	0	0	0	.600	.600
	Barney Brown	5	5	0	2	0	0	0	0	.400	.400
	Willie Foster *	2	5	1	2	0	0	0	0	.400	.400
	Satchel Paige *	5	6	0	2	1	0	0	0	.333	.500
Catchers	Josh Gibson *	12	37	8	17	4	1	0	8	.459	.622
	Ted Radcliffe	3	10	1	3	0	0	1	2	.300	.600
	Roy Campanella *	2	10	1	3	0	0	0	0	.300	.300
1st Basemen	Doc Dennis	3	12	2	4	1	0	0	0	.333	.417
	Buck Leonard *	13	48	9	15	1	1	3	14	.313	.563
2nd Basemen	Ray Neil	3	10	3	6	1	1	0	2	.600	.900
	Sam Bankhead	4	14	4	5	1	0	0	3	.357	.429
	Jesse Williams	2	9	1	3	0	1	0	4	.333	.556
	Piper Davis	7	26	5	8	3	0	0	4	.308	.423
3rd Basemen	Ray Dandridge *	2	10	1	5	1	0	0	1	.500	.600
	Jud Wilson	3	11	2	5	0	0	0	5	.455	.455
	Howard Easterling	5	21	4	8	0	0	0	4	.381	.381
	Alec Radcliffe	13	50	7	16	2	1	0	9	.340	.420
	Minnie Minoso *	4	13	1	4	2	0	0	0	.308	.462
Shortstops	Rabbit Martinez *	5	11	2	6	0	0	0	3	.545	.545
	Artie Wilson *	7	26	7	11	0	0	0	2	.423	.423
	Willie Wells *	9	35	7	12	6	1	0	5	.343	.571
Left Fielders	Jose Colas	2	9	0	3	0	0	0	3	.333	.333
	Vic Harris	4	10	2	3	1	0	0	0	.300	.400
Center Fielders	Neal Robinson	8	21	7	11	1	0	2	5	.524	.857
	Bill Wright *	4	16	4	7	2	0	0	2	.438	.563
	Willard Brown *	3	10	2	3	0	0	0	0	.300	.300
Right Fielders	Ted Strong	3	10	1	5	1	1	0	1	.500	.800
	Henry Milton	3	10	2	3	0	0	0	0	.300	.300
TOTALS	Pitchers		165	12	32	4	2	1	8	.194	.261
	Catchers		186	18	49	9	3	1	18	.263	.360
	First Basemen		205	30	54	6	2	5	33	.263	.385
	Second Basemen		199	27	56	13	2	1	31	.281	.382
	Third Basemen		206	24	61	8	3	0	31	.296	.364
	Shortstops		201	28	42	7	1	0	14	.209	.254
	Left Fielders		185	25	44	11	1	2	23	.238	.341
	Center Fielders		211	36	64	7	2	3	31	.303	.398
	Right Fielders		213	29	54	11	3	1	26	.254	.347
	Excluding pinchhitters and pinchrunners		1771	229	446	76	19	14	215	.257	.346

*Hall of Famers in various countries

All-Star Home Runs (1933–1953)

1933 Mule Suttles (West) off Sam Streeter

1934 none

1935 Slim Jones (East) off Ray Brown; Mule Suttles (West) off Martin Dihigo

1936 none

1937 Buck Leonard (East) off Ted Trent; Ted Strong (West) off Barney Brown (Strong's HR was inside-the-park)

1938 Neal Robinson (West) off Barney Brown (inside the park)

1939 (1st game), Neal Robinson (West) off Roy Partlow; Dan Wilson (West) off Roy Partlow

1939 (2nd game), none

1940 none

1941 Buck Leonard (East) off Ted Radcliffe

1942 (1st game), none

1942 (2nd game), none

1943 Buck Leonard (East) off Theolic Smith

1944 Ted Radcliffe (West) off Barney Morris

1945 none

1946 (1st game), none

1946 (2nd game), none

1947 (1st game), none

1947 (2nd game), none

1948 (1st game), none

1948 (2nd game), Luis Marquez (East) off Vibert Clarke

1949 none

1950 Junior Gilliam (East) off Vibert Clarke

1951 none

1952 none

1953 none

Vibert Clarke and Barney Brown each gave up two home runs

All-Star Trivia

Willie Foster pitched the only complete game in all-star history in 1933.

Of the starting nine for the first game, seven of the players were from the Chicago American Giants: Larry Brown, Steel Arm Davis, Willie Foster, Alec Radcliffe, Turkey Stearnes, Mule Suttles, and Willie Wells.

A record 10 Pittsburgh Crawfords appeared in the 1934 contest: Cool Papa Bell, Oscar Charleston, Jimmie Crutchfield, Rap Dixon, Josh Gibson, Vic Harris, Slim Jones, Harry Kincannon, Satchel Paige, Cy Perkins, and Ches Williams.

In 1935 Slim Jones became the only pitcher to hit a home run in all-star competition, when he slammed one off Ray Brown.

The first future major league players to appear in the East-West classic were Satchel Paige and Willard Brown in 1936, 12 years before the color barrier was broken.

In 1937 the Radcliffe brothers, Chicago American Giants' Alec (3b) and Cincinnati Tigers' Ted (c), became the first siblings to appear in the same East-West All-Star game.

Later, in 1943, Alec and Ted Radcliffe became the first brothers to represent the same team, the Chicago American Giants.

In 1939 the Negro Leagues played two all-star games, one in New York and the other in Chicago. This was 20 years before the Major Leagues would play two all-star games. In 1959 the first major league game was played at Forbes Field in Pittsburgh and the second at the Los Angeles Coliseum. In 1942 three East-West games were scheduled, but the third game, in Memphis, was rained out.

The Bankhead family had the most brothers—three—to play in all-star competition: Dan in four games, Fred in two, and Sam with nine appearances.

In the 1941 contest, the West team used 23 players. This record number of players included five pitchers, three pinch-hitters and one pinch-runner. The West squad lost 8–3.

A record 10 pitchers were used in the 1941 game.

The 1935 game showcased eight future Hall of Famers (as of this writing): Ray Dandridge, Leon Day, and

Martin Dihigo for the East; Cool Papa Bell, Oscar Charleston, Josh Gibson, Buck Leonard, and Willie Wells for the West. Satchel Paige did not appear in the game.

In the 1946 contest, held at Griffith Stadium in Washington DC, no player recorded an extra base hit.

The shortstops and third basemen are the only positions that failed to hit a home run in all-star history.

The shortest players in East-West history were Lloyd "Ducky" Davenport, Frank "Groundhog" Thompson, and Murray "Skeeter" Watkins at five feet, four inches.

The tallest players in East-West history were Slim Jones and Ted Strong, both at six feet, six inches.

The oldest player-manager to perform was Biz Mackey in the July 27, 1947, contest. He received a ceremonial walk in his only plate appearance to celebrate his 50th birthday.

Based on available information, the youngest performer in an all-star game was Connie Johnson. Johnson was 17 years old when he made an appearance in the 1940 game for the Toledo-Indianapolis Crawfords.

The versatile Ted "Double Duty" Radcliffe lived up to his name by pitching in three games and catching in three all-star games.

Catchers Quincy Trouppe, Josh Gibson, and Roy Campanella also played other positions. Trouppe played left field in the 1938 game, Gibson played left field in the 1934 game, and Campy played the hot corner in the 1944 contest.

Junior Gilliam is the only man in baseball history to hit a home run in both Negro League (8–20–50, Comiskey Park) and Major League (8–3–59, Los Angeles Park) all-star games.

In the 1947 game at Yankee Stadium, Artie Wilson, the last .400 hitter in Negro League history, went 4 for 4 and scored four runs.

The second all-star game of 1948, played at Yankee Stadium featured the most future major leaguers, 14: Joe Black, Bob Boyd, Willard Brown, Vibert Clarke, George Crowe, Luke Easter, Junior Gilliam, Sam

Hairston, Monte Irvin, Luis Marquez, Minnie Minoso, Quincy Trouppe, Roberto Vargas, and Artie Wilson.

The 1950 all-star game featured the most future major league pitchers, 4: starters Joe Black and Vibert Clarke, and relievers Connie Johnson and Pat Scantlebury.

The 1953 game featured the last Hall of Famer to play in an East-West all-star classic: Ernie Banks.

Jonas Gaines is the only pitcher with no earned runs or walks to pitch more than nine innings.

Alec Radcliffe played on the most winning teams: 8.

Buck Leonard played on the most losing teams: 7.

Sammy T. Hughes played for four different Elite Giant franchises: Nashville, Columbus, Washington and Baltimore.

First Shutout: 1934, East over West, 1–0.

First Game with No Extra-Base Hits: 1946 (1), East over West, 5 to 3, at Griffith Stadium, Washington DC.

First Extra Inning Game: 1935, West over East, 11–8, 11 innings.

First Night Game: 1942, August 18, Municipal Stadium, Cleveland OH.

Earliest Date for Game: July 27 in 1941 and 1947 (1)
Latest Date for Game: September 10, 1933.

Lowest Attendance: 1953, 10,000 estimated fans
Highest Attendance: 1943, 51,723 fans

Future Major Leaguers Who Appeared in East-West All-Star Games

1936 Satchel Paige, Willard Brown (2)

1937 Willard Brown

1938 Quincy Trouppe

1940 Bus Clarkson, Connie Johnson (2)

1941 Dan Bankhead, Satchel Paige (2)

1942 Willard Brown, Sam Jethroe, Satchel Paige (3)

1943 Willard Brown, Satchel Paige (2)

1944 Sam Jethroe, Artie Wilson (2)

1945 Roy Campanella, Jackie Robinson, Quincy Trouppe (3)

1946 Artie Wilson, Sam Jethroe, Quincy Trouppe, Vibert Clarke, Larry Doby, Monte Irvin, Pat Scantlebury,
      Dan Bankhead (8)

1947 Monte Irvin, Minnie Minoso, Artie Wilson, Sam Jethroe, Quincy Trouppe, Dan Bankhead, Bob Boyd,
      Vibert Clarke, Joe Black, Luis Marquez (10)

1948 Luis Marquez, Minnie Minoso, Luke Easter, Monte Irvin, Junior Gilliam, Artie Wilson, Willard Brown,
      Bob Boyd, Quincy Trouppe, Roberto Vargas, Sam Hairston, Vibert Clarke, George Crowe, Joe Black (14)

1949 Bus Clarkson, Junior Gilliam, Pat Scantlebury, Bob Boyd, Willard Brown (5)

1950 Junior Gilliam, Joe Black, Pat Scantlebury, Vibert Clarke, Connie Johnson (5)

1951 Milt Smith, Vibert Clarke, Jay Heard (3)

1952 Winn "Pop" Durham

1953 Ernie Banks, Pancho Herrera (2)

1954 John Kennedy, Pancho Herrera, Hank Mason (3)

1955 J. C. Hartman, Lou Johnson, Satchel Paige (3)

All-Stars and Their Major League Debuts

1. Jackie Robinson, **Brooklyn Dodgers**, April 15, 1947
2. Larry Doby, **Cleveland Indians**, July 5, 1947
3. Willard Brown, **St. Louis Browns**, July 19, 1947
4. Dan Bankhead, Brooklyn Dodgers, August 26, 1947
5. Roy Campanella, Brooklyn Dodgers, April 20, 1948
6. Satchel Paige, Cleveland Indians, July 9, 1948
7. Minnie Minoso, Cleveland Indians, April 19, 1949
8. Don Newcombe, Brooklyn Dodgers, May 20, 1949
9. Monte Irvin, **New York Giants**, July 8, 1949
10. Luke Easter, Cleveland Indians, August 11, 1949
11. Sam Jethroe, **Boston Braves**, April 18, 1950
12. Luis Marquez, Boston Braves, April 18, 1951
13. Artie Wilson, New York Giants, April 18, 1951
14. Harry Simpson, Cleveland Indians, April 21, 1951
15. Willie Mays, New York Giants, May 25, 1951
16. Sam Hairston, **Chicago White Sox**, July 21, 1951
17. Bob Boyd, Chicago White Sox, September 8, 1951
18. George Crowe, Boston Braves, April 16, 1952
19. Bus Clarkson, Boston Braves, April 30, 1952
20. Quincy Trouppe, Cleveland Indians, April 30, 1952
21. Joe Black, Brooklyn Dodgers, May 1, 1952
22. Dave Pope, Cleveland Indians, July 1, 1952
23. Junior Gilliam, Brooklyn Dodgers, April 14, 1953
24. Connie Johnson, Chicago White Sox, April 1, 1953
25. Ernie Banks, **Chicago Cubs**, September 17, 1953
26. Jay Heard, **Baltimore Orioles**, April 24, 1954
27. Winn "Pop" Durham, Baltimore Orioles, September 10, 1954
28. Roberto Vargas, **Milwaukee Braves**, April 17, 1955
29. Milt Smith, **Cincinnati Reds**, July 21, 1955
30. Vibert Clarke, **Washington Senators**, September 4, 1955
31. Pat Scantlebury, Cincinnati Reds, April 19, 1956
32. John Kennedy, **Philadelphia Phillies**, April 22, 1957
33. Pancho Herrera, Philadelphia Phillies, April 15, 1958
34. Hank Mason, Philadelphia Phillies, September 12, 1958
35. J. C. Hartman, **Houston Colt .45's**, July 21, 1962

Boldface indicates the player was the first East-West player to play for a particular Major League team

Sapphire Superstars of the Negro Leagues and Major Leagues

Listed below are players who participated in both Negro League and Major League All-Star games, along with their all-star years.

Ernie Banks

NL—1953, Kansas City Monarchs

ML—1955-62, 1965, 1967, 1969, Chicago Cubs

LEAGUE	G	AB	R	H	D	T	HR	RBI	AVG.	SLG.
Negro Leagues	1	4	0	0	0	0	0	1	.000	.000
Major Leagues	13	33	4	10	3	1	1	3	.303	.545

Roy Campanella

NL—1941, 1944-45—Baltimore Elite Giants

ML—1949-56—Brooklyn Dodgers

LEAGUE	G	AB	R	H	D	T	HR	RBI	AVG.	SLG.
Negro Leagues	3	11	2	4	0	0	0	0	.364	.364
Major Leagues	7	20	1	2	0	0	0	0	.100	.100

Larry Doby

NL—1946 (2) Newark Eagles

ML—1949 to 1955, Cleveland Indians

LEAGUE	G	AB	R	H	D	T	HR	RBI	AVG.	SLG.
Negro Leagues	2	7	2	3	0	0	0	1	.429	.429
Major Leagues	6	10	2	3	1	0	1	1	.300	.700

Junior Gilliam

NL—1948 (2), 1949-50—Baltimore Elite Giants

ML—1956, 1959—Brooklyn and Los Angeles Dodgers

LEAGUE	G	AB	R	H	D	T	HR	RBI	AVG.	SLG.
Negro Leagues	4	13	2	3	0	0	1	2	.231	.462
Major Leagues	1	2	1	1	0	0	1	1	.500	2.000

Minnie Minoso

NL—1947 (2), 1948 (2)—New York Cubans

ML—1951-54, 1957, 1960—Chicago White Sox; 1959—Cleveland Indians

LEAGUE	G	AB	R	H	D	T	HR	RBI	AVG.	SLG.
Negro Leagues	4	13	2	3	0	0	1	2	.308	.462
Major Leagues	8	20	2	6	2	0	0	2	.300	.400

Jackie Robinson

NL—1945, Kansas City Monarchs

ML—1949-54—Brooklyn Dodgers

LEAGUE	G	AB	R	H	D	T	HR	RBI	AVG.	SLG.
Negro Leagues	1	5	0	0	0	0	0	0	.000	.000
Major Leagues	6	18	7	6	2	0	1	4	.333	.611

Satchel Paige

NL—1934, 1936—Pittsburgh Crawfords; 1941-43—Kansas City Monarchs

ML—1953—St. Louis Browns

LEAGUE	G	IP	R	H	ER	K	BB	W	L	ERA
Negro Leagues	1	15	10	4	1	13	3	2	1	0.60
Major Leagues	1	1	3	2	2	0	1	0	0	18.00

TOTAL BATTING	G	AB	R	H	D	T	HR	RBI	AVG.	SLG.
Negro Leaguers	15	53	8	13	0	0	2	6	.245	.358
Major Leaguers	41	103	17	28	8	1	4	11	.272	.485

Fast Facts on the First Game

The first East-West All-Star game was held on September 10, 1933, at Comiskey Park, Chicago, Illinois

Ticket prices for the first East-West game:
> $1.50 for box seats
> $1.10 for general admission seats
> $0.55 for bleacher seats

Game time for the first East-West classic was 2:30 PM, with an attendance of 19,568.

In the first all-star game, the top vote getter among all players was Oscar Charleston with 43,793 votes; the leading vote getter among pitchers was Willie Foster with 40,637 votes.

First Strikeout: Sam Streeter (Pittsburgh Crawfords) struck out Turkey Stearnes (Chicago American Giants) in the first inning (swinging).

First Double Play: Richard Lundy (Philadelphia Stars) hit into a double play in the second inning (Willie Wells, ss, to Leroy Morney, 2b. to Mule Suttles, 1b).

First Walk Issued: Willie Foster (American Giants) issued the first base-on-balls to Vic Harris (Homestead Grays) in the third inning.

First Hit: Sam Bankhead (Nashville Elite Giants) hit a single in the third inning.

First Double: Willie Wells (Chicago American Giants) doubled in the fourth inning.

First Triple: Larry Brown (Chicago American Giants) tripled in the fifth inning.

First Home Run: Mule Suttles (Chicago American Giants) homered in the fourth inning.

First Run Scored: Sam Bankhead (Nashville Elite Giants) scored in the third inning.

First RBI: Turkey Stearnes (American Giants) drove in Bankhead with a single in the third inning

First Stolen Base: Rap Dixon (Philadelphia Stars) stole third in the fourth inning.

First Double Steal: In the fourth inning, Rap Dixon (Philadelphia Stars) stole third base and Oscar Charleston (Pittsburgh Crawfords) stole second.

And Josh Gibson (Homestead Grays) made the last out in the first East-West Classic.

Latin American Players in the East-West Game

CUBA (18 PLAYERS)
Dave Amaro
Juan Armenteros
Harry Blanco
Alex Crespo
Martin Dihigo
Verdes Drake
Claro Duany
Pedro Formental
Raul Galata
Silvio Garcia
Rene Gonzalez
Pancho Herrera
Rogelio Linares
Cando Lopez
Alejandro Oms
Luis Tiant, Sr.
Orlando Varona
Gilberto Varona

PUERTO RICO (3 PLAYERS)
Jose Burgos
Pancho Coimbre
Luis Marquez

PANAMA (3 PLAYERS)
Vibert Clarke
Leon Kellman
Pat Scantlebury

DOMINICAN REPUBLIC
Horacio "Rabbit" Martinez

Financial Statements, 1942–1953

Tenth Annual East-West Baseball Classic, Comiskey Park, Chicago, Ill., Sunday, August 16, 1942
Score: East 5 – West 2

ATTENDANCE			TOTAL	TAX	NET
5,416	Box Seats	$1.65	$ 8,936.40	$,812.40	$ 8,124.00
33,278	Grand Stand	1.10	36,605.80	3,327.80	33,278.00
5,000	Bleachers	.55	2,750.00	250.00	2,500.00
663	Grand Stand Comps	.40	265.20	66.30	198.90
272	Box Seat Exchanges	.55	149.60	13.60	136.00
540	Tax Tickets	.10	54.00	54.00	
44,897					
	EXCHANGES				
	272 Box Seats	.55	149.60	13.60	136.00
	282 Grand Stand	.55	155.10	14.10	141.00
	554		$48,916.10	$4,538.20	$44,377.90

Comiskey Park Statement

Total Park Revenue		$15,279.88	
	Less Expenses		
	Ticket Printing	$ 232.50	
	Park Expense	792.00	
	Park Rental	9,717.18	
	Total Expenses	$10,028.68	($10,028.68)

Net Balance from Comiskey Park to Negro National and American Leagues	$ 33,636.22
Balance from Comiskey Park to both Leagues	$33,636.22

General Promotion Expenses — Both Leagues

Posters and "2" sheets	$205.00
Poster distribution	110.00
Frank Young — Publicity	750.00
Hall and Harrison	600.00
Posey and Young	120.00
Singer	10.00
Sound truck	42.00
Rain Insurance	219.00
Baseballs	73.44
Radio Stations	197.50
Ads — Bee and World	40.00
Signs — Tickets and Sound Truck	12.00
Corner Signs	145.00
Umpires	60.00
Advance Ticket Sellers	60.00
Police	70.00
Scorers	20.00
Clubhouse	10.00
Press Refreshments	10.90
J. T. Harris — Ticket Distribution	20.00
Stamps	13.50
Stationary and Envelopes	13.20

Tickets	6.60		
Phone	21.82		
Telegrams	3.54		
Mimeographing	4.50		
Stenographer	5.00		
H. & H. Press	3.50		
Miscellaneous	.74		
Total Promotion Expense	$2,847.04		($ 2,847.04)
		Balance	$30,789.18
5% Balance — Newspapers			
Pittsburgh Courier	769.75		
Chicago Defender	769.75		($ 1,539.46)
		Net Balance	$29,249.72
10% Net balance to League Presidents			
Dr. J. B. Martin	1,462.49		
Thomas T. Wilson	1,462.48		$2,924.97

Balance to be divided between both leagues   **$26,324.75**

Balance to be divided between both Leagues		$26,324.75
One-half to Negro American League	$13,162.38	
One-half to Negro National League	$13,162.37	

NEGRO NATIONAL LEAGUE SHARE		$13,162.57
Expenses—Negro National league		
Players— 18 [$200 each]	$900.00	
Sporting Goods	26.50	
Umpires transportation	67.94	
Umpires meals, hotels, cabs	44.70	
[Dave] Barnhill—Transportation to Dayton	12.50	
Phone Calls	10.00	
[Cum] Posey—Transportation	26.00	
Cabs for Players	43.65	

	Total	$1,131.29	1,131.29
	Balance		$12,031.09
	5% League Treasury		601.55
	Net Balance		$11,429.54

EACH CLUB'S SHARE—NEGRO NATIONAL LEAGUE [6 clubs] $1,904.92

RECAPITULATION—East—West Baseball Classic—Sunday, August 16, 1942

Total Receipts—Itemized		$48,916.10	
Park Expense—Itemized	$15,279.88		
General Promotion Expense—Itemized	2,847.04		
5% Net Balance—Courier-Defender	1,539.46		
10% Net Balance—League Presidents	2,924.97		
Total	$22,591.35	22,591.35	
Balance		$26,324.75	
One—Half to Each League		$13,162.37	

Eleventh Annual East vs. West Baseball Classic, Comiskey Park, Chicago, Ill., Sunday, August 1, 1943
Score: West 2-East
Weather-Perfect

ATTENDANCE			TOTAL	TAX	NET
5,595	Box Seats	$1.65	$9,231.25	$839.25	$8,392.50
35,402	Grandstand	1.10	38,942.20	3,540.20	35,402.00
5,000	Bleachers	.55	2,750.00	250.00	2,500.00
474	Grandstand Comps	.40	189.60	47.40	142.20
400	Tax Tickets	.10	40.00	40.00	—
46,871					
	EXCHANGES				
	100 Grandstand	.55	55.00	5.00	50.00
			$51,208.55	$4,721.85	$46,486.70

Comiskey Park Statement

Park Rental	$10,045.32		
Park Expense			
(Including Tickets)	1,260.12		
Total Park expense	11,305.44		$11,305.44

Balance from Comiskey Park to Negro National and Negro American Leagues. $35,181.28

Balance from Comiskey Park to Both Leagues $35,181.25

General Promotion Expenses—Both Leagues

Stamps	$13.00
Telephone Call—Tom Wilson	7.50
Mentrell Parker—Signs	7.50
Rain Insurance	221.40
Telegrams	1.41
Baseballs	72.00
Local Phone Calls	4.00
Chicago World Newspaper	20.00
Chicago Bee	20.00
Phone Call—Ernest Wright	1.80
Sayre—Adv. service (Posting)	45.00
Sound Truck	20.00
H. George Davenport—signs	6.00
Sound Truck Speaker	10.00
Local Calls	6.00
Policemen	65.00
Stamps for News Release	8.00
South Side Dist. Agency	120.00
Globe Posters	148.00
John C. Hamberlain—Car and service	10.00
Two week Ticket Sale—Rosette Frooks	100.00
South Center Dept.—Dif. on Ticket Sales	33.95
H.G. Hall and Wm. Harrison	600.00
H. George Davenport—Corner Signs	150.00
H. & H. Press—Stationery	7.25
Postage	.64
Long Distance Calls	5.05
Local Calls	5.00
Posey and Simmons	120.00
Saperstein—Publicity	70.00
Error in computing total	25.30

Total General Promotion Expense	$2,553.80			$2,553.80
			Balance	$32,627.46
5% Balance—Newspapers				
Pittsburgh Courier		815.68		
Chicago Defender		815.69		1,631.37
			Net Balance	$30,996.09
10% Net Balance to League Presidents				
Dr. J. B. Martin		1,549.80		
Thomas T. Wilson		1,549.81		3,099.61

Balance to be divided between both leagues $27,896.48

Share to each league 13,948.24

Financial Report Eleventh Annual East vs West Game Chicago, Illinois—August 1, 1943

Cash Received after Government Tax, Park Rental & Park Expense had been deducted		$35,181.26
Local Expense Sheet attached		2,553.80
Disbursement of the top		$32,627.46
Pittsburgh Courier 815.68		
Chicago Defender 815.69		1,631.37
		$30,996.09
Thomas T. Wilson	1,549.80 1/2	
Dr. J. B. Martin	1,549.80 1/2	3,099.61
		$27,896.48
Negro National League 13,948.24		
Negro American League 13,948.24		$27,896.48
		$00,000.00

Shares & Disbursements Negro American League

DEDUCTIONS

Chicago		$268.57
Supplies Sullivan	44.63	
Railroad Fare	38.94	
Players (5)	125.00	
Hotel Expense	60.00	
Kansas City		531.30
Railroad Fare	71.30	
Satchel Paige	300.00	
Players (4)	100.00	
Hotel expense	60.00	
Birmingham		345.20
Railroad Fare	160.20	
Players (5)	125.00	
Hotel Expense	60.00	
Cincinnati		114.11
Railroad Fare	40.11	
Players (2)	50.00	
Hotel Expense	24.00	
Cleveland		110.54
Railroad Fare	36.54	
Players (2)	50.00	
Hotel Expense	24.00	
Memphis		276.35
Railroad Fare	91.35	
Players (5)	125.00	
Hotel Expense	60.00	

Umpires		75.00
	Walker	50.00
	Blueitt	25.00
Total Deductions		$1,721.07

NEGRO AMERICAN LEAGUE SHARE

		$13,948.24
Less Expense		1,721.07
Balance 1/6		12,227.17
Each Team Share		2,037.86
Less for club room boy		1.67
Each Club's share		2,036.19

Chicago	2,036.19 − 268.57 = 2,304.76
Kansas City	2,036.19 − 541.30 = 2,577.49
Birmingham	2,036.19 − 345.20 = 2,381.39
Cincinnati	2,036.19 − 114.11 = 2,150.30
Cleveland	2,036.19
Less [Roy] Sparrow	10.00
Announcer	1.00
	$2,025.19 + 110.54 = 2,135.73*
Memphis	2,036.19 + 276.35 = 2,312.54*

Umpires	75.00
Sparrow	10.00
Announcer	1.00

TOTAL	$13,948.21
Plus Fractions 1/2 on 6 Shares = .03	.03
	$13,948.24

*Note expenses for Memphis and Cleveland were ADDED to their shares.

Negro American League and Negro National League East-West Game, July 29, 1945, Chicago, Ill.

Paid Admissions			32,762
Gross Gate			$70,096.58
Park Rental	$12,318.76		
Park Expense	1,638.75		
Gov't Tax	11,864.07		
TOTAL	$25,821.58		$25,821.58
Net Receipts			$44,275.00

Promotional Expenses:
Telegrams	3.49
Telephone	2.85
Transport tickets	1.00
Telephone Philadelphia	3.35
Bronzeville, Chicago World &	120.00
Bell & H. Press	8.50
Signs for Park & sound truck	29.00
Sound truck	40.00
Announcer	20.00
Stamps	3.30
Baseballs	87.00
Police	220.00

Signs—Stamps (Hall)	15.00	
Special Police	40.00	
Street Signs	300.00	
Postage Enve. (Harrison)	8.16	
Harrison	500.00	
Hall	500.00	
Secretaries	120.00	
	$2,021.65	
	1,250.00	
	3,271.65	
	100.00	
	3,371.65	3,371.65
Balance after Expenses		40,903.35
10% Presidents share		4,090.34
		36,813.01
5% for the Courier and Defender		1,840.65
		34,972.36
Each League's share		$17,486.18

East West Game Report, Sunday, July 29, 1945

SALE

5,563	Box Seats @	$3.00	$16,689.00
26,101	Grand Stand Seats @	2.00	52,202.00
1,098	Bleacher Seats @	1.00	1,098.00
326	Tax @	.33	107.58
33,088	TOTAL CASH		70,096.58

DISTRIBUTION

Park Rental	$12,318.76
Game Expense	1,638.75
Federal Tax	11,864.07
Net – East–West Share	44,275.00
TOTAL	70,096.58

EAST & WEST NET · 44,275.00

Expense for promotion

Telegrams	$3.49
Telephone long distance	2.85
local	1.00
Ed Gottlieb	3.35
Bronzeville Magazine—2 ads	40.00
Chicago Bee—2 ads	40.00
Chicago World—2 ads	40.00
H. H. Press (working Press Passers)	8.50
H. Geo. Davenport for signs Ball	
Park and Sound Truck	29.00
Sound Truck Engineering Corp.	40.00
Announcer Sound Truck	20.00
Stamps	3.30
Baseballs	87.00
Police for lunch	220.00
H. G. Hall for ticket on sale sign and stamps	15.00

Special police for H. G. Hall	40.00
H. Geo. Davenport for corner signs	300.00
Wm. P. Harrison for envelopes & Postage	8.16
H. G. Hall for Promotion	500.00
Wm. P. Harrison for Promotion	500.00
East West Secretaries—$60.00 each	120.00
Official Scorer & care of Press Box	100.00
A.M. Saperstein, Publicity	1,250.00
Total expense from net gate off top	$3,371.65
Total net gate—both leagues	$44,275.00
Less—total expense Off Top	3,371.65
BALANCE	$40,903.35
Less - 10%—2 President's Shares	4,090.34 divided by 2 equals $2,045.17 ea. President's Share
BALANCE	$36,813.01
Less - 5%—Defender & Courier	1,840.65 divided by 2 equals $920.32 1/2—ea. Paper's share
BALANCE	$34,972.36 divided by 2 equals $17,486.18—ea. League's share

EXPENSE SHEET NEGRO AMERICAN LEAGUE

Taxicab to get 1st Base Mitt	$4.00
Bat Boys	2.00
Club House Man	15.00
First aid & Lemons	4.66
Trainer Club House	10.00
Announcer Ball Park	20.00
Umpire Ward (Cincinnati)	75.00
Umpire Blueitt (Chicago)	50.00
K. City Players Expense	132.40
Cincinnati Players Expense	98.62
Memphis Players Expense	148.23
Cleveland Players Expense	243.20
Ernest Wright for Bats	36.00
Birmingham Players Expense	122.97
Chicago Players Expense	139.40
22 Players & Coaches @ $100.00 each	2,200.00
TOTAL EXPENSE—WEST	3,301.48
American League Share	$17,486.18
Less expense	3,301.48
BALANCE	$14,184.70 divided by 6 equals $2,364.11 Each Share

EACH'S TEAM'S SHARE As Follows:

Kansas City	$2,896.51
Cincinnati	2,662.73
Memphis	2,812.34
Cleveland	3,143.31
Birmingham	2,787.08
Chicago	3,003.51
TOTAL	17,305.48
Miscellaneous Expense	180.56
TOTAL	$17,486.14
Plus 4 cents due Dr. Martin	.04
GRAND TOTAL	$17,486.18

Negro National League and Negro American League All Star Game, August 15, 1946, Griffith Stadium, Wash., D. C.

Paid Admissions		15,009
Gross Gate		$30,494.40

Park Rental	$6,337.50		
Gov't Tax	5,144.33		
Park Expense	1,179.06		
TOTAL		$12,660.89	
Net Receipts			$17,833.51
Promotional Expense	$585.00		
Salaries 2 secretaries	125.00		
Press Party	71.44		
Travel Clark & Office	121.00		
Radio & Bulletin	155.00		
Stamps	33.82		
Miscellaneous	61.52		
Newspaper Advert.	605.02		
Added Expenses	414.03		
Operational Expenses	408.00	$2,2579.85	
Col. & White Papers	872.65		
Dr. Martin Expense	75.00		
Clark & Carter	800.00	$1,747.65	
TOTAL			4,327.48
Balance after Expenses			13,506.03
Each League's Share		$6,753.01	

East West Game Report, Sunday August 18, 1946

SALE

5,044 Box Seats at $3.00		$15,132.00
35,048 Grand Stand seats at 2.00		70,096.00
1,382 Bleacher Seats at 1.00		1,382.00
181 Pass tickets at .50		90.50
345 Tax tickets at .33		113.85
CASH TOTAL		$86,814.35

DISTRIBUTION

Park Rental		$14,985.17
Game Expense		2,178.16
Gov't Tax		14,710.36
Net East West Share		54,940.66
TOTAL		86,814.35

EXPENSE FOR PROMOTION

Telephone calls, stamps register	$ 23.30
Arcus Ticket Co. (Printers)	305.66
Chicago Bee	40.00
Chicago World Newspaper	40.00
Bronzeville Magazine	40.00
Working Press passes & photo passes	16.00
George Davenport signs	373.00
Decoration of park	50.00
Band	296.00

Balls six dozen	73.44	
Sound truck	80.00	
Radio	72.00	
Arcus Ticket Co. (tax tickets)	8.85	
Policemen	300.00	
Official Announcer	25.00	
Registers & Policeman (Mr. Little)	23.49	
For newspapers (Saperstein)	1,250.00	
W. P. Harrison	750.00	
W. M. Little	750.00	
Press Tickets	38.00	
Mr. Harrison	21.40	
2 Dozen balls	24.52	
Extra Balls	12.50	
TOTAL EXPENSE		4,613.16
Balance After Expenses		50,327.50
10% presidents share		5,032.75
		45,294.75
5% for the Courier and Defender		2,264.73
		43,030.02
Official Scorer Frank Young		100.00
		42,930.02
Two Secretaries		120.00
		42,810.02

Each League's Share 1/2 of the above $21,405.01

Negro American League East-West Game Cash and Disbursements, August 18, 1946

Negro American League Shares (Chicago)			$21,405.01
(Washington)			6,753.01
		TOTAL	28,158.02
Teams share and expenses			28,157.98
		Surplus	.04

TEAMS SHARE—NEGRO AMERICAN LEAGUE

Birmingham	$4,524.11
Clowns	4,189.22
Kansas City	4,804.21
Cleveland	5,035.95
Memphis	5,036.55
Chicago	4,393.68
TOTAL	$27,983.72

Expenses—Negro American League

Blueitt—Umpire	$50.00		
Rogan—Umpire	91.26	Teams Share	$27,983.72
Wilbur Hayes—Good Will	10.00	League Exp.	174.26
Bat Boy	1.00	TOTAL	$28,157.98
Clubhouseman	10.00		
1 Doz. Balls (Posey)	12.00		
	$174.26		

East-West Cash Received and Disbursements (Both Leagues), August 18, 1946—Chicago

Total Cash Received—Both Leagues			$54,940.65
Expenses	E. W. G.		4,613.16
	Balance		$50,327.50

PRES.	Thomas T. Wilson, N. N. L.	$2,516.38 (10%)	5,032.75
	Dr. J. B. Martin, N. A. L.	2,516.37 Balance	$45,294.75
NEWSPAPERS	Chicago Defender	$1,132.37 (5%)	
	Pittsburgh Courier	1,132.36	2,264.75
	Balance		$43,030.02
	Frank Young Scorer & Press Box		100.00
	Balance		$42,930.02
SEC'YS	Frank Young—N. A. L.	$60.00	
	Curtis Leak—N. N. L.	60.00	120.00
	Balance		$42,810.02
	Each League		$21,405.01

Negro National League and Negro American League East West Game; Chicago, Ill., July 27, 1947

5,965	Boxes at $3.00	17,895.00
34,949	Grand stand at $2.00	69,898.00
947	Bleacher at $1.00	947.00
84	Res. G. S. Exc. At $1.00	84.00
492	Pass tickets at 33 c	162.36
526	Pass tickets at .50	263.00
42,963	Total Cash	89,249.36

Distribution

Park Rental	$15,347.89
Game Expense	2,394.44
Federal Tax	15,115.46
The Two Leagues Received	56,391.59
Total	89,249.36

Gross Gate		$56,391.57
Promotion Cost		5,135.02
	Balance	51,256.55
10% President share:		
Pres. Johnson	$2,562.55	
President J. B.	2,562.54	5,125.65
	Balance	46,130.90
5% to Nespapers (Newspapers)		
Courier	1,153.27	
Defender	1,153.27	2,306.54
	Balance	43,824.36
Secretaries		
Young	$60.00	
Leak	$60.00	120.00
	Balance	43,704.36
Oficial [official] Scorer Young		100.00
	Balance	43,604.36
Each Leagu's [League's] share 1/2 of above		21,802.18

Per Curtis A. Leak, Secretary

See Dan Burley's article, dated 9 September 1947, in the New York Amsterdam News, for comments of the 1947 East-West expense report.

Negro National League and Negro American League All Star Game, July 29, 1947, Polo Grounds, New York, N.Y.

SOLD		PRICE	CASH	TAX	TOTAL
3,645	Boxes	$2.00	6,087.15	1,202.85	7,290.00
28,838	G.S.	1.25	29,991.52	6,055.98	36,047.50
1,001	Bl.	.60	500.50	100.10	600.60
481	Ad.	.75	298.22	62.55	360.75
	Press	.21		59.01	59.01
281	''	.49	137.69		137.69
34,246					
Totals			37,015.08	7,480.47	44,495.55
			Gross Gate		44,495.55

Government Tax	7,480.47	
Park Rental	9,253.77	
Park Expense	1,752.56	
Park Lights	1,000.00	
	19,486.80	19,486.80
Balance to both leagues		25,008.75
Promotional cost as per attached sheet		5,113.45
Balance		19,859.30
5% to promoter for promotional cost		994.76
Balance		18,864.54
1/2 to Each League		
Negro American League	9,432.27	
Negro National League	9,432.27	
		18,854.54

Per: Curtis A. Leak, Secretary

All Star Game, Polo Grounds, July 29, 1947

EXPENSES

850 placards distribution	10 each	$ 85.00
500 '' ''	5 ''	25.00
150 '' ''	10 ''	15.00
500 2-sheets Distribution	30 ''	150.00
Rain insurance $2,000 coverage		351.00
Liability Insurance 34,502 on basis of .588 per 100		202.87
Photographs		15.00
Printing plycards & posters		271.00
Advertising signs		73.44
Rick Hurt Expenses (stamps, telephone, etc.)		10.00
Baseballs 8 Dozen $16.00		128.00
Sound Wagon		135.00
White Newspapers		500.00
Colored Newspapers		300.00
Colored Adds—Age		30.00
Voice		40.32
Amsterdam News		175.00
Hurt Colored Newspapers		300.00
Radio Joe Bostic		150.00
Spanish Newspaper		25.00

Carboards	3.43	
Press Refreshments	16.50	
Tickets for President Johnson (Cuban office)	36.00	
" " " " Curtis "	12.00	
" " Forbes Broadcast	12.00	
Polo Grounds Advance sale man July 27	10.50	
Pete Hoffman Polo Grounds Secretary Advance Sales	100.00	
Club House Man	10.00	
Police Tips and other help	50.00	
Watchers	30.00	
Ball Chasers	6.00	
Ball Watcher	5.00	
Bat Boy	3.00	
2 Extra Umpires	50.00	
Announcer	10.00	
Scorer (Age)	25.00	
Various calls to Chicago in connection with game	18.25	
Mr. Dival (Tickets Cubans office)	50.00	
Miss. Leak (" Yanks office)	50.00	
Cadets	100.00	3,579.31
League Secretary	50.00	
Tickets Printed	450.78	
Photos	15.00	
Additional tickets	18.36	
Promotional cost	1,000.00	
Complete Total		5,113.45

Negro National League and Negro American League East-West Game, Chicago, Ill., August 22, 1948

10,974	Boxes at $3.00	$32,922.00
25,234	Grand Stands at $2.00	50,468.00
891	Bleacher seats at 1.00	891.00
37,099		
219	Exchanges	219.00
386	Pass tickets	128.80
480	Comp. Passes	240.00
	Total Cash	84,868.80

Distribution

Park Expense	2,845.98
Park Rental 20%	13,678.29
Federal Tax	14,362.17
City Admission Tax	2,115.20
Two Leagues received	51,867.16
	84,868.80

Balance to both leagues:			51,867.16
10% presidents shares:	2,593.35		
	2,593.35	5,186.71	
Promotional cost as per attached statement		5,077.36	10,264.07
	Balance		41,603.09
Each league's share 1/2 of the above			20,801.54
Plus president share			2,593.35
	Total in full		23,394.89

Negro American League and Negro National League East-West Game, Chicago, Ill, Comiskey Park; August 22, 1948

PROMOTION EXPENSES

Band	$358.00
Decorations of park	100.00
Street signs	325.00
World paper	50.00
Argus Ticket Co.	349.78
H. & H. Press badges, etc.	8.75
Baseballs 9 dozen	154.22
Signs for sign truck	12.00
Announcer	35.00
Policeman	300.00
Sound truck	80.00
Watchers (4)	40.00
Radio Stations (3)	150.00
Chicago Defender	600.00
Office expense	18.25
Daily papers	600.00
Mr. Harrison	750.00
Telephone & Postage	26.35
Police protection	100.00
Dr. Martin's Man for tickets	800.00
Two secretaries	120.00
Scorer	100.00
TOTAL	**$5,077.36**

East West Game, Negro American League, Comiskey Park, Chicago; August 22, 1948

Negro American League Share	$20,801.54
Teams transportation and food	1,005.93
Balance	19,795.61
League Expencies [*sic*]	1,375.75
Balance	18,419.86
Ball Players	3,600.00
Balance	14,819.86
East Ball Players	1,700.00
Balance	13,119.86
1/6 or Each Team Share	$2,186.64

Transportation and Food

Kansas City	$170.00	Kansas City	$3,256.64
Memphis	185.00	Memphis	3,256.64
Indianapolis	138.00	Birmingham	3,298.72
Cleveland	145.69	Indianapolis	3,124.64
Birmingham	212.08	Chicago	3,241.80
Chicago	155.16	Cleveland	3,232.33
Total	$1,005.93	Total	$19,410.77

League Expencies [sic]

Lowe & Campbell . . . Bats, Catchers Outfit	$95.93
Club House Man	10.00
Jesse Holt . . . Trainer or Physical Director	15.00
Bat and Ball Boy	2.00

Ball players tickets . . . Chicago to New York	907.82
Umpires Blueitt and West	100.00
Umpire Blueitt to New York	50.00
Blueitt Expense to New York	25.00
Gift Watch to J. L. Wilkerson [Wilkinson] .Kansas City, Mo	95.00
Umpire Expense—West	50.00
Wilbur Hayes	5.00
Total	1,375.75

Total Teams Share		$19,410.77
League Expencies [sic]		1,375.75
Coach Carter from Memphis		15.00
	Total—	$20,801.52
Total League Share		$20,801.54
		.02 over

Dr. J. B. Martin, Pres. N. A. L.
East West Game Cash Received and Expenditures, Comiskey Park, Chicago, Ill., August 22, 1948

Total cash received both leagues		$51,867.16
John H. Johnson, NNL—5%—$2,593.36		
J.B. Martin, NAL —5%—$2,593.35		$5,186.71
Balance		46,680.45
East West Game Expencies [sic]		5,077.36
Balance		41,603.09
Both Leagues, 1/2 of each league share		20,801.54

East West Game Expencies [sic]

Omar's Band	$358.00
Decorating Park	100.00
Street Signs	325.00
Chicago World	50.00
Argus Ticket Co.	349.78
H & H Press, Badges, Press & Photographers	8.75
Lowe & Campbell . . . 9 doz. balls	154.22
Signs for Sound Truck	12.00
Official Announcer	35.00
Policemens	300.00
Sound truck	80.00
Four gate watchers	40.00
Three Radio Stations	150.00
Newspapers (Chicago Defender)	600.00
Daily Papers	600.00
J.B. Martin Office expencies [sic] (Stamps, etc.)	18.26
Mr. Harrison's Expencies [sic]	750.00
Telephone, postage	26.35
Police protection	100.00
Dr. J.B. Martin's ticket selling	800.00
Secretaries (Young & Curtis)	120.00
Young official scorer	100.00
	$5,077.36

J.B. Martin, Pres. N.A.L.

JBM:rss

Negro National League and Negro American League All Star Game, August 24th. 1948, Yankee Stadium, New York, N.Y.

CASH STATEMENT

		NET	TAX
902	Box Chairs at $3.00	$2255.00	451.00
2,900	Box Chairs at $2.00	4676.00	924.00
8,914	Grand Stand Adm. at $1.25	2270.56	1871.94
453	Exch. at .75	244.62	95.15
818	Bleacher Adm. at .60	409.00	81.80

Press Gate

98 at $4.00			49.00
122 at 1.25		35.38	25.62
		$26,890.56	$3,498.49

Less 25% for Rental	4,222.64
	$12,667.92
Less Park Expenses	2,292.30
Net to Pres. Johnson	$10,375.62
Prom. Cost, attached sheet	$3,316.38
Balance	7,059.24
10% Presidents Share	$705.92
Balance	$6,355.32
10% Promotional Cost	635.33
	$5,717.99
1/2 to each league	$2,858.99
Total to Negro American League	$2,958.99
President's Share	352.96
	$3,211.95
Total to Negro National League	$2,858.99
President's Share	352.96
	$3,211.95

Per: Curtis A. Leak, Secretary

Yankee Stadium, August 24th, 1948, National League All Stars vs American League All Stars

PROMOTION EXPENSES

Sandwich Man Advertising	$ 35.00
Printing 1500 Placards	190.00
Printing 500 2 sheets	100.00
Shipping expencies [*sic*] above sheets and placards	20.00
Liability Insurance on 14,107 Attendance 588%	82.94
Property Damage Ins. Policy on $16,890.50	28.38
Rain Insurance No. 50001 (on $2,000)	232.60
Distribution of Placards	150.00
Distribution of 2 sheets	150.00
Tickets for clubs 78 at $3.00 ea.	234.00
80 1.25 ea.	100.00
Printing of Hand Bills	57.12
Distribution of Hand Bills 3 boys @ 50 cents ea.	1.50
Printing Signs	163.20
2 oil cloth signs	6.00

Printing 2000 envelopes	20.00
1000 requisition cards	15.00
Stamps 2400 at 1 cent	24.00
Stamps .03	15.25
2 trips to Newark	5.00
Paper Memo	2.40
Storage for signs	2.00
Baseballs 6 dozen	105.00
News paper ads: New York Age (2 weeks)	30.00
Amsterdam News (2 weeks)	191.10
Pittsburgh Courier (1 week)	19.50
Announcer	10.00
Scorer	10.00
Watchers	22.00
Ball Chasers	7.00
Press Box Refreshments	6.50
Telegrams	8.64
Telephones	7.25
Steno on releases	9.00
Sound Wagon	133.00
Newspaper Publicity: La Prensa	15.00
Lester Bromborg	300.00
Lacey [Sam Lacy]	100.00
Radio Publicity Burley [Dan]	200.00
Joe Bistic [Bostic]	100.00
Park Tips (Mr. McManus)	50.00
Cadets	125.00
Advance Sale Offices: Yankees & Cubans	50.00
Secretary Cubans Office Mailing List	25.00
Colored Newspapers	150.00
Ticket paid for and uncalled for	18.00
Complete Total	$3,316.38

East-West Game Expenses, Chicago, Illinois, August 14, 1949

Arcus Ticket Co.	$ 377.77
Two catchers outfit	18.20
Omar O. Crittenden's Band and Majorettes	329.00
Six dozen baseballs	102.82
Float for Bud Billikin [Billiken] Parade	250.00
Sound System Billikin [Billiken] Parade	50.00
Three Radios	120.00
Two girls on Float, Bud Billikin [Billiken] Parade	20.00
Announcer on float Bud Billikin [Billiken] Parade	17.50
Two Newspapers (World and Crusader)	100.00
Street Signs	325.00
Sound truck	80.00
East West Game Ticket Seller	750.00
Decorating Park	100.00
Policeman at Park	300.00
Four gate watchers at Park	40.00
Daily Papers	642.00
Office expense, telephone, telegrams, stamps, etc.	22.00
Official Scorer	25.00
Clubhouse man for East and West	20.00

H & H Press, Press and Photographer badge		9.75
Jesse Holt, Trainer		15.00
Signs for sound Truck		12.00
Police Escoree, for A. B. Chandler		20.00
Automobile for A. B. Chandler		5.00
Three ball and bat boys		3.00
Official Announcer		25.00
Umpires		230.00
		$4,109.04
Ed Gottleib, Telephone — Telegram		10.00
		$4,119.04

Financial Statement, East West Game played at Comiskey Park, Chicago, Illinois, August 14, 1949

Negro American League Share	$37,309.62

DISBURSEMENTS

Memphis' Share	$2,888.56
New York's Share	2,963.82
Chicago's share	2,866.91
Birmingham's Share	2,956.90
Kansas City's Share	2,869.34
Cleveland's Share	2,665.03
Houston's Share	2,723.41
Baltimore's Share	3,866.55
Philadelphia's Share	2,771.41
Indianapolis's Share	2,767.30
Fred McCrary, Umpire expense	61.25
Frank Duncan, Umpire expense	44.81
Mark Van Buren, Umpire expense	20.74
Presidents Share 10% Net	3,319.05
Chicago Defender	602.71
Pittsburgh Courier	602.71
East West Game Expenses (As listed on Page 1)	4,119.04
	$37,309.56
Negro American League Share	$37,309.62
Negro American League Disbursements	37,309.56
	.06

Dr. J. B. Martin
League President — Secretary

Negro American League 19th Annual E-W Game, August 12, 1951

Number paid admissions 14,161			$32,511.91
Federal Tax	$5,558.90		
City	808.59		$6,367.49
		Net	$26,144.42
Park Rental	$5228.88		
Expense	2,369.70		$7,598.58
		Net	$18,545.84
Expense Promotion			$3,196.00
			$15,349.84

5% to Saperstein		$767.49
		$14,582.35
10% to Dr. Martin		$1,458.24
		$13,124.11
5% to Pittsburgh Courier and Chicago Defender		$656.20
		$12,467.91

TRANSPORTATION

Kansas City	$107.28		
Birmingham	110.72		
Philadelphia	196.64		
Memphis	148.28		
New Orleans	166.36		
Clowns	109.67		
Chicago	298.35		
Baltimore	92.48		$1,229.78
			$11,238.13
Each Club $400.00 for Players (18 Players)			$3,200.00
			$8,038.13
Each Club (1/8)			$1,004.77

1952 20th Annual East-West Game

Number paid Admissions	14,122		$31,860.79
Federal Tax			$5,280.02
City Tax			797.42
			$25,783.35
Park Rental			$5,156.67
Park Expense		1,316.34	6,473.01
			$19,310.34
A. M. Saperstein		$1,002.73	
Promotion Expense, Dr. J. B. Martin			1,969.34
			2,972.07
			$16,338.27
5% to Mr. Saperstein			816.91
			$15,521.36
10% to Dr. J. B. Martin			1,552.14
			$13,969.22
Pittsburgh Courier	$349.23		
Chicago Defender	$349.23		698.46
			$13,270.76
Transportation			987.03
			$12,283.73
Each Club $400 for Players			2,400.00
			$9,883.73
1/6 to each club			$1,647.25

Expense
East–West Game, August 16, 1953

Paid Admissions	$11,013.58
Promotion Expense, Dr. J. B. Martin	2,576.79
	$8,436.79
10% to Promotion	843.68
	$7,593.11
10% to President	759.11
	$6,834.00
5% for Newspapers	341.70
	$6,492.30
Each Club $400.00 for Players [four clubs]	1,600.00
	$4,892.30
1/4 to Each Club	$1,223.07

Promotion Expenses

Crusader Newspaper	$50.00
Telephone and Telegrams	14.20
Postage Stamps	8.12
Veterans Sign Co.	124.00
For selling tickets	350.00
Bud Billiken Parade	75.00
Sound Truck—4 Days	150.00
H & H Press Photographers & Press Passes Printed	8.75
Ray Gray	400.00
Commercial Broadcasters	300.00
Al Benson	423.72
2 Gate Watchers	20.00
4 Umpires	60.00
4 Doz. Baseballs at $19.00 a dozen	76.00
Omar Crittendon Band	294.00
Wendell Smith	50.00
Official Scorer	25.00
Club House	20.00
Mr. Bryant and 2 Ball Chasers	8.00
Man Accompanying Sound Truck Man	20.00
Radio Station WIND (Bob Elson)	100.00
Total	$2,576.79

All-Time All-Star Teams

As selected by various players, managers, writers, historians and newspapers. The years given are the years the teams were selected or the active years of the player or other person naming the teams.

Pos.	Pittsburgh Courier 1925	Pittsburgh Courier 1952—1st team	Pittsburgh Courier 1952—2nd team	Dick Clark, historian All-Time All-Stars	Frank Forbes, TSN, 1957
c	Biz Mackey	Biz Mackey	Roy Campanella	Josh Gibson	Josh Gibson
c	Julio Rojo	Josh Gibson	Bruce Petway	Biz Mackey	Biz Mackey
1b	George Carr	Buck Leonard	Ben Taylor	Buck Leonard	Ben Taylor
2b	Frank Warfield	Jackie Robinson	Bingo DeMoss	Bingo DeMoss	Bill Monroe
3b	Judy Johnson	Oliver Marcell	Judy Johnson	Jud Wilson	Oliver Marcell
ss	Dick Lundy	Pop Lloyd	Willie Wells	Pop Lloyd	Pop Lloyd
of	Chaney White	Cool Papa Bell	Pete Hill	Turkey Stearnes	Spots Poles
of	Oscar Charleston	Oscar Charleston	Monte Irvin	Oscar Charleston	Oscar Charleston
of	Rap Dixon	Cristobal Torriente	Chino Smith	Cristobal Torriente	Cristobal Torrienti
p	Rats Henderson	Joe Williams	Dave Brown	Wilber Rogan	Smokey Joe Williams
p	Nip Winters	Satchel Paige	Dick Redding	Satchel Paige	Jose Mendez
p	Phil Cockrell	Bullet Rogan	Nip Winters	Smokey Joe Williams	Frank Wickware
p	Rube Currie	John Donaldson	Dizzy Dismukes	Leon Day	Slim Jones
p	Oscal Levis	Willie Foster	Don Newcombe		Pat Dougherty
mgr	Pop Lloyd	Rube Foster	Cum Posey	C. I. Taylor	
coach		Dizzy Dismukes	C. I. Taylor	Martin Dihigo, util.	Martin Dihigo, util
coach		Danny McClellan	Dave Malarcher		Scotty Bowman, util.

Pos.	Rollo Wilson, writer 1929	Don Delieghbur, writer 1944	Art Carter's 1944 Negro Baseball Yearbook	Art Carter's 1945 Negro Baseball Yearbook	William E. Clark, writer New York Age, 1937	Frazier Robinson 1942–50
c	Buck Ewing	Josh Gibson	Roy Campanella	Josh Gibson	Biz Mackey	Josh Gibson
c	Biz Mackey	Roy Campanella				
1b	Jud Wilson	Buck Leonard	Buck Leonard	George Giles	George Carr	Buck Leonard
2b	George Scales	Ray Dandridge	Ray Dandridge	Jesse Douglas	Frank Warfield	Bonnie Serrell
3b	Judy Johnson	Splo Spearman	Parnell Woods	Parnell Woods	Martin Dihigo	Ray Dandridge
ss	Dick Lundy	Frank Austin	Frank Austin	Avelino Canizares	Dick Lundy	Monte Irvin
of	Vic Harris	Pancho Coimbre	Cool Papa Bell	Gene Benson	Fats Jenkins	Willard Brown
of	Rap Dixon	Gene Benson	Johnny Davis	Sam Jethroe	Oscar Charleston	Cool Papa Bell
of	Chino Smith	Johnny Davis	Ed Steele	Bill Wright	Spots Poles	Bill Wright
p	Laymon Yokely	Ray Brown	George Jefferson	George Jefferson	Dave Brown	Satchel Paige
p	Porter Charleston	Bill Ricks	Gentry Jessup	Willie Jefferson	Nip Winters	Hilton Smith
p	Connie Rector	Barney Morris	Ray Brown	Roy Welmaker	Satchel Paige	Leon Day
p	Martin Dihigo, util	Terris McDuffie	Alfred Saylor		Pop Lloyd, util	Connie Johnson
mgr	Pop Lloyd				John Beckwith, util	

Pos.	Cum Posey,	Cum Posey,	Cum Posey,	Cum Posey,	Cum Posey,	Cum Posey,
c	Biz Mackey	Biz Mackey	T. J. Young	Biz Mackey	T. J. Young	Josh Gibson
c	John Beckwith	Josh Gibson		Josh Gibson	Josh Gibson	Robert Clarke
1b	Rev Cannady	Oscar Charleston	Mule Suttles	Oscar Charleston	Buck Leonard	Buck Leonard
2b	Frank Warfield	Newt Allen	Willie Wells	Rev Cannady	Sammy T. Hughes	Sammy T. Hughes
3b	Dave Malarcher	Jud Wilson	Jud Wilson	Jud Wilson	George Scales	Jud Wilson
ss	Dobie Moore	Dick Lundy	Dick Lundy	Willie Wells	Jake Stephens	Ches Williams
of	Cristobal Torriente	Martin Dihigo	Fats Jenkins	Vic Harris	Jerry Benjamin	Vic Harris
of	Oscar Charleston	Cool Papa Bell	Cool Papa Bell	Cool Papa Bell	Ray Brown	Turkey Stearnes
of	Hurley McNair	Dink Mothell	Roy Parnell	Rap Dixon	Turkey Stearnes	Rap Dixon
p	Army Cooper	Ted Radcliffe		Satchel Paige	Luis Tiant	Satchel Paige

Pos.	Cum Posey,	Cum Posey,	Cum Posey,	Cum Posey,	Cum Posey,	Cum Posey,
p	Bullet Rogan	Sam Streeter	Bert Hunter	Slim Jones	Satchel Paige	Leroy Matlock
p	Joe Williams	Willie Foster	Willie Foster	Ray Brown	Slim Jones	
p	Rats Henderson			George Britt		
p	George Harney			Bill Holland		
util		Mule Suttles	Ches Williams	George Scales		Martin Dihigo
util				Turkey Stearnes		Jimmie Crutchfield

Pos.	Cum Posey, owner 1936—1st team	Cum Posey, owner 1936—2nd team	Cum Posey, owner 1938	Dan Burley Amsterdam News 1944—1st team	Dan Burley Amsterdam News 1944—2nd team
c	Josh Gibson	Frank Duncan	Josh Gibson	Josh Gibson	Thad Christopher
c				Roy Campanella	Louis Louden
1b	Buck Leonard	Jud Wilson	Buck Leonard	Buck Leonard	Jim West
2b	Sammy T. Hughes	Rev Cannady	Sammy T. Hughes	Ray Dandridge	Blue Perez
3b	Ray Dandridge	Pat Patterson	Ray Dandridge	Clyde Spearman	Felton Snow
ss	Willie Wells	Ches Williams	No selection	Frank Austin	Tommy Butts
of	Wild Bill Wright	Roy Parnell	Wild Bill Wright	Pancho Coimbre	Ed Stone
of	Sam Bankhead	Cool Papa Bell	Fats Jenkins	Gene Benson	Henry Kimbro
of	Vic Harris	Ed Stone	Neal Robinson	Johnny Davis	Cool Papa Bell
p	Satchel Paige	Neck Stanley	Ray Brown	Ray Brown	Barney Morris
p	Martin Dihigo	Leon Day	Barney Brown	Bill Ricks	Vic Greenidge
p	Leroy Matlock	Satchel Paige	Hilton Smith	Andy Porter	Terris McDuffie
p		Bill Holland			
util			Vic Harris		

Pos.	Ed Bolden 1910–50	Oscar Charleston 1915–54	Monte Irvin 1937–48	Max Manning 1938–49	Buck Leonard 1933–50	Sam Lacy, writer 1930–1999
c	Louis Santop	Louis Santop	Josh Gibson	Josh Gibson	Josh Gibson	Biz Mackey
c	Josh Gibson	Josh Gibson			Biz Mackey	Josh Gibson
1b	Buck Leonard	Ben Taylor	Buck Leonard	Buck Leonard	Buck Leonard	Buck Leonard
2b	Frank Warfield	Bingo DeMoss	Sammy T. Hughes	Dickie Seay	Sammy T. Hughes	Pop Lloyd
3b	Ray Dandridge	Oliver Marcell	Ray Dandridge	Ray Dandridge	Judy Johnson	Ray Dandridge
ss	Pop Lloyd	Pop Lloyd	Willie Wells	Willie Wells	Willie Wells	Dick Lundy
of	Chaney White	Cristobal Torrienti	Oscar Charleston	Martin Dihigo	Bill Wright	Pete Hill
of	Oscar Charleston	Rap Dixon	Cool Papa Bell	Cool Papa Bell	Cool Papa Bell	Cool Papa Bell
of	Martin Dihigo	Martin Dihigo	Cristobal Torrienti	Bill Wright	Turkey Stearnes	Oscar Charleston
p	Satchel Paige	Satchel Paige	Satchel Paige	Satchel Paige	Satchel Paige	Satchel Paige
p	Bullet Rogan	Bullet Rogan	Slim Jones	Leon Day	Ray Brown	Hilton Smith
p	Dick Redding	Dizzy Dismukes			Ted Trent	Joe Williams
p	Joe Williams					
mgr	Rube Foster		Rube Foster	Biz Mackey	Vic Harris	Rube Foster

Pos.	Jud Wilson 1922–45	Dewitt Smallwood 1951–54	Jim LaMarque 1942–51	Herman Horn 1951–54
c	Biz Mackey	Buster Haywood	Frank Duncan	Roy Campanella
1b	Mule Suttles	Buck O'Neil	Buck O'Neil	Buck O'Neil
2b	Martin Dihigo	Charlie Neal	Bonnie Serrell	Newt Allen
3b	Dick Lundy	Hank Baylis	Herb Souell	Ray Dandridge
ss	Willie Wells	Jesse Williams	Jesse Williams	Newt Joseph
of	Turkey Stearnes	Oscar Charleston	Willie Simms	Monte Irvin
of	Cool Papa Bell	Willie Mays	Willard Brown	Willie Mays
of	Cristobal Torrenti	Hank Aaron	Ted Strong	Hank Aaron
p	Satchel Paige	Bullet Rogan	Satchel Paige	Satchel Paige
p	Smokey Joe Williams	Jim LaMarque	Hilton Smith	Bill Beverly

Pos.	Jud Wilson 1922–45	Dewitt Smallwood 1951–54	Jim LaMarque 1942–51	Herman Horn 1951–54
p	Slim Jones		Gene Richardson	
			Gene Collins	
mgr		Buster Haywood	Buck O'Neil	Buck O'Neil

Pos.	Lonnie Summers 1938–51	Art Pennington 1940–51	Bubba Hyde 1927–51	Willie Grace 1942–50	Bob Boyd 1946–50	Sherwood Brewer 1946–60
c	Josh Gibson	Josh Gibson	Larry Brown	Josh Gibson	Quincy Trouppe	Josh Gibson
1b	Jim West	Buck Leonard	George Giles	Buck Leonard	Buck Leonard	Buck Leonard
2b	Sammy T. Hughes	Bonnie Serrell	Newt Allen	Newt Allen	Jackie Robinson	Piper Davis
3b	Ray Dandridge	Ray Dandridge	Alex Radcliffe	Judy Johnson	Ray Dandridge	Ray Dandridge
ss	Willie Wells	Willie Wells	Willie Wells	Willie Wells	Artie Wilson	Willie Wells
of	Henry Kimbro	Willard Brown	Willard Brown	Willard Brown	Henry Kimbro	Willard Brown
of	Cool Papa Bell	Cool Papa Bell	Turkey Stearnes	Cool Papa Bell	Cool Papa Bell	Cool Papa Bell
of	Bill Wright	Sam Bankhead	Hank Thompson	Willie Mays	Larry Doby	Oscar Charleston
p	Satchel Paige	Satchel Paige	Satchel Paige	Satchel Paige	Satchel Paige	Satchel Paige
p	Leroy Matlock	Ted Radcliffe	Willie Foster	Martin Dihigo	Verdell Mathis	Hilton Smith
mgr	Winfred Welch	Candy Jim Taylor	Willie Wells	Candy Jim Taylor	Buck O'Neil	Buck O'Neil

Pos.	Buck O'Neil, 1937–55 —1st team	Buck O'Neil, 1937–55 —2nd team	Sam Hairston 1945–50	Marlin Carter 1932–50	Willie Pat Patterson 1945–55	Red Moore 1935–42
c	Josh Gibson	Biz Mackey	Josh Gibson	Josh Gibson	Josh Gibson	Josh Gibson
1b	Buck Leonard	Luke Easter	Buck Leonard	Buck Leonard	Buck Leonard	Buck Leonard
2b	Newt Allen	Dickie Seay	Jackie Robinson	George Scales	Johnnie Cowan	Sammy T. Hughes
3b	Ray Dandridge	Oliver Marcell	Ray Dandridge	Judy Johnson	Marlin Carter	Ray Dandridge
ss	Willie Wells	Pop Lloyd	Ernie Banks	Willie Wells	Artie Wilson	Willie Wells
of	Turkey Stearnes	Ted Strong	Willard Brown	Willard Brown	Jimmie Crutchfield	Monte Irvin
of	Oscar Charleston	Cool Papa Bell	Willie Mays	Cool Papa Bell	Cool Papa Bell	Cool Papa Bell
of	Mule Suttles	Wild Bill Wright	Hank Aaron	Sam Bankhead	Ed Steele	Turkey Stearnes
p	Satchel Paige	Bullet Rogan	Satchel Paige	Satchel Paige	Satchel Paige	Satchel Paige
p	Joe Williams	Leon Day	Bullet Rogan	Bullet Rogan	Leon Day	Leon Day
p	Hilton Smith	Willie Foster				
mgr	Rube Foster	Candy Jim Taylor	Buck O'Neil	Andy Cooper	Oscar Charleston	Oscar Charleston

Pos.	Quincy Trouppe 1930–49	Ted Radcliffe 1928–50	Wild Bill Wright 1932–45	Jim Cohen 1948–52	Ernie Johnson 1949–53	Cool Papa Bell 1922–46
c	Josh Gibson	Biz Mackey	Josh Gibson	Joe Greene	Josh Gibson	Biz Mackey
c	Biz Mackey	Josh Gibson				
1b	Buck Leonard	George Giles	Buck Leonard	Buck Leonard	Bob Boyd	Oscar Charleston
2b	George Scales	Newt Allen	Sammy T. Hughes	Junior Gilliam	Jackie Robinson	Sammy T. Hughes
3b	Ray Dandridge	Alec Radcliffe	Ray Dandridge	Herb Souell	Alex Radcliffe	Judy Johnson
ss	Pop Lloyd	Willie Wells	Willie Wells	Pee Wee Butts	Ernie Banks	Willie Wells
of	Chino Smith	Turkey Stearnes	Turkey Stearnes	Willard Brown	Willard Brown	Monte Irvin
of	Cristobal Torrienti	Cool Papa Bell	Cool Papa Bell	Bob Thurman	Carl Long	Turkey Stearnes
of	Oscar Charleston	Willard Brown	Oscar Charleston	Hank Thompson	Hank Aaron	Rap Dixon
p	Hilton Smith	Hilton Smith	Luis Tiant	Leon Day	Satchel Paige	Ted Trent
p	Dick Redding	Satchel Paige	Bullet Rogan	Vibert Clarke	Ted Richardson	Willie Foster
p	Bullet Rogan	Ray Brown				
p	Ray Brown	Willie Foster				
mgr	Rube Foster	Bingo DeMoss	Candy Jim Taylor	Winfred Welch	Buck O'Neil	

Pos.	Bill Cash 1943–50	Louis Santop 1909–31	Tex Burnett, 1921–46	Leon Day 1934–50	Dick Powell, 1938–51	Al Moses, writer 1948
c	Josh Gibson	Josh Gibson	Josh Gibson	Leon Ruffin	Josh Gibson	Biz Mackey
c	Biz Mackey					Josh Gibson
1b	Buck Leonard	Buck Leonard	Buck Leonard	Buck Leonard	Martin Dihigo	Buck Leonard
2b	Bonnie Serrell	Sammy T. Hughes	Deke Mothel	Larry Doby	Sammy T. Hughes	Bingo DeMoss
3b	Ray Dandridge	George Scales	Jud Wilson	Ray Dandridge	Oliver Marcell	Ray Dandridge
ss	Jessie Williams	Willie Wells	Willie Wells	Willie Wells	Dick Lundy	Pop Lloyd
of	Gene Benson	Bill Wright	Jerry Benjamin	Martin Dihigo	Jose Mesa	Carlos Torrienti
of	Cool Papa Bell	Cool Papa Bell	Ray Brown	Cool Papa Bell	Oscar Charleston	Oscar Charleston
of	Mule Suttles	Sam Bankhead	Fats Jenkins	Mule Suttles	Rap Dixon	Rap Dixon
p	Hilton Smith	Satchel Paige	Slim Jones	Satchel Paige	Smokey Joe Williams	Dave Brown
p	Barney Brown	Chet Brewer	Chet Brewer	Hilton Smith	Jonas Gaines	Smokey Joe Williams
p			Ray Brown			Dick Redding
p			Bill Holland			Satchel Paige
mgr	Oscar Charleston	Pop Lloyd		Biz Mackey	Candy Jim Taylor	Rube Foster

Pos.	James Riley's player survey All-Stars–1st team	James Riley's player survey All-Stars–2nd team	James Riley's player survey All-Stars–3rd team	Larry Lester's player survey 1993 All-Stars–1st	Larry Lester's player survey 1993 All-Stars–2nd	John Bissant 1934–47
c	Josh Gibson	Biz Mackey	Roy Campanella	Josh Gibson	Biz Mackey	Larry Brown
1b	Buck Leonard	Ben Taylor	Mule Suttles	Buck Leonard	Mule Suttles	Buck Leonard
2b	Martin Dihigo	Bingo DeMoss	Newt Allen	Piper Davis	Newt Allen	Chester Williams
3b	Ray Dandridge	Judy Johnson	Oliver Marcell	Ray Dandridge	Judy Johnson	Alex Radcliffe
ss	Pop Lloyd	Willie Wells	Dick Lundy	Willie Wells	Artie Wilson	Willie Wells
of	Oscar Charleston	Monte Irvin	Sam Jethroe	Oscar Charleston	Sam Jethroe	Sam Bankhead
of	Cool Papa Bell	Turkey Stearnes	Willard Brown	Cool Papa Bell	Willard Brown	Cool Papa Bell
of	Cristobal Torriente	Pete Hill	Clint Thomas	Turkey Stearnes	Martin Dihigo	Nat Rogers
p	Satchel Paige	Smokey Joe Williams	Willie Foster	Satchel Paige	Smokey Joe Williams	Satchel Paige
p				Leon Day	Bullet Rogan	Willie Foster
p				Hilton Smith	Ray Brown	
mgr	Rube Foster	C. I. Taylor	Vic Harris	Buck O'Neil	Candy Jim Taylor	

Pos.	Tweed Webb, writer 1922–1990	Bobby Robinson 1925–42	Lester Lockett 1937–50	Robert Peterson, Only the Ball was White—1st team	Robert Peterson, Only the Ball was White—2nd team	Robert Peterson, Only the Ball was White—3rd team
c	Biz Mackey	Larry Brown	Josh Gibson	Biz Mackey	Josh Gibson	Bruce Petway
c		Frank Duncan Sr.				
1b	Ben Taylor	Mule Suttles	Buck Leonard	Buck Leonard	Ben Taylor	Mule Suttles
2b	Bingo DeMoss	Bingo DeMoss	Sammy T. Hughes	Bingo DeMoss	Newt Allen	Sammy T. Hughes
3b	Dave Malarcher	Dave Malarcher	Ray Dandridge	Ray Dandridge	Judy Johnson	Dave Malarcher
ss	Pop Lloyd	Willie Wells	Willie Wells	Pop Lloyd	Willie Wells	Dick Lundy
of	Mule Suttles	Cristobal Torriente	Henry Kimbro	Oscar Charleston	Cool Papa Bell	Spot Poles
of	Cool Papa Bell	Cool Papa Bell	Cool Papa Bell	Martin Dihigo	Pete Hill	Turkey Stearnes
of	Oscar Charleston	John Henry Russell	Sam Bankhead	Cristobal Torriente	Rap Dixon	Chaney White
p	Smokey Joe Williams	Ted Trent	Satchel Paige	Smokey Joe Williams	Dick Redding	Bullet Rogan
p	Satchel Paige	Bullet Rogan	Verdell Mathis	John Donaldson	Willie Foster	Dave Brown

Notes

INTRODUCTION

1. Seventy-Fifth Anniversary banquet speech at the Negro Leagues Baseball Museum in Kansas City, Missouri, 29 October 1995.

2. O'Neil, Wulf, and Conrads, *I Was Right on Time*, 121–23.

3. Sam Lacy, telephone interview, 8 November 1996.

THE GUIDING LIGHT OF MODERN NEGRO BASEBALL

1. This title was bestowed on Greenlee by writer Don de Leighbur, in an article about Greenlee's new venture into the United States League. *Kansas City Call*, 8 September 1944.

2. Richard Powell, telephone interview, 24 October 1997.

3. William Augustus Greenlee headstone, Allegheny Cemetery, Pittsburgh PA.

4. Greenlee headstone.

5. *Pittsburgh Post-Gazette,* 10 October 1932.

6. *Pittsburgh Courier,* 25 March 1925.

7. Teenie Harris, telephone interview, 8 December 1996.

8. Charles Greenlee, interview by Rob Ruck, 18 June 1980, University of Pittsburgh, Archives of Industrial Society, Hillman Library.

9. Harris interview, 8 December 1996.

10. Greenlee interview, 18 June 1980.

11. *Pittsburgh Post-Gazette,* 10 october 1932.

12. Greenlee interview, 18 June 1980.

13. Harris interview, 8 December 1996.

14. Harris interview, 8 December 1996.

15. *Pittsburgh Courier,* 18 July 1931.

16. *Pittsburgh Courier,* 13 August 1932.

17. *Pittsburgh Courier,* 6 August 1932.

18. *Pittsburgh Courier,* 24 February 1934.

19. *Pittsburgh Courier,* 12 July 1952.

20. *Pittsburgh Courier,* 27 February 1932.

21. *Pittsburgh Sun-Telegraph,* 28 April 1932.

22. *Pittsburgh Courier,* 7 May 1932.

23. *Pittsburgh Sun-Telegraph,* 30 April 1932.

24. *Pittsburgh Courier,* 7 May 1932.

25. *Pittsburgh Courier,* 21 May 1932.

26. *Pittsburgh Courier,* 9 July 1932.

27. The Wilberforce football team were National Black Football Champions in 1931. From 1923 to 1927, their star running back was Harry "Wu Fang" Ward, who also pitched for the collegiate team and would umpire in the 1945 East-West All-Star Game.

28. Ruck, *Sandlot Seasons,* 156.

29. *Pittsburgh Post-Gazette,* 5 May 1932.

30. *Pittsburgh Courier,* 20 August 1932.

31. *Pittsburgh Courier,* 17 September 1932.

32. The Kansas City Monarchs had been the first professional team to use a portable lighting system, on April 30, 1930, in Enid, Oklahoma, against the Phillips University Haymakers at Alton Stadium. The portable lights would become a fixture at Monarchs games played in Kansas City, Missouri. Monarchs owner J. L. Wilkinson had experimented previously with lights in the early 1920s with his semipro All Nations team. The lights proved to be financial bonanza in the post-depression years for Wilkinson, as he often rented out his mobile lights to minor league clubs. Major League Baseball would not install stadium lights until 1935, five years later, in Cincinnati's Crosley Field. The Reds would play seven night games, one against each National League team. Despite its critics, night baseball has become a national tradition.

33. *Pittsburgh Courier,* 20 August 1932.

34. *Pittsburgh Courier,* 4 March 1933.

35. *Pittsburgh Courier,* November 1932.

36. *Pittsburgh Courier,* 7 January 1933.

37. *Pittsburgh Courier,* 21 July 1934.

38. *Pittsburgh Courier,* 12 July 1952.

39. Historians often conclude that the 1935 team, with five future Hall of Famers in Satchel Paige, Oscar Charleston, Cool Papa Bell, Josh Gibson, and Judy Johnson—at the time the highest representation from any Negro League team—was perhaps the greatest assemblage of talent ever.

40. *Pittsburgh Courier,* 10 December 1938.

41. *Pittsburgh Courier,* 8 April 1939.

42. *Chicago Defender,* 14 August 1937.

43. Joseph Rainey was a former newspaper writer and Pennsylvania state commissioner. Rainey later became president of the Philadelphia chapter of the NAACP and in 1948 spoke out against police chief Eugene "Bull" Connor's civil rights policy at a racially mixed crowd attending the Southern Negro Youth Conference in Birmingham, Alabama. The Manleys also offered William H. Hastie, once a federal judge and later dean of the Howard University Law School, an opportunity to be commissioner. He declined. Overmyer, *Effa Manley,* 149.

44. *Pittsburgh Courier,* 8 May 1943.

45. *Pittsburgh Courier,* 8 May 1932.

46. *Pittsburgh Courier,* 8 May 1932.

47. *Pittsburgh Courier,* 6 January 1945.

48. *New York Amsterdam News,* 31 March 1945.

1933

1. *Pittsburgh Courier,* 15 August 1942.

2. The Loendi Club, founded on August 13, 1897, was named for a river in Africa. It was considered the city's elite black male club, along with the Monticellos. It was located on 93 Fulton (now Fullerton) Street, in the Hill District. At one time, Cum Posey was president of the club. Glasco, "Take Care of Business," 177.

3. *Pittsburgh Courier,* 15 August 1942.

4. *Pittsburgh Courier,* 15 August 1942.

5. *Pittsburgh Courier,* 15 August 1942.

6. Lester Lockett, interview with author, 29 October 1995.

7. The black newspapers were often the only voice of the black underclass. For further study of the role of the black newspaper and the integration of baseball, see William Simons, "Jackie Robinson and the American Mind: Journalistic Perceptions of the Reintegration of Baseball," *Journal of Sport History* (spring 1985); Donald L. Deardorrff, "The Black Press Played a Key Role in Integrating Baseball," *St. Louis Journalism Review* (July/August 1994); Bill Weaver, "The Black Press and the Assault on Professional Baseball's Color Line," *Phylon* (winter 1979); and Patrick Washburn, "The Pittsburgh Courier's Double V Campaign in 1942," *American Journalism* (1986). For books on the black press, see Reisler, *Black Writers/Black Baseball;* Roland E. Wolseley, *Black Press, USA* (Ames: Iowa State University Press, 1971); and Christopher C. De Santis, *Langston Hughes and the Chicago Defender* (Urbana: University of Illinois Press, 1995).

8. Woods and Liddell, *I, Too, Sing America,* unnumbered pages.

9. In 1904, Dr. Mary Bethune became founding president of Bethune-Cookman College in Daytona Beach, Florida, and later president of the National Council of Negro Women.

10. *Pittsburgh Post-Gazette,* 26 April 1932.

11. *Chicago Defender,* 1 July 1933.

12. *Chicago Defender,* 1 July 1933.

13. *Philadelphia Tribune,* 5 August 1944.

1934

1. *Pittsburgh Courier,* 11 August 1934.

2. *Philadelphia Tribune,* 25 September 1943.

3. *Kansas City Call,* 26 October 1934.

4. *Kansas City Call,* 19 October 1934.

5. Jimmie Crutchfield, interview with author, 25 November 1991. Crutchfield had a great memory.

6. *Chicago Defender,* 27 October 1934.

7. The Monarchs' sojourn to Wichita became the beginning of the second major midwestern baseball tournament, the National Baseball Congress Tournament. The Denver Post Tournament was the first, in 1933. Starting in 1935, this tournament, sponsored by Ray Dumont (a close friend of Monarchs owner J. L. Wilkinson), offered $10,000 for first place, twice the bounty of the Denver tourney. In the tournament's initial year, the crown was won by the Bismarck team of North Dakota, led by former Monarchs pitchers Satchel Paige, Chet Brewer, and Hilton Smith with catcher Quincy Trouppe.

8. Despite writer Young's claim of the East-West game as "just an ordinary game" (*Kansas City Call,* 27 July 1934), the game of games would become the highlight of the season for black baseball. In fact, Cool Papa Bell responded: "I can see more good baseball prospects this year than at any time in my career. It is my firm belief that the East-West game last year encouraged these youngsters. To my mind, the game is the best thing ever offered to the public, the players and club owners. I am for it."

Young's claims of commercialism were perhaps confused with Major League Baseball's commitment to donate all-star game proceeds to charity or to a players' pension fund. Negro League financiers were not assured of a profit at this early stage of the promotion, and therefore possible donations were uncommitted at this time.

A review of the voting results reveals that players receiving the most votes were selected to the game. Although the Monarchs were not in the league this year (they were barnstorming instead), league officials chose to allow public voting of the popular Monarchs for the benefit of the game.

1935

1. *New York Age,* 19 January 1935.

2. This was the first all-star game to use black umpires. In 1922 *Chicago Defender* sportswriter Fay Young, official scorer for several East-West All-Star Games, asked his readers in an August 19 editorial for their opinions on hiring black umpires. The response was overwhelming, with readers in favor of hiring

black umpires. One response was from Ed O'Malley, writer for the *Los Angeles Times*, who recommended W. W. (Billy) Donaldson, from the Pacific Coast League. Donaldson would later umpire in the 1936 and 1937 East-West games.

The following year, 1923, the Negro National League signed its first black umpires. Billy Donaldson of Los Angeles, B. E. Gholston (Cuban League) of Oakland, California, Leon Augustine and Lucian Snaer of New Orleans, Caesar Jamison of New York, and William Embry of Vincennes, Indiana, completed the magnificent seven crew. Former Chicago American Giants pitcher Tom Johnson was named as a reserve. *Kansas City Call*, 20 April 1923.

On April 28, 1923, in Kansas City, Missouri, Donaldson and Gholston made history as the first black umpires to officiate a Negro League game. *Kansas City Call*, 20 April 1923.

3. *New York Age*, 5 October 1935.

4. *New York Age*, 11 May 1935.

5. Paige, *Satchel Paige's Own Story*, 52.

6. *Kansas City Call*, 11 October 1935.

7. *Pittsburgh Courier*, 19 October 1935.

8. *Kansas City Call*, 18 October 1935.

9. *Kansas City Call*, 25 October 1935.

10. Sam Lacy, *Baltimore Afro-American* writer, who covered the 1935 game, recalls: "Suttles hit some prodigious home runs. Long suckers! Mule Suttles hit home runs as high as they were far. He and Josh were different. Josh and Buck [Leonard] hit line drive home runs. But Mule Suttles and John Beckwith hit home runs that went up in the air like sky rockets. They went as high in distance as they went far. When I said prodigious, I mean prodigious!" Telephone interview, 8 November 1996.

11. Future Hall of Famer Martin Dihigo may have been weak from his crash into the outfield fence in an earlier attempt to catch Josh Gibson's double. Dihigo's heroic play was described by Dan Burley in an August 17 article in the *Chicago Defender*, "Here's How the West Made History at Comiskey Park": "Gibson drove the ball on a line against the left center field wall, 400 feet away and Dihigo, racing for the catch, slammed into the wall. He crumpled to the grass as Gibson slowed up at second base. The entire playing cast rushed out to the side of the stricken player. The crowd sat in stunned silence as doctors, photographers and newspapermen ran to where Dihigo lay. Later, the player recovered and continued in the game."

1936

1. *Chicago Defender*, 29 August 1936.

2. *Chicago Defender*, 29 August 1936.

3. *Chicago Defender*, 29 August 1936.

4. *Philadelphia Tribune*, 30 July 1936.

5. *Philadelphia Tribune*, 30 July 1936.

6. *Philadelphia Tribune*, 30 July 1936.

7. *Kansas City Call*, 13 March 1936.

8. *Philadelphia Tribune*, 12 March 1936.

9. *Philadelphia Tribune*, 12 March 1936.

10. *New York Age*, 18 January 1936.

11. *Philadelphia Tribune*, 12 March 1936.

12. *Kansas City Call*, 13 March 1936.

13. *Philadelphia Tribune*, 3 December 1936.

14. *New York Age*, 27 June 1936.

15. *Kansas City Call*, 11 December 1936.

16. *Kansas City Call*, 14 August 1936.

17. Buck Leonard fondly remembers playing with Cool Papa in Denver: "We played on an all star team in the 1936 *Denver Post* Tournament in Denver, Colorado. He won the stolen base award in this event. We won the tournament seven games to no losses. In this tournament he was the fastest thing I have ever seen on the bases."

Leonard added: "We roomed together on the Grays for a few years. He had arthritis and I did too. After a hard game we had a little bottle of gin with lemons and sugar. We would take a couple of swallows before going to bed at night."

Leonard continued: "He had everything a player needed. A needle and thread, a safety pin, a piece of string, corn medicine, iodine, pocket knife, face cream, and extra razor blades. He could shave in the baseball bus while it was moving."

"He was the nicest fellow I have ever known on or off the playing field," Leonard remembered, "in baseball or out of baseball. He was tops!" Letter to author, 25 May 1972.

1937

1. *New York Age*, 26 August 1937.

2. *New York Daily Worker*, 16 September 1937.

3. Peterson, *Only the Ball Was White*, 130.

4. *Kansas City Call*, 30 April 1937. Dihigo and Salazar were identified as the architects behind the raids. Salazar never returned to play in the Negro Leagues, spending the remainder of his career playing winters in Cuba and summers in Mexico. In 1954 he was elected to the Mexican Hall of Fame. Dihigo was forced to play in Mexico and Cuba until 1945, when the New York Cubans asked him to return and manage their ballclub, where he made his last

East-West appearance. Dihigo was later elected to halls of fame in the United States, Cuba, and Mexico.

5. *New York Age*, 29 May 1937.

6. "My Greatest Day in Baseball," as told to Ernest Mehl, *Chicago Daily News*, 13 March 1943. For additional reading on the 1937 season in Santo Domingo, see Ruck, *The Tropic of Baseball*, 37–40. For further insight on the dictator Generalissimo Dr. Rafael L. Trujillo, see German E. Ornes, *Trujillo: Little Caesar of the Caribbean* (New York: Thomas Nelson, 1958).

7. *Denver Post*, 10 August 1937.

8. *Chicago Defender*, 21 August 1937.

9. Rogosin, *Invisible Men*, 140–41.

1938

1. *Chicago Defender*, 30 July 1938.

2. *Chicago Defender*, 30 July 1938.

3. *Chicago Defender*, 30 July 1938.

4. *Chicago Defender*, 30 July 1938.

5. *Washington Afro-American*, 20 August 1938.

6. *Washington Afro-American*, 20 August 1938.

7. *New York Age*, 13 August 1938.

8. *New York Age*, 13 August 1938.

9. *Washington Afro-American*, 20 August 1938.

10. *Pittsburgh Courier*, 14 January 1939.

11. *Philadelphia Tribune*, 11 November 1944.

12. Gilbert, *Baseball and the Color Line*, 129.

13. *Pittsburgh Courier*, 10 December 1938.

14. *Washington Afro-American*, 17 September 1938.

1939

1. Traditionally, the first-place winner played the weaker fourth-place team to increase the chances to compete for the league title.

2. Until now, the term *organized baseball* had always meant Major League Baseball.

3. Players routinely borrowed against future paychecks.

4. *New York Amsterdam News*, 11 November 1939.

5. *New York Amsterdam News*, 10 June 1939.

6. *New York Amsterdam News*, 28 July 1939.

7. Ritter, *Lost Ballparks*, 190. The Associated Press dispatch (4 May 1994) read: "The St. Louis major league baseball teams, the Cardinals and Browns, have discontinued their old policy of restricting Negroes to the bleachers and pavilion at Sportsman's Park. Negroes may now purchase seats in the grandstand."

8. *New York Daily Worker*, 30 July 1939.

9. *New York Daily Worker*, 30 July 1939.

10. *New York Daily Worker*, 30 July 1939.

11. *New York Daily Worker*, 30 July 1939.

12. *New York Daily Worker*, 30 July 1939.

13. *New York Daily Worker*, 30 July 1939.

14. *Pittsburgh Courier*, 5 August 1939.

15. *Pittsburgh Courier*, 12 August 1939.

16. *Pittsburgh Courier*, 12 August 1939.

17. *Pittsburgh Courier*, 5 August 1939.

18. *Pittsburgh Courier*, 5 August 1939.

19. *Pittsburgh Courier*, 5 August 1939.

20. *Pittsburgh Courier*, 5 August 1939.

21. *Pittsburgh Courier*, 5 August 1939.

22. *Pittsburgh Courier*, 5 August 1939.

23. Lester Rodney, telephone interview, 31 October 1997.

24. *New York Times*, 25 August 1939 and 27 August 1939.

1940

1. *New York Age*, 25 May 1940.

2. Effa Manley, letter to writer Art Carter, 15 August 1940.

3. *Baltimore Afro-American*, 2 February 1940.

4. *Pittsburgh Courier*, 12 February 1940.

5. William Marshall is currently director of special collections and archives at the University of Kentucky and author of the book *Baseball's Pivotal Years* (Lexington: University of Kentucky Press, 1999).

6. Overmyer, *Effa Manley*, 6.

7. Overmyer, *Effa Manley*, 7.

8. Abe Manley was threatening to use players currently under contract to rival American League teams if the Monarchs did not force Paige to report to the Eagles. Earlier, Paige had sent a letter to Effa Manley requesting permission to join the club and play in the East-West game. The letter below shows Paige's willingness to report; however, Paige never appeared in a Newark Eagles uniform. It is not known whether Abe or Effa Manley responded to Paige's letter. The letter was written on letterhead from the Angelus Hotel in Vancouver, British Columbia, Canada.

July 24–40

Dear Mrs. Manley

Just a few lines to let you hear from me. Listen Mrs. Manley make [*sic*] this means more to you my coming now playing in the East and West game that is if it is possible I can come and pitch in the East and West game. Really I want to do something for you. Now don't be angry with me. Just tell me what you will give me to finish the season with you and send me a ticket on the plane and I will come and finish the season with you, that is if it will do you any good. If this is OK please answer this letter at Tacoma Washington I am at the Victoria Hotel on Broadway. Just let me know what you will give one month and play in the East and West game and send me a ticket on the plane and I will come straight there. I am tired of out here. See if you get this letter. Please answer at once.

Tacoma Washington
Victoria Hotel
On Broadway,
Satchell Paige

9. Besides Paige, George Giles (one game), Norman Robinson (one game), Byron "Mex" Johnson (one game), and Herb Souell (five games) were the East-West all-stars on the Satchel Paige All-Stars. Other players included pitchers Ed Barnes, Walter "Big Train" Johnson, and Johnny Markham; catchers Paul Hardy and Frazier Robinson (Norm's brother); second baseman Jesse Douglass; outfielders Bill Brown, Fred Daniels, Leandy Young, and Everett Marcell; with manager Newt Joseph.

1941

1. *Philadelphia Tribune,* 14 August 1941.
2. *Philadelphia Tribune,* 10 April 1941.
3. *Newark Afro-American,* 26 July 1941.
4. *Newark Afro-American,* 26 July 1941.
5. Bolton, *Before the Game Was Color Blind,* 66.
6. *Philadelphia Tribune,* 7 August 1941.
7. Irvin, *Nice Guys Finish First,* 64–66.
8. *Chicago Defender,* 6 September 1941.
9. *Chicago Defender,* 6 September 1941.

1942

1. Major League Baseball business was included for the first time as the war depleted club rosters, raising the question of possible integration of teams. The race issue became more urgent as owners struggled to put quality squads on the field. War sympathizers become socially conscious and, more importantly, provided an opportunity for patriotic concerns or propaganda.
2. *New York Daily Worker,* 4 February 1942.
3. *Pittsburgh Courier,* 30 May 1942.
4. *Pittsburgh Courier,* 30 May 1942.
5. Copies of Indianapolis Clowns stationery from various years consistently list Syd Pollock as owner. Hunter Campbell's name never appeared on the stationery in any administrative capacity. Nor was he mentioned in any promotional material mailed to clubs by Pol-

lock. If Campbell was indeed the owner, he didn't respond to Wendell Smith's allegations. Pollock's son, Alan, who died on January 10, 1999, at age 56, confirmed that his father was sole owner of various teams using the Clowns moniker.

6. Although several books have been written about Jackie Robinson, little is known about Californian Nate Moreland. Moreland was a teammate of Robinson at Muir Tech High School and Pasadena Junior College, where he was a catcher. He later completed his education at Redlands University, pitching for the college team instead of catching. Moreland was also a Golden Gloves boxing champion and threw the javelin in junior college. After graduation, he joined the 1940 Baltimore Elite Giants and won 14 games against 5 losses. His battery mate was Robinson's future Dodgers teammate Roy Campanella. Subsequent years found Moreland pitching for several teams in Mexico and a teammate again of Robinson with the 1945 Kansas City Monarchs. Moreland threw an above-average fastball plus a darting slider. He averaged roughly three strikeouts a game but walked just as many. When he was at the top of his game, he retired most batters on ground balls. At six feet two inches and around 200 pounds, he was often compared to Don Newcombe but never quite filled Newk's potential. John McReynolds, Nate Moreland presentation at SABR Allan Roth Chapter, 5 April 1997.
7. *New York Daily Worker,* 23 March 1942.
8. *Pittsburgh Courier,* 8 August 1942.
9. *Pittsburgh Courier,* 29 August 1942.
10. *New York Daily Worker,* 25 May 1942.
11. *Chicago Daily News,* 25 May 1942.
12. *Chicago Herald American,* 25 May 1942.
13. Buck O'Neil, telephone interview, 17 March 1998.
14. *Washington Post,* 1 June 1942.
15. The $250 fine was reported as the stiffest fine to date by the league president. *Pittsburgh Courier,* 15 August 1942.
16. *New York Daily Worker,* 8 June 1942.
17. *New York Daily Worker,* 18 June 1942.
18. Rodney interview, 31 October 1997.
19. *New York Daily Worker,* 15 July 1942.
20. *Louisville Courier Journal,* editorial by Tommy Fitzgerald, 12 April 1942.
21. *Los Angeles Times,* 17 July 1942.
22. *Los Angeles Times,* 17 July 1942.
23. *Los Angeles Times,* 17 July 1942.
24. *Los Angeles Times,* 17 July 1942.
25. *Cleveland Call-Post,* 24 July 1942.

26. *Cleveland Call-Post*, 24 July 1942.

27. *New York Daily Worker*, 28 July 1942.

28. *Pittsburgh Courier*, 22 August 1942.

29. *Pittsburgh Courier*, 8 August 1942.

30. *Pittsburgh Courier*, 22 August 1942.

31. *Pittsburgh Courier*, 22 August 1942.

32. *Pittsburgh Courier*, 17 September 1942.

33. *Cleveland Call-Post*, 2 September 1942.

34. *New York Daily Worker*, 19 September 1942.

35. *New York Daily Worker*, 2 December 1942.

36. *Cleveland Call-Post*, 22 August 1942.

37. O'Neil interview, 18 March 1998.

38. Riley, *Dandy, Day and the Devil*, 66.

39. *Pittsburgh Courier*, 22 August 1942.

1943

1. *Pittsburgh Courier*, 23 January 1943.

2. *Philadelphia Tribune*, 8 July 1944.

3. *Philadelphia Tribune*, 15 May 1943.

4. *Pittsburgh Courier*, 27 February 1943.

5. *Pittsburgh Courier*, 27 February 1943. The Senators' roster included pitcher Alex Carrasquel, from Caracas, Venezuela, and outfielder Roberto Ortiz, from Camaguey, Cuba. Carrasquel debuted with the Senators in 1939, while Ortiz joined Washington in 1941.

6. *Pittsburgh Courier*, 11 December 1943.

7. *Pittsburgh Courier*, 11 December 1943.

8. *Pittsburgh Courier*, 11 December 1943.

9. *Pittsburgh Courier*, 11 December 1943.

10. *Pittsburgh Courier*, 11 December 1943.

11. *Pittsburgh Courier*, 11 December 1943.

12. *Pittsburgh Courier*, 11 December 1943.

13. *Pittsburgh Courier*, 11 December 1943.

14. *Pittsburgh Courier*, 11 December 1943.

15. *Philadelphia Tribune*, 25 March 1944.

16. *Philadelphia Tribune*, 25 March 1944.

1944

1. *Pittsburgh Courier*, 6 May 1944.

2. *Philadelphia Tribune*, 22 July 1944.

3. *Philadelphia Tribune*, 25 March 1944.

4. *Philadelphia Tribune*, 25 March 1944.

5. Carter, *Negro Baseball Pictorial Yearbook*, 5.

6. Rodney interview, 31 October 1997.

7. *Pittsburgh Courier*, 2 December 1944.

8. *Baltimore Afro-American*, 19 August 1944.

9. *Kansas City Call*, 18 August 1944.

10. Earlier in the season, the Negro National League voted to reject Greenlee's application for a franchise. Cum Posey (league secretary) and Sonnyman Jackson, owners of the Homestead Grays, felt that another team at Forbes Field would infringe on the territorial rights of the Grays. Although the Grays played the majority of their games at Griffith Stadium in Washington DC, Posey and Jackson conveniently called Pittsburgh their home field.

11. According to financial reports from the league office in 1943, Paige was paid $300 of the $531.30 allocated to the Kansas City Monarchs who participated in the game. After railroad and hotel expenses were deducted, the four Monarchs split the remaining $100. Players on the West squad netted earnings of $25 each, much less than the $100 reported to the public.

12. Willie Simms, telephone interview, 9 July 1997.

13. *Philadelphia Tribune*, 10 June 1944.

14. *Philadelphia Tribune*, 10 June 1944.

15. The submarine pitcher Porter "Ankle-ball" Moss was fatally shot by Johnny Easley of Camden, Tennessee, on July 16, a Sunday, aboard a train traveling about 50 miles outside of Nashville. As the Memphis bus was being repaired, the team was forced to travel by train to play a doubleheader that afternoon.

In an interview by John Erardi of the *Cincinnati Enquirer* (4 April 1993), Moss's teammate Verdell Mathis recalled the incident:

No sooner had the ballplayers wedged themselves into the front car than an intoxicated man began giving a hard time to some of the young women. Moss said, "Why don't you go and sit down and leave these women alone?" Well this guy didn't like that, but he didn't say anything and got up and walked to the back of the car. I was glad to see him go, because I had just said to my buddy Larry Brown, "This guy is packing a pistol."

Porter got up—not to follow the guy—but to go back and talk to some of our guys who were standing between the cars. Next thing you know, an argument starts up and guys start backing up. One of our guys, a second baseman named Fred Bankhead, kicked at the guy, but he missed. Right about then, the train pulled into the next station. When the train came to a stop, this guy jumped off, wheeled and fired a shot that just missed the conductor and hit Moss right under his heart.

Moss was in a lot of pain. . . . We carried him to the baggage department and laid him down. We were told there was a doctor at the next station. When we got there, he said he wouldn't treat Moss because he was colored. We had to go on to the next stop in Jackson, Tennessee, where there was an ambulance waiting for us. It was an hour farther down the line. By then, Moss had lost too much blood. The doctors operated, but he died that next day.

Mathis added, "Moss was a college-educated man and had a fine life in front of him. The police finally caught up with the guy who shot Moss. . . . He was sentenced to 10 years in prison. That's better than what Moss got."

1945

1. Rodney interview, 31 October 1997.

2. *New York Amsterdam News,* 24 March 1945.

3. *New York Amsterdam News,* 7 April 1945, quoting the *New York Daily News.*

4. *New York Amsterdam News,* 7 April 1945.

5. *New York Amsterdam News,* 7 April 1945.

6. Tygiel, *Baseball's Great Experiment,* 44.

7. In an article entitled "You Could Almost Have a Negro All-Star Game," Jackie Robinson reported to writer Steve Gelman that "Sam Jethroe, Marv Williams and myself had a tryout with the Red Sox. I don't think the Red Sox or any other team had three players put on a demonstration the way we did. Everything worked just right. At bat, we were bouncing balls off the fence like it was handball. We were fielding like we never did before. Jethroe was running faster than he ever did and catching balls in the outfield that he never caught again. We were told they never saw anybody do so well in a tryout and that's the last thing we were told." *Sport* (July 1960), 89.

Earlier, Robinson told reporter Frank Wake-field, 'I know that the Red Sox are a prejudiced club. They were when I went to Fenway Park for a trial from the Kansas City Monarchs. Sam Jethroe, Marv Williams and myself put on a pre-game batting show in Fenway Park that day that they're still talking about." Robinson added, "The Sox could have had all of us for very little. But they were a prejudiced club then, and they are now." *Buffalo Evening News,* 20 April 1959.

8. *San Antonio Express, San Antonio Light,* 2 April 1945; *San Antonio Register,* 6 April 1945.

9. *Pittsburgh Courier,* 14 May 1938.

10. *New York Amsterdam News,* 14 April 1945, quoting the *Herald-Tribune.*

11. Rodney interview, 31 October 1997.

12. *People's Voice* (New York), 14 April 1945.

13. *People's Voice* (New York), 14 April 1945.

14. *New York Amsterdam News,* 14 April 1945.

15. *People's Voice* (New York), 14 April 1945.

16. *New York Amsterdam News,* 14 April 1945.

17. Rodney interview, 31 October 1997.

18. *Pittsburgh Courier,* 28 April 1945.

19. *New York Post,* 8 May 1945.

20. *New York Post,* 8 May 1945. Rickey's comment was based on misinformation about the black leagues. From the Manuscript Division in the Library of Congress, writer Arthur Mann, in his paper "The Negro and Baseball: The National Game Faces a Racial Challenge Long Ignored," quotes Rickey as saying, "They are the poorest excuse for the word league, and by comparison with organized baseball, which they understandably try to copy, they are not leagues at all. I failed to find a constitution or a set of bylaws. I failed to find a single player under contract, and learned that players of all teams became free agents at the end of each season."

Rickey was only correct in his assessment that the Negro Leagues try to emulate the major leagues. Like major league teams, the black teams were incorporated with charters filed with their appropriate states. Team records show that all players were under one-year contracts and thereby were free agents at the end of the season.

21. Buck Leonard, interview with author, 12 July 1994.

22. *Chicago Defender,* 30 July 1945.

23. *New York Times,* 8 May 1945.

24. Robinson, *I Never Had It Made,* 41.

25. Carter, *Negro Baseball Pictorial Yearbook,* 29.

26. Kenny Washington had been an outstanding shortstop for Lincoln High School in Los Angeles. Washington repeated as winner of the Babe Ruth Bat award, given annually to the city's top prep batter. His senior year, he beat out Bobby Doerr, future second baseman for the Boston Red Sox and later a Hall of Famer, for the award. During his freshman year at UCLA, Washington led the conference with a batting average of .429. *Pittsburgh Courier,* 15 August 1942.

27. Wendell Smith Collection, National Baseball Hall of Fame, Cooperstown NY.

28. Wendell Smith Collection, National Baseball Hall of Fame, Cooperstown NY.

29. Wendell Smith Collection, National Baseball Hall of Fame, Cooperstown NY.

30. Sammie Haynes, a catcher with the 1945 Kansas City Monarchs, recalled the events that forced Serrell to leave the team: "Serrell was our regular shortstop. He had a skin disorder. A bad rash, that tormented him a lot. It made

him very sensitive to criticism. The truth is, when they brought Jackie in at Buffalo Stadium down there in Houston, they had to make a decision [as] to where they were gonna to play Jackie. Dizzy [Dismukes, the club's traveling secretary] said they were gonna to play him at short because that is what was advertised. So we have to make the change. So what they did they put Bill [Jesse] Williams at second base and Bonnie Serrell at first base. Serrell had played first base in spring training. He could play anywhere. OK! So what happen, Bonnie didn't like it. Bonnie was really the team star at the time. We got to San Antonio and stopped at a service station. He got off the bus and went to the back of the bus where the luggage was kept, you know. Bonnie took his suitcase out and suitroll, took his Kansas City uniform off and said, 'I'm gone' and headed to Mexico. He was pissed off. He never came back. That's what actually happened. Frank Duncan and Dizzy didn't have the presence of mind to put Jackie at first base. We didn't have a good first baseman. Back then we had Lee Moody and a few other guys. [Buck O'Neil was in the Navy.] We had a great double-play combination in Williams and Serrell. Boy, they were tough! Perfect, you know what I mean! So that move made second base weaker, because Bill had played shortstop all of his life. And Bonnie knew how good he was. They would not put him back at second base but Bonnie got mad and left. Now that's the truth!" Interview with author, Cleveland OH, 7 July 1997.

31. Carter, *Negro Baseball Pictorial Yearbook*, 28.

32. *New York Amsterdam News,* 3 November 1945.

33. *Michigan Chronicle,* 3 November 1945.

34. *Pittsburgh Courier,* 29 December 1945.

35. *Pittsburgh Courier,* 3 November 1945.

36. *New York Amsterdam News,* 27 October 1945.

37. *New York Amsterdam News,* 27 October 1945.

38. This was Jackie Robinson's only East-West all-star appearance. In *Ebony* magazine, he recalled the perils of traveling in the Negro Leagues:

When I look back at what I had to go through in black baseball, I can only marvel at the many black players who stuck it out in Jim Crow leagues because they had nowhere else to go.

Finding satisfactory or even passable eat-ing places was almost a daily problem. There were no hotels (for black players) in many of the places we played. Sometimes there was [a] hotel for blacks with no eating facilities. No one ever thought of trying to get accommodations at white hotels. "What's Wrong with Negro Baseball," *Ebony,* 1 June 1948, 17

39. The *New York Amsterdam News* gave its version of the low attendance, blaming Office of Defense Transportation regulations and bans against wartime travel for civilians for the sharp falling off in attendance at this famous spectacle. In addition, the game was what some called a "sleeper" shot. In other words, the operators kept quiet about the game for fear of government interference. As a result, many fans didn't know it was going to be played this year. *New York Amsterdam News,* 4 August 1945.

1946
1. Dodson, "The Integration of Negroes in Baseball," *Journal of Educational Sociology* (October 1954): 74–75.

2. *New York Amsterdam News,* 26 January 1946.

3. Albert B. "Happy" Chandler Papers, Report for Submission to National and American Leagues, 27 August 1946, University of Kentucky, 19–20. Major league teams rented Yankee Stadium and the Polo Grounds in New York, Comiskey Park and Wrigley Field in Chicago, Crosley Field in Cincinnati, Griffith Stadium in Washington DC, Municipal Stadium in Cleveland, Rickwood Field in Birmingham, Blues Stadium in Kansas City, Forbes Field in Pittsburgh, Shibe Park in Philadelphia, and Ruppert Stadium in Newark. The only exclusive black ballparks at this time were Martin Park, on Crump Boulevard and Danny Thomas Avenue in Memphis, and Bugle Field (owned by Hispanic Washington Senators scout Joe Cambria), on Biddle Street and Edison Highway in Baltimore. Typical major league parks contracted for a guarantee of $1,000 against a percentage of the gross, usually 25 percent. Booking agents were normally paid between 10 and 15 percent of the gate. With the Yankees and Giants of New York monopolizing rental agreements, Branch Rickey, president of the Brooklyn Dodgers, was unable to rent out Ebbets Field. The rental boycott may have prompted Rickey to create a black circuit, the United States League, in 1945.

4. Pappas, "Outside the Lines," 2. Pappas did an excellent job in summarizing Chandler's

Report for Submission to National and American Leagues.

5. Pappas, "Outside the Lines," 2.

6. Rodney interview, 31 October 1997.

7. *Pittsburgh Courier*, 6 April 1946.

8. *Cleveland Call-Post*, 13 April 1946.

9. *Pittsburgh Courier*, 6 April 1946.

10. *Cleveland Call-Post*, 8 June 1946.

11. Larry Gerlach, email from University of Utah, 6 April 1996.

12. *Baltimore Afro-American*, 20 June 1931.

13. *Baltimore Afro-American*, 27 June 1931.

14. Griffith Stadium would host the first East-West game played under the lights.

15. Willie Grace, telephone interview, 27 October 1997.

16. Jim Robinson, letter to author, 5 May 1996.

1947

1. *Chicago Defender*, 26 July 1947.

2. *Brooklyn Eagle*, 18 February 1948.

3. Among those attending the East-West game was Charles Graham, owner of the San Francisco Seals. Graham expressed his concerns about the team's weakness at first base, third base, and center field. Among the players Graham considered signing were Cleveland outfielder Sam Jethroe, Indianapolis Clowns first baseman Goose Tatum, Baltimore Elite Giants first baseman Johnny Washington, Birmingham Black Barons second baseman Piper Davis, and Black Barons shortstop Artie Wilson. Graham announced, "We'll hire any Negro player who really can help us." Graham did not sign any players from the East-West game. *Chicago Defender*, 9 August 1947.

4. Frank A. Young, the author of this article, offered his comments about the between-inning antics of King Tut, saying: "Fans were entertained by King Tut of the Indianapolis Clowns before and during the East vs. West classic. However there are thousands who did not approve of King Tut's crap shooting stunt or his shimmy in the grass skirt. He could have left that part of his act at home. The East vs. West classic is a high class sport event. Let's keep it that way." *Chicago Defender*, 2 August 1947.

5. On July 17, Hank Thompson became the third Negro League player in the majors. In his St. Louis debut, he went hitless in 4 at bats, with an error, at second base against the Philadelphia Athletics. The hapless Browns lost 16–2, after the Athletics scored nine runs in the ninth. Thompson spent 37 frustrating days with the Browns and hit only .256 in 78 at bats, playing 27 games, mostly at second base.

Meanwhile, Willard Brown became the first black player to hit a home run in the American League. On August 13, pinch-hitting for Joe Schultz, Brown drilled an inside-the-park homer off Detroit Tigers pitcher Hal Newhouser. However, the fantasy trip was over after only 21 games. Hitting less than his weight, a .179 batting average, Brown was released. The struggling St. Louis Browns, who two years earlier had signed an one-armed outfielder named Pete Gray before considering a black athlete, were not satisfied with Brown's chilly style of play.

6. This was the second East-West night, but the first in New York.

1948

1. *Philadelphia Tribune*, 7 August 1941.

2. *New York Amsterdam News*, 3 January 1948.

3. *New York Amsterdam News*, 3 January 1948.

4. *New York Amsterdam News*, 3 January 1948.

5. *New York Amsterdam News*, 24 January 1948.

6. *New York Amsterdam News*, 24 January 1948.

7. *New York Amsterdam News*, 7 February 1948.

8. *New York Amsterdam News*, 28 February 1948.

9. *New York Amsterdam News*, 28 February 1948.

10. *New York Amsterdam News*, 28 February 1948.

11. *New York Amsterdam News*, 6 March 1948.

12. *New York Amsterdam News*, 22 May 1948.

13. Rodney interview, 31 October 1997.

14. *New York Amsterdam News*, 24 January 1948.

15. Young's reference to Paige's drawing 51,000 fans was to Paige's second major league start for the St. Louis Browns, against the Chicago White Sox in Comiskey Park, on Friday the 13th. Good luck was in store for White Sox officials as a reported 15,000 fans were turned away from the capacity crowd of 51,013, at the time the largest crowd in White Sox history. Paige pitched a shutout, 5–0, for his fourth win against one defeat, putting the Indians back into first place. Following the game, the Indians announced that Paige would no longer pitch in relief and would take his place in the starting rotation.

Paige's first starting assignment came 10 days earlier, in Cleveland, on August 3. He defeated the Washington Senators, 5–3, before the largest crowd to ever attend a night game in baseball history, 72,434 fans. Following his first shutout victory, Paige pitched his second major league shutout on August 20, a three-hitter, for a 1–0 victory over the White Sox before a standing room, record-breaking crowd of 78,382 screaming fans. That record attendance for a night game still stands today.

Speaking of attendance, Mrs. Effa Manley, co-owner of the Newark Eagles, sounded off after the Paige game in an article written by Lillian Scott of the *Chicago Defender*. The article, entitled "Hotter Than Horse Radish: Calls Negro Fans Damn Fools," ripped the fans, the black press, and white baseball. Because of the lack of support by the black community, she was threatening to disband or sell her club.

Having lost money the last few years had caused her great concern. In 1946 she told a reporter that the Newark Eagles' total attendance for the year was 120,293 fans. The previous year, because Larry Doby went to the Cleveland Indians, attendance had dipped to 57,119 fans for the season. "You know figures don't lie," cried Effa. "And this year, up to the first week of September only 32,000 had attended the Eagles home games. Part of this [was] due to bad weather," she added.

Realizing the end of black baseball was near, Manley stated for the *Chicago Defender,* 18 September 1948: "After seeing Paige draw more people in one game than the Eagles had drawn so far this season only begs the question of 'How long will Negro league baseball survive?'"

16. Major league owners frequently cited the Negro Leagues as Class C status to justify getting top caliber players at less than market value. To address the hidden agenda of the "gentlemen's agreement," the owners used this myth of inferior talent to defend their decisions for not signing black players. Substantive evidence indicates that in many cases the black players were as equally talented as their white counterparts. The following table shows the impact Negro League players had, winning several batting and pitching categories in the top three minor league affiliations, from 1946 to 1955. Starting with Jackie Robinson's first season in the minors, he led a Triple A division in runs scored and won the batting title. A year earlier, as a Kansas City Monarch, Robinson was not among the top five batters for the Negro American League batting title. As regularly stated by Robinson's Monarchs team-

mates, the 26-year old was not the best player on the team. Additionally, note that although future Hall of Famer Ray Dandridge did not win the American Association's batting title in 1950 (he finished second), he was named their Most Valuable Player. Finally, you will find at the lower minor league classifications, former Negro Leaguers winning more than their proportionate share of individual awards and titles and setting records.

See the chapter for 1953 for the impact Negro League players had in winning major major league titles.

17. Despite having a brilliant spring training, Roy Campanella was assigned to St. Paul to help gate attendance. It was only after the Dodgers' regular catcher Bruce Edwards was injured that the Dodgers were forced to bring a Negro League veteran up to the parent club.

Earlier, in an exhibition game on April 18, Campanella made his first appearance in the seventh inning at catcher, replacing the Dodgers' future regular first baseman, Gil Hodges.

Before 62,369 fans, the Dodgers played the New York Yankees at Yankee Stadium. According to the *New York Amsterdam News* of April 24, 1948, it was estimated that 42 percent of the fans who came to see Robinson, Campy, and Newcombe were African-Americans.

1949

1. *Chicago Herald American,* 1 December 1948.

2. Tom Baird, letter to Fresco Thompson, 20 January 1949, Kansas Collection, University of Kansas.

3. *New York Amsterdam News,* 6 March 1948.

4. Lacy's father, Samuel Erskine, never missed an Opening Day at Griffith Stadium. He arrived early to see the parade of players, cheerleaders, and marching band. The younger Lacy remembered his father waiting in the long lines and recalled, "And then it happened! One of the white players,—I won't say which one—just gave him this nasty look and, as he passed by, spat right in his face. Right in that nice old man's face. That hurt my father terribly. And you know, as big a fan as he had been, he never went to another game as long as he lived, which was seven more years." Fimrite, "Sam Lacy," 93.

5. The Newark Eagles would become the Houston Eagles to start the 1949 season. Earlier in the year, Effa Manley had made her

NEGRO LEAGUER	RANK	YEAR	LEAGUE	H	R	D	T	HR	RBI	SB	AVE.	WINS	K'S	ERA
Jackie Robinson	AAA	1946	International		113						.349			
Dan Bankhead	AAA	1949	International										176	
Sam Jethroe	AAA	1949	International	207	154	19								
Artie Wilson	AAA	1949	Pacific Coast							47	.348			
Ray Dandridge	AAA	1950	American Assoc.	195										
Jim Pendleton	AAA	1950	American Assoc.				19							
Artie Wilson	AAA	1950	Pacific Coast	264	168									
Harry Simpson	AAA	1950	Pacific Coast				19		156					
George Crowe	AAA	1951	American Assoc.	189		41			119					
Jim Pendleton	AAA	1951	American Assoc.		116									
Jim Gilliam	AAA	1951	International		117									
Sam Jones	AAA	1951	Pacific Coast										246	
Bob Boyd	AAA	1951	Pacific Coast							41				
Billy Bruton	AAA	1952	American Assoc.	211	130									
Dave Pope	AAA	1952	American Assoc.				14				.352			
Bob Boyd	AAA	1952	Pacific Coast				18				.320			
Bob Wilson	AAA	1952	Pacific Coast	216										
Sam Jethroe	AAA	1953	American Assoc.		137									
Artie Wilson	AAA	1953	Pacific Coast				14							
George Crowe	AAA	1954	American Assoc.	197		38			128					
Sam Jethroe	AAA	1955	International							24				
Bob Wilson	AAA	1955	International	190		41								
Dave Hoskins	AA	1952	Texas									22		
Jose Santiago	AA	1953	Texas									21		1.59
Bill Greason	AA	1953	Texas									16		
Bob Boyd	AA	1955	Texas	197										
Harry Simpson	A	1949	Eastern		125			31	120					
Al Smith	A	1949	Eastern					17						
Sam Jones	A	1950	Eastern										160	
George Crowe	A	1950	Eastern	185		43					.353			
Dave Pope	A	1950	Eastern					18						
Dave Pope	A	1951	Eastern		113		13							
Jose Santiago	A	1951	Eastern									21		
Billy Bruton	A	1951	Western					27						
Connie Johnson	A	1952	Western										233	
Hank Aaron	A	1953	South Atlantic	108	115	36			125		.362			
Sam Hairston	A	1953	Western				42				.350			
Al Pinkston	A	1954	South Atlantic	180							.363			

final effort to save her club, and others, from folding, in a statement to the Negro Publishers Association:

Organized Negro baseball today, stands at the crossroads. The success or failure of the teams to draw this year may determine the future of our Negro Leagues. The past two seasons have seen our Negro fans desert our ballparks to follow the exploits of Jackie Robinson and Roy Campanella of Brooklyn and Larry Doby of the Cleveland Indians.

This season the trend of our fans still is toward the major league parks, and unless a real campaign is launched to retain their interest in Negro baseball, our Negro Leagues may be unable to continue operating. It is this situation which impels me to release to The Negro publishers this statement as an individual who has owned a team in organized Negro baseball for the past 15 years. I am firmly convinced that if organized Negro baseball is to be saved, the Negro press will have to save it. This poses the question "Is Negro baseball worth saving?"

The answer to that question can be found in the number of players who were developed in our league and are now making good in the Majors. It is hardly necessary for me to remind that Robinson, Campanella, Doby and Paige and Newcombe are all products of organized Negro baseball. If Negro fans want to see our boys in the majors after the present group have ended their careers, then it is necessary that they support our Negro leagues, which discover and develop players capable of playing in the majors.

If we fail to support our Negro leagues in this crucial period we may be hastening the day when no Negro's will be playing in the majors. The boys cannot make the jump from sandlot baseball into the big leagues without going through a period of development such as they are given in the Negro leagues. It is also evident that there will not be a sufficient number of our boys scattered throughout the minor league chains to meet the situation. At present we have 10 clubs in the Negro American League, and eight in the American Association that employ about 350 ball players, all being paid substantial salaries receiving training and competition that inspires them to give their best. This is the only practical source for futures Robinsons and Dobys.

I believe that some affirmative steps must be taken by those of us who want Negro baseball to survive.

I have been associated with professional baseball in the front office operation for the past 15 years and I have observed a great number of things which I believe must be brought to the attention of the general public.

When Negro ballplayers were first signed by the major leagues teams, principally the Brooklyn Dodgers, the owners of the teams in the Negro National League, now defunct, and the Negro American League shuddered with fear. They were stunned. Nothing was paid for the players' contracts and no one appeared to be willing to make any issue of the "steals." Most owners felt that to raise the question would be to make it appear that because of a selfish interest in money, the opportunity of some young man was being thwarted.

Even when Larry Doby of the Newark Eagles, the team which my husband, Abe, owned and in which I was active as business manager, the management of the Cleveland Indians made a promise to me which was not kept. I of course, remember the arrangements very well, but the major league team president ignores even my inquiries which seek only a courteous reply.

The problem was not only mine. It involved every owner in the Negro Leagues and will continue to confront them until they unite in a common purpose. They must intent first, to provide entertainment and employment for our people; secondly, they must want to protect the future of Negro Baseball for what it must mean to the world, and thirdly, they must want to protect that investment, time and energies.

Fortunately, I have no monetary interest in baseball now. The Eagles were sold to Houston, Texas, and therefore my interest at this point is only in the future of the sport. I have no selfish interest.

It was only last winter that Branch Rickey signed Monte Irvin who was a rightfielder for the Newark Eagles. He made no effort to contact us as the owners of the team which developed Monte since his first attempts in professional baseball. If it had not been for our action, through our attorney, we would have been by-passed and ignored.

However, by exerting our rights, we prevailed upon Mr. Rickey through officials in the major leagues, to withdraw his contractual arrangement with Irvin, and we ultimately sold him to the New York Giants. The result was best for everyone concerned. The Eagles were paid for Irvin's contract. Irvin was assigned to Jersey City in the International League (which he is leading in batting) instead of St. Paul, Minn., where the Dodgers were planning to send him. Because Irvin's home is closer to Jersey City he was happier, and because he was the first Negro in the Giants chain his opportunities are greater than they would been with the Brooklyn.

This incident is a page out of a long story. It was significant because a wave of contract signing opened, and we even read in the newspapers about a fight between two major league teams over a Negro ball player. Wasn't that news!

My point is this: Some steps must be taken to establish a firm relationship between the major leagues and the present Negro Baseball Leagues.

Unless something is done we are now seeing the last crop of Negro players in the big leagues. They have killed themselves off, because at the same time, Negro professional baseball is being killed.

We must never lose sight of the fact that the origin of Negro baseball as it is presently constituted was born of discrimination. We would never have had all-Negro teams, or even all Negro audiences if it had not been for the Jim Crow practices all of us have sought to eliminate.

If the signing of Negro baseball players means a step in that direction, we must not let it's [sic] very accomplishment be the factor which will defeat us for all time. We are at the crossroads. The future of Negro baseball is at stake.

The Negro press has a very definite responsibility in helping to preserve the leagues. If the sports writers on your publications will evidence the same enthusiasm toward our Negro baseball leagues . . . the

Negro players in the White major leagues, the future of Negro baseball will not be jeopardy. If they will give us the space, coverage, and buildup, the fans will give us the support necessary to make the Negro teams financially successful.

Newspapers, fans, owners, and everyone interested in the welfare of our people must get together on a common basis. We must do something and do it immediately. Otherwise Negro baseball is in great danger of folding . . . and that must NEVER happen.

6. The league leaders at the all-star break were Piper Davis, batting .406, followed by Baltimore's Lennie Pearson (.381) and Indianapolis's Len Pigg (.369) in the number two and three slots. Chicago's first baseman Lyman Bostock Sr. led in three departments: total bases (114), doubles (17), and runs batted in with an even 50. Kansas City's Bob Thurman had 12 thefts to lead in that department, while Junior Gilliam of Baltimore had scored the most runs with 48. Lonnie Summers was hitting .317 with 100 total bases and 37 RBIs, while leading the league in homers with six. In pitching, Isaiah Harris of Memphis was the leader with four wins against no losses.

1950
1. *Kansas City Call*, 17 February 1950.
2. *Kansas City Call*, 17 February 1950.
3. *Kansas City Call*, 17 February 1950.
4. *Kansas City Call*, 24 November 1950.
5. *Philadelphia Tribune*, 4 July 1950.
6. John Talmo, letter to author, 1996.
7. *Kansas City Call*, 28 July 1950.
8. *New York Times*, 10 July 1950.
9. *New York Times*, 8 August 1950.
10. *Kansas City Call*, 28 July 1950.
11. Bunch was unable to attend the game due to a family illness. *Kansas City Call*, 22 August 1950.

1951
1. Tom Baird, letter from Harry C. Jenkins, Boston Braves farm director, 9 March 1951, Kansas Collection, University of Kansas.

2. *Kansas City Call*, 22 December 1950.
3. Merrill Clifton, letter to author, 22 May 1987.
4. *Kansas City Call*, 6 July 1951.
5. Neft and Cohen, *The Sports Encyclopedia*, 274.
6. *Kansas City Call*, 20 July 1951.
7. *Kansas City Call*, 20 July 1951.

1952
1. *Kansas City Call*, 6 June 1952.
2. *Kansas City Call*, 4 January 1952.
3. Dewey Griggs, letter to John Mullen, 25 May 1952.
4. Syd Pollock, letter to John Mullen, 27 May 1952.
5. Western Union telegram, 7:00 A.M., 29 May 1952.
6. Western Union telegram, 9:09 A.M., 28 May 1952.
7. *Kansas City Call*, 13 June 1952.
8. *Kansas City Call*, 13 June 1952.
9. *Kansas City Call*, 13 June 1952.
10. *Kansas City Call*, 12 September 1952.

1953
1. *Kansas City Call*, 25 September 1953.
2. *Kansas City Call*, 5 June 1953.
3. *Kansas City Call*, 26 June 1953.
4. *Kansas City Call*, 18 September 1953.
5. *Kansas City Call*, 17 April 1953.
6. *Kansas City Call*, 29 May 1953.
7. *Delta Democrat-Times* (Greenville MS), 24 April 1953.
8. *Kansas City Call*, 19 June 1953.
9. *Kansas City Call*, 26 June 1953.
10. Robert Cromie of the *Chicago Tribune* reported: "Ernie Banks, also of the Monarchs, who played the full game at shortstop for the West, went hitless in four times at bat, but lived up to advance notices in the field as he accepted seven chances without error and made one of the game's fielding gems with a spectacular stop of Verdes Drake's smash in the third inning, taking the ball on a short hop and throwing Drake out from deep short." *Chicago Tribune*, 17 August 1953.

Bibliography

BOOKS AND PERIODICALS

Bjarkman, Peter C. *Baseball with a Latin Beat: A History of the Latin American Game.* Jefferson NC: McFarland & Company, 1994.

Bolton, Todd. *Before the Game Was Color Blind.* Cleveland: Society for American Baseball, The National Pastime, 1992.

Bruce, Janet. *The Kansas City Monarchs: Champions of Black Baseball.* Lawrence: University of Kansas Press, 1985.

Carter, Art. *Negro Baseball Pictorial Yearbook.* Washington DC: Sepia Sports Publication, 1945 and 1946.

Clark, Dick, and Larry Lester. *The Negro Leagues Book.* Cleveland: Society for American Baseball Research, 1994.

Cowan, Tom, and Jack Maguire. *Timelines of African-American History: 500 Years of Black Achievement.* New York: Perigee Books, 1994.

Craft, David. *The Negro Leagues: 40 Years of Black Professional Baseball in Words and Pictures.* Avenel NJ: Crescent Books, 1993.

Dodson, Dan W. "The Integration of Negroes in Baseball." *Journal of Educational Sociology* (October 1954).

Fimrite, Ron. "Sam Lacy: Black Crusader." *Sports Illustrated,* 29 October 1990.

Gelman, Steve. "You Could Almost Have a Negro All-Star Game." *Sport* (July 1960).

Gilbert, Tom. *Baseball and the Color Line.* New York: Franklin Watts, 1995.

Glasco, Laurence. "Take Care of Business: The Black Entrepreneurial Elite in Turn-of-the-Century Pittsburgh." *Pittsburgh History* (winter 1995/96).

Harley, Sharon. *The Timetables of African-American History.* New York: Simon & Schuster, 1995.

Holway, John B. *Blackball Stars: Negro League Pioneers.* Westport CT: Meckler Books, 1988. Reprint, New York: Carroll & Graf, 1992.

———. *Black Diamonds: Life in the Negro Leagues from the Men Who Lived It.* Westport CT: Meckler Books, 1989. Reprint, New York: Stadium Books, 1991.

———. *Voices from the Great Black Baseball Leagues.* New York: Dodd, Mead Company, 1975. Reprint, New York: Decapo, 1993.

Hornsby Jr., Alton. *Milestones in 20th-Century African-American History.* Detroit: Visible Ink, 1993.

Hughes, Langston. *Langston Hughes and the Chicago Defender.* Edited by Christopher C. DeSantis. Urbana: University of Illinois Press, 1995.

Irvin, Monte, with James A. Riley. *Nice Guys Finish First.* New York: Carroll & Graf, 1996.

Lacy, Sam, with Moses J. Newson. *Fighting for Fairness: The Life Story of Hall of Fame Sportswriter Sam Lacy.* Centreville MD: Tidewater, 1998.

Lenburg, Jeff. *Baseball's All-Star Game: A Game-by-Game Guide.* Jefferson NC: McFarland & Company, 1986.

Leonard, Buck, with James A. Riley. *Buck Leonard: The Black Lou Gehrig, An Autobiography.* New York: Carroll & Graf, 1995.

Neft, David S., and Richard M. Cohen. *The Sports Encyclopedia: Baseball.* New York: St. Martin's Griffin, 1997.

O'Neil, Buck, with Steve Wulf and David Conrads. *I Was Right On Time.* New York: Simon & Schuster, 1996.

Overmyer, James. *Effa Manley and the Newark Eagles.* Metuchen NJ: Scarecrow Books, 1993.

Paige, Leroy (Satchel), as told to Hal Lebovitz. *Pitchin' Man: Satchel Paige's Own Story.* N.p., 1948.

Pappas, Doug. "Outside the Lines," SABR *Business of Baseball Committee Newsletter* (summer 1996).

Peterson, Robert. *Only The Ball Was White: A History of Legendary Black Players and All-Black Professional Teams.* Englewood Cliffs NJ: Prentice-Hall, 1970. Reprint, New York: McGraw-Hill, 1984 and 1992.

Press, David P. *A Multicultural Portrait of Professional Sports.* North Bellmore NY: Marshall Cavendish, 1993.

Reisler, Jim. *Black Writers/Black Baseball: An Anthology of Articles from Black Sportswriters Who Covered the Negro Leagues.* Jefferson NC: McFarland & Company, 1994.

Riley, James A. *Dandy, Day, and the Devil: A Trilogy of Negro League Baseball.* Cocoa FL: TK Publishers, 1987.

Ritter, Lawrence S. *Lost Ballparks.* New York: Viking Studio Books, 1992.

Robinson, Jackie, with Alfred Duckett. *I Never Had It Made.* New York: G. P. Putnam's Sons, 1972.

———, with Wendell Smith. *My Own Story.* New York: Greenberg, 1948.

Rogosin, Donn. *Invisible Men: Life in the Negro*

Leagues. New York: G. P. Putnam's Sons, 1972.

Ruck, Rob. *Sandlot Seasons: Black Sport in Pittsburgh.* Urbana: University of Illinois Press, 1986.

————. *The Tropic of Baseball: Baseball in the Dominican Republic.* Ferry Lane West CT: Meckler, 1991.

Trouppe, Quincy. *Twenty Years Too Soon.* Los Angeles: Sands Enterprises, 1977. Reprint, St. Louis: Missouri Historical Society Press, 1995.

Tygiel, Jules. *Baseball's Great Experiment: Jackie Robinson and His Legacy.* New York: Oxford Press, 1983. Reprint, New York: Oxford Press, 1993.

Van Hyning, Thomas E. *Puerto Rico's Winter Leagues: A History of Major League Baseball's Launching Pad.* Jefferson NC: McFarland & Company, 1995.

Wiggins, David K. *Glory Bound: Black Athletes in White America.* Syracuse NY: Syracuse University Press, 1998.

Woods, Paula L., and Felix H. Liddell. *I, Too, Sing America: The African American Book of Days.* New York: Workman, 1992.

NEWSPAPERS

Anderson Independent-Tribune (South Carolina)
Baltimore Afro-American
Brooklyn Eagle
Catholic Register (Denver)
Chicago Daily News
Chicago Defender
Chicago Herald American
Cincinnati Enquirer
Cleveland Call-Post
Cleveland Plain Dealer
Delta Democrat-Times (Greenville MS)
Denver Post
Erie Herald Dispatch
Erie Post-Dispatch
Kansas City Call
Los Angeles Times
Louisville Courier Journal
Michigan Chronicle
New Jersey Herald News
New York Amsterdam News
New York Daily Mirror
New York Daily News
New York Daily Worker
New York Post
New York Times
Newark Afro-American
People's Voice (New York)

Philadelphia Tribune
Pittsburgh Courier
Pittsburgh Post-Gazette
Pittsburgh Sun-Telegraph
Washington Afro-American
Washington Post

PUBLIC RECORDS

New York City, New York. "Report of the Mayor's Committee on Baseball to Mayor F. H. LaGuardia," by John H. Johnson, chairman, 31 October 1945.

U.S. Congress, House, Committee on the Judiciary. "Study of Monopoly Power: Organized Baseball, in Hearings before the Subcommittee on Study of Monopoly Power of the Committee of the Judiciary," 82d Congress, 1st Session, 1951.

ARCHIVES

National Baseball Hall of Fame and Museum, Cooperstown, New York
Black Archives of Mid-America, Kansas City, Missouri
Spencer Research Center, University of Kansas, Lawrence, Kansas
Author's correspondence file

RECORDED INTERVIEWS

Gene Benson
Chet Brewer
Bill Cash
Jim Cohen
Jimmie Crutchfield
Ross Davis
Lou Dials
Larry Doby
Willie Grace
Teenie Harris
Albert Haywood
Monte Irvin
Sam Jethroe
Byron Johnson
Connie Johnson
Ernie Johnson
Sam Lacy
Jim LaMarque
Rufus Lewis
Bob Motley
Buck O'Neil
Dick Powell
Ted Radcliffe
Lester Rodney
Quincy Trouppe
Jesse H. Williams